Anthropomorphic Depictions of God: The Concept of God in Judaic, Christian and Islamic Traditions

Representing the Unrepresentable

❦

TO MY LATE PARENTS: RAZIA AND ABBAS SHAH

May Allah SWT grant them Jannah

AND TO HAMMAD, SUMAYYAH AND SOHAIB

Hoping that they continue searching for meanings

ANTHROPOMORPHIC DEPICTIONS *of* GOD

•

The CONCEPT OF GOD IN JUDAIC, CHRISTIAN AND ISLAMIC TRADITIONS

Representing the Unrepresentable

ZULFIQAR ALI SHAH

THE INTERNATIONAL INSTITUTE OF ISLAMIC THOUGHT

LONDON • WASHINGTON

THE INTERNATIONAL INSTITUTE OF ISLAMIC THOUGHT
P.O. BOX 669, HERNDON, VA 20172, USA
www.iiit.org

LONDON OFFICE
P.O. BOX 126, RICHMOND, SURREY, TW9 2UD, UK
www.iiituk.com

ISBN 978-1-56564-575-2 *limp*
ISBN 978-1-56564-576-9 *cased*

Design and layout by Shiraz Khan
Printed in Malta by Gutenberg Press Ltd

CONTENTS

CONTENTS

Endorsements

BINYAMIN ABRAHAMOV
Professor, Department of Arabic, Bar Ilan University

Erudite, showing impressive mastery of the various sources used, very vast, comprehensive and promising academic discussions of the conclusions drawn.

MUMTAZ AHMAD
President, International Islamic University, Islamabad

This is arguably one of the most important works in recent years on the study of anthropomorphism and transcendence in the comparative perspectives of the Bible and the Qur'an. Zulfiqar Ali Shah has written a truly scholarly, and yet accessible book that opens up new avenues of research in comparative religion and invites both scholars and religious leaders to reconsider the theological formulations that lie at the center of the line that separates the idea of absolute monotheism from that of anthropomorphism. Closely argued and lucidly written, this book will surely provide a rewarding reading experience to both scholars and lay educated readers.

IHSAN BAGBY
Associate Professor, University of Kentucky

A well-researched and thought-provoking work that masterfully surveys the thinking of theologians and philosophers in the Christian, Jewish and Muslim tradition on the issue of anthropomorphism. There is much here for all people to learn and ponder.

CHARLES E. BUTTERWORTH
Professor Emeritus, Department of Government and Politics, University of Maryland

Zulfiqar Ali Shah has read widely, very widely, in seeking to understand Hebrew Scriptures and their Christian counterparts. His reading leads him at times to fault both sets of Scriptures rather than their followers – a position that is surely in tension with the teaching of the Qur'an and that will intrigue the adherents of all three revealed traditions. The boldness of the exposition as well as its vast scope will challenge many a reader and provide fruitful material for all those interested in the comparative study of religion. These features, combined with Ali Shah's clear and lucid prose and the over-all appealing manner in which the book has been prepared, make it one to be examined and pondered.

CHARLES L. COHEN
Director, Lubar Institute for the Study of the Abrahamic Religions, University of Wisconsin-Madison

The growing recognition that the fullest appreciation of Jewish and Christian theological discourses requires setting them in dialogue with Islam as well as with each other is an extremely important and relatively recent development. By examining classic Jewish, Christian, and

Islamic sources concerning God's unity and transcendence, Zulfiqar Ali Shah makes a major contribution to both debates about anthropomorphic depictions of God within the Abrahamic religions, and, by virtue of his comparative method, to the larger "trialogue" itself. This work presents a worthy challenge to scholars and theologians of all three traditions.

FREDERICK MATHEWSON DENNY
Emeritus Professor, Department of Religious Studies, University of Colorado, Boulder

Zulfiqar Ali Shah's comprehensive, penetrating and masterly study of anthropomorphism across the landscape of Abrahamic traditions is a must-read for students and professional scholars, as well as all readers dedicated to constructively balancing the intellectual and spiritual dimensions of life.

JOHN L. ESPOSITO
University Professor and Professor of Islamic Studies, Georgetown University

[This work] is a masterful, thought-provoking, and insightful study by Zulfiqar Ali Shah of anthropomorphism in the conceptions of God in the Bible and the Qur'an that will be welcomed by scholars and students and all who are interested in the Abrahamic traditions.

KHALED ABOU EL FADL
Omar and Azmeralda Alfi Professor of Law, Chair of Islamic Studies Program, UCLA School of Law

I am in awe of Zulfiqar Shah's work! His exposition on anthropomorphism and transcendence in Judaism, Christianity, and Islam is not only learned, rigorous, and erudite, but also profound and inspiring. Every student of comparative religion, and every person of faith ought to read and reflect upon this book. I for one after completing this book, feel compelled to read it again. And this time with greater relish.

WILLIAM A. GRAHAM
Dean of The Faculty of Divinity, Harvard Divinity School, John Lord O'Brian Professor of Divinity, and Murray A. Albertson Professor of Middle Eastern Studies (Faculty of Arts And Sciences)

Zulfiqar Ali Shah's book is an extensive undertaking that is encyclopedic in its scope and ambitious in its aims. Although written with a view to demonstrating the relative superiority of the Qur'anic and Muslim understanding of the transcendent God, the book's lengthy treatments of corresponding biblical, Jewish, and Christian understandings seem largely fair, balanced and thorough. Scholars dealing with concepts of God in the three traditions will have to come to terms with this work in the future.

STEWART GUTHRIE
Professor Emeritus of Anthropology, Fordham University

The book as a whole is scholarly, engages a topic of great interest to scholars of religion, and is very well written. The opening chapter, 'Anthropomorphism: Background, Criticism, and Defining Categories', is an excellent compendium on the nature of anthropomorphism together with an excellent introduction (detailed in later chapters) to its manifestation in particular religions, primarily the Abrahamic ones. As a locus of these two related but distinct accomplishments, the chapter is one of the best I know.

YVONNE HADDAD
Professor of the History of Islam and Christian-Muslim Relations, Center for Muslim-Christian Understanding

An important and timely contribution on a topic that has engaged participants in interfaith polemics as well as dialogue for centuries.

SHEIKH HAMZA YUSUF HANSON
Founder, Zaytuna College, CA

This is an extremely important topic and critical to the understanding of Western faiths and the current crisis of disbelief. Idolatry is the great sin of Judaism and Islam, and yet many of the greatest theologians have missed the idolatry of the very conception of God as mental image. The image of God that a mind holds is invariably idolatrous; hence this subject is an essential one for anyone today who takes God seriously, whether an atheist or theist. The atheist because the god he imagines he doesn't believe in probably doesn't exist, and the theist because the God he believes in through some mental image probably doesn't exist either.

JOHN HICK
Emeritus Professor, University of Birmingham, UK and the Claremont Graduate University, California

Anthropomorphism in our scriptures is a very important question for Christians as well as for Muslims and Jews, and we must all be grateful for this thoroughly researched and clearly written new treatment of the subject. I am glad to be able to recommend it.

SHERMAN A. JACKSON
King Faisal Chair of Islamic Thought and Culture, The University of Southern California

This book takes in a wide range of sources, scholars and issues, all of which stood at the very core of theological debate in pre-modern Islam and continue, albeit in attenuated form, to animate theological thinking and discussions among Muslims today. Ali Shah pulls no punches in this text, stating his positions clearly and directing his critique with unfailing candor. This, alongside the wealth of information it provides, is almost certain to gain this book a wide readership and to spawn serious, constructive and seminal debate.

JOHN KELSAY
Distinguished Research Scholar (Religion), Florida State University, Tallahassee

I am glad to see Zulfiqar Ali Shah's comparative study of anthropomorphism and transcendence in print. The topic is an important one, and readers willing to invest the time will find the analysis challenging. One need not agree with the author's conclusions regarding the relative superiority of Islam on this matter in order to appreciate his contributions. The book is a welcome addition to conversations in comparative religious thought.

DANIEL C. MAGUIRE
Professor, Marquette University

Zulfiqar Ali Shah has written a masterly book that proves that true scholarship can foster dialogue, not by shying from differences, but by facing them squarely and clarifying them. He does this with a passion for fairness and objectivity that is exemplary.

DONALD W. MITCHELL
Professor of Philosophy, Purdue University. Editor CLARITAS, Journal of Dialogue and Culture

This book is an extremely important contribution to the comparative study of the attribution of anthropomorphic qualities and characteristics to God in the Hebrew Bible, the New Testament and the Qur'an as well as later thought in all three Abrahamic traditions. The encyclopedic scope of this book reflects the impressive breadth and depth of the author's scholarship. Deserving special attention is the author's comprehensive treatment of Islam's theological safeguarding of the unity and transcendence of God that is clarifying, engaging and challenging. Therefore, this comprehensive and sympathetic work adds a significant and welcome voice to both scholarship and interfaith dialogue.

EBRAHIM MOOSA
Professor of Religion and Islamic Studies, Department of Religion, Duke University, Durham, NC

This study on anthropomorphism and transcendence in the Bible and the Qur'an is a timely intervention in an ongoing theological conversation. It comes at a time when both understanding between Christians and Muslims holds promise while misunderstanding between these communities threatens global peace. This book is a tour de force and relevant to students of Islam and comparative religion. The author has painstakingly and intelligently excavated the archives of religious thought in order to render, to make available insights that show how each tradition is distinct as well as similar. A must read for the contemporary student of theology.

JACOB NEUSNER
Distinguished Service Professor of The History and Theology of Judaism
Senior Fellow, Institute of Advanced Theology Bard College, Annandale-on-Hudson, New York

The chapter on Judaism is well researched and solid.

IRFAN A. OMAR
Associate Professor, Department of Theology, Marquette University

This book is based on meticulous research and presents a comparative view of the three monotheistic traditions focusing on "anthropomorphism" and "transcendence" in the Hebrew Bible, the New Testament, and the Qur'an. It is unique in its undertaking as it attempts to address the subject matter in light of contemporary debates about God while remaining attentive to the hermeneutical as well as theological perspectives that underlie those debates. The author utilizes all the available scholarly methodologies and approaches and more; the end result is a re-examination and reframing of key issues to help the modern reader navigate through them with relative ease. It is a welcome addition to the growing library of works that seek to discover paths of convergence and divergence within the Judeo-Christian-Islamic heritage.

ANDREW RIPPIN
Former Dean of Humanities, Professor of Islamic History, Specialist in the Qur'an and the History of Its Interpretation, University of Victoria, British Columbia

Clearly the result of many years of reading, reflection and writing, Scripture and God in the Judeo Christian and Islamic Traditions goes to the heart of theological reflections on the nature of God. By elucidating the differences and the similarities in the way God is conceived, Zulfiqar Ali Shah has produced a perceptive study from which readers will benefit greatly.

Extensively documented and lucidly written, the book provides a stimulating summary of theological articulations and controversies ranging from ancient times down to the present day.

ABDULLAH SAEED
The Sultan of Oman Professor of Arab and Islamic Studies, and Director of the National Centre of Excellence for Islamic Studies and Asia Institute, University of Melbourne

A major contribution to our understanding of anthropomorphic conceptions of God in the Abrahamic traditions. The author's mastery of the material, his depth of analysis and his ability to ask hard questions and skillful addressing of them are evident throughout the work. A must read for students of Islamic thought.

OMID SAFI
Professor of Religious Studies, University of North Carolina

This is a powerful study, simultaneously an analysis and a devastating critique of anthropomorphism in Abrahamic traditions. The author, a pious and observant Muslim, moves through Islam, Judaism, and Christianity in arguing for the devastating consequence of an anthropomorphized understanding of God for the contemporary world.

CAROLINE SEYMOUR-JORN
Associate Professor, Comparative Literature Program, University of Wisconsin, Milwaukee

This exploration of anthropomorphism in Jewish, Christian and Muslim scriptures is well researched and clearly expounded. This study provides a useful historical synopsis of anthropological, sociological and philosophical understandings of religion, and of the various religious concepts of transcendence and immanence of God. While I differ with some of Ali Shah's overarching conclusions, I find that this text generates a fascinating comparison of the three Abrahamic scriptural traditions with regard to conceptions and descriptions of deity. Moreover, it is clearly written and accessible, and thus it will therefore be of great interest to both students and scholars of comparative religions.

MUZAMMIL H. SIDDIQI
Chairman, Fiqh Council of North America

This is an extremely important work. The author brings out very clearly what unites Islam with its other Abrahamic traditions, namely, Judaism and Christianity and what sets it apart. Monotheism (*Tawḥīd*) is the hallmark of Islam and in a unique way it brings home the point that God (Allah) is neither an abstract reality nor an anthropomorphic being. "There is nothing like unto Him and He is All Hearing and All Seeing" (Qur'an 42:11) We are thankful to Ali Shah for presenting his thesis with careful research and high standard of scholarship.

THE MOST REVEREND RICHARD J. SKLBA
Vicar General/Auxiliary Bishop of Milwaukee, Wisconsin

Rarely has the precise point of debate between Islam and Christianity been so carefully and extensively articulated. Ali Shah has studied the classic Christian theological sources of Scripture and the early Church Councils in order to sharpen his comprehension of the key areas for mutual understanding and radical disagreement between these two major world religious traditions. This is a profound work. His thesis is simply that Christianity's conviction regarding Jesus the Christ as incarnate Logos, divine Person and perfect Image of the Father renders the God of Christianity as essentially corporeal. It remains a conclusion which in his judgment cannot be logically overcome, even though Catholic Christianity has long struggled with its tension between the final triumph of the Risen Christ, the sacramental system of God at work in the world and the apophatic approach of the holy mystics. Shah's work now awaits a similar study of equal erudition from the Christian perspective in order to bring the points of legitimate disagreement, especially in areas of Christology, to the table of fruitful theological interreligious dialogue.

JANE I. SMITH
Associate Dean for Faculty and Academic Affairs, Harvard Divinity School

A valuable contribution to the comparative study of the scriptures of Judaism, Christianity and Islam. Zulfiqar Ali Shah has shed important light on the influence of text on respective believers' perception of God.

TAMARA SONN
Kenan Professor of Humanities, Department of Religious Studies, College of William and Mary, Williamsburg. Editor-in-Chief, Oxford Bibliographies Online: Islamic Studies. *Co-Editor-in-Chief,* Religion Compass

Zulfiqar Ali Shah's study provides profound insight into Muslim perceptions of divine transcendence. While anthropomorphism is inevitable in human efforts to describe the divine, Shah maintains that the Qur'an's explicit insistence on divine incomparability protects Muslims from excesses in this regard. His conclusion that Islam's relatively greater emphasis on divine transcendence precludes as well the alienation he observes in the secular West provides a worthy challenge for Jews and Christians.

MERLIN SWARTZ
Professor Emeritus of Religion (Islamic Studies), Boston University

Despite differences with Z. A. Shah on certain matters of detail, he has performed a remarkable service to the scholarly community by his in-depth and fair-minded examination of anthropomorphic conceptions of God in the Bible and the Qur'an. I applaud his efforts and commend his impressive work to the world of scholarship for serious study and reflection.

ELLIOT R. WOLFSON
Abraham Lieberman Professor of Hebrew and Judaic Studies, New York University

Zulfiqar Ali Shah's study is an honest assessment of one of the most perplexing shadows of monotheism as it has expressed itself in the history of the three Abrahamic faiths. The author painstakingly examines the anthropomorphic depictions of God in the Jewish, Christian, and Islamic scriptural traditions. He correctly notes that at the textual level the Qur'an is the most consistently and severely anti-anthropomorphic, upholding a more rigorous notion of divine transcendence. Beyond the historical value of this book as an exegetical work of comparative religion, it can be read as an important theological composition. The tension between a God who is wholly other and thus resistant to any human characterization, on one hand, and the basic psychological need on the part of human beings to portray God anthropomorphically, on the other hand, continues to be at the heart of religious faith and devotion. God may be without image, but in the absence of image it is hard to imagine how to worship God. In that respect, if monotheism is to persist as a vibrant force, there must always be an idolatrous element expressed in the anthropomorphic representation of the deity. And yet precisely because this is so, we must always refine our beliefs so that we are not ensnared in representing the unrepresentable and imaging the imageless by the fabrication of images that, literally speaking, are false. Rather than expanding the analogical imagination in envisioning transcendence, the spiritual demand of the hour, the epochal duty, is the need to overcome it. Zulfiqar Ali Shah's book has contributed significantly to this conversation.

MARK E. WORKMAN
Provost and Vice President for Academic Affairs, University of North Florida

Zulfiqar Ali Shah's monumental work, reflects equally the deep erudition and profound humanity of its author. It is a work that beneficially could be read by people of all faiths, who will discover in this rich text not only what makes certain faiths distinct from one another, but just as importantly, what it is that binds people of different faiths together in their common quest for absolute meaning and purpose.

JOHN VOLL
Professor of Islamic History and Associate Director of the Prince Alwaleed bin Talal Center for Muslim-Christian Understanding, Georgetown University

In a time when inter-faith relations are of great global significance, this volume provides an important analysis of shared visions and diversities of views held by Jews, Christians, and Muslims. I hope this book is widely read.

PUBLISHER'S FOREWORD

ZULFIQAR ALI SHAH'S *Anthropomorphic Depictions of God: The Concept of God in Judaic, Christian and Islamic Traditions* is an extensive and meticulous exposition of the issues of anthropomorphism and corporealism (the description of God in human terms or form) in the three Abrahamic Faiths, as viewed through the texts of the Hebrew Bible, the New Testament and the Qur'an. It is, in addition, a detailed examination of later developments in theological thought, scriptural interpretation, and exegetical criticism, with regards to anthropomorphism, and how these have significantly influenced perceptions of God by followers of all three Traditions.

Throughout history Christianity and Judaism have tried to make sense of God, accepting anthropomorphic images (whether verbal or physical) of the Divine, yet disagreeing as to what these mean, whilst at the same time attempting to save the transcendent God from notions of corporeality and anthropomorphism. The author addresses the worldview of both faiths, and fundamentally how each has chosen to framework its own understanding of, and encounter with, God – how each views God's personality and nature – and how much of this has been the result of scripture and how much supplemental additions of later theological debate, absorption of Hellenistic philosophy, and church decrees of later centuries.

Muslims too have historically debated the few mildly anthropomorphic expressions contained in the Qur'an, albeit strictly confining discourse to issues of metaphorical versus literal interpretation, whilst simultaneously taking an unequivocal anti-anthropomorphic stance to safeguard Islam's concept of a unique, transcendent and monotheistic God. The author examines in great detail Islamic theological discourse on the Ninety-Nine Names of God and what these have meant in relation to God's essence and attributes, situating this analysis in its proper historical setting. He also explains the importance and impact of *Sūrah al-Ikhlāṣ* (Qur'an 112) and its maxim "there is none like unto Him [God]" as setting the benchmark for pure monotheism and *tawḥīd* and governing all aspects of debate.

As secularism and modern philosophy debate whether God is dead, the issue of anthropomorphism, in the author's opinion, has become of immense importance, primarily because he connects this directly to the decline of religion and belief in God in the first instance, and the general degeneration of spiritual thinking in the second. Religion to modern man, now simply reduced to the question of whether God exists or not, has become largely irrelevant, forgetting that religion's primary goal was to solve the problem of meaning in this life and answer questions relating to life after death, and not to satisfy man's immediate needs. It is the contention of this book that a crude, anthropomorphic or corporeal notion of God is partly to blame, standing resolute between modern intellectual thought and belief in God, and that at best this has weakened the authority of God and religion and at worst annihilated it in favor of a more meaningless view of existence.

Seeking God is an intellectual as much as it is a spiritual exercise, although the term intellectual would sound strange to modern ears. Past civilizations sought God, whether in the heavens, in nature, or in themselves. Whatever the case there was an acute understanding that the business of life was to prepare for death, and it is this search which at length led to varying depictions of God in anthropomorphic terms. The question of whether the attribution of qualities and characteristics elevated or degraded mankind's final perception of the Transcendent Being, depended on the nature or complexity of the anthropomorphism(s) involved. The ultimate rendering one could argue found meaning in the desire to bring God within reach of our own selves, on this earthly plane, defining the framework of man's own understanding of Him and how He was to be worshipped.

Eventually, the historical and seemingly irresistible progression of anthropomorphism was to reach a pinnacle of sorts, interestingly in Christianity, culminating in the veneration of a triune deity, a God walking alive amongst humanity and encompassing man's own field of vision.

Islam differed markedly. The Qur'an categorically denies any ascription to God of human tendencies, bridging the gap between man and the divine whilst simultaneously maintaining God's transcendence, otherliness, and Oneness. Man could 'know' God through worship and communication, through His names and attributes, and through following His messenger, in a way that would allow an intensely close and personal relationship with the Deity without compromising transcendence. God was certainly not 'unknowable' because of His uniqueness as some critics of Islam would have it. God in other words was not perceived through outer form but spiritual realization of an infinite Reality.

The intellectual strength of Islamic theology was remarkable. Fuelled by the simple idea of "there is none like unto Him [God]" and ever on guard against opening the door to *shirk* (associating partners with God), the centuries that followed witnessed theologians entering into complex and lengthy debate, not only with scholars of other faiths but also Hellenistic philosophers, countering the many convoluted questions raised with regards to the nature and even appearance of God. Despite minor expressions of anthropomorphism contained in the Qur'an (i.e. God's hand, face) and the various clashes which resulted, primarily over as to how these were to be interpreted by Muslims, Islamic exegesis and discourse remained historically and heavily anti-anthropomorphic.

This study analyzes in great detail many of these issues to ultimately chart the reasons why an almost unfettered anthropomorphism was able, even allowed, to develop in rabbinic thought and church Christologies, within essentially a transcendent conception of the Deity, to gain in due course general acceptance and authority. The author has made great efforts to treat Judaic, Christian, and Islamic literature systematically in this careful investigation and as such evidence is not only taken from many scriptural passages but also sources authored by members of each faith as well as respected critics. The issue of anthropomorphism is surveyed thoroughly and dispassionately through the lense of each tradition to give readers a clear understanding of the scriptural, theological, political, historical, and philosophical issues involved, and the significance of later developments in thought down the centuries: broadly summed up as the often heated tug-of-war between an essentially anthropomorphic versus the return to a more purely transcendent concept of the Divine. What we are left with is a work of remarkable value, significantly increasing our own understanding of current and historical complexities and controversies, surrounding this vital issue which after all addresses the key question of "who to worship?" and the impact of which is felt today.

Written in a clear and lucid style, the book will benefit both general and specialist readers alike, increasing their awareness of the question of anthropomorphism and corporealism as well as the God paradigm of Islam, Judaism and Christianity.

This study is being published to widen discourse, invite scholars to respond, and hopefully pave the way for further research. Since it deals with some critical and difficult issues, doubtless readers may agree with some of the issues raised, and disagree with others, but it is hoped that for the most part both general and specialist readers will benefit from the perspective offered and the overall issues examined in the book.

Where dates are cited according to the Islamic calendar (hijrah) they are labelled AH. Otherwise they follow the Gregorian calendar and labelled CE where necessary. Arabic words are italicized except for those which have entered common usage. Diacritical marks have been added only to those Arabic names not considered modern. English translations taken from Arabic references are those of the author.

The IIIT, established in 1981, has served as a major center to facilitate serious scholarly efforts based on Islamic vision, values and principles. The Institute's programs of research, seminars and conferences during the last thirty years have resulted in the publication of more than four hundred titles in English and Arabic, many of which have been translated into other major languages.

We express our thanks and gratitude to the author for his cooperation throughout the various stages of production. We would also like to thank the editorial and production team at the IIIT London Office and all those who were directly or indirectly involved in the completion of this book including, Shiraz Khan, Dr. Maryam Mahmood, Tahira Hadi, and Salma Mirza. May God reward them for all their efforts.

IIIT LONDON OFFICE
Safar 1433 AH / January 2012 CE

FOREWORD

I AM VERY GLAD TO WRITE a foreword to this quite brilliant study of Anthropomorphism and Transcendence in the Bible and Qur'an. For seven years I was privileged to work closely with Zulfiqar Ali Shah as supervisor of the doctoral thesis on which this book is based. Both I, and colleagues who shared with me in the task of supervision were deeply impressed by the thoroughness of Dr. Shah's research and the range of scholarship covered. All three examiners spoke in the highest terms of his thesis and I am delighted that it will now be available to other scholars.

The book contains a thorough overview of Jewish understandings of the authority and significance of the Torah and of the later writings which make up the Hebrew Bible. It covers both Orthodox and Reformed perspectives and ranges across the centuries.

Christian understandings of the New Testament are treated with equal care and the book contains a careful study of the development of Christian doctrine leading up to the Councils of Nicea and Chalcedon as well as exploring modern attempts to reinterpret the classical doctrinal statements.

The Qur'an is equally thoroughly discussed as one would expect from a person who not only learned to recite it by heart as a child, but who has subsequently gone on to academic work in Islamic and Religious Studies in Pakistan, Britain and the USA.

The great virtue of this book is that it is fair to each of the traditions that it covers. All claims made are carefully documented both by reference to the original sources and to academic debates about them. A powerful case is made that belief in the unity and transcendence of God is better safeguarded in the Qur'anic tradition than in the earlier scriptures where an anthropomorphic understanding of God is often presented in the Hebrew Bible and in traditional understandings of Christology.

As a Christian theologian I would wish to argue that within contemporary Christianity anthropomorphism is often criticized and that appeal can also be made to apophatic, mystical and analogical interpretations of classical doctrines which seek to avoid anthropomorphic understandings. However, I have to acknowledge that Zulfiqar Ali Shah succeeds in showing that this is not the most natural reading of the scriptures themselves nor the most natural understanding of the Christological doctrines derived from them.

This is a challenging book which Jewish, Christian, and Islamic scholars will all benefit from reading.

THE REV. DR. PAUL BADHAM

Professor of Theology and Religious Studies
University of Wales, Lampeter

PREFACE

IN RESPONSE TO THE CREATION STORY found in the Bible someone once quipped, "God created humans in his image and then humans turned around and returned the favor." That there is great truth in this aphorism is well demonstrated by Dr. Zulfiqar Ali Shah's magisterial study of the tendencies toward anthropomorphism and transcendence in the Jewish, Christian, and Islamic theological traditions. Encyclopedic in scope and fastidious in its documentation, Dr. Shah has produced a definitive work that thoroughly and comprehensively engages the human tendency to on the one hand conceive of a God who is transcendent, omnipotent, and wholly other than humans, but on the other to portray this God using all means of anthropomorphic attribution. From the God of the biblical Old Testament who walks, talks, and expresses a full range of human emotions to the Christian assertion that God was incarnated in human form to the theological struggles between the Muʿtazilites and Ashʿarites, the difficulty of talking about a transcendent deity in anything other than anthropomorphic terms has been a central issue for all three Abrahamic faiths.

But this is more than just a theological conundrum. The ability (and even the necessity) to anthropomorphize God has too often gone beyond the mere attempt to talk about God and has instead led to a disturbing tendency to enlist God in support of human agendas and prejudices, and this latter with ethically disastrous results. The very human God of the Old Testament who favors one nation over all others authorizes the wanton slaughter of the indigenous Canaanites under the leadership of Joshua in history's first-recorded genocide simply because the Canaanites happen to be living on land God had promised to his chosen people, a paradigm that plays out again in early American history as largely Christian European colonialists begin making an appeal to the biblical conquest narrative as a source of divine authorization to remove the indigenous inhabitants of North America from the new "promised land" in the doctrine known as Manifest Destiny. Of course, recent history should not be ignored in this regard as God has become enlisted as the pre-eminent supporter of an aggressive U.S. foreign policy designed to extend western hegemony over many parts of the world – not the least of which are the oil-rich lands of the Middle East – via the deployment of "shock and awe" military campaigns. And in some cases those reacting to the effects of these policies (though they undoubtedly have legitimate grievances) have enlisted God in support of spectacular displays of violence. These examples could be multiplied many times over but the problem is clear. When one talks about God in human terms it is all-too-easy to enlist God in support of human concerns.

So while it may not be possible to engage in meaningful God-talk without resorting to anthropomorphic categories, we must try to resist the tendency to fully reduce God to human form and thereby invert the divine/human relationship by "recreating God in our image." Interestingly, the Islamic tradition might do this the best with its overt rejection of Christian incarnational theology – perhaps the supreme example of anthropomorphism – and Islam's emphasis on utter human submission to the will of an overarching divine unity. It appears to me that one of the motivating factors behind Islamic thinking is the attempt to restore the divine/human relationship to its proper structure – humans living according to the divine plan, not God supporting human agendas.

I recently heard a Methodist pastor preach a sermon on a day that was being celebrated as Trinity Sunday in the Christian liturgical calendar. Preaching such a sermon was a difficult prospect for this pastor because she is an avowedly non-Trinitarian Christian. Feeling compelled, however, to address the doctrine of the Trinity, she said that she interpreted the trinitarian concept to be nothing more than an assertion of God's greatness and magnitude, that God is more than or greater than what can be conceived in a single concept. After the service I approached her and with tongue in cheek congratulated her on having become a Muslim. Shocked at my comment, she replied, "What did I say?!" I responded that her metaphorical rather than literal understanding of the meaning of the Trinity was not very different from the Muslim assertion of *Allāhu akbar* (God is greater than...). As she thought about this she seemed rather willing to accept a Muslim (if not Muslim) identity. More importantly, she understood the inherent problem with conceiving of God too much within human terms.

In a world of violence and injustice, much of it perpetrated in the name of God, perhaps the way forward is by coming to recognize the level to which we humans have for millennia been recreating God in our image and allow this to motivate us to work to restore the divine/human relationship to its proper place. This will not happen without first understanding how we got to where we are today. Dr. Shah has done us all a great service by providing us with the most comprehensive history ever written on the development of the tension between anthropomorphism and transcendence in the Jewish, Christian, and Islamic traditions. We will be well served by knowing this rich, complex, and fascinating history as we struggle to move forward toward a brighter future.

ROBERT F. SHEDINGER

Associate Professor of Religion
Luther College, Decorah, IA

INTRODUCTION

THIS BOOK IS THE CULMINATION of a long and complex journey, full of the twists and turns that make up the narrative of life. I was born into a conservative Muslim family in which the words Allah (SWT),* Muhammad (ṢAAS)** and the Qur'an were highly revered and held deeply sacred. Pushed to memorize the Arabic text of the Qur'an at a young age, without incidentally understanding a word of it, it increasingly seemed to me by the time I reached middle school, that the words Allah, Qur'an, and Muhammad were an impediment to my fun, and gradually a clear sense of resentment began to present itself in my mind. These frustrations became compounded as I entered my teen years and the passions of youth began to assert themselves. I felt that Allah was too intrusive, Muhammad rather invasive, and that Islamic manners were a hindrance to my freedom and autonomy.

College afforded the freedom I so deeply longed for. But, just as every action has an equal and opposite reaction, so it was in my case, as this new found freedom caused the pendulum of religion to swing during these heady college years firmly in the other direction. At this time I had somehow fallen into the habit of watching western movies, which opened a whole new horizon for me, and not surprisingly levels of fascination with the Western world and its civilization and values, grew swiftly. And just as the fragmented Muslim society of Pakistan, I surmised, was the product of Islamic religion, likewise, I reasoned, Western civilization must have been the product of

---

*(SWT) – *Subḥānahu wa Taʿālā*: May He be praised and may His transcendence be affirmed. Said when referring to God.

**(ṢAAS) – *Ṣallā Allāhu ʿalayhi wa sallam.* May the peace and blessings of God be upon him. Said whenever the name of Prophet Muhammad is mentioned.

Christianity and Judaism. This new found love and sheer appreciation for Western civilization brought me exuberantly to the doors of the only Catholic Church that stood on the college premises. There I met its gentle priest who presented me with a copy of the Holy Bible and offered the 'Jesus solution' as the ticket to salvation and Paradise. Now, the Bible was quite different from the Qur'an both in its language, style and exhortations and to me it felt more like a storybook with real people, genealogies, dates, places and history. More importantly, there was a sense of continuity, consistency and completeness *vis-à-vis* some of the prophetic stories it presented, quite familiar to me as a Muslim. Where I had been ruffled by what I perceived to be missing links, lack of historical and geographical details and continuity in the Qur'anic accounts, the Bible seemed to have filled the vacuum very well.

Then things took an interesting turn. During one of his surprise visits to my lodgings, my father happened to see a copy of the Bible lying innocuously in my room and was appalled. He began to insist that I learn the Qur'an before exploring the Bible further and enlisted the help of some family friends to try and make of me a conscious rather than a traditional Muslim. These individuals were more open than my parents to questions, discourse and debate, and the gist of their discussions revolved around the fact that Islam was the only true religion, the sole gateway to salvation and Paradise, that Christianity and Judaism were considered corrupted faiths due to the historical corruptions of their scripture, and that Christianity had utterly compromised the monotheistic legacy of the prophets by introducing a Trinitarian fallacy etc. Furthermore, how could God they very logically reasoned, be said to have a "Son" when He did not beget? How could He save humanity when He was unable to save His own "Son" from Jewish and Roman persecution? How could someone remain in the womb of their mother for nine months, be given birth to, eat, drink, have normal human needs and yet still be called God Almighty? Abraham, Isaac, Jacob, Moses and Jesus, they pointed out, were not Jewish or Christian but in reality Muslim prophets; and Islam was the only faith which God had ever revealed since the creation of Adam.

This level of debate and these forceful questions brought me to the pragmatic question of what Islam truly entails. During the discussions it appeared that for some, Islam largely revolved around acts of worship such as the five daily prayers, fasting, alms giving, Hajj, whilst for others the focus was more upon regulations such as dress codes, dietary laws, social norms, customs and values. It also seemed to me that there existed no single agreed upon definition of what Islam truly was and that in its many facets it represented everything that life had to offer but, one could not quite put one's finger on, or pinpoint exactly to, what it was. Islam I surmised was different things to different people. One of the less assertive teachers described it as the divine guidance regulating human relationships. To him, Islam denoted a voluntary submission to the commandments of Allah, the Wise, Omnipotent, Omniscient, Merciful Creator and Compassionate God, for the sake of peace in this world and eternal happiness in the life to come. He focused more upon the moral values Islam sought to inculcate, such as honesty, truthfulness, trustworthiness etc. as well as social values which it sought to promote, such as caring for and about others, fair dealing, human equality, safeguarding one's sexuality etc. moving Islam away from the realm of outward observance such as performance of the daily prayers, Qur'anic recitation, dress code or dietry restrictions to something more inwardly sacred. He summed up his differences with the others by stating that the essence of the Islamic faith was essentially human interaction, how one treated the other. Put simply treat others the way you wish to be treated. This was the overarching goal with the rest of Islamic teachings subservient to it. His seemingly benign statement startled everybody. Was Pakistan an Islamic country then? Without hesitation he declared that Pakistan was a Muslim country but not an Islamic country. Islam and Muslims were two different animals. Pakistan, he observed, needed implementation of the Islamic Shariʿah to become an Islamic state. Further, he argued, the inherited man-made laws of the old colonial empire and the modern West were the real sources of Pakistan's internal fiasco. The Qur'an if we followed it would guarantee prosperity, as well as economic, social, political and legal justice. To others his interpretation of Islam carried political overtones.

The college pre-med program was exhausting. My frustrations were intensified by the complete absence of Muslim names from the course books assigned for the various scientific disciplines under study including chemistry, biology and physics. It seemed to indicate that Muslims had made little or no contributions to modern science and technology. My curiosity about this scholarly void was often met with supernatural, spiritual, moral, epistemological and, at times, absurd answers. The golden era of the Islamic civilization was overemphasized. Or, rather strangely, it was argued that Islam was a religion of eternity, and it was more important to focus upon eternal salvation rather than the material gains of this temporal existence, Western faiths and civilization had fallen into the trap of becoming too materialistic achieving material success at the price of the hereafter etc. This seemed like a hollow excuse to me for there was too much talk about the grave and what would happen six foot under while the most pressing issues and problems of this earthly existence were conveniently being ignored. No convincing answer was given *vis-à-vis* lack of scientific development, technology, political stability and institutionalization, in Pakistan in particular and the Muslim world in general. I was introduced to a college professor of Islamic Studies to pacify my concerns.

The professor was adamant about Islam's superiority over other faiths/religions. He informed me that Muslims had ruled two thirds of the then known world for thirteen consecutive centuries. The Islamic caliphate had continued from 632 CE to 1923, when the Ottoman Caliphate, the longest continuous dynasty in human history, was formally abolished by Mustafa Kemal (Ataturk). During its golden age and at the height of its power, the Muslim world had made incredible strides in scientific knowledge and achievement and indeed all forms of knowledge, whilst pre-Renaissance Europe remained mired in fragmented city states in what was termed the dark ages. In fact, not only had Islam as a faith come as an empire but it had also come as the great herald of knowledge; a knowledge which the world had not experienced before, and which gave new life to Greek scholarship. Other extant faiths had failed in this regard. Ironically it was only when humanistic secularism held sway in Europe and after the Islamic catalyst had swept into the continent did the West develop the knowledge and expertise for which it is the envy of the world today. Whereas, it was only when Muslims had turned away from their faith, failing to abide by the teachings of the Qur'an did their era of backwardness and decline begin to take shape. So I learned that Muslims had been connoisseurs of geo-politics, law, science, philosophy and many other fields for centuries, whilst at the same time Christian Europe had been paralyzed in the quagmire of internal strife and the anti-science stance of Church dogmatism. Today's modern scientific, political and social progress was largely the result of Renaissance thought and the Enlightenment rather than Judeo-Christian religious traditions.

Renaissance thinkers were more liberals than traditional Christians and were in turn influenced by the medieval Muslim scientists and philosophers of the Islamic world, scholarly giants such as Ibn Sīnā, al-Ṭusī, Ibn Rushd and al-Fārābī. During medieval times, I was amazed to learn, Arabic had in fact been the lingua franca of science, medicine and philosophy. Scientific Arabic manuscripts had been translated into Latin and English all the way to 17th century England. Further, the majority of the American Founding Fathers such as George Washington, John Adams and Thomas Jefferson had been against traditional Christianity. They denied Jesus' divinity, did not believe in the Trinity, refused biblical inerrancy, disapproved of Church hierarchy and also questioned traditional Christian political concepts such as submission to the authorities as a religious duty. They envisioned a non-Christian, non-religious liberal United States of America with a complete wall standing between the Church and State. Many of the Founding Fathers were influenced by Roger Bacon, John Locke, Robert Boyle and other English thinkers who in turn were influenced by Muslim philosophers such as Ibn Ṭufayl, al-Fārābī and Ibn Rushd.

I came to the conclusion that the present decline of Muslims had not been due to Islam but rather their betrayal of it and that Islam cannot play second fiddle in our lives but requires sincere devotion. One of the symptoms of this decline has been the intellectual bankruptcy of Muslims as enscapulated by a centuries long stagnation in Muslim critical thinking. For far too long now the faith's religious leadership has sought to punish thinking outside of the box, without regard for the serious socio-political consequences which have resulted. Further, analytical reasoning has been replaced by mere imitation; the Shariʿah has been used as a form of control rather than a force for justice, to coerce people into socio-political conformity; and there has been a complete disconnection between the original Islamic legacy and modern Muslim institutions. Such is the state of affairs that ironically it is Muslims who now require a Renaissance/Reformation of their own reversing the present day decline, and it is the Qur'an which miraculously transformed seventh century desert Bedouins into harbingers of empire, which has the potential to bring this about. Unlike earlier and other scriptures it has remained unchanged for the last fourteen centuries. I realized that if Muslims adhered sincerely to the teachings of the Qur'an and the Qur'anic principle of using reason, then Allah would support them just as He had done so in the past.

Going back to my meeting with the Catholic priest it was interesting to note that he held an altogether different assessment of the situation. He regarded the success of the West as largely being due to Christian faith and values, while Muslim failure was seen to have been the result of the backward teachings of the Qur'an. It seemed to echo socio-political and economic realities. Further, I was told that the Christian God was a loving deity, loving enough to die for the sins of mankind, while Allah was a wrathful God, enough to punish people for small mistakes. The priest's message was a simple, easy and attractive one: accept the trinity and believe that Jesus as the Son of God died for your sins, and you will receive salvation and be saved for eternity. The Christian road to Paradise seemed a lot easier than the Islamic one! I was perplexed for years. For further exploration of the subject, I joined the International Islamic University in Islamabad, a newly established institution whose patron was the then (now late) President of Pakistan, General M. Ziaul Haq.

The University had a diverse international faculty with specializations ranging from Qur'anic Exegesis, Hadith Sciences, theology, philosophy, comparative religions, law, Arabic language and much more. The higher level World Religions courses, led to theological discussions and term papers which brought old memories of the Catholic priest to the surface. I now perceived that Christian theology and views on salvation were not that simple or as straightforward as I had originally imagined. For a start, the historical aspects of Christian scripture and Christian dogma were fairly complex and convoluted. The triune conception of the Deity, the Chalcedonian formula of Jesus being a perfect man and a perfect God, the two nature theories of Jesus, the simultaneously Almighty Creator and mercilessly crucified Jesus, all such fundamental Christian concepts now appeared utterly confusing. In stark contrast, the history of Islamic scripture and the Islamic God paradigm seemed simple, straightforward and logical. Had the priest oversimplified Christian theology, or had the course book authors missed the mark? Were the Muslim professors showing bias concerning Christian and Jewish theological discourses? A sense of objectivity, my appreciation for Western civilization, and a respect for the gentle priest demanded that I find out for myself. I decided to take a different route i.e. through understanding Christianity from believing Christians rather than outsiders. I established contact with the leadership of an influential Church in Islamabad.

This priest was far more educated, articulate and daring. To him, the Church came before the scriptures, selecting the very books of the Christian New Testament. One would be at a loss, he stated, to understand, comprehend or truly believe the scriptures without the help of the Church, its traditions and teachings. Further, important terms such as the "trinity", "Divine Person or Persons" and the "Divine Substance" were not scriptural terminologies. They had been introduced to Christian thought by the Church Councils in conformity with the spirit of the scriptures. There were three co-equal, co-eternal, autonomous "Persons" in the Godhead but, God was One. Likewise, acceptance of Jesus was a precondition to understanding the Christian mysteries such as the Trinity, divine persons and nature, as well as the necessary corollaries to it.

These lengthy and contorted commentaries left me confused and impatient. How could I believe in something so incomprehensible I asked? God was unknowable, mysterious and arcane, replied the priest. Why did the Old Testament not mention Jesus' incarnation or the triune God even once? The answer was labyrinthine. The Old Testament addressed Jesus with the title "Lord"; the Trinity was meant whenever God used the plural "us" i.e. "Let us make man" etc.; God the Father was transcendent; it was God the Son who appeared to Abraham, who ate and drank, who wrestled with Jacob, rested and was refreshed, incidents the Old Testament mentions in relation to God. The theophanous and anthropomorphic passages of the Old Testament were proofs of Jesus' incarnation. And, the Old Testament "I AM" statements were proofs of Jesus' divinity. His crucifixion and resurrection proved that Jesus was God Almighty. Jesus reconciled humanity with God. He paid with his blood for our sins. The theological complexities were compounding with every additional question, discussion and meeting that was held.

Islamabad was host to an annual book fair which drew people from all over. There I came across a group of missionaries, mostly physicians from the USA. They were Protestants with a visible preference for the scriptures over the Church. Their God consisted of the three independent "Persons", each one of them equally and eternally God, the three autonomous modes of existence, consciousness and will united in the essence. It seemed as if there were three equal gods and the Godhead was an aggregate of them. One of them differed with the others and insisted that it was the same one God coming in different modes: Father, Son and the Holy Spirit. The variety of their biblical interpretations regarding the Christian God paradigm was quite obvious. The Bible was the inerrant Word of God to some, inspired not inerrant to others and divinely inspired but culturally conditioned to the few. Such an obvious difference of opinion regarding the fundamental doctrinal issues, among an otherwise congenial group of missionaries, was truly amazing. Consult the theologians and not the preachers, was their sincere advice to me. The group graciously put me in touch with a Protestant theologian.

During my Master's at IIUI, I concentrated mostly upon the comparative study of Jewish, Christian and Islamic theology. The program also exposed me to some international conferences on world religions. I was lucky to meet with Professor Houston Smith and Professor Ninian Smart during one of these conferences in Rome. My theological instincts were enthusiastically encouraged and appreciated by Professor Smith. As a competent teacher, he simplified for me many complicated theological concepts in a matter of a few hours. To my surprise, he was quite uncomfortable about traditional Christian theology especially in its incarnation garb and hesitated delving deeply into it. He proved to be a Christian without conventional Christianity, and further promised to help me with admission to some leading theological programs in the US; with his recommendations, I obtained acceptance letters from Harvard Divinity School, Pennsylvania University's Religious Studies program and some other schools.

Meanwhile I had joined IIUI's Comparative Religions department as a full time lecturer. The university's study leave formalities for a new employee were quite stringent. While in the final preparations of my intended travel, I was suddenly involved in a life threatening car accident. The impact of a head on collision left me paralyzed from the neck down with multiple injuries all over my body. Unable to move any part of my body except the head I was left wondering about my destiny. The long months of complete helplessness, sheer dependence upon others, and a sense of total despair brought me face to face with the ultimate questions I had hitherto shrugged off. What was this life all about? Where did I come from? What was the purpose of my existence? Who was directing my life affairs? Where was I headed to? What was true happiness?

Mostly staring at the roof in a lonely hospital room, I was left to ponder upon these painful realities. Many worthy and unworthy thoughts crossed my mind during these long tiring months. Why would Allah, the Most Merciful and Compassionate, strike me with such a dismantling blow? How could I beseech Him to give me another chance by curing me of this disability? The doctors had already indicated that my spinal cord injury could be life threatening. Was it a result of me not searching for the true God? Could Jesus be the true God and save me at this difficult juncture of my life? Whom should I call to? God the Father whom Jesus cried to on the Cross or Jesus himself? What could the Holy Spirit do for me now? There were times when these mere thoughts bothered me a great deal. I felt that I was committing *shirk* by associating partners with the One and Only Allah, the true Master.

This was also a time of deep reflection upon the realities of life. What about my degrees, accounts, articles and everything else that I had cared so much about? Were they of any use to me now? All the modern theories of the origins of religion and God, discussions on atheism, agnosticism, relativism, pragmatism and skepticism etc. at once became utterly irrelevant. Suddenly the issue of life after death became of great interest. I sincerely promised to myself and God that I would truly search for the meanings if given the chance.

After almost two years of a slow but miraculous recovery I was finally able to stand up and walk. In spite of some health challenges, my life started getting back to normal. By now the TOEFL and GRE scores, university admissions and visa papers were outmoded. I applied to Saint David's University College, University of Wales, mostly because of its strong theology program and teaching opportunities. The academic environment at the University of Wales was quite different to that of the academic institutes in Pakistan, with a different teaching methodology, research tools, approaches and processes. There was openness, boldness, fairness and objectivity. Further, faith as such was in a more dramatic climate of suspicion, attacks and bewilderment than initially envisaged. It was clear that organized Christianity had become visibly weakened while the traditional notions of God were fast disappearing. The God Who was very much with me, was radically absent from the society at large, at least so it seemed to me. The gulf between the sacred and the profane was quite wide. The dichotomous bifurcation of faith and reality and a personal sense of loss and alienation were quite apparent. After the initial cultural shock and a few months' work with an advisor, I transferred my work to a Professor Paul Badham, an accomplished author and a renowned Christian theologian. This scholarly soul made it clear to me from the outset that objectivity (not subjectivity) would be the ruling standard. No claims were to be made without proper documentation and substantiation. Scholarly Jewish and Christian sources were to be depended upon while addressing issues connected with these traditions, and respectable Western sources were to be explored while discussing matters related to the Qur'an and its God paradigm. This methodology was essential to shun any possibility of suspicions of bias, prejudice and bigotry. This was what the sensitive nature of the subject demanded. Professor John Kelsay of Florida State University, a profuse author and an expert on Islam, was requested to co-supervise the thesis which he readily accepted. I was extremely pleased that Professor Ian Richard Netton, Head of the Department of Arabic and Middle Eastern Studies at the University of Leeds, chaired the viva committee as the external examiner. Professor Netton, originally of Jewish origins, was a prolific writer on a variety of Islamic subjects such as philosophy, theology, Sufism, Arabic and Islamic bibliography, comparative textuality and semiotics. It added a great deal to the validity and significance of my work.

This book is the result of seven long years of research, discussions, debates and friendly fire engagements. In the first chapter I discuss the problems of atheism, skepticism and anthropomorphism, give an account of the historical background and define the relevant categories. The second chapter traces issues related to the authenticity, authority, textual purity and validity of the Hebrew Bible, and the Christian Old Testament. It continues by exploring the transcendental and anthropomorphic tendencies contained within the text of the Hebrew Bible with some significant discussions of the same in Rabbinic theology. The third chapter explores some of the crucial points related to the origins, compilation, canonization, authority, authenticity, reliability and textual purity of the New Testament. The crux of the chapter deals with the multiple Christologies which exist, i.e., the New Testament theologies and their historical development. It culminates in some contemporary traditional as well as liberal interpretations of Christology. The fourth chapter delves into several significant and controversial matters connected with the historical authenticity, authority and purity of the Qur'anic text. It culminates in an excursion into the transcendental and anthropomorphic tendencies in the Qur'an. It also explores some of the main Islamic sects in relation to their anthropomorphic, literal or metaphorical dispositions. The book ends with a conclusion and bibliography.

It is my fervent wish that this study generates positive scholastic and general debate and dialogue between followers of the three Semitic traditions. These traditions enjoy many commonalities with some fundamental distinctions. These distinctions represent the variety of perspectives, historical contexts, cultural settings and realities which they have faced over the centuries. These distinctions must not be ignored but discussed with a sense of understanding and composure to enhance mutual respect, appreciation, coexistence and tolerance. Such dialogue and debate could spell the return of the Abrahamic God to the consciousness of modern alienated man, who is sorely in need of God's moral commandments and spiritual guidance.

I would like to sincerely thank Fr. Phil Reifenberg and Rabbi Marc Berkson of Milwaukee, WI, for their valuable suggestions, observations and comments. I would also like to thank the International Institute of Islamic Thought (IIIT) for making this publication possible. My sincere gratitude also goes to Tahira Hadi of IIIT London Office for her thorough copyediting of a cumbersome text and to Riyad al-Yemani for his professional support. I would finally like to express my earnest thanks and gratitude to Shiraz Khan for her wonderful contributions to this work. I am indebted to her in so many ways. This work would have not been what it is without her countless efforts.

ZULFIQAR ALI SHAH

Milwaukee, Wi, October 21, 2010

CHAPTER I

Anthropomorphism: Background, Criticism and Defining Categories

"IS GOD DEAD?" asked *Time* magazine in its April 8, 1960 issue. Yes, "God is dead," responded three American scholars: Thomas Altizer of Emory University in Atlanta, William Hamilton of Colgate-Rochester Divinity School, and Paul Van Buren of Temple University. This bold response to a very extraordinary question proved to be the birth of what is known as "The Death of God" school, a movement marking one culmination of a centuries old study into the existence and nature of the "Transcendent God" of theism.

This chapter examines the claimed origins of religion and the rise of anthropomorphism: its ancient connotations, its historical development down the centuries, and what it has meant to followers of different faiths, as well as to philosophers, scholars and theologians. I am deeply indebted to Stewart Guthrie, Professor Emeritus of Anthropology, Fordham University, New York, a world authority on anthropomorphism, whose work I draw heavily upon in this chapter. Also examined will be the various levels of criticism directed towards its application to God, where it collides with corporealism, incarnation and mystical interpretation, and where it has been considered appropriate to use in reference to 'knowing' God, strictly qualified of course and hemmed in by carefully defined parameters.

Confident sounding claims concerning the death of God are neither unusual nor are they new. For centuries, philosophers, intellectuals, and scientists have viewed the theistic conception of God as too confusing, complicated and indeed inconsequential, arguing that the idea of a transcendental God and his institutions have become irrelevant to man and his surroundings. This postulation is implied in many philosophical and scientific writings. In the relatively modern age, to speak of "the death of God" is to invoke the name of Friedrich Nietzsche (1844–1900), famed German philosopher and nihilist, who stated these very words at the end of the nineteenth century. Writing on the various stages of development which ultimately led man – in Europe anyway – to the shared cultural belief that God was dead, Nietzsche first pointed to the many gods worshipped by ancient humanity. These in turn gave way to the jealous, biblical God of the Old Testament who declares, "There is but one God! Thou shalt have no other gods before me!" All the other gods, wrote Nietzsche, then laughed and shook upon their thrones, exclaiming an interesting secret: "Is it not just divinity that there are Gods, but no God?"[1] expiring from their laughter.

The multiple deities of ancient times, according to Nietzsche, connected usefully with human needs or natural forces. The one God who replaced them however, transcended human will and was too intrusive, disturbing, and involved in human affairs. This God, wrote Nietzsche "beheld everything I use, and also man: that God had to die! Man cannot endure that such a witness should live."[2] Commenting on Nietzsche's observations, religious ethics scholar Paul Ramsey explains that such a conception of God "was too much God with us, God in human, all-too-human form. He mixed too much in human affairs, even manifesting himself in this miserable flesh. In a sense, God's fellow-humanity killed him." Furthermore, "After the gods made in man's image, the God who proposed to make and remake man in his own image, that God too had to die."[3]

So, this "death of God" solution was necessary to liberate man from the unlimited restrictions, or so-called religious interpretations of man and the universe, imposed in the name of God upon the scientific and cultural products of men. This death, wrote German-Jewish philosopher Karl Löwith, "demands of the man who wills himself, to whom no God says what he must do, that he transcend man at the same time as he is freed from God."[4] This view considered men as autonomous and unlimited creators of their culture and destiny. Whereas in the past humanity would accomplish this task by projecting its fears and aspirations into the cosmos through the creation of gods, now it achieves this autonomy through science and philosophy. In other words, science and rationalism have effectively killed God removing the need for Him in the development of human culture and activity. So important is this line of thought that it is the belief of James C. Livingston, a scholar of modern religious thought, that the outcome of this development has been "the death of the ultimate ground and support of all traditional values. For over two thousand years men have derived their 'thou shalt' and 'thou shalt not' from God, but that is now coming to an end."[5]

In poetic and prophetic terms, Nietzsche meant to represent the numerous critics of a theistic understanding of God, who for many centuries had asserted that the traditional, official, and transcendent God of theism had lost authority over the world and His usefulness to it. "In man the consciousness of an ultimate in the traditional sense has died."[6] Meaning that the God who once upon a time was worshipped as Creator of the universe, was no longer accepted as such and so regarded as neither the Creator of man nor his surroundings. Ironically, it was man who now created God, in his, that is man's, own image.

Projection theories or claims concerning the human origins of notions relating to the divine are not recent. They can be traced back to the Greek philosopher-poet Xenophanes (570–470 BC), around six hundred years before Jesus Christ. Criticizing the anthropomorphism of Homer and Hesiod in their portrayal of gods, Xenophanes wrote:

> if oxen (and horses) and lions...could draw with hands and create works of art like those made by men, horses would draw pictures of gods like horses, and oxen of gods like oxen...Aethiopians have gods with snub noses and black hair, Thracians have gods with gray eyes and red hair.[7]

It has long been claimed that the origins of religion and the worship of gods has stemmed from man's inner desires as well as attempts to explain and control the natural environment around him, particularly its disturbing and puzzling phenomena. In the words of Cicero, "In this medley of conflicting opinions, one thing is certain. Though it is possible that they are all of them false, it is impossible that more than one of them is true."[8] The "Awe," according to Cicero, evoked in man by terrifying natural phenomena and attempts to comprehend a greater power, was pivotal in helping to produce conflicting religious opinions and images of the divine.

Writing in the fifteenth century, Francis Bacon (1561–1626), virtually substantiated Cicero's observations by noting that human understanding relied upon causes that related "clearly to the nature of man rather than to the nature of the universe." These significant observations were hallmarks of a new era: the era of science. Bacon, regarded by many as the leading philosopher of modern science and a prophet of empiricism, maintained that man anthropomorphizes. Under the now famous heading "idols and false notions"[9] he classified anthropomorphism into four separate kinds: idols of the tribe, cave, marketplace, and theater. Bacon believed that tribal idols were based on the

> false assumption that the sense of man is the measure of things. On [the] contrary, all perceptions as well of the sense as of the mind are according to the measure of the individual and not according to the measure of the universe. And human understanding is like a false mirror, which, receiving rays irregularly, distorts and discolors the nature of things by mingling its own nature with it.[10]

Bacon held that human perceptions depend on and are motivated by human feelings. He pinpointed to the human tendency to anthropomorphize as a fundamental weakness of the human thought process, and its major stumbling block.

In the sixteenth century, French writer Bernard Fontenelle (1657–1757), renewed the old Ciceriаn approach by proposing a universal evolutionary framework for the development of human thought and culture. Fontenelle believed that even the most ancient and crude centuries had had their philosophers. And these ancient philosophers had used the same anthropomorphic method as ours to explain the unseen and unknown by recourse to the seen and known, though they had used crude images and metaphors vastly different from our sophisticated technological symbols and images. Fontenelle stated that, "This philosophy of the first centuries revolved on a principle so natural that even today our philosophy has none other...we explain... unknown natural things by those which we have before our eyes, and that we carry over to natural science...those things furnished us by experience."[11]

Natural forces beyond human control lead people to imagine beings that are more powerful than themselves, able to significantly affect human lives and destinies. Furthermore, the very diversity of natural forces explains the multitude of primitive divinities worshipped, these gods the products of human thought and circumstances being thus anthropomorphic in nature. Therefore, the nature as well as qualities and attributes of these gods, change accordingly with changes in human thought pattern and culture. Primitive people ascribed rudimentary attributes to their gods i.e. physical bodies, corporeal attributes and crude anthropomorphic qualities. The more educated and sophisticated groups likewise described their gods in more developed forms and categories i.e. love, compassion, spiritual existence and transcendentalism. Hence, the conception of a god or gods in any given society reflected that society's culture and sophistication.

Seventeenth-century philosopher Benedict de Spinoza (1632–1677) followed Bacon in criticizing the human tendency of anthropocentrism and anthropomorphism. He regarded our perceptions of the world as extending from our views regarding ourselves. As we do things for certain ends, we perceive nature working for specific ends. Yet when humans "cannot learn such causes from external causes," Spinoza wrote, "they are compelled to turn to considering themselves, and reflecting what end would have induced them personally to bring about the given event, and thus they necessarily judge other natures by their own."[12] Therefore, gods and other transcendental beings are simply the mere creation of human imagination. They are seen to exist only in the imaginative world of man.

David Hume (1711–1776), Scottish philosopher and economist, pioneered this line of approach in the modern age. He provided a more detailed account of the anthropomorphic nature of the divine. According to his thinking, notions about the divine did not spring from reason but from the natural uncertainties of life and out of fear of the future. The resulting invented divine entity provided man with a framework of meaning boosting his confidence against uncertainty related anxieties and concerns for happiness. As a result, man was allowed to feel an artificial sense of orderliness and security in a world full of disorderliness and insecurities. Viewing the idea of God in evolutionary terms, Hume rejected the theory of an original monotheism and considered the earliest form of religion to be idolatry or polytheism; the origin of the idea of God resulted as man personified his hopes and fears into the cosmos, then worshipped gods created in his own image.

After placing the world of ideas in the realm of human experience and impressions, Hume argued that even refined and abstract ideas of the divine or God sprang only from human senses and experiences. Man's worries about the uncertainties of the future included

> the anxious concern for happiness, the dread of future misery, the terror of death, the thirst for revenge, the appetite for food and other necessaries. Agitated by hopes and fears of this nature, especially the latter, men scrutinize, with trembling curiosity, the course of future causes, and examine the various and contrary events of human life.[13]

This sheer anxiety leads humanity to imagine and formulate ideas about powers governing them: "These unknown causes, then, become the constant object of our hope and fear; and while the passions are kept in perpetual alarm by an anxious expectation of the events, the imagination is equally employed in forming ideas of those powers, on which we have so entire a dependence."[14]

This anthropomorphic tendency of modeling all unknown powers after familiar human categories is the foundational source of man's belief in the divine. Neither is it limited to primitive man but is also the case for modern believers who like his ancestors, harbors the same tendencies. Ask any contemporary believer

> why he believes in an omnipotent creator of the world; he will never mention the beauty of final causes, of which he is wholly ignorant: He will not hold out his hand, and bid you contemplate the suppleness and variety of joints in his fingers, their bending all one way...To these he has been long accustomed; and he beholds

> them with listlessness and unconcern. He will tell you of the sudden and unexpected death of such a one: The fall and bruise of such another: The excessive drought of this season: The cold and rains of another. This he ascribes to the immediate operation of providence: And such events, as, with good reasoners, are the chief difficulties in admitting a supreme intelligence, are with him the sole arguments for it.[15]

David Hume placed this anthropomorphic principle that originated with Xenophanes in a systematically coherent epistemological context. His analysis guides and serves as a point of reference for many modern scholars of religious philosophy and sociology who share his assumptions: Auguste Comte, Ludwig Feuerbach, Edward Tylor, Sigmund Freud, Thomas De Quincy, Robert Browning, Matthew Arnold, Gerard Manley Hopkins, Emily Brontë, Jean-Paul Sartre, Maurice Merleau Ponty, Albert Camus, A.J. Ayer, and E. D. Klemke, for example.

Auguste Marie Francois Comte (1798–1857), the father of modern sociology, rejected like Hume and other modern philosophers and idealists, transcendental metaphysics and theology. Emphasizing the intimate relationship that existed between ideas and society and the evolutionary nature of human thought, Comte applied his Law of the Three Stages (theological, metaphysical, and positive related to societal development) to human religious thought: the theological-military, the metaphysical-feudal, and the positive-industrial. Comte located the idea of the divine in the first and primitive stage (theological) of mankind. He further subdivided this age into three main periods, i.e.: fetichism, polytheism, and monotheism. The first stage "allowed free exercise to that tendency of our nature by which man conceives of all external bodies as animated by a life analogous to his own, with difference of mere intensity."[16] Its motive, as Hume already observed, was to try to apprehend and make some sense of unknown effects. After the idea originated in the anthropomorphic nature of mankind, it developed into polytheism, passing through the Egyptian, Greek, Roman, and Judaic cultures, to reach the third stage to become modified into monotheism.[17]

Many scholars do not originate certain ideas, but expand upon already existing one, and as a result, are distinguished by their profound influence on the history of subsequent thought. They provide other genius writers with the spark that, in the words of Isaiah Berlin, "sets on fire the long-accumulated fuel."[18] Ludwig Feuerbach (1804–1872) German philosopher, anthropologist and atheist, was one such scholar. Feuerbach developed what he termed the true anthropological essence of religion and gods to its ultimate dimension, and provided philosophers like Marx and Engels with many crucial and seminal ideas. Engels proclaimed himself a Feuerbachian after reading Feuerbach's *Essence of Christianity*: "One must himself have experienced the liberating effect of this book to get an idea of it," he wrote.[19] Richard Wagner saw in Feuerbach "the ideal exponent of the radical release of the individual."[20] Karl Marx, perhaps rightly, marveled that Feuerbach's work "consists in the dissolution of the religious world into its secular basis...[resolving] the religious essence into the human."[21]

Feuerbach noted that "What distinguishes man from the brutes is the awareness of a distinctive human nature transcending individuality." Man has reason, will, and affection, yet man cannot escape his nature: "Not even in our imagination can we transcend human nature; and to the 'higher' beings in which we believe we can attribute nothing better than human characteristics." Therefore, the "religious object of adoration is nothing but the objectified nature of him who adores,"[22] because

> the object of a subject is nothing else than this subject's own nature objectified. Such are a man's thoughts and moral character, such is his God; so much worth as man has, so much and no more has his God. Man's being conscious of God is man's being conscious of himself, knowledge of God is man's knowledge of himself. By their God you know men, and by knowing men you know their god; the two are identical. God is the manifested inward nature, the expressed self of man; religion is the solemn unveiling of man's hidden treasures, the revelation of his most intimate thoughts, the open confession of what he secretly loves.[23]

Feuerbach further argued that if divine predicates are merely anthropomorphic as is often observed, then the subject of them is also merely an anthropomorphism. Human attributes such as love, goodness, and personality are also attributed to the existing God. These attributions, as well as the very belief there is a God, are also anthropomorphisms. Furthermore, God is the highest concept humans could possibly attain.[24] In Feuerbach's doctrine, "*Theology is anthropology*... the object of religion, which in Greek we call *theos* and in our language God, expresses nothing other than the deified essence of man, so that the history of religion... is nothing other than the history of man."[25]

Feuerbach, like Hume and others, maintained that the idea of God originated in human needs, desires, wishes, and shortcomings in life: "The foundation of religion is a feeling of dependency; the first object of that feeling is nature; thus nature is the first object of religion." By projecting his feelings onto natural phenomena, man creates his own gods and then worships them. Therefore, "To live in projected dream-images is the essence of religion. Religion sacrifices reality to the projected dream: the 'Beyond' is merely the 'Here' reflected in the mirror of imagination."[26] Also like Hume, Feuerbach viewed religion as anthropomorphism but differed from him in that he located it in the inner self of man rather than in the external world around him. By promises of a better life in the hereafter, argued Feuerbach, religion provides people "an escape mechanism, which prevents men from going after a better life in a straight line. Religion is as bad as opium."[27] A phrase later echoed by Marx.

Feuerbach's anthropomorphic interpretations of religion render religious thought as mere wishful thinking, a means of human self-consciousness and childish error. In other words, religion stems from man's cognitive confusion and not from a supra-terrestrial transcendent being called God. Feuerbach concludes that man comes first and God ranks second. Therefore religions must recognize this historical and ethical reality. "*Homo homini Deus est*–man's God is Man. This is the highest law of ethics. THIS IS THE TURNING POINT OF WORLD HISTORY."[28]

No doubt Feuerbach's interpretations of the divine and religion resulted in a turning point in subsequent influential philosophical thinking. Karl Marx followed Feuerbach's thesis but replaced Feuerbach's "man" with "society and state," declaring religion to be "the imaginative realization of the human essence, because that essence has no true reality...It is the opium of the people."[29]

In the nineteenth century, Charles Darwin's newly developed theory of natural selection also touched upon religion, refuting the traditional theistic view of God as the Creator and Designer, and nature as the manifestation of purpose, design, and immutability. This, according to American botanist Asa Gray, was an "atheistical" step.[30] Adam Sedgwick, one of the founders of modern geology, a former teacher of Darwin, and a man of faith, whilst also stating that he roared with laughter at parts of Darwin's work, criticized Darwin, writing to him that, "It is the crown and glory of organic science that it does, through final cause, link material to moral...You have ignored this link... you have done your best...to break it. Were it possible (which, thank God, it is not) to break it, humanity, in my mind, would suffer a damage that might brutalize it, and sink the human race into a lower grade of degradation than any into which it has fallen since its written records tell us of its history."[31]

In the *Descent of Man*, Darwin theorized that "The Simiadae then branched off into two great stems, the New World and Old World monkeys; and from the latter, at a remote period, Man, the wonder and glory of the Universe, proceeded."[32] He emphatically advocated an evolutionary theory of human and cosmic origins. Such an interpretation of man and his universe certainly countered orthodox metaphysics.[33]

Biblical metaphysics is based on the concept of a loving God who created man in a unique fashion. The Christian worldview revolves around the concept of a fallen human nature, divine intervention through atoning sacrifice, and resultant redemption through the crucifixion and resurrection of Jesus Christ. Darwin's worldview and interpretation of nature as autonomous, self-directing, and evolutionary undermined the traditional Christian worldview more than the scientific revolutions of Copernicus, Galileo, and Newton. Darwin's theories challenged and effectively shook the foundations of Christian metaphysics. With Darwin's evolutionism, every need for a God as the original source of creation and the sole maintainer of this universe ceased to exist. If creation was regarded as having evolved naturally from primitive origins and to be constantly evolving through the process of natural selection without any external divine intervention, then it stood to reason that God was not required for its existence, sustenance and continuity.

Evolutionary theory became extremely popular in almost all other disciplines aside from biology. It caused uproar in religious circles and not surprisingly, received a heated response from theologians. Despite opposition from religious establishments, evolutionary theory became the guiding principle in all leading disciplines of the nineteenth century. And in terms of God, the result was monumental, for empirical scientists, anthropologists, philologists, psychologists, sociologists, and naturalists of the time broke the moral theological link between this utilitarian sphere and a heavenly God. Instead they searched for God in this their own world: in nature, the human soul, the psyche, and human society. All of them, almost unanimously, were able to locate God in the human experience: i.e., in the mental process by which man acquires ideas and is influenced by his emotions. "We cannot take a step towards constructing an idea of God," argued H. Spencer, the famous nineteenth century anthropologist, "without the ascription of human attributes."[34]

Edward Tylor (1823–1917), considered by many to be the founder of the science of social anthropology, advocated an evolutionary/developmental rather than a degradation theory of religion. Traditional theistic scholars have all along argued that the original stage in religious thinking had been that of monotheism; polytheism being the result of a degradation of human religious thought. Tylor argued that it was the other way around. Recognizing the survival of earlier cultural elements in new cultures, Tylor defined these elements as "processes, customs, opinions...carried on by force of habit into a new state of society...and they thus remain as proofs and examples of an older condition of culture out of which a newer has been evolved." Tylor propounded a plausible theory of "animism," in which "the conception of the human soul is the very '*fons et origo*' of the conception of the spirit and deity in general."[35] Animism, to Tylor, was the primary formation of religious beliefs that developed into modern higher forms of religion. He argued that such a belief stemmed from man's efforts to explain dream experiences and the phenomenon of death. Tylor believed that animism of the lower tribes could have easily continued had man not risen from his savage conditions. Therefore, instead of a lofty divine origin, religious phenomenon had rather originated in the confused cognitive experiences of primitive savages only later developing into higher forms such as polytheism, henotheism, and monotheism.

French sociologist Emile Durkheim (1858–1917) and Austrian father of psychoanalysis Sigmund Freud (1856–1939) agreed with Tylor that religion was no longer "true" in the literal sense of the statements it made about the world and gods. They also agreed that human beings anthropomorphize, and that religion results from this process. However they disagreed with Tylor that religion originated in mere speculation. Freud argued that men were not inspired to create their first system of the universe by pure speculative curiosity. The practical need for controlling the world around them must have played its part. Instead, "Animism came to primitive man naturally and as a matter of course... primitive man transposed the structural conditions of his own mind into the external world."[36] It is our responsibility to "ask where the inner force of those doctrines lies and to what it is that they owe their efficacy, independent as it is of recognition by reason."[37] Durkheim thought religion to be a sociological problem, while Freud took it as a psychological problem.

Freud argued that belief in God and religion was an illusion, a childhood experience of an exalted father figure, and a projection of desires, fears, and a sense of helplessness (echoing Hume and Feuerbach) into the cosmos. In other words, religion was not unreal or a lie, for it was a reality but of the unconscious experience of infancy that needed to be decoded by psychoanalysis. Freud differed with past philosophers, poets, and psychologists by giving a new interpretation to the unconscious experience. To Freud, the unconscious was the repressed conscious incapable of consciousness. The dynamic content of this unconscious was wishes, desires, and dreams. In his *Interpretation of Dreams,* Freud defined a wish as "a current in apparatus, issuing from pain [=accumulation of excitation] and striving for pleasure [=diminution of excitation through gratification], we call a wish."[38] Every dream is a wish-fulfilment and a key to understanding neurosis. He further argued that the wish and not speculation or reason was the basis of all psychic activities: "Man's judgments of value follow directly his wishes for happiness [and]...accordingly, they are an attempt to support his illusions with arguments."[39] Freud believed man to be surrounded by relentless, unfriendly, and untamed forces of nature:

> There are the elements, which seem to mock at all human control: the earth, which quakes and is torn apart and buries all human life and its works; water, which deluges and drowns everything in a turmoil; storms...diseases...and finally there is the painful riddle of death, against which no medicine has yet been found, nor probably will be. With these forces nature rises up against us, majestic, cruel and inexorable; she brings to our mind once more our weakness and helplessness, which we thought to escape through the work of civilization.[40]

Chief among these strategies of civilization is religion. Freud declares: "I have tried to show that religious ideas have arisen from the same need as have all the other achievements of civilization." Therefore religion serves as a palliative when life comes down hard on us, when we are hurt, disappointed, and dismayed. In reality, it does not solve our problems but offers simply a psychological mechanism of shunning problems and finding artificial solace in unseen powers and unconscious experiences. Freud believed that man's childhood experience provided the clue, in that the helpless small child received protection from his parents. Similarly, wrote Freud, "a man makes the forces of nature not only into persons with whom he can associate as he would with his equals – that would not do justice to the overpowering impression which those forces make on him – but he gives them the character of a father."[41]

Therefore, God, in reality, is nothing but the reappearance of childhood unconscious experience and the projection of a father figure into the cosmos because "the root of every form of religion," to Freud, was "longing for the father."[42] In *Civilization and Its Discontents,* Freud elaborated this point further. He argued that even though religious need originates in childhood helplessness, it does not stop there. It is "permanently sustained by fear of superior power of Fate.

...The origin of religious attitude can be traced back in clear outlines as far as the feeling of infantile helplessness. There may be something further behind that, but for the present it is wrapped in obscurity."[43]

The decisive element of Freudian theory is the substitution of psychology for metaphysics, and as Stan Draenos, a York University social scientist, observes, "The transformation of metaphysics into metapsychology substitutes an immanent 'within' for a transcendent 'beyond' as the ground of self-understanding."[44] With this brief statement Draenos puts the point of our discussion into a nutshell. The origins of transcendent divinity lie in the inner feelings and experiences of man and not in heavenly realms.

Freud, like Durkheim, connected his theory with "totemism" (an ancient system of belief in which humans are said to have kinship with a spirit-being symbolized in a totem) to give it a historical perspective. Scottish social anthropologist James G. Frazer and Durkheim explained that in "primitive" tribes this totem played two vital roles: a) providing tribesmen with protection, help, guidance, and warnings about troubles, and b) referring to an animal or plant species emblematic of a specific group, notably a clan. Clan members, respected, revered, and protected the totem animal by establishing a taboo around it and strictly observing two laws in connection with it: that of no killing of the totem animal and no sex to take place between clan members. Violations of these laws were punishable by death. Totemism, the primitive religious experience was based upon unconscious reasons, or as Freud put it, a "product of the conditions involved in the Oedipus complex."[45]

Freud explained this complex as a subconscious sexual desire on the part of the child for the parent of the opposite sex. This occurred as a process of transition with the helpless child entering society and becoming aware of the limits of the father's abilities and powers as well as his own (the child's) sexual desires. At which point the child's attitude towards the father "takes on a hostile coloring and changes into a wish to get rid of the father in order to take his place with the mother."[46] The pre-oedipal identification with the father helped repress these feelings.

The Totem, then, was simply a substitute for the father: what "is sacred was originally nothing but the perpetuated will of the primeval father."[47] Thus, to discover the origins of religion Freud pointed to Totemism as the foundation of man's primordial, simplistic and ancient religious thought. How he applied the concept to religion was to surmise that once upon a time primitive people lived a horde life where the father ruled over the younger males of the group, keeping all the females for himself, with other males' wishes being repressed by sexual restrictions. One day the sons united and killed the father doing what would have been impossible on an individual level. And it was in this primeval murder that Freud looked for the clues to the origins of morality:

> The violent primal father had doubtless been the feared and envied model of each one of the company of brothers, and in the act of devouring him they accomplished their identification with him, and each one of them acquired a portion of his strength. The totem meal, which is perhaps mankind's earliest festival, would thus be a repetition and commemoration of so many things: of social organization, of moral restrictions and of religion.[48]

Freud advocated that religion was a powerful and durable reality because "the store of religious ideas includes not only wish-fulfillments but important historical recollections. This concurrent of past and present must give religion a truly incomparable wealth of power."[49] Yet he still viewed religion as an illusion, and believed that people of the modern scientific era should abandon it. Freud contended that as a psychologist studies the development of man, he is forced to reach the conclusion that religion is comparable to childhood neurosis and that mankind will eventually surmount this neurotic phase just as many children grow out of theirs.

Commenting on Freud's theory, Karen Armstrong observes that to Freud:

> Religion belonged to the infancy of the human race; it had been a necessary stage in the transition from childhood to maturity. It had promoted ethical values which were essential to society. Now that humanity had come of age, however, it should be left behind.

> Science, the new logos, could take God's place. It could provide a new basis for morality and help us to face our fears. Freud was emphatic about his faith in science, which seemed almost religious in its intensity...[50]

Sigmund Freud then made this "comfort theory"[51] of anthropomorphism the clearest source of the divine, reducing religion to mere feelings of infantile helplessness and childish, unconscious, or subconscious experiences, worthy of elimination when humanity had come of age and 'grown up.' Hence religion was viewed as something infantile, to be discarded on reaching mental maturity. This perspective of religion and God revolutionized subsequent thought, anthropomorphizing God and bringing Him down from the realms of heaven to the world of man.

Another revolutionary perspective on religion came in the middle of the nineteenth century when the long historical battle between men of faith on the one hand, and philosophers, scientists, empiricists, social scientists, and general skeptics of religion on the other, reached a decisive point: the application of Darwin's theory of evolution by anthropologists and social scientists to the study of the developmental stages of religion. Supposing the idea of the divine to have originated in the world of man, many scholars applied extensive research to locating the exact origin of the idea of God and religion. Although some like Austrian linguist and anthropologist Father Wilhelm Schmidt used their research findings to prove that primitive religion everywhere had begun with an essentially monotheistic concept of god, they were nevertheless in the minority. The great majority of anthropologists, psychologists, sociologists, and even some so-called theologians, contended that the origins of religion lay in the simple forms of primitive cultures, in animism, fetishism, and totemism, claiming that these had developed in turn into higher forms of religion such as polytheism, monolatry, monotheism, and finally into the ethical monotheism of modern religions such as Judaism, Christianity, and Islam which comprise the bulk of belief today.

Despite their differences, they largely agreed on one point, that God does not have an objective reality of his own. He depends upon human needs, aspirations, and fears for His existence. The word "God" they asserted was merely a reification, personification, or projection of forces found in the external, internal, and social world of man. In other words discourse about God was basically a discourse about man, or in Feuerbach's words, and as discussed, "Theology is anthropology".[52]

This essential understanding of the divine continued into the twentieth century. American anthropologist Franz Boas saw most religions as a "dogmatized development" of anthropomorphism.[53] Anthropologist Claude Lévi-Strauss argued that "religion consists in a humanization of natural laws" and an "anthropomorphization of nature."[54] In sum, anthropomorphism was thought to be, and still is, in the words of R. J. Zwi Werblowsky of the Hebrew University of Jerusalem, a "central problem" both in theology, the history of religions, and religious philosophy.[55] Nigerian scholar E. Bolaji Idowu observed that anthropomorphism has "always been a concomitant of religion, all religions, every faith. In the purest religion... there can be no way of avoiding anthropomorphism."[56] According to anthropologist Stewart Guthrie "religion *is* anthropomorphism."[57]

In light of these observations, and when we examine the known faith traditions of the world, we see that anthropomorphism is embedded in the scriptures of almost all with varying degrees. Theologians of most of these traditions vainly try to eliminate anthropomorphism from their scriptures, but very often, scriptural text refuses such treatment. As it is impossible to discuss all the religious traditions within the limited scope of this work, we confine our observations to the three developed Semitic religions that claim their origin in the Abrahamic faith: Judaism, Christianity, and Islam. In the Hebrew Bible or Old Testament, God is shown to possess manifest human qualities, both mental and physical, as befits his proposal to make "man in our image." In the New Testament He is given a completely human form, in Jesus. Despite the many concerted efforts of some Jewish scholars and church fathers (as explored in later chapters) to stem this, the concept of a physically humanlike God has persisted in both the traditions. Most Muslims, like their Jewish and Christian counterparts, try to avoid anthropomorphisms, but the struggle is chronic, though not exactly as crude as in Judaism and Christianity. The cause, in the opinion of R. Strothmann in his article "Tashbih" in *The Shorter Encyclopaedia of Islam,* is to be found in the Qur'an, "which strongly emphasizes the absolute uniqueness of God and yet at the same time plainly describes him in the language of anthropomorphism, giving him a face, eyes, and hands and talking of his speaking and sitting."[58]

Because of the pervasive nature of such anthropomorphism some theologians like W. J. Duggan have called it "indispensable."[59] The late philosopher F. B. Jevons argued that it "has characterized religion from the beginning [and] characterizes it to the end."[60] Other prominent scholars like Hugo Meynell, a Catholic philosopher,[61] and Frederick Ferré, a professional theologian, have tried to defend anthropomorphism and resolve the paradox by analogy, faith, or any other possible means to save and advocate the validity of religion. For instance, Ferré, in his article "In Praise of Anthropomorphism," re-evaluated this "deep seated antagonism to anthropomorphism in discourse about God, and to offer reasons to praise rather than bury such a speech." He argued that anthropomorphism is "*not necessarily demeaning* religiously to the Most High [that is, we need not think Him mean or petty, for example] but also is *necessarily not avoidable* logically if the language of either the believer or the philosopher is not to be emptied of all content."[62] On the other hand, Stewart Elliott Guthrie, a Fordham University anthropologist observes, "Ferré's praise, however, amounts to admitting once more that if we cannot say anything anthropomorphic about God, we cannot say anything at all...This, however, merely makes a virtue of necessity."[63]

Despite the pervasiveness and defense of a few scholars, anthropomorphism continues to be an "anathema,"[64] American philosopher Humphrey Palmer observed, stuck to religion. For German theologian and philosopher Paul Tillich (1868–1965) traditional Christian names for God, such as Father and Lord were all too anthropomorphic. Names such as these made of the divinity a perfect heavenly person living somewhere above the world.[65] Tillich viewed the word 'religion' to be derogatory,[66] and found even the name 'God' objectionable because it made the deity an object among other worldly objects:

> The concept of a "Personal God" interfering with natural events, or being "an independent cause of natural events," makes God a

> natural object beside others, an object among others, a being among beings (maybe the highest) but nevertheless a being. This indeed is not only the destruction of the physical system but even more the destruction of any meaningful idea of God.[67]

In an effort to avoid anthropomorphism, Tillich created new names for the deity: "Being-itself," "Ground of Being," "the Unconditional," and others as preferable to the term God. Karen Armstrong observes that a century earlier, "Feuerbach had made a similar claim when he had said that God was inseparable from normal human psychology, and that now this atheism had been transformed into a new theism."[68] In short, religion, according to Tillich, is "directedness of the spirit toward the unconditional meaning."[69] The name of this infinite and inexhaustible depth and ground of "all being is God. That depth is what the word god means. And if that word has not much meaning for you, translate it, and speak of the depths of your life, of the source of your being, of your ultimate concern, of what you take seriously without any reservation."[70]

Few scholars or theologians accept Tillich's definition of God. Rene Williamson, a modern American political scientist, argues that the "Christian God is a person, a living person," whereas Tillich's is "devoid of color and power...bloodless", He fails to impress or convince the ordinary believer.[71] Guthrie observed that in, "Trying to eliminate the disease, however, he kills the patient." Guthrie also argued that, "Like birdshot fired at a flock in general, it hits nothing at all. The less anthropomorphic Tillich makes God, the more God becomes incomprehensible."[72]

Many scholars it would seem prefer a somewhat anthropomorphic notion of God to an obscure, unintelligible, and non-personal God. Swinburne, for instance, begins his book with the observation "By a theist I understand a man who believes that there is a God. By a 'God' he understands something like a person."[73] Comparative religion scholars and philosophers such as S. G. F. Brandon,[74] Kai Nielsen,[75] and A. Gallus agree with German philosopher Karl Jaspers that "if religion is demythologized, it is no longer religion."[76] Moshe Greenburg, a Hebrew University biblical scholar, well summarized the situation when he noted "Contemplative thinkers among Jews, Christians, and Moslems have always recognized the predominance of anthropomorphism as the mode of religious perception and discourse and have declared it an obstacle to true knowledge of God."[77] Finally, Guthrie observes that "Most theologians admit that to eliminate anthropomorphism is to eliminate religion. The religion cannot be extricated from anthropomorphism suggests that anthropomorphism is even more than its matrix. Rather, religion looks like anthropomorphism, part and parcel."[78]

On the other hand religion which retains an anthropomorphic understanding of God has been criticized and refuted by many scholars, philosophers, and scientists of modern times. In addition to scientific developments or scientific metaphysics, and a mechanical interpretation of nature, such apathy towards religion can partly be attributed to the over-anthropomorphic nature of theistic notions of God. English novelist W. M. Thackeray, commenting on nineteenth century English cultural critics and poets such as Thomas De Quincy, Robert Browning, Matthew Arnold, Gerard Manley Hopkins, and Emily Brontë, once remarked that they were "a set of people living without God in the world."[79] French existentialist philosopher Jean-Paul Sartre (1905–1980) rejected God. French phenomenological philosopher Maurice Merleau Ponty (1908–1961), French Nobel Prize winner philosopher and journalist Albert Camus (1913–1960), and Logical Positivists like A. J. Ayer (1910–1991), advocated heroic atheism.

Physicist Steven Weinberg,[80] astronomer Sandra Faber,[81] biologist S. E. Luria,[82] paleontologist Stephen Jay Gould,[83] and philosophers like E. D. Klemke[84] etc., have all accepted a world without God. Celebrated astronomer and philosopher Sandra Faber, for instance, winner of the Heineman Prize and the Harvard Centennial Medal has asserted that,

> the universe was created out of some natural process, and our appearance in it was totally a natural result of physical laws in our particular portion of it... or what we call our universe. Implicit in the question...is that there is some motive power that has a purpose beyond human existence. I do not believe in that...[and]... ultimately I agree with Weinberg that it is completely pointless from [a] human perspective.[85]

Cornell professor of natural history, William Provine, encapsulates the position of almost all biologists and indeed most scientists of our time when he remarks:

> Everything proceeds purely by materialistic and mechanistic process...modern science directly implies that the world is organized strictly in accordance with mechanistic principles. There are no purposive principles whatever in nature. There are no gods and no designing forces that are rationally detectable. The frequently made assertion that modern biology and the assumptions of Judeo-Christian tradition are fully compatible is false.[86]

The idea of God as an external agency governing the universe leaves American philosopher E. D. Klemke "cold. It would not be mine...I, for one, am glad that the universe has no meaning, for there is man all the more glorious."[87] What Feuerbach envisioned a century ago is today fully accomplished. Finally, theologian Thomas Altizer (b.1927) following Nietzsche proclaims the apparent "good news" of God's death, arguing that "Only by accepting and even willing the death of God in our experience can we be liberated from a transcendent beyond, an alien beyond which has been emptied and darkened by God's self alienation in Christ."[88] Altizer is fairly mystical here. However, William Hamilton of Colgate-Rochester Divinity School is not so. His is a forthright clinical analysis bluntly stating that secular man does not need God for anything and wants to find his own solutions in the world.

Literary critic Joseph Hillis Miller (b.1928) has accurately characterized the current situation with regard to God and religion:

> The lines of connection between us and God have broken down, or God himself has slipped away from the places where he used to be. He no longer inheres in the world as the force binding together all men and all things. As a result the nineteenth and twentieth centuries seem to many writers a time when God is no more present and not yet again present, and can only be experienced negatively, as a terrifying absence.[89]

Furthermore, Miller considered cities to be a "literal representation of the progressive humanization of the world." He saw no room for God in the city, and wondered if man excluded God by building great cities, or whether cities were built because God had disappeared. In any case, he wrote, life in the city is the most common way that men have experienced most directly what it means to live without God in the world.[90]

Despite the brave front, there exists a strong sense of alienation, isolation, subjectivism, relativism and nihilism in modern man. In the words of Dostoyevsky, "If there is no God, then everything is permitted."[91] Religious values do not currently bind, in general. Moral values are not ultimate but fairly relative, disappearing, at least in the United States and Europe, with unprecedented speed, while family values are diminishing in most parts of the developed world.

A new cultural-values survey of 2,000 American adults undertaken in March of 2007 by the polling firm Fabrizio, McLaughlin & Associates for the Culture and Media Institute revealed that a strong majority, 74 percent, believed moral values in America to be weaker than they were 20 years ago. Almost half, 48 percent, agreed that values were much weaker than they were 20 years ago.[92] Most Americans blamed entertainment media for the sharp decline in moral values. The agreement was quite remarkable across political and religious groups. This sentiment was shared by Republicans (86 percent) and Democrats (68 percent); conservatives (80 percent) and liberals (64 percent); even religious types identified as orthodox (82 percent) and mostly secular progressives (62 percent).

A detailed survey by the Pew Forum on Religion & Public Life conducted from May 8 to August 13, 2007 showed that:

> More than one-quarter of American adults (28%) have left the faith in which they were raised in favor of another religion – or no religion at all. If change in affiliation from one type of Protestantism to another is included, 44% of adults have either switched religious affiliation, moved from being unaffiliated with any religion to being affiliated with a particular faith, or dropped any connection to a specific religious tradition altogether.[93]

On March 9, 2009 a CNN survey revealed that America was "becoming less Christian."[94] The findings pointed out that the US had become a less Christian nation in 2009 than it had been 20 years ago. Christianity had not been losing to other faith traditions but to rejection of religion altogether. In 2009 seventy five percent of Americans identified themselves as Christians according to the American Religious Identification Survey from Trinity College, Hartford, Connecticut. In 1990, the figure was 86 percent. The survey also showed that one in five Americans denied having any religious identity while one in four explicitly stated that they intended not to have any religious funeral. Erosion of religion it would appear is a nationwide trend.

Whilst it could be argued that the number of evangelical churches and their attendance has increased in the past decades, this is deceptive, for the increase is disproportionate to the loss of church members in the mainstream Protestant and Catholic churches. Additionally being religious and moral in contemporary America or Europe is substantially different from the practice some twenty years ago. Many Christian dogmas such as the Trinity, Incarnation, and Original Sin as well as moral values such as sexual decency, protection of life, and family dignity are frequently compromised, or interpreted in such a fashion as to become a different animal. The modern idea of God is not as awe inspiring as it was in past centuries, and modern man has distanced himself from the transcendent God of theism. Consequently, and as Miller states, "We are alienated from God; we have alienated ourselves from nature; we are alienated from our fellow men; and finally, we are alienated from ourselves, the buried life we never seem able to reach. The result is a radical sense of inner nothingness."[95] God-conscious people do of course exist in the world, but the vast majority present the exact picture mentioned in the Qur'an when it says: "And be ye not like those who forgot God, and He made them forget themselves"(59:19).

Hence what has been discussed alludes to two distinct charges levelled against a theistic understanding of God. The first is that of anthropomorphism. Advocates of this charge against religion (whilst not denying God's existence) contend that any material description of God is conditioned by and derived from man's understanding of his own nature. Those who, since Xenophanes, have pressed this charge have maintained that God transcends this material world and is solely different from human beings; therefore, any description of Him in terms of human nature, no matter how greatly qualified, will distort His perfection and will be worse than no description of Him at all.

The other charge is that of 'invention'. The supporters of this charge contend that God is fictional with no real existence. He depends ontologically on human beings for they invent him by a cosmic projection of their nature, characteristics, and qualities. Guthrie noted that people who say religion anthropomorphizes usually mean that it attributes human characteristics to gods, or that, in claiming gods exist, it attributes human characteristics to nature. In the former meaning, religion makes gods humanlike in crediting them with the capacity for symbolic action. In the latter religion makes nature humanlike by seeing gods there.[96]

To understand the depth and reality of the charge we need to define the related terms of anthropomorphism and transcendence.

ANTHROPOMORPHISM

Anthropomorphism derives from the Greek *anthropos* (human being) and *morphe* (form). As a term it is relatively modern being developed in the eighteenth century. A general definition of anthropomorphism could be: an inveterate tendency to project human qualities into natural phenomena, consciously or not,[97] or, the description of non-material, 'spiritual' entities in physical, and specifically human, form.[98]

Used in its religious sense, the term denotes a universal human tendency to experience, express, and appeal to the divine in human shapes or categories. Anthropomorphism can denote the ascription to God of a human form or member.[99] In its wider sense, the term has been used to include attribution of any kind of human characteristics, activities, emotions, or feelings to God. It is sometimes broadly defined as forming religious concepts and ideas in human terms, according to shapes and metaphors of this world and human experience of it.[100] Essential to anthropomorphism is the description of God and formulation of the concepts pertaining to Him in human forms and categories.

There are two major forms of anthropomorphism. The first, in which appeal is made to physical or corporeal traits of the deity, is termed "physical anthropomorphism." The second refers to ascription of human emotions like love, hate, desire, anger, and repentance to God and has been termed "mental, psychical, or psychological anthropomorphism." Social thinker and author John Ruskin (1819–1900) called it "anthropopathism," from the Greek *anthropos* (man) and *pathein* (suffering). Both forms allude to the same notion that divine functions, qualities, attributes, and characters derive from human life and experience. The theistic notion of a personal God with personal qualities and attributes is thought to be the ultimate source of anthropomorphism. In contrast to this mood of imagination is "theriomorphism," a tendency to describe and embody the divine being in forms and categories borrowed wholly or partly from the animal world.

Various scholars have given two standard explanations for anthropomorphism: the "theory of comfort" and the "theory of familiarity". The "comfort theory" postulates that human beings feel comfortable when seeing human faces in a non-human world, and fear of the unknown causes this wish fulfillment and cognitive confusion. The "familiarity theory" holds that the human self is man's mirror to the external world. The knowledge of oneself is the most authentic and the easiest of all sources of human knowledge. This would explain projecting human faces, qualities, and characters in the realms of heaven because humanity is naturally acquainted with these anthropomorphic traits.

Each of the theories has several versions. The "theory of familiarity" has two chief versions which Guthrie terms "confusion" and "analogy." He further observes that these versions

> are on a continuum. They share the notion that anthropomorphism consists in extending models of what we know to what we do not know. They differ in that the confusion version assumes this extension is involuntary, unconscious, and indiscriminate, while [the] analogy version assumes it is voluntary, conscious, and discriminating.[101]

We have already seen examples of confusion theory in the discussions on Feuerbach, Freud, Spinoza, and Comte, and analogy theory, to some extent, in discussions of Hume and Fontenelle.

St. Thomas Aquinas (1224–1274) successfully advocated the religious version of analogy theory. However, the "comfort theory" is also widespread, and closely relates to the wishful thinking theory of religion, as seen in Feuerbach and Freud. Freud argued that human beings humanize nature so that they "can breath freely, can feel at home..."[102] Anthropologist Leslie White (1900–1975) argued that the anthropomorphic philosophy is that of "wish and will projected from the human mind."[103] It has sustained man with illusions and provided him with courage, comfort, consolation, and confidence. Each of these theories, Guthrie observes, "has a little truth but neither is sufficient."[104] Indeed, both are problematic, and neither of them a good reflection upon religious phenomenon when analyzed in detail.

The charge of anthropomorphism directed at religion, as in its original form first levelled by Xenophanes of Colophon, only denotes ascription to the deity of a bodily figure. Not much consideration was given by Xenophanes or his successors to the attribution of intellectual as well as moral attributes and qualities to God that might be akin to those of human beings. Consequently, Christian apologists like Justin Martyr, who although believing in the theistic conception of a personal God and the Christian concept of divine incarnation in the figure of a historical man, yet nevertheless levelled this charge against pagan religions and the polytheism of the time. K. Latourette, a modern church historian, observed that church fathers, "excoriated the immoralities ascribed to gods by the current myths, pilloried the follies and inconsistencies in polytheistic worship, and poured scorn on the anthropomorphic conceptions and images of the gods."[105] In the fourth century, the charge of anthropomorphism was directed by orthodox fathers toward a group of African Christians who maintained that God Himself had suffered a painful death on the cross. In consequent history the charge was repeatedly made to repudiate various religious traditions who viewed God in corporeal terms.

Medieval philosophers and theologians like al-Fārābī (870–950) and Rabbi Moses Maimonides (1135–1204) further developed God's non-corporeality to cover various aspects of God's intellectual and moral attributes. Interestingly, anthropomorphism never became a serious weapon against God, or even religion as a whole, except after the Enlightenment, because it was the intellectual movement of this 'age of reason', as it is often called, which negatively effected man's attitude towards God. Although, the change of direction, perspective, and emphasis is too complex to be traced here, three inherent factors of the pre-Enlightenment period can be identified as having laid the foundations for this decline. Firstly, the power struggle which developed between the Church and the educated elite; secondly, issues with Christian incarnation theology, especially its popular version; and thirdly the use of personal images of God in popular piety.

Empirical scientists and scholars, in an effort to restrict the compass of God and religion, and thereby the Church's influence and interpretations of man and his surroundings, promoted the charge of excessive visual imagery or physical anthropomorphism against religion, extending it to cover all aspects of God deemed comparable to that of human beings. Accusations of anthropomorphism were pressed so hard that the exercise became a virtual witch-hunt with any divine quality or attribute, no matter how moral or spiritual, if linked to the human realm, being dubbed as sheer anthropomorphism. Pushed beyond its limits the accusation ultimately lost all credible meaning stripped of its real context to become merely a term of reproach or vehicle for the expression of dislike. Things deteriorated to such a state that English theist James Martineau (1805–1900) was forced to declare, "you can scarcely recognize any quality, however spiritual, as common to the Divine and the human nature, without incurring the imputation of 'anthropomorphism'." A term which "when fastened upon a belief, is apparently supposed to make an end of it for every one above a 'philistine'."[106] Little has changed. Despite several modern efforts to prevent this hysterical imputation, as seen above, the situation today is no different to that observed by Martineau.

INCARNATION

Incarnation is a species of anthropomorphism. Whereas anthropomorphism allows description of God in human categories, with human characteristics, without His emerging in human form, the term "incarnation" specifically alludes to the representation of a human being as the true image of God. Jewish studies scholar Jacob Neusner defines incarnation as: "The representation of God in the flesh, as corporeal, consubstantial in emotion and virtue with human beings, and sharing in the modes and means of actions carried out by mortals,"[107] This is more perhaps a definition of the popular Christian concept of incarnation, but Christianity is not an isolated case. The idea that God or gods have incarnated in this sense is quite widespread in the history of religions. Philosophical theologian Brian Hebblethwaite writes:

> ...it constitutes a third, incarnational, strand alongside the numinous and the mystical strands in the religious experience of mankind. The Christian doctrine of Incarnation represents this strand in its most highly developed form. The central Christian doctrine states that God, in one of the modes of his triune being and without in any way ceasing to be God, has revealed himself to mankind for their salvation by coming amongst them as man. The man Jesus is held to be the incarnate Word or Son of God. Taken into God's eternity and glorified at the resurrection, the incarnate one remains for ever the ultimate focus of God-man encounter; for he not only, as God incarnate, mediates God to man, but also, in his perfect humanity, represents man to God.[108]

This definition differs slightly to the popularly understood Christian interpretation of the incarnation of God in Christ. Meaning that it represents a more intellectual than popular trend in Christianity, where literal rather than metaphorical interpretations are more common. In popular Christianity, God is represented as human flesh, in the person of the historical Jesus Christ, and moreover is presented in corporeal forms said to have suffered a physical and agonizing death as atonement for man's sins under the doctrine of salvation. The Christian theological doctrine of Jesus as simultaneously a complete God and a complete man represents corporealism and anthropomorphism in perhaps its purest form, although many Christian theologians claim otherwise. Yet this is a pivotal aspect of Christian theology, for if God is believed to have become fully incarnate in human flesh (that is, in the historical person of Christ) and is believed to have experienced human limitations to the extreme point of having experienced pain and an agonizing death, then surely we have in front of us nothing less than the strongest case of corporealism.

This notion of God as having suffered death has seemingly contributed to the 'death of God' theology mentioned in the opening of this chapter, and underscored His irrelevance to modern culture and society. The reasoning is clear. A God that forsakes Jesus on the cross is a God that modern man no longer trusts. What guarantee does man have that this same God will not forsake him when man needs Him most? A God that is unable to forgive a simple mistake, the transgression of Adam having eaten of the forbidden apple, requiring that atonement be made through the violent bloodshed of an innocent righteous man, is a God that modern man has serious doubts about especially with regards to His justice, loving nature, and validity. A God that is unable to eliminate or even subdue sin despite this blood atonement, is a God that becomes irrelevant to the modern culture of relativism and logical positivism. Such a God makes no sense and is too mysterious, paradoxical, and anthropomorphic to be taken seriously. Ironically, and in a sense, the death of God in the human conscious was already set in motion, and is in fact the inevitable outcome of, his physical (in the form of Jesus Christ incarnate) death at the hands of the Romans. In short, the humanization of the divine has ironically resulted in the divinization of the human.

Having discarded what he dismissively perceives to be outmoded and unwarranted notions of the Divine, man is left seeking his own solutions to life's varying problems, using the tools of his knowledge and institutions, and without looking to the transcendental realms for assistance or guidance. The old cognitive confusion of imploring God during times of need have now been cast aside in favor of solutions provided by science and technology.

The subject of incarnation will be examined in more detail in Chapter 3. For now suffice it to say that whenever God is portrayed in corporeal terms and categories, or shown engaged in activities practiced in the manner and style and emotion of human beings then we have in front of us a clear case of incarnation.

The incarnation of God is manifested in two primary ways: (a) in the form of individuals such as kings, emperors, imams, or other human personalities etc., a common phenomenon in various religious traditions including Hinduism, certain Greek religions, certain traditions of Judaism, as well as some extreme Shiite sects, as will be seen in Chapters 2 and 4. (b) As the second person of the Trinity *logos*, thought to personally adopt a human mortal personality and live on earth for a specific period of time in history. It is an understanding of incarnation unique to Christianity among the Semitic religions and is derived from the Christian conviction that the union of the divine with humanity was realized in the person of Jesus Christ, a notion quite controversial even among Christians, as will be discussed in Chapter 3.

Having introduced, defined, and given a brief background of the term anthropomorphism, I will now examine the essentials of the charge that religion by nature is anthropomorphic, and that being anthropomorphic, God has no reality of His own outside the world of man. Before looking more deeply into the main theme and crux of this work (the study of anthropomorphism and transcendence in the Bible and the Qur'an), we need to first establish the boundaries or parameters of the charge of anthropomorphism levelled at religion, and estimate the grounds of its sheer dislike by many modern scholars.

The nature of the problem can be located in the assertion that any attribute, quality, or category present in the human sphere is to be disqualified from being referred to God. This qualification goes too far. An extreme application of this perspective would strip God of all meaning and relevance in terms of our human faculties and the sensory world around us. In almost all theistic traditions God, seen as Great and Almighty, is accepted as the source of all creation, and as such, it is religion that has tackled historically and to the present, issues of humanity's origins, destiny, and longing for immortality. Science and technology although resolving many of the problems of our physical realm are unable to provide satisfactory answers to the most basic, and at the same time most ultimate, questions facing humanity: who are we?, where do we come from?, what is our purpose?, what happens after death? etc. Furthermore, science and technology are not a panacea for all ills and are unable to provide solutions to many of the problems and conditions humanity faces. In contrast, human beings depend upon God for their origin, existence, being, and continuity. There is worldly outward knowledge and then there is knowledge of the soul, the inner world of man. Naturally (and it is a universal fact) human beings long to know their source of existence and being. Nothing is so important to man as man himself, his existence, his being, his consciousness and his outward and inner experiences. Therefore, it is natural and appropriate for humanity to reflect and think about the unknown God through whatever is certain, familiar and known to it, to establish a viable relationship with the Creator. We try to project on our Creator the best that is in ourselves, for we give this great value, and this approach results from our inadequacies and not from divine necessities or shortcomings.

When we project upon God what we consider to be the highest qualities and characteristics of man, this in no way means that we are degrading our idea of God or ascribing personality to Him. For mankind also understands that God is the definite perfect Being, absolutely other than man by His very nature, and that these qualities that we ascribe to Him are imperfectly held within us but perfectly and in their most complete way held by Him. If we show mercy He is the Most Merciful, and so on and so forth. It is in this vein that we use personality as the gateway of our knowledge of the Divine. Human beings, observed John Calvin (1509–1564),

> must therefore borrow comparisons from known objects, in order to enable us to understand those which are unknown to us; for God loves very differently from men, that is, more fully and perfectly, and although he surpasses all human affections, yet nothing that is disorderly belongs to him.[109]

Philosophical theist Ian Thomas Ramsey (1915–1972), Ferré, theologian John Macquarrie (1919–2007),[110] and many others have developed this thought further to show that these known comparisons or religious images serve as conceptual models albeit with some definite qualifiers.

Ramsey viewed religious language in terms of "models and qualifiers" that function in "logically odd" ways to stimulate "discernment situations" noting that for the religious man "God" is

> a key word, an irreducible posit, an ultimate of explanation expressive of the kind of commitment he professes. It is to be talked about in terms of the object-language over which it presides, but only when this object-language is qualified; in which case this qualified object-language becomes also currency for the odd discernment with which religious commitment, when it is not bigotry or fanaticism, will necessarily be associated.[111]

Ramsey argued that, "We should expect religious language... to be constructed from object language which has been given appropriately strange qualifications..." This odd object-language has "a distinctive significance, and we might even conclude in the end that the odder the language the more it matters to us."[112] Furthermore, a religious assertion such as 'God is loving' claims that we can model God in terms of "loving" situations. He also wrote that the assertion is logically incomplete and should be qualified with "infinitely" or "all," as in "God is infinitely loving," or "God is all-loving." He concluded that,

> special positioning can nevertheless be reached from ordinary language, to which words like "love" belong, once this ordinary language has been appropriately qualified, as by the word "infinite." Here then is a method by which not only are problems overcome, but where at every point we plot and map our theological phrases with reference to a characteristically religious situation: one of worship, wonder, awe.[113]

Ferré argued for the use of conceptual models in considering theistic images in their speculative function:

> In all logical respects... anthropomorphic theistic imagery can function on its speculative side as a vivid metaphysical model. It can give conceptual definiteness to the ultimate nature of things

> by picturing all of reality as constituting either creature or Creator, each with specific characteristics; it can suggest patterns and unity in the totality of things in terms of its representation of the various relations between the entities so pictured; and it can give a sense of intelligibility, an aura of meaning and familiarity, by virtue of the appeal to personal purpose, volitional power, and moral principle as the ultimate explanatory categories.[114]

Ferré concluded that the theistic model as religious imagery is a kind of symbolism that may, for those who adopt it, "overcome the threat of the arbitrary on its valuational side as well as to meet the cognitive challenge of strangeness and disconnection on its theoretical side." The model portrays the best as also most relevant, and shows "'brute fact' not to be just 'brutal' but, rather, to display the propriety that is its final vindication. And so theoretical and practical reason rejoin one another once more, at the upper reaches of the search for understanding." Therefore to Ferré, "anthropomorphic theistic imagery has a reasonable claim on any who judge the success of ultimate imagery, in part at least, in terms of its capacity to stimulate and sustain valuational fullness in the lives of those who adopt it."[115]

Moreover, historically and ontologically, God existed from eternity, long before human beings could speculate about Him. The personality of God should have been the origin of human understandings of their own personalities. St. Thomas Aquinas observed that the word 'God' was primarily used for the Creator and derivatively of creatures. The word symbolizes perfection and absoluteness which flows from God to His creatures. He noted that we apply it first "to creatures because we know them first. That...is why it has a way of signifying that is appropriate to creatures."[116] Furthermore:

> All words used metaphorically of God apply primarily to creatures and secondarily to God. When used of God they signify merely a certain parallelism between God and creature. When we speak metaphorically of a meadow as 'smiling' we only mean that it shows its best when it flowers, just as a man shows at his best when he smiles: there is a parallel between them. In the same way,

> if we speak of God as a 'lion' we only mean that, like a lion, he is mighty in his deeds. It is obvious that the meaning of such a word as applied to God depends on and is secondary to the meaning it has when used of creatures.[117]

Notre Dame University professor of philosophy Ralph M. McInerny explained St. Thomas's position by observing that:

> The names common to God and creatures, like "being" said of what falls into the various genera, happens to be such that the perfection from which the name is imposed to signify is in each of the things, but according to a scale of greater and lesser perfection, a magis et minus which will be revealed in the various rationes of the common name. Thus there will be participation per prius et posterius or, in the case of the divine names, God will have the perfection essentialiter, be one in substance with truth, for example, and creatures will be true per participationem.[118]

Dutch theologian Herman Bavinck (1854–1921) observed that "All virtues primarily are in God, and only then in his creature. He possesses them *per essentiam*, those only *per participationem*. The metaphors we are using to describe the divine are true in so far as they rest on the truth of God himself."[119] He believed that God made humans theomorphous, (referring to the bestowal of divine attributes on humanity) which justified our speaking of Him anthropomorphically.[120] The observations of both Bavinck and Aquinas should be qualified with the stipulation that God created the theomorphus in a spiritual and moral sense and not in a corporeal sense; therefore, although our only choice is to find some common ground and language to have a useful relationship with and experience of the divine, this experience should only be expressed in spiritual imagery terms and not in concrete material or gross corporeal imagery. By this is meant that only those metaphors or anthropomorphic expressions should be used of God that do not violate His transcendence, His great uniqueness, His utter difference from His creatures. Further, only those phrases of the commonly used object-language should be allowed of Him that do not make Him fully resemble His creatures and are appropriate to His exalted majesty. Bearing in mind of course that even these can only ever be superficial as compared to His perfection. In addition and needless to say this metaphorical commonality must only ever be seen as a vehicle to facilitate communication and in no way, shape or form to denote absolute resemblance. Only in God's case are these images, attributes, and names in absolute form, while in the human sphere they are just relative.

Once this is understood and the development of the reasoning process with regards to expressing God in appropriate human categories and terms for communication purposes, is appreciated, the allegation of anthropomorphism in its negative sense, as found in some developed theistic understandings of God, would lose its foundation. J. R. Illingworth, the famous nineteenth century English theologian, observed that human belief "in a personal God, from whatever source it is derived, must obviously be interpreted through his consciousness of his own personality."[121] As man's idea of personality in most cases derives from and is interpreted in terms of man's consciousness of his own personality, all personal, theistic notions of God in a sense would have to be somewhat anthropomorphic and should not be regarded, as religious reformer Theodore Parker (1810–1860) did, "a phantom of the brain that has no existence independent of ourselves."[122] Some scholars would disagree with Parker. In fact, religion by its very nature is somewhat anthropomorphic and even "in its highest and most transcendental effort...can never escape from anthropomorphism."[123] This anthropomorphic tendency is intrinsic to and connected with human limitations, and not with the divine sphere or Being.

Discourse about God in appropriate personal terms is particularly symbolic and metaphorical in nature. Without tracing the historical roots of this approach, it is enough to quote Aquinas's classical position. He asserted that God provides for all things in accordance with their nature and abilities. Human beings use senses to access the world of intelligence. Consequently, the Scriptures imply metaphors taken from bodily things to communicate spiritual truths. In addition, "no word can be used literally of God... every word used of God is taken from our speech about creatures...but...are used metaphorically of God, as when we call him a 'rock' or a 'lion'."[124] Aquinas elaborated on establishing content by analogy:

> Some words that signify what has come forth from God to creatures do so in such a way in which that part of the meaning of the word is the imperfect way in which the creatures share in the divine perfection. Thus it is part of the meaning of 'rock' that it has its being in a merely material way. Such words can be used of God only metaphorically. There are other words, however, that simply mean certain perfections without any indication of how these perfections are possessed – words, for example, like 'being', 'good', 'living' and so on. These words can be used literally of God.[125]

Muslim Aristotelian Averroes (1126–1198) preceded Aquinas, and distinguished between univocal, equivocal, and analogous predication.[126] The Fourth Lateran Council (1215) rejected the former two kinds whilst accepting the third, the analogous concept, which became a fundamental in Christian circles.[127] Martin Luther (1483–1546) disagreed with Aquinas's interpretation of metaphor, and argued that when Christ is called a 'rock' the old word 'rock' acquires a completely new sense. Although Luther defended the correlation between God-talk and human experience, between *cognitio dei et hominis,* he did not deny that God-talk is somewhat symbolic. The example that "Christ is a flower," meant to Luther "that Christ is a flower but not 'a natural one.'"[128]

John Calvin (1509–1564) worked tirelessly to establish the metaphorical nature of the biblical language and tried extensively to explain these metaphors in his commentaries. Bavinck,[129] Ramsey,[130] Harry Kuitert, Just van Es,[131] Janet Soskice,[132] and many others agree that God-talk is symbolic and metaphorical in nature. These "symbolic elements," argued the Scottish theologian John Macquarrie, "in theological language preserve the mystery and transcendence of God, and acknowledge that he is characterized by an 'otherness' that goes beyond the grasp of rational thought. Such symbols are evocative rather than straightforwardly descriptive."[133] Janet Soskice, the Cambridge philosophical theologian, argued that in religious and in all language the distinction between literal and metaphorical is determined by the context and use alone. She observed that "what we call 'literal' usage is accustomed usage and that metaphorical usages which begin their careers outside the standard lexicon may gradually become lexicalized."[134]

In caution it should be said that religious language or God-talk is metaphorical in nature but should not allow anybody to violate the basic rules of language or spirit of the text itself to invent something not present in the text. The spirit of the text must be maintained. Metaphors should be based upon standard language usages and not upon mere excuses of subjective agency or unverifiable suppositions. They should be found from within the textual context and not arbitrarily invented to substantiate certain preconceived thoughts or claims, or to add something to the scripture.

We conclude this part of the discussion with Guthrie, who observed:

> There is no religion without relationship, no relationship without significant communication, no significant communication without language, and no language without likeness. For the most rudimentary communication, humans may gesture; but even gesture depends on human likeness such as smiling, frowning, eating, and breathing. In any case, communication requires some commonality in context, in communicative system, and in content. Fully human relationships require language in some form. Any god worth talking about – that is, any god we can talk with – must be at least so like us as to share our language and its context. A shared language already is more than all humans have in common.[135]

Religion, by its very nature, is communicative as Clifford James Geertz, the American anthropologist[136] Robert Neelly Bellah, the American sociologist,[137] and many others point out.[138] Austrian born Jewish philosopher, M. Buber, describes God as one who speaks and communicates, "whom men trust because he addresses them by word and calls them."[139] To Buber, "God is the Being that is directly, most nearly, and lastingly, over against us, that may properly only be addressed, not expressed."[140] The Oxford philosopher Richard Swinburne's God is a person and language is fundamental to persons for communication.[141] Barbara Krasner, a contemporary psychiatrist, also pinpoints living and ongoing communication.[142] Even to Feuerbach, "the essential act of religion...is prayer."[143] Guthrie gave a detailed account of such a communicative process.[144] Therefore, there is no choice for religious believers as well as the scriptures but to communicate. For the communication to be meaningful and appropriate to the profundity of religious experience, it has to be personal and hence somewhat anthropomorphic.

Although scientists starting with Bacon[145] have always disliked anthropomorphisms and have tried to minimize if not possibly eliminate them, anthropomorphism in this minor sense is intrinsic to all human achievements and endeavors including science and philosophy.[146] Philosophers of science like Robert McCauley,[147] scholars of religion like E. Thomas Lawson, and sociologists of science like Barry Barnes all argue that science is the "most elaborated and systematized of all forms of knowledge, and the least anthropomorphic."[148] On the other hand, primatologist Linda Fedigan believes that although the fundamental achievement of science is the "realization that we are not the center of, nor the prototype for, all else in the universe, [that] while anthropo-morphism is to be avoided or minimized, it will not be eliminated."[149] Philosophers like Percy Nunn argue that the very notion of matter in physics is anthropomorphic. Anthropomorphism, to London professor of education T. P. Nunn, is

> too deeply rooted in human nature to be easily suppressed. The average student of physics today is probably still at heart an anthropomorphist. He takes his science to be a hunt after causes [that] convey into the transactions between material bodies features of the traffic between man's mind and his environment.[150]

Brightman observes that "all knowledge, scientific, philosophical, or religious, must be based on human experience and reason; hence, anthropomorphism is unavoidable. The question should be: what kind of anthropomorphism, critical or uncritical?"[151]

Guthrie conducted a comprehensive survey of various branches of science to conclude that anthropomorphism occurs even in the most systematically self-critical and technical domains of thought. His survey seemed to support Nietzsche's claim "that it does so fundamentally, intrinsically, and inevitably." However, Guthrie, along with other philosophers and scientists, including Bacon, agree that "at least egregious anthropomorphism can in principle largely be eliminated and that doing so improves our understanding of the world." Guthrie noted that although philosophers and scientists are wary of anthropomorphism, and "most now regard it as unalloyed error, they are as prone to it as the rest of us." And, "while modern reflection tends to diminish it, some forms, generally judged inoffensive, survive. Anthropomorphism, then, though fundamental neither to philosophy nor to science, criticized by both and evidently antithetical at least to science, continues to appear in them."[152]

Now, if scientists and empiricists render the religious conception of God anthropomorphic merely because it is limited by the conditions of human personality or controlled by the experience and thoughts provided by human personality, then the world, as the English philosopher and politician A. Balfour puts it, "presented to us by science can no more be perceived or imagined than the Deity as represented to us by Theology."[153] Balfour maintained that the epistemological foundations of science were just as open to doubt as were the foundations of theology. In the words of Martineau:

> In every doctrine, therefore, it is still from our microcosm that we have to interpret macrocosm: and from the type of our humanity, as presented in self-knowledge, there is no more escape for the pantheist or materialist, than for the theist. Modify them as you may, all casual conceptions are born from within, as reflections or reductions of our personal, animal, or physical activity: and the severest science is, in this sense, just as anthropomorphic as the most ideal theology.[154]

Man is at a loss to perceive the deity but in three possible forms: personal, animal, and physical, or as mind, life, and matter; the only question arising being as to which one of these forms he would choose. He can construe the deity in terms of His highest attributes and, thus, allow for extremely strong feelings of reverence and dependence upon Him, or by the middling qualities man shares with some other organisms; or by the lowest characteristics man shares with every physical thing. The first choice will be classed as *anthropomorphism*; the second as *biomorphism* (describing God in organic, biological and natural life categories) or *zoomorphism* (in animal form or imagery); and the third as *hylomorphism* (as matter or substance).[155] And 'anthropomorphism', perhaps, will be a better choice than the empiricists' choice of *hylomorphism*. Therefore, it would not be objectionable to describe religion as anthropomorphic; but we may condemn any particular form of anthropomorphism as narrow, trite, or degrading.[156] The degrading anthropomorphisms will be those expressions used without proper qualifiers and precautions, so as to make God look like a human being or assign to God any attribute or quality inappropriate or incompatible with His Infinitude, Majesty, Absoluteness, Perfection, or in other words His 'Otherness and Transcendence.'

Due limits must be maintained between what is human and what is Divine. Blurring the demarcation lines between humanity and divinity will confuse the nature, significance, and essence of the divine thereby degrading the Deity and, in reality, the very essence of the religious experience. Metaphorical or seemingly anthropomorphic expressions should be used to provide human imagination with a kind of modality, but the imagination should be alerted not to go too far or overstep its bounds because God transcends all human modalities and conceptions and cannot be fully grasped or conceptualized by any material model or figure. He cannot be and must not be reduced to the categories of human thinking and must not be modeled on a blown-up anthropocentrism or physical anthropomorphism. He is by His very nature unknown to us in His essence. Therefore none of the above categories of minor or seemingly anthropomorphic expressions, as Macquarrie argued, "can be taken literally. This means that they have to be both affirmed and denied, so that theological language has a paradoxical character."[157] A healthy tension should be maintained between the affirmation and the denial process of even such minor anthropomorphic expressions. Intelligible concepts and models should be developed to articulate and bring home the idea of the creator God, but this must be done with the greatest care so as to not fall into the trap of sheer abstraction or sheer anthropomorphism or corporealism. Both extremes would infringe upon the transcendence and mystery of God. Such extreme notions would fail to reach the depths of human beings and they would be at a loss to create a proper response. A sense of mystery and ineffability is absolutely essential for the proper man-God relationship.

TRANSCENDENCE

Transcendence, on the other hand, is the term most commonly used to signify God's continuous providential guidance to, and independence of, this material world by emphasizing His separation from and elevation above this world. Transcendence is the most significant attribute of all the divine attributes, for the other-worldliness of divinity and supernaturalism rests upon it. God is beyond this utilitarian sphere of time and space since He is the creator of this spatio-temporal cosmos. Moreover, the term transcendence denotes that God Himself and notions about His existence, Absoluteness, Power, and Authority are not humanly created conceptions, so cannot be dispensed with as meaningless and empty terms, as contended by empiricists. In contrast, God and His revelation are the fundamental sources and ground of meaningfulness in this world.

The etymology of the word 'transcendence' has its origin in the Latin root *scando* which means 'I climb'; when to this root, prepositions like *as, de, and trans* are added, we get the words i.e., 'ascend', 'descend' and 'transcend'. Thus, the word 'transcend' will literally mean "something has climbed out of something,"[158] or something has "risen above" and "went beyond" something. This definition presupposes two things: a difference between the one which transcends and that which is transcended. It also presupposes a relationship or relevance between them. As a metaphor, the term transcendence has been used to convey a number of varied though related meanings;[159] therefore, the precise significance of the term in any particular work would be determined from the context in which it is used. In this enterprise, the term will be used for God, His uniqueness and otherness, and to denote His unique mode of relationship to the world with the exclusion of corporealism.

God transcends the world not in the sense that He is out of the world, but in the sense that "He stands over against all finite beings" and is "not identical with or His power not exhausted by the realm of finite being."[160] He is never non-being like finite beings. God "transcends structure," the unbreakable necessities, both spatially and temporally, and is free in relation to all of them. To Karl Paul Reinhold Niebuhr, American Protestant theologian, this freedom of God means that He neither resembles any created structures nor is a product of any such structure. He cannot be explained or comprehended fully by these structures or, in the words of Tillich, by "the world of polarities and finitude."[161] These finite structures are neither self-sufficient nor self-explaining, while God is self-sufficient as well as self-explaining. He is self-explaining through acts of creation and revelation. Moreover, He is the source of explanation and meaning for the finitude and hence, as the transcendent and unique reference, solves their problem of meaning. Without such a transcendental reference human life will be nothing but "meaninglessness and absurdity, a pointless and empty burden silly to be endured."[162]

In short, God's transcendence, to quote Karl Heim, the German professor of dogmatics, "means that he is not a member of the series, nor is he the series itself, but rather its Lord."[163] He is the creator "who makes finite and relative existence possible...and is the source of all reality."[164] He is the Absolute, the Perfect, the Almighty, the Omniscient, the Omnipresent, the Holy, the Eternal and the highly impressive transcendental other. The "Other" who differs from all that is usual and familiar to this world of senses. As Illingworth observes, He "sustains all finite beings in existence, or in other words imparts to them all the reality that they possess, while transcending them as immeasurably as the creator ever must transcend the creature. He is our infinite and absolute Other. He is all that what we are not."[165] Consequently, God's existence or authority does not depend on our feelings or emotions. He exists independent of the whole material world and is not subject to the limitations of whatsoever is other than Him.

TRANSCENDENCE: A PHILOSOPHICAL INTERPRETATION

It needs to be made clear that the religious/theological concept of 'transcendence' as discussed above is different to the interpretation given to it by philosophers. Their notion of transcendence contrasts sharply with their concept of divine immanence. In their efforts to press Gods' unity and oneness, and to purify His being from all human attributes or characteristics, philosophers go so far as even to cut His entire relationship with, and in some cases direct authority over, this world of perception. This extreme notion of transcendence, which started life with the Pythagoreans and Platonists, permeating through Philo and Neo-Platonists to a great number of philosophers and theologians from all three traditions, identifies God with that source of divine reality from whom all other realities emanate wittingly or unwittingly as the light emanates from the sun.

To Plato this world and all it contains was nothing but a copy of the "Ideas" existing in a higher realm. Behind these 'Ideas' of the higher realm was the "Ultimate Idea": the Idea of Good. Speusippus, the successor of Plato as the head of the Old Academy, developed Plato's philosophy of Ideas into the notion of the absolute transcendence of the supreme First Principle.[166] Philo, a Jewish theologian and philosopher of Alexandria, incorporated this emphatic doctrine of divine transcendence into religious theology to avoid the anthropomorphic notion of deity presented by the scriptures, and to insist instead upon man's total inability to perceive God's essence. The scope of this work does not allow further discussion on this.

IMMANENCE

The term 'immanence' denotes God's presence in this world and is thought to directly oppose the term 'transcendence.' 'Immanence' derives from the Latin base *manere*, meaning to stay or to remain. The addition of the preposition 'in' renders the meaning of 'staying in' or 'remaining within.' It is worth noticing that what stays in something or remains within something is distinguishable and distinct from that which it stays in; otherwise, one will merely be a part of the other. Keeping this fact in mind, it can be argued that the term 'immanence' is not a polar opposite of the term 'transcendence.' In a sense the transcendence of God presupposes a relationship of God with the world. He transcends, while necessitating His "otherness" from it. God, as Niebuhr observed, "is certainly in the structures and temporal processes just as the human person is 'in' its organism. But both the human and the divine person possess a freedom over and above the processes and structures."[167] (Freedom to Niebuhr means neither being identifiable nor created by any created structure). Therefore, the transcendent God is related to this world of senses as the original and only source of its creation and existence, as the Creator and the Sustainer. He stays within the world of the material and is immanent in every aspect of its existence by means of His eternal power, knowledge, authority, protection, love, and many other infinite and absolute attributes and qualities, but ontologically is wholly 'other' than the world. Therefore, when contrasting transcendence, or surpassing nature, with immanence or the indwelling presence of God, we only describe in inadequate human language two aspects of one and the self-same Being which differ from each other.[168] This is probably why J. R. Illingworth maintained that both transcendence and immanence are "not alternatives but correlatives."[169] Both supplement each other as each contains some elements of the other.

Such a theistic understanding of 'transcendence' is central to the Semitic religions (Judaism, Christianity, and Islam). The belief in such a transcendent God sinks deep into the personalities of those who believe in Him and shapes their whole life. This belief is not something they can keep to themselves; there is a kind of compulsion and urgency behind it. All activities of true believers seem to be molded into and dictated by the particular kind of belief they possess regarding the 'Transcendent', because to them He is the sole source of their very existence, the One Unified, Perfect being that, though distinct from the cosmos, is the source of it, and continues to sustain and providentially guide it.

The approaches adopted by followers of these Semitic traditions with regards to anthropomorphic and corporeal depictions of this "transcendent" God are different to certain degrees. Jewish Scripture (the Hebrew Bible, Old Testament) is inundated with anthropomorphic expressions and depictions of God, though medieval Jewish theologians and philosophers like Saadia ibn Joseph (Saadia Gaon) (882–942), Moses Maimonides (1135–1204), and many modern scholars of our times have tried to eliminate or at least minimize these scriptural anthropomorphisms by various methods of interpretation. On the other hand, the pervasiveness of anthropomorphism in the Hebrew Bible makes such intellectual attempts superficial. Christianity's dogma of the person of Christ and "Incarnation" is also anthropomorphic. In spite of ample emphasis in the Christian tradition upon the transcendence of God and His uniqueness, the presence of dogmas like "Incarnation" and the frequent usage of expressions like the Father, the Son, God in human form, God on earth, Mother of God, and the face and hands of God etc. leave tinges of corporealism in the human mind. Islam emphasizes God's transcendence and its scripture keenly protects the transcendent God from any shade of corporealism and physical anthropomorphism being ascribed to Him, for "... there is none like unto Him" (Qur'an, 112:4).

I conclude this chapter by reference to its opening statement "Is God Dead?"

> The form of the questions that often arise concerning the nature of Divinity is revealing in this connection. It is usually something like "is there a God?" or "does God exist?" or "is God a reality?" or "what is God like?"; in any such form they are really "leading questions", since they imply that God can properly be considered as one factor in our situation among others; that God "as He is in Himself" – to use an admittedly but inevitably equivocal phrase – can be objectivised distinctively, like the objects of our perceptions and imaginations; that He is not even as real as those objects unless He can be brought into comparison with them; in short, that God is a relativity like everything else we can perceive or know.[170]

The next chapter explores in detail transcendental and anthropomorphic tendencies and expressions contained in the Bible, both the Old and the New Testaments.

NOTES

[1] Friedrich Nietzsche, "Thus Spoke Zarathustra," *The Philosophy of Nietzsche* (New York: Modern Library, 1954), part III, ch.52, p.190.

[2] Nietzsche, "Thus Spoke Zarathustra," part IV, ch.67, pp.264–67.

[3] Paul Ramsey, in his preface to Gabriel Vahanian, *The Death of God* (New York: George Braziller, 1961), p.XIX.

[4] Karl Löwith, *From Hegel to Nietzsche: The Revolution in Nineteenth Century Thought* (New York: Columbia University Press, 1964), p.322.

[5] James C. Livingston, *Modern Christian Thought* (New York: Macmillan, 1971), p.196.

[6] Paul Tillich, *A History of Christian Thought, from its Judaic and Hellenistic Origins to Existentialism* (New York: Simon and Schuster, 1972), p.497.

[7] This is an oft-repeated statement quoted in the majority of works on Greek thought. For instance see John M. Robinson, *Introduction to Early Greek Philosophy* (Boston: Houghton Mifflin, 1968), p.52.

[8] Marcus T. Cicero, *On the Nature of the Gods*, H. C. P. McGregor, trans. (Harmondsworth: Penguin, 1972), p.71.

[9] Francis Bacon, *The New Organon and Related Writings*, Fulton H. Anderson, ed. (New York: Liberal Arts Press, 1960), p.52.

[10] Ibid., p.48.

[11] J. Samuel Preus, *Explaining Religion* (London: Yale University Press, 1987), pp.43–44.

[12] Benedict de Spinoza, *The Chief Works of Benedict de Spinoza: On the Improvement of the Understanding; The Ethics; Correspondence*, R. H. M. Elwes, trans. (New York: Dover, 1955), p.75.

[13] David Hume, *The Natural History of Religion*, H. E. Root, ed. (Stanford: Stanford University Press, 1957), vol. II, p.28.

[14] Ibid., vol. III, p.29.

[15] Ibid., p.50.

[16] Auguste Comte, *The Positive Philosophy* (New York: D. Appleton & Company, 1854) vol. II, p.186.

[17] Auguste Comte, *The Positive Philosophy*, with a new Introduction by Abraham S. Blumberg (New York: AMS Press, 1974), p.545, 559.
[18] Isaiah Berlin, *Karl Marx: His Life and Environment* (Oxford: Oxford University Press, 1963), p.76.
[19] Friedrich Engels, *Ludwig Feuerbach and the Outcome of Classical German Philosophy* (New York: International Publishers, 1941), p.18.
[20] Richard Wagner, *My Life* (New York: Dodd Mead, 1911), vol.1, p.522.
[21] Karl Marx, "Theses on Feuerbach," *Ludwig Feuerbach and the Outcome of Classical German Philosophy*, Friedrich Engels (New York: International Publishers, 1941), p.83.
[22] Ludwig Feuerbach, *The Essence of Christianity*, E. G. Waring, F. W. Strothmann, eds. (New York: Frederick Unger, 1957), p.7, 9, 11.
[23] Ibid., pp.10–11.
[24] Ibid., pp.1–2, 14.
[25] Ludwig Feuerbach, *Lectures On the Essence of Religion*, Ralph Manheim, trans. (New York: Harper & Row, 1967), p.17.
[26] Feuerbach, *The Essence of Christianity*, p.49.
[27] Ibid., p.47.
[28] Ibid., p.65.
[29] Karl Marx, "Contribution to the Criticism of Hegel's Philosophy," quoted in Henri De Lubac, *The Drama of Atheist Humanism*, M. Riley, trans. and ed. (New York: Sheed & Ward, 1950), pp.15–16.
[30] Livingston, *Modern Christian Thought*, p.230.
[31] Tess Cosslett, *Science and Religion in the Nineteenth Century* (Cambridge: Cambridge University Press, 1984), p.87; Livingston, *Modern Christian Thought*, p.230.
[32] Charles Darwin, *The Descent of Man* (New York: Appleton & Co., 1962), p.528.
[33] Livingston, *Modern Christian Thought*, p.228.
[34] Herbert Spencer, *Illustrations of Universal Progress* (New York: D. Appleton & Co., 1870), p.442.
[35] Edward B. Tylor, *Primitive Culture: Researches into the Development of Mythology, Philosophy, Religion, Language, Art and Cultures* (New York: Holt & Co., 1883), vol.1, pp.26–27, vol.2, p.247.
[36] Sigmund Freud, *Totem and Taboo: Some Points of Agreement Between the Mental Lives of Savages and Neurotics*, J. Starchey, trans. (New York: W. W. Norton, 1955), p.91.

[37] Sigmund Freud, *The Future of an Illusion* (New York: W. W. Norton, 1961), p.29.

[38] Sigmund Freud, *The Interpretation of Dreams*, A. A. Brill, trans. (New York: Modern Library, 1950), p.450.

[39] Sigmund Freud, *Civilization and Its Discontents*, James Starchey, trans. (New York: W. W. Norton, 1961), p.92.

[40] Freud, *The Future of an Illusion*, pp.15–16.

[41] Ibid., p.17.

[42] Ibid., p.30.

[43] Freud, *Civilization and Its Discontents*, p.19; and see also Freud, *The Future of an Illusion*, pp.23–24.

[44] Stan Draenos, *Freud's Odyssey: Psychoanalysis and the End of Metaphysics* (New Haven: Yale University Press, 1982), p.80.

[45] Freud, *Totem and Taboo*, p.132.

[46] Sigmund Freud, *The Ego and the ID*, John Riviere, trans. (London: Hogarth, 1927), pp.40–41.

[47] Sigmund Freud, *Moses and Monotheism*, Katherine Jones, trans. (New York: Vintage, 1967), p.156.

[48] Freud, *Totem and Taboo*, pp.141–142.

[49] Freud, *The Future of an Illusion*, p.42.

[50] Karen Armstrong, *A History of God: The 4,000 Year Quest of Judaism, Christianity, and Islam* (New York: Ballantine Books, 1994), p.357.

[51] Stewart Guthrie, *Faces in the Clouds: A New Theory of Religion* (Oxford: Oxford University Press, 1995). The terms "comfort theory" and "familiarity theory" have been coined by Professor Stewart Guthrie.

[52] Feuerbach, *Lectures On the Essence of Religion*, p.17.

[53] Franz Boas, "Anthropology," *Encyclopedia of the Social Sciences* (New York: Macmillan, 1935), p.94.

[54] Claude Lévi-Strauss, *The Savage Mind* (Chicago: University of Chicago Press, 1966), p.221.

[55] R. J. Zwi Werblowsky, "Anthropomorphism," *The Encyclopedia of Religion*, Mircea Eliade, ed. (New York: Macmillan, 1987), vol.1, p.317.

[56] Emanuel B. Idowu, *African Traditional Religion: A Definition* (London: S.C.M Press, 1973), p.59.

[57] Stewart Guthrie, *Faces in the Clouds*, p.178.

[58] Hamilton A. R. Gibb, Johannes H. Kramers, eds., *The Shorter Encyclopaedia of Islam* (Leiden: E. J. Brill, 1953), p.583; Kees Wagtendonk, "Images in Islam:

Discussion of a Paradox," *Effigies Dei: Essays on the History of Religion*, D. Plas, ed. (New York: Brill, 1987), pp.112–129, all provide further details.

[59] W. J. Duggan, "Anthropomorphism," *Encyclopedic Dictionary of Religion*, Paul Kevin Meagher, Thomas C. O'Brien, Sister Consuelo M. Aherne, eds. (Washington: Corpus Publications, 1979), p.195.

[60] Frank B. Jevons, "Anthropomorphism," *Encyclopedia of Religion and Ethics*, James Hastings, ed. (New York: Charles Scribner's Sons, 1913), pp.573–74.

[61] See Hugo Meynell, "The Intelligibility of the Universe," *Reason and Religion*, S. C. Brown, ed. (Ithaca: Cornell University Press, 1977), pp.23–43; also see his *The Intelligible Universe* (New York: Macmillan, 1982).

[62] Fredrick Ferré, "In Praise of Anthropomorphism," *International Journal for Philosophy of Religion* (1984), vol.16, no.3, p.206, 208.

[63] Guthrie, *Faces in the Clouds*, p.183; I am indebted mostly to Guthrie in this discussion.

[64] Humphrey Palmer, *Analogy* (New York: St. Martin's Press, 1973), p.36.

[65] Paul Tillich, *Systematic Theology* (Chicago: Chicago University Press, 1951), vol.1, p.245.

[66] Paul Tillich, *What is Religion?*, James L. Adams, trans. (New York: Harper & Row, 1973), p.127.

[67] Paul Tillich, *Theology and Culture* (New York; Oxford: Galaxy Books, 1964), p.129.

[68] Armstrong, *History of God*, p.383.

[69] Tillich, *Theology and Culture*, p.72.

[70] Paul Tillich, *The Shaking of the Foundations* (New York: Scribner's Sons, 1948), p.63.

[71] Rene de Visme Williamson, *Politics and Protestant Theology: An Interpretation of Tillich, Barth, Bonhoeffer, and Brunner* (Baton Rouge: Louisiana State University Press, 1976), pp.5–9.

[72] Guthrie, *Faces in the Clouds*, p.182, 183.

[73] Richard Swinburne, *The Coherence of Theism* (Oxford: Clarendon Press, 1977), p.1.

[74] Samuel G. F. Brandon, ed., "Anthropomorphism," *Dictionary of Comparative Religion* (New York: Scribner's Sons, 1970), p.86.

[75] Kai Nielsen, "Empiricism, Theoretical Constructs, and God," *Journal of Religion* (1974), vol.54, p.199; also see his *Skepticism* (London: St. Martin's Press, 1973).

[76] Alexander Gallus, "A Biofunctional Theory of Religion," *Current Anthropology* (1972), vol.13, p.546.

[77] Moshe Greenberg, "Comments" [on "A Cognitive Theory of Religion" by Stewart Guthrie], *Current Anthropology* (1980), vol.21, p.196.
[78] Guthrie, *Faces in the Clouds*, p.185.
[79] William M. Thackery, *Letters and Private Papers*, G. N. Ray, ed. (Cambridge: Harvard University Press, 1945), vol.2, p.309.
[80] See Steven Weinberg, *The First Three Minutes: A Modern View of the Origin of the Universe* (New York: Basic Books, 1977), pp.101ff.
[81] See Alan Lightman, Roberta Brawer, *Origins: The Lives and Worlds of Modern Cosmologists* (Cambridge: Harvard University Press, 1990), pp.340ff.
[82] Salvador E. Luria, *Life: The Unfinished Experiment* (New York: Scribner's Sons, 1973), pp.148ff.
[83] Stephen J. Gould, *Ever Since Darwin* (New York: W. W. Norton, 1977), pp.12f.
[84] E. D. Klemke, "Living Without Appeal," *The Meaning of Life* (New York: Oxford University Press, 1999).
[85] Lightman, Brawer, *Origins: The Lives and Worlds of Modern Cosmologists*, p.340.
[86] See William Provine, "Evolution and the Foundation of Ethics," *Science, Technology and Social Progress,* Steven L. Goldman, ed. (Bethlehem, PA: Lehigh University Press, 1989), p.261.
[87] Klemke, "Living Without Appeal," pp.169–72.
[88] Thomas J. J. Altizer, *The Gospel of Christian Atheism* (London: Collins, 1966), p.136.
[89] Joseph H. Miller, *The Disappearance of God: Five Nineteenth Century Writers* (Cambridge: Harvard University Press, 1975), p.2.
[90] Ibid., p.5.
[91] Kevine J. Vanhoozer, *Is There a Meaning in This Text?* (Michigan: Zondervan, 1998), p.368.
[92] http://www.washingtontimes.com/news/2007/mar/14/20070314–095357–6808r/
[93] http://religions.pewforum.org/reports
[94] http://www.cnn.com/2009/LIVING/wayoflife/03/09/us.religion.less.christian/
[95] Miller, *The Disappearance of God*, p.8.
[96] Guthrie, *Faces in the Clouds*, p.177.
[97] Philip P. Wiener, *Dictionary of the History of Ideas* (New York: Charles Scribners' Sons, 1972), pp.1–87.
[98] Eliade, *The Encyclopedia of Religion*, vol.1, pp.316–17.
[99] James Martineau, *A Study of Religion: Its Sources and Contents* (Oxford: Clarendon Press, 1888), vol.1, p.313.

[100] Jacob Neusner, *The Incarnation of God: The Character of Divinity in Formative Judaism* (Philadelphia: Fortress Press, 1988), p.11.
[101] Guthrie, *Faces in the Clouds*, p.65.
[102] Freud, *The Future of an Illusion*, p.23.
[103] Leslie White, *The Science of Culture: A Study of Man and Civilization* (New York: Macmillan, 1964), p.111.
[104] Guthrie, *Faces in the Clouds*, p.73.
[105] Kenneth Latourette, *A History of Christianity* (New York: Harper, 1953), p.105.
[106] Martineau, *A Study of Religion*, vol.1, p.314.
[107] Neusner, *The Incarnation of God*, p.12.
[108] Alan Richardson, John Bowden, eds., "Incarnation," *The Westminster Dictionary of Christian Theology* (Philadelphia: The Westminster Press, 1983), p.289.
[109] John Calvin, *Commentary on the Book of the Prophet Isaiah*, W. Pringle, trans. (Michigan: William B. Eerdman, 1948), vol.3, p.302.
[110] Ian T. Ramsey, "Some Traditional Characterizations of God: Models and Qualifiers," *Religious Language: An Empirical Placing of Theological Phrases* (New York: MacMillan, 1963), ch.2, pp.55–102; also see Archbishop of Canterbury Michael Ramsey, ed., *Lambeth Essays on Faith* (London: The Society for Promoting Christian Knowledge SPCK, 1969); Frederic Ferré, *Basic Modern Philosophy of Religion* (New York: Charles Scribner's Sons, 1967), ch.12, 13, pp.335–71; and John Macquarrie, *God-Talk: An Examination of the Language and Logic of Theology* (London: S.C.M Press, 1967), ch.9, 10; and his *Thinking about God* (New York: Harper & Row, 1975), part 1, pp.3–27.
[111] Ramsey, *Religious Language*, p.53.
[112] Ibid., p.54.
[113] Ibid., p.102.
[114] Ferré, *Basic Modern Philosophy of Religion*, pp.379–80.
[115] Ibid., p.358.
[116] Palmer, *Analogy*, p.175.
[117] Ibid., p.174.
[118] Ralph M. McInerny, *The Logic of Analogy: An Interpretation of St. Thomas* (The Hague: Martinus Nijhoff, 1961), pp.124–25.
[119] Marjo C. A. Korpel, *A Rift in the Clouds: Ugaritic and Hebrew Descriptions of the Divine* (Munster: UGARIT-Verlag, 1990), p.11; see for the original Herman Bavinck, *Gereformeerde Dogmatiek*, 4th edn. (Kampen: Kok, 1928), vol.2, p.75.

[120] Korpel, *A Rift in the Clouds*, p.11.
[121] John R. Illingworth, *Personality, Human and Divine* (London: Macmillan, 1899), p.54.
[122] Theodore Parker, *Discourse of Matters Pertaining to Religion* (Boston: C. C. Little J. Brown, 1842), Book 11, p.165.
[123] Lewis R. Farnel, *Attributes of God* (Oxford: Clarendon Press, 1925), p.21.
[124] St. Thomas Aquinas, *Summa Theologiae*, H. Mcabe, trans. (New York: McGraw-Hill, 1964), vol.3, pp.57–59.
[125] Ibid.
[126] See Averroes, *Averroes' Middle Commentaries on Aristotle's Categories and De Interpretatione*. Translated with notes and Introductions by Charles E. Butterworth (St. Augustine's Press, 1998). Abū al-Walīd Muḥammad ibn Aḥmad ibn Rushd, *Faṣl al-Maqāl fī mā bayn al-Ḥikmah wa al-Sharīʿah min al-Ittiṣāl*, 2nd edn. (Cairo: Dār al-Maʿārif, 1983); for English source see Majid Fakhry, *A History of Islamic Philosophy* (New York; London: Columbia University Press, 1970), pp.302ff. Also *Averroes Decisive Treatise and Epistle Dedicatory*. Translation, with introductions and notes, by Charles E. Butterworth (Brigham Young University, 2002).
[127] See details in Hampus Lyttkens, *The Analogy Between God and The World: An Investigation of its Background and Interpretation of its Use by Thomas of Aquino* (Uppsala: Almquist and Wiksells Boktwyckeri AB, 1952); George Klubertanz, *St. Thomas Aquinas on Analogy: A Textual Analysis and Systematic Synthesis* (Chicago: Loyola University Press, 1960); Eric L. Mascall, *Existence and Analogy* (London: Darton, Longman & Todd, 1966).
[128] Korpel, *A Rift in the Clouds*, p.7.
[129] See Ibid.
[130] Ramsey, *Religious Language*; also his *Models and Mystery* (Oxford: Oxford University Press, 1964); also see Jerry H. Gill, ed., *Christian Empiricism* (London: SPKC, 1974).
[131] See Korpel, *A Rift in the Clouds*, pp.17–23; also see Ian G. Barbour, *Models and Paradigms* (London: S.C.M Press, 1974), p.14ff.
[132] Janet M. Soskice, *Metaphor and Religious Language* (Oxford: Oxford University Press, 1985); also her paper "Myths, Metaphor and Narrative Theology," *Recent Developments in the Philosophy of Language* (Utrecht: Oxford University Press, 1988), pp.130–55.
[133] Macquarrie, *Thinking About God*, p.13.
[134] Soskice, *Metaphor*, p.83.
[135] Guthrie, *Faces in the Clouds*, p.199.

[136] Clifford Geertz, "Religion as a Cultural System," *Anthropological Approaches to the Study of Religion*, Michael Banton, ed. (London: Tavistock Publications, 1966), pp.4ff.
[137] Robert Bellah, "Civil Religion in America," *Daedalus, Journal of the American Academy of Arts and Sciences*, (Winter, 1967), vol.96, pp.1–21.
[138] See Stanley J. Tambiah, *Magic, Science, Religion, and the Scope of Rationality* (Cambridge: Cambridge University Press, 1990), p.6; Raymond Firth, *Tikopia Ritual and Belief* (Boston: Beacon Press, 1967), p.12; Paul Ricoeur, "Philosophy and Religious Language," *Journal of Religion* (1974), vol.54, pp.71–85.
[139] Martin Buber, *The Prophetic Faith* (New York: Harper & Brothers, 1960), p.35.
[140] Martin Buber, *Between Man and Man*, R.G. Smith, trans. (Boston: Beacon Press, 1961), pp.80–81.
[141] Swinburne, *The Coherence of Theism*, p.101.
[142] Barbara R. Krasner, "Sublime Anthropomorphism: The Significance of Jewish Mysticism for Personal and Communal Existence," Ph.D. Dissertation, Temple University (Ann Arbor: University Microfilms International, 1975).
[143] Feuerbach, *The Essence of Christianity*, p.193.
[144] Guthrie, *Faces in the Clouds*, pp.199ff; I am fully indebted to Guthrie in this discussion.
[145] Bacon, *The New Organon*, pp.52f.
[146] See John A. Wheeler, "Foreword," *The Anthropic Cosmological Principle*, J. D. Barrow, Frank J. Tipler (Oxford: Oxford University Press, 1986); also Joseph Agassi, "Anthropomorphism in Science," *Dictionary of the History of Ideas*, Philip P. Wiener, ed. (New York: Charles Scribner's Sons, 1973); and also Guthrie, *Faces in the Clouds*, ch.6, pp.152–76.
[147] E. Thomas Lawson, Robert N. McCauley, *Rethinking Religion: Connecting Cognition and Culture* (Cambridge: Cambridge University Press, 1990), p.162.
[148] Barry Barnes, *Scientific Knowledge and Sociological Theory* (London: Routledge and Kegan Paul, 1974), p.VIII.
[149] Linda M. Fedigan, *Primitive Paradigms: Sex Roles and Social Bonds* (Montreal: Eden Press, 1982), pp.16–17.
[150] T. Percy Nunn, "Anthropomorphism in Physics," *Proceedings of the British Academy*, [Annual Philosophical Lecture, Henriette Hertz Trust] (London: Oxford University Press, 1927), p.15.
[151] Edgar S. Brightman, "Anthropomorphism," *Collier's Encyclopedia* (New York: Crowell-Collier Educational Corporation, 1965), p.314.
[152] Guthrie, *Faces in the Clouds*, p.176.

[153] Quoted from John R. Illingworth, *Divine Transcendence* (London: Macmillan, 1911), p.220; see more detailed discussions in Guthrie, "Anthropomorphism in Philosophy and Science," *Faces in the Clouds*, ch.6, pp.152–76.
[154] Martineau, *A Study of Religion*, vol.1, p.317.
[155] Terms taken from Ibid.
[156] Farnel, *Attributes of God*, p.22.
[157] Macquarrie, *Thinking About God*, p.13.
[158] See Sabapathy Kulandran, *The Concept of Transcendence* (Madras: The Christian Literary Society, 1981), p.1.
[159] Van Harvey, *A Handbook of Theological Terms* (New York: Macmillan, 1964), p.242.
[160] Ibid.
[161] Tillich, *Systematic Theology*, vol.1, p.18.
[162] Herbert W. Richardson, ed., *Transcendence* (Boston: Beacon Press, 1969), p.114.
[163] Karl Heim, *God Transcendent* (London: James Nisbet & Co., 1935), p.16f.
[164] Illingworth, *Divine Transcendence*, p.13.
[165] Ibid., p.16.
[166] David Winston, *Philo of Alexandria* (New York: Paulist Press, 1981), p.22.
[167] Charles W. Kegley, ed., *Reinhold Niebhur, His Religious, Social and Political Thought* (New York: Macmillan, 1956), p.299.
[168] Illingworth, *Divine Transcendence*, p.13.
[169] Ibid., p.72.
[170] Lord Northbourne, "Intellectual Freedom", *Studies in Comparative Religion*, vol. 5, no.1. (Winter, 1971) © World Wisdom, Inc.

CHAPTER 2

Transcendental and Anthropomorphic Tendencies in the Hebrew Bible

THE UNDERSTANDING OF GOD distinctive to the Hebrew Bible and hence to Judaic tradition is an amalgamation of anthropomorphic and transcendental tendencies. Emphasis upon the former however runs deep, and to such a level that God in the ancient biblical period is presented in manifest anthropomorphic terms, with ascription of human qualities and attributes so clear, that even the Ten Commandments are said to have been written by the "finger of God". Some of the anthropomorphisms employed are crude and blatant, portraying God as embodying human physical characteristics and feelings, even acting much like a human being (details being quite graphic in certain places) leaving the theological problem of how to interpret them, their impact, and whether to regard them as objectionable or not. These and other elements are explored in this chapter.

In the Bible God appears in human form, eats, drinks, rests and is refreshed. For example, in a well known biblical encounter, God wrestles with Jacob, dislocates Jacob's thigh and is even shown to be weak, unable to physically dominate Jacob, to the point of finally asking Jacob to let Him go as the dawn breaks.

Theophany (meaning appearance of God) is thus a common occurrence in the Hebrew Bible. Many biblical theophanies are either concrete anthropomorphisms, or subcategories of physical anthropomorphism, such as envisioned anthropomorphism. And many of these theophanies portray God's utter closeness to human beings, for the most part in terms of human form, but with varying degrees of explicitness and human embodiment. So, most human organs are ascribed to God with the exception of sexuality. There are times when God is depicted in transcendental anthropomorphisms where He is portrayed in human shapes and qualities yet residing in the heavens. He is enthroned on a special throne, rides cherubim, plants a garden, studies Torah, presides over a divine council and even speaks to people directly from this heavenly sphere. Some of the anthropomorphic expressions are figurative or metaphorical in nature as they render themselves to linguistically accepted metaphorical interpretations. Many however are not, being corporeal and anthropomorphic through and through. Unfortunately numerous biblical scholars muddle these concrete and literally corporeal phrases by attempting to give them figurative or representational interpretations through recourse to some very arbitrary means. So, for instance, we have scholars attempting to synthetically impose their own sophisticated and developed understandings of God and His nature onto the text of the Hebrew Bible, an approach which completely defies the original intent as well as context of the script.

The origins of Biblical anthropomorphism lie in the Book of Genesis, the first book of the Jewish Torah and the Christian Bible. In verse 1:26 God is said to proclaim "*na'aseh 'adam beselmenu kidemutenu*", meaning, "Let us make man in our image after our likeness." Many orthodox exegetes try to interprete this verse spiritually, claiming that the image and likeness mentioned in the verse refer not to a physical but to a spiritual aspect. However, the original Hebrew words defy any such interpretation. The Hebrew words *tzelem* (image) and *demute* (likeness) denote the outward form and not inward spiritual attributes. Howard Eilberg-Schwartz has no hesitation in confessing that this passage in Genesis presupposes

> a resemblance between the human body and divine form. The use of the word "image" (*selem*), which most interpreters construe to mean a physical likeness, supports this view. Furthermore, in Genesis 5:1–3, the term "image" and "likeness" are used to describe the resemblance between Adam and his son Seth. The use of the terminology here suggests that humanity resembles God in the same way that Seth resembles Adam, including their physical characteristics.[1]

Therefore the Hebrew God looks like man and very often acts like man. This idea of a God-man resemblance abounds in the Hebrew Bible together with anthropomorphic imagery. Thus God, like man, is "mutable", freely "localized in space and time," moves, changes and reacts to changes. Esther J. Hamori observes:

> The God of the Hebrew Bible is profoundly anthropomorphic, mutable, free and able to be localized in space and time, able to move, change and be influenced to change. In biblical texts, this includes both intrinsic and extrinsic change...The Israelite God is hardly the immutable, atemporal God of classical theism.2

Further, the God of the Hebrew Bible also changes His mind as well as His decisions. For instance the prophet Moses is recorded as having made God repent of certain evil decisions so causing God to change His mind. At times God appears as tribalistic with racist undertones, and at others a real estate agent more concerned with property rights than worship. Very often He represents the Hebrews' aspirations and national agenda projecting in a sense their failures, dreams and fears into the cosmos. Thus in the Hebrew God what we have is not the absolute transcendent and perfect God of theism but rather an imperfect, corporeal and finite God, a product of His very finite creators, those who recorded the Old Testament.

Ethical monotheism was not the predominant concern of the early Hebrews. Henotheism is perhaps the best term to denote a patriarchal understanding of God. Monolatry or Mono-Yahwism replaces henotheism with the arrival of Moses who at the same time seems to be sowing the seeds of biblical monotheism although not in the strict sense of the term. His Yahweh is a jealous God though his universe is not free from the existence of other gods. Moreover, his Yahweh is not free from anthropomorphic attributes and qualities seemingly boldly presented in anthropomorphic as well as physical terms. The anthropomorphic tendency is quite visible even in the case of later prophets, who championed strict monotheism and offered vehement opposition to idolatry and graven images. Their God is not presented in crude material terms, but is still visibly corporeal and anthropomorphic i.e., a reflection of the idea that God created man in His own image and likeness. There are many biblical statements which if taken at face value present God in transcendental terms. On the other hand, God's transcendence is not carefully protected against possible exploitation and compromise. So, the same Bible which categorically differentiates God from mortals, also on many occasions portrays Him very much like mortals with mortal qualities and attributes. There appears to be a tension between anthropomorphism and transcendence throughout the Hebrew Bible but that tension is not quite decisive in eliminating the anthropomorphic depictions of God. Moreover, the Jewish community at large did not seem troubled by the presence of these anthropomorphic expressions in their scripture, until the onslaught of Greek philosophy especially in the first century BC. Even later Rabbinic thought, though not without exceptions, appears to be accepting of biblical anthropomorphisms. Hellenistic thought moved a number of Jewish scholars to interpret anthropomorphic expressions figuratively. For instance, Aristobulus (150 BC) and Philo Judaeus (20 BC–40 CE) championed allegorical interpretation to eliminate anthropomorphic passages, so much so that Philo completely stripped his God of all ascription of attributes.

Later in medieval times Saadia Gaon (882–942), Bahya ibn Paquda (1040), and Judah ha-Levi (1075–1141) vehemently opposed biblical anthropomorphisms. Finally we come to Moses Maimonides (1135–1204) who propounded the dogma of God's incorporeality and declared its deniers as idolaters and heretics. The medieval Jewish philosophers seem to have been really bothered by these anthropomorphic expressions, and this was mostly due to the polemic offensive of Muslim speculative theologians against them. Despite the authoritative esteem with which Maimonides was, and is, held among many Jews, his intellectualization of the Hebrew God failed to receive acceptance from among his coreligionists who rejected his incorporeal deity. They regarded his Hellenistic doctrine to be antithetical to the historically authenticated and scripturally mandated anthropomorphic tradition of Jewry at large.

The history of God in the Hebrew Bible seems to be progressive, with conflicting anthropomorphic tendencies reflected throughout this progressive process. This paradoxically simmering tension, with regards to the transcendental and anthropomorphic tendencies characterized of

God, poses a problem. However, it would not be an issue were the Bible to be accepted as a composite work of many generations, a multiplicity of biblical writers, whose differing worldviews, dispositions and cultural milieus reveal themselves in the text, and so explain the tension. If, on the other hand we view the Bible as the Word of God verbatim given to Jews through the prophetic offices of Moses and other Hebrew prophets we are left with manifold challenges. For instance, if God is entirely capable (as of course He is) of expressing His will and intent in idioms most appropriate to His majesty and grandeur then needless to say His authentic Word does not need artificial and arbitrary allegorical tools to convey His true intent to the recipients of His Word. In sum the conflicting tension in the Hebrew Bible is reflective of the competing tendencies, thought patterns, worldviews, and metaphysics of the Hebrew Bible's compilers and little more. The Hebrew Bible itself is best witness to this claim, so we turn next to its study for the proof.

THE BIBLE: AN INTRODUCTION

Along with the Qur'an, the Bible is perhaps ranked one of the most read, distributed and discussed books in the world. Read for nearly two thousand years or more it has been a force, molding, shaping and reshaping the lives and views of millions into its own thought patterns. Some of its readers have taken it literally and others figuratively or symbolically. Some have related themselves to it, and revered it as the fountainhead of their faith and tradition, whilst others have read it to criticize it or study it as a powerful force which has led to or helped to create a number of great civilizations and cultures. Whatever the case, the fact remains that the Bible has without doubt, been part and parcel of various human religious, educational, political and social institutions, in different capacities since its compilation, or canonization, centuries ago. So vast is the work connected with it, says Geddes MacGregor, that "even if an international commission were set up with unlimited funds to investigate the work, a complete inventory of it would be impossible."[3]

The word "Bible" is derived from the Greek "biblos," which itself is a translation of the Hebrew *Sepharim* meaning "books". As a general term it can be used for any book venerated as "Sacred" by its followers but as a specific term "the Bible" denotes the books which are acknowledged as canonical by the Christian Church.

The Bible consists of two main parts, commonly referred to as the Old Testament and the New Testament. Both form part of the Christian Canon but the Old Testament is specifically the sacred scripture of the Jews who refer to it as the "Hebrew Bible" or just the Bible rather than Old Testament, as this designation implies a new testament based on events the Jews believe never happened. For Christians, on the other hand, the Hebrew Bible is traditionally accepted as heavenly inspired along with the New Testament and hence authoritative in shaping their religious teachings and practices.

The Hebrew (or Jewish) Bible differs from the Old Testament of the Catholic Bible in a number of respects, and this concerns the number and order of the books that comprise it. Most importantly the Hebrew Bible excludes the twelve books of the Apocrypha, which are accepted by Catholics as canonical and part of their compilation of the Bible. Like the Jews, the Protestants also do not treat these Apocryphal works as canonical, or heavenly inspired, and so do not include them. However the order of the books in the Protestant Old Testament differs from that of the Hebrew Bible.

The Jews divide their Bible into three main categories comprising a total of 39 books: the Law or *Torah*, the Prophets or *Neve'im* and the Writings or *Ketuvim*. These three sections are collectively known as *TaNaKh*, which is an acronym derived from a combination of the first letters of each section in their Hebrew terminology (*Torah, Neve'im, and Ketuvim*).

The Law or Torah comprises the *Chumash* (five) or the *Pentateuch*, the five "Books of Moses": Genesis, Exodus, Leviticus, Numbers, Deuteronomy.

The "Prophets" fall into two further subdivisions: the "Former Prophets" (four historical books) comprising Joshua, Judges, Samuel (I & II) and Kings (I & II) and the "Latter Prophets" comprising Isaiah, Jeremiah, Ezekiel and "The Books of the Twelve Prophets": Hosea, Nahum, Joel, Habakkuk, Amos, Zephaniah, Obadiah, Haggai, Jonah, Zechariah, Micah, and Malachi.

The third section "Writing" or *Hagiographa* contains the rest of the books: Psalms, Proverbs, Job, Lamentations, Ecclesiastes, Song of Songs, Ezra-Nehemiah, Chronicles (I & II) Daniel, Ruth and Esther.

This threefold division of the Hebrew Bible is simply a reflection of its historical development and in no way or form represents any topical or stylistic classification or categorization. It is frequently believed to correspond to the three historical stages during which the books of each section received canonical recognition. Although all three parts of the scripture were believed to be inspired and their significance and authority determined by their respective positions in this tripartite division, the Pentateuch stands in a special class with its author Moses considered as the fountainhead of the rest of the books. Therefore,

> the prophets are transmitters of a continuous tradition beginning with Moses; the Prophets and the Hagiographa explain the Pentateuch. Thus all the rest of [the] books, with no detraction from their divine inspiration and authority, are an authority of the second rank; they repeat, reinforce, amplify, and explain the Law, but are never independent of it.[4]

In view of this conspicuous position of the Torah it is pertinent to discuss the status and authority of the "Law" or "Pentateuch" in Judaic tradition.

THE "LAW" OR THE "TORAH": SIGNIFICANCE AND AUTHORITY

The term "Torah" separates the Pentateuch from the other two sections of the Hebrew Bible. It means "teaching", "doctrine", or "instruction" and is often used to refer to all the body of laws. The term in a wider sense is also applied to scriptures as a whole and to biblical legislation in contrast to rabbinical enactments.

The Torah is the most important and authoritative book in Jewish faith. It received this recognition from Numbers 8:1, "And the Lord spoke unto Moses" and also from Deuteronomy 31:9, "And Moses wrote this law"; (see also Exodus 20:1, 32:16; Leviticus 1:1, 4:1; Numbers 1:1, 2:1, etc.) In view of its divine origin and Mosaic authorship, the Torah has been held in great esteem throughout Jewish history. The Rabbinical tradition declared it to exist even prior to its revelation to Moses. To the Rabbis the Torah existed even before the world was created. It is regarded as one of the six or seven things that were created before the creation of anything in the world and it even preceded the throne of God's glory. The "Torah which God had kept by him in heaven for nine hundred and seventy-four generations was a hidden treasure."[5] God consulted the Torah in regard to the creation of the world as an architect consults a blue print.

It is evident from these quotations that Rabbinic Judaism had a strong belief in the Torah being the preexistent "Word of God" given to Moses in a mode of direct revelation. They also had no doubt whatsoever about the physical Mosaic authorship of the Torah, "And who wrote them? Moses wrote his own book (The Torah) and the sections concerning Balaam and Job."[6] Otto Eissfeldt summarizes the point in the following words:

> Moses was from an early date regarded as the compiler, or more correctly as the mediator, of the laws of the Pentateuch which issued from God himself. The name used in the New Testament clearly with reference to the whole Pentateuch – *the Book of Moses* – is certainly to be understood as meaning that Moses was the compiler of the Pentateuch. Explicit references to this conception may be found in Philo ..., in Josephus, and in the Talmud (bab. Baba Batra 14b), where it is said that Moses wrote the five books named after him. Philo and Josephus explicitly attribute to Moses also the conclusion which relates his death (Deut. xxxiv, 5–12), whereas the Talmud regards this as having been written by Joshua. The Jewish tradition concerning the compilation of the Pentateuch was taken over by the Christian church.[7]

In addition to this, the rabbinic sources contended that God's whole revelation was not comprised in the written Torah but also in the Oral

Torah, the Talmud, which Moses received side by side with the Written Torah on Mount Sinai and which was orally carried and conveyed through subsequent generations.

The medieval Jewish scholars maintained the same position *vis-à-vis* the divine provenance of the Torah and the resulting authoritative and binding nature of the Bible in general and the Dual Torah in particular. There is a popular saying concerning Moses Maimonides that "from Moses to Moses there was none like Moses".[8] This medieval philosopher and Rabbi argued in his introduction to the "Mishneh Torah" ("Repetition of the Torah") that:

> All the precepts which Moses received on Sinai were given together with their interpretation, as it is said, "And I will give to you the table of stone, and the law, and the commandment" (Exodus 24:12). "The Law" refers to the Written Law: "the commandments" to its interpretation... This commandment refers to that which is called the Oral Law. The whole of the Law was written by Moses, our Teacher, before his death in his own hand.[9]

In his letter to Joseph Ibn Gabir, he declared that "the Torah in its totality has been given to us by the Lord through Moses."[10] This greatest of the Jewish scholars of the Middle Ages formulated "Thirteen Principles" which a Jew must believe in order to be a Jew. The Eighth Fundamental Principle is comprised of the following words:

> [T]hat the Torah came from God. We are to believe that the whole Torah was given to us through Moses, our Teacher, entirely from God. When we call the Torah "God's Word" we speak metaphorically. We do not know exactly how it reached us, but only that it came to us through Moses who acted like a secretary taking dictation. He wrote down the events of the time and the commandments, for which reason he is called "Lawgiver."[11]

To Maimonides, the entire Hebrew Bible was the inerrant Word of God. He argues:

> There is no distinction between a verse of Scripture like "The sons of Ham were Cush and Mizraim" (Genesis 10:6), or "His Wife's name was Mehatable and his concubine was Timna" (Genesis 36:39, 36:12) and one like "I am the Lord your God" (Exodus 20:2) or "Hear, O Israel" (Deuteronomy 6:4). All came from God, and all are the Torah of God, perfect, pure, holy, and true. Anyone who says Moses wrote some passages on his own is regarded by our sages as an atheist or worst kind of heretic, because he tries to distinguish essence from accident in Torah. Such a heretic claims that some historical passages or stories are trivial inventions of Moses and not Divine Revelation.[12]

These words are crystal clear and forceful enough to speak for themselves. Jews of the Middle Ages held a strong belief in the divine origin and Mosaic authorship of the entire Torah, as well as belief in its infallibility, immutability, and eternity. Saᶜad ibn Manṣūr ibn Kammūnah, a 13th century Jewish philosopher, wrote a famous treatise which argued that the law would neither be abolished nor changed nor substituted for something other than itself.[13] This belief in the Torah's infallibility, supernatural origin and permanent credibility was so deep held in the hearts of medieval Jewish scholars that they closed all doors to and denied all the possibilities of progressive revelation. They held with Maimonides that "it will neither be abrogated nor superseded, neither supplemented nor abridged. Never shall it be supplanted by another divine revelation containing positive and negative duties."[14] They also maintained, as Maimonides observed, that "To the Torah, Oral and Written, nothing must be added nor any thing taken from it."[15] And this view continued to be maintained by Jews till the beginning of our era. Even in today's world of scientific naturalism and cosmic pessimism, this is what a reformed Jew has to say about the significance of the Torah:

> The teachings of the Torah are the most sacred legacy and inspiration of the Jewish people. They are so fundamental that they are recited in public reading every week of every year. The five books are divided into segments or portions, one of which is to be

> read on each successive Sabbath. Usually, the first words of each portion are chosen as the title, so that every week of the Jewish year can be identified by its Torah portion....since no object in Jewish life is more precious than a Torah.[16]

He further informs us that "A Torah can never be deliberately destroyed. If it becomes too brittle or too fragile to use, it is buried in the earth just like a deceased person."[17]

Though voices against such a literal view of the Torah have included Christian scholars like Clementine Homilies, St. Jerome, and Theodore of Mopsuestia (d. c. 428) and some Jewish scholars like Isaac ibn Yashush, Rashi, David Kimhi and Abraham ibn Ezra (d. 1167) in the twelfth century, continuing with Carlstadt, Andreas Masius (1574) in the sixteenth, and Isaac de la Payrere (1655), and Richard Simon, Thomas Hobbes and then Spinoza in the seventeenth century, it was only in the age of reason in the eighteenth century that the stage was set for the loss of biblical authority as inspired Scripture.

Finally it was in the nineteenth and early twentieth century that biblical scholars like Julius Wellhausen (1844–1918) were able to analyze, oppose and finally shatter the idea of the divine and supernatural origin of the Torah and Mosaic authorship of it. At present, claims R. E. Friedman, "there is hardly a biblical scholar in the world actively working on the problem who would claim that the Five Books of Moses were written by Moses – or by any one person."[18]

Contemporary Jews and the Authority of the Torah

Though significant results were achieved by the as mentioned scholars of the sixteenth and seventeenth centuries, yet nobody attempted to differentiate clearly between various component parts of the Pentateuch. This process started with H. B. Witter whose *Jura Israelitarum in Palastinam* appeared in 1711. He pointed out the usage of different divine names in the Book of Genesis. Jean Astruc (born in 1684) identified these sources as one which used the divine name "Elohim", and the other which used the divine name "Jehovah". Eichhorn in his *Einleitung in das Alte Testament* (first edition 1780–3) proved that there existed two main strands and hence two sources for the ancient writings. English scholar Alexander Geddes and German scholar J. S. Vater developed "*the fragment hypothesis*" picturing the Pentateuch as a collection of fragments. Hupfeld in his book *Die Quellen der Genesis und die Art ihrer Zusammensetzung*, inaugurated a new phase in the history of Pentateuchal criticism. He identified three narrative strands in the Pentateuch.

As a result of biblical scholars Wilhelm Vatke's *Die Religion des Alten Testament I* (1835) and Karl H. Graf's *Die geschichtlichen Bucher des Alten Testaments* (1866), two independent research works, a historical or documentary hypothesis about the different sources of the Pentateuch came into the limelight. Vatke sought to trace from the biblical narration the historical development of the ancient Hebrew religion while Graf worked on the text itself so as to find which of the texts must have preceded or followed others. They identified four different source documents; J (the document associated with the divine name Yahweh or Jehovah), E (the one associated with Elohim, the Hebrew word for God), P (the passages emphasizing the legal aspects and the functions of priests), and D (the source responsible for composing the book of Deuteronomy). J. Wellhausen combined the research of his predecessors and propounded the "Documentary Hypothesis," which brought a revolution in the field of biblical research in general and Pentateuch studies in particular. Since then most critics of the Pentateuch argue that it is a composite work, produced at different intervals, with contradictions, inconsistencies and different literary styles, and as such it cannot be the work of one individual (Moses) as has been claimed for centuries. Opposition to the critical study or examination of the Bible comes from the Church as well as Judaism, but the new scholarship has impacted on followers of both religions resulting in schism with respect to the authority of the Torah. At present there are three main groups among those of the Jewish faith, each having a different view with regards to the authority of the Torah.

Reform or Progressive Judaism

Reform Judaism, which appeared in nineteenth century Germany, recognizes the validity of the critical study of the Bible and accepts the picture of the Torah or Pentateuch which has emerged as a result of modern historical and critical research and investigation. The movement of Reform Judaism can be further divided into two main categories: the "Classical" and the "Radical". The Classical Reform movement does not dispense with the traditional concept of the Torah altogether. These reformers attempt rather to reinterpret and adapt it to new requirements:

> The emphasis at the outset was on adaptability, not on total rejection. The early Reformers understood very well that Jewish law was central to Jewish life. They acknowledged the need to discontinue the observance of antiquated commandments, but they staunchly defended the necessity of the legal process in determining Jewish belief and practice.[19]

The Classical Reform movement ended in 1881 when radical trends within the movement got a chance to dominate it. The outcome, the Radical Reform Judaism movement, practically dispensed with the concept of "Torah," having lost faith in its divine origin. In the words of M. M. Kaplan, one of the pioneers of modern Jewish thought:

> With critical and historical research proving that the Pentateuch is a composite document which began to function as a single code not earlier than in the days of Ezra, the laws and institutions contained in the Pentateuch are deprived at one blow of the infallibility and permanent validity which traditional Judaism was wont to ascribe to them.[20]

Contrary to the traditional view, Radical Reformers give more importance to Jewish history, the Jewish people, Jewish civilization etc. and see Judaism as a constantly evolving organism rather than something revealed and static. Judaism, observes J. Neusner, "has a history, that history is single and unitary; and it has always been leading to its present outcome: Reformed Judaism."[21] This means that "the origin of the reliable definition of Judaism lies not in revealed records of God's will but in human accounts of humanity's works."[22]

For Radical Reform Judaism the source of religious authority, observes Danzger, is "the ethical and universalistic teachings of the prophets. Because conscience is a reflection of the Godhead for Reform, the ultimate authority is man's own conscience, guided by the moral and ethical teachings of the Bible."[23] This perhaps is the reason why the Reformers are more concerned with philosophy than the Torah. Even the term "Torah" is missing from their vocabulary. This is evident from the language used in the historic Pittsburgh platform which declared:

> We recognize in the Mosaic legislation a system of training the Jewish people for its mission during its national life in Palestine, and today we accept as binding only its moral laws and maintain only such ceremonies as elevate and sanctify our lives, but reject all such as are not adapted to the views and habits of modern civilization... We hold that all such Mosaic and rabbinical laws as regular diet, priestly purity, and dress... Their observance in our days is apt rather to obstruct than to further modern spiritual elevation.[24]

One cannot imagine a more forthright declaration addressed to the age which refutes or transforms the authority of the Written as well the Oral Torah. Commenting on this revolution, Greenstein observes that

> the principle of earlier Reform had been a commitment to evolution in Jewish law, not revolution. Classical Reform tried to adapt Jewish law to new conditions while still retaining the principle. The Pittsburgh Platform abandoned that effort altogether. Halakah, the Hebrew word for "Jewish law," disappeared from Reform vocabulary.[25]

This trend continued in Reform circles till the early 1930s. In 1930 the Columbus Platform replaced the Pittsburgh Platform. It emphasized the evolution of Jewish law and life rather than revolution. It renewed the approach of Classical Reformers *vis-à-vis* the Torah and continues to be popular among Reform Jews today.

Orthodox or Traditional Judaism

Orthodox Judaism, contrary to popular impression, is not a monolithic movement. Orthodoxy spans a range of complexity with regards to beliefs, customs, practices and political views. However, there is one thing common among them: the Orthodox do not see Judaism as a constantly changing organism or as a human construct. They believe that the Torah was revealed on Sinai and is supernatural and eternal and in no way man-made or subject to change. Jacob Neusner defines orthodoxy as "all Jews who believe that God revealed the dual Torah at Sinai, and that Jews must carry out the requirements of Jewish law contained in the Torah as interpreted by the sages through time."[26] Therefore, the Orthodox or traditionalists are in line with the position held by the generality of Jewry at large for centuries. They maintain that the Torah is the word of God and by definition truth itself. They further maintain that the Torah

> being given by God, must carry meaning in every word and not even one letter can be superfluous. One may not understand everything, but that is human shortcoming. If modern scientific knowledge appears to contradict the biblical word, then either our present-day science will prove to be in error or we do not understand the Bible properly.[27]

So to Orthodoxy the Torah constitutes facts that are divinely oriented and above all doubt. As the facts of nature leave no room for any kind of doubt, so does the Torah. This view of the essential truthfulness or absolute inerrancy of the Torah also attended to its natural corollary that the Torah teachings are directed, precise and full of divine wisdom. Human beings may not deny them even if they are at a loss to grasp the meanings. In short the religious authority in orthodoxy is the Written as well as the Oral Torah (Talmud) along with the subsequent rabbinic traditions and not (as in Reform Judaism) the history of the Jewish people. Greenstein observes that

> in more recent times, this appeal to authenticity through traditional sources has persuaded portions of [the] Orthodox

community to define its theological stance as "Torah-true" Judaism. They perceive themselves as guardians of the Torah and its commandments with the duty to preserve them and follow them regardless of changing times or circumstances.[28]

Conservative Judaism

Conservative Judaism is a "counter-Reform" movement and is a mixture of both the above discussed views. Conservative Jews maintain their belief in the revealed nature of the Dual Torah, but do not seal the door of revelation with the rabbinical period. They believe in a continuity of revelation in Jewish tradition. This middle position espouses both the previous views, for it holds that God revealed the written Torah, which was supplemented by "the ongoing revelation manifesting itself throughout history in the spirit of the Jewish people."[29]

To the Conservatives, Jewish tradition, culture, customs, and the practices and value schemes of the Jewish people, are quite significant. It is their belief that Judaism is a tradition that includes not only the written and oral Torah, the Mishna and the Talmud, but also the historical practices of Jews, the traditions of the entire Jewish civilization. Robert Gordis summarizes the fundamental postulates of Conservative Judaism in the following words: "The maintenance of the twin principles of authority and development in Jewish law... together with the emphasis upon the worldwide peoplehood of Israel – these are the basic postulates of Conservative Judaism."[30] This emphasis upon the catholic Israel does not imply lack of faith in the Torah. The Torah to the Conservatives is the word of God and divinely inspired. Such a strong faith in the validity of the Torah is clear from the words of Isaac Leeser, 'the founder of Conservatism' in the United States. He wrote in the preface to his English version of the Bible, "the translator believes in the Scriptures as they have been handed down to us, as also in the truth and authenticity of prophecies and their literal fulfillment."[31] Conservatives would allow application of biblical criticism to the Hebrew Bible with the exception of the Pentateuch. Morris Raphall, for instance, "differentiated between the Five Books of Moses and the rest of the Scriptures. It was not possible, he believed, to apply the same measure of analysis to both. Whoever undertook the criticism of the Pentateuch would touch the basis of Judaism."[32]

In light of what has been discussed thus far, it may be asserted that although modern biblical criticism has left its traces in and imprint on modern Judaic thought and has caused some Jews to revise their faith in the supernatural origin and binding nature of the Torah, many Jews maintain a strong belief in the divine origin and nature of the Torah. They believe in its essential facticity and venerate it as the true "word of God". In case of the Orthodox, the Torah is the inerrant and infallible Word of God in its literal sense. None of the Jewish groups, even Reformism in its radical form, has rejected its validity altogether. The phrase, all Scripture (Written + Oral), only Five Books of Moses, not five books of Moses in its entirety, but just the beliefs along with the ethical and moral teachings, will, perhaps, be fitting to convey the position regarding the Torah of the traditionalists, conservatives and reformists consecutively. Therefore, a student who intends to learn about the authentic Jewish concept of God, or transcendence or anthropomorphism, and compare these to their counterparts in other traditions,would have no choice but to go to the Hebrew Bible in general and the Five books of Moses in particular, because the Torah, whatsoever may be the claims and findings of modern research, enjoys authoritative and authentic status among Jewry at large. This assertion may be substantiated by the words of one of the best known Conservative Jewish scholars, Kohut, who observes, "to us the Pentateuch is *noli me tangere!* Hands off! We disclaim all honour of handling the sharp knife which cuts the Bible into a thousand pieces."[33]

THE HEBREW BIBLE AND CHRISTIANITY

The Christian Scriptures consist of two Testaments, the Old and the New. What Christians regard as the Old Testament, an intrinsic part of Christianity since the very beginning of the faith, is for Judaism the Hebrew Bible. So, in reality the original Christian Bible, which was used by Jesus and his followers, was the Hebrew Bible of the Jewish community. It was treated as "Sacred Scripture" and enjoyed absolute canonical authority. Thus, the Holy book for Jesus as well as for the early founders of the Christian faith, was not the New Testament but the Hebrew Bible of Judaism. Though perhaps we should qualify this by noting that the New Testament and Early Church quotations from the Old Testament seem to have been almost always made from the Greek Septuagint (ancient Greek translation of the Hebrew Bible) and therefore the Bible for the first Christians also included the apocrypha which was almost invariably in all Christian Bibles until the Protestant Reformation. Since the New Testament books, observes Grant,

> which reflect the life of early Christians are written exclusively in Greek, it is not surprising that most of the Old Testament quotations in them are derived from the Greek Old Testament, the Septuagint; but sometimes, for example in the Gospel of Matthew, some of the quotations seem to be based on different renderings of the Hebrew text. Recent archaeological discoveries have shown that the Septuagint was in circulation even in Palestine, and that its text was somewhat different from that found in the major, later manuscripts. Undoubtedly the Palestinian Greek manuscripts underwent a good deal of correction on the ground of comparison with Hebrew texts, and it may be that New Testament passages which seem to be closer to the Hebrew than to the Septuagint are based on corrected Septuagint texts.[34]

The Old Testament enjoyed this authoritative status even when need was felt to add the Christian Gospels to it, which were the first books to be added to the Hebrew Bible as supplementary scriptures. The issue of the New Testament canon will be addressed at length in the next chapter. However, it must be noted that throughout the long centuries of the formative period of Christianity it was the Hebrew Bible and not the New Testament which was fully in the canon. Some of the New Testament books obtained their place in the canon gradually while the Old Testament books were accepted as canonical from the beginning.

It is beyond doubt therefore that the Hebrew Scripture was the original Sacred Book of the Christian faith. Indeed for the first four centuries it remained the only canonical Scripture (before the complete canonization of the New Testament), and has been in the Christian Bible since the Church's canon was first formulated. The question arises as to the relationship of the Hebrew Bible with the Christian faith and its doctrines. Is the Hebrew Bible in conformity with Christian doctrines, and further, is it accepted by all Christians as authoritative and binding? Could the findings of anyone studying the text of the Old Testament for instance be equally applicable to the Christian faith as they would be to the Jewish one? The answer to these important and valid questions is extremely difficult. What is required is a thorough discussion of Christian responses to the Old Testament. Nevertheless, we can gain an impression of what some Christians at least feel about this complex situation. John Bright for instance states:

> The Old Testament... is different. It was not in the first instance a document of the Christian faith at all, but of the faith of Israel. It contains much that is strange to Christian belief and that has never been practiced by Christians, together with not a little that may even be offensive to Christian sentiments. How is this ancient book, which presents a religion by no means identical with the Christian religion, to be appealed to by the church as normative over Christian belief and Christian conduct?[35]

Bright further points out what could be offensive to Christians when he tells us that

> there is much in the Old Testament – and it ought frankly to be admitted – that offends the Christian's conscience. Its heroes are not always heroes, and are almost never saints. They lust, they brawl, and commit the grossest immorality; they plot, they kill, or seek to kill. And often enough their conduct receives no whisper of rebuke: it is just recorded. How are the stories of such things in any way a guide for the faith and conduct of the Christian? How shall he learn from them the nature of his God and of the duty that his God requires of him? Many a sincere Christian has, explicitly or tacitly, asked that question. Scarcely a part of the Old Testament is exempt from it. Not even the prophets![36]

Giving as example the well known story of David and Bethsheba, Bright further elaborates that

> it is an altogether sordid tale of lust, adultery, treachery, and murder, and many a reader has been shocked by it. How can such a story possibly be said to speak any authoritative word to the Christian with regard to his faith, or in any way furnish guidance for his conduct? Certainly it provides him with no example to follow – unless it be an example of what he ought under no circumstances to do.[37]

In view of this complex situation it is entirely justifiable to ask the question, in what sense is the Old Testament authoritative for Christians in matters of faith and practice? Do Christians differentiate between the two Testaments and assign the Old Testament a position second in rank to the position and authority of the New? And if what the Old Testament comprises of, was and is not identical to the Christian faith and cannot work as the fountainhead of its doctrines, why was it and why is it a part of the Bible today, accepted by the Church as the legitimate authority in matters of faith and practice? Why are pastors and evangelists of modern times reading and quoting the Old Testament in their sermons and services?

The Christian response to these significant questions is interesting, and can be classified into three main categories.

(i) The Marcionist Response

'Get rid of the Old Testament' was the solution typified by Marcion (in around CE 140). Marcion (100–160), the son of a Christian bishop in *Pontus,* found the Old Testament to be absolutely different from the Christian faith and therefore completely separated the two Testaments in his canon, rejecting the Hebrew Bible entirely. Marcion, observes Grant, "believed that the earliest apostles had distorted the original tradition in order to make it relevant to their earliest hearers."[38] His canon consisted of the *Gospel* (Luke, without interpolations) and *Apostle* (Paul, without interpolations and without the Pastoral Epistles). He is classified by some as a Gnostic and an extreme dualist while others, disputing the degree to which he was influenced by Gnosticism, do accept that his systematic effort to justify the devaluation of Hebrew Scripture was an outcome of Gnostic teachings that swept over the ancient world.

Marcion believed that there were two gods in existence. One, the Creator and Just God of the Old Testament, and the second the good God who loved and redeemed humanity from the angry and jealous God of the Old Testament. It was this latter good God who in his opinion sent Jesus to be crucified as atonement to satisfy the justice of the Old Testament God. Carmichael observes that the

> redemption in Christ was to him in no way to be understood in terms of Judaism or the Scriptures of Judaism, in which he found much to offend him. The God of the Old Testament is another and inferior being, the Demiurge-creator, the vindictive God of the law, wholly opposed to the Gracious God revealed in the Gospel.[39]

For Marcion redemption meant redemption from the Law (Old Testament). He had no reservation in declaring that as the book of a different and hostile god, the Old Testament had no place in the Christian scheme of divine revelation or Christian Canon.

Marcion further maintained that both Jesus and Paul had held the same views about the Old Testament, but that their teachings had been corrupted by the apostles. Marcion's radical views were well accepted among his followers. The Church, on the other hand, rejected his views and declared him a heretic because, in the words of Irenaeus, "he persuaded his disciples that he was more trustworthy than the apostles who transmitted the gospel."[40]

Though the Christian Church roundly rejected this solution and persecuted Marcion's followers, his teachings nevertheless maintained their corporate existence until the fifth century. In modern times, a Marcion-like attitude re-emerged in the Liberal period of the late nineteenth century, with Goethe, Schelling, Feuerbach and Schleiermacher being just a few examples of Christian Marcionite tendencies. Friedrich Schleiermacher (1786–1834), accepted as the father of modern Protestant theology during the nineteenth and for about half the twentieth century, made a systematic effort to draw a stark line and pinpoint the gulf which lay between Old Testament theology and that of the New Testament by placing Old Testament theology on a par with heathenism. He contended that "The relations of Christianity to Judaism and Heathenism are the same, inasmuch as the transition from either of these to Christianity is a transition to another religion."[41] Though he did not object to the Old Testament being printed in the Bible, he did feel that its addition to the New Testament would be more appropriate in the form of a sort of appendix and not as something of equal rank and authority for "The Old Testament Scriptures do not ... share the normative dignity or the inspiration of the New."[42] The proponents of this trend argued that there existed no bond of continuity or internal relationship between Judaism and Christianity. The two faith traditions followed two very different deities, that of the Old and New Testaments, with very different schemes of salvation.

The Marcionist strain has survived in Christianity down to the present day. Although people like Friedrich Delitzsch are accused of Nazism, anti-Semitism, and their views on the Old Testament are often discarded as biased and sick, the views of scholars like A. Harnack, one of the great historians of dogma, are not given the same treatment. Harnack like Marcion concluded that "the Old Testament should be removed from the Christian canon."[43]

(ii) The Official Response

Although the Church from the very beginning accepted the Old Testament as "Holy Scripture", meaning the word of God, and hence authoritative and canonical, this does not mean that the early Church Fathers were unaware of the problem of incongruity and strangeness inherent in the texts of the two Testaments. For, as Origen observes, if someone

> points out to us the stories of Lot's daughters and their apparently unlawful intercourse with their father, or of Abraham's two wives, or of two sisters who married Jacob, or the two maidservants who increased the number of his sons, what else can we answer than that these are certain mysteries and types of spiritual matters, but that we do not know of what sort they are?[44]

Men like Celsus, Porphyry and others did point out the existence of immoralities as well as anthropomorphisms contained in the Old Testament, identifying several passages to indicate the human aspect of the Hebrew Bible. The Fathers, on the other hand, could not declare the Old Testament to be manmade and hence unauthoritative for they believed that it had been divinely inspired and entrusted by God through His only Begotten Son Jesus Christ. They reasoned to themselves that it was the normative Scripture which Jesus had in fact followed and thus urged others to look to this as the key to understanding his person. To discard the Old Testament was tantamount to discarding the person of Jesus Christ, an act which would have risked the entire faith. Ipso facto, the Church Fathers retained the normativeness of the Old Scriptures by appealing to "allegory" and "typology".

The school of Alexandria in the shape of two of its theologians and philosophers, Clement (155–215) and Origen (185–254), advocated this allegorical recourse which, later on, came to be adopted by other Fathers including, Ambrose and Augustine. Origen saw numerous difficulties with the literal textual sense of the Scriptures arguing that many people misunderstood the Old Testament because "they understand Scripture not according to their spiritual meaning but according to the sound of the letter."[45] According to R. E. Brown:

> Many of the Church Fathers, e.g., Origen, thought that the literal sense was what the words said independently of the author's intent. Thus was Christ spoken of as "the lion of Judah," the literal sense for these Fathers would be that he was an animal. That is why some of them rejected the literal sense of Scripture.[46]

Origen argued that

> the law has twofold interpretation, one literal and the other spiritual... It is consistent with this when Paul [2 Corinthians 3:6] also says that 'the letter kills,' which is the equivalent of literal interpretation; whereas 'the spirit gives life' which means the same as the spiritual interpretation.[47]

Charles J. Scalise observes:

> Though Origen takes Paul's contrast between "the letter and the spirit" and Paul's use of allegory as scriptural points of departure, his view of "the letter and the spirit" dramatically alters the Pauline perspective. For Paul, the "historical pattern" of the Old Testament story is explicitly preserved, even in the few places where an allegorical approach is explicitly used (e.g., the story of Sarah and Hagar in Galatians 4:22–26). For Origen, however, though much of the Scripture is viewed as historical, the historicity of Scripture is itself unimportant; what matters is the spiritual meaning of Scripture developed by the method of allegory.[48]

Hanson observes that to Origen "History... is meaningless unless a parable is derived from it, unless it is made into an allegory."[49]

Origen, following Neo-Platonistic tendencies and using a word pattern from Paul (1 Thessalonians 5:23), introduced what came to be his famous threefold distinctive meanings of the Scripture corresponding to the supposed trichotomy of man's nature: body, soul and spirit. First among these, he contended, was "the somatic" literal or philological meaning of the text which everybody can understand. Second was "the psychic" moral or tropological meaning, the existential application of the biblical text to one's own situation, and the third "the pneumatic" spiritual or mystical meaning which could be grasped only by those who were mystically perfect. He argued that "all [Scripture] has a spiritual meaning but not all a bodily meaning."[50] He observed that certain passages do not make sense at all if not understood allegorically. "Now what man of intelligence will believe that the first, second, and third day, and evening and the morning existed without the sun, moon, and stars?"[51] Therefore, Origen interpreted them thoroughly and allegorically. Bigg, Wolfson, and J. Danielou argue that Origen derived this method of interpretation from Philo. Bigg observes that "his rules of procedure, his playing with words and numbers and proper names, his boundless extravagance are learned, not from the New Testament, but through Philo from the puerile Rabbinical schools."[52] Grant, on the other hand, argues that it was not "Philonic, but derived from Origen's studies of Greek grammar and rhetoric."[53]

Origen went so far in his allegorism that all Scripture became, as Bigg observes, "transparent beneath his touch; the 'crannies in the wall' multiply and widen, till the wall itself disappears."[54] By this "exegetical suicide"[55] as Hanson characterizes it, the Alexandrians, argues Bigg:

> found symbols where there was no symbol; they treated symbols not as indications, as harbingers, but as proofs. Thus they undertook to demonstrate Christian doctrine by passages which in the belief of the Jew were not Messianic at all, or, if Messianic, had not been fulfilled. They neglected the difference between before and after.[56]

In short they "found in the Old Testament what they already possessed, what they could not have found unless they had possessed it. But at any rate they found nothing more."[57] Through this "dangerous" and "delusive" method, as Bigg characterizes it,[58] they abandoned too quickly the grammatical and historical sense of the text, such that the text, argues Scalise, lost "its capacity to exercise hermeneutical control over interpretation through its literal sense."[59]

The school of Antioch represented by Theophilus of Antioch (115–188), Diodorus of Tarsus (d. 393), Theodor of Mopsuestia (350–428) Chrysostom (354–407) and Theodoret (386–458), was more sober in its approach to the Scriptures than its rival the Alexandria School. These Antiochian interpreters, observes Mickelsen:

> all emphasized historical interpretation; yet this stress was no wooden literalism, for they made full use of typology. The school of Alexandria felt that the literal meaning of the text did not include its metaphorical meaning, but the school of Antioch insisted that the literal meaning cannot exclude metaphor.[60]

These early fathers tried to solve problems raised by Marcion and others by typology and allegory. D. B. Stevick observes:

> Insofar as the Fathers recognized problems and discrepancies in the text of Holy Scripture (as many of them did), they seem able

> to accept some ingenious reconciling explanation or to shift to allegorical exegesis. That is, they would observe the problem passage and then say that the apparent difficulty concealed a mystery: This number stood for one thing; this river was a symbol of something else; and this person was a type of still another thing. Put them together as an allegory, and the problem passage becomes a revelation of great truth.[61]

Other fathers like Jerome (347–419) and Augustine (354–430) followed Origen in allegorism. Though Jerome in his later life tried to get away from allegory, he did not fully succeed. Farrar observes that "He flatters himself that he succeeded himself in steering safely between the Scylla of allegory and the Charybdis of literalism, whereas in reality his 'multiple sense' and 'whole forests of spiritual meanings' are not worth one verse of the original."[62] Augustine, in the name of having sound principles for interpretation, himself allegorized extensively. From 600 to 1200, allegory, observes Mickelsen, "had a real hold upon the minds of medieval theologians."[63] Brunner observes that "the rank growth of the allegorical method of Biblical exposition made it impossible to maintain the Bible text as normative, as compared with the ecclesiastical development of doctrine." By means of allegorical exposition the Scholastics, says Brunner, ""prove", with the help of Scripture, all that they wish to prove."[64] The outcome was, as John Bright puts it:

> a wholesale and uncontrolled allegorizing of Scripture, specifically the Old Testament. This did not confine itself to difficult or morally offensive passages, or to passages that tell of something that seems unnatural or improbable, or to places where Scripture contradicts, or seems to contradict, other Scripture; it extended itself almost everywhere. Scarcely a text but yielded hidden and unsuspected riches to the interpreter's ingenuity.[65]

By means of this wholesale allegorizing, the Church was able to save the Old Testament as the Sacred Scripture which, according to them, propounded Christian meanings in each of its texts. The Roman

Catholic Church, the heir of this tendency, has traditionally been and still is more inclined and hospitable to the allegorical "mystical" meanings of the text than most Protestant churches.

Many Protestants, following the pattern of Reformers like Luther and Calvin, reject allegory in principle. Luther scolded those who used the allegorical method of interpretation and rejected it altogether. In his "Preface to the Old Testament" he writes:

> There are some who have little regard for the Old Testament... They think they have enough in the New Testament and assert that only a spiritual sense is to be sought in the Old Testament. Origen, Jerome, and many other distinguished people have held this view. But Christ says in John (5:39), "search the Scriptures, for it is they that bear witness to me."[66]

He further argues:

> The Holy Spirit is the simplest writer and advisor in heaven and on earth. That is why his words could have no more than the one simplest meaning which we call written one, or the literal meaning of the tongue... But one should not therefore say that Scripture or God's Word has more than one meaning.[67]

Calvin called allegorical interpretations an invention of the Devil, something "puerile" and "farfetched" meant to undermine the authority of Scripture.[68] By emphasizing the plain historico-philological sense of the text, both Luther and Calvin emphasized the authority of the Scripture and dispensed with "Tradition" with its accepted mystical meanings, "the exotic jungle of fanciful interpretation."[69] Luther gave profoundly Christological interpretations to the Hebrew Bible and urged Christians to search Christ and the gospel in the Old Testament.

Since the Reformation period, the trend to find Christological as well as typological meanings in the Old Testament has been quite pervasive in influential Protestant circles, and is still popular among a number of scholars especially in Europe and the UK. Karl Barth, Wilhelm Vischer, O. Procksch, A. B. Davidson, and R. V. G. Tasker are examples. Vischer, for instance, argues that, "the Bible is the Holy Scripture only insofar as it speaks of Christ Jesus."[70] It is the only "dogma which for the Christian binds the testament together; the Old Testament telling us what the Christ is and the New Testament telling us who He is."[71] Procksch contends that "the figure of Jesus Christ has the Old Testament as its background. He is the fulfillment of the Old Testament prophecies: without him the Old Testament is a torso."[72] Bright remarks that:

> The normative element in the Old Testament, and its abiding authority as the Word of God, rests not in its laws and customs, its institutions and ancient patterns of thinking..., but in that structure of theology which undergirds each of its texts and which is caught up in the New Testament and announced as fulfilled in Jesus Christ.[73]

This approach, though rejecting the allegorical sense and advocating a plain literal or grammmatico-historical meaning of the text, seems to do a similar injustice. All these methods supply the Old Testament with meanings and results in advance. The result is that writers merely quote the Old Testament to prove what they think should be proven by it. Somewhat like their Catholic friends, Protestants, in the name of finding Christological meanings, approach the Old Testament with preconceived, set ideas, as well as hard and fast assumptions, superimposing these assumptions onto the text of the Old Testament itself and in the process perhaps consciously disregarding its plain meanings. The practical outcome not surprisingly is the same, a disguised sort of allegory. Worth mentioning here is the fact that the Protestant approach to the Scriptures has probably caused more confusion and diversity of interpretation than that of the Roman Catholics. For Catholicism the Church is the final authority determining the validity of interpretation. No interpretation can be given to, and no meaning interpolated from the Scriptures, which contravenes the Church's dogmas and teachings. Protestantism, on the other hand, exercises individualism. Protestants shrink from official church-dictated meanings of biblical text and give every individual Bible reader the right to find meanings for him/herself. Predictably, this has resulted in such a diversity of biblical interpretation that often it seems we are left with nothing but a heap of confusion, with biblical text meaning simply what each individual interpreter takes it to mean.

(iii) The Liberalist Response

This solution was advocated by liberal theologians during the nineteenth century. Accepting the validity of Wellhausen's theory of an evolutionary development in the Old Testament, they not only looked at the Bible as a historically conditioned book but also recognized its human aspect as a whole, something which had largely been ignored by orthodoxy over the centuries. The liberal writers observed that the Old Testament had over time evolved from primitive to more developed forms and had gone through a fundamental change during this developmental process. They accepted the person of Jesus along with his teachings as their point of orientation and looked into the Old Testament from that perspective. As the New Testament is the only record of Jesus and his teachings, they therefore based their value judgment on the principles of the New Testament. By imposing these principles on the Old Testament, they separated passages of a normative nature from primitive, immoral, outgrown, and non-Christian ones contained within it, without denying the Old Testament's authority. A. B. Davidson, for example, argues that we must neither deny all authority to the Old Testament in favor of the New nor place the Old Testament on the same level as the New, but study the Old Testament in view of "its climax in the New Testament."[74] E. Sellin maintains that "the Old Testament Canon is significant for the Old Testament theologian only in so far as it was accepted by Jesus and his apostles. That is to say, Old Testament theology is only interested in the line which was fulfilled in the Gospel."[75] F. W. Farrar informs us:

> Is it not enough that, to us, the test of God's word is the teaching of Him who is the Word of God? Is it not an absolutely plain and simple rule that anything in the Bible which teaches or seems to teach anything which is not in accordance with the love, the gentleness, the truthfulness, the purity of Christ's Gospel, is not God's word to us, however clearly it stands on the Bible page?[76]

This liberal approach to the Old Testament was unique in the sense that it neither fully followed Marcionism, nor the official, traditional solutions. Rather it assimilated thoughts from both camps without following any of the tendencies in toto. The position of the Liberalists was and still is quite complicated. Whilst they attempt to honor the Old Testament with historical and religious importance, they simultaneously cut it into a thousand pieces, treating some elements as binding and others as insignificant. Such an approach is in effect tantamount to their imposing their own authority upon the text of the Old Testament and determining which of the text should be religiously significant and which should be ignored as irrelevant. Through this approach, of which A. Harnack and H. Gunkel are good examples (as mentioned earlier), the liberals brought to modern Christianity "at least the camel's nose of Marcionism."[77] The result was that large parts of the Old Testament lost their importance as well as practical authority, and the effective liberal canon became a rather small one, usually containing the life and teachings of Jesus and some other biblical passages which might add some moral or spiritual point of view to these teachings.

It is justifiable to ask whether the Old Testament is divinely inspired or not. If the answer is yes, then it follows logically that it cannot be taken in parts. Either the Old Testament is fully inspired and authoritative in its entirety, or it is not authoritative at all. In fact, Jesus' person and his teachings cannot be taken as the yardstick to determine authoritative passages from non-binding ones in the Old Testament due to historical reasons. The Old Testament existed historically before the person of Jesus Christ. And he followed it as Scripture (as is commonly held) and did not change it or cut it into pieces. On the other hand, the true facts about his historical life and teachings are themselves problems of great magnitude, as will be seen in the next chapter. The solution put forward by liberals not surprisingly encountered problems and limitations similar to those of Marcionism and the Orthodoxy, and the individual interpreter's understandings were again to play a vital role in interpreting the accepted passages of the Old Testament. This ultimately lead to individualism and very often to mutual contradiction, confusion and utter subjectivism.

It is clear from the above discussion that mainstream Christianity has preserved the Old Testament as something sacred and canonical and an intrinsic and inseparable part of its Holy Scripture whilst at the same time maintaining that it has been superseded by the New Testament. In this Christianity's view of the Old Testament differs sharply to that of Judaism, which latter regards the Old Testament as sacred and unsuperseded. Theoretically the Old Testament is regarded as authoritative by Christianity and a part of its Holy Scripture, practically however, it is the New Testament which enjoys unitary, undisputed and unsuperseded authority. Christians read, understand, evaluate and explain the Old Testament in light of the New Testament and as a result accept its validity only to the degree that its teachings accord with those of the New. In doing so modern Christianity toes the line delineated by early Church Fathers such as Irenaeus, Tertullian and Origen. Although these Fathers clearly subordinated the Old Testament to the New Testament since the early part of the second century, one can also see similar mixed and confused views concerning the real significance and authority of the Old Testament in the very early Christian Church dating back to the first century. Harnack summarizes the situation of the time in the following words:

> The fact of the New Testament being placed on a level with the Old proved the most effective means of preserving to the latter its canonical authority, which had been so often assailed in the second century.... The immediate result of this investigation was not only a theological exposition of the Old Testament, but also a theory which ceased to view the two Testaments as of equal authority and subordinated the Old to the New. This result, which can be plainly seen in Irenaeus, Tertullian, and Origen, led to exceedingly important consequences. It gave some degree of insight into statements, hitherto completely unintelligible, in certain New Testament writings, and it caused the Church to reflect upon a question that had as yet been raised only by heretics, viz., what are the marks which distinguished Christianity from the Old Testament religion?[78]

The Early Church, like most modern Christians today, could not completely reject or accept the Old Testament. It also harbored contradictory views about the Old Testament, as Harnack observes:

> An historical examination imperceptibly arose; but the old notion of the inspiration of the Old Testament confined it to the narrowest limits, and in fact always continued to forbid it; for, as before, appeal was constantly made to the Old Testament as a Christian book which contained all the truths of religion in perfect form. Nevertheless the conception of the Old Testament was here and there full of contradiction.[79]

AUTHORITY IN CHRISTIANITY

In light of the discussion so far, it becomes clear that were, for instance, a student to examine anthropomorphic and transcendental tendencies in the Bible as a whole, he/she may find themselves not doing justice to Christian readers, for the validity of the findings taken from the Old Testament may not be accepted by a great many Christians, as not all of them take the whole Bible as binding. The student would in fact have to study the New Testament to explore Christian views on anthropomorphism and transcendence because the New Testament alone is the claimed primary authority for most Christians. In this case would they accept the text of the New Testament as binding?

(1) The Catholic Church maintains that the Scripture does not only contain the Word of God, but is the Word of God and hence final authority. It also maintains that alongside the Scripture, the Church's ongoing tradition, the rule of faith, is also authoritative. The Scripture and the Tradition are accepted with equal piety and reverence.

"Tradition" in the past was nothing but the Church or the decisions of the Vatican, and no one was allowed to oppose or reject these. It was stated in the Council of Trent in 1546 that, "No one... shall presume to interpret Sacred Scripture contrary to the sense which the Holy Mother Church – to whom it belongs to judge the true sense and interpretation of Holy Scripture – both held and continues to hold..."[80] This belief found its climax in the dogma of "Papal Infallibility", when the Pope speaks *ex cathedra*, defined at the Vatican Council of 1870 as "when the Pope speaks *ex cathedra*; that is, when in his character of 'pastor and doctor of all Christians,' he 'defines a doctrine regarding faith and morals,' he is possessed of infallibility."[81] This doctrine was applied in 1950 to the bodily assumption of the Virgin Mary (the taking up of the Virgin Mary into Heaven at the end of her life). "When the dogma of Mary's assumption was declared in 1950", observes G. C. Berkouwer, "the absence of any reference to it in Scripture was acknowledged. But, it was added, 'The Catholic Church teaches that there are two sources of revelation from which we can derive divine truth, the written Word of God and unwritten tradition. We know Mary's ascension into heaven through tradition.'"[82] In modern Catholic theory, the Scripture, the "Tradition" or the Church in the figure of the Pope, are all considered authorities, but practically this means the Pope or the Church, as Loofs a responsible theologian of the Vatican states, "Neither the Holy Scripture nor the Divine tradition, but the teaching Church, which infallibly expounds both sources of truth ... is for us the first rule of faith."[83]

In recent times, especially after the Second Vatican Council of 1959, this view has been slightly modified to give a strong accent to the scriptures. As an outcome of this unexpected Council, which has created unprecedented tensions within the Roman Catholic Church in the twentieth century, the two sources of authority previously held independent were closely interconnected. The Council declared that both the Scripture and sacred traditions are "like a mirror in which the pilgrim Church on earth looks at God...until she is brought to see Him as He is, face to face."[84] To fully understand the Scripture:

> Christian scholars must be ever mindful of the findings which the Spirit-guided Church has already achieved, above all, those which the magisterium has guaranteed. This perfect accord with the insights of the Church's living tradition is the best guide that anyone can have in studying God's word.[85]

In short the final guarantee of correctness and truth lies with the Church. The gist of this new theological standpoint is that though the Scripture is all authority its true interpretation can only be achieved by the tradition and with the help of the Holy Spirit. And Rome is quite sure it has both of them.

Some observers have rightly pointed out that though the recent shift is significant it "does not make much difference because a tradition that interprets can very subtly become a tradition that creates truth."[86] It will easily be apparent that although the Scriptures are acknowledged as the final authority in matters of doctrine, in practice this seems mere lip service to them. The authority of the Scriptures is closely linked with the 'tradition' of which the church is the sole repository. Therefore, the end product remains the same, the Church's certain authority over the Scriptures (or at least in effect it seems to be), and this authority is manifested through the Church's sole right to declare an interpretation of the Scriptures as traditional. The Church's official stamp guarantees the validity of the interpretation and finally assumes binding and authoritative status.

(2) One dominant trend in Protestantism, as exemplified for instance in classical Lutheranism, neither gives the Church nor Tradition equal authority with the Scripture. These Protestants do not accept the Church as infallible but following Luther, subordinate the Church to Scripture in matters of faith. The Church, argued Luther, "cannot create articles of faith; she can only recognize and confess them as a slave does the seal of his lord."[87] Calvin, debating the Romanists, argued:

> For if the Christian Church has been from the beginning founded on the writings of the prophets and the preaching of the apostles, wherever the doctrine is found, the approbation of it has preceded the formation of Church, since without it the Church itself had never existed.[88]

Therefore, "Those persons betray great folly who wish it to be demonstrated to infidels that the Scripture is the Word of God, which cannot be known without faith."[89] He concluded:

> Let it be considered, then, as an undeniable truth, that they who have been inwardly taught by the Spirit feel an entire acquiescence in the Scripture, and that it is self-authenticated, carrying with it its own evidence, and ought not to be made the subject of demonstration and arguments from reason; but it obtains the credit which it deserves with us by the testimony of the Spirit.[90]

To many Protestants today, the Word of God alone in its "Grammatical, historical meaning" or the "meaning of the tongue or of language" in which it is understood by everyone, and not the doctrine of the Church, has the ultimate authority. Although this is overtly claimed, the reality, as has already been seen, is that final authority ends up in the individual interpreting that Scripture.

Luther himself, in spite of his principle of Verbal Inspiration, made distinctions between different passages of the Scripture. He accepted some of them as binding and others as non-binding. For instance, he rejected the Apocryphal books of the Old Testament and described James as a "right straw Epistle." To him "it is not the Bible that counts but Christ therein contained."[91] Other Reformers like Calvin, on the other hand, seemed to maintain the traditional and authoritative view of the Scripture.

Scholars like C. A. Briggs state that "the theory of a literal inspiration and inerrancy was not held by the Reformers."[92] On the other hand, Warfield, Brunner, Harris and many others argue otherwise, maintaining that the Reformers did hold a literal view concerning the inerrancy of the Scriptures. Harris remarks that "Most students of the Reformation will be astonished at the suggestion that Calvin believed anything else."[93] Brunner notes:

> Calvin is already moving away from Luther toward the doctrine of verbal inspiration. His doctrine of the Bible is entirely the traditional, formally authoritative, view. From the end of the sixteenth century onwards there was no other "principle of Scripture" than this formal authoritarian one. Whatever development took place after this culminated in the most strict and most carefully formulated doctrine of Verbal Inspiration...[94]

Today, the situation, especially in academic circles, is quite different. "Historical and Literary Criticism" in biblical studies or "Lower", and "Higher" biblical criticism, as briefly mentioned earlier, has brought about substantial changes in a great many biblical scholars' attitude towards the Scriptures. Lower criticism refers to attempts to determine what a text originally said before it was altered, and is concerned with the transmission and preservation of the biblical text, whilst higher criticism refers to attempts to establish the authorship, date, and place of composition of the original text. Starting with Jean Astruc's (1753) discovery of the variation of the divine names in *Genesis*, the hypothesis or the documentary theory was developed (generally stating that the Pentateuch was derived from different narratives) and modified by German scholars like Eichhorn (d. 1827) and Hupfeld (1853). Higher criticism was given its classical form by Karl H. Graf (1866) and Julius Wellhausen (1876 and 1878). In England this approach found expression through the edited work of Benjamin Jowett *Essays and Reviews* published in February of 1860. In his long essay "On the Interpretation of Scripture" Jowett set his own principles of scriptural interpretation. They were taken as outrageous at the time but are still viable and serve as a charter for modern critical biblical scholarship.

Jowett's guiding principle was "*Interpret the Scripture like any other book.*" The real meanings of the Scripture were the meanings intended by the author and by the text itself. Jowett argued:

> The book itself remains as at the first unchanged amid the changing interpretations of it. The office of the interpreter is not to add another, but to recover the original one: the meaning, that is, of the words as they struck on the ears or flashed before the eyes of those who first heard and read them. He has to transfer himself to another age to imagine that he is a disciple of Christ or Paul; to disengage himself from all that follows. The history of Christendom is nothing to him.... All the after thoughts of theology are nothing to him.... The greater part of his learning is knowledge of the text itself; he has no delight in voluminous literature which has overgrown it.[95]

He further observed that "we have no reason to attribute to the Prophet or Evangelist any second or hidden sense different from that which appears on the surface."[96] He denied infallibility to biblical writers and believed in "*progressive revelation.*" This, to him, was the solution to rectify biblical immoralities. "For what is progressive is necessarily imperfect in its earlier stages, and even erring to those who come after....Scripture itself points the way to answer the moral objections to Scripture."[97] Since then this approach has been the dominant trend in almost all the universities of the western world though not without resistance.

In the nineteenth century William Robertson Smith, editor of the *Encyclopedia Britannica*, advocated the principles of the historical criticism of the Bible, publishing articles by Wellhausen within it. He was put on trial and expelled from his chair. In the same century, John Colenso, a South African Anglican bishop, was condemned as "the wicked bishop" and his works drew three hundred responses within twenty years. In the twenty-first century, however, we witness a quite different situation. Even the Catholic Church, the age long opponent of such investigation into biblical data, has joined the majority of biblical scholarship. In 1943 Pope Pius XII issued an encyclical letter, *Divino Afflante Spiritu,* which promoted biblical studies opening, the door for such investigation in Catholic circles. It has been called "a Magna Carta for biblical progress." The Pope concluded writing:

> Let the interpreter then, with all care and without neglecting any light derived from recent research endeavor to determine the peculiar character and circumstances of the sacred writer, the age in which he lived, the sources written or oral to which he had recourse and the forms of expression he employed.[98]

Since then the approach has been adopted universally in most academic institutions.

This approach, as we have seen, presupposes that in all books of the Bible there is only one meaning that matters and that is the meaning intended by the original human author. One needs to explore to the best of his/her ability the original historical and cultural setting of the individual author of each book or passage and study his thought to discern what it was that he believed and wanted to say. Theologians such as Kahler, Schlatter, v. Oettingen, Ritschl, Harnack, Bultmann, Joseph Stevens Buckminister, Moses Stuart, Andrews Norton, and Morton Smith are just a few examples of this approach.

Conclusion

As we have seen, the Hebrew Bible is comprised of different books, as well as approaches, trends, styles, focuses and directions. More importantly, it does not easily yield to a systematic theological treatment specifically *vis-à-vis* anthropomorphism and transcendence. Its original text is non-existent. In addition, in the case of the Old Testament one becomes lost in the ocean of allegorical interpretations, and occult and mystical meanings, ascribed to its text by countless followers, especially the Christians, spanning centuries. Of these, what is one to accept and what to reject? What is the criterion to be used to prove the authenticity or invalidity of any given meaning or interpretation? Jewish interpretations are not accepted by Christians and vice versa. Catholic interpretations differ from the Protestants and a very wide diversity of interpretations exists within Protestantism itself. The diversity of the interpretations concerning the same text is fascinating. In this process of interpretation and allegorization, the text, the assumed original revelation, seems to be completely enveloped in fanciful allegorical categories, foreign to the original linguistic and contextual meanings. Consequently the text itself very often suffers violence and injustice. Furthermore, it does not seem to provide meanings by itself, but is provided with meanings by its interpreters. Instead of being an authority itself, the Bible, especially the Hebrew part of it, seems to surrender to the authority and mercy of interpreters. History is witness to the strange and often absurd garb into which the biblical text has been attired. Due to the diversity of interpreters and their backgrounds, the meaning and understanding of biblical texts has itself become alarmingly diversified. This diversity and lack of unity necessitates a return to the text of the Bible itself.

To avoid all such intricacies and confusion I propose, for the purpose of this treatise, to treat the Bible as the Word of God and authoritative. Claims with regards to the Bible's divine origin and inspiration should be tantamount to claims concerning its full authority, a view held for centuries by the majority of its followers. The Bible should be the primary source used to study the beliefs of its followers and to compare such beliefs with those of other faith traditions. Moreover, I suggest that the revelation, or the Word of God, if it is so, in itself should be quite competent to convey its message and spirit without any need for external human help. God, the author and source of that Word, is the Wise, the Knowledgeable, and the Powerful. He has all the means and power to communicate His message in clear, intelligible, and logical terms to the recipients of His revelation. It is my belief that God does not need finite beings of very limited knowledge, wisdom, and resources to hijack His word in the name of a highly subjective agency i.e., the Holy Spirit. People should not be allowed to say or prove from the biblical text whatever they want to say or prove, using by way of excuse the metaphorical nature of the biblical language. I would like to point out that this is in no way meant to cast doubt on the intention, sincerity or piety of the text's interpreters, rather my intention is simply to respect the Word of God if one believes the Bible to be so. The Word of God is the text of the Scriptures and all the rest is the word of man, whatever position or status he/she may enjoy in the tradition. Let the Word of God speak objectively for itself, this should be the criterion for any comparisons.

THE HEBREW BIBLE AND THE TRANSCENDENCE OF GOD

God the Almighty and All-Powerful is the Hero of the Hebrew Bible. At the same time the Hebrew Bible's understanding, representation and concept of God appears to be complex and often confusing. In the text of the Hebrew Bible, God is presented as the Transcendent Reality and at the same time is often described in concrete anthropomorphic and corporeal terms. These two polar tendencies or strands go side by side in the entire Hebrew Bible. Though the biblical text shows visible efforts made by the classical prophets to reduce the usage of anthropomorphic expressions and to lay more and more emphasis on the transcendental elements of the deity, there is hardly a page in the Old Testament in which anthropo-morphism or its vestiges cannot be found. This is why even Jewish biblical scholars, like S. T. Katz, feel no hesitation in admitting that, "Anthropomorphisms abound in the Bible."[99] P. van Imschoot, a contemporary biblical scholar, observes that, "There are many anthropomorphisms in all the Old Testament books. They abound in the narratives attributed to the Yahwist and in the works of most of the prophets, who have nevertheless, a very high idea of God."[100]

Considering the diversity of the biblical writers' backgrounds and confusions about the Hebrew Bible's interpretations, it is interesting to note that, as a whole, the biblical God is more transcendent than anthropomorphic and more homogeneous than contradictory or heterogeneous, as compared to the deities of neighboring cultures and nations of the time. This tendency becomes more interesting when examined in light of the historical fact that the Bible is not a continuous revelation to a single person, nor the product of a single writer, but a collection of different books and volumes compiled in various places spanning a period of more than a millennium. There is a manifest progressive element in the theistic notions of the Hebrew Bible. Various kinds of concepts can be located in regard to the deity in various parts of the Old Testament (Hebrew Bible). Animism, polytheism, henotheism, monolatry, national monotheism and universal and ethical monotheism, all these 'isms' are reported to have been practiced by the Israelites during the various stages and periods of their early history and overlooked in most cases if not sanctioned by the biblical writers. This is one reason why it has been observed that, "one could not speak of Old Testament theology (in the singular), for the Old Testament exhibits not one theology but many."[101] Perhaps this is also one of the leading factors that explains the fact that, "In recent discussion of the beginnings of Israel's religion no subject has received more attention than belief in God."[102]

Evidently most of the western anthropologists, psychologists, sociologists and scientists, discussed in chapter 1, who have interpreted religion either as a psychological illusion or a sociological need, are clearly interacting with, and reacting to, the anthropomorphic and progressive concept of God as presented by a majority of the Old Testament writers. Indeed amongst the Scriptures of all the developed religions, like Judaism, Christianity and Islam, it is the Hebrew Bible which depicts God in the most anthropomorphic and corporeal terms. Undoubtedly Christian incarnational theology is one culmination and climax of this anthropomorphic and corporeal concept of God, whilst interestingly, (as discussed in chapter 3), the Christian New Testament does not contain many anthropomorphic expressions. In reality anthropomorphic incarnational theology is but one interpretation of the New Testament material though it is the most popular among Christian believers. There are many Christologies and theologies in the New Testament. The Qur'anic theology is ultra transcendental and does not lend itself to an evolutionary scheme of progressive development from animism to polytheism to monolatry to monotheism. Qur'anic theology is transcendental and monotheistic through and through. It also seems that many of the scholars of religious phenomenon discussed earlier, and exponents of various theories of the origin of religion, did not have access to the Qur'anic concept of the deity nor the linguistic tools to comprehend it. Their understanding of metaphysics might have been a little different had they had the opportunity or the tools to study the Qur'anic concept of God. We turn next to the Hebrew Bible to examine the nature of the tension existing between the transcendental and anthropomorphic tendencies.

The Unity of God and The Hebrew Bible

The unity of God or monotheism

> is the belief in one unique god to the exclusion of any other divinity. Its absolute and exclusive character distinguishes it [monotheism] from monolatry which is the belief of a group of men in god, recognized as the only legitimate god of the group, but who concede the existence of other divinities adored by other peoples.[103]

The Hebrew Bible in its present set up contains many passages that can be interpreted as explicitly or tacitly advocating the unity of God. The first verse of the Bible declares that only One God and no one else created the universe. "In the beginning God created the heaven and the earth" (Genesis1:1). The verse manifestly declares the oneness of God the Creator who created heaven and earth and all that is in them in six days by His all-powerful word. In spite of the anthropomorphic conception of God, the Yahweh of this biblical account is the absolute master of man and his surroundings and is presented as the only God. The Hebrews, from the very beginning, took the existence of God for granted. As A. B. Davidson observes, "it never occurred to any prophet or writer of the Old Testament to prove the existence of God. To do so might well have seemed an absurdity. For all the Old Testament prophets and writers move among ideas that presuppose God's existence."[104]

Genesis aside, one of the next immense statements made in the Bible with regards to God's oneness is the first of the Ten Commandments taught by God to Moses, one of the great figures of the Hebrew Bible, in order for him to convey them to the Hebrews. Moses is additionally required to make sure that the Israelites put them into practice. The first and the foremost Commandment reads, "Hear, O Israel: The Lord our God is one Lord: And thou shall love the Lord thy God with all thine heart: These commandments that I give you today are to be on your hearts. And thou shalt teach them diligently unto thy children..." (Deuteronomy 6:4–7). Nothing, says Abraham J. Heschel, "in Jewish life is more hallowed than the saying of the Shema: Hear, O Israel, the Lord is our God, the Lord is One." He further argues that this monotheism was

> not attained by means of numerical reduction, by bringing down the multitude of deities to the smallest possible number. One means unique. The minimum of knowledge is the knowledge of God's uniqueness. His being unique is an aspect of His being ineffable.[105]

Hermann Cohen observes that:

> In the "Hear, O Israel" this uniqueness is designated by the word Ehad... throughout the development of religion unity was realized as uniqueness, and this significance of the unity of God as uniqueness brought about the recognition of the uniqueness of God's being, in comparison with which all other beings vanish and become nothing. Only God is being... This, to be sure, makes

> anthropomorphism unavoidable, and the decline of Jewish thought into myth would have been unavoidable if the *fight against anthropomorphism* had not proved from the very beginning of the oral teaching to be the very soul of Jewish religious education. It is perhaps possible to say that this fight already played a role in the compilation of the canon of Scripture... God is not that which is, nor is he only the one, but the Unique One that is.[106]

W. G. Plaut, on the other hand, translates the verse of *Shema* as: "Hear, O Israel! The LORD is our God, the LORD alone." This translation is identical with that of the New Revised Standard Version of the Bible. In this translation, Plaut observes that

> two affirmations are made: that the Divinity is Israel's God, and two, that it is He alone and no one else. Other translations render "The Lord our God, the Lord is One" (stressing the unity of God) or "The Lord our God is one Lord" (that is, neither divisible nor to be coupled with other deities, like Zeus with Jupiter).[107]

In "Exodus" God is reported to have given the commandments to Moses in the following words:

> And God spake all these words, saying, I am the Lord thy God, which have brought thee out of the land of Egypt, out of the house of bondage. Thou shalt have no other gods before me. Thou shall not make unto thee any graven image, or any likeness of anything that is in heaven above, or that is in the earth beneath, or that is in the water under the earth: Thou shalt not bow down thyself to them, nor serve them: for I the Lord thy God am a jealous God, visiting the iniquity of the fathers upon the children unto the third and fourth generation of them that hate me. (Exodus 20:1–5)

The jealousy of God is very often mentioned in the Hebrew Bible. "Ye shall not go after other gods, of the gods of people who are round about you; (For the Lord thy God is a Jealous God among you) lest the anger of the Lord thy God be kindled against thee, and destroy thee from off the face of the earth" (Deuteronomy 6:14–15). This theme is so pervasive in the entire Hebrew Bible (Deuteronomy 4:24, 5:9, 6:15; Exodus 20:4–5; Joshua 24:19 etc.) that Imschoot argues that, "jealousy is a trait completely characteristic of Yahweh, since in the Old Testament it most frequently expresses the exclusive character of the God of Israel."[108]

The *Midrash* (a form of rabbinic literature) translates the first part of this commandment as follows: "You shall have none of those (whom others call) gods before Me."[109] Plaut observes:

> The prohibition of the sculptured images for purpose of adoration stresses the incorporeality of God. "You saw no shape when the Lord your God spoke to you at Horeb out of the fire", Deuteronomy 5:15 reminds the people. The worship of images is proscribed in the most urgent and vivid terms: nothing, but absolutely nothing, is permitted that might lead to idolatry....This meant, however, that, in ages when the arts served primarily the goals of religion, sculpture and painting found no fertile soil amongst the Jewish people. Instead, Judaism directed its creative powers towards the inner life, the vision of souls rather than the eye, the invisible rather than the visible, the intangible rather than the sensual.[110]

In view of the great significance of this commandment, Ibn Ezra, the great Jewish mediaeval scholar, used to say that this commandment must not be transgressed even in one's thought.

Contrary to these explanations, some modern scholars do not see in the First Commandment the affirmation of God's unity, uniqueness and transcendence. Following methods of biblical criticism, they date this commandment far later than Moses' times.[111] They also argue that it may prove monolatry or mono-Yahwism rather than strict monotheism. Robin Lane Fox, for instance, contends:

> Before we find early monotheism in the first commandment, we have to date it (it might be as late as the seventh or sixth century) and also be sure that we can translate it. Its dating is extremely

> difficult, although Hosea might seem to presuppose it too: chapter 8 of his book appears to connect idolatry and foreign worship with a blindness to God's law (8:1, 8:12). However, this law seems to be something more general than our First Commandment, and Hosea himself does not deny that other gods exist.[112]

Furthermore, there is no consensus among scholarship about the exact translation of the First Commandment. Many biblical scholars argue that this Commandment is neither historically authentic nor categorical or precisely directed in its meanings. Fox states:

> As for the First Commandment, the translation of its Hebrew is also not certain. Perhaps originally it meant 'Thou shalt have no other gods before my face' (no idols in Yahweh's temple), or 'before me', in preference to me, but on any view, 'the claim for Yahweh's exclusiveness, that Yahweh alone has existence, is not contained in the First Commandment'. The text need only have been saying that Yahweh is Israel's Number One among other lesser divinities. Monotheism, the much stronger belief that only one god exists anywhere, was not revealed on Sinai's peaks.[113]

T. J. Meek asserts:

> There is no certainty of course that this command originated with Moses or that it was known in his day...However, the most we can claim for Moses in it is monolatry. Neither here nor anywhere else does he deny the existence of gods other than Yahweh, nor does he assert the sole existence of Yahweh, and not having done that, he cannot be called a monotheist. Even O. E. James, who is an anthropologist as well as an Old Testament scholar, with decided leaning towards the theory of primitive monotheism, has to acknowledge that the command asserts nothing more than monolatry and not pure monotheism, and so conservative a churchman as late Bishop Gore has to concede that it neither proves nor disproves either monolatry or monotheism.[114]

G. Von Rad:

> The problem of monotheism in ancient Israel is admittedly connected with the first commandment, in so far as Israel's monotheism was to some extent a realization which was not granted to her without the long discipline of the first commandment. Still, it is necessary to keep the two questions as far as possible distinct, for the first commandment has initially nothing to do with monotheism: on the contrary, as the way it is formulated shows, it is only comprehensible in the light of a background which the historian of religion designates as polytheism. Even the way in which Jahweh introduces himself, "I am Jahweh, your God," presupposes a situation of polytheism. For many a generation there existed in Israel a worship of Jahweh which, from the point of view of the first commandment, must undoubtedly be taken as legitimate, though it was not monotheistic. It is therefore called henotheism or monolatry.[115]

K. Armstrong:

> When they recite the Shema today, Jews give it a monotheistic interpretation: Yahweh our God is One and unique. The Deuteronomist had not yet reached this perspective. "Yahweh ehad" did not mean God is One, but that Yahweh was the only deity whom it was permitted to worship. Other gods were still a threat: their cults were attractive and could lure Israelites from Yahweh, who was a jealous God.[116]

She further observes:

> The Israelites did not believe that Yahweh, the God of Sinai, was the only God, but promised, in their covenant, that they will ignore all other deities and worship him alone. It is very difficult to find a single monotheistic statement in the whole of the Pentateuch. Even the Ten Commandments delivered on Mount Sinai take the existence of other gods for granted: "There shall be no strange gods for you before my face."[117]

Such an interpretation of the First Commandment seems more in line with the biblical data (as we will see later in the chapter). It is sufficient meantime to quote the work of Cristoph Uehlinger who has shown that "With regard to the situation in the kingdom of *Israel*, we have ...archaeological, inscriptional and iconographical evidence which clearly points to the use of anthropomorphic cultic statuary by Israelites to a degree similar to their neighbors."[118] Yehweh was "worshipped in the form of an anthropomorphic cult statue both in the central state temples of Israel (Samaria) and Judah (Jerusalem)."[119] The strong emphasis upon Yahweh's jealousy also implies belief in monolatry. One cannot be jealous of people being devoted to a non-existent entity. Jealousy implies a rival for one's affections and goes well with the idea that Israel ought to be loyal to Yahweh and not to the gods of other nations.

Historically speaking, Jews from antiquity to modern times, have held the First Commandment to mean emphasis upon the unity of Yahweh. Traditional Jews had always argued that the Hebrew religion had been monotheistic from the very beginning and such an understanding was the theme of the entire corpus of the Rabbinic/ Midrashic literature. Even ancient Jewish philosophers and historians, such as Philo, Jubilees and Josephus, had maintained similar views about the ancient Hebraic religion. Almost all of them had contended that Abraham believed in monotheism and following him, the patriarchs were monotheists. Though the philosophers disagreed with the rabbinical traditions in maintaining that Abraham was a convert to monotheism; nevertheless; like Rabbinic Judaism, they saw in Abraham the origin of Hebrew monotheism. In the words of Jubilees: "He was thus the first to boldly declare that, God, creator of the universe, is one, in that, if any other being contributed aught to man's welfare, each did so by His command and not in virtue of its own inherent power."[120] Philo and Josephus held similar views. Biblical texts like Exodus 3:6, 16 and 4:5 were frequently quoted to substantiate the claim that the God of Moses was also the God of Abraham and other patriarchs. The Bible reports that God said to Moses "I am the God of thy father, the God of Abraham, the God of Isaac, and the God of Jacob. And Moses hid his face; for he was afraid to look upon God" (Exodus3:6). God ordered Moses "Go, and gather the elders of Israel together, and say unto them, The Lord God of your fathers, the God of Abraham, of Isaac, and of Jacob, appeared unto me, saying, I have surely visited you, and seen that which is done to you in Egypt" (Exodus 3:16, see also Genesis 26:24, 28:13, 32:10, 43:23, 49:24–25).

In modern times A. Alt, while drawing attention to Palmyrene and Nabataean inscriptions, informs us that three such gods who were not bound to any locality and were worshipped in patriarchal times – the God or Shield of Abraham, the Fear of Isaac (Genesis 31:42), the Mighty One of Jacob (Genesis 49:24) – were fused to produce the God of Abraham, Isaac, and Jacob, and identified with Yahweh.[121] Following Alt's theory Spieser, J. P. Hyatt, R. de Vaux and C. A. Simpson have contended that the Patriarchs (especially Abraham) were monotheists.[122] A. B. Davidson, discussing the peculiarity of the patriarchal religion, observes that

> this peculiarity, if it cannot be called Monotheism, forms at least a high vantage ground from which a march towards Monotheism may commence. And it is probable that we see in the patriarchal names just referred to, particularly in El Shaddai, the advance in the family of Abraham towards both the unity and the spirituality of God. He who called God El Shaddai, and worshipped Him as the 'Almighty,' might not have the abstract and general conception in his mind that He was the only powerful Being existing. But, at least to him He was the supreme power in heaven and in earth, and He had given him His fellowship, and was condescending to guide his life.[123]

He concludes arguing that there may be a difference of emphasis "But the doctrines were the same from the beginning."[124]

Davidson seems to be indulging more in speculation than substantiation of his claims from the data of the Hebrew Bible itself, for the names mentioned, like *El Shaddai*, do not prove that the patriarchs believed in monotheism or the spirituality of the Deity as he contends. K. Armstrong, after a good discussion of biblical narration, argues that it is wrong to assume that the three patriarchs of Israel – Abraham, his son Isaac and his grandson Jacob – were monotheists, that they believed in only one God. This does not seem to have been the case. Indeed, it is probably more accurate to call these early Hebrews pagans who shared many of the religious beliefs of their neighbors in Canaan. They would certainly have believed in the existence of such deities as Marduk, Baal and Anat. They may not all have worshipped the same deity: It is possible that the God of Abraham, the "Fear" or "Kinsman" of Isaac and the "Mighty One" of Jacob were three separate gods. We can go further. It is highly likely that Abraham's God was El, the High God of Canaan. The deity introduces himself to Abraham as El Shaddai (El of the Mountain), which was one of El's traditional titles. Elsewhere he is called El Elyon (The Most High God) or El of Bethel.[125]

Ignatius Hunt explains that:

> The accounts in Genesis 12–50 were written up in their final form many centuries after the events narrated had taken place. In the meantime the Hebrew religion had greatly developed, and great advances had been made, at least by those who served as Israel's spokesmen. Many crudities, and other defects of the ancient traditions were corrected and at times omitted, recast, or transformed in keeping with a more refined outlook. This is common in religious development.[126]

After posing a number of questions regarding these biblical narrations Hunt concludes, that "With the advent of archaeology and the discovery of sources of texts, the religious milieu of the patriarchs is now seen as completely polytheistic."[127] A. Lods' conclusions are very much the same.[128] Hans Kung views patriarchal religion as henotheism:

> Thus nowadays there is agreement among the critical exegetes that neither the exalted ethic of Bible nor strict monotheism will have prevailed as early as the time of patriarchs. From a historical perspective, Abraham was certainly a henotheist, someone who

> presupposed the existence of a number of gods but who accepted only the one God, his God, as the supreme and binding authority.[129]

In light of the available biblical data, polytheism, or in the extreme case henotheism, rather than monotheism, would appear to be a better alternative with regard to the patriarch's understanding of God. The Biblical text portrays patriarchs as worshipping other gods besides Yahweh. "Thus says the Lord, the God of Israel: Long ago your ancestors – Terah and his sons Abraham and Nahor – lived beyond the Euphrates and served other gods" (Joshua 24:3). It also says:

> Now therefore revere the Lord, and serve him in sincerity and in faithfulness; put away the gods that your ancestors served beyond the River and in Egypt, and serve the Lord. Now if you are unwilling to serve the Lord, choose this day whom you will serve, whether the gods your ancestors served in the region beyond the River or the gods of Amorites in whose land you are living; but as for me and my household, we will serve the Lord. (Joshua 24:15)

Moreover, we are told that God made Himself known to the patriarchs with the old name of "El Shaddi" and to Moses with the name of Yahweh. "I appeared to Abraham, to Isaac, and to Jacob, as El Shaddi but by my name Yahweh I did not make myself known to them" (Exodus 6:2–3). El Shaddai means the God of the Mountain, or The Rock, or the Mighty One etc. and occurs in the Pentateuch several times (Genesis 17:1, 28:3, 35:11, 43:14, 48:3). The Bible also uses other personal names for God, such as *El-Elyon* (God most high), *El Roi* (God of vision) or *El Olam* (The Eternal God). The patriarchs are reported to have addressed God with these names and also with the word "*Elohim*", the word most often used in the Hebrew Bible to designate God (about 2,000 times). Elohim is a plural word and in many early passages is used straightforwardly in the plural sense. For example: "Now I know that the Lord is greater than all gods (elohim)..." (Exodus 18:11, also see 12:12, 34:15; Deuteronomy 10:17). In view of these facts, it may certainly be concluded that elohim, the plural word, was later used as if it were singular while retaining its original format. The frequent usage of these names also suggests that the original god of Israel was El as Mark S. Smith contends. This reconstruction, he argues,

> may be inferred from two pieces of information. First the name of Israel is not a Yahwistic name with the divine element of Yahweh, but an El name, with the element el. This fact would suggest that El was the original chief god of the group named Israel. Second, Genesis 49:24–25 presents a series of El epithets separate from the mention of Yahweh in verse 18... Similarly, Deuteronomy 32:8–9 casts Yahweh in the role of one of the sons of El, here called elyon: "When the Most High (elyon) gave to the nations their inheritance, when he separated humanity, he fixed the boundaries of the people according to the number of divine beings. For Yahweh's portion is his people, Jacob his allotted heritage."[130]

Furthermore, the variety and diversity of these names also suggest that originally there was a belief in many "Els". Many of the personal names, observes Rowley,

> which we find in Israel testify to the polytheistic background out of which they emerged. Alt has argued that each of the patriarchs, Abraham, Isaac, and Jacob, had their own special God. Moreover, while in the Old Testament Shaddi, El, Elyon, and Yahweh are all equated and identified, it is hardly to be denied that they were once regarded as separate deities.[131]

The claims of patriarchal monotheism therefore would seem to be less of a reality than polytheism or henotheism.

In contrast to this, D. Nielsen argues that the word *elohim* originally was not a plural word, but is the noun '*elah*' with mimation (that is the addition of an 'm').[132] Davidson contends that though the word is plural it is but "a plural of that sort called the plural of *majesty* or *eminence*, more accurately the plural of *fullness* or *greatness*. It is common in the East to use the plural to express the idea of the singular in an intensified form."[133] According to Davidson, elohim does not imply a polytheistic tone or background. Hermann Cohen argues that "the intention of this word in the plural form could not be plurality, but, as its connection with the singular form proves, singularity."[134] Moreover, Davidson sees its origin in prehistoric animism or spiritism from where, as he contends, the ancient Israelites developed their practical monotheism. Having said this, Davidson also confesses that the word in itself does not imply monotheism and neither do the other related names: "Such names as *El-Elyon, El-Shaddai*, do not of themselves imply Monotheism, inasmuch as one God Most High, or Almighty, might exist though there were minor gods..."[135] In light of the passages mentioned earlier where it has been straightforwardly used as a plural (see also Deuteronomy 10:17; 11:24; 3 Kings 11:5), and other passages where (with a weakened meaning) it has been employed to refer to beings belonging to the divine sphere but having lesser importance or intensity (Jacob 1:6, 2:1), what becomes more evident is the word's plurality rather than singularity. Therefore, it is more convincing to agree with R. Smend, E. Meyer, Otto Eissfeldt, W. Eichrodt, and many others who maintain that the word elohim "is a vestige of the polytheism of the ancient Hebrews: gradually they fused the many local divinities which they adored into one single god and came to use the plural as singular to designate the unique God."[136]

Monotheism also asserts that God transcends nature, and is not identical with or part of it. The transcendence of God is one of the crucial traits of monotheism. Hence Yahweh is said to be the Most High God (Genesis 14:18–20) who is "The Lord God of heaven" (Genesis 24:7) who dwells in celestial heights (Genesis 19:24, 21:17, 24:7). Abraham is reported to have said to the King of Sodom: "I have lifted up mine hand unto the most high God, the possessor of heaven and earth" (Genesis 14:22). In Genesis 14 alone, the phrase "Most High God" has been used four times (Genesis 14:18,19, 20, 22; also see Numbers 24:16; Deuteronomy 32:8). Psalm 7:17 reads: "I will praise the Lord according to his righteousness: and will sing praise to the name of the Lord most high." God is exalted in the earth: "Be still, and know that I am God: I will be exalted among the heathen, I will be exalted in the earth" (Psalm 46:10). He is exalted because he dwells on high

(Isaiah 33:5). God rides in His eminence through the skies: "There is none like unto the God of Jesh-u-run, who rideth upon the heaven in thy help, and in his excellency on the sky. The eternal God is thy refuge..." (Deuteronomy 33:26, 27). From passages like these Davidson maintains that to the Hebrews "God and the world were always distinct. God was not involved in the process of nature. These processes were caused by God, but were quite distinct from God."[137]

The God of the Hebrew Bible is also "The Holy" *qados*. "There is none holy as the Lord: for there is none besides thee: neither is there any rock like our God" (1 Samuel 2:2; also see 2 Samuel 7:22; Isaiah 1:4, 10:17, 40:25, 30:11–12; Joshua 24:19; Habakkuk 3:3; Jacob 6:10). The governing principle or the motto of the so-called "Holiness Code" (a term used in biblical criticism to refer to Leviticus 17-26, so-called due to its much repeated use of the word Holy) is: "You shall be holy, for I the Lord your God am holy" (Leviticus 19:2). Robert C. Dentan observes that

> the word "holy" has become almost [an] epitome of the whole character of the God of Israel. On the one hand, in its original metaphysical sense, it speaks of its inexpressible remoteness from everything created, his absolute otherness to everything that is, and of his ineffable power, manifest in the violent forces of nature, that summons all the nature to kneel before him in reverent awe. But, on the other hand, it speaks with equal clarity of the moral purity of his being, which excludes the ugly, the cruel, the irresponsible and the arbitrary, and makes him of "purer eyes than to behold evil" (Habakkuk 1:13). When the several "Isaiahs" who produced the Book of Isaiah speak so regularly of Yahweh as the "Holy One" (Isaiah 57:15) – "the Holy One of Israel" (Isaiah 1:4, 41:14)...it is in both these senses, the metaphysical and the moral, that they use the term, but the major stress has come to be on the latter.[138]

Biblical scholars such as Dentan and Baab stress that the name "Holy" emphasizes the apartness and otherness of God. It is evident from this discussion that a great many Old Testament theologians interpret the holiness of the Hebrew God as His transcendence over, and otherness from, the world. They seem to argue that a developed concept of the divine transcendence is implied in the Hebrew Bible's usage of the term "Holy" for God. Katz and Hermann Cohen are just a few examples of this tendency. It is worth noting, however, that all these intellectual and philosophical interpretations of the title "Holy" are probably reflections of the interpreters' own backgrounds and on key points no substantial support is found in the biblical data. Such lofty claims of God's incomparability, immutability, and otherness cannot be proven from the material attributed either to Moses or to many other biblical writers, as will be seen later in this chapter.

Monotheism also declares that God is different from human beings and is not comparable or similar to them. His ways are not the ways of mortals. Thus the Bible says: "God is not a man, that he should lie; neither the son of man, that he should repent: hath he said, and shall not do it? Or hath he spoken, and shall he not make it good?" (Numbers 23:19). Also:

> For who in the skies can be compared to the Lord? Who among the heavenly beings is like the Lord, a God feared in the council of the holy ones, great and awesome above all that are around him? O Lord God of hosts who is as mighty as you O Lord? Your faithfulness surrounds you. You rule the raging of the sea; when its waves rise, you still them...The heavens are yours, the earth also is yours; the world and all that is in it – you have founded them. (Psalm 89:6–11)

All other gods are made of wood and stone, "the work of men's hands, wood and stone, which neither see, nor hear, nor eat, nor smell" (Deuteronomy 4:28). But nobody can see Him and survive: "And he said, Thou canst not see my face: for there shall no man see me, and live" (Exodus 33:20).

Most of the passages emphasizing God's incomparability are from later writings. The polemics against polytheism and idolatry and the stress on the otherness and transcendence of God increase noticeably in the later prophets such as Isaiah, Hosea, Nahum and others:

> All nations before him are as nothing; and they are counted to him less than nothing, and vanity. To whom then will ye liken God? Or what likeness will ye compare unto him? The workman melteth a graven image, and the goldsmith spreadeth it over with gold, and casteth silver chains. He that is so impoverished that he hath no oblation chooseth a tree that will not rot; he seeketh unto him a cunning workman to prepare a graven image, that shall not be moved. Have ye not known? Have ye not heard? Hath it not been told you from the beginning? Have ye not understood from the foundations of the earth? It is he that sitteth upon the circle of the earth, and the inhabitants thereof are as grasshoppers; that stretcheth out the heavens as a curtain, and spreadeth them out as a tent to dwell in: That bringeth the princes to nothing; he maketh the judges of the earth as vanity. (Isaiah 40:17–23)

"Thus says the Lord, the King of Israel and his Redeemer, the Lord of hosts: I am the first and I am the last; besides me there is no god. Who is like me? Let them proclaim it..." (Second Isaiah 44:6–7).

Here in these prophets the actual denial of the worship of other gods and existence is seen. Isaiah explains the absurdity of idol worship in the following strong words:

> All who make idols are nothing, and the things they delight in do not profit; their witnesses neither see nor know. And so they will be put to shame. Who would fashion a god or cast an image that can do no good?...The ironsmith fashions it and works it over the coals, shaping it with hammer, and forging it with his strong arms; he becomes hungry and his strength fails, he drinks no water and is faint. The carpenter stretches a line, marks it out with a stylus, fashions it with planes, and marks it with a compass, he makes it in human form, with human beauty, to be set up in a shrine...Then he makes a god and worships it, makes it a carved image and bows down before it. Half of it he burns in the fire...The rest of it he makes into a god, his idol, bows down to it and worships it; he prays to it and says, "Save me, for you are my god!" They do not know, nor they comprehend, for their eyes are shut, so they cannot

> see, and their minds as well, so that they cannot understand. (Second Isaiah 44:9–19; also see 44:6–8, 43:10–14, 45:12–13)

He further ridicules the idol worshippers by saying:

> To whom will you liken me and make me equal, and compare me, as though we were alike? Those who lavish gold from the purse, and weigh out silver in the scales – they hire a goldsmith, who makes it into a god; then they fall down and worship! They lift it to their shoulders, they carry it, they set it in its place, and it stands there; it cannot move from its place. If one cries out to it, it does not answer or save anyone from trouble...for I am God and there is no other; I am God and there is no one like me... (Second Isaiah 46:5–9; also 45:21–25, 55:7–19)

God is not made of any material thing but is a spirit: "Now the Egyptians are men, and not God; and their horses flesh, and not spirit" (Isaiah 31:3).

Contrary to these ideas of the transcendence and otherness of God there are many passages in the Hebrew Bible that portray God as part of this world of nature. Despite being the "Most High", according to Exodus 15:17, He has a sanctuary on the mountain built with His own hands: "You brought them in and planted them on the mountain of your own possession, the place, O Lord, that you made your abode, the sanctuary, O Lord, that your hands have established." Psalm 76:1–2 specifies His dwelling place: "In Judah God is known, his name is great in Israel. His abode has been established in Salem, his dwelling place in Zion." Zion is His eternal dwelling place: "Rise up, O Lord, and go to your resting place...For the Lord has chosen Zion; he has desired it for his habitation: This is my resting place forever; here I will reside, for I have desired it" (Psalm 132:8–12–13). In addition to Zion, He dwells on holy mountains, on Sinai, Horeb, the heights of Seir (Judges 5:4). His epithet "*s'dy* or Shaddy" probably means "Mountain-dweller" as De Moor has shown.[139] Korpel has observed that "The idea of God dwelling on a mountain [*hr*], or hill [*qb`h*] occurs throughout the Old Testament. In 2 Kings 20:23, 28 it is expressly stated that YHWH is a mountain god [*'ihy hrym*] and *not* a god of plains [*`mqym*]. Most theophanies also took place on a mountain."[140] God also has his abodes in ancient sanctuaries, such as Bethel (Genesis 28:16–17, 31:13), Barsabee (Genesis 21:33) and later in the temple of Jerusalem (Jeremiah 7:4).

Archaeological investigations have proven that in ancient Israel there existed numerous sanctuaries founded for Yahweh at various sites. Although Solomon is reported to have said: "But will God indeed dwell on the earth? Even heaven and the highest heaven cannot contain you" (1 Kings 8:27), in the same chapter we also have him saying:

> And when the priests came out of the holy place, a cloud filled the house of the Lord, so that the priests could not stand to minister because of the cloud; for the glory of the Lord filled the house of the Lord. Then Solomon said, "The Lord has said that he would dwell in thick darkness. I have built you an exalted house, a place for you to dwell in forever." (1 king 8:10–13)

Before these sanctuaries were built, Yahweh lived only in a tent and a tabernacle: "I have not lived in a house since the day I brought up the people of Israel from Egypt to this day, but I have been moving about in a tent and a tabernacle" (2 Samuel 7:6–7). Several verses show that Yahweh was believed to be enthroned between Cherubim (2 Samuel 6:2) and was present only at a place where His ark was located:

> When the ark of the covenant of the Lord came into the camp, all Israel gave a mighty shout, so that the earth resounded. When the Philistines heard the noise of the shouting, they said: "What does this great shouting in the camp of the Hebrews mean?" When they learned that the ark of the Lord had come to the camp, the Philistines were afraid, for they said: "Gods have come to the camp." (1 Samuel 4:5–6)

The King James version translates the last verse as "for they said, God is come into the camp."

A. Lods has identified four stages of development regarding the idea of Yahweh's dwelling. In the early settlement days of the Israelites it was believed that Yahweh dwelt in the *desert of the south* (Judges 5:4).

A new concept however evolved when people had settled down in Palestine. They believed that Yahweh was the *God of the land of Canaan*. Palestine was the only abode of Yahweh. The people who lived on the frontiers of the chosen land were "nigh unto Jahweh".[141] To be banished was to be "driven out from the face of Jahweh." He could not be worshipped in foreign lands:

> He cannot be worshipped in any other country: a foreign soil, belonging to other gods, permeated with their effluvia, is unclean in the eyes of the God of Israel. Hence in order to obtain the help of Jahweh in a foreign country, it is necessary either to make a vow to him, that is, to promise him a sacrifice, a vow which can only be paid on returning to Palestine, as Absolem did, or to have recourse to the more original method of Naaman, the Aramean general whom Elisha healed of his leprosy: he carried off into his own country two mules' load of earth from the land of Canaan, and set up an alter which was thus land of Jahweh (2 Kings: 17).[142]

In the third stage a distinct belief evolved that Yahweh lived in the *sanctuaries of the land of Canaan*. His full presence was felt only in this sacred enclosure. This belief persisted even among the great prophets who otherwise had a relatively developed concept of the Deity. According to Ezekiel the destruction of the temple in 586 would have not been possible had Yahweh not abandoned his sanctuary. "The whole priestly legislation is unintelligible unless it is recognized that the post-exilic Jews believed in a real though mysterious presence of the God of the heavens within the Holy of Holies of the second temple."[143]

It was only in the fourth stage that the belief appeared that Yahweh dwelt in heaven (Exodus 24:10; Ezekiel 1:26, 10:1; Psalm135:7; Deuteronomy 28:12 etc.). This thought of Yahweh as dwelling in heaven, argues Lods:

> did not necessarily involve the abandonment of terrestrial limits which popular belief imposed upon him. It is possible that the God of Israel was thought of as reigning only in that part of the heavens corresponding to the land of Canaan, in "the heaven of Jacob," as a poet of that period expresses it (Deuteronomy xxxiii. 28).

> However, such a representation would suggest a more superhuman, less material conception of the nature of Jahweh and one which would hormonize better with the increasing recognition of the wider extent of his kingdom.[144]

Surprisingly, Davidson derives altogether different conclusions from the above quoted passages i.e. the universality of Israel's God:

> We cannot say that from the time of Israel's becoming a nation any belief in a local limitation of God can be traced. The sanctuaries scattered up and down the country were hardly places where, having manifested Himself, He was held to have authorized His worship. Such facts as that men, e.g. Gideon, Saul, etc. reared an alter anywhere, and that Absalom who in exile in Geshur outside of Palestine made a vow to Jehovah, show that they conceive of Jehovah as without local limitations.[145]

Davidson, after this fascinating interpretation, cannot deny the fact that Yahweh, according to these passages, seems closely bound to the soil itself. Such a bondage is not universality but a definite limitation. In light of passages such as Judges 11:23 where Jephthah fights the Moabites to contain them to the territory given to them by their god saying: "Should you not possess what your god Chemosh gives you to possess?" and in light of passages such as 1 Samuel 26:19, all claims of Yahweh's universality until the time of later prophets in or after the eighth century BC lose ground. They clearly connect Yahweh's divinity to the land of Palestine.

Moreover, although the term 'holy' does imply the transcendence of God, its usage by the ancient Hebrews may not be equivalent to our understanding of the term, i.e. a full-fledged concept of the transcendence of God. In addition, prevailing popular belief among the ancient Hebrews with regards to the existence and power of other deities over different nations is another factor extremely detrimental to the idea of a transcendent God. Finally, manifestations of God in nature (theophanies) and in human form are also indicative of the fact that the ancient Hebrews' concept of God was rather primitive. That God can

> give visible evidence of his presence on earth is a conviction taken as much for granted by Israel as by other nations. Their sharing the common view on this point is shown by the fact that they regard it as perfectly possible for the deity to manifest himself both in the forces of Nature and in human form.[146]

From the earliest Old Testament writings to the latest, God is depicted as appearing in the guise of various natural phenomena, i.e. a thunderstorm (Exodus 19:9 ff, 20:18 ff; Deuteronomy 5:21, 33:2; Judges 5:4 ff; Psalm 18:8 ff, 68:8 ff, 77:17 ff, 97:2 ff), riding upon storm-clouds (Psalm 18:1; Isaiah 19:1, 66:15; Habakkuk 3:8), causing His voice to resound in thunder (Exodus 19:19, 20:18; 1 Samuel 7:10; Amos 1:2; Isaiah 30:27; Job 37:5), shooting fire from the heavens with burning breath or a tongue of flame (Psalm 18:9; Isaiah 30:27), etc. The vivid description of the Sinai theophany is another concrete example of this in practice:

> On the morning of the third day there was thunder and lightning, as well as a thick cloud on the mountain, and a blast of a trumpet so loud that all the people who were in the camp trembled. Moses brought the people out of the camp to meet God. They took their stand at the foot of the mountain. Now Mount Sinai was wrapped in smoke, because the Lord had descended upon it in fire; the smoke went up like the smoke of a kiln, while the whole mountain shook violently. As the blast of the trumpet grew louder and louder, Moses would speak and God would answer him in thunder. When the Lord descended upon Mount Sinai, to the top of the mountain, the Lord summoned Moses to the top of the mountain, and Moses went up. (Exodus 19:16–21)

Also, "When all the people witnessed the thunder and lightning, the sound of the trumpet, and the mountain smoking, they were afraid and trembled and stood at distance, and said to Moses, 'You speak to us, and we will listen; but do not let God speak to us, or we will die'" (Exodus 20:18–20). Exodus 24:9 narrates that Moses and seventy of the elders of Israel "went up, and they saw the God of Israel. Under his feet there was something like a pavement of sapphire stone..."

Eichrodt observes that "It can, however, hardly be disputed that the original narrative is concerned with an actual vision of God."[147] He also warns against a common tendency of coloring the old traditions with higher concepts presented by the later narration:

> It is not permissible to evade the force of such passages by playing off against them others according to which Israel indeed heard the voice of God at Horeb, but did not see any form. Such a procedure would be valid only on the historically untenable assumption that the total of statements in the Old Testament must provide a unified 'corpus of doctrine'. On the contrary one thing of which we can be sure is that at different periods Israel produced differing statements about the nature of God's relationship with the world, and that there was therefore unquestionably an advance to a deeper knowledge of God.[148]

The same warning should be repeated *vis-à-vis* anthropomorphic passages in the Hebrew Bible.

In monotheism, God is not subject to the variations and limitations of a material and mortal life. Many verses of the Hebrew Bible describe Yahweh as "the living God, and an everlasting king. At his wrath the earth quakes, and the nations cannot endure his indignation" (Jeremiah10:10). Joshua says to the Israelites: "By this you shall know that among you is the living God who without fail will drive out from before you the Cananites...the ark of the covenant of the Lord of all the earth is going to pass before you into Jordan" (Joshua 3:10–11). The writer of Psalms (42:2) finds consolation in the fact that God is living: "My soul thirsts for God, for the living God." "My heart and my flesh give a shout of joy for the living God" (Psalm 84:2). David has the confidence to face Goliath because his God is the living God (1 Samuel 17:26, 36). In view of passages like these Baab observes that the most typical word for identifying the God of the Old Testament is the word "living." Baab observes that: "The living God is, of course, a creating and a creative God....Holiness in association with personal and spiritual traits denotes the transcendent power which enables God to act as God, and not as man, in creating both the world and human beings."[149] Psalm 93 is full of praises of God's majesty:

> The Lord is King, he is robed in majesty; the Lord is robed, he is girded with strength. He has established the world; it shall never be moved; your throne is established from of old; you are from everlasting...More majestic than the thunders of mighty waters, more majestic than the waves of the sea, majestic on high is the Lord. Your decrees are very sure; holiness befits your house, O Lord, forevermore. (Psalm 93:1–5)

Unlike mortals God neither slumbers nor sleeps (Psalm 121:4). He does not grow weary: "The Lord is the everlasting God, the Creator of the ends of the earth. He does not faint or grow weary, his understanding is unsearchable" (Isaiah 40:28). He does not repent as mortals do (1 Samuel 15:29; Numbers 23:19). He is Omnipotent, so much so that His words are realities: "so shall my word be that goes out of my mouth; it shall not return to me empty, but it shall accomplish that which I purpose, and succeed in the thing for which I sent it" (Isaiah 55:11). "I am God...there is no one who can deliver from my hand; I work and who can hinder it?" (Isaiah 43:13). He is the Most High (Genesis 14:18–20–22), the Omnipresent: "The whole earth is full of His glory", the Omniscient (Jeremiah 11:20): "O Lord of hosts, that judgest righteously, that triest the reins and the heart...", the eternal: "I am the first and I am the last; besides me there is no god" (Isaiah 44:6 also 41:4), the immortal, the immutable: "For I the Lord do not change" (Malachi 3:6), the sublime, the spirit, the all-forgiving: (Isaiah 55:7).

All these sketched attributes and qualities are often related to Yahweh. They express the fact that He is not subject to the limitations of mortals. However, it is worth noting that these attributes, terms and notions about God's absolute qualities are not always used in absolute terms or in an absolute sense, for there are times when they are marked with explicit reservations or qualifications, as we shall see later in the chapter. Suffice it to say and as already noted, the usage of these terms in their absolute sense most often occurs with later prophets like Isaiah. Early writing reports concerning God's repentance (Exodus 32:10–14) and His wrestling with Jacob (Genesis 32:24–30) for instance, pose serious threats to the idea of His omnipotence. In the same vein, His advice that "the blood shall be a sign for you on the houses where you live: when I see the blood, I will pass over you, and no plague shall destroy you when I strike the land of Egypt" (Exodus 12:13), and other verses of this nature, (i.e. Genesis 18:21) also put his omniscience in jeopardy. The list continues, we have for instance the idea that God "rested" on the seventh day after the work of creation (Exodus 20:11) with, in addition, passages like Psalms 44:24 going against the claims of Deutero-Isaiah that God does not weary. These claims are in themselves completely nullified in light of the creation passage where the word "*nwh* meaning rest" is specifically used for God. Korpel has observed that "It is noteworthy that the first verb is a general term which occurs frequently with human beings as the subject, but also with insects"[150] (see Exodus 23:14; Deuteronomy 15:14 'man'; Exodus 10:14 'locusts'). Moreover, in view of the passages where God is reported to have ordered the destruction of everything (1 Samuel 15:3; 2 Samuel 7:6), His mercy and righteousness are shown to be restricted. Even traditional Jews understand and recognize the difficulties caused by the presence of such daring passages in the Hebrew Bible. S. T. Katz, for instance, while discussing God's omnipresence, omniscience and omnipotence, observes: "Another fundamental question about the biblical view of God is whether the Godhead is subject to restriction. Biblical teaching seems to imply that such a limitation exists..."[151]

In light of these issues it becomes evident that there are different narrative strands regarding the biblical Deity that occur side by side in the Hebrew Bible. Not surprisingly, the existence of so many polar strands has left biblical scholarship divided and confused. Scholars have drawn widely varying and contradictory conclusions *vis-à-vis* the original Hebrew concept of God, with some biblical scholars, in view of the many passages that delineate Yahweh (God) in relatively transcendental categories, arguing that the Israelites were originally a monotheistic nation and their monotheism was authentic and original, not something secondary but a fundamental expression of Hebrew culture. Y. Kaufmann contends that the Israelite religion

> was an original creation of the people of Israel. It was absolutely different from anything the pagan world ever knew; its monotheistic world view had no antecedents in paganism. Nor was it a

> theological doctrine conceived and nurtured in limited circles or schools: nor a concept that finds occasional expression in this or that passage or stratum of the Bible. It was the fundamental idea of a national culture, and informed every aspect of the culture from its very beginning.[152]

H. Cohen maintains that, "Monotheism is not the thought of one man, but the whole Jewish national spirit..."[153] According to Leo Baeck:

> Only in Israel did an ethical monotheism exist, and wherever else it is found later, it has been derived directly or indirectly from Israel. The nature of this religion was conditioned by the existence of the people of Israel, and so it became one of the nations that have a mission to fulfill.[154]

Hans Kung, on the other hand, rightly observes that "Yehezkel Kaufmann, who ignores the results of historical-critical research, does not answer one question. Was it like this from the beginning?"[155] As we have already discussed at length views regarding the patriarchal understanding of God, it should come as no surprise to see W. F. Albright also disagreeing with Kaufmann and other Jewish thinkers, disputing the idea of Hebrew monotheism being a fundamental and natural idea outcome of Israelite national culture. Albright, for instance, shows that the Israelites borrowed and adapted heavily, and greatly, from the neighboring Canaanite culture, maintaining that the simplistic picture being presented to us of the Hebrew religion is in fact not so, rather, "we can state definitely that it does not support the extreme position of the late Yehezkel Kaufmann, who maintained in his great "History of the Faith of Israel" that Mosaic monotheism was a phenomenon entirely peculiar to Israel."[156] However, he does agree with Kaufmann in suggesting the *Mosaic* origin and age of monotheism as opposed to the purely Israelite. Kaufmann, for example, strongly advocates that:

> With Moses the sin of idolatry particularly as a national sin – comes into existence. Before, idolatry was nowhere interdicted and

> punished. The stories depicting idolatry as a national sin presuppose the existence of a monotheistic people. Since such stories begin only with Moses, we infer that it was in his time that the great transformation took place. By making Israel enter a covenant with one God, he made it a monotheistic people that alone among men was punishable for the sin of idolatry.[157]

Similarly, Albright argues that:

> The only time in the history of ancient Near East when we find monotheism in the leading cultural centers, Egypt and Babylonia, is about the fourteenth century BC; it is also then that we find the closest approach to monotheism in Syria and Asia Minor. Since it is now an historical commonplace that we find similar ideas emerging simultaneously in different parts of a given cultural continuum, we should expect to find Israelite monotheism somehow emerging at the same time.[158]

He further argues that the God of Moses was a creator God unrelated to any deity, and not bound to any geographical area or setting or any natural phenomenon. Though conceived anthropomorphically He was not represented in material or unexalted forms. All the human attributes and characteristics of the Hebrew God were exalted. Albright concludes observing that "It was indeed Moses who was the principal architect of Israelite monotheism."[159] In *Archaeology and the Religion of Israel*, emphasizing the historicity of Mosaic traditions, Albright observes:

> The Mosaic tradition is so consistent, so well attested by different pentateuchal documents, and so congruent with our independent knowledge of the religious development of the Near East in the late second millennium BC, that only hypercritical pseudo-rationalism can reject its essential historicity.[160]

Albright has used the term "monotheism" in its very broad sense and not in its refined, modern and philosophically developed sense. He himself has observed:

> Was Moses a true monotheist? If by "monotheist" is meant a thinker with views specifically like those of Philo Judaeus or Rabbi Aqiba, of St. Paul...of Mordecai Kaplan or H. N. Wieman, Moses was not one. If, on the other hand, the term "monotheist" means one who teaches the existence of only one God, the creator of everything, the source of justice, who is equally powerful in Egypt, in the desert, and in Palestine, who has no sexuality and no mythology, who is human in form but cannot be seen by human eye and cannot be represented in any form – then the founder of Yahwism was certainly a monotheist.[161]

Meek criticizes such a usage of the term "monotheist" observing:

> Albright protests against giving a Unitarian definition to the word "monotheism," but the only acceptable use of the word is in its dictionary sense, and it is Albright and his kind, rather than his opponents, as he affirms, who are "highly misleading" when they read into a word a meaning it cannot and should not bear.[162]

H. W. Robinson also warns against such a broad usage of the term:

> Yet the very term 'monotheism,' together with all other metaphysical attributes, such as omnipotence, omnipresence, immanence, and eternity, can be misleading. Such terms suggest modern and intellectualistic categories. They conceal the gradual development of an intuition, and substitute for it a process of ratiocination never found in the Old Testament.[163]

Meek further rejects Albright's arguments stating: "There was no great, onrushing movement toward monotheism in the Near East in the fourteenth century, such as Albright affirms. There is no evidence that Syria and Asia Minor were more monotheistic then than at any other period."[164]

Many modern scholars of the Bible conform to Albright's position and maintain the Mosaic origin of Hebrew monotheism. G. E. Wright, J. Bright, I. Engnell, E. Jacob are a few examples. E. Jacob, for instance, noted:

> One cannot speak of evolution within the faith of Israel towards monotheism, for from the moment when Israel becomes conscious of being the people chosen by one God it is in practice a monotheistic people; and so one can speak with Albright, to name only one of the most recent and illustrious historians, of the monotheism of Moses, on condition that by this term there is understood a conviction of faith and not a result of reflection.[165]

The definition of Albright, on the other hand, is not acceptable to many contemporary scholars who see in it significant flaws and shortcomings. H. H. Rowley for instance adds:

> Most of the elements of this definition are irrelevant to the question of monotheism, and of the one vital element there is no evidence. For no where in the Pentateuch is Moses credited with the formal denial that any other gods exist, such as we find in Deutero-Isaiah, save in passages such as Deuteronomy 4:35, 4:39, 32:39, which quite certainly did not issue from Moses.[166]

There is no evidence that Moses worshipped many gods and was a polytheist (like a number of his followers), yet according to the biblical narration, there exists no proof that he was a monotheist, in the sense that he clearly denied the existence of more than one God. On the other hand there is every evidence that he worshipped only Yahweh and denied any association with Him, though without universalizing him. This fact has led scholars like T. J. Meek, S. R. Driver, and R. Kittle to conclude that Moses was a 'henotheist'. Meek observes:

> It is hard to find any evidence that Moses either believed or taught that Yahweh was the only existing God, and that He was therefore not only the God of Israel but of all men. On the other hand, it does not seem sufficient to note that at Sinai it was affirmed that Yahweh was alone the legitimate object of Israelite worship, and that there was no denial of the existence of other gods.[167]

He also notes:

> The new thing that came with Moses was not the worship of Yahweh to the exclusion of all other gods, but the united allegiance of a number of tribes to Yahweh as their confederate god, Yahweh being to the confederacy as a whole what the tribal god was to the tribe. This is monolatry and is quite like the monolatry that we noted in Babylonia, Assyria, Egypt, and elsewhere in the ancient world...[168]

S. R. Driver and Kittle conclude that the Mosaic religion can be described as ethical henotheism.[169]

A. Lods holds Moses' religion as monolatry, "for the god whom Moses sought to win over to his people was not a universal god like that of Islam: he had a proper name, Jahweh, local centers of worship, and an essential national character, he was and chose to be the God of Israel." He further argues that

> the Israelites, when they emerge into the full light of history and up to the time of the great prophets, although Jahwist, were not monotheists. They only worshipped one national god, Jahweh; but they believed in the existence and power of other gods: they were monolaters. But monolatry is a form of polytheism.[170]

The charge of polytheism, henotheism and monolatry is too much for scholars like Rowley, Baab, Bright, F. James, Th. C. Vriezen and a good number of other contemporary scholars to accept *vis-à-vis* Moses. Baab stresses:

> We must reject the easy evolutionism which sorts out the records, arranges them in neat piles on the basis of decisions as to dates, and finds a convincing illustration of development from animism to absolute monotheism, with all the stages from polydaemonism to henotheism in between.[171]

He further argues that:

> The concept of the oneness of God was not reached primarily through logical analysis by Hebrew thinkers; their approach was

> pragmatically religious and experience centered. The life and social experience of the community, with its inner tensions and its relations to other groups, made up the historical ground for the achievement of monotheism. The great doctrine of modern Judaism as of biblical Judaism, drawn from Deuteronomy – "Listen, O Israel; the Lord is our God, the Lord alone" (6:4) – was not formulated except as the result of prolonged and decisive acquaintance with this particular Deity. Undoubtedly the leadership of Moses, the work of the great prophets, and the faith of the many anonymous believers in ancient Israel helped to shape this doctrine.[172]

Bright strongly rejects the progressive theory too: "Certainly Israel's faith was no polytheism. Nor will henotheism or monolatry do, for though the existence of other gods was not expressly denied, neither was their status as gods tolerantly granted."[173] F. James concludes that "The actual evidence regarding him (i.e. Moses) points more towards his having been a monotheist than a henotheist."[174] G. Fohrer expresses the concept more carefully when he states that:

> Mosaic Yahwism therefore knew nothing of a theoretical monotheism that denies the existence of other gods. Neither is the oft-used term "henotheism" appropriate, since it refers to belief in several individual gods who alternately rank supreme. It would be more correct to speak of monoyahwism or practical monotheism.[175]

Th. C. Vriezen fully agrees with Fohrer in describing the Mosaic religion as "monoYahwism" rather than monolatry or henotheism.[176]

H. H. Rowley presents a relatively more elaborate and careful view concerning the Mosaic religion as it is portrayed in the Bible. He maintains that "if Moses was less than a monotheist he was more than a henotheist."[177] He recognizes that Yahweh shared the name with the Canaanite's deity, but had a unique character of his own:

> I do not take the view that the work of Moses is to be resolved into the mere mediation to Israel of the religion of the Kenites. The

> divine name Yahweh was probably taken over, and the forms of the religion; but a new spirit was given to the religion and a new level to its demands. The sense of Yahweh's election of Israel, of His deliverance, of His claims upon her obedience, were all new, and through the truly prophetic personality of Moses it was established on a higher basis than the Kenite's religion had reached.[178]

The gods worshipped by the Israelites were identified with Yahweh and ceased to be counted against him. "This is not monotheism, and there is no reason to attribute universalism to Moses. Yet here we have surely sccds of both."[179] Yahweh, according to Rowley, was not restricted to a single area or people:

> He could be active in Egypt or in Palestine as freely as in His chosen seat. A God who could thus be active wherever He wished, and beside whom no other gods counted, was not a tribal or national god, and certainly not merely one of a host of gods. His "onliness" might not be affirmed; but His uniqueness is manifest. If He is not the only God, He is certainly more than one example – even the most important example – of the categories of gods. Among all gods He alone mattered, and He could do with Israel or with any other people what He would.

Rowley draws from here a conservative conclusion:

> This is not monotheism, and it is unwise to exaggerate it into monotheism. Nevertheless, it was incipient monotheism and incipient universalism, so that when full monotheism was achieved in Israel it came not by natural evolution out of something fundamentally different, but by the development of its own particular character.[180]

Dentan's views are very similar to that of Rowley's. He observes:

> The views of scholars today vary all the way from that which regards Moses, or even Abraham, as monotheists, to another that

> sees monotheism as emerging only with Second Isaiah, or, in less theoretical form, with Amos. The truth is probably to be found in a mediating position that sees the germ of monotheism present in early times, with the full flower coming at the end of the Old Testament period.[181]

Such an interpretation of Hebraic monotheism is neither new nor specific to Rowley or Dentan only. It has been held by a number of scholars like E. Konig, P. Volz, A. B. Davidson, B. Bascheit, N. K. Gottwald and G. W. Anderson. One would have to resort to far-fetched interpretations and several twists to a variety of biblical passages, as cited above, to fully agree with this view on the Mosaic understanding of God. Rowley's view in substance is very close to the Albright school. He, like Albright and others, leans towards the traditional standpoint. For Albright and almost all 'right-wing' scholars, "the significance of Moses' achievement for the religion of Israel is an established fact; and many of them still view him, if not as the man who taught monotheism, at any rate as the founder of Israel's religion."[182] Even those scholars who deny monotheism to Moses recognize him as one of the leading factors towards this end. A. Lods for instance asserts:

> The principle laid down by Moses was that of 'monolatry': in everything that concerns the nation. Yahweh is the only Elohim to whom Israel has the right to appeal. Yahweh is a jealous God. This rigorous exclusivism was, however, one of the roots of the theoretic monotheism of the Jewish period.[183]

Whilst we may agree that Moses played a significant role in putting the Israelites on the track of monotheism, we may disagree as to labeling him the hero of Hebraic monotheism as far as the biblical data is concerned. Our concern here is not a comparison of the Mosaic concept of the deity with that of the Canaanite's or indeed other primitive societies of that time, but rather to focus on monotheism as the term itself denotes. Moses, according to available biblical data, does not seem to deny the existence of other gods. Further, his portrayals of God are corporeal and anthropomorphic through and through. This representation of God as well as lack of stand against other gods, does not sit well with the notion of a transcendent, monotheistic God. All things considered, this context, as well as the issues outlined concerning the historicity and translation of the First Commandment, leave a great many issues unresolved in terms of Moses being a monotheist. Therefore, in light of the biblical data, Mose's monolatry is more evident than his leaning towards monotheism in the strict sense of the term. Monolatry, on the other hand, is an idea detrimental to the Unity, Oneness and Transcendence of God as the terms are understood today. Therefore we conclude this section with the observation that the Hebrew Bible's early concept of God is neither monotheistic nor transcendental in the developed sense of these terms. Furthermore, ethical monotheism and thc transcendence of God are vaguely stated but not well defined or protected against violations and compromises, and the depiction of the deity is anthropomorphic and corporeal. Finally, this tendency is as pervasive in the later prophets as it is in the early writings, though with a relative degree of sophistication and refinement.

Anthropomorphism and the Hebrew Bible

A great majority of biblical scholars, especially after the 19th century evolutionary approach to religion and Wellhausen's evolutionary presuppositions in the field of the history of religion, disagree with the theory of original biblical monotheism or a transcendental deity. They see in the Hebrew Bible an evolution of the idea of God. They contend that the developmental process starts with animism, then anthropomorphic and corporeal concepts of the Deity, gradually developing, as a result of the Davidic monarchy and finally after the Babylonian exile, into a full fledged monotheism. M. Kaplan, A. Lods, I. G. Matthew, T. J. Meek, J. Barr, H. H. Rowley, W. Eichrodt, Morton Smith, and Mark S. Smith are just a few amongst those who represent this position. A. Lods, for instance, asserts that "Israel only attained to monotheism in the eighth century and to a clear and conscious monotheism only in the sixth, and that by a slow process of internal development whose stages we can trace."[184] Causse attributes the beginning of monotheism to Elijah, while I. G. Matthew thinks that it was Amos who laid the foundations of ethical monotheism. Pfeiffer absolutely denies any real monotheism before Deutero-Isaiah. He observes that "We can only speak of monotheism in the Old Testament before Second Isaiah by using the word in some other sense than the belief that there is only one god."[185] M. M. Kaplan observes that:

> The traditional belief that the Jewish religion has remained the same since it was promulgated at Sinai is quite untenable and is being superseded by the evolutionary conception of its origin and growth. According to that conception, the complex of ideas and practices centering about the belief in God underwent gradual but thorough-going changes.[186]

Following this evolutionary approach, Kaplan, a well-known modern Jewish thinker, concludes that the Hebrews, like other primitive people, were originally polytheists worshipping multiple anthropomorphic and corporeal deities. In the second stage of the developmental process, they reached the belief in a national God, Yahweh, worthy of worship and all other acts of obedience, but still conceived of in anthropomorphic terms. "They retained the survivals of animism."[187] Yahweh would fight their battles, take care of all their needs, and in turn they would conform to His laws and be loyal to Him. At this stage, there existed no thought of denying the validity of other gods for other nations. It is in the third stage, especially with the victories of David, that Yahweh's oneness is achieved:

> By this time the God of Israel is no longer conceived merely as a god, or as the principal god, but as God, the creator of the world and of all that it contains, the one Being who is sui generis, whose power is manifest both in the ordinary and in the extraordinary manifestations of nature and whose will governs the life of every created being.[188]

Still, even at this later stage of the developmental process, we do not have monotheism in the strict sense of the term:

> The religion of canonical Prophets is not quite identical with what is commonly understood by the term "monotheism." That term

> usually designates the outcome of an intellectual development which could not possibly have been carried on in early Israel. God, as monotheism conceives him, is a metaphysical being whose traits and attributes have nothing in common with anything in human experience. When we say that God is all-knowing, or all-good, it is with the qualification that we are using terminology which in strictness is totally inapplicable to God. Why then do we use it? Simply because we have none better. No such sophistication could ever form part of the Prophet's Idea of the God of Israel.[189]

In the final and fourth stage, real monotheism and transcendence was achieved by denying the ascription to God of human corporeal and anthropomorphic terms and the negation of those attributes and qualities which were thought as unworthy of His being. The Jewish religion passed through this stage "of its existence from about the beginning of the common era down to modern times."[190] Therefore, argues Kaplan, "to ascribe to traditional Jewish religion the urge to teach the nations the formal truth of monotheism is to convey an entirely wrong impression of what the Jews conceived to be their place in the world."[191] The concept of such a transcendent Deity was forced upon Jewish thought by the circumstances in which they found themselves:

> Until Judaism was compelled to reckon with the challenge of Aristotelian philosophy, the philosophic difficulty of ascribing form to God in no way disturbed rabbinic thought. Even the question of Gods' omnipresence did not trouble them greatly. Although they assumed that God was omnipresent, they nevertheless held the idea of God as moving from place to place, and of heaven as his principal abode. Certain as it was that God was a being perceptible not merely to the mind but also to the senses, traditional Jewish religion could, for practical purposes, afford to leave unsolved the question about the form and substance of the divine nature and its relationship to the visible world. Hence the vagueness and the contradictions which abound in the traditional conception of God with regard to his spatial relationship to the physical universe.[192]

It was in medieval Jewish theology "when the anthropomorphic conceptions of God in the Bible were found to clash with the more intellectualized conceptions of God developed in Greek philosophy, there arose the need for reinterpretation."[193] Such a development in the Jewish concept of God was a result of evolution; a product of Jewish civilization and culture; and not in any way or form a supernatural intrusion or event. Therefore:

> The Jewish quality of the religion of the Jews will not depend on claims to supernatural origin or claims to being more rational or more ethical than other religions. Its uniqueness will consist chiefly in the fact that it will be lived by Jews, and will be expressed by them through such cultural media as Jewish civilization will produce.[194]

To Kaplan and other modern Jewish scholars like Rabbis Solomon Goldman and Herman Lissauer, "what a person understands about God or any other reality is the result of patient, persistent searching and not a miraculous intervention from a supernatural source."[195] This group of Jewish "clerical apostles", to use B. J. Heller's term, have eliminated the traditional vital God idea from their purview and program. Such an idea of God is a part of the ancient Jewish civilization and primitive in nature. As a result this belief can be dispelled and dispensed away with in modern times. To the above mentioned Reformists "Judaism primarily is and was a culture and a civilization. God and religion played a part in it, but were not synonymous with the whole of it. Significant as it may have been to the Jewish scheme in the past, it is not essential to it in the present."[196] They do not accept the long held doctrine that "*Israel's ideal life was Israel's Scripture*" and God; they believe Israel's ideal life was and is Israel itself. Rabbi Herman Lissauer frankly admits:

> I am not sure whether we may properly use the term God since our meaning of the term is so different from our fathers. We don't hold any belief in God as an 'externalized, individualized, personal being.' When we speak the word God, it is purely in poetical

> meaning, and as a symbol for the idea. I have defined God as 'the advancing totality of our highest ideals.'...We deal with man and not with God. Our great difficulty is to find in Jewish life and literature any expression of this view, and we are compelled to interpret even the 'Sh'ma Yisrael' in order to enable us to voice the one expression which every Jew uses as a watchword.[197]

This account of the concept of God on the part of some leading modern Jewish thinkers echoes and bears close resemblance to modern humanism placing emphasis upon man as the architect of his destiny and in effect the creator of God, as discussed in the previous chapter. This secular humanist phenomenon, divorcing God from the high position traditionally accorded Him by the Hebrew Bible, may be connected to the diversity of ideas concerning God found in the Hebrew Bible, and perhaps most notably, the bold, corporeal, and anthropomorphic depictions of Him prevailing in many biblical writings.

It should be apparent by now that biblical passages such as the First Commandment most quoted to prove original biblical monotheism and the transcendence of God, as well as classical arguments long cited as evidence, are in fact not fully accepted as proving monotheistic transcendence, and this by virtually all biblical scholars, including to some degree, those of Judaism. I feel no hesitation in attributing these problematic multiple theories concerning the God concept or monotheism in the Hebrew Bible to the biblical text itself. In fact, a thorough, systematic, and honest treatment of biblical passages, as they are recapitulated and expressed in the Hebrew Bible in its present shape, would reveal that the idea of monotheism and God's absolute transcendence was probably one of the most perplexing ideas the Israelites had to wrestle with throughout their ancient history. Monotheism penetrated the minds and souls of the Hebrews gradually and slowly. The five books attributed to Moses describe God in relatively transcendental and monotheistic terms, yet these same books give clear indications of the existence and presence of other gods of other nations, legitimize their worship in the lands of those nations, limit Yahweh's territory, power, and sovereignty to the land of Canaan, give detailed information about his sanctuaries and dwelling places, portray patriarchs as well as known Israelite figures as idolatrous, and depict God in naive anthropomorphic and corporeal terms.

Examining these aspects of the biblical text in detail, a modern scholar would easily unearth the unusual tension prevailing with respect to the unity, unicity, and uniqueness of God. On the one hand, the unity and uniqueness of Yahweh is emphasized, whilst on the other it is seriously undermined, by showcasing not only the existence of other gods but also through God Almighty's recognition of their existence by appointing other nations to them while keeping Israel for Himself. "When the Most High apportioned the nations, when he set up the divisions of mankind, He fixed the boundaries of the people according to the members of the sons of God. But Yahweh's own allotment is His people, Jacob His apportioned property" (Dueteronomy 32:9). A contemporary Jewish biblical scholar comments on this passage by observing that:

> Faith in YAHWEH's triumphant majesty facilitated acceptance of the principle that YAHWEH was the supreme deity, that he had appointed other gods to govern the non-Israelite peoples of the world but retained himself rulership of Israel and ultimate jurisdiction in the council of heavenly beings.[198]

In this perspective then Yahweh is not the universal God of mankind, but a national God of Israel; one God among many differing gods (ascribed for other nations) with the exception of His being unique among them: "Who is like unto thee, O Lord, among other gods?" (Exodus15:11). Such texts, argues Marjo Christina Korpel, "prove that initially the Israelites did not deny the existence of other deities and they therefore cannot be termed pure monotheists."[199]

The belief in the existence, power, and rule of other gods, besides God Himself, is detrimental to the concept of the true unity, unicity, uniqueness, and transcendence of God; therefore, the above quoted passages and others like I Samuel 26:19 and Judges 11:23–24, that assert the existence of other gods, are in conflict with the monotheistic and transcendental concept of God. Moreover the Hebrew Bible allows worship of these gods, as A. Lods point out:

> The worship of "strange gods," as they were called, was regarded as perfectly legitimate within the limits of their respective territories. The view which placed the true God in sharp opposition to the false gods, God over against the "non-gods", and the true religion in contrast with the worship of lies, was still unknown.[200]

So the Bible portrays patriarchs as serving other gods, without denouncing them as patriarchs due to this act of ignorance (for instance see Joshua 24:2,14,15; Judges 5:7–9). Aaron, who according to the Bible, was made the prophet and spokesman of Moses to the Israelites, whom God promised to stand with his mouth and teach him what to do (Exodus 4:15–16), is reported to have made the golden calf and allowed his people to worship it (Exodus 32:22–35). King Solomon is reported to have gone after other gods due to the influence of his foreign wives (I Kings 11:1–16). The Israelites are often depicted as engaged in the worship of other gods like Asherah and Baal. Morton Smith notes:

> Solomon's worship of Yahweh was not exclusive; he built high places to Moabite, Sidonian, and Amonite gods and worshipped others, too. And there is no evidence that his subjects were more Yahwist than the King. When the northern tribes broke away from Solomon's son, Rehoboam, about 925 BC and set up the separate kingdom of "Israel" in central and northern Palestine, as opposed to "judah" in the south, the first king, of Israel, Jeroboam, showed his devotion to Yahweh by endowing the shrines of Bethel and Dan with golden images of the deity in the form of a bull calf.[201]

In view of these facts, it has already been suggested that, "up to the eighth century, the Israelites believed firmly in the existence of many other deities beside their national God."[202] Morton Smith argues that the fundamental change in attitude towards the worship of Yahweh took place in the reign of King Asa (died c. 875). "Evidently, from this period on there was a newly important element in the situation: the demand that Israel worship Yahweh and Yahweh alone."[203] On the other hand, we know from the text of the Hebrew Bible that the worship of other gods was still prevalent amongst the Israelites as late as the time of Jeremiah in the seventh century. Jeremiah admonishes his people saying:

> Then the cities of Judah and the inhabitants of Jerusalem will go and cry out to the gods to whom they make offerings, but they will never save them in the time of their trouble. For your gods have become as many as your towns, O Judah; and as many as the streets of Jerusalem are the alters you have set to shame, alters to make offerings to baal. (Jeremiah 11:12–13)

Smith observes that:

> In spite of the Yahwist revolutions of the ninth century, the cult of the various Baals continued. It was evidently popular in the eighth century, when Hosea denounced it, and still popular at the end of the seventh century, when denounced by Zephaniah and Jeremiah. The prophets, Jeremiah said, prophesied by Baal and the people swore by him. Jerusalem had as many alters to him as it had street corners – perhaps an exaggeration. Sacrifices and incense were commonly offered to him. Nor were the baals Yahweh's only competitors. Judea had as many gods as it had cities. When another Yahwist reformation was put through in the time of King Josiah (621 BC) the priests throughout Judea had to be stopped from burning incense on the high places, not only to Baal, but also to the sun, the moon, the planets, and all the host of heaven; around Jerusalem the high places of "the Satyres" and of the gods Ashtoreth, Kemosh, and Milkom had to be destroyed; and the temple of Yahweh itself had to be purged of the vessels of Baal, Asherah, and the host of the heaven, the chariots of the sun, and the houses of the sacred "prostitutes" where the women wove coverings for the pillar which symbolized the goddess Asherah. Josiah's reforms seem to have had little success with the masses and to have died with him in 609, for the later prophecies of Jeremiah and Ezekiel are full of denunciations of Judean worship of other gods than Yahweh. Such complaints are not to be

> dismissed as mere exaggeration; the evidence of archaeology supports them.[204]

He further argues that only "with the appearance of the beginnings of synagogue worship – a type of worship quite different from the sacrificial cult of the temples – the Yahweh alone party became in effect a new religion, and a new kind of religion."[205]

The emergence of an Israelite monotheism involved perplexing and numerous factors, elements, and features, and developed over various stages. It was most probably the Babylonian Exile which gave impetus to the idea of a strict, universal, and ethical monotheism. W. Eichrodt, van Rad, D. M. G. Stalker, Fohrer, B. Lang, Halpern, Mark S. Smith are just a few of the scholars who follow this line of approach. They emphasize the crucial role played by the exile experience in determining the nature of Israelite monotheism. Texts dating to the Exile, explains M. S. Smith, "are the first to attest to unambiguous expressions of Israelite monotheism. Second Isaiah (Isaiah 45:5–7) gave voice to the monotheistic ideal that Yahweh was the only deity in the cosmos. Not only are the other deities powerless; these are nonexistent."[206]

As far as the textual data is concerned, monotheism and the idea of God's transcendence were scarcely hallmarks of Israel's earliest history. Monotheism emerged as a result of the differentiation between Yahweh and other gods and the convergence of their characteristics and attributes to the Israelite Deity. "Monotheism", argues M.S. Smith, "was hardly a feature of Israel's earliest history. By the sole token, convergence was an early development that anticipates the later emergence of monolatry and monotheism."[207] He further states that three levels of development in early Israel bear on convergence. The first reflects Israel's Cananite heritage, features in this category include El, Baal, Asherah, and their imagery and titles, and the cultic practices of the Asherah, high places, and devotion to the dead. The second level involves features that Israel shared with its first millennium neighbors: the rise of the new national deity, the presence of a consort goddess, and the small number of attested deities compared with second-millennium West Semitic cultures. Third, there are characteristics specific to Israelite culture, such as the new god, Yahweh, the traditions of a separate origin and a southern sanctuary, the aniconic requirement, and decreased anthropomorphism. Any of the features in this third category might be invoked to help explain convergence. This long process of convergence, for Smith, was an evolution and a revolution at the same time:

> It was an "evolution" in two respects. Monolatry grew out of an early, limited Israelite polytheism that was not strictly discontinuous with that of its Iron Age neighbors. Furthermore, adherence to one deity was a changing reality within the periods of the judges and the monarchy in Israel. While evolutionary in character, Israelite monolatry was also "revolutionary" in a number of respects. The process of differentiation and the eventual displacement of Baal from Israel's national cult distinguished Israel's religion from the religions of its neighbors...Israelite insistence on a single deity eventually distinguished Israel from the surrounding cultures, as far as textual data indicate.[208]

According to these biblical scholars, the united Davidic monarchy played a decisive role in uniting the Israelites to the worship of Yahweh alone. Conversely, scholars like Albright, G. Mendenhall, J. Bright, and others, who believe in the existence of an early pure Yahwism, argue that the monarchy had a negative effect upon the religion of Israel for it was at this time that pollution occurred through the worship of Baal and other deities. Mark Smith, criticizing this line of approach, argues that "The pure form of Yahwism that Mendenhall and Bright envision was perhaps an ideal achieved rarely, if ever, before the exile – if even then." He further argues that

> the monarchy was not a villain of Israelite religion that Mendenhall and Bright make it out to be. Indeed, the monarchy made several religious contributions crucial to the development of monolatry. In short, Mendenhall and Bright stand much of Israel's religious development on its head.[209]

It is difficult to determine the authenticity of the narration attributed to Moses or other patriarchs, as Morton Smith and others have shown.

The reason is very simple and straightforward. The present Hebrew Bible has gone through a lengthy process of editing, party politics, correction and transmission. Therefore, it is extremely difficult to say with certainty what religious beliefs these patriarchs originally held. As far as biblical textual data is concerned, the view emphasizing progressive revelation seems the more probable, virtually having become a classic as Hans Kung observes. On the bases of most recent research

> present-day scholars assume that polytheism was widespread in Israel down to the Babylonian exile. In other words...it was only after long controversies that strict biblical monotheism was able to establish itself. From our present perspective we have to begin from 'a chain of successive revolutions in the direction of monotheism following relatively rapidly after one another'.[210]

He summarizes this classic view by observing that it was the ninth century, the early monarchical period, which witnessed the battle against Baal and the emphasis upon Yahweh instead of Baal:

> The eighth century saw the beginning of the 'Yahweh alone movement,' which was first in a minority: only this one God is to be worshipped in Israel, no matter what gods other peoples worship...In the seventh century this sole worship of Yahweh became established. The existence of other gods outside Israel was not still denied, but in Israel, the exclusive people of the covenant, Yahweh was to be worshipped exclusively, in exclusive worship (and not Baal or later Zeus); there was a reform program under King Josiah with a purification and centralization of the cult and the declaration that the new cultic order was the law of the state. The sixth century, finally, saw the further development of the sole worship of Yahweh to the point of strict monotheism, which now denied the existence of other gods: the conquest of Jerusalem by the Babylonians was interpreted as punishment for going astray into polytheism, and a redaction of the old writings was undertaken in a strictly monotheistic direction.[211]

This manifest progressive feature of the Hebrew Bible is proof that it is a historically conditioned account of the efforts on the part of finite human beings to understand and perceive God. These efforts seem to be as limited as the limitations of the societies they first appeared in. God, as He is portrayed by many theistic traditions in their developed form, is formless, eternal, immutable, and everlasting. In any case why would God portray Himself in categories inappropriate to His Majesty just because the understanding of the ancient Hebrews was a primitive one? Why would He have to sanction the worship or existence of other gods which are in reality non-existent? This could only muddy waters as to His transcendence, and sow the seeds of confusion. The answer that makes sense is that He did not do so but human agency makes it appear to be so. By this I mean that these issues cannot be resolved if we take the Hebrew Bible to be, in its present shape, the direct, unchanged, pristine revelation or Word of God, verbatim, to the Hebrew prophets. On the other hand, the difficulties can be grasped and mitigated if we recognize the decisive role played by human agency in the final outcome of these writings. The latter alternative will free God of a number of accusations and avert the finger of blame for all the subsequent confusion.

In addition to the flaws contained in the Hebrew Bible with respect to monotheism, there is additional evidence in the text of the Bible indicating that the ancient biblical concept of God was primitive in nature. There are, of course, passages in the Hebrew Bible that emphasize God's transcendence, incorporeality, and otherness, as discussed above (Isaiah 31:3; Job 10:4; Hosea 11:9; Psalm 121:4; Isaiah 40:28). But the passages portraying him in anthropomorphic and corporeal terms and categories outweigh the transcendental passages, so much so and so vividly in fact that it has been argued that "All the evidence suggests that from the outset Yahweh was conceived in human form."[212] Korpel observes that early Israelite traditions attribute "a visible human form to God."[213] Indeed, a majority of mortal, human, physical and mental categories appear to be present in the Hebrew God: God has a body; in the plains of Mamre, He appears to Abraham in a mythico-anthropomorphic form; Abraham bows down towards the ground, offers God water, requests Him to let him wash His feet, fetches

Him a morsel of bread and God responds to Abraham's request and does eat:

> And the Lord appeared to him in the plains of Mamre; and he sat in the tent door in the heat of the day. And he lifted up his eyes and looked, and, lo, three men stood by him; and when he saw them, he ran to meet them from the tent door, and bowed himself to the ground. And said, My Lord, if now I have found favor in your sight, pass not away, I beseech you, from your servant. Let a little water, I beseech you, be fetched, and wash your feet, and rest yourselves under the tree. And I will fetch a morsel of bread, and you comfort your hearts; after that you shall pass on; seeing that you are come to your servant. And they said, So do, as you have said. And Abraham hurried to the tent to Sarah, and said, Make ready quickly three measures of fine meal, knead it, and make cakes. And Abraham ran to the herd, and fetched a calf tender and good, and gave it to a young man; and he hurried to prepare it. And he took butter, and milk, and the calf which he had prepared, and set it before them; and he stood by them under the tree, and they ate. (Genesis 18:1–8)

There are several interpretations given to this passage to avoid the idea of the presence of God with Abraham. One traditional explanation is that all three were angels.[214] But the biblical text itself refutes such interpretations. Only two of the angels, the Bible tells us, went to Sodom while Abraham was still standing with God. On the basis of this evidence, Friedman observes that "from the text it has been argued that the third visitor is God."[215] Esther Hamori after a detailed analysis of Genesis 18:1–33 concludes that the text is so crystal clear that it does not leave any room for any other interpretation but to confess that "Yahweh appears as a man, with such anthropomorphic realism that Abraham does not recognize him until Yahweh's verbal self-revelation."[216] There is no metaphor in the text and it must be taken literally. "Yahweh arrives, washes up, rests, eats, and speaks with Abraham and Sarah, all in entirely concrete human form."[217]

Likewise, Genesis 32:25–33 portrays God in the most graphic corporeal terms. God wrestles with Jacob in an absolutely physical form, so much so that Jacob does not even recognize until the last moments of the match that his opponent is in reality Almighty God. During the fight God touches the hollow of Jacob's thigh and dislocates it. These are without doubt physical acts. The passage reads:

> And Jacob was left alone; and there wrestled a man with him until the breaking of the day. And when he saw that he prevailed not against him, he touched the hollow of his thigh; and the hollow of Jacob's thigh was out of joint, as he wrestled with him. And he said, Let me go, for the day breaks. And he said, I will not let you go, except you bless me. And he said to him, What is your name? And he said, Jacob. And he said, Your name shall be called no more Jacob, but Israel; for as a prince you have power with God and with men, and have prevailed. And Jacob asked him, and said, Tell me, I beg you, your name. And he said, Why is it that you ask after my name? And he blessed him there. And Jacob called the name of the place Peniel; for I have seen God face to face, and my life is preserved. And as he passed over Peniel the sun rose upon him, and he limped upon his thigh. Therefore the people of Israel do not eat of the sinew of the vein, which is in the hollow of the thigh, to this day; because he touched the hollow of Jacob's thigh in the sinew of the vein. (Genesis 32:25–33)

According to Esther Hamori the text is

> blunt and concise regarding what follows: "a man (*ʿis*) wrestled with him." The ensuing description leaves no room for ambiguity regarding the man's physical form. He cannot prevail against Jacob – that is, he is not supernaturally strong, but is fully tied to the realistic human form. He therefore resorts to dislocating Jacob's hip. Yet even now he is not stronger than Jacob, but rather must ask to be let go! It is clear that he is in physical form concretely a man, and not simply a disguised divinity with superhuman strength.[218]

Moreover the man blesses Jacob and Jacob has no further questions about the man's identity. He immediately claims that he has seen God face to face. The place is called "Peniel". The man also gives a new name to Jacob. "The giving of a new name does reflect his divine nature, but moreover, the '*is* names Jacob *Yisra'el*, or 'God strives.'"[219] Hamori has extensively analyzed the traditional interpretations of this passage and shown their absurd nature. Stephen Geller throws light upon the passage's complexity: "This is a famously enigmatic story. The weird struggle in darkness and blessing in the twilight of dawn tempt normally sober exegetes to flights of allegory, often disguised as psychological symbolism... Others despair of ever finding coherent meaning in it."[220]

This passage is nothing short of blasphemy and utterly defies logic. Are we seriously expected to believe that God who is Omnipotent, Creator of the universe, is so helplessly weak that He cannot overcome a feeble human being like Jacob even after dislocating his hip? The whole narrative is a complete affront to the majesty of God Almighty, and without doubt the handiwork of an audacious and blasphemous scribe. We can barely trust the nonsense contained in this so-called wrestling match passage which was certainly neither revealed nor inspired by God.

In Exodus 33 Moses is allowed to see the back part of God and speak face to face to Him: "And the Lord spake unto Moses face to face, as a man speaketh unto his friend" (Exodus 33:11):

> And he said, You cannot see my face; for no man shall see me and live. And the Lord said, Behold, there is a place by me, and you shall stand upon a rock; And it shall come to pass, while my glory passes by, that I will put you in a cleft of the rock, and will cover you with my hand while I pass by; And I will take away my hand, and you shall see my back; but my face shall not be seen. (Exodus 33:20–23)

James Barr describes this passage as "the most sophisticated and delicate discussion of the seeing of God by man in the OT."[221] This is a strange conclusion for the point here is not the possibility of seeing or not seeing God but the fact of divine holiness, for no man can see God and survive. God's holiness is incompatible with human sinfulness and impurity. The preceding chapter, Exodus 32, throws light upon the

Israelites' sinful act of fashioning and worshipping the golden calf. As Barr states:

> in this chapter the problem is not really the problem of anthropomorphism as such... It seems clear that the passage was written for its context, that is, to follow immediately after the incident of the sin of Israel in making the golden calf...The danger is that if he goes with them personally, he will consume them clearly, because of their rebelliousness.[222]

So therefore the problem here is not with the anthropomorphism or the transcendence of God, rather, the issue is connected with sin and atonement regarding God's presence and vision. As Moses did not participate in the golden calf transgression, he is shielded by God's hand and placed in the cleft of a rock so that he can withstand the overbearing radiance of God's glory and see Him. The passage shows God's special grace upon and intimacy with the person of Moses to the exclusion of the other Israelites. Moreover, Moses here is not shown asking something new, for other righteous Israelites have also seen God's glory quite often (Exodus 16:10, 24:9–11, 33:11). The preceeding verses show that Moses had already had an intimate dialogue with God "face to face" as a person speaks to a friend. The passage shows Moses' closeness to God. In Numbers 12:8 God confirms that he spoke to Moses "mouth to mouth."

In addition to Moses, the elders of Israel had also seen God, "Then went up Moses, and Aaron, Nadab, and Abihu, and seventy of the elders of Israel: And they saw the God of Israel: and there was under his feet as it were a paved work of a sapphire stone ..." (Exodus 24:9–10). Despite figurative interpretations by the Jewish philosopher Saadia and others, that what was actually seen was some form created by God rather than the great God Himself, this is not what the text says. The words clearly state, "they saw the God of Israel". Howard Eilberg-Schwartz observes that this passage "lends itself more readily to literal reading. Indeed, the myth goes out of its way to emphasize that the Israelite leaders saw God, repeating the idea two times."[223] Samuel Terrien admits that, "In this narrative, on the contrary, the setting is topographically concrete, the human witnesses are many, and the visual perception of Godhead, twice affirmed (vss. 10 and 11), is made even more explicitly sensorial by its sequential climax 'they ate and drank'."[224]

The passage also depicts God as having feet, a theme also presented in several other biblical passages (Nahum1:3; Habakkuk 3:5; Zechariah 14:4). There is a tendency among traditional biblical scholars to interpret theophanies (appearances of God) such as Exodus 33:23 as transcendental anthropomorphisms or something metaphorical in nature, and they attempt to equate these theophanies with anthropomorphic expressions such as God's hand, face, eyes etc. and give them metaphorical explanation. James Barr has shown that such tendency is flawed as the theophanies are not metaphorical in nature at all, rather thoroughly physical and depict God in embodied human form. He observes that:

> In contrast with all this, it is in the theophanies where God lets himself be seen that there is a real attempt to grapple with the form of his appearance. Indeed, for Hebrew thought 'form' and 'appearance' may be taken as correlative, and where there is no 'appearance' a passage is of only secondary importance for the idea of form.[225]

God it is written has a head (Isaiah 59:17; Psalm 110:7), and the hair of His head is like pure wool (Daniel 7:9). His face is mentioned around 236 times.[226] Whilst metaphorical meaning can be ascribed most of the time, sometimes the text is fairly literal and anthropomorphic as seen in the case of Moses. God hides His face. This particular phrase occurs over thirty times in the Hebrew Bible:[227] "And I shall leave them, and I shall hide my face from them... and they will say in that day, 'Is it not because our God is not among us that these evils have found us?'" (Deuteronomy 31:17; also Deuteronomy 32:20). Some of these passages are metaphorical in nature but a good number of them are inescapably anthropomorphic. Not surprisingly, therefore, it has been observed that, "Originally... the Israelites did believe that God could reveal himself with a human face."[228]

God's eyes are mentioned 200 times. He has a nose (Genesis 8:21) such that there issues "a smoke out of his nostrils" (Psalm 18:8), and he has a sense of smell (Exodus 25:6, 29:18; I Samuel 2:18), and Ezekiel 20:41 where He likes and is pleased with sweet odor. Given these bold and daringly descriptive passages, it has been observed that:

> According to the Old Testament, God also has a nose ['P]. Genesis 8:21 and other comparable texts state that he can smell and likes the pleasant odor of agreeable sacrifices. Therefore his people burn incense "under his nose" according to the archaic verse Deuteronomy 33:10. It would seem that such an expression still presupposes a fairly literal, anthropomorphic image of God.[229]

These and other anthropomorphic expressions in Deuteronomy seriously call into question M. Weinfeld's theory that Deuteronomy and the Deuteronomic school are vigorously against the conceiving of God in anthropomorphic terms.[230]

Further, God's ear is mentioned frequently (Numbers 11:1; II Samuel 22:7; Psalm 86:1). God is said to have a mouth, "With him will I speak mouth to mouth even apparently" (Numbers 12:8); he has lips, a tongue and breath "his lips are full of indignation, and his tongue as a devouring fire and his breath, as an overflowing stream" (Isaiah 30:27–28). He has teeth "he gnasheth upon me with his teeth" (Job 16:9); he has a back "I will shew them the back and not the face" (Jeremiah 18:17). God's hand is mentioned almost as frequently as his face and eyes. Although a good number of these expressions can be understood in an allegorical and non-mythological sense, some passages are, however, far too anthropomorphic. They ascribe a right and left hand to God, "Thy Lord said unto my Lord, Sit thou at my right hand" (Psalm 110:1), "Thy right hand, O Lord, is become glorious in power: thy right hand, O Lord, hath dashed in pieces the enemy" (Exodus15:6), "I saw the Lord sitting on his throne, and all the host of heaven standing by him on his right hand and on his left" (I Kings 22:19). He has the name of Zion written on his palm, "Behold I have graven thee upon the palms of my hand" (Isaiah 49:16). He gives to Moses, on Sinai, two tablets of stone "written with the finger of God" (Exodus 31:18). God has arms (Isaiah 30:30; Jeremiah 27:5), he stretches his arm, he claps (Ezekiel 21:17), Amos sees him with a plumline in his hand "behold, the Lord stood upon a wall made by a plumline, with a plumline in his hand" (Amos 7:7). Howard Eillberg-Schwartz makes an important observation regarding the historical theophanies of Amos, Ezekial and others. He argues that to

> say the body is simply a metaphor like 'God is a lion' or 'God the rock' is to fail to take seriously the distinctive context in which images of the body are used...The ancient Judaic sources after all have special significance. They depict the exceptional cases of religious leaders who were privileged to see God...The point is that when they described seeing God, they evoked a human form. The image of the human body is thus of a different order than other metaphors that are used to refer to God. The comparison of God to a lion does not conjure up the image of a lion because this image is not used in contexts that describe God sightings. But when Moses is said to have seen the divine back, and Isaiah the divine robe, and Ezekiel the divine figure, the sources evoke a human image. The human body, then, is the privileged image for imagining what it might be like to gaze on the deity. In the texts of ancient Israel, then, we are dealing with at least two kinds of God images: (1) visual descriptions of what is seen when a character looks upon God and (2) conceptual representations that describe God in contexts in which seeing does not take place.[231]

Jeffrey J. Niehaus confirms the fact that biblical theophanies are "cast in a mode of historical reportage."[232] It is worth noting also that when God is portrayed as coming in thunder, lightening or behind clouds, this does not mean that He does not have a physical human form or body but rather that sinful Hebrews are not allowed to look at his radiant glory with their immoral eyes, which is only the purview of the righteous among them, who can still physically gaze at God's glorified majestic form. Binyamin Uffenheimer states that the "dispute between these traditions relates to the question whether it is *permitted* to see Him, though all agreed that it is *possible* to see Him."[233]

In sum and given the numerous descriptive passages involved, we can only conclude that the God of the Hebrew Bible is neither incorporeal nor invisible. The bare facts are that a) He has appeared to many people (very often unexpectedly) at different times, and b) He has often appeared in human form leading to widespread confusion as to His identity, for many in the encounter have mistaken Him for an ordinary human being.

Therefore it becomes evident, taking these passages of the Hebrew Bible together, that the concept of God in the Hebrew Bible, at least as presented by its different writers, is clearly an anthropomorphic one. Although some of the passages can undoubtedly be explained away metaphorically, the overall picture is such that given the very vivid, graphic, and detailed nature of most of the depictions of the deity, it is almost impossible to believe that certain writers of the Hebrew Bible did not have an anthropomorphic and corporeal deity in mind. Such in fact is the resemblance of God to the human physical form that almost all the major organs and parts of the human body are ascribed to God with certain exceptions, i.e. legs, buttocks, toes, sexual organs etc. The Israelite, observes A. Lods:

> went still further in this assimilation of God to man: they ascribed to Jahweh bodily organs which in man are the seat of organs of expression of feelings or thoughts: Jahweh had eyes, ears, a mouth, nostrils, hands, a heart, bowels, his breath was long or short (quiet or disturbed). These were not metaphors.[234]

Furthermore, at times these anthropomorphic expressions are so naive as to leave no room for any metaphorical interpretation to be ascribed to them. As Katz observes, even "if one explains these terms as being nothing but picturesque expressions, intended to awaken within man a sense of the real presence of God and His works, nonetheless they remain personifications."[235] According to Fahrer, they prove that Yahweh was "conceived solely as having human form."[236]

In addition the anthropomorphic concept of God is as much abundant in the Torah (the so-called five books of Moses), as it is in the later classical prophets. Isaiah for instance, a stalwart of universal monotheism, does not feel any hesitation in portraying God in anthropomorphic and corporeal terms saying:

> In the year that king Uzziah died I saw also the Lord sitting upon a throne, high and lifted up, and his train filled the temple. Above it stood the seraphims: each one had six wings; with twain he covered his face, and with twain he covered his feet, and with twain he did fly.... Then said I, Woe is me! for I am undone; because I am a man of unclean lips, and I dwell in the midst of a people of unclean lips: for mine eyes have seen the King, the Lord of hosts. (Isaiah 6:1–5)

In this passage Isaiah sees God with his own physical, not imaginative, eyes. He sees God's transcendent *anthropos*.[237] J. J. M. Roberts after detailed analysis of the visual elements in this passage concludes that "Isaiah claims to have seen with his own eyes Israel's God sitting enthroned as a king on a high and lofty throne."[238]

Ezekiel 1:1–28 also reports God as enthroned transcendent *anthropos* with radiant luminosity. Rimmon Kasher observes that "there is perhaps no other biblical prophet whose God is so corporeal as Ezekiel."[239] Ezekiel's physical breakdown in the face of God is proof that the experience is not a visionary but a very real physical one.

Amos, the proposed originator of ethical and pure monotheism, claims to have seen the Lord standing on a wall with a plumline in His hand, as mentioned earlier (Amos 7:7). It is a striking fact, observes Eichrodt,

> that in prophetic visions too the human manifestation of Yahweh frequently recurs, even if, with greater reticence, it is rather suggested than described; and the same anthropomorphism persists in eschatological word pictures...It will be better to revert to an observation made earlier, namely that the immediate proximity and reality of God, which for us are all too easily obscured by spiritualizing concepts, are outstanding features of the Old Testament revelation, and compel men to clothe the divine presence in human form.[240]

A. Lods observes:

> Another feature of the "theology" of ancient Judaism, which has often been noted, was what is known as the "transcendence" which it attributed to God. The term cannot here be taken in its strictly philosophical sense, or it will give rise to false conclusions: the Jews of this period did not think that because God was a spirit he could have no relation to the world of matter, or that he was outside the visible universe. Ezekiel and the priestly historian tell of the appearances of God to man, and sometimes make use of distinctly anthropomorphic expressions to describe divine activity.[241]

This alludes to the fact that an anthropomorphic and corporeal concept of God was not thought to be a problem at all even by those classical prophets who roundly rejected idolatry, graven images, and a material representation of God. Hence it has been suggested that:

> The anthropopathic and anthropomorphic conception of Jahweh was an advance on the naturalistic and theriomorphic representations: this explains why the great prophets, far from opposing this mode of conceiving of Jahweh, commonly made use of the metaphors which served to express it.[242]

Moreover, the anthropopathic (attribution of human passions/ emotions to a deity) descriptions of God are prevalent throughout the Hebrew Bible and substantiate, as discussed, the theme of pervasive anthropomorphism. Some of these attributes and actions are inevitable for God's perception as a living, personal, active, close, and loving God. Such attributes are congenial to His absolute majesty and perfection while others are undoubtedly inappropriate to His omniscience, omnipotence, omnipresence, and absolute perfection. These qualities are too human to be ascribed to the true God, the source of all perfection. It is natural for God to have eternal life, ceaseless mercy, unparalleled, unmatched and surpassing love, infinite knowledge, unlimited and unprecedented power, unsurpassed authority and all other attributes of goodness and perfection in absolute terms. These are the terms and attributes essential to produce in human beings a profound and appropriate response to their Creator. But the attribution of traits such as weeping, sleeping, crying, roaring, repenting, doing evil, walking etc. are too anthropomorphic and terrestrial to be believed of, or ascribed to, any celestial being, let alone God. They transmogrify the majesty, awesomeness and mystery of God and transmute the resultant response.

These anthropopathic passages, when studied in light of the pictorial passages cited above, leave little room for doubt that the majority of biblical writers and narrators held an anthropomorphic concept of the deity and that very often they speak of God as of a man. Ironically, the God who it is said created man in His own image and likeness seems very often to be created in man's own image and physical likeness. And indeed, such are some of the characteristics and categories ascribed to God by several biblical writers that an honorable and dignified human being would disdain their being ascribed to him (meaning man), let alone to God.

The following verses of the Hebrew Bible substantiate the claim. God fears (Deuteronomy 32:27), He weeps, wails, laments, "For the mountains will I take up a weeping and wailing, and for the habitations of the wilderness a lamentation" (Jeremiah 9:10). "Therefore will I howl for Moab, and I will cry out for Moab; mine heart shall mourn for the men of Kirheres. O vine of Sibmah, I will weep for thee with the weeping of jazer" (Jeremiah 48:31–32). Extraordinarily God does "evil". This happens not only as a reaction to the sins of man, but also as a non-causal action. Moreover, He is shown to repent His planned evil when Moses reminds Him of his promises with the patriarch:

> And Moses besought the Lord his God, and said, Lord why doth thy wrath wax hot against thy people...wherefore should the Egyptians speak, and say, For mischief did he bring them out, to slay them in the mountains...Turn from thy fierce wrath, and repent of this evil against thy people.... And the Lord repented of the evil which he thought to do unto his people. (Exodus 32: 11–14)

Commenting on similar passages a contemporary American scholar has observed that, "The God of Moses was a God with hands, with feet, with the organs of speech. A God of passion, of hatred, of revenge, of affection, of repentance; a God who made mistakes – in other words, an immense and powerful man."[243] Though it is sometimes stated that God is not a man and therefore need not repent "for he is not a man, that he should repent", (I Samuel 15:29), yet nevertheless, in the same chapter he is made to repent, "and the Lord repented that he had made Saul king over Israel" (I Samuel 15:35). In fact throughout the Hebrew Bible God is made to repent very often, "And it repented the Lord that he had made man on the earth, and it grieved him at heart" (Genesis 6:6; and also Amos 7:6). This is not perfection but imperfection. It is not appropriate for the All-Wise, All-Knowing God to repent of what He plans or does because His plans are eternally based on His absolute knowledge and He has all the power in the world to execute them accordingly. Friedman rightly observes that "This is a curious way to speak about God. The concept of God regretting something is strange enough. If God is all-knowing, how could He possibly regret any past action? Did He not know when He did it what the results would be?"[244]

Not only does God repent, but He also wrestles with Jacob and Jacob prevails, as mentioned earlier,

> for as a prince hast thou power with God and with man, and hast prevailed. And Jacob asked him, and said, Tell me, I pray thee, thy name. And he said, Wherefore is it that thou dost ask after my name? And he blessed him there. And Jacob called the name of the place Peniel: for I have seen God face to face, and my life is preserved. (Genesis 32:28–30)

Friedman notes that, "After all, it is not just a story of a man having contact with divinity. It is a story of a man having a *fight* with divinity."[245] He further argues: "Adam disobeys God. Abraham questions God. Jacob fights God. Humans are confronting their creator, and they are increasing their participation in the arena of divine prerogatives."[246] In addition to this powerlessness, God walks (Genesis 3:8), sleeps (Psalm 44:23), "in [the] Old Testament God is supposed to take his rest at certain times."[247] He awakes "Then the Lord awoke as one out of sleep, and like a mighty man that shouteth by reason of wine" (Psalm 78:65). If God made man in His own image and in His likeness (Genesis 1:26) are we to infer from this that our basic experiences, emotive responses, characteristics, both positive and negative are a mirror of God's? Of course the verse requires a metaphorical reading but subsequent biblical passages seem to belie this. Ingersoll argues, that:

> No one can read the Pentateuch without coming to the conclusion that the author supposed that man was created in the physical likeness of the Deity. God said "Go to, let us go down;" "God smelled a sweet savor;" "God repented him that he had made a man;" "and God said;" "walked;" and "talked;" and "rested." All these expressions are inconsistent with any other idea than that the person using them regarded God as having the form of man.[248]

Anthropomorphism and the Rabbinic Mind

In addition to the Written Torah, the Oral Torah or Talmud is very important to Judaic tradition and a central text of mainstream Judaism. Rabbinic authorities believed that God had revealed the Oral Torah or Law to Moses just as He had revealed the Written Torah and this is what the term *Halakha LeMoshe MiSinai* exactly means. The Oral Torah was transmitted meticulously through continuous chains of narrators and well preserved orally though not compiled into an earlier written form until later like the Written Torah. Lawrence Shiffman observes that the Oral Torah or Talmudic "material became the new scripture of Judaism, and the authority of the Bible was now defined in terms of how it was interpreted in the rabbinic tradition. Scripture had been displaced by Talmud." [249] The rabbis, observes Friedman, with the help of this doctrine of the "Oral Torah" "placed their own traditions and rulings on a par with the Bible."[250] The scholars differ over when and how this metamorphosis took place but not many of them differ with regards to the outcome. In a classic work on rabbinic Judaism, Ephraim Urbach has observed that the tradition of the fathers, the enactments, and the decrees, became the Torah alongside the Written Torah. The expositions of the Sages possessed decisive authority and deserved at least the same place in the scale of religious values as the Written Torah, and in truth transcended it.[251] This doctrine, remarks Neusner, became "the central myth of rabbinic civilization."[252]

The Oral Torah or Talmud echoed the Written Torah in preserving the anthropomorphic and corporeal depictions of the Divine contained in the latter. In fact, the rabbinic authorities, with rare exception, emboldened the corporealism of the Written Torah and made it so graphic that the Talmudic God becomes nothing short of a complete human being with excessive human limitations. Some efforts have been made by rabbis such as Rabbi Simon b. Judah, Rabbi Judah b. Ilai, Rabbi Joshua b. Levi and Rabbi Zeira (the student of Hisda of Huna) to remove or mitigate biblical anthropomorphism from rabbinic literature but they have been part of a tiny minority. Some of these Rabbis have placed particles such as "as it were" or "as though it were possible" before anthropomorphic biblical expressions to mitigate their intensity. Many actions, appearances, and attributes, repugnant to the concept of a transcendent and absolute Deity, were ascribed to intermediary beings and angels. In these circumstances, observes Jacob B. Agus:

> their legal training came to the aid of the sages. Accustomed to weigh the full significance of each word in the Torah, they applied the same method to the Scriptural verses which imply the Lord's presence with men. The verb shochon, "to dwell," was thus turned into a noun, shechinah, "presence," implying that an emanation from the Supreme Being or a special effulgence of divine radiance was made to dwell in certain places...[253]

Such interpretations had their own peculiar difficulties and problems. The terms, states S. Schechter:

> which were accepted in order to weaken or nullify anthropomorphic expressions were afterwards hypostatised and invested with a semi-independent existence, or personified as the creatures of God. This will explain the fact that, along with the allegorizing tendency, there is also a marked tendency in the opposite direction, insisting on the literal sense of the world of the Bible, and even exaggerating the corporeal terms.[254]

The rabbinic mind faced two choices in describing God, i.e. personification (hypostatization) or anthropomorphism and corporealism. They seem to have clearly opted for the second option. As a result, the "God of rabbinic Judaism", notes R. M. Seltzer:

> was as anthropomorphic as the God of the Bible, but in different ways. He studies Torah, he dresses in a prayer shawl; he prays to himself... Qualified by "as it were," the human qualities that the rabbis identify as godly lead them to depict a fatherly deity, intimate and personal, loving without compromising his ethical rigor, a God who weeps when he must punish.[255]

The following Talmudic passages substantiate the points made. God prays:

> R. Johanan says in the name of R. Jose: How do we know that the Holy One, blessed be He, says prayers? Because it says: Even them will I bring to My holy mountain and make them joyful in My house of prayer. It is not said, 'their prayer', but 'My prayer'; hence [you learn] that the Holy One, blessed be He, says prayers. What does He pray? — R. Zutra b. Tobi said in the name of Rab: 'May it be My will that My mercy may suppress My anger, and that My mercy may prevail over My [other] attributes, so that I may deal with My children in the attribute of mercy and, on their behalf, stop short of the limit of strict justice'.[256]

Some Rabbis are regarded as spiritually so elevated that God seeks their blessings:

> It was taught: R. Ishmael b. Elisha says: I once entered into the innermost part [of the Sanctuary] to offer incense and saw Akathriel Jah, the Lord of Hosts, seated upon a high and exalted throne. He said to me: Ishmael, My son, bless Me! I replied: May it be Thy will that Thy mercy may suppress Thy anger and Thy mercy may prevail over Thy other attributes, so that Thou mayest deal with Thy children according to the attribute of mercy and

> mayest, on their behalf, stop short of the limit of strict justice! And He nodded to me with His head.[257]

Talmudic passages such as these met with vehement opposition and ridicule from non-Jewish writers and were dubbed as blasphemous. Both the Geonic era (539–1038 CE) and post Geonic era rabbis responded to such attacks by interpreting Akathriel Jah as an angel or the Light of Glory. Arthur Marmorstein notes that such an effort would not have succeeded anyway as the

> ancient readers saw in this name God Himself. Besides, the older as well as the younger Haggadah preserved numerous traces of a religious conception in which God is spoken of or imagined as a visible figure. Rabbis in the Middle Ages still adhered to such a presentation of religious teaching. The Midrash depicts the Hebrews as seeing God as a warrior or as a learned scribe. The Hebrews on the Red Sea were able to point at God with their fingers, 'They beheld His image as a man is able to look his friend in the face.' [258]

God wears traditional Tefillin, "I will take away My hand, and thou shalt see My back. R. Hama b. Bizana said in the name of R. Simon the Pious: This teaches us that the Holy One, blessed be He, showed Moses the knot of the tefillin."[259]

God follows a fixed day schedule and sports with Leviathan:

> Yet Rab Judah said in the name of Rab: 'The day consists of twelve hours; during the first three hours the Holy One, blessed be He, is occupying Himself with the Torah, during the second three He sits in judgment on the whole world, and when He sees that the world is so guilty as to deserve destruction, He transfers Himself from the seat of Justice to the seat of Mercy; during the third quarter, He is feeding the whole world, from the horned buffalo to the brood of vermin; during the fourth quarter He is sporting with the leviathan, as it is said, There is leviathan, whom Thou hast formed to sport therewith'? Said R. Nahman b. Isaac: Yes, He sports with His creatures, but does not laugh at His creatures...[260]

God also has a night schedule and he listens to songs:

> And what does He do by night? — If you like you may say, the kind of thing He does by day; or it may be said that He rides a light cherub, and floats in eighteen thousand worlds; for it is said, The chariots of God are myriads, even thousands shinan... He sits and listens to the song of the Hayyoth, as it is said, By the day the Lord will command His loving kindness and in the night His song shall be with me.[261]

According to certain other rabbis God has some extra work to do at night:

> R. Eliezer says: The night has three watches, and at each watch the Holy One, blessed be He, sits and roars like a lion. For it is written: The Lord does roar from on high, and raise His voice from His holy habitation; 'roaring He doth roar' because of his fold. R. Isaac b. Samuel says in the name of Rab: The night has three watches, and at each watch the Holy One, blessed be He, sits and roars like a lion and says: Woe to the children, on account of whose sins I destroyed My house and burnt My temple and exiled them among the nations of the world.[262]

> It has been taught: R. Jose says, I was once travelling on the road, and I entered into one of the ruins of Jerusalem in order to pray. Elijah of blessed memory appeared and waited for me at the door... He said to me...My son, what sound did you hear in this ruin? I replied: I heard a divine voice, cooing like a dove, and saying: Woe to the children, on account of whose sins I destroyed My house and burnt My temple and exiled them among the nations of the world! And he said to me: By your life and by your head! Not in this moment alone does it so exclaim, but thrice each day does it exclaim thus! And more than that, whenever the Israelites go into the synagogues and schoolhouses and respond: 'May His great name be blessed!' the Holy One, blessed be He, shakes His head and says: Happy is the king who is thus praised

> in this house! Woe to the father who had to banish his children, and woe to the children who had to be banished from the table of their father! [263]

The rabbinic sages project a myth of repeated divine lamentations over the destruction of the Temple in Jerusalem and the dispersal of the Israelites:

> R. Kattina said...When the Holy One, blessed be He, calls to mind His children, who are plunged in suffering among the nations of the world, He lets fall two tears into the ocean, and the sound is heard from one end of the world to the other, and that is the rumbling...R. Kattina, for his own part, said: [God] clasps His hands, as it says: I will also smite my hands together, and I will satisfy my fury. R. Nathan said: [God] emits a sigh, as it is said: I will satisfy my fury upon them and I will be eased. And the Rabbis said: He treads upon the firmament, as it says: He giveth a noise as they that tread grapes against all the inhabitants of the earth. R. Aha b. Jacob says: He presses his feet together beneath the throne of glory, as it says: Thus saith the Lord, the heaven is my throne and the earth is my foot-stool.[264]

God weeps over the destiny of Israel and the destruction of His temple in secret chambers:

> But if ye will not hear it, My soul shall weep in secret for the pride. R. Samuel b. Inia said in the name of Rab: The Holy One, blessed be He, has a place and its name is 'Secret'... But is there any weeping in the presence of the Holy One, blessed be He? For behold R. Papa said: There is no grief in the Presence of the Holy One blessed be He; for it is said: Honour and majesty are before Him; strength and beauty are His sanctuary! There is no contradiction; the one case [refers to] the inner chambers, the other case [refers to] the outer chambers. But behold it is written: And in that day did the Lord, the God of Hosts, call to weeping and to lamentation, and to baldness, and to girding with sackcloth! The

> destruction of the Temple is different, for even the angels of peace wept [over it]; for it is said: Behold for their altar they cried without; the angels of peace wept bitterly.[265]

God daily weeps over three failures:

> And mine eye shall drop tears and tears, and run down with tears, because the Lord's flock is carried away captive. R. Eleazar said: Wherefore these three [expressions of] 'tears'? One for the first Temple, and one for the second Temple, and one for Israel, who have become exiled from their place.[266]

> Our Rabbis taught: Over three the Holy One, blessed be He, weeps every day: over him who is able to occupy himself with [the study of] the Torah and does not; and over him who is unable to occupy himself with [the study of] the Torah and does; and over a leader who domineers over the community.[267]

Rabbinical recognition of the blasphemous nature of these daring statements concerning God is evidenced from their own confessions that "if Scripture did not speak thus, the tongue that says this should be cut to ribbons."[268] Nevertheless they have continued to repeat the myth of divine sorrow, pain and lamentation as if this were an integral part of the scriptural portrayal of God:

> 'My eye, My eye flows with tears' (Lamentations 1:16). R. Levi said: (This verse may be) compared to a doctor whose eye ailed him. He said, 'Let my (good) eye weep for my (bad) eye'. Similarly, Israel is called the eye of the Holy One, blessed be He, as it is said, 'For all men's eyes will turn to the Lord, along with (like) the tribes of Israel' (literally, 'For to the Lord is the eye of man, and all the tribes of Israel') (Zechariah 9:1). The Holy One, blessed be He, said, as it were (kivyakhol), 'Let My eye weep for My eye'.[269]

Commenting on this vividly anthropomorphic interpretation of a scriptural passage, Michael Fishbane notes that:

God is the speaker of the verse, and His lament is over one of His eyes which has been damaged—this being the people of Israel. Indeed, instead of the biblical lament marking the absence of God from the nation, it now underscores His active presence, expressed through tears and lamentation. For R. Levi, therefore, the wound of the people is construed as a wound for God Himself, since Israel is mythically transformed into part of the corpus dei—'for the Lord has a human eye'. The qualification kivyakhol at the end does not undermine this point, but rather fixes attention on the fact that this mythopoeic teaching has been derived from Scripture. Through such theology, the borders between history and myth collapse.[270]

R. Ishmael ascends to the heaven and sees God crying:

At that moment...the Omnipresent would cry, and five rivers of tears flowed from its fingers into the Great Sea, making the whole earth quake; as it is written, "The foundations of the earth will shudder; the earth will be rent in ruin; the earth will split asunder; the earth will bend and buckle; the earth will totter and tilt" (Isaiah 24:18–20)—five times, corresponding to the five fingers of the great right arm.[271]

Finally God himself comes to appease Jerusalem and is judged through fire. According to Fishbane:

Perhaps with such extraordinary judgements in mind, recriminations could be made which take ancient rabbinic theology to the brink. Thus the Palestinian Amora R. Reuben (a contemporary of R. Isaac Nappaḥa) transmitted a statement of R. Ḥanina bar Ḥama, with all due caution but with no doubt about the point: 'If Scripture did not say so, one could not say this—"For YHWH is judged through fire" (Isaiah 66:16); (note that) Scripture does not say "(YHWH) judges (shopheṭ)" but "is judged (nishpaṭ)"—not more and not less. A more complete inversion of the theme of God's salvific judgement than this portrayal of divine punishment and purgation is hard to find.[272]

The rabbinic God is an absolutely corporeal diety with countless human limitations, and the rabbinic theological conception of God in no way or form resembles the Omnipotent, Omniscient, Omnipresent, and independent God of monotheistic transcendental theology. Rather, evidence would appear to suggest that the rabbinic concept of God is a reflection of Judaic religious and political aspirations, with God's destiny being paired off with Judaic destiny: He suffers with their suffering and laments their failures. This lamenting and weeping deity can hardly be said to be the Omnipotent God of the universe:

> R. Aba said to R. Nahman b. Isaac: Since the day of the destruction of the temple, there is no laughter for the Holy One, blessed be He. Whence do we know that there is not? Shall we say from the verse, And on that day did the Lord, the God of Hosts, call to weeping and lamentation? But this refers to that day and no more. Shall we then say, from this verse: If I forget thee, O Jerusalem, let my right hand forget her cunning, let my tongue cleave to the roof of my mouth if I do not remember thee? But this, too, excludes forgetfulness, but not laughter. Hence, [it is known] from the verse, I have long time held my peace, I have been still, and refrained myself, now will I cry. What then does God do in the fourth quarter? He sits and instructs the school children, as it is said, Whom shall one teach knowledge, and whom shall one make to understand the message? Them that are weaned from the milk. Who instructed them theretofore? If you like, you may say Metatron, or it may be said that God did this as well as other things.[273]

God is frequently depicted as crying. For example, He requests Jeremiah to summon an embassy of Patriarchs like Abraham, Isaac and Jacob to console Him:

> 'for they know how to cry'. Soon a procession of lamentation and mourning moved towards the Temple—a cortege involving Abraham, Isaac, Jacob, and Moses. And when the Holy One, blessed be He, saw them (approach), at once, "On that day, YHWH,

> God of hosts, summoned to crying and lamenting, to tonsuring and girding with sackcloth" (Isaiah 22: 12); and if Scripture did not say so, it would be forbidden to say it. And they went crying from one gate to another, like a person "whose dead (relative) lies before him"; and the Holy One, blessed be He, was lamenting and saying, "Woe to the king who was successful in his youth (*shebe-qaṭnuto hitzliaḥ*), but who, in his old age (*be-ziqnuto*), was not successful".[274]

These portrayals and assertions of God's supposed historical failures, weaknesses and personal lamentings are nothing short of blasphemy. The powerful sovereign of the universe is depicted as a helpless king unable to protect His children, defend His sanctuary, establish His services etc. and lamenting openly due to His broken pride. He weeps in inner chambers and needs human patriarchal consolation in private to avoid other nations' mockery. These utterly physical anthropomorphisms and realistic corporeal manifestations of God are not the result of human or language limitations but rather truly reflect the authors' understanding of the deity. A. E. Suffrin rightly observes that "When we turn to the Rabbinic writings from about the 3rd cent. A.D. onwards, however, we meet with gross anthropomorphisms... It not only wrote human history as it ought or ought not to have happened, but explored the seven heavens and revealed the Deity."[275] He further remarks that:

> Putting together the passages from the Talmud and Midrashim, we find in plain prose that on the highest heaven is the throne of Glory, on the back of which is engraved the image of Jacob... Metatron is close to the deity... Behind the throne stands Sandalphon, whose height is a distance of a walk of 500 years, and who binds chaplets for the Deity...God is occupied with studying 24 books of the Bible by day, and the six sedarim of the Mishna by night... There are schools in heaven after the Rabbinic model, where Rabbis in their order discuss the Halakha, and God studies with them... Every day He promulgates a new Halakha... He wears phylacteries... of which Moses saw the knot... At the

> Exodus from Egypt every servant girl saw God bodily and could point Him out with her finger. When God descended on Sinai, He was wrapped in the Rabbinic tallith... He has His own synagogue. He prays to Himself that His mercy should overcome His wrath... He weeps daily over Jerusalem... The last three hours of the day He sports with Leviathan...[276]

This perhaps explains the reason why Gedaliahu Stroumsa argues that the corporeal nature of biblical expressions was widely recognized by rabbinic thinkers, and that in antiquity, God not only had "human feelings, but also a body of gigantic or cosmic dimensions."[277]

Arthur Marmorstein, on the other hand, does not consider anthropomorphism to be a problem at all. He claims anthropomorphism to be a higher level of religious understanding:

> Paganism was far removed from anthropomorphism, it cherished the lower stage of theriomorphism... The religion of Israel was from the very beginning free from this false doctrine... Without anthropomorphism the ordinary man with his narrow vision and limited intelligence would not have been able to grasp the belief in God, in His omnipotence and eternity, His universal knowledge and presence.[278]

He further argues that:

> In this respect the teachers of the Haggadah stand not much below the prophets; they attain in many respects the height of the prophetic conception of God. The treatment of the anthropomorphism in the Bible had from of old been a subject of dispute between opposing schools. The history of this spiritual conflict goes back very far. If this is borne in mind the contradictions between the scholars in Haggadah become much more intelligible. One has only to think of the attitude of R. Akiba and of R. Ishmael to this problem. No harm is done to religion if one designates it as anthropomorphic. All higher religious systems are of this nature.[279]

Marmorstein attempts to solve all the problems posed by rabbinic anthropomorphism by asserting a hypothesis which states that since ancient times two schools existed among the rabbis, the allegorists and the literalists. By qualifying anthropomorphisms by various qualifiers, the rabbis, according to Marmorstein, allegorized and hence overcame anthropomorphisms. On the other hand, the literalists took these anthropomorphisms literally, enlarging them and adding to their vitality. He then explains away some of the anthropomorphic passages as a reaction and endeavors to respond to the polemics directed against Israel in the rabbinic period.[280] Schechter contends that arguments in favor of rabbinic anthropomorphisms and their allegorical interpretations are as shallow as Marmorstein.[281]

Max Kadushin strongly rejects any such hypothesis and argues that:

> The whole hypothesis, indeed, falls to the ground as soon as we examine its central thesis – the division into two schools. In the attempt to maintain this division, Marmorstein is forced, in a number of instances, to change around the proponents of opinion, often solely on the basis of his thesis.[282]

Biblical writers and rabbinic thinkers did not view anthropomorphic descriptions of the Deity as a problem, and a great majority of them did not consider it wrong to ascribe to God characteristics and qualities altogether human and corporeal. Kadushin rightly argues that:

> To ascribe to the Rabbis any sort of stand on anthropomorphism is to do violence, therefore, to rabbinic thought. Indeed, this entire discussion only shows that when we employ the terms of classical philosophy even in an attempt to clarify rabbinic ideas, we are no longer within the rabbinic universe of discourse.[283]

He further asserts that "Whatever the Rabbis do, they do not really qualify or mitigate either biblical anthropomorphisms or their own. The very problem of anthropomorphism did not exist for them."[284] This is probably the reason that most rabbinic writings seem not to worry much about gross anthropomorphisms.

Moreover, the problem, as noted in chapter one, is not really one of minor or mild anthropomorphisms such as seeing, watching, loving etc. for these are essential for the communication between God and man. The difficulty occurs when we come to concrete anthropomorphisms which go beyond the purpose of modality and depict God as a human-like figure. In the *Genesis Rabbah*, ca. 400–450, it is reported that R. Hoshaiah said: "When the Holy One, blessed be he, came to create the first man, the ministering angels mistook him [for God, since man was in God's image,] and wanted to say before him, 'Holy', [holy is the Lord of hosts]."[285] According to Said R. Hiyya the Elder, God had appeared to the Israelites through every manner of deed and condition:

> he appeared to them at the sea as a heroic soldier, carrying out battles in behalf of Israel... he had appeared to them at Sinai in the form of a teacher who was teaching Torah and standing in awe... he had appeared to them in the time of Daniel as an elder, teaching Torah, for it is appropriate for Torah to go forth from the mouth of sages... he had appeared to them in the time of Solomon as a youth, in accord with the practices of that generation...[286]

J. Nuesner observes that, "Both passages constitute allusions to God's corporeality and refer to God's capacity to take on human traits of mind, and soul and spirit as well as of outward form."[287] Daniel J. Silver notes that:

> Midrash necessarily emphasized the immanence, even the humanness, of God... God is not an idea, but an intimate. Midrash often depicts God as one of the folk. God participates in the exile, cries over Israel's anguish, bends down to hear prayer, rejoices with a bride at her wedding, puts on tefillin and joins in public prayer. The Midrash innocently and happily speaks of God as father, friend, shepherd, lover, and avenger. One episode may picture God as guardian protecting Israel, another as sage teaching Torah, still another as shepherd shielding his flock...[288]

In explaining Exodus 15:3 which states, "The Lord is a man of war; the Lord is his name", the Talmud has no hesitation in portraying God as a real man. "The word 'man' signifies none other than the Holy One, blessed be He, as it is said: The Lord is a man of war."[289] At another place the Talmud reports:

> R. Johanan said: What is meant by, I saw by night, and beheld a man riding upon a red horse, and he stood among the myrtle trees that were in the bottom, etc.? What means, 'I saw by night'? — The Holy One, blessed be He, wished to turn the whole world into night, 'but behold, A man riding'. 'Man' can refer to none but the Holy One, blessed be He, as it is written, The Lord is a man of war: the Lord is his name; 'upon a red horse' — the Holy One, blessed be He, wished to turn the whole world to blood; but as soon as he looked upon Hananiah, Mishael and Azariah his anger was appeased, for it is written, and he stood among [hadasim] the myrtle trees that were in the deep. Now 'hadasim' refers but to the righteous, as it is written, And he brought up Hadassah; and 'deep' refers to Babylon, as it is said, that sayeth to the deep, Be dry, and I will dry up thy rivers. Straightway He who was filled with wrath was partially calmed, and then completely pacified.[290]

Given the graphic nature of many Talmudic passages such as these even the otherwise cautious Schechter is forced to point out that there is an awareness by rabbis of the danger of losing God 'in the world':

> Eager, however, as the Rabbis were to establish this communication between God and the world, they were always on their guard not to permit him to be lost in the world, or to be confused with man. Hence the marked tendency, both in the Targumim and in the Agadah, to explain away or to mitigate certain expressions in the Bible, investing the deity with corporeal qualities.[291]

How deep does this awareness really go? The same Schechter also observes that the God of the rabbis:

> acts as best man at the wedding of Adam and Eve; he mourns over the world like a father over the death of his son when the sins of

> ten generations make its destruction by the deluge imminent; he visits Abraham on his sick-bed; he condoles with Isaac after the death of Abraham; he "himself in his glory" is occupied in doing the last honors to Moses, who would otherwise have remained unburied, as no man knew his grave; he teaches Torah to Israel, and to this very day he keeps school in heaven for those who died in their infancy... Like man he also feels, so to speak, embarrassed in the presence of the conceited and overbearing, and says, I and the proud cannot dwell in the same place. Nay, it would seem that the Rabbis felt an actual delight in heaping human qualities upon God whenever opportunity is offered by Scripture.[292]

Nuesner writes:

> God figures in the canon of the Judaism of the dual Torah as premise, presence, person, and, at the end, personality. God is represented not solely in abstract terms of attributes (e.g., merciful, loving) but in concrete terms of relationships with the world, humanity, and Israel. The theological discourse of the dual Torah may be classified in four parts: first comes discourse which presupposes God as premise; second is the recognition of God as a presence; third, God appears as a person; and fourth, God personally participates in the here and now of everyday discourse.[293]

He concludes that "out of the material of the final stage of the canon of the Judaism of the dual Torah, we can compose something very like a gospel of God incarnate on earth."[294] This to Nuesner is "divinity in the form of humanity, however the relations between the one and the other are sorted out. And that is what, in a narrowly descriptive framework, incarnation, as a species of the genus anthropomorphism, means." [295]

On the other hand, apologetics like Silver, Schechter and Kaufmann try to explain away rabbinic anthropomorphism and corporealism as simply efforts to maintain and stress the immanence of God, contending that the problem of anthropomorphism and corporealism was in fact foreign to indigenous Judaism. There are two key problems here, the first is that they forget to consider, and as we have already seen, God's immanence does not necessarily require expression in concrete anthropomorphisms and corporealism. That is, God does not have to literally weep or cry or repent to emphasize His mercy and love. Neither does immanence require Him in any way, shape or form to have a fixed schedule of study, undertake sport, or be the best man at anything. Secondly, anthropomorphism and to some extent corporealism, have historically very much existed alongside almost all stages of ancient Judaic thought with very few exceptions. Therefore, it would appear that it is perhaps the concept of immanence, in the strict sense of the term, and not anthropomorphism that seems foreign to indigenous Judaism. Kadushin observes that "the very idea of immanence is foreign to rabbinic thought."[296] G. F. Moore argues that the Palestinian masters were innocent of an abstract, transcendent God. To him, imputation to the rabbis of the concept of transcendence is an abuse of philosophical terminology.[297] Kadushin rightly points out that:

> The problem of anthropomorphism is indeed foreign to indigenous Judaism, but foreign in a far more radical manner than Kaufmann conceives it to be. Such problems are not in any sense within the rabbinic universe of discourse, not even by implication, and are not to be injected there even for the purpose of analysis.[298]

Their interpretations and stories are, argues Kadushin, "thoroughly and completely anthropomorphic, and they tell of actions done by God and emotions felt by Him in terms entirely human."[299] The same trend continued in the later generations. Suffrin observes that:

> A more hideous form of anthropomorphism meets us in the period of the Gaonim (7th-10th cent.)... The most monstrous book of this period was the Shiʿur Koma, 'Estimation of the Height,' of which we possess only two fragments – a greater one in the book of Raziel, and a lesser in the Alphabet of R. 'Akiba. In it the Deity is described as a huge being in human shape and out of all proportion. The measurement of each member, such as the neck,

> the beard, the right and left eyes, the upper and lower lips, the ankles, etc. is given in parasangs. Only 'those parasangs are not like ours, for a heavenly parasang measures a million cubits, each cubit four spans, and each span reaches from one end of the world to the other.' 'And,' says the book of Raziel, 'blessed is he who knows these measurements, for he has a share in the world to come.'[300]

The Karaites (Karaite Judaism being a movement distinct from Rabbinic Judaism), Saadia Gaon (882–942), Sherira (d. 1002), and Hai (d. 1032), vigorously opposed such anthropomorphisms and interpreted them figuratively. Interestingly, most of the known Karaites including Saadia, were contemporaries of al-Ashʿarī, the Muʿtazilites, and other well known Muslim theologians and apologetics (discussed in chapter 4), and were most probably influenced by Islamic transcen-dental thought as many western scholars have observed. Wolfson for instance notes, "The need of explaining scriptural anthropomorphisms became all the greater to spokesmen of Judaism under Muslim rule during that period in view of the fact that in Muslim literature Jews were represented as anthropomorphists."[301] The Karaites (meaning "readers" of the Hebrew scripture) believed in original Judaism and denied rabbinic/Talmudic authority partly due to the anthropomor-phisms this indulged in. Karaites such as Salmon ben Yeruhim for instance, snapped at some of the daring anthropomorphic expressions found in post-scriptural rabbinic writings to show, as Wolfson observes:

> that the rabbis had an anthropomorphic conception of God. Of post-Talmudic literature he explicitly mentions the mystical works Sefer Shem ben Noah, Otiyyot de-Rabbi Akiba, and Shiʿur Komah, and quotes from other works of the same type without mentioning them by title.[302]

The Karaites explained most biblical anthropomorphisms figura-tively, for example, the phrase God creating man in His own image (Genesis 1:26–7) was explained as "by way of conferring honor."[303] The movement was very much influenced by Greek rational thought, as well as coming very close to Muslim rationalists with regards to their conception of the Deity. The Karaites, Jacob B. Agus informs us:

> ventured into the field of philosophical speculations, in advance of their rabbinic brethren, identifying themselves completely with the Mutazilite school of thought among the Arabs. In common with the Moslem theologians, they elaborated a rationalistic theology, which emphasized the principles of God's unity, incorporeality, man's freedom and God's justice.[304]

There was so much identification that, to I. Husik, the works of one group can be credited to the other.[305]

Saadia opposed Karaite rejection of rabbinic/Talmudic authority, defending traditional rabbinic thought by emphasizing the figurative nature of the anthropomorphic expressions and hence the figurative interpretations employed. Notably, his translation of the scripture into the Arabic language, eliminated all anthropomorphic expressions by the figurative method. For instance referring to Moses' plea (Exodus 33) to behold the glory of God, and God's response that Moses could see the back of God but not His face, Saadia explained:

> I wish to say in explanation of this entire passage that the Creator possesses an effulgence which He created and showed to the prophets in order that they might be convinced that the words they hear are indeed from the Creator. When one of them sees it, he declares, "I have seen the glory of God." Some, too, speaking figuratively, say, "I saw God"... But when they perceive this light, they cannot endure contemplating it, because of its tremendous potency and splendor...[306]

Similarly, Daniel saw not God but the same created form which the rabbis called *Shekinah*. He further argued that "If we were to speak of Him in true language, we should have to forego and reject such assertions as the following – that He hears and sees, that He loves and wills, with the result that we should be left with nothing but His existence alone..."[307] In addition to this, and like the Muʿtazilites

(Muslim anti-attributists), he established the internal unity of God in the sense of His simplicity. Clearly there exist a great many similarities and borrowings from Islamic Rationalists, especially the Muʿtazilites, and as Neusner and others have observed, figurative interpretations of scriptural anthropomorphisms, were mostly due to them.[308] Wolfson notes that such a

> conception of internal unity or absolute simplicity was not derived by the Arabic-speaking Jews directly from Scripture, for the unity of God in Scripture meant only numerical unity. It was the Muʿtazilite stressing of internal unity or absolute simplicity that led them to interpret scriptural unity in that sense.[309]

Saadia was later followed by many other rabbis such as, Bahya (1270–1340), Chasdai Crescas (1340–1410) and Joseph Albo (1380–1444), who favored allegorical interpretation of anthropomorphic passages of the Hebrew Bible.

Yet it was in the twelfth-century Jewish philosopher, rabbi and physician, Moses b. Maimon (1135–1204), "a proud son of *aljamas* of Muslim Spain", and physician to the Muslim governor of Egypt, Ayyub, in whom Jewish rationalism received its classic formulation. Maimonides stressed the transcendence, incomparability and absolute otherness of God, interpreting biblical anthropomorphisms thoroughly and figuratively. In this area, argues O'Leary, Maimonides "reproduces the substance of that already associated with al-Farabi and Ibn Sina put into a Jewish form."[310] He also observes that "the teaching of Maimonides shows a somewhat modified form of the system already developed by al-Farabi and Ibn Sina adapted to Jewish beliefs."[311] Lawrence V. Berman no less, famous Stanford professor of Judaic Studies, declares Maimonides as "the Disciple of al-Farabi."[312] Berman declares that "doubtless, there were many intellectuals who accepted the Alfarabian view and tried to understand Islam and Christianity from its perspective, but no one else in a major work attempted to apply his theory in detail to a particular religious tradition."[313]

In his *The Guide for the Perplexed*, Maimonides, according to Berman, "appears as a theologian in the Alfarabian sense and here the

Alfarabian point of view is clearly felt."[314] In the *Guide* Maimonides asserts in philosophical language the spirituality of God and mitigates biblical anthropomorphisms by *via negativa* meaning that God cannot be known by human categories but by negative attributes i.e. God does not commit evil, God is not finite, in other words stripping God of all positive attributes. He argues for the complete "rejection of essential attributes in reference to God."[315] After a detailed discussion of various attributes Maimonides concludes:

> Consider all these and similar attributes, and you will find that they cannot be employed in reference to God. He is not a magnitude that any quality resulting from quantity as such could be possessed by Him; He is not affected by external influences, and therefore does not posses any quality resulting from emotion. He is not subject to physical conditions, and therefore does not possess strength or similar qualities... Hence it follows that no attribute coming under the head of quality in its widest sense, can be predicated of God... are clearly inadmissible in reference to God, for they imply composition, which... is out of question as regards the Creator...He is absolutely One.[316]

Maimonides saw in literalism the source of error. "The adherence to the literal sense of the text of Holy Writ is the source of all this error..."[317] He further argued that

> the negative attributes of God are the true attributes: they do not include any incorrect notions or any deficiency whatever in reference to God, while positive attributes imply polytheism, and are inadequate... we cannot describe the Creator by any means except by negative attributes.[318]

So Maimonides' God is existing but not in existence, living but not in life, knowing but not in knowledge, etc.:

> It is known that existence is an accident appertaining to all things, and therefore an element superadded to their essence. This must

> evidently be the case as regards everything the existence of which is due to some cause; its existence is an element superadded to its essence. But as regards a being whose existence is not due to any cause – God alone is that being, for His existence, as we have said, is absolute – existence and essence are perfectly identical; He is not a substance to which existence is joined as an accident, as an additional element. His existence is always absolute, and has never been a new element or an accident to Him. Consequently God exists without possessing the attribute of existence. Similarly He lives, without possessing the attribute of life; knows without possessing the attribute of knowledge...[319]

He concluded by observing that

> every attribute predicated of God either denotes the quality of an action, or – when the attribute is intended to convey some idea of the Divine Being itself, and not of His actions – the negation of the opposite... All we understand is the fact that He exists, that He is a Being to whom none of His creatures is similar, who has nothing in common with them, who does not include plurality. ... Praised be He! In the contemplation of His essence, our comprehension and knowledge prove insufficient... in the endeavor to extol Him in words, all our efforts in speech are mere weakness and failure![320]

Maimonide's transcendental Deity did not seem to be resembling either the original biblical Deity nor the rabbinic one, and was in no way a development upon them. Its philosophical nature and foreign color was quite obvious. Therefore, his *Guide*, observes Agus, "was severely criticized, occasionally banned, more frequently permitted only for those over thirty. It was not included in the curriculum of study in the great *yeshivoth*, but the adventurous souls who dared to think for themselves regarded the *Guide* as their Bible."[321] His Creed of the thirteen essentials of faith, writes Suffrin, "has never been favorably accepted; and, although it is printed in some prayer-books, it is never recited publicly."[322] His path, argues Guthrie, ended "in obscurity and never has been the mainstream of Jewish belief."[323] Modern Jewish thinker, Franz Rosenzweig (1886–1929), observes that the negative theology

> dismembered and abolished the existing assertions about God's "attributes,"... This path leads from an existing Aught to Nought; at its end atheism and mysticism can shake hands. We do not take this path, but rather the opposite one from Nought to Aught. Our goal is not a negative concept, but on the contrary a highly positive one.[324]

Kadushin contends that the whole "Medieval Jewish philosophy is neither a continuation of that development nor in line with it. Rabbinic thought alone has its roots firmly in the Bible, and it alone remains united with the Bible in a living bond."[325] And rabbinic thought is undoubtedly anthropomorphic and in certain cases quite corporeal.

Biblical scholars and theologians, without denying the presence of crude and other forms of anthropomorphisms contained in the Bible, try to explain away some of the reasons why they feel their mention to be necessary. The first and most commonly cited cause is the assumption that the human mind is unable to represent God as He is in Himself. The second reason claims to be the lack of a philosophical spirit in ancient people such that they had no choice but to perceive of the Deity as a living, active, personal and individual God, this perception requiring an anthropomorphic depiction. The third reason is said to be the practical nature of the Hebrew people, their boldness and the linguistic structure of their language. Thus some theologians like Franz Rosenzweig do not see any problem with depicting God in anthropomorphic terms. Rosenzweig regards authentic revelation as the vehicle of transcendence, and views human experience of God as "incommunicable, and he who speaks of it makes himself ridiculous."[326] Still he argues that, "though man is not God and recognizes his limits, he can still address God in meaningful language, with the Divinity doing the same in relation to man." Given a situation like this Rosenzweig fails to see "why human language to and about God, even anthropomorphic, should be considered inauthentic or impermissible, given the revelatory situation which exists between God and humankind."[327] Thus, he argues, "it is not human illusion if Scripture speaks of God's countenance and even of his separate bodily parts. There is no other way to express the Truth."[328]

All very well, but if, as traditionally believed, the Hebrew Bible is the true revelation or inspiration of God, the Word of God verbatim as is commonly held, then how is it, we may ask, that God the Creator of human nature and the Revealer of His Will, is suddenly regarded as being incapable of informing people in proper terms and categories of what He is and how He should be represented? Why would He resort to the use of crude and naive anthropomorphic expressions to explain Himself when He has afterall endowed human beings with the capacity and capability to recognize the fundamental facts and truths about Himself as the Ultimate Reality and Truth? As Rosenzweig himself observes: "Truth is not God. God is Truth."[329]

In point of fact, it is the very existence of such terminology that points to biblical scripture being the outcome of human agency. Meaning that the very assumption of progressive or evolutionary revelation and existence of crude anthropomorphic expressions (rather too simply explained away as being a result of man's inability to know God or represent Him in non-anthropomorphic and appropriate terms) forces the inevitable conclusion that these parts of the Bible are not divine revelation but man's own words and representations. Human limitation and inability to grasp the essence of God should not be used as an excuse to depict God in concrete human forms and shapes; in the forms and qualities which all agree are not there in Him. In actual fact it is entirely possible to emphasize God's love, mercy and concern without making Him weep or cry. The Torah's significance can be stressed in many other ways than claiming God reads its 24 books throughout the day and the Mishna during the night. One fails to make sense of or understand the bizarre connection between God's daily, three hourly, sport schedule with the Leviathan and the excuses made that human beings are unable to understand Him! Ironically the whole matter if anything seems to have become skewed in entirely the other direction, with human beings knowing/focusing on far too many details regarding God, down to His personal schedule even, eclipsing any sense of His greatness and majesty. Proper communication and retention of the mystery that is God does not need or allow for such crude familiarity. The transcendent God is far above these limitations or depictions.

In addition, the non-philosophical nature of a person or a nation does not require that God be represented in terms, categories, and characteristics that are altogether inappropriate and detrimental to the very definition and concept of His transcendence and unicity. Moreover and as discussed, this is reinforced by the fact that using the same Hebrew language, individuals from the same nation and culture have perceived and represented God in transcendental, non-corporeal, non-anthropomorphic terms. Meaning that had anthropomorphism been intrinsic to the nature of the language, or a practical requirement of the Hebrews, or even part of the boldness of the Hebrew nation, then it would have been an inclusively universal phenomenon. But it is not. So why do it? Ironically the same scholars who maintain that the patriarchs, or Moses, or at least the great prophets, were monotheists in the strict sense of the term, also at the same justify the use of primitive, crude expressions to visualize and understand God, providing explanations to make some sense out of them. But strictly speaking we can't have it both ways. For if, as these scholars maintain, the nature or boldness of ancient figures like Moses or other prophets, did not stop them from holding a high concept of God, then this should not and cannot be a leading factor behind the crude anthropomorphisms of the biblical narrative. The same can be said with regards to the nature of primitive societies in terms of their concept of God.

The problem lies in the fact that the Bible is considered to be the word of God verbatim, and not the work of primitive Hebrew people or the Hebrew nation. Yet, the remoteness of societies, the limitations of language structure and construction, or any other factor, could only have a bearing were human agency to be involved, for God does not and cannot misrepresent the facts or conceal the truth.

Further, these causes cannot realistically be cited as the only reasons to explain biblical anthropomorphisms. Room should be left for other rational suggestions, reasons, and foundations to explain the presence and vividness of crudely realistic human anthropomorphisms as well as biblical confusion and discrepancies. In fact the major reason, and explanation for the existence of the latter would be to accept the role played by human agency in the compilation and transmission of the Hebrew Bible, and this in fact is being widely recognized in our times. What is clearly apparent is that the writers, redactors and compilers of the Hebrew Bible created a biblical God in their own image and in their own likeness.

In summary, and projecting these conclusions and reasoning to our own times, we may safely assert that it is the Hebrew Bible's core understanding of God and the progressive or evolutionary nature of its God-concept that could be factors attributing to modern man's reckless and heedless attitude towards the transcendent God of traditional religion. Furthermore, biblical data does not seem to disprove the projection theory (discussed earlier) in categorical terms, but rather underscore it, for the human element is so dominant in several parts of the Bible that it seems clear that authorship can only be ascribed to human beings, imposing their own images, qualities, and categories upon God and conceiving of Him as like themselves.

We leave the last word to Robin Lane Fox who puts it rather succinctly: "In scripture this God is not revealing himself: human authors are creating him, as he is supposed to have created them, 'after their own image'."[330]

NOTES

[1] Howard Eilberg-Schwartz, *God's Phallus, and Other Problems For Men and Monotheism* (Boston: Beacon Press, 1994), p.205.

[2] See Esther J. Hamori, *When Gods Were Men, The Embodied God in Biblical and Near Eastern Literature* (New York: Walter de Gruyter, 2008), p.51.

[3] Geddes MacGregor, *The Bible in the Making* (New York: J. B. Lippencott, 1959), p.301.

[4] George Moore, *Judaism* (Cambridge: Harvard University Press, 1970), vol.1, p.239.

[5] Ibid., vol.1, p.247.

[6] "Tractate Baba Bathra," [ch.14b], quoted from Harry Gersh, *The Sacred Books of the Jews* (New York: Stein and Day Publishers, 1968), p.2.

[7] Otto Eissfeldt, *The Old Testament: An Introduction*, P. R. Ackroyd, trans. (New York: Harper & Row, 1965), p.158.

[8] Moses Maimonides, *The Guide for the Perplexed*, M. Friedlander, trans., 2nd edn. (New York: Dover Publication Inc., 1956), p. XXV.

[9] Isadore Twersky, *A Maimonides Reader* (New York: Behrman House, 1972), p.35.

[10] Ibid., p.480.

[11] Ibid., p.420.

[12] Ibid., pp.420–21.

[13] See Moshe Perlmann, *Ibn Kammūna's Examination of the Three Faiths: A Thirteenth Century Essay in Comparative Study of Religion* (Berkeley, LA: University of California, 1971).

[14] Twersky, *A Maimonides Reader*, p.446.

[15] Ibid., p.421.

[16] Howard Greenstein, *Judaism: An Eternal Covenant* (Philadelphia: Fortress Press, 1983), p.18.

[17] Ibid., p.19.

[18] Richard E. Friedman, *Who Wrote the Bible?* (New Jersey: Prentice Hall, 1978), p.28.

[19] Greenstein, *Judaism*, p.111.

[20] Mordecai M. Kaplan, *Judaism as a Civilization: Toward a Reconstruction of American-Jewish Life*, 2nd edn. (New York: Schocken Books, 1967), p.104.

[21] Jacob Neusner, *Death and Birth of Judaism* (New York: Basic Books, 1987), p.97.

[22] Ibid., p.101.

[23] M. Herbert Danzger, *Returning to Tradition* (New Haven; London: Yale University Press, 1989), p.166.

[24] Jakob J. Petuchowski, "Reformed Judaism," *Encyclopedia Judaica* (Jerusalem: Keter Publishing House, 1971), vol.4, p.36.

[25] Greenstein, *Judaism*, p.113.

[26] Neusner, *Death and Birth of Judaism*, p.118.

[27] W. Gunther Plaut, *The Torah, A Modern Commentary* (New York: Union of American Hebrew Congregations, 1981), p. XVIII.

[28] Greenstein, *Judaism*, p.144; see also Joseph L. Blau, *Modern Varieties of Judaism* (New York: Columbia University Press, 1966), pp.64–73, 79.

[29] Neusner, *Death and Birth of Judaism*, p.140.

[30] Greenstein, *Judaism*, p.121.

[31] Moshe Davis, *The Emergence of Conservative Judaism* (Philadelphia: The Jewish Publication Society, 1963), p.293.

[32] Ibid., p.295.
[33] Ibid., p.296.
[34] Robert McQueen Grant, *The Formation of the New Testament* (New York: Harper & Row, 1965), p.14.
[35] John Bright, *The Authority of the Old Testament* (New York: Abingdon Press, 1967), p.53.
[36] Ibid., p.55.
[37] Ibid., p.153.
[38] Grant, *The Formation of the New Testament*, p.9.
[39] Bright, *The Authority of the Old Testament*, p.62.
[40] Robert McQueen Grant, ed., *Gnosticism: An Anthology* (London: Collins, 1961), p.45.
[41] Friedrich Schleiermacher, *The Christian Faith*, [2nd edn. of *Der Christliche Glaube*], H. R. Mackintosh, J. S. Stewart, trans. and eds. (Edinburgh: T & T Clark, 1928), pp.60–62.
[42] Ibid., pp.608–11.
[43] James A. Senders, "Torah and Paul," *God's Christ and His People*, Jacob Jervell, Wayne A. Meeks, eds. (Oslo: Universitetsforlaget, 1977), p.133.
[44] Rowan A. Greer, trans., *Origen: An Exhortation to Martyrdom, Prayer and Selected Works* [The Classics of Western Spirituality Series] (New Jersey: Paulest Press, 1979), p.180.
[45] Ibid.
[46] Raymond Brown, "The Literal Sense of Scripture," *The New Jerome Biblical Commentary*, Raymond Brown, Joseph Fitzmeyer, Jerome Murphy, eds. (New Jersey: Prentice-Hall, 1968), p.607.
[47] Henry Chadwick, trans., *Origen: Contra Celsum* (Cambridge: Cambridge University Press, 1965), vol. VII, p.411.
[48] Charles Scalise, "Origen and the Sensus Literalis," *Origen of Alexandria, His World and His Legacy*, Charles Kannengiesser, W. L. Peterson, eds. (Notre Dame, Indiana: University of Notre Dame Press, 1988), pp.121–22.
[49] Richard P. C. Hanson, *Allegory and Event*, (London: S.C.M Press, 1959), p.280.
[50] George W. Butterworth, trans., *Origen on First Principles* (London: SPCK, 1936), vol. IV, p.297.
[51] Ibid., p.288.
[52] Charles Bigg, *The Christian Platonists of Alexandria: The 1886 Bampton Lectures* (Oxford: Clarendon Press, 1968), p.185.

[53] Robert McQueen Grant, *The Letter and the Spirit* (London: SPCK, 1957), p.101.

[54] Bigg, *The Christian Platonists of Alexandria*, p.184.

[55] Hanson, *Allegory and Event*, p.258.

[56] Bigg, *The Christian Platonists of Alexandria*, p.188.

[57] Ibid.

[58] Ibid., p.187.

[59] Scalise, "Origen and the Sensus Literalis," p.129.

[60] A. Berkeley Mickelsen, *Interpreting the Bible* (Michigan: Wm. B. Eerdmans Publishing, 1963), p.33.

[61] Daniel B. Stevick, *Beyond Fundamentalism* (Richmond, USA: John Knox Press, 1964), p.86.

[62] Frederic W. Farrar, *History of Interpretation*, [Bampton Lectures] (New York: E. P. Dutton & Co., 1886), [reprinted by Baker Book House, Michigan, 1961], p.233.

[63] Mickelsen, *Interpreting the Bible*, p.36.

[64] Emil Brunner, *The Christian Doctrine of God*, Olive Wyon, trans., 11th edn. (Philadelphia: The Westminster, 1974), vol.1, p.108.

[65] Bright, *The Authority of the Old Testament*, pp.80–81.

[66] Timothy F. Lull, ed., *Martin Luther's Basic Theological Writings* (Philadelphia: Fortress Press, 1989), p.118.

[67] Ibid., pp.78–79.

[68] Bright, *The Authority of the Old Testament*, pp.82 ff.

[69] Ibid., p.81.

[70] Wilhelm Vischer, *The Witness of the Old Testament to Christ*, A. B. Crabtree, trans. (London: Lutterworth Press, 1949), vol.1, p.14.

[71] Harold H. Rowley, *The Old Testament and Modern Study: A Generation of Discovery and Research* (Oxford: Clarendon Press, 1967), ch. XI, p.337.

[72] Ibid., p.331.

[73] Bright, *The Authority of the Old Testament*, pp.155–56.

[74] Rowley, *The Old Testament and Modern Study*, p.315.

[75] Ibid., p.328.

[76] Farrar, *History of Interpretation*, p.431.

[77] Bright, *The Authority of the Old Testament*, p.101.

[78] Adolf V. Harnack, *History of Dogma*, Neil Buchanan, trans. (New York: Dover Publications, 1961), vol.2, p.64.

[79] Ibid., pp.64–65.

[80] John E. Steinmueller, *A Companion to Scripture Studies*, 2nd edn. (New York: Joseph F. Wagner Inc., 1941), vol.1, p.394.
[81] George P. Fisher, *History of Christian Doctrine* (New York: AMS Press, 1901), pp.542–43.
[82] Gerrit C. Berkouwer, *The Second Vatican Council and the New Catholicism*, Lewis B. Smedes, trans. (Michigan: Eerdmans, 1965), p.108.
[83] Brunner, *The Christian Doctrine of God*, vol.1, p.108.
[84] John H. Miller, ed., *Vatican II: An Interfaith Appraisal* (London: University of Notre Dame Press, 1966), p.49.
[85] Ibid., p.59.
[86] Ibid., p.108.
[87] Bright, *The Authority of Old the Testament*, p.34.
[88] John Calvin, *Institutes of the Christian Religion*, John Allen, trans., 6th American edn. (Philadelphia: Presbyterian Board of Christian Education, 1932), pp.75–76.
[89] Ibid., pp.90 f.
[90] Ibid., pp.79 f.
[91] Robert L. Harris, *Inspiration and Canonicity of the Bible*, 5th edn. (Michigan: Zondervan, 1973), p.75.
[92] Ibid., p.73.
[93] Ibid., p.75.
[94] Brunner, *The Christian Doctrine of God*, vol.1, p.111.
[95] Livingston, *Modern Christian Thought*, p.217.
[96] Ibid.
[97] Ibid., p.218.
[98] Friedman, *Who Wrote the Bible?*, p.27.
[99] Steven T. Katz, *Jewish Ideas and Concepts* (New York: Schocken Books, 1977), p.15.
[100] Paul V. Imschoot, *Theology of the Old Testament*, Kathryn Sullivan, F. Bucks, trans. (New York: Descleev Company, 1954), p.27.
[101] Bright, *The Authority of Old the Testament*, p.117.
[102] Harold H. Rowley, *From Moses to Qumran: Studies in the Old Testament* (New York: Books for Libraries Press, 1971), p.286.
[103] Imschoot, *Theology of the Old Testament*, p.30.
[104] Andrew B. Davidson, *The Theology of the Old Testament*, S. D. F. Salmond, ed. (New York: Charles Scribner's, 1904), pp.30–31.
[105] Abraham J. Heschel, *Between God and Man, An Interpretation of Judaism*, F. A. Rothschild, ed. (New York: Free Press, 1959), pp.104–05.

[106] Hermann Cohen, *Religion of Reason: Out of the Sources of Judaism*, Simon Kaplan, trans., introduced by Leo Strauss (New York: Frederik Ungar Publishing Co., 1972), pp.41–42.
[107] Plaut, *The Torah*, p.1366.
[108] Imschoot, *Theology of the Old Testament*, p.81.
[109] Plaut, *The Torah*, p.541.
[110] Ibid., p.14.
[111] See for details in connection with the date Adolphe Lods, *Israel, From its Beginnings to the Middle of the Eighth Century* (London: Routledge & Kegan Paul, 1948), pp.315 f.
[112] Robin L. Fox, *The Unauthorized Version: Truth and Fiction in the Bible* (New York: Penguin Books, 1992), p.154.
[113] Ibid., p.155.
[114] Teophile J. Meek, *Hebrew Origins* (New York: Harper & Row, 1960), pp.208–09. Meek also argues, that "The Lutheran Church is one of our more conservative denominations and yet one of its theological professor, Harold L. Creager, writes concerning the First Commandment in its official organ, *The Lutheran Church Quarterly*: "In neither case [of two possible translations, "in addition to" and "in preference to"], of course, is any teaching here of monotheism, but only of henotheism. The possibility of worshipping other gods, either along with Jehovah or as entirely displacing him, is directly conceived." Identical are the views of other leading conservative scholars."
[115] Gehhard V. Rad, *Old Testament Theology*, D. M. G. Stalker, trans. (New York: Harper, 1962), pp.210–11.
[116] Armstrong, *A History of God*, p.51.
[117] Ibid., p.23
[118] Christoph Uehlinger, "Anthropomorphic Cult Statuary in Iron Age Palestine and the Search for Yahweh's Cult Images," *The Image and the Book*, Karel van der Toorn, ed. (Leuvan: Peeters, 1997), p.152.
[119] Ibid., p.153.
[120] Quoted from Geza Vermes, *Scripture and Tradition in Judaism* (Leiden: E. J. Brill, 1973), p.85. Also see John V. Seters, *Abraham in History and Tradition* (New Haven: Yale University Press, 1975); Robert E. Clements, *Abraham and David* (London: S.C.M. Press, 1967).
[121] Rowley, *From Moses to Qumran*, p.286.
[122] Ibid., p.46. Simpson, for instance, argues that, "Momentary monotheism was a characteristic of primitive Jahvism from the first, necessary because of the very

nature of the religion." Cuthbert A. Simpson, *The Early Traditions of Israel: A Critical Analysis of the Pre-Deuteronomic Narrative of the Hexateuch* (Oxford: Basil Blackwell, 1948), p.425. Roland de Vaux observes that "Genesis tells the history of the ancestors of Israel, the line of Patriarchs Abraham, Isaac, and Jacob, from whom were born the Twelve Tribes. They acknowledge the same God, who will become the God of Israel." Roland de Vaux, *The Bible and the Ancient Near East* (New York: Doubleday, 1971), p.51.

[123] Davidson, *The Theology of the Old Testament*, p.62.

[124] Ibid., p.67.

[125] Armstrong, *A History of God*, p.14.

[126] Ignatius Hunt, *The World of the Patriarchs* (New Jersey: Prentice-Hall, 1967), p.67.

[127] Ibid., p.68.

[128] Lods, *Israel*, pp.256–57.

[129] Hans Kung, *Judaism, Between Yesterday and Tomorrow*, John Bowden, trans. (New York: Crossroad, 1992), p.9.

[130] Mark S. Smith, *The Early History of God* (New York: Harper & Row, 1990), p.7.

[131] Rowley, *From Moses to Qumran*, pp.45–46.

[132] See Imschoot, *Theology of the Old Testament*, p.12.

[133] Davidson, *The Theology of the Old Testament*, p.41.

[134] Cohen, *Religion of Reason*, p.38.

[135] Ibid., p.42.

[136] Imschoot, *Theology of the Old Testament*, p.12.

[137] Davidson, *The Theology of the Old Testament*, p.32.

[138] Robert C. Dentan, *The Knowledge of God in Ancient Israel* (New York: The Seabury Press, 1968), p.165. To Imschoot, "Holiness" of Yahweh presented by the biblical text does not lay as much stress upon the moral perfection of God as it does upon the transcendence and otherness of God. He observes: "Although the God of Israel has always been a moral God, as many old accounts and ancient theophoric names attest, the holiness which characterizes Him does not denote, in all the texts, Yahweh's moral perfection. Several-and this is largely true of the oldest ones-denote only the "numinous" aspect... The "numinous" embraces several elements: it is "the wholly other", that is to say, that which is totally different from and above all being, that which is powerful and majestic, mysterious and terrifying, but at the same time fascinating." Imschoot, *Theology of the Old Testament*, pp.44–45.

[139] Johannes C. de Moor, *The Rise of Yahwism: The Roots of Israelite Monotheism* (Leuvan: Peeters Press, 1990), pp.125 ff.
[140] Korpel, *A Rift in the Clouds*, p.380; See also James Barr, "Theophany and Anthropomorphism in the Old Testament," in *Supplements to Vetus Testamentum* (Leiden: E. J. Brill, 1960), vol.17, pp.31–38.
[141] Lods, Israel, p:452
[142] Lods, *Israel*, pp.451–52.
[143] Ibid., p.452.
[144] Ibid., pp.253–54.
[145] Davidson, *The Theology of the Old Testament*, p.112.
[146] Walther Eichrodt, *Theology of the Old Testament*, J. A. Baker, trans. (Philadelphia; Pennsylvania: The Westminster Press, 1961), vol.2, p.16.
[147] Ibid., p.19.
[148] Ibid., p.21.
[149] Otto Baab, *The Theology of the Old Testament* (New York: Abingdon Press, 1969), p.48.
[150] Korpel, *A Rift in the Clouds*, p.210.
[151] Katz, *Jewish Ideas and Concepts*, p.155.
[152] Yehezkel Kaufmann, *The Religion of Israel*, Moshe Greenberg, trans. (Chicago: The University of Chicago Press, 1960), p.2.
[153] Cohen, *Religion of Reason*, p.36.
[154] Leo Baeck, *The Essence of Judaism*, Victor Grubenweiser, trans. (New York: Schocken Books, 1961), p.61.
[155] Kung, *Judaism*, p.27.
[156] William F. Albright, *Yahweh and the Gods of Canaan* (New York: Doubleday, 1968), p.206.
[157] Kaufmann, *The Religion of Israel*, p.230.
[158] William F. Albright, "Archaeology Confronts Biblical Criticism," *The American Scholar* (April, 1938), vol. VII, p.186.
[159] William F. Albright, *From the Stone Age to Christianity*, 2nd edn. (Baltimore: The Johns Hopkins Press, 1967), p.264.
[160] Albright, *Yahweh and the Gods of Canaan*, p.206.
[161] William F. Albright, *Archaeology and the Religion of Israel* (Baltimore: The John Hopkins Press, 1968), p.96.
[162] Meek, *Hebrew Origins*, p.207.
[163] Harold W. Robinson, ed., *Record and Revelation: Essays on the Old Testament* (Oxford: The Clarendon Press, 1951), p.308.

[164] Meek, *Hebrew Origins*, p.205.
[165] Edmond Jacob, *Theology of the Old Testament*, A. W. Heathcote, P. J. Allcock, trans. (London: Hodder and Stoughton, 1958), p.66.
[166] Rowley, *From Moses to Qumran*, p.42.
[167] Harold H. Rowley, *The Faith of Israel: Aspects of Old Testament Thought* (London: S.C.M. Press, 1956), p.71.
[168] Meek, *Hebrew Origins*, p.216.
[169] See Rowley, *The Faith of Israel*, p.43; See S. R. Driver, *An Introduction to the Literature of the Old Testament* (Gloucester: Peter Smith, 1972).
[170] Lods, *Israel*, p.257.
[171] Baab, *The Theology of the Old Testament*, p.48.
[172] Ibid., pp.48–49.
[173] Rowley, *From Moses to Qumran*, p.44.
[174] Ibid.
[175] Georg Fohrer, Ernst Sellin, *Introduction to the Old Testament*, David E. Green, trans. (New York: Abingdon Press, 1968), p.78.
[176] Theodorus C. Vriezen, *The Religion of Ancient Israel* (Philadelphia: The Westminster Press, 1967), p.82.
[177] Rowley, *From Moses to Qumran*, p.44.
[178] Ibid., p.59.
[179] Ibid., p.60.
[180] Ibid., p.61.
[181] Dentan, *The Knowledge of God in Ancient Israel*, p.134.
[182] Vriezen, *The Religion of Ancient Israel*, p.135.
[183] Robinson, *Record and Revelation*, pp.205–06; Meek, *Hebrew Origins*, p.215.
[184] Lods, *Israel*, p.257.
[185] Rowley, *From Moses to Qumran*, p.35.
[186] Kaplan, *Judaism as a Civilization*, p.352.
[187] Ibid.
[188] Ibid., p.353.
[189] Ibid., pp.357–58.
[190] Ibid., p.368.
[191] Ibid., p.372. Leo Baeck disagrees with such a claim and argues that "Only in Israel did an ethical monotheism exist, and wherever else it is found later, it has been derived directly or indirectly from Israel." *The Essence of Judaism*, p.61.
[192] Kaplan, *Judaism as a Civilization*, p.371–72.

[193] Ibid., p.382.

[194] Ibid., p.385; See also Mordecai M. Kaplan's, *The Future of the American Jew* (New York: Reconstructionist Press, 1957); and his *The Meaning of God in Modern Jewish Religion* (New York: Reconstructionist Press, 1962).

[195] Greenstein, *Judaism*, p.136.

[196] Bernard J. Heller, *Modern Jewish Thought*, J. B. Agus, ed. (New York: ARNO Press, 1973), p.339.

[197] Ibid., pp.340–41.

[198] Robert M. Seltzer, *Jewish People, Jewish Thought* (New York: Macmillan, 1980), p.38.

[199] Korpel, *A Rift in the Clouds*, p.272.

[200] Lods, *Israel*, p.454.

[201] Morton Smith, *Palestinian Parties and Politics that Shaped the Old Testament* (New York: Columbia University Press, 1971), pp.22–23.

[202] Lods, *Israel*, p.454.

[203] Smith, *Palestinian Parties*, p.23.

[204] Ibid., pp.23–24.

[205] Ibid., p.53.

[206] Ibid., p.152.

[207] Ibid., p.154.

[208] Ibid., p.156.

[209] Ibid., p.155.

[210] Kung, *Judaism*, p.28.

[211] Ibid., pp.28–29.

[212] Fohrer, *Introduction to the Old Testament*, p.169.

[213] Korpel, *A Rift in the Clouds*, p.95.

[214] See Hamori, *When Gods Were Men*, pp.5–13.

[215] Richard E. Friedman, *The Disappearance of God* (Boston; New York; London: Little, Brown & Co., 1995), p.11.

[216] Hamori, *When Gods Were Men*, p.13.

[217] Ibid., p.11.

[218] Ibid., p.23.

[219] Ibid.

[220] Stephen Geller, "The Struggle at the Jabbok: The Use of Enigma in a Biblical Narrative," *JANES (Journal of the Near Eastern Society)* (1982), vol.14, p.38.

[221] Barr, "Theophany and Anthropomorphism in the Old Testament," p.35.

[222] Ibid., pp.35–36.
[223] Eilberg-Schwartz, *God's Phallus*, p.69.
[224] Samuel Terrien, *The Elusive Presence* (San Francisco: Harper & Row, 1978), p.135.
[225] Barr, "Theophany and Anthropomorphism in the Old Testament," p.1.
[226] M. D. Fowler, "The Meaning of *lipne* YHWH in the Old Testament," *ZAW 99* (Berlin, 1987), p.384; and Korpel, *A Rift in the Clouds*, p.102.
[227] See Richard E. Friedman, "The Biblical Expression *master panim*," *Hebrew Annual Review* (1977), vol.1, pp.139–47; and Samuel Balentine, *The Hidden God: The Hiding of the Face in the Old Testament* (New York: Oxford University Press, 1983). It is interesting to see the psychological theories and interpretations of Erich Fromm and Dale Patrick. See Erich Fromm, *You Shall Be As Gods* (Greenwich; Connecticut: Fawcett Premier, 1966); and Dale Patrick, *The Rendering of God in the Old Testament* (Philadelphia: Fortress Press, 1981).
[228] Korpel, *A Rift in the Clouds*, p.102.
[229] Ibid., p.105.
[230] See Moshe Weinfeld, *Deuteronomy and Deuteronomic School* (Oxford: Oxford University Press, 1972), p.191.
[231] Eilberg-Schwartz, *God's Phallus*, pp.75–76.
[232] Jeffrey J. Niehaus, *God at Sinai: Covenant & Theophany in the Bible and Ancient Near East* (Michigan: Zondervan, 1995), pp.3–4.
[233] Benjamin Uffenheimer, "Myth and Reality in Ancient Israel," *The Origins and Diversity of Axial Age*, S. N. Eisenstadt, ed. (Albany: State University of New York Press, 1986), p.149.
[234] Lods, *Israel*, p.457.
[235] Katz, *Jewish Ideas and Concepts*, p.89.
[236] Fohrer, *Introduction to the Old Testament*, p.78.
[237] See Hans Wildberger, *Isaiah 1–12, A Commentary*, Thomas H. Trapp, trans. (Minneapolis: Fortress Press, 1991), p.260.
[238] J. J. M. Roberts, "The Visual Elements in Isaiah's Vision in Light of Judaean and Near Eastern Sources," *From Babel to Babylon: Essays on Biblical History and Literature in Honour of Brian Peckham*, J. R. Wood, John E. Harvey, Mark Leuchter, eds. (New York: T & T Clark, 2006), p.200.
[239] Rimmon Kasher, "Anthropomorphism, Holiness and Cult: A New Look at Ezekiel 40–48," *ZAW 110* (1998), p.192.
[240] Eichrodt, *Theology of the Old Testament*, vol.2, p.21.

[241] Adolphe Lods, *The Prophets and the Rise of Judaism* (Connecticut: Greenwood Press, 1971), p.323.
[242] Ibid., p.459.
[243] Robert Ingersoll, *Some Mistakes of Moses* (New York: Prometheus Books, 1986), pp.92–93.
[244] Friedman, *The Disappearance of God*, p.104.
[245] Ibid., p.37.
[246] Ibid., p.38.
[247] Korpel, *A Rift in the Clouds*, p.210. For more details see Trygge N. D. Mettinger, *In Search of God: The Meaning and Message of the Everlasting Names* (Philadelphia: Fortress Press, 1988), pp.88–91; and Thomas H. McAlpine, *Human and Divine Sleep in the Old Testament* (Sheffield: JSOT, 1987), pp.191–99.
[248] Ingersoll, *Some Mistakes of Moses*, pp.93–94.
[249] Lawrence Schiffman, *From Text to Tradition: A History of Second Temple and Rabbinic Judaism* (New Jersey: KTAV Publishing House Inc., 1991), p.267.
[250] Friedman, *The Disappearance of God*, p.121.
[251] Efraim Urbach, *The Sages, Their Concepts and Beliefs* (Massachusetts: Magnes Press Hebrew University, 1975), pp.304–08.
[252] Jacob Neusner, ed., *Understanding Rabbinic Judaism: From Talmud to Modern Times* (New York: KTAV Publishing House Inc., 1974), p.6.
[253] Jacob B. Agus, *The Evolution of Jewish Thought* (New York: ARNO Press, 1973), p.71.
[254] Ibid.
[255] Seltzer, *Jewish People, Jewish Thought*, p.290.
[256] Talmud – Mas. Berachoth 7a.
[257] Ibid.
[258] Arthur Marmorstein, *The Old Rabbinic Doctrine of God: Essays in Anthropomorphism* (London: Oxford University Press, 1937), p.50.
[259] Talmud – Mas. Berachoth 7a.
[260] Talmud – Mas. Avodah Zarah 3b.
[261] Ibid.
[262] Talmud – Mas. Berachoth 3a.
[263] Ibid.
[264] Talmud – Mas. Berachoth 59a.
[265] Talmud – Mas. Chagigah 5b.
[266] Ibid.

267 Ibid.

268 Michael Fishbane, *Biblical Myth and Rabbinic Mythmaking* (Oxford: Oxford University Press, 2003), p.164.

269 Ibid., p.165.

270 Ibid., p.166.

271 Ibid., p.167.

272 Ibid., p.169.

273 Talmud – Mas. Avodah Zarah 3b.

274 Fishbane, *Biblical Myth and Rabbinic Mythmaking*, pp.171–72.

275 A. E. Suffrin, "God," [Jewish Concept], James Hastings, *Encyclopedia of Religion and Ethics*, John A. Selbie, ed. (Edinburgh: Kessinger Publishing, 1925–1940), vol.6, p.295.

276 Hastings, *Encyclopedia of Religion and Ethics*, pp.295–96; see for a more detailed study of the issue Marmorstein, *The Old Rabbinic Doctrine of God*, section "The Attributes of God," pp.148–217.

277 Gedaliahu G. Stroumsa, "Form(s) of God: Some notes on Metatron and Christ," *Harvard Theological Review* (1983), vol.76, no.3, p.269.

278 Arthur Marmorstein, *Studies in Jewish Theology*, J. Rabbinowitz, M. S. Lew, eds. (New York: Books for Libraries Press, 1972), pp.108–09.

279 Ibid., pp.107–08.

280 Ibid., pp.71 ff.

281 Soloman Schechter, *Aspects of Rabbinic Theology: Major Concepts of the Talmud* (New York: Schocken Books, 1961), pp.36 ff.

282 Max Kadushin, *The Rabbinic Mind*, 3rd edn. (New York: Bloch Publishing Co., 1972).

283 Ibid., p.280.

284 Ibid.

285 Neusner, *The Incarnation of God*, p.15.

286 Ibid., p.16.

287 Ibid., p.17.

288 Daniel J. Silver, *A History of Judaism* (New York: Basic Books Inc., 1974), vol.1, pp.308–09.

289 Soncino Talmud – Mas. Sotah 42b, Davka Judaic Classics Software.

290 Talmud – Mas. Sanhedrin 93a.

291 Schechter, *Aspects of Rabbinic Theology*, p.35.

292 Ibid., p.36, 37.

[293] Neusner, *The Incarnation of God*, p.19.
[294] Ibid.
[295] Ibid., p.15.
[296] Kadushin, *The Rabbinic Mind*, pp.278–79.
[297] Moore, *Judaism*, vol.1, pp.421–23.
[298] Kadushin, *The Rabbinic Mind*, p.283.
[299] Ibid., p.141.
[300] Suffrin, *Encyclopedia*, p.296. For an Islamic interpretation of the Rabbinic theology see Abū Muḥammad ʿAlī ibn Aḥmad ibn Ḥazm al-Ẓāhirī, *Al-Faṣl fī al-Milal wa al-Ahwā' wa al-Niḥal* (Cairo: Maktabah al-Salām al-ʿĀlamiyyah, n.d.), vol.1, pp.161 ff.
[301] Harry A. Wolfson, *Repercussions of the Kalam in Jewish Philosophy* (London: Harvard University Press, 1979), p.41. For an Islamic source regarding this issue see Ali Sami al-Nashshar and al-Sharbini, *al-Fikr al-Yahūdī wa Ta'aththurihi bi al-Falsafah al-Islāmiyyah* (Alexandria: Dār al-Maʿārif, 1972).
[302] Wolfson, *Repercussions of the Kalam in Jewish Philosophy*, pp.44–45.
[303] Ibid., p.44.
[304] Agus, *The Evolution of Jewish Thought*, pp.157–58.
[305] Isaac Husik, *A History of Medieval Jewish Philosophy* (New York: Simon & Schuster, 1930), vol. XXV.
[306] Agus, *The Evolution of Jewish Thought*, p.164.
[307] Ibid., p.162.
[308] See Neusner, *Understanding Rabbinic Judaism*, pp.147 ff.
[309] Wolfson, *Repercussions of the Kalam in Jewish Philosophy*, p.3.
[310] De Lacy O'Leary, *Arabic Thought and Its Place in History* (London: Routledge & Kegan Paul Ltd., 1968), p.266; for Ibn Sīnā and al-Fārābī's treatment of the issue see Ian R. Netton, *Allah Transcendent: Studies in the Structure and Semiotics of Islamic Philosophy, Theology and Cosmology* (London: Psychology Press, 1994; New York: Routledge, 1989); also Oliver Leaman, *An Introduction to Medieval Islamic Philosophy* (Cambridge: Cambridge University Press, 1985); David B. Burrel, *Knowing the Unknowable God: Ibn Sina, Maimonides, Aquinas* (Notre Dame, Indiana: University of Notre Dame Press, 1986).
[311] O'Leary, *Arabic Thought and Its Place in History*, p.267.
[312] See Lawrence V. Berman, "Maimonides, the Disciple of Alfarabi," *Israel Oriental Studies* (1974), vol.4, pp.154–78.
[313] Lawrence V. Berman, "Maimonides, the Disciple of Alfarabi," *Maimonides, A*

Collection of Critical Essays, Joseph A. Buijs, ed. (Notre Dame, Indiana: University of Notre Dame Press, 1988), p.196.

[314] Buijs, *Maimonides*, p.200.

[315] Maimonides, *The Guide for the Perplexed*, p.68.

[316] Ibid., pp.70–71.

[317] Ibid., p.69.

[318] Ibid., p.81.

[319] Ibid., p.80.

[320] Ibid., p.83.

[321] Agus, *Evolution of Jewish Thought*, p.206.

[322] Suffrin, *Encyclopedia*, p.298.

[323] Guthrie, Steward, *Faces in the Clouds*, p.180; Donald Crosby argues that *via negativa* is still an important theme in Judaism. See his *Interpretive Theories of Religion* (The Hague: Mouton Publishers, 1981).

[324] Franz Rosenzweig, *The Star of Redemption*, W. W. Hallo, trans. (Notre Dame, Indiana: University of Notre Dame Press, 1985), p.23.

[325] Kadushin, *The Rabbinic Mind*, p.337.

[326] Kaufman, *The Religion of Israel*, p.43.

[327] Katz, *Jewish Ideas and Concepts*, p.55; also see Martin Buber, "Religion and Reality," *Eclipes of God: Studies in the Relation Between Religion and Philosophy* (New York: Harper & Brothers, 1952), pp.14–15.

[328] Rosenzweig, *The Star of Redemption*, p.422; also see Nahum Glatzer, *Franz Rosenzweig: His Life and Thought* (New York: Schocken Books, 1973); Bernard Martin, ed., *Great 20th Century Jewish philosophers* (New York: Macmillan, 1970); Julius Guttman, *Philosophies of Judaism*, David W. Silverman, trans. (New York: Holt, Rinehart and Winston, 1964).

[329] Rosenzweig, *The Star of Redemption*, p.385.

[330] Fox, *The Unauthorized Version*, p.360.

CHAPTER 3

Anthropomorphism & Transcendence in the New Testament

CHRISTIANITY INHERITED the Hebrew Bible from Judaism but not without difficulty. From early on an almost built-in contradiction began to emerge, with some of the early Church Fathers, especially the Alexandrian Platonists, struggling to reconcile and interpret biblical anthropomorphisms with a Platonic conception of God as a spirit, and the spirit as immaterial, ideal, and absolute. Many of these Fathers viewed biblical anthropomorphisms as incompatible with the divine majesty and mystery of God, and tried to eliminate them by allegorical interpretations. Clement of Alexandria, for instance, allowed neither human form nor human passions to describe God, the Father, pointing to biblical anthropomorphisms as simply metaphors adapted to the limitations of human understanding. To Clement God was formless and nameless and also, as Bigg observes, unknowable:

> We know not what He is, only what He is not. He has absolutely no predicates, no genus, no differentia, no species. He is neither unit nor number; He has neither accident not substance. Names denote either qualities or relations; God has neither... These are but honorable phrases which we may use, not because they really describe the Eternal, but that our understanding may have something to lean upon.[1]

Thus, where the Hebrew Bible mentioned God's hands, feet, mouth, eyes, etc. or His entrance into or exit out of a tent, or indeed any other anthropomorphic attribute or quality, these were reasoned away with the explanation that none of the expressions intended any human form, passion or likeness. To Clement, divine reverence required an allegorical meaning and interpretation to be given to biblical passages such as these. Origen was no less emphatic on the issue of anthropomorphism, stating that, "the most impious doctrines are implied by the belief that God is corporeal; and He will be thought to be divisible, material, and corruptible."[2] Origen's God was Mind and hence incorporeal:

> Being incorporeal God is independent of the laws of Space and Time, omniscient, omnipresent, unchanging, incomprehensible. His dwelling-place is the thick darkness. 'How unsearchable are His judgments, and His ways past finding out.' He has in a sense no titles, and His fittest name is He That Is.[3]

Origen was not unaware of the fact that, "even before the corporeal coming of Christ, many passages of Scripture seem to say that God is in a corporeal place..."[4] Through his allegorical interpretations Origen wanted to "persuade the reader in every way to hear the sacred Scripture in a more lofty and spiritual sense, when it appears to teach that God is in a place."[5]

St. Augustine, the mystical theologians especially, and many others, also insisted upon the ineffability and utter transcendence of God, the Father. However, despite the clear preference for this transcendental or Platonistic model, it was the peculiar incarnation concept of God which gradually came to supersede it and which popular orthodox Christianity has cherished down the centuries until today. In 543, Origen and his views were condemned by a synod in Constantinople and the condemnation was ratified by the Fifth General Council of 553.[6]

In the Bible, as we have it today, it is the New Testament which is distinctive to Christianity representing those books which the Church regards as expressions of its faith. The distinctively Christian understanding of God is based on the claim that God is most fully revealed through what Christians claim is His self-revelation in the life, teaching, death, and resurrection of Jesus Christ. William Blake notes astutely that, "The final revelation of Christianity is, therefore, not that Jesus is

God, but that God is Jesus."[7] I. R. Netton confirms the point by observing that, "The *traditional* Christian theological paradigm, of course, despite much debate, was that Jesus' 'self-consciousness was always consciously of Himself as God.'"[8] If the essence of Christianity is that God has revealed Himself most fully in the language and reality of a human life, it inevitably follows that the Christian understanding of God is essentially and literally corporeal and anthropomorphic. To claim that the historical human person, Jesus of Nazareth, was simultaneously God and man requires as its necessary condition that divinity is able to find self-expression and self-exposure through the "form of a man" which is what the two Greek words "morphe" and "anthropos" translate to. To show that this is really implied in the claims of historic Christianity, it is necessary to emphasize two things: first, that the New Testament documents are essentially focused on the life and works of Jesus Christ as the center of the Christian religion; and second, that the historic formulations of Christian doctrine – as set out by the early Christian Fathers, and recognized as normative by subsequent generations of Christians – teach a doctrine of salvation which makes it necessary that Christ be truly God and truly man and truly one. This popular incarnational theology is corporeal through and through, as we will be examined in this chapter.

The New Testament consists of twenty-seven books made up of the Gospels, Acts of the Apostles, the Epistles, and the Book of Revelation. It is highly valued by all divisions of Christianity – Roman Catholic, Protestant, Eastern, Orthodox. The term New Testament stands in contrast to the term Old Testament to denote the inauguration of "a new covenant that has made the first old" (Hebrews 8:13). Christians refer to the Hebrew Bible as the Old Testament because to them, it is associated with the history of the "old covenant", made by Yahweh in the past with the Israelites in the wilderness. Christians refer to their specific portion in the present Bible as the New Testament because, they believe, they are the foundation documents of the "new covenant", the covenant inaugurated and fulfilled by the works of Jesus, the Christ.

The central pivot of all New Testament writings is Jesus Christ. However, although crucial information about his life, teachings, death, and resurrection, are contained in the books, none of them in fact were written by him or under his supervision. Philip Schaff notes that " ...the Lord chose none of his apostles, with the single exception of Paul, from the ranks of the learned; he did not train them to literary authorship, nor gave them, throughout his earthly life, a single express command to labor in that way."[9] There is a consensus among biblical scholars regarding this issue, "whereas we possess documents originally written by Paul", observes J. Jeremias, "not a single line has come down to us from Jesus' own hand."[10] These books were the product of later generations and are commonly accepted as the earliest, classical responses to the many-faceted aspects of Christ's life and existence. R.M. Grant observes that the New Testament

> is the basic collection of the books of the Christian Church. Its contents, unlike those of the Old Testament, were produced within the span of a single century, under the auspices of disciples of Jesus or their immediate successors. The collection is unlike the Koran in that it contains not a word written by the founder of the community, though his spoken words are recorded by evangelists and apostles and reflected in almost all the documents.[11]

As stated, the New Testament is composed of twenty-seven books written by different authors at various places, communities, and times. It consists of the four widely known Gospels (the three Synoptic Gospels – the term commonly used for Matthew, Mark, and Luke since the nineteenth century – and the Gospel of John); the Acts of the Apostles; fourteen Pauline Epistles (the Greater as well as Pastoral) i.e., Romans, Corinthians I & II, Galatians, Ephesians, Philippians, Colossians, Thessalonians I & II, Timothy I & II, Titus, Philemon and Hebrews; and the seven "Catholic" (meaning "universally accepted") Epistles i.e., the letters of James, Peter I & II, John I, II & III, Jude; and finally the book of Revelation.

The New Testament in its present shape, number, and order, was not available to the early Christians for centuries after the departure of Jesus and his disciples. Clarke comments that the New Testament writings were "written for the special needs of particular groups of people, and the idea of combining them into one authoritative volume was late and not in the mind of the authors. Christians, therefore, and the Christian Church might conceivably have gone on indefinitely without Christian scriptures."[12] One of the leading factors may have been the existence of an already compiled Hebrew Bible. "Throughout the whole patristic age", observes Kelly, "as indeed in all subsequent Christian centuries, the Old Testament was accepted as the word of God, the unimpeachable sourcebook of saving doctrine."[13] The compilation, collection, and identification of this particular group of writings (the canonization process) as a distinct and authoritative entity resulted from a complex development within the Christian Church. It took the Church 367 years to produce a list of writings and a canon that would contain all the present day (New Testament) canonical writings. The oldest indisputable witness to the New Testament canon is Athanasius, fourth century bishop of Alexandria, known for his role at the First Council of Nicaea. In his Easter letter of 367 he wrote:

> Forasmuch as some have taken in hand, to reduce into order for themselves the books termed apocryphal, and to mix them up with the divinely inspired scriptures... it seemed good to me also... to set before you the books included in the Canon, and handed down and accredited as Divine.[14]

The list that follows this prologue contains the twenty-seven books of the present New Testament though not in the same order. According to Athanasius these books were, "the springs of salvation, so that he that is thirsty can fill himself with the (divine) responses in them; in these alone is the good news of the teaching of the true religion proclaimed."[15]

New Testament scholars differ widely over the process of the compilation and history of the New Testament canon – authors, places, sources, dates. However, traditional or Orthodox scholars declare the New Testament to be the absolutely authentic and inspired work of the disciples, attributing almost all the New Testament writings to either the disciples or the immediate apostles. The time in which they lived is known as the apostolic age, the first century CE. For instance, R. L. Harris states: "It seems clear that the New Testament books arose in the latter half of the first century A.D., and almost all of them were clearly known, reverenced, canonized, and collected well before a hundred years had passed."[16] Philip Schaff is more specific regarding the issue: "Nearly all the books of the New Testament were written between the years 50 and 70, at least twenty years after the resurrection of Christ, and the founding of the church; and the Gospel and Epistles of John still later." He concludes that, "Hence seven and twenty books by apostles and apostolic men, [were] written under the special influence and direction of the Holy Spirit."[17]

Scholars following this line of thought claim that Jesus was the personal Word of God, the eternal *Logos*, and hence the ultimate authority. Further, Jesus assigned this divine authority to his twelve disciples (Matthew 10:2–5) after his resurrection (Matthew 28:19–20, Mark 16:15–16); the Church was "built upon the foundation of the apostles and prophets" (Ephesians 2:20) whom Christ had promised to guide unto "all the truth" (John 16:13) by the assistance of the Holy Spirit. The apostles, like Luke and Mark, derive their authority from their masters who for their part represent the authority of Christ. Therefore, the entire collection of the New Testament is said to derive its authenticity and authority from the ultimate divine authority of Jesus Christ himself. Harris points out that: "The Lord Jesus did not, in prophecy, give us a list of the twenty-seven New Testament books. He did, however, give us a list of the inspired authors. Upon them the Church of Christ is founded, and by them the Word was written."[18] In the words of H.T. Fowler:

> Jesus strove to set religion free from the tyranny of the written law, meticulously interpreted by the scribes. He left no written word, but instead, living men whom he had inspired by his own life and word to claim direct access to God as Father and to trust in the power and guidance of the Spirit.[19]

In short, argues Geisler, "God is the source of canonicity."[20] This view of apostolic authority and New Testament authorship was common among the early Christian Fathers. For instance Irenaeus, the second century (180) bishop of what is now known as Lyons, believed that the apostolic authority issued from the fact that the apostles were endowed with the Comforter, the Holy Spirit, as Jesus had promised them at the time of his resurrection. Jesus had also assigned them the responsibility to preach his word to the ends of the earth. Given these aspects, apostolic writings carried the stamp of authentic divinity in the form of Jesus as well as the Holy Spirit. Irenaeus attributed the ultimate authorship of all the four Gospels to the immediate disciples of Jesus.

It was common practice with the early Fathers to ascribe the Markan and Lucan Gospels to their respective masters, Peter and Paul, hence insinuating Mark and Luke's firsthand knowledge of the historical Jesus event and their Gospels' perfect historical accuracy. The same trend is pervasive among present day orthodox/traditional scholars. P. Schaff, R. L. Harris, B. B. Warfield, Charles Hodge and N. Geisler are just a few examples. They contend that the canonicity of Mark, Luke or any other books not directly authored by the known apostles, is not dependent upon anything except that the apostles authorized and approved of them.

However, there exists a different line of approach taken by Papias, a second century bishop of Hierapolis. Though not suspicious of the intention or sincerity of Mark, he does raise some questions about the direct authority and order of the Gospel of Mark, observing that:

> The elder [John] used to say, Mark, having become Peter's interpreter, wrote accurately all that he remembered; though he did not [record] in order that which was either said or done by Christ. For he neither heard the Lord nor followed him; but subsequently, as I said [attached himself to] Peter, who used to frame his teachings to meet the [immediate] wants [of his hearers]; and not as making a connected narrative of the Lord's discourses.[21]

It is difficult to fully accommodate these traditional claims of apostolic authorship and authority for most of the New Testament books in light of the findings of modern scholarship and what these have proven. The fact of the matter is, as Westcott notes: "The recognition of the Apostolic writings as authoritative and complete was partial and progressive."[22]

Contemporary critical scholars, following form-criticism, redaction criticism, literary criticism, and a historical approach to the New Testament, disagree with the traditional view of the authenticity and divine nature of New Testament writings. It is their contention that the New Testament books are not the works of the immediate disciples of Jesus, but rather writings compiled long after their lifetimes by authors mostly unknown to us. Hans Conzelmann for example states that, "the circumstances of composition (author, time, place, occasion, and any of the more specific circumstances) are not known for any of the New Testament writings other than Paul's letters."[23] These scholars further assert, that Jesus never asked his disciples to put anything in writing. After his resurrection the disciples were occupied with preaching to those around them, concerning the end of the world and the arrival of the Kingdom of God, and therefore were least interested in writing the words of Jesus: "The time is fulfilled, and the kingdom of God is at hand" (Mark 1:15). The first Christians, states R. L. Fox,

> were people of faith, not textual fundamentalists: to hear Peter or Paul was to hear a man with a conviction, not a Bible, and a new message which old texts were quoted to back up. We can take this message back to within four years of Jesus' death through the personal testimony of Paul: he 'received,' he tells the Christians in Corinth, that 'Christ died for our sins in accordance with the scripture, that he was buried, that he was raised on the third day in accordance with the scripture,' and he then appeared to Peter and then to others in a sequence which does not match the stories of the appearances in our Gospels.[24]

In the words of J. D. Crossan, "Jesus left behind him thinkers not memorizers, disciples not reciters, people not parrots."[25]

The disciples also waited the second coming, the '*Parousia*' of the risen Lord and expected his return at any moment. D. Nineham notes:

> Since the early Christians thus believed themselves to be living in a comparatively short interim period before the end of the world, their energies were naturally concentrated on practical tasks, on

> bringing others to a realization of the situation and on the attempt to maintain and deepen their own relationship with the exalted Lord so that when he came to establish his kingdom finally, they would be worthy to be members of it. Consequently, they will have had little leisure, even had they had aptitude, for antiquarian research into Christ's earthly life; nor would they have thought it worthwhile, seeing that they do not look forward to any posterity who might be expected to profit from the result of it.[26]

Moreover, the belief that the eschatological and prophetic Spirit of God was operative among them, led the first Christians to focus more on oral transmission and preaching rather than writing of the message. Even Paul, who actually did write the letters attributed to him, did so because he could not personally reach the places they were being sent to (see 1 Thessalonians 2:17, 3:10 or 1 Corinthians 4:14–21). Otherwise, he appears to have valued spoken words and personal presence over the written word.

Consequently, the word or the tradition, was orally transmitted until the second generation, when with the passage of time enthusiasm concerning Jesus' second coming cooled. When his delay caused a number of problems, the books began to be written. F. R. Crownfield remarks that even when they were compiled, "it was not with any thought that they would eventually become a part of Scripture, in supplement to the ancient Scriptures which Christians now call the Old Testament."[27] J. Jeremias observes that, "It was more than thirty years after his death before anyone began to write down what he [Jesus] said in an ordered sequence, and by that time his sayings had long been translated into Greek. It was inevitable that during this long period of oral transmission alterations took place in the tradition..."[28] During this interval new sayings came into being and were added to the old corpus. Jeremias notes:

> The seven letters of Christ to the seven churches in Asia Minor (Rev. 2–3) and other sayings of the exalted Lord handed down in the first person (e.g. Rev. 1.17–20; 16.15; 22.12 ff.) allow the conclusion that early Christian prophets addressed congregations

> in words of encouragement, admonition, censure and promise, using the name of Christ in the first person. Prophetic sayings of this kind found their way into the tradition about Jesus and became fused with the words that he had spoken during his lifetime. The discourses of Jesus in the Gospel of John provide an example of this development; to a considerable degree they are homilies on sayings of Jesus composed in the first person.[29]

In Hans Kung's opinion

> the *Gospels emerged* in a process of about fifty to sixty years... The disciples at first passed on orally what he had said and done. At the same time, like any narrator, they themselves changed the emphasis, selected, clarified, interpreted, extended, in each case in the light of their own personal inclination and the needs of their hearers. There may have been from the beginning a straightforward narrative of the work, teaching and fate of Jesus. The evangelists – certainly not all directly disciples of Jesus, but witnesses of the original apostolic tradition – collected everything very much later: the stories and sayings of Jesus orally transmitted and now partly fixed in writing, not as they might have been kept in civic archives of Jerusalem or Galilee, but as were used in the religious life of the early Christians, in sermons, catechetics and worship.[30]

Therefore the New Testament writers were not merely biographers reporting historical events in their original form. They were responding to a particular "living situation" (*Sitz im Leben*) meaning that they had an axe to grind. They were theologians of their time and had a message to share. Kung observes:

> The evangelists – undoubtedly not merely collectors and transmitters, as people once thought, but absolutely original theologians with their own conception of the message – arranged the Jesus narratives and Jesus sayings according to their own plan and at their own discretion... The evangelists – themselves

> certainly...engaged in missionary work and in catechizing – arranged the traditional texts to suit the needs of their communities. They interpreted them in the light of the Easter events, expanded them and adapted them where they thought it necessary. Hence, despite all their common features, the different Gospels each acquired a different profile of the one Jesus.[31]

John Hick puts the point in a nutshell:

> None of the writers was an eye-witness of the life that they depict. The Gospels are secondary and tertiary portraits dependent on oral and written traditions which had developed over a number of decades, the original first-hand memories of Jesus being variously preserved, winnowed, developed, distorted, magnified and overlaid through the interplay of many factors including the universal tendency increasingly to exalt one's leader-figure, the delight of the ancient world in the marvelous, opposition to the mainstream of Judaism from which the church had now been separated, an intensification of faith under persecution, factional polemics within different streams of the Christian community itself, and a policy of presenting events in Jesus' life as fulfillments of ancient prophecy or as exemplifying accepted religious themes.[32]

Clearly, explains Hick, "the attempt to form a picture of the life that lay forty to sixty or seventy years behind the written Gospels cannot yield a great deal in the way of fully assured results."[33] Howard Kee observes that unlike our times the historians and writers of the first century, "were not interested simply in reporting events of the past, but saw their role as providing the meaning of those past events for readers in the present."[34] Therefore, during these sixty years or so, the Gospels were developed, in the words of Paula Fredricksen, "from oral to written; from Aramaic to Greek; from the End of time to the middle of time; from Jewish to Gentile; from Galilee and Judea to the Empire..."[35]

Given facts and findings such as these (of oral transmission, the Easter experience, missionary zeal, and the compilation of Jesus' sayings after a period of 30 to 60 years), many modern scholars doubt the authenticity and integrity of most of the New Testament books. According to Ernst Kasemann,

> the individual sayings and stories it must be said that from their first appearance they were used in the service of the community's preaching and were indeed preserved for the very reason. It was not historical but kerygmatic interest which handed them on. From this standpoint it becomes comprehensible that this tradition, or at least the overwhelming mass of it, cannot be called authentic. Only a few words of the Sermon on the Mount and of the conflict with the Pharisees, a number of parables, and some scattered material of various kinds go back with any real degree of probability to the Jesus of history...The preaching about him has almost entirely supplanted his own preaching, as can be seen most clearly of all in the completely unhistorical Gospel of John.[36]

John Hick claims that:

> The identifiable consensus begins with a distinction between the historical Jesus of Nazareth and the post-Easter development of the church's mingled memories and interpretations of him. And it is a basic premise of modern New Testament scholarship that we have access to the former only through the latter.[37]

G. Zuntz asserts that people of ancient times had a different attitude towards the text of an author, an attitude altogether different from that of ours in the modern age,

> an attitude of mind... prevailed among Christians of all classes and all denominations. The common respect for the sacredness of the Word, with them, was not an incentive to preserve the text in its original purity. On the contrary, the strange fact has long since been observed that devotion to the founder and His apostles did not prevent the Christians of that age from interfering with their transmitted utterances. The reliance of the believers upon the continuing action of the Spirit easily led them to regard the letter

> less highly; the two appeared to be at variance, the urge to interpolate what was felt to be true was not always resisted.[38]

Bultmann has claimed that the early Church did neither perceive nor make a distinction between the pre-Easter sayings of Jesus and the post-Easter utterances of Christian prophets which were accepted as the words of the Risen Lord and were sometimes intentionally and at other times unintentionally, retrojected into Jesus' mouth or into settings in Jesus' earthly life.[39] M.E. Boring has made the case that a substantial number of the early Christian prophet's sayings found their way into the Synoptic Gospels.[40] H. Boers explains:

> The question of whether a particular saying was actually pronounced by Jesus is not only impossible to answer but, from the point of view of the developing Christian religion, irrelevant. What was important about Jesus for the developing Christian religion was not so much the concrete facts of his life but the impact he had made on his followers, as reflected in the tradition of his life and teachings and in the legends of his birth and childhood.[41]

Thus, in the opinion of scholars like Boring and Boers, a great chasm was fixed between what Jesus viewed and presented himself and the way the early church interpreted him, as Christ, Lord, or Son of God. It is possible then to perceive of these books as merely interpretations of the Christ event, they do not provide us with exact and accurate information concerning what Jesus preached about himself and what he really was. Therefore, according to H. Conzelmann, "The historical and substantive presupposition for modern research into the life of Jesus is emancipation from traditional Christological dogma on the basis of the principle of reason."[42]

On the other hand, there are scholars who view the matter differently, and to them the early Christians were no innovators. I. H. Marshall suggests:

> It is clear that the basic sayings of Jesus was *modified* both in the tradition and by the Evangelists in order to re-express its

> significance for new situations; it is by no means obvious that this basic tradition was created by the early church. Similarly, it is unlikely that the stories about Jesus and the narrative setting for his teaching are [all] products of the church's *Sitz im Leben*. The fact that such material was found to be congenial for use in the church's situation is no proof it was created for this purpose.[43]

Richard A. Burridge, who has carefully discussed the biographical genre of the Gospels by comparing it with forms of biographies from the Graeco-Roman world, argues that, "If the early church had not been interested in the person and earthly life of Jesus, it would not have produced *Bioi,* with their narrative structure and chronological framework, but discourses of the risen Christ, like the Gnostic 'gospels', instead."[44] Bilezikian maintains that "the very existence of the Gospel, and that of Matthew and Luke after Mark, bears witness to the importance attached to the historical Jesus by the early church."[45]

Some of these scholars contend that Jesus used various mnemonic devices to make his teachings memorable as well as memorizable. In Jeremias and M. Black's opinion, there had been a relatively fixed Aramaic tradition from an early date behind much of Jesus' sayings, the statements attributed to Jesus by the present day Gospels, which in the case of the Synoptics Gospels, seems authentic to Jeremias:

> Nevertheless, we can say in conclusion that the linguistic and stylistic evidence... shows so much faithfulness and such respect towards the tradition of the sayings of Jesus that we are justified in drawing up the following principle of method: In the synoptic tradition it is the inauthenticity, and not the authenticity, of the sayings of Jesus that must be demonstrated.[46]

Many scholars do not share Jeremias's optimism. It is argued that Jesus enjoyed tremendous reverence among his early followers. Therefore his words, deeds and sayings were faithfully preserved and memorized like the Jewish Talmud. Birger Gerhardsson has discussed the issue at length, stating that:

> During the first four centuries of our era the oral Torah tradition of the Jewish rabbis grew enormously. And it was still being handed down orally. If one wonders how it was possible for such a huge body of text material to be preserved and passed on orally, one must consider the rabbis' pedagogical methods and technique employed in oral transmission.[47]

He pinpointed methods like memorization, text and commentary, didactic and poetic devices, repetition, recitation and the art of writing, as instrumental in this aspect. From here he contended that "Jesus taught in parables and logia, in all probability he taught his hearers these texts... Jesus presented *meshalim* for his hearers, and the disciples were the first to memorize them, to ponder them, and to discuss together what they meant."[48] Therefore, he claims that "there is a historical justification, based on sound historical judgments, for concluding that there is an unbroken path which leads from Jesus' teaching in *meshalim* to the early church's methodical handing on of Jesus texts, a transmission carried on for *its own sake.*"[49]

Space does not allow for a detailed discussion of Gerhardsson's thesis, however, it may be sufficient to quote E. P. Sanders who demonstrates that

> the Christian tradition – at least in Papias' generation – was not passed down and spread in the systematic manner which Gerhardsson describes as having taken place in Rabbinic Judaism. In sum, then, we see that there were probably significant differences between the Christian and Jewish method of transmission, although there may also have been significant similarities.[50]

In short, to this group of scholars, the Gospel material is not inauthentic, and there is no great gulf between the historical Jesus' sayings and the post-Easter portrayal of him in the Gospels. The only difference is that Jesus proclaimed that God was about to act decisively and after his crucifixion, whereas the first century Apostolic preachings or kerygma proclaimed that God had already acted so. Therefore Jesus' historical message is deemed to be exactly what the post Jesus Gospel materials contain. Ben Witherington concludes: "Thus, the alleged chasm between the speech event of the historical Jesus and the post-Easter speaking about Jesus probably never existed."[51]

From a historical perspective it may be noted that no actual proof exists of any written collection of the original Aramaic sayings of Jesus, or any notes or Gospel for that matter. E. G. Goodspeed has discussed at length the issue of the original language of the Gospels and concluded like many others that, "Certain it is that from the time Christianity really entered the Greek world it instinctively went about recording itself in writing – first letters, and then books."[52] There is also no proof that the disciples took notes of Jesus' sayings or tried to preserve them, whether verbatim or in any other systematic way such as those employed by rabbinical Judaism. Further, E. P. Sanders has already shown that any such supposition cannot be substantiated by historical facts. Indeed the sheer existence of numerous compositions and structures of Jesus' sayings, as well as their early Greek translations, demonstrates the validity of the assertion. Martin Dibelius' *From Tradition to Gospels*, Bultmann's *History of the Synoptic Tradition*, and E. P. Sanders' *The Tendencies of the Synoptic Tradition* are still useful references to elaborate the point. Even the earliest forms of Christian literature, Paul's letters for instance, contain virtually nothing but a very few sayings of Jesus (as discussed later in the chapter). B. Gerhardsson recognizes that, "It is certain that Paul does not quote the earthly Jesus very often in his Epistles, nor does he discuss such material."[53] Historical-critical study of the New Testament points to the chronological gap that exists between the Gospel writers and Jesus' own times. Not forgetting also the spatial one, for they wrote at places where Jesus' disciples or contemporaries were virtually absent. The writers' acceptance of Jesus as Lord and his central position in their writings does not necessarily mean that their accounts regarding him are accurate. Rather these credentials only prove that they were believers and preachers with good news to share.

Having said this however, it does not seem plausible that the early Church would concoct the entire incident, for there would have to be some basis in the historical person of Jesus, and the idea of his simply being a myth does not hold water. Proponents of the non-existence of Jesus theory, i.e. Arthur Drews, William B. Smith, and George A. Well, merely indulge in speculation, for documentary and other evidence (reliable Christian and non-Christian) suggests otherwise. Our point of contention is the precise accuracy of the accounts. The earliest Christian writers were perhaps heir to a variety of oral traditions and the latter were probably circulating in the community regarding Jesus' virgin birth, miracles, and preaching. It would appear that these traditions were selected, colored, modified and added to, in light of the so-called resurrected Jesus or Easter experience and early Church proclamations about it (kerygma). G. N. Stanton comments:

> Perhaps we will never know *precisely* the influences at work in the earliest christological reflections of the church. To claim that the christological beliefs of the primitive church have not left their mark upon the gospel traditions would be to fly in the face of clear evidence to the contrary. But we may be sure that traditions about the life and character of Jesus played an important part not only in the preaching of the primitive church, but also in its christological reflection: both began with Jesus of Nazareth.[54]

It must be pointed out that although the historical figure of Jesus of Nazareth may have formed the beginning point for the primitive church, this does not mean that the Jesus who actually existed was identical to the church's later teachings about him. Howard C. Kee is probably right when he observes that, "What we are dealing with in the gospel tradition is not objective historical evidence that has become overlaid with the claims of Christian faith, but with the evidence that in its entirety stems from the witness of faith at various stages of development."[55]

Caught in the middle of all these developments, one can attempt to locate the basic realities connected with the earthly life of Jesus despite their being overlaid with kerygmatic interpretations and mythical portrayals. Peeling off these mythical layers to determine fact from fallacy, or misconception, is possible by a New Testament scholar, well versed in the cultural context of these writings as well as first century Jewish and Hellenistic thought. Whereas scholars in the past, typically the period between 1910–1970, would contend that we know virtually nothing about the historical Jesus, this kind of trend has presently given way to a more positive approach. E. P. Sanders observes that "in recent decades we have grown more confident."[56] Sanders claims that now "There are no substantial doubts about the general course of Jesus' life: when and where he lived, approximately when and where he died, and the sort of thing he did during his public activity."[57] Many modern scholars like John Hick, James Dunn, N.T. Wright and J. L. Houlden would agree with most parts of this description.

This does not mean however that a consensus exists among New Testament scholars as to how and where to situate Jesus in the first century Jewish context. Paul Badham explains:

> This does not mean that modern scholarship endorses every aspect of the traditional picture of Jesus. Historical and literary criticism constantly reminds us of the inevitable limits of our knowledge as we look back over long centuries. But whereas an earlier generation of scholars tended to say that unless we know something for certain we should not claim to know it at all, the modern view recognizes that uncertainty is present in all historical reconstructions of the past and need be no bar to reasonable confidence in what seems the most probable interpretation of what lies behind the narrative.[58]

John Hick reminds us:

> Scholars have listed such generally agreed points as that Jesus was a Galilean Jew, son of a woman called Mary; that he was baptized by John the Baptist; that he preached and healed and exorcized; that he called disciples and spoke of there being twelve; that he largely confined his activity to Israel; that he was crucified outside Jerusalem by the Roman authorities; and that after his death his followers continued as an identifiable movement. Beyond this an unavoidable element of conjectural interpretation goes into our mental pictures of Jesus.[59]

This tells us how limited our knowledge about the historical Jesus actually is. It should seem apparent by now that kerygmatic interpretations of the Christ-event are at the very foundation of the Gospels. This orientation, states Hans Kung,

> and peculiar character of the Gospels do not merely render impossible a biography of Jesus. They make any dispassionate, historical interpretation of the texts more difficult. Of course no serious scholar assumes today, as people did at the beginning of Gospel criticism, that the disciples deliberately falsified the story of Jesus. They did not arbitrarily invent his deeds and words. They were simply convinced that they now knew better than in Jesus' lifetime who he really was and what he really signified. Hence they had no hesitation in following the custom of the time and placing everything that had to be said in regard to him under his personal authority: both by putting certain sayings into his mouth and by shaping certain stories in the light of his image as a whole.[60]

J. D. Crossan stresses:

> The Gospels are neither histories nor biographies even within the ancient tolerances for those genres. They are what they were eventually called, Gospels or good newses, and thereby comes a double warning. "Good" is always such within some individual's or community's opinion or interpretation. And "news" is not a word we usually pluralize again as "newses".[61]

H. Riesenfeld's arguments concerning the rigid formulation and careful memorization of early Christian traditions, analogous to the Jewish method of that time, do not seem convincing in light of the long period of mere oral transmission which prevailed and the freedom with which material was handled by the earliest Christian community. Stephen Neill observes:

> No one is likely to deny that a tradition which is being handed on by word of mouth will undergo modification. This is bound to happen, unless the tradition has been rigidly formulated, and has

> been learned by heart with careful safeguards against the intrusion of error. Most of us would, I think, be inclined to agree that, in the story of the coin in the fish's mouth, and of Peter walking on the water in Matthew 14, an element of imaginative enlargement has at some point or other been added to the original tradition. Again, the variation of the forms in which sayings of Jesus appear, as between one Gospel and another, suggests that there was freedom of interpretation, even in this most sacred area of the tradition, which did not demand exact verbal fidelity.[62]

Neill continues:

> But there is a vast difference between recognition of this kind of flexibility, of this creative working of the community on existing traditions, and the idea that the community simply invented and read back into the life of Jesus things that he had never done, and words that he had never said. When carried to its extreme, this method suggests that the anonymous community had far greater creative power than the Jesus of Nazareth, faith in whom had called the community into being.[63]

Moreover, theological interests have always played a vital role in the transmission of Christian texts. The first century of transmission is no exception as Helmut Koester observes:

> The problems for the reconstruction of the textual history of the canonical Gospels in the first century of transmission are immense.... Textual critics of classical texts know that the first century of their transmission is the period in which the most serious corruptions occurred. Textual critics of the New Testament writings have been surprisingly naive in this respect.[64]

Origen, in the second century, had to undertake a great deal of textual criticism. Bigg observes that:

> He devoted much time and labor to the text of the New Testament, which was already disfigured by corruptions, 'some arising

> from the carelessness of scribes, some from the evil licence of emendation, some from arbitrary omissions or interpolations.' Already the records were perverted in numberless passages...[65]

In the opinion of R. L. Fox, "A critical history of Christian thought could not possibly begin to have been written until after 1500 because of forgeries by Christians themselves. The same danger besets the New Testament."[66]

If we examine these comments in light of the crucial differences that exist between *The Revised Version* of the Bible and the *King James Version* over several theologically important passages such as, 1 John 5:7–8, it becomes evident that theological interests caused several insertions to be introduced into the text of the New Testament after it had been canonized, or declared the Divine Scripture and the Word of God. Fox rightly observes that, "There is a thin and difficult line between a saying (perhaps largely authentic) which Christians inserted into an existing Gospel and those sayings which a Gospeller ascribed implausibly to Jesus himself."[67] If this is the case with the text after its having been declared the Word of God, and note despite the severe warnings of punishment given at the end of the Canon for tampering with it (see Revelation 22:18–19: "If any man shall add unto these things, God shall add unto him the plagues that are written in this book: And if any man shall take away from the words of the book of this prophecy, God shall take away his part out of the book of life, and out of the holy city, and from the things which are written in this book"), then what are we supposed to make of the oral traditions and their text in the first century when these were not even taken as Holy Scripture?

Interestingly, in the first century Christian Church the terms, 'Holy Scriptures', 'Divine Oracles' or the 'Holy Word' were implied for the Old Testament only. The words of Jesus were notably prefaced with the expressions, "the words of our Lord Jesus" or "the Lord saith". An example of this tendency among first century Christians can be seen in the so-called first Epistle of Clement of Rome. Scholars have shown that the epistle, or letter, is an authentic Church of Rome document dating to around 96 CE which fact brings us even closer to the world of the New Testament and its cultural and theological settings. Of significance is that in the Epistle the writer always alludes to the Old Testament writings as the Holy Scriptures but, as Grant observes, "never refers to the New Testament writings as scripture."[68] Fox summarizes the situation in the following words:

> This anonymous letter twice refers directly to 'words of the Lord Jesus', but neither reference is an exact quotation of a saying found in any one of our Gospels. The author is also unaware of any written New Testament and restrained in his use of scripture. He urged Corinth to consult its epistle from the 'blessed apostle Paul' and apparently alluded elsewhere to other Pauline epistles, as if he already knew them in a collection. He certainly knew our Epistle to the Hebrews, though not its anonymous author. However when he mentioned Paul's Romans 1:29, he continued with a quotation from Psalm 50, introduced by the phrase 'For the scripture says...' It seems that Paul's epistles were not quite the same as scripture in his mind: it is striking that he quotes clusters of sayings from Jesus only twice, whereas he referred over a hundred times to verses in Hebrew scripture. Christianity, for this author, is certainly not yet a 'religion of the book' with its own closed body of texts.[69]

Geisler and Nix disagree with such a depiction of the Epistle asserting that, "This contains several quotations from the New Testament, including the synoptic gospels. His citations are more precise than those attributed to Barnabas, but they still lack modern precision."[70] What Geisler and Nix recognize by "lack of modern precision" is exactly the point raised by the scholars of "form criticism", who classify biblical passages and textual units by their literay styles and attempt to trace them back to their possible historical contexts and periods. Concerning the issue of precision, John Ferguson observes even about Clement of Alexandria (Christian theologian c.150) that, "He turns next to New Testament and can still startle us by throwing in a phrase from Homer in the middle of his scriptural citations."[71]

The earliest Christian writings are that of St. Paul as Bornkamm and others have shown. Bornkamm states:

> All the letters, without exception, were composed towards the end of his career and within a relatively short span of time. They cover

> a period of no more than six or seven years when he worked as a missionary before being taken prisoner on his last visit to Jerusalem (ca. A.D. 56–57), after which he probably died a martyr's death in Rome in the early sixties, during the reign of Nero.[72]

A. Schweitzer comments that for these letters "we have to place a period of about twelve years, which are probably the years A.D. 52–64, but possibly from 50–62, if not still earlier."[73] Modern scholarship agrees with dating genuine Pauline letters to the years between 49–62 CE as T. G. A. Baker has shown.

It is interesting to note that Paul is quite silent in his writings about the historical settings which seem to be fundamental to the whole gospel narrative of Jesus' life and does not quote from Jesus except once. H. Anderson rightly points out that "if Paul were our only source, we would know nothing of Jesus' parables, the Sermon on the Mount, or the Lord's prayer."[74] According to Victor P. Furnish:

> It is striking, however, how little use the apostle actually makes of Jesus' teachings. For example, he invokes none of the parables which later on were given such prominence in the Synoptic Gospels. Moreover, he has very little to say about the Reign of God, even though that is a fundamental theme in both the sayings and parable traditions. True, not all of Paul's letters have survived, and we have no transcripts of his actual preaching. Yet the sources we do have probably give us an accurate picture... Paul focuses his attention neither on the teachings of Jesus nor on Jesus' Palestinian ministry. His attention is focused, rather, on Jesus the crucified Messiah and the risen Lord.[75]

John Hick observes that "Paul fits Jesus into his own theology with little regard to the historical figure."[76]

Burridge, on the other hand, argues that, "Because Paul says little about the person of Jesus in his epistles does not necessarily mean that he was not interested in his earthly ministry; it might be because he is writing epistles and not *Bioi*."[77] It is beyond the scope of this book to discuss and review the evidence as to how far the Gospels could be treated as *Bioi* (ancient biographies). Whatever the case, the issues discussed highlight the fact that the parables, sayings of Jesus, and the Gospels, were neither transmitted in a rigid, organized or systematic method nor written or accepted as Holy Scripture in the Christian circles of the middle first century. This complete silence on the part of Paul, observes Grasser, "is an unexplained riddle."[78] According to Francois Bovon:

> We must learn to consider the gospels of the New Testament canon, in the form in which they existed before 180 C.E., in the same light in which we consider the apocrypha. At this earlier time the gospels were what the apocrypha never ceased to be. Like the apocrypha, the gospels of the New Testament were not yet canonical; they did not circulate together [for example, only Luke and John are present in Papyrus 45], and when they did, they did not always appear in the same sequence [for example, the order Matthew, John, Luke, Mark in Codex Bezae].[79]

The Gospel's composition and collection was not the end of the oral tradition of Jesus' sayings. The oral tradition can be traced until well into the second century, in the Apostolic Fathers, and perhaps in Justin, who of course was well aware of the Gospels and in fact used them in his writings. M. Wiles states:

> For a long time, even after many of the New Testament writings had been written, the method of oral transmission continued to be regarded as the basic way in which the substance of the Christian Gospel was to be learned and passed on. Papias, bishop of Hierapolis in Asia Minor in the first half of the second century, is not unrepresentative of his age in preferring to the written record of books a living and abiding voice, a continuous chain of remembered teaching which could be traced back to 'the commandments given by the Lord to faith, and reaching us from the Truth himself'. The overall picture to be found in the writings of Justin Martyr and the other apologists contemporary with him is fundamentally similar; their conception of Christianity is the

> teaching of Jesus spreading its way around the world through the medium of the preaching first of the apostles and then of those who came after them.[80]

Papias of Hierapolis (c. 130–140), who has been credited with being the author of *Exposition of the Lord's Oracles* which survives in fragments only, states what is thought to be a classical example of the continued exaltation of oral tradition: "I did not think that I could get so much from the contents of books as from the utterances of the living and abiding voice."[81] In short,

> the general illiteracy of the first Christians, the expectation of an imminent parousia, and the high regard for Spirit-inspired prophetic utterance together ensured that the first generation of Christians would be itinerant, charismatic-type prophetic figures rather than scholarly authors of written works. Their social circumstances and their activity mutually served to prevent their producing written works.[82]

When the Gospel literature started to be compiled, it was perhaps Mark who took the initiative. In fact, observes Burridge, "out of 661 verses in Mark's gospel, around 90 per cent occur in Matthew too, and about half are also in Luke."[83] The old hypothesis that Mark made use of Matthew and Luke was challenged by Lachmann in 1835 in an article entitled "De Ordine Narrationum in Evangeliis Synoptics" [The Order of the Narration of Events in the Synoptic Gospels]. Hermann Weisse (1801–1866) furthered it by two acutely penetrating remarks i.e., the fuller account of various events in Mark than that in Matthew and Luke, and Mark's addition of vivid touches. He further observed that Matthew and Luke must have made use of another written collection of Jesus' sayings from which much of the material common between them was derived. Here in Weisse one can see the embryonic stage of the 'Two-Source' theory of the composition of the Gospels which by the end of the century dominated the field of New Testament studies. B. H. Streeter (1874–1937) developed a "Four-document" theory of the origins of the Gospels asserting:

> It is assumed that a hypothesis which reduces the number of sources to a minimum is more scientific... But a plurality of sources is historically more probable. In particular, if Mark is the old Roman Gospel, it is antecedently to be expected that the other Gospels conserve the specific traditions of Jerusalem, Caesarea and Antioch.[84]

By the end of the century the priority of Mark and of the "Two-source" theory was looked upon as the assured result of the historical-critical approach to New Testament study, and any attempt to replace it with alternate views was vehemently opposed and scholarly rebuked by known authorities in the field. By 1919 Martin Dibelius could write that "the two-source theory is better able than any other to explain the synoptic problem."[85] Burridge observes that "the current consensus among gospel scholars about the complex overlapping between the gospels is that Mark wrote first; Matthew and Luke used Mark and another source, 'Q', plus their own material; and that John was written independently of the other three, probably last of all."[86] Mark is said to have been written shortly before the destruction of Jerusalem between the years 65 and 75 CE as Baker contends, or by the end of the seventies as Crossan argues; Matthew around 90 CE and Luke as early as the nineties, most probably 85 CE (both after the destruction). By comparison with the Synoptics, the Gospel of John, observes Hans Kung, "has a completely different character in both the literary and theological sense... Undoubtedly too it was the last Gospel to be written (as David Friedrich Strauss discovered early in the nineteenth century). It could have been written about the year 100."[87] The earliest extant fragment, argues Crossan, "of John is dated to about 125 C.E."[88]

In addition to the late compilation of the Gospels we also have the case that when Christian literature started to be compiled, it was not only the books later regarded as canonical that were in circulation or accepted as authoritative but others too. Luke's beginning verse pinpoints the situation:

> Forasmuch as many have taken in hand to set forth in order a declaration of those things which are most surely believed among

> us, even as they delivered them unto us, which from the beginning were eyewitnesses, and ministers of the word; it seemed good to me also, having had perfect understanding of all things from the very first, to write unto thee in order, most excellent Theophilus, that thou mightest know the certainty of those things, wherein thou hast been instructed. (Luke 1:1–4)

In other words quite a few other gospels were also in circulation, the Gospel of the Hebrews for instance (which, according to Jerome, some called "the true Matthew"), the Gospel According to the Egyptians, the Gospel of Peter, the Gospel of Thomas, the Gospel of Philip, the Gospel of the Ebionites, and others. Helmut Koester summarizes the situation: "the number of gospels in circulation must have been much larger, at least a good dozen of which we at least have some pieces, and everybody could and did rewrite, edit, revise, and combine, however he saw fit."[89] Some of these Gospels were frequently quoted by the early fathers, like Clement and Papias, and were later declared Apocryphal or unlawful. Fox observes that, "At the turn of the century, the Christian intellectual Clement of Alexandria still cited the Gospel of the Egyptians and interpreted a saying of Jesus from it, although he knew very well that it was not one of four."[90]

On the whole, then, it can be stated that during the first half of the second century, the four Gospels of the present New Testament as well as other Christian literature like Paul's epistles were extant, but the idea of a close canon or New Testament was not present. No doubt the traces of the idea of a Christian Scripture steadily became clearer during this period and the presuppositions of the formation of the canon can be evaluated. But the crystal clear idea of the Christian canon was not the work of orthodoxy but a reaction and response to the pressure of heretics (like Marcion), Montanists and Gnostics and their heretical teachings. As B. M. Metzger observes: "Various external circumstances assisted in the process of canonization of the New Testament books. The emergence of heretical sects having their own sacred books made it imperative for the church to determine the limits of the canon."[91]

The great majority of New Testament scholars, especially since the last century (after publication of the works of D. de Bruyne and A. von

Harnack), have postulated that Marcion was responsible for creating the canon. In his book *Antitheses*, Marcion contrasted his own ethical dualism (discussed in chapter 2) as based on New Testaments texts, with other New Testament texts and with passages from the Old Testament. He rejected the Old Testament altogether and set up a list of writings to be recognized as Scripture by his followers. It was comprised of a form of the Gospel of Luke and 10 of the Pauline Epistles (excluding the three Pastoral Epistles). The mainstream Church could not accept this short canon and in reaction was forced to define more carefully the list of books that it recognized as Divine Scriptures.

J. N. D. Kelly, on the other hand, disagrees with Harnack and others by observing that the Church already had its own roughly defined collection of books which it was beginning to treat as scriptures by the time of Marcion. Therefore the claim that Marcion was the originator of the Catholic canon is "an extravagant point of view." Kelly however fails to prove the point of the Church's own initiative in canonizing the Christian books with the exclusion of many others. Moreover, he himself recognizes the fact that

> if the idea of a specifically Christian canon was deeply rooted in the Church's own convictions and practice, Marcion played an important part in the practical emergence of one. What none of the great ecclesiastical centers, so far as we know, had done, and what his initiative seems to have provoked them to do, was to delimit their lists of authorized Christian books in a public, official way. The influence of Montanism...worked in the same direction.[92]

Furthermore, the Montanist controversy of the "Spirit" was another factor in narrowing down the list of divine writings. In the early Christian congregations the Spirit had been accorded a central role. When the Montanists tried to exploit this belief in the Spirit to rationalize some of their extravagant assertions, the Church emphasized the authority of the written Word (the Scriptures) to counter them.

A decisive element in the canonization process of the New Testament came in the second century during conflict with another group known as the 'Gnostics'. This group claimed to have a special knowledge of what Jesus had really taught, alleging that ordinary Christian teachings were little more than what Jesus and the disciples had taught publicly, but that their knowledge consisted of what Jesus had taught his close associates in private. To refute their claims and occult teachings, the Church focused on the sacred writings and their apostolic authority.

The first list which has come down to us from the Church is what is known as the "Muratorian" fragment, first published by Milanese scholar L. A. Muratori (1672–1750) in 1740. Previously thought of as a second century western text this is nowadays thought to represent a fourth-century eastern text. From this and other ancient manuscripts like the Codex Alexandrinus, the Codex Sinaiticus and the Codex Vaticanus, it becomes manifest that until the third and fourth century, the limits of the canon were regarded by all as fluid. These old manuscripts included in their New Testament certain works such as Hermas' "The Shepherd" and the "Epistle of Barnabas" (no more a part of the present New Testament), while omitting other canonical ones like the Epistles of James, the Epistles of Peter and Hebrews. Eusebius of Caesarea (d. 340) an important witness to the state of the canon in the various Christian communities of his era, classified extant Christian writings into three categories: (1) *Homologoumena* or "agreed upon" – this referred to the universally accepted books which were the four Gospels, Acts, a fourteen-item Pauline corpus, 1 Peter, 1 John, and "if it seems correct," Revelation; (2) *Antilegomena* or "the disputed" – referring to books whose canonicity was disputed. Under this he lists five of the seven Catholic Epistles i.e. Epistle of James, Jude, second Epistle of Peter and the second and third Epistles of John. These were accepted by the majority and rejected by a minority. A subset of the "disputed" ones was not accepted by the majority and these were the Acts of Paul, the Apocalypse of Peter, the Shepherd of Hermas, the Letter of Barnabas, the Didache and "if it seems correct" Revelation; (3) The *Atopa Pante Kai Dusebe* or "the altogether absurd and impious works".[93] Most of the apocryphal gospels are listed under this category. It was Athanasius's Easter letter of 367 that settled the discussion of the internal limits of the New Testament canon within the eastern church, yet not with absolute success. In the fourth century Hebrews was generally accepted in the East and rejected in the West. The Apocalypse was generally accepted in the West and rejected in the East.

The canon in the West was closed in the fifth century under the influence of St. Augustine and Jerome. For the Greek church in the East the question was settled by Constantine. He ordered Eusebius to prepare 50 copies of the Scriptures to be used in the new capital. In this way the 27 New Testament books included in these copies obtained a semi-official recognition. The Syrian church still had some reservations about 2 Peter, 2–3 John, Jude, and Revelation. The fifth-century Syrian Jacobite manuscript Peshitta contained only 22 books. In the sixth and seventh century the influence of the Vulgate (4th century Latin version of the bible) and Constantinople prevailed and all 27 books of the New Testament were recognized by the church. The western Syrian Bible of the sixth and seventh century, the Philoxenian and Harklian versions, contained the same 27 books accepted in the East as well as in the West, though the eastern Syrian Church observes Metzger, "having lost contact with the rest of Christendom, continued much longer to hold to the shorter canon."[94]

Though the issue of the New Testament canon was settled in the fifth century, Eusebius's distinction between the *homologoumena* and *antilegomena* did not disappear completely from the Church. During the Middle Ages, Hebrews and the Catholic Epistles, except 1 Peter and 1 John, were still the subject of some controversy. Luther, for instance, severely censured Hebrews, Jude, 2 Peter and called James "a straw epistle". He relegated some other canonical books to second place. In spite of these differences, all the Catholic as well as Protestant New Testament copies contain all 27 canonical writings.

It is important to note Kelly's observation that:

> The main point to be observed is that the fixation of the finally agreed list of books, and of the order in which they were to be arranged, was the result of a very gradual process...By gradual stages, however, the Church both in East and West arrived at a common mind as to its sacred books. The first official document which prescribes the twenty-seven books of our New Testament as alone canonical is Athanasius's Easter Letter for the year 367, but the process was not everywhere complete until at least a century and a half later.[95]

Now when we read the New Testament as a book what we are in fact reading, as R. L. Fox puts it, is "a list of books which some of the Christian's bishops approved and asserted more than three hundred years after Jesus's death...Three centuries are a very long time: do these late listings really create a unity with such an authority that it directs our understanding?"[96] Obviously, it would be implausible to cite the protection, guidance and comforting work of the Holy Spirit to the exclusion of human beings with all their human limitations behind the very letters of the New Testament books. In Fox's view:

> Even an atheist can see the difference between one of the turgid or most sectarian alternative Gospels and one of the recognized four: as for the others, even early Christians who respected our four could quote sayings from some of the other Gospels too. As for the rest of the New Testament, it was never agreed definitively, unless the entire Syriac, Ethiopic and Greek Orthodox Churches are disqualified from a share in the Holy Spirit, along with the bulk of those Christians who wrote in Greek throughout the first seven centuries of Church history and made such subtle contributions to Christian theology.[97]

Therefore, the only solid conclusion one can reach is that the authors, compilers, and canonizers were after all simple human beings. In addition, it is pertinent to note as S. Neill does that, "Whatever view we may hold of the inspiration of the New Testament, we are bound to admit that it has been immune from none of the chances, the perils, and the corruptions which have assailed all other manuscript traditions of similar length."[98] He further argues:

> In regard to the text of almost all ancient authors this is certain that none of them presents what the author himself can possibly have written...We cannot rule out the possibility that the same may be true of the New Testament, and that in certain passages, which are likely to be very few, nothing but the inspired guesswork will take us back to the original.[99]

Just the expressions 'Canonical writings' or 'Canon of Scriptures,' in the words of Matthew Arnold,

> recall a time when degrees of value were still felt, and all parts of the Bible did not stand on the same footing, and were not taken equally. There was a time when books were read as part of the Bible which are no Bible now; there was a time when books which are in every Bible now, were by many disallowed as genuine parts of the Bible... And so far from their finally getting where they now are after a thorough trial of their claims, and with indisputable propriety, they got placed there by the force of circumstances, by chance or by routine, rather than on their merits.[100]

It is also not the case that once the Canon was established nobody had any problems with it. Rather, "the whole discussion died out, not because the matter was sifted and settled and a perfect Canon of Scripture deliberately formed; it died out as medieval ignorance deepened, and because there was no longer knowledge or criticism enough left in the world to keep such a discussion alive."[101]

Since the eighteenth century onward however, this discussion has once again ignited, though its emphasis and tone is a little different.

THE CONTEMPORARY CHRISTIAN STANDPOINT

Christians are divided on the issue of their Scripture's origin and authority. Some, particularly in certain Evangelical traditions, enthusiastically advocate the infallibility, inerrancy and verbal inspiration of the Bible. Their logic is palpable. If God the Omniscient, the Omnipresent, the Omnipotent, is regarded as author of the scriptural text, then it follows that the text should be entirely free of any mistakes and errors, whether in content or form. If however, Scripture is found to contain errors, whether by the unintentional or indiscernible will of its authors or not, we are left with a critical problem, for God's power and perfection does not allow for errors to exist in His written work.

According to B. B. Warfield, a staunch exponent of Scriptural Inerrancy, the scriptures are, "not as man's report to us of what God says, but as the very Word of God itself, spoken by God himself through human lips and pens."[102] He further argues that each word of the text is "at one and the same time the consciously self-chosen word of the writer and the divinely-inspired word of the Spirit."[103] To affirm the doctrine of the inerrancy of Scripture, in 1978 an International Conference on Biblical Inerrancy was held in the USA, and its roughly 300 attendees formulated what is known as "The Chicago Statement on Biblical Inerrancy", viewing biblical Scripture as wholly inerrant: "Being wholly and verbally God-given, Scripture is without error or fault in all its teachings, no less in what it states about God's acts in creation, about the events of world history, and about its own literary origins under God, than in its witness to God's saving grace in individual lives."[104] G. L. Archer is more specific when he states that, "We must therefore conclude that any event or fact related in Scripture – whether it pertains to doctrine, science, or history – is to be accepted by the Christian as totally reliable and trustworthy, no matter what modern scientists or philosophers may think of it."[105]

Such Evangelists, often called Fundamentalists, also hold the view that biblical Scripture should be understood literally. O. B. Greene, for instance, argues that, "Jesus dies a literal death. He was buried – not figuratively or spiritually, but literally, in a literal tomb. And He literally rose again – bodily, as He had declared He would and it had been prophesied."[106] Nevertheless, although a literal reading of biblical Scripture is often emphasized, it is not always followed through, meaning that there is a common tendency to interpret the text in a way to fit a presupposed scheme, theology or eschatology, sometimes leading to full-scale exegetical exploitation.

Furthermore, we also have the matter that biblical Scripture would need to be accepted in its totality to avoid doubt being cast on its authority as well as absolute truthfulness in issues fundamental to the Christian faith. If Paul, as Francis Schaeffer argues, "is wrong in this factual statement about Eve's coming from Adam [1 Corinthians 11:8], there is no reason to have certainty in the authority of any New Testament factual statement, including the factual statement that Christ rose physically from the dead."[107] Therefore any criticism of scriptural text or belief in a limited or "virtual" inerrancy would be appalling, for it would not only negate the Scripture's self-testimony, but appear to cast doubt on the pivotal doctrine of the Christian faith and the perfect knowledge and authority of Jesus. J. I. Packer observes that "Christ does not judge Scripture; He obeys it and fulfills it. By word and deed He endorses the authority of the whole of it. Certainly, He is the final authority for Christians; that is precisely why Christians are bound to acknowledge the authority of Scripture. Christ teaches them to do so."[108]

Christian fundamentalists thereby prove the inerrancy and plenary inspiration of the Scripture by appealing to the character of its witnesses, contending that Jesus and his apostles maintained the doctrine of biblical sufficiency and inerrancy, therefore it must be so. They are not isolated in this, for Church history and tradition is also witness to this line of thought. According to Gaussens:

> With the single exception of Theodore of Mopsuestia...it has been found impossible to produce, in the long course of the first eight centuries of Christianity, a single doctor who has disowned the plenary inspiration of the Scriptures, unless it be in the bosom of the most violent heresies that have tormented the Christian Church.[109]

The point is supported by J. N. D. Kelly's observation that:

> It goes without saying that the fathers envisaged the whole of the Bible as inspired. It was not a collection of disparate segments, some of divine origin and others of merely human fabrication. Irenaeus, for example, is not surprised at its frequent obscurity, 'seeing it is spiritual in its entirety'; while Gregory of Nyssa understands St. Paul to imply that everything contained in Scripture is the deliverance of the Holy Spirit. Even Theodore of Mopsuestia, who distinguished between the special inspiration of the prophets and the inferior grace of 'prudence' granted to Solomon, was not really an exception, for he was satisfied that all

> the authors of both the Testaments wrote under the influence of one and the same Spirit. Origen, indeed, and Gregory of Nazianzus after him, could perceive the activity of wisdom in the most trifling verbal minutiae, even in the solecisms, of the sacred books.

Kelly further notes:

> This attitude was fairly widespread, and although some of the fathers elaborated it more than others, their general view was that Scripture was not only exempt from error but contained nothing that was superfluous. 'There is not one jot or title', declared Origen, 'written in the Bible which does not accomplish its special work for those capable of using it.' In similar vein Jerome stated that 'in the divine Scriptures every word, syllable, accent and point is packed with meaning'; those who slighted the commonplace contents of *Philemon* were simply failing, through ignorance, to appreciate the power and wisdom they concealed. According to Chrysostom, even the chronological figures and the catalogues of names included in Scripture have their profound value; and he devoted two homilies to the salutations in *Romans 16* in the hope of convincing his auditors that treasures of wisdom lie hid in every word spoken by the Spirit.[110]

Kelly concludes that with the exception of Augustine and Theodore, "The majority were content to accept the fact of the inspiration of the sacred writers, without examining further the manner or the degree of its impact upon them."[111]

However such a claim may be anachronistic, for according to Canon Charles Smyth, "nobody really believed in the verbal inspiration of the Holy Scriptures until the geologists began to question it in the nineteenth century."[112] The Scriptures are not the infallible and inerrant Word of God, containing absolute truth about everything in the world. They are records of God's revelation and good for Christian faith. Long before modern times St. Augustine commented, "We do not read in the Gospel of the Lord's having said: I send you a Comforter to teach you about the course of the sun and moon. What he sought to produce was

Christians, not astronomers."[113] Augustine further analyzed the prophetic vision into three principal categories: corporal, spiritual and intellectual.[114] Writing about the scriptural depiction of the paradise of Eden, St. Augustine observed,

> a number of interpreters give a symbolic meaning to the whole of that paradise, in which dwelt the first parents of mankind, according to the truthful narrative of holy Scripture. They give a spiritual reference to those fruit-bearing trees, and the others, turning them into symbols of virtues and moral qualities. They take it for granted that those were not visible and material objects, but were thus described in speech or writing to stand for spiritual and moral truths.[115]

Augustine approves this line of approach to the Scriptures by arguing that, "This is the kind of thing that can be said by way of allegorical interpretation of paradise; and there may be other more valuable lines of interpretation. There is no prohibition against such exegesis, provided that we also believe in the truth of the story as a faithful record of historical fact."[116] Christian history is replete with allegorical interpretations of the Scriptures as seen in the previous chapter.

Modern Christian responses to biblical Scripture have taken so many forms that space does not allows us to dwell on them. However, one of the most frequently discussed responses is that of Rudolf Bultmann. To Bultmann the New Testament cosmology is "essentially mythical in character."[117] Its world view and the event of 'redemption' which is the subject of its preaching is obsolete. A "blind acceptance of the New Testament mythology would be arbitrary, and to press for its acceptance as an article of faith would be to reduce faith to works."[118] Modern man's knowledge and mastery of the world has advanced to such a degree that he is no longer interested in this pre-scientific and mythical eschatology, "Man's knowledge and mastery of the world have advanced to such an extent through science and technology that it is no longer possible for anyone seriously to hold the New Testament view of the world – in fact there is no one who does."[119] If Christians want to save the truth and message of the New Testament, "the only way is to demythologize it."[120] The New Testament itself invites such a revolutionary process, "the principal demand for the criticism of mythology comes from a curious contradiction which runs right through the New Testament."[121]

The demythologization of the Scriptures can be achieved only through "an existentialist interpretation" of the New Testament. Bultmann and his school have given a great deal of thought to hermeneutics and scriptural interpretation. They believe that the Christian Gospel is the proclamation of something God has done once and for all in the early decades of our era. That *kerygma*, as Bultmann calls it, of the New Testament can be made fully intelligible and acceptable today once interpreted by appropriate hermeneutic techniques apart from mythology. This *kerygma* will offer "man an understanding of himself which will challenge him to a genuine existential decision."[122]

Scholars following the existential approach do not view the Bible as the Word of God but view biblical Scripture as a unique place where the believer encounters the Word of God. To them only Christ is the Word of God and the Scriptures are perceived as fallible, finite and a human witness/response to Christ. The Scriptures become the Word of God only because God uses them to reveal Himself. The spoken word, states Brunner, "is an indirect revelation when it bears witness to the real revelation: Jesus Christ, the personal self-manifestation of God, Emmanuel."[123] Therefore, the

> Scriptures – first of all the testimony of the Apostle to Christ – is the "crib wherein Christ lieth" (Luther). It is a "word" inspired by the Spirit of God; yet at the same time it is a human message; its "human character" means that it is colored by the frailty and imperfection of all that is human.[124]

This is all very well but leaves unanswered the biggest question: how in the world is anyone to know the true "Word of God" when the sole source of information for that Word, that is the Scripture, is imperfect and unauthentic to begin with? Further, how could the Holy Spirit or Divine Providence preserve and guard the text and truths of certain parts of the Scripture whilst letting others be disfigured by imperfect human beings?

Continuing on with subtleties such as these, for Paul Tillich the Scripture is less revelation than a record of revelation; revelation takes place in a dialectical encounter between God and man. The Scriptural text is the report of such an encounter:

> The Bible is a document of the divine self-manifestation and of the way in which human beings have received it...The basic error of fundamentalism is that it overlooks the contribution of the receptive side in revelatory situation and consequently identifies one individual and conditioned form of receiving the divine with the divine itself.[125]

This throws up yet other questions not answered, what are the other forms and ways of receiving the divine and how authentic and objective are they? Would they not lead us to sheer subjectivity? What would be the methods and tools of verifying the authenticity and rationality of such forms or claims?

Liberal Christians seem to answer many of these questions by not believing in the literal doctrine of a divine dictation of the Scriptures. For them the Scriptures are an outstanding expression of man's hopes, aspirations and fears. The authors of these so-called 'sacred' books were mere human beings whose thought patterns were influenced and conditioned by their cultural limitations. This approach paves the way for liberals to possibly disagree with biblical authors, should in their opinion modern times and understandings demand it, even in religious matters. D. Nineham, for instance, argues that as soon as

> we look closely at individual New Testament writers and the way they articulate their feelings and their understanding of the new situation, the element of variety and strangeness become much more apparent, and it becomes clear that the variety derives from the fact that the writers have come from a variety of backgrounds, each with its own mythology and terminology, each dominated by its distinctive religious outlook, fears and aspirations.[126]

So these scribes were not infallible stenographers putting into writing whatever God dictated to them or whatever the Spirit inspired them. They were "at best honest, but simple-minded and ill-educated, primitives",[127] who were trying to make some sense out of the unusual event of Christ. Their account of Christ's event is not the inerrant Word of God but is "precisely history and story – history embedded in a context of interpretative story."[128] The "story" was not critically examined in the previous generations because, as states C. S. Lewis, the Middle Ages were "the ages of authority", and he goes on,

> if their culture is regarded as a response to environment, then the element in that environment to which it responded more vigorously were manuscript. Every writer if he possibly can, bases himself on an earlier writer, follows an auctour: preferably a Latin one. This is one of the things that differentiates that period...from our modern civilization.[129]

To tell the same story is the "embarrassment of the modern scholar"[130] because it lacks "consistency appropriate to unified dogmatic theory."[131] Therefore, Dennis Nineham advises Christians to approach the Scriptures

> in an altogether more relaxed spirit, not anxiously asking 'what has it to say to me immediately?', but distancing it, allowing fully for its 'pastness', accepting it without anxiety as an ancient story about God and the world, told by people who regarded the world as a phenomenon of at most some five thousand year's duration and believed in God's constant saving interventions in its affairs from creation day to Doomsday.[132]

It is no more a 'sacred' book and Christians should not feel guilty about it. Fr. Thomas Williams writes:

> The discarding of the old bottle and the provision of the new has been interpreted by some Christians as a denial that there is any wine at all. That is because they have imagined that God can be

> contained within the limits of a definition as though wireless waves were identical with a certain type of receiving set.[133]

The question is worth repeating, if the wireless waves are not fully transmitted and authentically communicated through the receiving set, what else is there to authentically inform us and appropriately convey to us the nature and function of the waves and how could we benefit from such a source of communication? Discarding the old bottle is quite different from discarding the only bottle available.

In short, according to Nineham, "Liturgists, quite as much as dogmatic theologians, need to free themselves from what has rightly been called 'the curse of the canon'."[134]

Richard Swinburne's approach is quite interesting. He agrees with many that we cannot take the Bible literally, commenting:

> Of course if we are misguided enough to interpret the Bible in terms of the 'original meaning' of the text, that original meaning is often false: there is scientific, historical, moral, and theological falsity in the Bible, if it is so interpreted. This evident fact led many liberal-minded theologians of the twentieth century to cease to talk of the Bible being 'true', but to speak rather of it being 'useful' or 'insightful' if read in accord with some rule or other of interpretation; and there have evolved as many ways of interpreting as there have been theologians to do the interpreting. And saying this sort of thing about the Bible hardly gives it special status – the same could be said of any great work of literature. A general fog settled over 'hermeneutics.'[135]

However, he further argues:

> And yet the rules are there, sanctified by centuries of use by those who claimed in accord with Christian tradition that the Bible was 'true'. If we wish to take seriously claims for the truth of the Bible, we must understand it in the way that both philosophical rules for interpreting other texts, and so many of those who interpreted the Bible or laid down the rules for doing so in previous centuries,

> suggest; and that includes their admission that it contains deeper truths which future generations wiser than themselves might detect by using their rules.[136]

Swinburne, I think, is quite aware of the limitations of these centuries-old rules of interpretation and can appreciate the problems involved in applying and following those rules without further elaborations and modifications.

Any modification less than a frank confession of the fact that the writers of these books were imperfect, primitive human beings, trying to understand and interpret the multi-faceted Christ event to the best of their ability, probably would not work in our times. It goes without saying that such a response and interpretation face the limitations of their writers and cannot be equated with or labeled as the inerrant Word of God Himself. The existence of this variety of writers and interpretations are the main source of the contradictory nature of the Christological doctrines.

Christology: Corporealism & Anthropomorphism

Jesus historically existed among the Jewish people, respected their Scripture, thought of himself as a fulfillment of their law, struggled with the Jewish religious hierarchy and claimed to be sent to the lost sheep of the house of Israel. There may have been features distinctive to Jesus' understanding of God and His transcendence, but the concept as a whole would probably not be at odds with Judaic understanding of the Deity. The earliest Christians would perforce have obviously inherited the themes of divine transcendence and monotheism from the developed Judaism around them, meaning that the unity, uniqueness and sublimity of the Creator God must have been the indisputable premise of the original Church's faith tradition. One can deduce from available historical data that the Church has used the same transcendental monotheistic premise against the polytheists, Gnostic emanationists and Marcionite dualists to refute their monotheistic violations.

Like Clement of Alexandria, many of the Church Fathers insisted that the Hebrew Bible's anthropomorphic expressions be understood and taken metaphorically. So, for instance, Saint Basil of Caesarea

(330–379) interpreted God turning "His face" as God leaving one alone in difficulties, Gregory of Nazianzus interpreted God's "face" as His oversight, Theodoret as His benevolence and restoration of freedom, and John of Damascus as His display and self-revelation through countless works.

The New Testament in contrast contains very few anthropomorphic expressions. It does refer to the finger of God (Luke 11:20), mouth of God (Matthew 4:4), sight of God (Luke 16:15), earth being the footstool of God (Matthew 5:35) etc., and almost all of these expressions can be interpreted metaphorically. Despite this, many church fathers held a corporeal and anthropomorphic concept of the Deity. Bigg notes that, "In the view of the *Homilies*, the Valentinians, Melito..., Tertullian *Adv. Praxeam* 7, God is corporeal. Even Irenaeus finds the image of God in the body of man... Anthropomorphism lingered on long in the East."[137] Two centuries after Clement, St. Augustine was still wrestling with the strong anthropomorphic and corporeal tendency seemingly entrenched among Christians as well as the Church itself. Christians, R. J. Teske observed, "think of God in a human form and suppose that he is such."[138]

This is in addition to the fact that the New Testament is not centered on God Almighty. It is Christocentric. Burridge has shown by manual analysis of the four Gospels that God the Almighty/Father occupies a sum total of just 2.5% of the Gospels while the rest of the Gospels are concerned with Jesus in various capacities i.e. his person, teachings, his disciples, his recipients, his dialogue with Jewish leaders etc. (Mark gives only a 0.2% place to the verbs whose subject is God/Father in his Gospel, with Matthew 0.6%, Luke 1.1% and John 0.6%).[139] Charles Gore pointed to this fact a long time ago observing that "Christianity is faith in a certain person Jesus Christ, and by faith in Him is meant such unreserved self-committal as is only possible, because faith in Jesus is understood to be faith in God, and union with Jesus union with God."[140]

There is, then, a tremendous concentration on one man, Jesus of Nazareth. He is described in different terms, concepts and ways. He is addressed as the Son of man, Son of God, the Word, the Prophet, the Messiah, the Kyrios or Lord and perhaps even as God. According to S. C. Guthrie:

> All the doctrines of the Christian faith are related to Christ as spokes to the hub of a wheel. We could not talk about who God is, how we know Him, what He is like and what He wants with us, without talking about the revelation of himself, His will and work in Christ...Everything else Christians believe stands or falls with what they believe about Jesus.[141]

Had there been no concentration on Jesus' person, or had the New Testament been systematic or uniform with regard to the nature of the above descriptions, there might perhaps have been no need for critical study or discussion of anthropomorphism in the New Testament. But as it is, the New Testament writers are so obsessed with the Christ event that they seem to reflect upon every other thing, even God, through this mirror. There is a merger of divinity and humanity in the person of the historical Jesus, so much so that to traditional Christians Jesus is at once a complete God and a complete human being. This incarnation, the diffusion of divinity and humanity in a feeble human being, is the climax of divine corporealism and anthropomorphic realism. Moreover, there exits such a diversity of descriptions with regard to Jesus that it is extremely difficult to render him into one uniform, universally agreed upon figure or concept. Therefore, Christology, or the significance of Jesus and his relationship with God Almighty, will form the basic area of our study of anthropomorphism in the New Testament.

There are many Christologies in the New Testament. The fundamental issue in connection with the transcendence of God and anthropomorphism is the Christology of the person i.e. the doctrine of Christ's person and divinity. Modern scholarship is more widely divided on the issue of Christ's divinity as well as interpretations of the person of Jesus, than Christians of past generations. Almost all of the old christological issues and trends, often declared heresies by the Church teachings, could virtually be traced, finding boisterous expressions in many modern Christological discussions and debates. Many of the old Christological heresies are virtually incorporated into contemporary Christian thought without much hesitation or blame.

It has been customary for Christians until the late nineteenth century to believe in the divinity of Jesus Christ. The Church as well as the general Christian population (as discussed later in the chapter) have always contended that Jesus proclaimed himself to be the Son of God, the second person of a divine Trinity, who lived a completely mortal (yet sinless) life amongst humanity. In this God in Christ, traditional incarnational theology, we reach the apex of an anthropomorphic and corporeal conception of the deity. If God becomes incarnate as flesh in the person of Christ, eating, drinking, sleeping, feeling grieved and eventually being crucified, then in this physical embodiment we have the strongest case for the reality of divine corporeality in its purest sense. The main problem with traditional Christianity throughout the centuries has been how to maintain the transcendence of God and at the same time attain salvation through the incarnation and crucifixion of Christ as God. This is an awkward paradox from which there is no escape. Reason defies it.

Astonishingly, even in this day and age, there are scholars who maintain that although Jesus was divine and in fact conscious of his identity, nevertheless this incarnation somehow does not lead to the fact of polytheism or divine corporeality. This would seem to be at variance with human reason. The proofs given for Jesus' divinity concern reference to four aspects: what Jesus said, what he did, what others said about him, and what others did about him. Many modern evangelists try to prove Jesus' absolute divinity through the Gospels' "I am" statements, such as John 8:57 and Mark 14:62 corroborated by Matthew 26 and Luke 22. In the Synoptic Gospels Jesus is tried for blasphemy having been accused by his enemies (Mark 14:53–65; Matthew 26:57–68; Luke 22:63:71). Caiaphas, the Jewish High Priest, demands Jesus to identify himself (Matthew 9:2–6; Mark 2:7; Luke 5:21). Responding to Caiaphas' question, "Are you the Christ, the Son of the Blessed One?" Jesus reportedly answers: "I am; and you shall see the son of man sitting at the right hand of power, and coming with the clouds of heaven" (Mark 14:62). The Evangelists contend that Jesus, in response to the High Priest's inquiry, used the divine *I am* statement of Exodus 3:14:

> Then Moses said to God, "Behold, I am going to the sons of Israel, and I will say to them, 'The God of your fathers has sent me to

> you.' Now they may say to me, 'What is His name?' What shall I say to them?" God said to Moses, "I AM WHO I AM"; and He said, "Thus you shall say to the sons of Israel, 'I AM has sent me to you.'" (Exodus 3:13–14)

Wayne Grudem argues that the

> Jewish leaders recognized at once that he was not speaking in riddles or uttering nonsense; when he said, "I am," he was repeating the very words God used when he identified himself to Moses as "I AM *who* I AM" ... When the Jews heard this unusual, emphatic, solemn statement, they knew that he was claiming to be God.[142]

Thus modern evangelists attempt to draw parallels between the Old Testament's use of the divine "I AM" statements and its use in the Gospel of John to insinuate that John by these parallels was declaring Jesus' divinity. For instance, Richard Bauckham contends:

> This [I am] sentence occurs as a divine declaration of unique identity seven times in the Hebrew Bible. ... It is certainly not accidental that, whereas in the Hebrew Bible there are seven occurrences of *ni hu* [the Hebrew version of "I am"] and two of the emphatic variation '*anoki anoki hu*', in John there are seven absolute 'I am' sayings, with the seventh repeated twice for the sake of an emphatic climax.[143]

It is also postulated by these evangelists that in using the title "Son of Man", and by claiming to come on the clouds of heavens and sit on the right hand of God, Jesus was in reality claiming that he was the God of Moses and Abraham. According to Bowman and Komoszewski, "it was one thing *to enter* God's presence and yet another *to sit* in it. But *to sit at God's right side* was another matter altogether. In the religious and cultural milieu of Jesus' day, to claim to sit at God's right hand was tantamount to claiming equality with God."[144] To Darrel Bock, Jesus' claim was "worse, in the leadership's view, than claiming the right to be able to walk into the Holy of Holies in the temple and live there!"[145]

According to the evangelists, these phrases and expressions were quite known to the first century Jewish community as the epithets of divinity, which is why Jesus was accused of blasphemy and ordered to be killed.

They also assert that to prove his divinity, Jesus prophesized that he would die on the cross and then be resurrected on the third day. Therefore, claim evangelists, resurrection itself is the direct proof of Jesus' divinity. For instance, Gary Habermas and Michael Licona[146] argue that Jesus was crucified in public. His disciples believed that he rose from the dead and appeared to them. Paul believed that Jesus was resurrected and appeared to him. Jesus' own skeptic brother James believed that Jesus appeared to him. Finally the tomb was empty when the disciples visited it. Habermas states that the "disciples were sure that Jesus' person had impinged on their visual field. This is what Paul claimed. Peter agreed. So did Jesus' brother James. Further, the tomb was no longer occupied by his body. As a result, they were changed forever."[147]

Hence evangelists regard the resurrection as an authenticated historical fact proving that Jesus was God and aware of his divine identity. R. E. Brown states that, "Jesus knew his own identity which involved a unique relationship to God that we call the divinity of the Son. Christians of later period were able to formulate Jesus' identity as "true God and true man,"....The idea that he was divine I find in most Gospel pages..."[148] Ben Witherington III, fully agrees with Brown's thesis. He writes:

> Material in the Synoptics hints that Jesus had a transcendent self-image amounting to more than a unique awareness of the Divine. If, however, one means by divine awareness something that suggests either that Jesus saw himself as the whole or exclusive representation of the Godhead or that he considered himself in a way that amounted to the rejection of the central tenet of Judaism, (i.e., monotheism), then the answer must be no. Jesus clearly prayed to a God he called *abba*, which excludes the idea that Jesus thought he was *abba*. Jesus' affirmation of monotheism seems clear (e.g., Mark 10:17–18; Matthew 23:9).[149]

He concludes affirming that

> the seeds of later christological development are found in the relationships, deeds, and words of Jesus, and that in these three ways Jesus indirectly expressed some of his self-understanding. In short, he may have been mysterious and elusive at times, but this was because he intended to tease his listeners into thought and ultimately into a response of faith or trust.[150]

D. M. Baillie goes further arguing:

> Indeed it seems alien to the New Testament writers, in all the varieties of their Christology, not only to say that Jesus *became* divine, but even to say He was or is divine. That is not how they would have put it, because in the world of the New Testament, even though it is written in Greek, the word God is a proper name, and no one could be divine except God Himself. Therefore it is more congenial to Christian theology to say that Jesus is God (with the further refinements of meaning provided by the doctrine of the Trinity) than to speak of Him as divine; and certainly it will not say that He became divine.[151]

The arguments used by evangelists as evidence of Jesus' divinity are both frivolous and precarious. Firstly, the four Gospels do not agree upon the exact words uttered by Jesus in response to the High Priest's inquiry. Matthew reports: "Jesus said to him, 'You have said so'" (Matthew 26:64); Mark reports: "And Jesus said, 'I am...'" (Mark 14: 62); Luke reports: "And he said to them, 'You say that I am'..." (Luke 22:67–72); and the Gospel of John gives a very different portrayal of the dialogue between Jesus and the High Priest! In fact, no question is asked about Jesus' Messianic role and no mention of the statement "I am" exists (John 18:20–22).

Hence, what this illustrates is that aside from Mark, the affirmative statement, "I am", does not occur in Jesus' dialogue with Caiaphas, and furthermore is either missing in the other three Gospels, or paraphrased as "you have said so" or "you say that I am." Evangelists have placed an awful lot of faith on this very common and simple verbal sentence drawing conclusions of immense consequence. For, dangerously ignoring the fact that it does not exist in three of the Gospels and that the word "am" in "I am" is nothing more than a verb of existence, they have built their very case for Jesus' divinity upon it.

Furthermore, in the Gospel of Mark the phrase does not denote Jesus' pure divinity (as claimed) in terms of his being exactly God or even like God. The question asked of Jesus was whether he considered himself to be Christ, the Son of the Blessed One, and his reported response was "I am". The most that anyone can prove or deduce from this "I am" statement is that Jesus affirmed his Messianic role, or close affinity with God, by it and nothing more. So to derive a divinity for Christ equal to that of God Himself, with no basis in the Gospel, and a two-word statement only, is not only astonishingly faulty reasoning but too far-fetched for belief.

In addition, there was no reason for Jesus to speak in riddles – with mysterious terms such as "I am" – throwing clarity to the winds, especially given the weight of what was at stake, the all important question of who to worship. He could have openly said, "I am Yahweh or Elohim, the God of Moses, David and Daniel. Worship me alone." Jesus was quite emphatic in asserting his mortal nature, his weaknesses, his dependence upon God and his subordination to Him, critical because trinitarianism denies this very obvious subordination. Given Jesus' clear assertions why on earth would he resort to a jumble of exotic statements, more resonant of Greek philosophical practice, to express something as significant as his supposed divinity?

The "I am" statement is a translation of the Greek phrase *ego eimi*. Significantly, this phrase is used many times in the New Testament for individuals other than Jesus. For instance, in Luke 1:19 the angel Gabriel uses *ego eimi*; in John 9:9, the blind man cured by Jesus uses the same "I am" phrase; in Act 10:21 Peter uses *ego eimi*, and so on. In other words mere usage of the phrase *ego eimi* does not qualify the one making it to be designated the equal of, or the great God Yahweh, the "I Am" of Exodus 3:14. In actual fact Jesus uses the phrase at least 27 times in the Bible without anyone attaching any significance to it and yet in only one instance do the Jews reportedly attempt to stone him for it, meaning that if the "I am" phrase was considered that blasphemous, surely Jesus would have been stoned a lot earlier. In John 8:12, 18, 24, 28, we have Jesus using *ego eimi* in front of the Pharisees. John 18 reports that soldiers of the chief priests and Pharisees went looking for Jesus in the Garden. Jesus asked them "Whom do you seek?" They replied, "Jesus of Nazareth." Jesus said to them, "I am he" (translation of *ego eimi* in John 18:4–5). The same soldiers and Pharisees were in attendance when Caiaphas and the Jewish council sought witnesses against Jesus to punish him for blasphemy. Again, if the phrase "I am" was considered to mean equality with God, and therefore ultimate blasphemy, surely Jesus' use of it would have been enough to convict him, and the High Priest would not have needed to look for false witnesses. His soldiers would have sufficed as evidence for Jesus' use of it. The fact is that the phrase simply means what it says it means at face value "I am the one" or "I am he" and the circular attempts of modern evangelists to convert it into something of far greater significance, having some tremendous esoteric meaning, is preposterous. The claim of godhood is momentous and could never be based on such a weak foundation.

There are other assertions which claim to prove the Divinity of Christ, one of these being that Jesus provided one proof – that he would die at the hands of the Jews and rise from the dead. This however is not substantiated by the gospel text. Jesus never claimed to die at the hands of the Jews *to prove his divinity*. It's a fallacious piece of reasoning and presupposes nothing – dying at the hands of anyone, and supposedly the Jews does not make one automatically God, and even were we to accept the assertion, it would not prove that Jesus was God Almighty. Jesus was not the first to be crucified historically and even on the day of the crucifixion there were others who were reportedly crucified with him.

In the same vein, Jesus' purported resurrection does not in itself prove him to be God Almighty and this is also not something unique to him. In fact biblical reports indicate that numerous other individuals were also either lifted up alive to heaven or resurrected after death. For instance, 2 King 2:11 reports that Elijah was raised up to heaven in front of the eyewitness Elisha. Genesis 5:24 reports that Enoch was raised up by God and that he walked with God. In contrast, there are no eyewitnesses for Jesus' resurrection. The alleged testimony given by Paul is of little historical value as Paul did not see Jesus' resurrection but claimed to see the light. Further, the reports of Jesus' appearances are inconsistent. How many times did Jesus return to the world after his death? Why is his second coming awaited so excitedly when he has already appeared several times after his crucifixion and supposed resurrection? Of note is also the fact that there no confirmations of his resurrection exist from any independent source of his time. The passage attributed to Josephus is a known interpolation. There is no other mention of Jesus in any historical document except later in the second century. Pliny's mention of Christians in his letter of c. 112 CE, deals with their illegal gatherings and not with Jesus' crucifixion. Additionally, it was God the Father who supposedly raised Jesus from the dead as Acts 2:24; Romans 6:4; I Corinthians 6:14; Galatians 1:1; Ephesians 1:20 make crystal clear. Many evangelists quote John 10:17–18 to insinuate that Jesus himself participated in his own resurrection: "The reason my Father loves me is that I lay down my life—only to take it up again. No one takes it from me, but I lay it down of my own accord. I have authority to lay it down and authority to take it up again. This command I received from my Father." Commenting on both the statement and its interpretation a) logic dictates that a person who is dead cannot by his own powers resurrect himself, for he cannot be dead and alive at the same time. b) Jesus' absolutely clear statement that "I have authority to lay it down and authority to take it up again. This command I received from my Father" (John 10:18) proves that his resurrection, even if accepted as a genuine historical fact, is a result of the Father's divinity and not the Son's.

The gospel crucifixion narratives bring us to the real question at hand, in terms of the subject of this book, and that is the corporeality of God in the New Testament. For these narratives impose limitations on God that only human beings are subject to. Did God die on the cross? Was it God who suffered the pangs of death or the human being on it? If God was truly dying on the cross then which God other than himself was he calling to? Was he calling upon himself when he cried out at being forsaken, "Eloi, Eloi, O My God, O My God" or was he calling to another God? How many Gods are out there? Was God nailed down on the cross, beaten and spat at? Was it God who cried, sought help and was buried by human hands? Are these limitations appropriate to the Majesty of God? Is it even plausible that the infinite could be finite and infinite at the same time, everlasting yet dead? The whole issue is at variance with human reason.

Textually, there exist numerous non-trivial discrepancies and inconsistencies within the crucifixion and resurrection narratives of the four Gospels. For instance (italics mine) Matthew reports that "... *toward the dawn* of the first day of the week, Mary Magdalene and the other Mary went to see the sepulchre" (28:1). Mark reports: "... Mary Magdalene, and Mary the mother of James, and Salome, bought spices... they went to the tomb *when the sun had risen*" (16:1–2). Luke reports: "*...at early dawn*, they went to the tomb..." (24:1); John reports: "... Mary Magdalene came to the tomb early, *while it was still dark...*" (20:1). There is a great deal of difference between early dawn and when the sun has risen. When the Sun rises there is no darkness, as John reports.

Matthew mentions that Mary Magdalene and the other Mary went to see the sepulcher. Mark reports that Mary Magdalene, and Mary the mother of James, and Salome visited the tomb. Luke mentions Mary Magdalene and Joanna and Mary the mother of James and the other women with them (24:10). John mentions Mary Magdalene only. Moreover, Matthew states that "an angel of the Lord descended from heaven" (28:2). Mark reports: "And entering the tomb, they saw a young man sitting on the right side, dressed in a white robe" (16:5), but Luke (24:4) and John (20:12) write of two angels. Matthew reports that after the earthquake the angel rolled back the stone (28:1). The other three Gospels report that by the time the women had reached the graveyard, the stone was already rolled back. The Synoptic account reports that Mary was reminded by the angel of Jesus' words about the resurrection, and she informed the disciples regarding the resurrection. John's Mary is distraught and thinks that Jesus' body has been stolen (20:2–4). Here the disciples mention no empty tomb.

The reports of Jesus' appearances are also conflicting in Matthew 28:8–9, Mark 16:9, Luke 24:9 and John 20:18. To believe Jesus to be

God or God to be Jesus it would appear is to base one's entire faith on a monumental claim which has little to recommend it aside from a few shaky texts of a contradictory nature and certain supposed incidents of questionable historicity. The rest is convoluted, to the point of absurd interpretation. Once again, the whole issue is at variance with human reason and deeply lacks coherence.

There are other facts that cannot be dismissed, downplayed, or simply ignored. For instance, ironically, Jesus never uses the word "God" for himself. Oft quoted passages as evidence such as John 1:1; 1:18; 20:28; Roman 9:5; Titus 2:13; Hebrews 1:8 and 2 Peter 1:1 are translated by various scholars in different ways and in no way or form attribute the word "God" to Jesus, neither by Jesus himself nor by any of the New Testament writers. So the claims of evangelists such as Wayne Grudem that there are "at least these seven clear passages in the New Testament that explicitly refer to Jesus as God"[152] are incorrect, for these passages are not "clear", fail to stand up to scrutiny, and are not accepted by the majority of New Testament scholars.

In fact with regards to Christ's divinity, "clear passages" is precisely what we do not have. It is valid to ask why Jesus or John did not speak plainly, choosing to hide behind riddles such as the "I AM" statements or Daniel's "Son of Man" phrase, to state Christ's divinity. This is out of character, for Jesus is quite emphatic in the Bible, and the gospel writers were crystal clear in depicting his great devotion to and sheer dependence on God (as an obedient servant and not as some sort of synthesis with Him), worshipping God, praying to Him, claiming to be sent by Him and even calling upon God for help at the most difficult juncture of his life. Hence given this and to reiterate why would Jesus resort to a smoke screen statement such as "I AM" to express his divinity? The primary question of Christ's divinity has not been answered or substantiated by evangelists, neither from scripture nor from their own strange reasoning process. Yet, ironically, it would seem that they hold all the cards when it comes to knowledge about Jesus for they claim to know more about him than what he seemingly knew about himself. The truth is that whatever one thinks one has learnt, this does not mean that one has learnt a true representation of this great man and prophet. A world of difference lies between actual biblical tenet and perceived notions based on opinion and faulty premise.

There are other scholars who although believing Jesus to be divine, God the Son, do recognize the fact that he did not explicitly proclaim his divinity. For instance Archbishop Michael Ramsey writes that, "Jesus did not claim deity for himself."[153] C. F. D. Moule observes that, "Any case for a "high" Christology that depended on the authenticity of the alleged claims of Jesus about himself, especially in the Fourth Gospel, would indeed be precarious."[154] James Dunn and even staunch upholders of traditional Christology like Brian Hebblethwaite and David Brown, have acknowledged the same theorizing that Jesus was not aware of his divine identity. Hebblethwaite states that, "it is no longer possible to defend the divinity of Jesus by reference to the claims of Jesus."[155] Brown recognizes that it is "impossible to base any claim for Christ's divinity on his consciousness..."[156]

On the other hand, some of these same scholars argue that Jesus was implicitly aware of his divine identity, and that he revealed this to his disciples by means of extraordinary actions such as his forgiveness of sins and radical approach to the Mosaic Law. C. F. D. Moule, Gerald O' Collins, James Dunn are good examples of this trend.

There are also other traditional scholars who use the concept of the "Christ-event" to justify the proper divinity of Jesus despite the fact that he did not proclaim it for himself. This elusive concept of kerygma and the Christ-event seems to have appeared first in R. Bultmann's existential interpretations of the New Testament myth, and has been widely utilized by scholars like John Knox. Knox argues that, "The Church is the distinctive Christian reality... And so I say again, the Incarnation originally took place, not within the limits of an individual's individual existence, but in the new communal reality, in principle co-extensive with mankind, of which he was the creative center."[157]

J. N. D. Kelly does not accept the idea that Jesus was aware of his divine identity. He sees a gulf between Jesus and the later Christian claims of his divinity. On the other hand, he insists upon essential continuity between later trinitarian christological developments and the initial New Testament as well as the Church's christology. In his words:

> The Trinitarianism of the New Testament is rarely explicit; but the frequency with which the triadic schema recurs ... suggests that this pattern was implicit in Christian theology from the start. If

> these gaps are filled in, however, we are entitled to assume with some confidence that what we have before us, at any rate in rough outline, is the doctrinal deposit, or the pattern of sound words, which was expounded in the apostolic Church since its inauguration and which constituted its distinctive message.[158]

It is strange to assume that the first generation of Christians is considered better equipped to understand Jesus than Jesus himself. In similar fashion modern day fundamentalists seem to be claiming their better aptitude to understand what Jesus must have been than the first Christians. Such interpretations only serve to substantiate the claims that Christianity consists of later responses to Jesus and not necessarily what he preached about God or about his person. John Hick rightly observes that "this kind of thinking, in which Christianity is no longer centered upon the person of Jesus but now upon the church, has moved a long way from the traditional belief that Jesus, the historical individual, was himself God the Son incarnate."[159] He argues that the

> 'soft' divinity, expressed in the 'son of God' metaphor, eventually developed into the 'hard' metaphysical claim that Jesus was God the Son, second person of a divine Trinity, incarnate. But to use the 'Christ-event' concept to validate this development involves arbitrarily stretching that highly flexible 'event' at least as far as the Council of Nicaea (325 CE), and preferably to include the Council of Chalcedon (451 CE).[160]

Thus Kelly and other scholars' line of approach insinuates that somehow the Church knew better than the man himself, meaning that they understood the true nature of Jesus whilst he lived ignorant of it. But, how in the world could Christ's followers be privy to such tremendous and significant knowledge yet he know nothing of it? This is pure speculation and defies logic. After careful discussion of other trends such as the Holy Spirit guiding the church to these theological developments, or the cosmic Christ or risen Lord, Hick concludes that

> none of these ways can relieve upholders of Jesus' deification of the task of justifying that momentous move. Such justification

> involves showing both that the process by which the deification came about is one that we can regard as valid, and that the resulting doctrine is in itself coherent and credible.[161]

Contrary to what has been observed with regards to the traditional view, many liberal scholars do not accept the theme of Jesus' divinity in its strict sense, maintaining that Jesus was not divine in the sense just discussed. They point to the fact that he neither claimed, nor was conscious of, the divinity of his person. Harnack, the Ritschlian historian of dogma, for instance roundly rejects notions of Christ's divinity and in this classical statement contends that, "The Gospel, as Jesus proclaimed it, has to do with the Father only and not with the Son. This is no paradox, nor, on the other hand, is it "rationalism," but the simple expression of the actual fact as the evangelists give it."[162] In other words, the Gospel is not about doctrines concerning Jesus but about the reality of God the Father, and obedience and worship to him. To Harnack, Jesus

> desired no other belief in his person and no other attachment to it than is contained in the keeping of his commandment. Even in the fourth Gospel, in which Jesus' person often seems to be raised above the contents of the Gospel, the idea is still clearly formulated: "If ye love me, keep my commandments." To lay down any "doctrine" about his person and his dignity independently of the Gospel was, then, quite outside his sphere of ideas. In the second place, he described the Lord of heaven and earth as his God and his Father; as the Greater, and as Him who is alone good. He is certain that everything which he has and everything which he is to accomplish comes from this Father. He prays to Him; he subjects himself to His will; he struggles hard to find out what it is and to fulfill it. Aim, strength, understanding, the issue, and the hard *must*, all come from the Father. This is what the Gospels say, and it cannot be turned and twisted. This feeling, praying, working, struggling, and suffering individual is a man who in the face of his God also associates himself with other men.[163]

It had been customary to suggest, as discussed, that Jesus did not disclose his true identity and message to the disciples because of their limitations. A. S. Peake for instance writes:

> It was far better that Jesus should lead them through intimate familiarity with Him, through watching His actions and listening to His words to form their own judgment of Him, rather than by premature disclosure to force the truth upon them before they were ready for it, and when they would inevitably have misunderstood it.[164]

To contend that Jesus intended his true message to be partially hidden or to be understood in the light of his death and resurrection, states Harnack,

> is desperate supposition. No! his message is simpler than the churches would like to think it; simpler, but for that very reason sterner and endowed with a greater claim to universality. A man cannot evade it by the subterfuge of saying that as he can make nothing of this "Christology" the message is not for him. Jesus directed men's attention to great questions; he promised them God's grace and mercy; he required them to decide whether they would have God or Mammon, an eternal or an earthly life, the soul or the body, humility or self-righteousness, love or selfishness, the truth or a lie.[165]

In short, Jesus did not hide anything but proclaimed a straight forward message, leading people to God by his actions, statements and even through his sufferings. He had no other creed other than the simple one of "do the will of God". "How great a departure from what he thought and enjoined is involved in putting a Christological creed in the forefront of the Gospel, and in teaching that before a man can approach it he must learn to think rightly about Christ. This is putting the cart before the horse."[166]

Harnack argues that this radical departure from Jesus' Gospel took place during the process of the Hellenization of the Gospel. It took place when Christianity entered the Greek world and became detached from the mother soil of Judaism. To Harnack, the apostle Paul was the chief agent of this transition. Paul perverted the Gospel of Jesus by giving new directions to it:

> Even in John we read: "If ye love me, keep my commandments." But the way in which Paul defined the theory of religion, the danger can certainly arise and did arise. No long period elapsed before it was taught in the Church that the all-important thing is to know how the person of Jesus was constituted, what sort of physical nature he had, and so on. Paul himself is far removed from this position, – "Whoso calleth Christ Lord speaketh by the Holy Ghost," – but the way he ordered his religious conceptions, as the outcome of his speculative ideas, unmistakably exercised an influence in a wrong direction.[167]

This perversion replaced God with Jesus and the message with the messenger. In the true Gospel of Jesus all things were directed towards worship of the One God and to keeping His commandments as embodied by his law and morality. The Pauline message redirected this focus towards the person of Jesus and salvation through him. What might have been a mystical twist in the beginning lead Christianity to a totally wrong direction. Harnack concludes observing:

> ...it is a perverse proceeding to make Christology the fundamental substance of the Gospel is shown by Christ's teaching, which is everywhere directed to the all-important point, and summarily confronts every man with his God.[168]

Following Harnack's lead, John Hick contends that Jesus' own cultural milieu and his first disciples' religious and historical background would not have allowed them to believe in a feeble man's divinity. Hick observes that "it is extremely unlikely that Jesus thought of himself, or that his first disciples thought of him, as God incarnate."[169] He stresses:

> If one has already accepted a form of orthodox christology one can reasonably interpret some of Jesus' words and actions, as

> presented by the Gospel writers, as implicitly supporting that belief. But it seems clear that one cannot justifiably arrive at the belief simply from the New Testament evidence as this has thus far been analyzed and interpreted by the scholarly community.[170]

Hick roundly rejects the notion that somehow Jesus directly or indirectly led his disciples to believe that he was the divine Logos in human flesh or acting in a dual capacity both as a complete God and a complete man. Many of the Gospel's Christological titles such as the son of man, son of God, or Lord were originally not loaded with divine implications, but were rather common place innocent titles meant to denote reverence and spiritual exaltation. Hick contends that

> it seems pretty clear that Jesus did not present himself as being God incarnate. He did not present himself as the second person of a divine trinity leading a human life. If in his lifetime he was called "son of God," as is entirely possible, it would be in the metaphorical sense that was familiar in the ancient world. In this sense, kings, emperors, pharaohs, wise men, and charismatic religious leaders were freely called sons of God, meaning that they were close to God, in the spirit of God, that they were servants and instruments of God. The ancient Hebrew kings were regularly enthroned as son of God in this metaphorical sense.[171]

It is easy to claim but hard to prove that a man who lived a very human life and who was human in every sense of the term – in that he had a natural birth (that is through the womb of a woman albeit virgin) and natural human limitations, ate, drank, grew in knowledge and wisdom, worshipped God, prayed to Him for guidance and help etc. – was at the same time the all powerful, Almighty God of the Universe. To Hick "it would require earth-shaking miracles, overturning the whole established secular world-view, to cause a historical individual to be regarded as being also God."[172]

Hick claims a kind of broad consensus among contemporary New Testament scholars to the effect that the historical Jesus never made any claims to divinity in the sense that later Christians made for him. Indeed,

Jesus in no way or form thought of himself as God Almighty or as the son of God incarnate:

> Divine incarnation, in the sense in which Christian theology has used the idea, requires that an eternally pre-existent element of Godhead, God the Son or the divine Logos, became incarnate as a human being. But it is *extremely* unlikely that the historical Jesus thought of himself in any such way. Indeed he would probably have rejected the idea as blasphemous; one of the sayings attributed to his, 'Why do you call me good? No one is good but God alone' (Mark 10. 18).[173]

Jesus' own understanding of himself could not have been anything other than as an eschatological prophet sent to the lost sheep of Israel. As such he confined his mission to a specific geographical area, focused upon the reformation of Jewish religious institutions and resisted the relentless onslaught of Roman hegemony and exploitation. The raison d'etre of Jesus' great existence, his true message, however became replaced with his person as the messenger, when Christianity entered the Graeco-Roman world, becoming heavily influenced by its systems and institutions. Hick notes that Jesus was simply

> fulfilling the unique role of the final prophet, come to proclaim a New Age, the divine kingdom that God was shortly to inaugurate on earth...to endure in the pluralistic world of the Roman empire and eventually to become its dominant structure of meaning: Jesus the eschatological prophet was transformed within Christian thought into God the Son come down from heaven to live a human life and save us by his atoning death.[174]

This message of salvation was a lot easier to digest than the austere one of salvation through hard work and discipline, following the commandments and working towards the rectification of political, economic and social injustices. It demanded less sacrifices, involved less struggles against the establishment, and was relatively acceptable to the Roman elite. Consequently it became the popular form of Christianity.

The fundamental role played by Paul in giving altogether new directions to Jesus' message has been emphasized by many nineteenth century biblical scholars such as Wellhausen. The core of the influential "Tubingen hypothesis" (a school of German Protestant theology that noted contradictions among the different gospels) was that Christianity owed far more to Paul than to Jesus. F. C. Baur, the founder of the "Tubingen School", argued that, "The history of the development of Christianity dates of course from the departure of Jesus from the world. But in Paul this history has a new beginning; from this point we are able to trace it not only in its external features, but also in its inner connection."[175] Paul had neither met with the historical Jesus, nor learned anything direct from him. His conversion narratives are quite legendary and inconsistent. His contact with the original disciples was minimal and at times hostile. Baur observed that "from the time of his conversion the apostle Paul went his own independent way, and avoided intentionally and on principle all contact with the older apostles."[176] Therefore it was the apostle Paul, concluded Baur, "in whom Gentile Christianity found in the course of these same movements, of which the proto-martyr Stephen is the center, its true herald, and logical founder and expositor."[177]

This influenced the famous nihilist scholar Nietzsche to observe first in his *The Dawn of Day* that

> the ship of Christianity threw overboard no inconsiderable part of its Jewish ballast, that it was able to sail into the waters of the heathen and actually did do so: this is due to the history of one single man, this apostle who was so greatly troubled in mind and so worthy of pity, but who was also very disagreeable to himself and to others.[178]

Then in his *The Antichrist* Nietzsche claimed that Paul was the great falsifier, disevangelist, forger out of hatred, the very opposite of a bringer of glad tidings:

> Paul is the incarnation of a type which is the reverse of that of the Saviour; he is the genius in hatred, in the standpoint of hatred, and

> in the relentless logic of hatred. And alas what did this dysevangelist not sacrifice to his hatred! Above all the Saviour himself: he nailed him to *his cross*. Christ's life, his example, his doctrine and death, the sense and the right of the gospel – not a vestige of all this was left, once this forger, prompted by his hatred, had understood it only that which could serve his purpose.[179]

He claimed that:

> The very word "Christianity" is a misunderstanding, – truth to tell, there never was more than one Christian, and he died on the Cross. The "gospel" *died* on the Cross. That which thenceforward was called "gospel" was the reverse of that "gospel" that Christ had lived: it was "evil tiding," a *dysevangel.*[180]

G. Bernard Shaw argued that:

> Paul succeeded in stealing the image of Christ crucified for the figure-head of his Salvationist vessel, with its Adam posing as the natural man, its doctrine of original sin, and its damnation avoidable only by faith in the sacrifice of the cross. In fact, no sooner had Jesus knocked over the dragon of superstition than Paul boldly set it on legs again in the name of Jesus.[181]

He concluded that, "Now it is evident that two religions having such contrary effects on mankind should not be confused as they are under a common name. There is not one word of Pauline Christianity in the characteristic utterances of Jesus."[182] In fact, "There has really never been a more monstrous imposition perpetrated than the imposition of the limitations of Paul's soul upon the soul of Jesus."[183] De Lagard, the champion of a "German religion" and "national church" traced the ironic development of Christianity back to the fact that "a man with no call whatsoever [Paul] attained to influence in the church."[184]

This negative attitude towards the apostle Paul is nothing new. Certain third century anonymous treatises such as "A False Proselyte", "Messenger of Satan" or "Persecutor of Faith" are enough to show the sense of negativity harbored by some Jewish-Christian opponents of Paul. G. Bornkamm has demonstrated that

> even in his own lifetime his opponents considered him as apostle without legitimation and a perverter of the Christian Gospel. In the subsequent history of the early church, too, there were two very different judgments. For a considerable period he continued to be sternly rejected by Jewish Christians as antagonistic to Peter and James the brother of the Lord; in these circles people did not even stop short of ranking him with Simon Magus, the chief of heretics (Pseudo-Clementine)...Even when, as in Acts, he was hailed as a great missionary or, as in the Pastorals, an attempt was made to preserve his teaching, and when in other parts of early Christian literature voices were raised in his honor, the lines along which theology evolved were different from his.[185]

Since the last century, polemics against the apostle have been observed in the writings of many critical Protestant researchers who, pointing to the wide gulf that existed between the historical Jesus and the Pauline post Easter Lord Jesus Christ, maintain that the Jesus of history must be understood in a Jewish monotheistic context. Further, the original Jesus message was changed into a religion of redemption, a strange mixture of some Judaic thought patterns amalgamated with Oriental polytheistic myths and views as mainly assimilated and transmitted by the Hellenistic mystery religions. These conclusions led many scholars to the oft-repeated slogan: "Back to the historical Jesus" or "Jesus, not Paul".

After the Second World War "Jesus, not Paul" became a virtual slogan in debates held between Christians and Jews. This transition enabled many educated Jews to claim Jesus as their own, whilst laying the blame for the gulf that existed between first and second century Judaism and orthodox Christianity at the doorstep of Paul. Martin Buber's *Two Types of Faith*,[186] Leo Baeck's *Romantic Religion*[187] and H. J. Schoeps' *Paul, The Theology of the Apostle in the Light of Jewish Religious History*[188] are examples of this trend. These scholars have argued that Paul was simultaneously a Jew and a Hellenist but that his

Jewish and Hellenistic identities were transformed by his Christian experience, explaining why he looks so different to Jewish and Hellenistic thought patterns in his epistles.

With the rise of the academic discipline of "comparative religion" or "the history of religions", emphasis was laid upon the religious experience of Paul instead of his theology. Certain parallels were observed between the language of Paul and that of the mystery cults and also between the sacramental practices in his churches and the rituals of the mysteries. Adolf Deissmann's illustration of caches of papyrus documents existing at the time of earliest Christianity has shown that Paul was not that much of a theologian as much as he was rather a representative of popular piety. Equally important was the discovery or recovery of the Dead Sea Scrolls and other early Christian and Jewish *apocalypses,* a number of books advocating the end of the present world and giving a mythological description of the messianic age or the kingdom of God at hand. Albert Schweitzer seized upon this framework of apocalyptic ideology to interpret Paul arguing that:

> Instead of the untenable notion that Paul had combined eschatological and Hellenistic ways of thinking we must now consider either a purely eschatological or a purely Hellenistic explanation of his teaching. I take the former alternative throughout. It assumes the complete agreement of the teaching of Paul with that of Jesus. The Hellenization of Christianity does not come in with Paul, but only after him.[189]

In this way Schweitzer breaks with the tradition of Reitzenstein, Bousset, Baur, Harnack and others who gave either Hellenistic or Jewish-Hellenistic interpretations to Paul. He contends that

> the conviction that through the death and resurrection of Jesus the proximate coming of the Messianic Kingdom with Jesus as its ruler was assured. It was this elementary teaching which formed the burden of the discourse when he journeyed as a missionary from place to place. To it he constantly recurs in his Letters. With this therefore, the exposition of Paulinism must logically begin. [190]

It was R. Bultmann's view of Paul which dominated the discipline in the 1950s and 1960s. Bultmann asserted that:

> The mythology of the New Testament is in essence that of Jewish apocalyptic and the Gnostic redemption myths. A common feature of them both is their basic dualism, according to which the present world and its human inhabitants are under the control of demoniac, satanic powers, and stand in need of redemption.[191]

Man alone cannot achieve redemption. "At the very point where man can do nothing, God steps in and acts – indeed he has acted already – on man's behalf."[192] This is what Paul's mysticism has emphasized:

> The Pauline catalogue of the fruits of the Spirit ("love, joy, peace, long-suffering, kindness, goodness, faithfulness, temperance", Gal. 5. 22) shows how faith, by detaching man from the world, makes him capable of fellowship in community. Now that he is delivered from anxiety and from the frustration which comes from clinging to the tangible realities of the visible world, man is free to enjoy fellowship with others.[193]

J. K. Riches observes that Bultmann's view of Paul was attractive as:

> Paul emerges not as the purveyor of arcane, pre-scientific myths, but as the father of a rich tradition of spirituality, including among its representatives Augustine (353–430), Luther, Pascal (1623–1662) and Kierkegaard, which charts and illumines the inwardness of men's and women's existence under God.[194]

Bultmann tried to give a Pauline reading of John to show that both were the apostles of a Christian inwardness (spirituality) that was effected by the kerygma or preaching of Christ, the Word. Though E. Kasemann, E. P. Sanders and others have differed with him over a number of issues their appraisals of Paul are quite favorable like those of Bultmann.

Regardless of these conjectures however, it is well to note that to be the herald of such a dramatic shift in emphasis, replacing God with the person of Jesus Christ no less, even the mystical as opposed to theological Paul was either directly misleading or being misunderstood by later generations. The Jesus of the Gospels, especially the Synoptic Gospels, is far removed from the Jesus of the Pauline epistles. The Gospel Jesus is a law observant Jewish reformer who focuses upon the twin principles of loving God and loving one's neighbor. He is a solace to the less fortunate, down trodden and oppressed people of his society. Unjust oppressors, usurpers, and the wealthy have no place in his kingdom. His world is divided into two main categories: good and evil. The good and the righteous, are not under the influence of Satan, but the people of God, children of the Most High. Salvation is contingent upon following the commandments of God and doing good deeds. When we come to the Pauline corpus however, a different man is depicted and the entire focus of his message changes with emphasis being placed instead on salvation through grace and redemption. The Pauline world is also classified into two categories: the redeemed and the condemned. The world is under the influence of Satan and destined to destruction except for those who believe in Christ, the risen Lord, and attain redemption through his atoning death. Pauline epistles introduce concepts such as original sin, salvation through grace and redemption, predestination and the supra-terrestrial spiritual existence of Jesus. Thus the Jesus of the Gospels is a very different figure to the one portrayed by Paul, including his spiritual community and powers. Even the Jesus who preaches through Paul's supposed sermons in Acts is very different to the one depicted in his epistles. This fact has led some New Testament scholars to theorize that the Acts of Paul is a later invention. Whether one accepts Paul as a cunning perverter or a sincere mystic, a creative follower of the essential teachings of Jesus or an introducer of Hellenistic or Gnostic inventions into Christianity, his role remains significant without doubt, for he was one of the determining factors if not the architect of the radical change which so alienated classical Christianity from the historical Jesus. The New Testament is the sole source of Christian understandings concerning Jesus and his mission, yet almost two thirds of it consists importantly of Pauline epistles as well as his supposed disciple Luke's Gospel and the Acts. The early church, especially in the gentile world, was heavily influenced by the Pauline faction, as was predominantly also it is worth noting, the most influential Church at Rome, which was significant in defining orthodoxy and then directing the later theological developments within Orthodox Christianity. This explains the reason why orthodoxy and Pauline Christianity are in fact two sides of the same coin, a reality which has led many modern New Testament scholars to disagree with the nineteenth century liberal interpretation and portrayal of Paul; the latter maintaining there clearly exists a sharp distinction and wide gap between the teachings of Jesus and those of Paul with the former failing to see it.

Scholars like J. G. Machen argue that Jesus' intimate friends and original disciples did not regard Paul as an innovator. They did not see Paul's emphasis upon the person of Christ and his insistence upon emancipation from the yoke of law as perversions from the original message of Jesus. This being the essence of the original Gospel message. Machen contends that if the Gospels are "trustworthy, then it will probably be admitted that Paul was a true disciple of Jesus. For the Gospels, taken as a whole, present a Jesus like in essential to that divine Lord who was sum and substance of the life of Paul."[195] We have already discussed the difficulties involved in accepting the Gospels as trustworthy and historically authentic documents giving us an accurate picture of the historical Jesus, as well as Paul's strange silence concerning the historical settings peculiar to the Gospel material. As discussed the idea of the Gospels portraying Jesus as divine and God in the traditional sense is again debatable. Any subjective reading of the Gospels, that is through the lense of divinity with preconceived notions and presuppositions concerning the divine, will yield passages that might support the Pauline understanding of Jesus as Lord. Any objective study of the Gospels however may oppose it. So discussion can be both subjective and objective meaning that the appraisal of Paul rests upon it would seem the inclination and disposition of the appraiser, dictated by one's taste and standpoint with regards to the Gospels and one's understanding of Paul's theology. All depends largely upon how one approaches the Gospel materials and how one interprets them – not an easy task!

The positive appraisal of Paul owes its success partly to the failures and disappointments faced by modern scholars in the field of study concerning the "Historical Jesus." Initially the "Rediscovery of the Historical Jesus" movement gathered great momentum, lasting for quite some time before eventually conceding defeat baffled by a jungle of diverse interpretations and conflicting portraits of Jesus. The remarks of Professor R. H. Lightfoot, British representative of Form Criticism, are a classical reflection of the outcome:

> It seems, then, that the form of the earthly no less of the heavenly Christ is for the most part hidden from us....And perhaps the more we ponder the matter, the more clearly we shall understand the reason for it, and therefore shall not wish it otherwise. For probably we are as little prepared for the one as for the other.[196]

The reason, to quote Edwyn Bevan, could be that:

> As a figure calculated to inspire men to heroic acts of self-sacrifice, it may be doubted whether the figure of Jesus, if detached from what Christians have believed about Him, is adequate. There are sayings which bid men give up everything for the Kingdom of Heaven's sake, but His own life, unless what Christians have believed is true, does not offer any single example of self-sacrifice....There is the Cross. Yes, but apart from the belief of the Church, it must be exceedingly doubtful whether Jesus incurred the suffering of the Cross voluntarily, with prevision of the destiny to which His action was leading.[197]

Aside from the New Testament (which itself is a result of Kerygma and not of history) we have no independent source detailing an account of the historical Jesus. The gospels are not the biographies of Jesus in the strict sense of the term, and were neither authorized by him nor cover the entire span of his life. Indeed, they barely deal with a few weeks of his presumed activity and this mostly in legendary and mythical form. Neither do the gospels present a systematic, objective, progressive or developmental account of Jesus' life. They are highly selective, follow a loose chronological framework, and focus resolutely on the theological significance and moralizing anthology of Jesus' supposed sayings and purported deeds. The gospel writers are faith driven preachers with an axe to grind and not dispassionate compilers of Jesus' biography. The gospel of John makes this fact abundantly clear (20:30–31). So, the gospels are neither historical biographies nor reliable narrations of the incidents they report. What they are is good news which is precisely what the word "gospel" means. So, according to Karl Barth,

> it is impossible from the study of the Gospels (which were never meant for such a purpose) to discover what Jesus was like as a human personality; and because, even if we could discover it, the result would be disappointing to those who expected to find a revelation there, since only a 'divine incognito', a veiling of God, was present in the human life of Jesus.[198]

Consequently, the attempts made to discover the historical Jesus and his message came to almost nothing. Christian scholarship resorted back to the Jesus of theology and interpreted the Christ statements of the New Testament through this lense. Martin Kahler stood at the beginning of the new movement; he brought to German Protestant theology the recognition that

> the Christian faith is related to Jesus of Nazareth as he was preached in the apostolic proclamation as the crucified and the risen one. The message of the apostles is the proclamation of a *kerygma* for which they have been commissioned by the appearances of the risen one....The reminiscences of the Jesus of history were preserved, shaped and interpreted within the framework of the proclamation of the risen one and this interpretation is the right and legitimate one for the Christian faith. The pendulum has now swung in the opposite direction: whereas the slogan used to be 'the pure Jesus of history', it is now 'the pure Christ of faith'.[199]

Bultmann adopted Kahler's approach and took it to its natural height. We have already seen in this chapter how Bultmann used the

"Christ myth" of the New Testament to formulate a Christian self-understanding by means of "existential interpretation". His existential approach effectively bracketed off the problematic historical Jesus from that of Christian theology and the latter was made an independent field completely divorced from the historical endeavors. The earthly Jesus was declared as identical to the exalted risen Lord and the Christian faith was assessed as the merger of the two constituent elements: the earthly and the heavenly.

This position is quite paradoxical and in a sense contradictory. It does not resolve the question of how much Christianity (in its traditional garb) is a human product and how much the religion manifestly preached by Jesus himself, or how much it is based on later Christian responses to the Jesus event. Either way the question of gospel authenticity and logical proof still remain, throwing into doubt the viability of any information contained therein. It is quite a herculean task to construct an entire faith based upon the premise of a feeble man being God and, in large part, the flimsy and subjective foundations of the Easter death and resurrection experience. Jesus was resurrected by God, as many other biblical figures had been raised in the presence of eyewitnesses (note as mentioned earlier there are no eyewitnesses for Jesus' resurrection). Jesus' resurrection and later appearances are not sufficient grounds to make the case that he was God or the second person of divinity. So what Christians believe and what actually took place in terms of the historical as opposed to theological Christ may be poles apart. However, despite its limitations, this approach has been adopted by a majority of English theologians, as H. Conzelmann observes:

> They thus reserve for themselves the possibility of drawing a continuous line from Jesus' understanding of himself to the faith of the community. Easter is no way ignored, but the content of the Easter faith, and with it the basic christological terms and titles, is traced back to Jesus' own teaching. The theology of the community appears as the working out of the legacy of the Risen Christ on the basis of his appearance....[200]

The entire Jesus event is therefore interpreted in light of his supposed incarnation and resurrection. Is this human imposition? Many English theologians have focused largely upon the Nicene and Chalcedonian interpretations of the Jesus event especially as understood by their original authors, the ancient Church Fathers. It is sufficient in this regard to quote A. M. Ramsey who observes that, "The theology of the Apostles sprang ... not from their own theorizing, but from certain historical events which led them to beliefs far removed from their own preconceived notions. The most significant of the events was the Resurrection."[201] Therefore, to Ramsey:

> The Resurrection is the true starting-place for the study of the making and meaning of the New Testament .... Jesus Christ had, it is true, taught and done great things: but He did not allow the disciples to rest in these things. He led them on to paradox, perplexity and darkness; and there he left them.... But His Resurrection threw its own light backwards upon the death and the ministry that went before; it illuminated the paradoxes and disclosed the unity of His words and deeds. As Scott Holland said: "In the resurrection it was not only the Lord who was raised from the dead. His life on earth rose with Him; it was lifted up into its real light."[202]

Therefore Ramsey and other English theologians understand Jesus of Galilee in light of the climax of Calvary, Easter and Pentecost. They argue that all the New Testament records were made by those writers who had already acknowledged Jesus as the risen Lord, God incarnate. Therefore any understanding of Jesus other than in terms of his incarnation and resurrection is regarded as going against the original intent of the New Testament. Yet whose intent are we discussing here? The disciples' or Jesus'? The question of explaining how the disciples would know Jesus better than Jesus himself remains unanswered. It is misguided religious intent and a desperate endeavor to build Christianity upon the foundations of the perplexity and confusion of the disciples rather than the true teachings of Jesus himself.

With this swinging of the pendulum in the other direction, views about Paul were also modified to a significant extent, as discussed earlier. Even a contemporary German scholar like Hans Kung is able to argue that

> only blindness to what Jesus himself willed, lived and suffered to the very roots or to what Paul urged with elemental force, in Jewish-hellenistic terminology, moved – like Jesus – by the prospect of the imminent end of all things: only blindness to all this can conceal the fact that the call "Back to Jesus" runs right through the Pauline letters and frustrates all attempts to turn the message into Jewish or Hellenistic ideology.[203]

Paul, according to Kung, spiritualized Jesus Christ. "It is not a question of another Jesus Christ but of a fundamentally changed relationship with him."[204]

Even amidst these changed circumstances and positive views of Paul the old and central theme of liberal theology can still be seen echoing in many modern scholars. Meaning that the theme of the wide gulf that exists between the Jesus of history and the Jesus of dogma is still being played out. The blame is now shifted from Paul to the later Church Fathers and Councils. For instance, K. Armstrong writes: "There has been much speculation about the exact nature of Jesus' mission. Very few of his actual words seem to have been recorded in the Gospels, and much of their material has been affected by later developments in the churches that were founded by St. Paul after his death."[205] To Armstrong Paul was too Jewish to call Jesus God. It was Paul's subjective and mystical experience that in a way forced Paul to describe Jesus in terms that were applied by some of his contemporaries to describe a god or a heavenly figure. Paul never called Jesus "God". He instead called him "the Son of God" in its reverential Jewish sense. Paul

> certainly did not believe that Jesus had been the incarnation of God Himself: he had simply possessed God's "powers" and "Spirit," which manifested God's activity on earth and were not to be identified with the inaccessible divine essence. Not surprisingly, in the Gentile world the new Christians did not always retain the sense of these subtle distinctions, so that eventually a

> man who had stressed his weak, mortal humanity was believed to have been divine.[206]

Armstrong further argues:

> After his [Jesus] death, his followers decided that Jesus had been divine. This did not happen immediately... the doctrine that Jesus had been God in human form was not finalized until the fourth century. The development of Christian belief in the Incarnation was a gradual, complex process. Jesus himself certainly never claimed to be God.[207]

R. A. Norris gives a somewhat similar account of the situation:

> It may well be the case that the earliest Christology simply proclaimed Jesus as the human being who had been marked out by the resurrection as the coming Messiah, that is, as the one through whom God would finally set things right. In such a Christology, the title "Son of God" would have referred not to any quality of divinity but to the fact that Jesus was called and set apart for a certain function in God's purposes. In fact, however, this way of understanding Jesus was generally supplanted as Christianity spread among Greek-speaking peoples in the Mediterranean world.[208]

Therefore, it is safe to argue that discussions regarding Paul, his mysticism, and theology, and also the role of the first Christians and evangelists in determining the direction of Christianity, all have undergone several changes in course in the past century. But the fundamental questions regarding the role of the historical Jesus in the outcome, of the significance of Paul and the Church in steering the later theological developments, and the relationship of later christological dogmas with the original message of Jesus, all remain by and large unanswered and so unresolved.

The dilemma of Christian thought is in essence that it wants to exalt Jesus to a level of pure divinity equal to God Almighty and to secure salvation through his redeeming death whilst, the Jesus of history and the Gospels dodges any such endeavor. In addition, Christian scholars and theologians want to maintain a transcendental monotheistic conception of God yet this is antithetical to the doctrines of incarnation and trinity. The entire history of Christian thought has been one of a tense struggle between these two contradictory tendencies. Of significance is the fact that the Jesus of history and the Gospels can survive the demise of incarnation and triune notions of his divinity whilst the Jesus of theology is doomed without them. Historical Christianity has paid a high price for establishing a metaphysical / romantic relationship with the Jesus of dogma – mostly at the expense of suspending logic and freedom. Logic and reason dictate that the historical Jesus was too much of a human being to serve as the atoning factor for humanity's sins and the Christ of faith and tradition too lofty a figure to be comprehended or explained by convoluted or simplistic logic and scriptural passages. Indeed, the Church has only been able to maintain the artifice of a Christ of faith theology by recourse to some extremely, if not extraordinary, artificial methods, self-contradictory presuppositions, and illogical inferences. The fundamental questions concerning the relationship of the historical Jesus with regards to the Logos, with God Almighty and the nature of Godhead, remain the same and will forever shadow the faith unless dealt with. Whenever efforts have been made to answer these questions however, the answers suggested have not been to the satisfaction of a great majority of the scholars in the field. None can deny the difficulties, doubts, and uncertainties involved in the issue, and whilst by no means have all the questions been answered with certainty, modern research has at least afforded us a better understanding and appreciation of the difficulties involved.

In addition, there are numerous developments in modern thought concerning Christology and Jesus' divinity which, to Albert C. Knudson, "make inevitable a revision of the traditional Christology. They call for a more historical, a more empirical, a more anthropocentric, a more ethical, a more personalistic approach to the problem. This is evident from the history of Christological thought during the past century."[209] Knudson summarizes the specific changes in the main three areas. Firstly, that Jesus was human not only in that he possessed a human soul, spirit and body, but in the sense that his personal ego and center was human. "This does not exclude his divinity, but it does mean the relinquishment of traditional theory that the human nature of Jesus was impersonal and that the ego or personal center of his being was constituted by the eternal Logos."[210] This can be seen even in the works of conservative theologians such as D. M. Baillie and careful ones like Mackintosh. The fifth century Cyril of Alexandria's familiar phrase, "the impersonal humanity of Christ" looks like 'Docetism' to Baillie and he recognizes that "few theologians now would defend the phrase or would hesitate to speak of Jesus as a man, a human person."[211] According to H. R. Mackintosh: "If we are not to trust our intuitive perception that the Christ we read of in the Gospels is an individual man, it is hard to say what perception could be trusted."[212]

Secondly, Jesus was unique in his sheer dependence upon the divine will and in his endowment with the Divine Spirit and not due to the complete union or fusion of the divine and human nature within him. Thirdly,

> divinity is to be ascribed to Jesus, not because he made this claim for himself, nor because he was possessed of omniscience and omnipotence, but because of his unique consciousness of oneness with God and because of his creative and redemptive agency in the founding of the kingdom of God.[213]

N. T. Wright does not "think that Jesus thought he was identified with the being that most people in our culture think is denoted by the word *god*."[214] To Wright high Christology is a form of docetism. Western orthodoxy at large and modern evangelicalism in particular has had too "long an overly lofty and detached view of God."[215] To Wright it is not the nature or divinity but the vocation that makes Jesus divine. He concludes saying that, "After twenty years of serious historical-Jesus study I still say the Christian creeds *ex animo*, but I now mean something very different by them, not least by the word *God* itself. The portrait has been redrawn."[216] How different is this approach from traditional claims that Charles Gore represented a few years ago, arguing that, "If we wish to account for the unique position which Jesus

Christ has held in religion it is only necessary to examine the claim which he is represented to have made for Himself in the earliest records which we possess."[217]

With these significant changes, and with especially the new emphasis on the humanity of Jesus many limitations came to be placed on his divine nature. The divinity of Jesus, according to many modern scholars, is grounded in the divine will rather than the divine nature, and in many modern works is explained as a heightened human experience rather than a divine consciousness alien to normal humanity. Jesus' divinity, in other words, was not his own self-consciousness about himself but rather a later development within the Church. It was the creative conception of the Church about what Jesus was and should have meant to his followers and to the world. The Church has retrospectively projected onto the historical Jesus the nature of his spiritual and moral significance, as it has regarded this, and affirmed with Paul and others that God was incarnated in him. Alfred Loisy once ironically remarked that, "Jesus proclaimed the Kingdom of God, but it was the Church that came."[218] This unique interpretation of the person of Jesus might have been relevant to a society where Neo Platonism and other Greek philosophies were a commonplace. These interpretations have become obsolete in modern societies and must be revised with the contention that these traditional Christological ideas are "obsolete even before we begin to revise them. A cobbler will no doubt be able to mend my shoes before I realize that there is anything wrong with them, but that does not mean to say that I cannot realize that they are letting the water in, even before I take them to him for repair."[219]

Moreover, the ancient Greek and Christian understanding of the term "*persona*" or "personality" has undergone significant changes in modern times. Karl Barth, for instance, disagrees with Boethius' (sixth century) classical definition that continued to be influential in the Middle Ages: *"naturae rationabilis individua substantia"* which really means an individual rational being. Quoting Aquinas' consciousness of the difficulties involved in the definition, Barth goes on to show how the modern concept of personality adds the attributes of "*self-consciousness*". The traditional doctrine of trinity (three Persons) or the Social Trinity would then be tantamount to tritheism as it would mean three distinct individuals and centers of consciousness, three self-conscious personal beings. Therefore Barth suggests dropping the term "three Persons" asserting:

> The ancient concept of Person, which is the only one in question here, had today become obsolete....Wherever ancient dogmatics, or Catholic dogmatics even today, speaks of "Person", we prefer to call Father, Son, and Holy Spirit in God the three individual modes of existence of the one God, consisting in their mutual relationship.[220]

Such an understanding of the term person and explanation of the concept of Trinity utterly demolishes the traditional Christian doctrine of the person of Christ and places significant limitations upon Jesus' divinity in the traditional sense. The popular traditional interpretations of Trinity would be tantamount to tritheism rather than monotheism. This is why Barth insists that, "It is to the one single essence of God, which is not to be tripled by the doctrine of the Trinity, but emphatically to be recognized in its unity, that there also belongs what we call today the "personality" of God."[221]

On the other hand Clement C. J. Webb does not see any radical change in the usage of the term "person" in modern times:

> The general history of the word Person with its derivatives in philosophical terminology may be said to have moved throughout on lines determined for it by the process whose result is summed up in the Boethian definition of *persona*. Within these lines there has been a continual oscillation... of independent and fundamentally unchangeable individuality, or the thought of social relationship and voluntary activity, suggested by the Latin word *persona*, has been uppermost.[222]

Webb notes three specific aspects of the term "personality" and labels them "as *incommunicability*, *self-consciousness*, and *will* respectively."[223] He argues that the Orthodox Church spoke of personality in God rather than the personality of God. It conceived of

God as comprising a unity of three personalities and not one personality. Consequently, to Webb the Divine Personality should be conceived as analogous to the collective personality of a state or nation. This is different from Barth's view and close to the Cappadocian fathers' analogy of three distinctive individual men alongside each other. This "ultra Cappadocian" movement, as Baillie names it, in modern Trinitarian thought has been influential in Anglican circles. Leonard Hodgson's *The Doctrine of the Trinity,* and F. D. Maurice are good examples of this influence. The central theme of this school is the "social" interpretation of the Trinity, and phrases such as "the social life of the Blessed Trinity" are frequently observed amongst its writers. The main contrast between Barthian interpretations and this school is that Barth speaks of one Person in three modes of existence while the other prefers to speak of three independent Persons in a kind of social unity. This "internal constitutive unity", as Hodgson says, or the unity in glory, as Moltmann argues, allows the possibility of three separate persons, i.e. centers of consciousness, but unites them in love.[224] On the other hand, Karl Rahner prefers "Sabellian Modalism" to what he calls the "vulgar tritheism" of Social Trinities. Gerald O'Collins and Mario Farrugia observe that "the inner life of the Trinity is so mysterious that any analogy will almost certainly run the risk of some error. It is better to edge towards a modalism that preserves monotheism than fall into vulgar tritheism."[225]

The fact of the matter is that like ancient Christian Fathers, as we shall shortly see, none of these schools and conservative theological approaches seem able to solve the central problem of Christian theology, and the one from which we started: the relationship of Jesus Christ's person with the transcendent, indivisible, impassable, unique, eternal and One God. These may be good speculative works, or guesses, but are definitely not satisfactory solutions. Whether one accepts the ultra Cappadocian movement's social Trinity or Barth's union Trinity one is still left unable to detach the Trinity from corporealism and concrete anthropomorphism. The incarnation of God in the human figure of Christ, whether in one mode of His existence or through one person of His Godhead, are crystal clear cases of corporealism. The difficulty lies in the insistence that traditional Christianity almost always places upon the person of Christ as being divine, the Second Person of the Trinity, and equal in all respects to God whilst simultaneously claiming Jesus' humanity as being equal in almost all respects (excepting sin) with mankind. This position is paradoxical, contradictory and defies logic. A fundamental tenet of Christianity, it nevertheless has little, if any, appeal to modern rational thought and as such is intelligible to modern man who scrutinizes particulars with rigorous criteria. Many modern Christian scholars and theologians do not seem ready to deny or denounce traditional claims but are yet at a loss as to how to prove their validity or even reasonability to the contemporary mind. Forced to resort to circular argument, they make claims without logically substantiating them and in doing so repeating, in many cases, opinions either discussed in early centuries or discarded as heretical. In neither case can the charges of anthropomorphism, corporealism and, in certain cases tritheism, be denied.

The source of this paradox is the New Testament. To understand the difficulties involved we need to study the New Testament Christological statements and how their themes were developed by the Church Fathers.

Christology and the New Testament

The central question "What think ye of Christ?" has been answered in a number of different ways by New Testament writers. He is referred to as a prophet: "And King Herod heard of him...and he said, That John the Baptist was risen from the dead... Others said, that it is Elias. And others said, that it is the prophet, or one of the prophets" (Mark 6:14–15). Matthew clearly names Jesus as the prophet: "And when he was to come into Jerusalem, all the city was moved, saying, who is this? And the multitude said, this is Jesus the prophet of Nazareth of Galilee" (Matthew 20:10–11, see also Acts 3:22, 7:37). In view of passages like these many scholars maintain that Jesus was a Jewish prophet, "a first-century apocalyptic prophet who expected the imminent end of his" (world).[226] Like Amos and Hosea, Jesus struggled to reform the Jewish religion and its tradition; he engaged with contemporary Judaism and its leaders, leveled fierce attacks against the Temple authorities and their selfish exploitation, and railed against the scribes and the Pharisees.

And like the Israelite prophets before him he suffered the consequences, his fate being sealed at the hands of the Roman authorities. It was only after his death that some of his enthusiastic followers exalted him, acclaiming the prophet of Galilee to be the Messiah, the Son of God and God's Anointed One. Shirley Jackson Case argues that Jesus was a prophet of God who

> lived in a relation to God that was essentially a mystical experience. But it was not the type of mysticism that evaporated in an orgy of emotions... On the contrary, the divine seizure was for the sake of increasing righteousness in the world and contributing to human welfare. Its end was to be the establishment of the Kingdom.[227]

Morton Scott Enslin argues that Jesus as the Prophet of Galilee fits very well into the grand scheme of the Gospels:

> As soon as this view of Jesus – a prophet sent from God – is recognized as the understanding of his first followers, who accepted wholeheartedly his own claim, many other elements in the gospel pages fall into place. There is a constant reference to his possession of a spirit which has come upon him and possessed him... the point of significance is that there would seem no attempt by anyone to deny that in the strictest and most literal sense of the word he was "inspired" by a spirit not his own.[228]

So Jesus who was originally a prophet, was raised and exalted to God's right hand. Joachim Jeremias observes that the

> unanimous verdict on him was that he was a prophet. There was a constant echo to this effect among the people (Mark 6.15 par.; 8.28 par.; Matt. 21.11, 46; Luke 7.16; John 4.19; 6.14; 7.40, 52; 9.17) and even – though coupled with skepticism – in Pharisaic circles (Luke 7.39; Mark 8.11 par.). According to Luke 24.19, Jesus' disciples, too, saw him as a prophet. Finally, it was as a false prophet that Jesus was arrested and accused. This is clear from the account of the mockery under Jewish confinement.[229]

He further argues that, "The tradition in which Jesus appears a prophet and bearer of the spirit must be an old one, as it cannot be traced back to the early church. Where possible, the earliest church avoided 'prophet' as a christological title, because it felt it to be inadequate."[230]

Geza Vermes maintains that Jesus was aware of his role as a prophet. Vermes argues that it was "not merely because of any dogmatic inadequacy, that the title ceased altogether to be applied to Jesus".[231] One of the reasons according to Vermes being that

> from the middle of the first century AD to the end of the first revolt these self-proclaimed wonder-workers found a ready following among the simple victims of the revolutionary activities of the Zealots. But as the promises remained unfulfilled and the miracles failed to materialize, and as the sarcasm and antipathy of their political opponents stripped the pretenders of their repute, the term 'prophet' applied to an individual between the years AD 50 and 70 not surprisingly acquired distinctly pejorative overtones in the bourgeois and aristocratic idiom of Pharisees and Sadducees.[232]

Vermes quotes many New Testament verses like Mark 6:15, 8:28, 14:65, Matthew 16:14, 21:11, 21:46, 26:68, Luke 7:39, 9:8, 9:19, 13:33, 24:19 etc. to conclude that, "No expert would deny that [the] Gospels portray Jesus as wearing the mantle of a prophet".[233] He further argues that according to many sayings reported in the Synoptic Gospels Jesus "not only thought of himself as a prophet, but also described to his prophetic destiny every unpleasantness that was to happen to him."[234] To Vermes,

> the belief professed by his contemporaries that Jesus was a charismatic prophet rings so authentic, especially in the light of Honi-Hanina cycle of traditions, that the correct historical question is not whether such an undogmatic Galilean concept was in vogue, but rather how, and under what influence, it was ever given an eschatological twist.[235]

The emphasis on the prophetic nature of Jesus' mission has increasingly been the focus of recent works, especially by scholars who study and locate Jesus against his Jewish background. M. Hengel, G. Theissen, G. Vermes, Bruce Chilton, E. P. Sanders and John Hick are just a few examples. E. P. Sanders, for instance, contends that certain unassailable facts about Jesus' life and mission locate him firmly within Jewish restoration eschatology. The fact that he was baptized by John the Baptist, was a Galilean preacher and healer who confined his activity to Israel, and engaged in controversy about the temple, called twelve disciples, and aroused substantial opposition among the Jewish people, all of these facts place him in the context of Jewish hopes for the restoration of the nation of Israel. Therefore, Sanders concludes, "Jesus saw himself as God's last messenger before the establishment of the kingdom."[236] John Hick contends that "Jesus' intense God-consciousness was of course inevitably structured in terms of the religious ideas of his own culture. The basic concept with which to understand his own existence in relation to God was that of prophet."[237]

The depiction of Jesus as a prophet is in line with many New Testament statements as well as Jewish prophetic history. Jesus was sent by God to reform the lost sheep of Israel and to proclaim the Kingdom of God. This portrayal of Jesus saves Christianity from the countless challenges of tritheism, corporealism and anthropomorphism constantly besieging it. It also provides humanity with a true model of socio-political reformation and spirituality. Yet for all that, the majority of conservative Christian scholars disagree with this description of Jesus. For instance, Charles Gore, a conservative Bishop who edited *Lux Mundi* in 1890, argued that "to represent our Lord only as a good man conscious of a message from God, like one of the Prophets or John the Baptist, is to do violence not to one Gospel only or to single passages in various Gospels, but to the general tenour of the Gospels as a whole."[238]

Others like H. Conzelmann, O. Cullmann, F. Hahn and R. H. Fuller have discussed the advantages and disadvantages of this title and seem to agree as to its inadequacy, while V. Taylor has qualified it as christologically "abortive".[239]

In conclusion, it is pertinent to quote Grillmeier who rightly observes:

The designation of Jesus as 'prophet' was only short-lived; it had a reference to Deut. 18.15, 18 and served to explain Jesus' mission to Jewish audiences (Acts 3.22; 7.37; John 6.14; 7.40). And even if the Fathers are right later in emphasizing that the transcendence of Christ is something more than a heightened prophetical office, this title nevertheless embraces his mission as revealer of the Father and teacher of men.[240]

Angel Christology

As early as the Synoptic Gospels, Christ is depicted as an angelic prince. "Whosoever therefore shall be ashamed of me and of my words in this adulterous and sinful generation; of him also shall the Son of man be ashamed, when he cometh in the glory of his Father with the holy angels" (Mark 8:38; also Matthew 13:41 ff; Mark 13:26 ff, 1:13; Luke 22:43; 1 Thessalonians 4:16). Grillmeier remarks:

One of the attempts of the primitive Christian period to express the transcendence of Christ is the so-called 'angel-christology' or the designation *Christos angelos*. It is so significant that attempts have been made to prove that it was the original christology, at least in Jewish-Christian circles. Jesus, it is held, was understood as an angel in the strict sense i.e. as a heavenly creature sent by God into the world. With the condemnation of Arianism this legitimate and original conception was stamped as heresy. It had to give place to the strict doctrine of two natures.[241]

M. Werner argues that the oft-quoted title Son of Man would be best interpreted if we assume "that this Messiah belonged to the (highest) celestial realm of the angels. This view is expressly confirmed by the sources."[242] He further argues that Paul's usage of the title *Kyrios* does not negate the fact. In Late Judaism and primitive Christianity the angels were invoked as *Kyrios*. Werner notes:

The history of the Primitive Christian doctrine of Christ as a high angelic being pursued its way in the post-apostolic period through successive stages. At first the very view gradually subsided of its

> own accord and became problematical. Then, already profoundly shaken within, it had to endure finally a decisive assault during the Arian dispute of the fourth century. In this conflict it was bitterly attacked by the representatives of the new doctrine of Christ, which had emerged in the interval, and at last it was proscribed and suppressed as erroneous doctrine.[243]

Grillmeier observes that, "We may point out the over-estimation of the *Christo angelos* idea, but within limits it is not to be denied as a historical fact. The sources testify that Christ was given the name 'angel' right up until the fourth century."[244]

Messianic Christology

Long before Jesus' advent the Jews had been expecting the Messiah. Jesus was given this title. He is the Christ, the Messiah, "And he saith unto them, but whom say ye that I am? And Peter answereth and saith unto him, Thou art the Christ. And he charged them that they should tell no man of him" (Mark 8:29–30). In Matthew 16:16–18 Jesus is said to have approved the title:

> He saith unto them, But whom say ye that I am? And Simon Peter answered and said, Thou art the Christ, the Son of the living God. And Jesus answered and said unto him, Blessed art thou, Simon Bar-Jonah: for flesh and blood hath not revealed it unto thee, but my Father which is in heaven. And I say also unto thee, That thou art Peter, and upon this rock I will build my church; and the gates of hell shall not prevail against it.

In a reply to the chief priest and the scribes, Luke (22:67–69) reports Jesus to have said: "Art thou the Christ? Tell us. And he said unto them, If I tell you, you will not believe: And if I also ask you, you will not answer me, nor let me go. Hereafter shall the Son of man sit on the right hand of the power of God." It is only in Mark 14:61–62 that Jesus is reported by the evangelist to have confessed being the Christ. "Again the high priest asked him, and said unto him, Art thou the Christ, the Son of the Blessed? And Jesus said, I am: and ye shall see The Son of

Man sitting on the right hand of power, and coming in the clouds of heaven."

The early Church extensively focused upon the Messianic role of Jesus and insisted that Jesus was conscious of his Messianic identity. However, it is baffling to notice that there is only one instance in the Synoptic Gospels where Jesus seemingly affirms that he is the expected Messiah. But, the one passage that confirms his Messianic identity (Mark 14:53–65) is of a dubious nature. B. Harvie Branscomb has shown its doubtful historical dependableness.[245] The evil spirits are portrayed as recognizing him as the Messiah. The healed ones declared him so. The disciples wished to proclaim him the Messiah but Jesus repeatedly demanded silence about this role until his resurrection. (Mark 9:9). Gunther Bornkamm is astonished by this fact:

> For this is the truly amazing thing, that there is in fact not a single certain proof of Jesus' claiming for himself one of the Messianic titles which tradition has ascribed to him... nowhere does this seem to be of any importance either in his preaching of the coming of the kingdom of God, or in his endeavour to make God's will a reality to us now...[246]

The New Testament scholars differ as to whether Jesus used the title "Christ or Messiah" or whether this was placed in his mouth by later writers. Many scholars such as Branscomb, conclude that Jesus considered himself a prophet and never made any claims about his Messianic identity. His followers identified him as the Messiah after the belief in his resurrection had been established. This explains the reason for the "Messianic Secret" of the Gospel of Mark. There was nothing about the Messianic role in the original tradition. It was later assumed that Jesus somehow had imposed a degree of silence upon the original disciples so as not to disclose his Messianic secret to the public. W. Wrede's famous work *Das Messiasgeheimnis in den Evangelien*[247] is a classical example of this approach. Prior to Wrede's analysis it was thought that Jesus' command to silence, as reported by Mark, was an integral part of the historical Jesus and was meant to circumvent high political expectations of his Messiahship and a gradual revelation of his identity. Wrede's study changed those perspectives altogether. He connected this secret motif to another element in Marks Gospel, the so-called "parable theory". This trend maintained that Jesus intended his teachings to be imported only to a handful of inner circle followers and hidden from the multitudes of lay people. Mark 1:35, 3:13 depicted Jesus as fleeing the crowd, Mark 1:29, 7:17, 9:28, 10:10, 13:3–4 portray him healing and teaching only a small band of close followers. Likewise his disciples had many difficulties in understanding his parables and teachings. To Wrede all these were part of the secrecy motives. The earliest Christians, in view of Jesus' humble earthly life, thought that he did not become the Messiah until his resurrection. The Easter experience exalted the heavenly Jesus. Gradually it became a tradition that in reality he had been the Messiah already during his life. This belief resulted in the secrecy motif to eliminate the tension between the reality that Jesus became Messiah only after his death and the notion that he was already so during his earthly life. The secrecy motif was the creation of the later evangelical circles. Martine Dibelius proposed an "apologetic" interpretation of the Messianic secrecy. He argued that Mark introduced this motif to explain the historical failures and lack of universal recognition of Jesus during his lifetime as expected of the Messiah. Many modern scholars are not convinced by the secrecy theory in its entirety. They contend that if it was an official stance or Mark's original intent then why would Jesus' command to silence be ignored later in the Gospel of Mark as reported by Mark 1:45 and 7:36. Therefore H. N. Roskam asserts that, "Wrede may have given the Messianic Secret in Mark's Gospel too wide a scope."[248]

Although some aspects of the "Messianic Secret" motif of Mark's theory has been questioned by a number of scholars, the ultimate results and conclusions drawn from that motif are still being followed by many liberal scholars. For instance Roskam maintains that Jesus' injunctions to silence as reported by Mark indicate that "Jesus had no ambition to assume political power: Mark's Jesus has no intentions to make the people believe that he will re-establish a free and independent Israel, nor does he have any ambition to mobilize the masses in preparation for a revolt."[249] This is very different from the traditional understanding of the Messianic role. Frances Young contends that

> we do not have the evidence available now to speculate realistically about Jesus' so-called Messianic consciousness. (If we were to try and read between the lines we might even speculate that Jesus regarded personal claims as a Satanic temptation.) Of course it remains true that the church's christological preaching must have some continuity with, and basis in, the mission of Jesus, but its content need not to be, and probably was not, identical.[250]

Bultmann contends that Jesus did not think of himself as the Messiah.[251] Bornkamm argues that "Jesus' history was originally a non-Messianic history, which was portrayed in the light of the Messianic faith of the Church only after Easter."[252] He further argues that, "we must not allow ourselves to be misled by the fact that the Gospels themselves contain many passages which are clearly Messianic. These should be regarded first of all as the Credo of the believers, and as the theology of the early Church."[253]

The Christian tradition is replete with the claims that Jesus was the Messiah and was conscious of his Messianic identity. Gospels are quoted extensively to substantiate the claim that Jesus was the Messiah and sooner or later confessed himself to be so. This modern analysis of the Messianic Secret levels an extremely serious blow to the tenet of Christology as well as to the Gospels. The Messianic Christology is not the high Christology of divine incarnation. Genuine Messianic expectations were prevalent during the pre and post Jesus era. What Christology can be trusted if the Messianic Christology was not the original understanding of Jesus himself? What truth can there be in the Gospels if they depict Jesus as the Messiah when Jesus did not consider himself to be so? Is Christianity a tradition of Jesus or a religion about Jesus? How far is it actually Jesus and his message and how far is it human imposition or inteference? Do the actions, sayings and approvals of Jesus constitute the core of the Christian message or is the Christian faith an accumulation of later Church reactions and interpretations of what Jesus was or should have been? Were the later Church authorities more qualified to understand Jesus than Jesus himself? How can we assign divine propriety to the later Church understandings of Jesus and his earthly life?

Many scholars contend that the historical Jesus did not fit into the image of the Messiah as depicted by the Old Testament. Jesus is not the son of David as claimed in the Gospels. His mother's genealogy does not connect him to David through Solomon. Joseph the Carpenter was his foster father and not his biological one. There is no mention in the Old Testament that the Messiah would be born to a virgin. The Hebrew term in Isaiah is "*alma*" which means a "young woman" and not a "virgin" as mistranslated by many Christian translators. According to Jeremiah 33:18 the Messiah is to build the Temple in Jerusalem. In contrast to this Jesus came when the Temple was still in existence. Jesus did not establish the religious laws of the land as predicted by Jeremiah 33:15. Additionally, the historical Jesus was a suffering figure while the Messiah was supposedly a triumphant one. The Messiah was supposed to bring the exiled to their homeland as Isaiah 11:11–12, Jeremiah 23:8, 30:3 and Hosea 3:4–5 manifestly indicate. Nothing of this sort took place during Jesus' life. Many traditional Christian scholars contend that Jesus will accomplish these predictions in his second coming. However, this poses the question as to whether Jesus was a Messiah during his first coming or whether he will become a Messiah in his second coming?

Ben Witherington III, on the other hand, argues that close scrutiny reveals that there is "no unified messianic secret motif in Mark."[254] He contends that in Mark 5:19–20 Jesus tells the man possessed by the devil to, "Go home to thy friends, and tell them how great things the Lord hath done for thee..." Verse 20 makes it clear that the man did "publish in Decapolis how great things Jesus had done for him." There also occurs a sort of publicity theme in some of the healing stories such as Mark 2:12; 3:3 ff. In addition, there is also the "more puzzling issue of why Mark records the disobedience to Jesus' command to silence in 1:25–28, 43–45, and 7:36–3 if he was really trying to impose a messianic secrecy motif on his material. Are we to think Mark is simply a bad editor of his source material despite considerable evidence to the contrary?"[255] Hoskyns and Davey observe that, "The Christology lies behind the aphorisms, not ahead of them; this means that at no point is the literary or historical critic able to detect in any stratum of the synoptic materiel that a Christological interpretation has been imposed upon an un-Christological history."[256] P. Stuhlmacher contends:

> The so-called Messianic secret is not simply ... a post-Easter theological construction, and in general it had nothing to do with the attempt after easter to hide the fact that Jesus' life had proceeded unmessianically and beginning at easter had first been put in the light of Messianism. It is a question much more of a characteristic of the work of Jesus himself.[257]

Ben Witherington concludes that "Jesus saw himself as the Messiah – the *Jewish mashiach*."[258]

It is easy to claim but hard to prove that Jesus fulfilled expectations of the Jewish Messiah. The Gospels records are so overlaid with later theology and beliefs that absolute certainty about anything is impossible. One fact is certain however, that the Jesus of history does not fit into the image of the Jewish Messiah in its entirety. The convoluted and elaborate Gospel attempts of modern evangelists to impose such an image upon the earthly Jesus are unconvincing and artificial. In the name of the spiritual Kingdom of God and of moral anthology, exotic meanings are imposed upon the simple and innocent texts of the Old and New Testaments, to derive meanings which these texts never intended and do not carry if taken at face value. Whilst these spiritual contortions may satisfy those who already believe, they are inadequate to convince the skeptical or to change historical realities.

The Son of Man Christology

Jesus' most favorite and frequently used title, as the evangelists report, is the Son of Man. The great significance of this Christological title is manifest from the fact that according to the Gospels it is the only designation Jesus has reportedly applied to himself. "For the Son of man shall come in the glory of his Father with his angels; and then he shall reward every man according to his works" (Matthew 16:27). "Jesus said unto them, the Son of man shall be betrayed into the hands of men: and they shall kill him, and the third day he shall be raised again" (Matthew17:22–23). The Son of Man passages occur so frequently in the Gospels that to enumerate them all is unnecessary, suffice it to say that they occur 69 times in the first three Gospels alone and over 80 times in the Gospels as a whole; see for instance Matthew 12:8, 26:64; Mark 8:38, 13:26, 14:62; Luke 22:69.

New Testament scholars differ over the origin, meanings and significance of the title. An overwhelming majority of biblical scholars look for its origins and significance in Judaic apocalyptic literature. H. E. Todt's *The Son of Man in the Synoptic Tradition* is a typical example of this approach.[259] The heading of the first chapter of this book reads: "The transcendent sovereignty of the Son of Man in Jewish apocalyptic literature." 1 Enoch 37–71 (the Similitudes), Daniel 7, and 4 Ezra 13 are the passages frequently quoted in connection with the meanings and implications of this title.

Scholars also differ as to whether Jesus used the title for himself or whether it was put into his mouth by the church. P. Vielhauer, for instance, argues that the term "the Son of Man" was originally used as a title for Jesus by the early Palestinian communities. It signified a supernatural, apocalyptic figure. It was not Jesus but the early Christians who used this term to designate Jesus. If "Jesus used it himself at all, it was only... with reference to a figure other than himself."[260] Bultmann and Bornkamm contend that Jesus did speak of the "Son of man or *bar enasha*" but his usage of the term was different from its later usages. Actually he was referring to someone other than himself.[261] Reference has been made above all to Luke 12.8, "Also I say unto you, Whosoever shall confess me before men, him shall the Son of man also confess before the angels of God." Bornkamm argues that,

> although the historical Jesus spoke most definitely of the coming Son of man and judge of the world in the sense of the contemporary apocalyptic hope, and did so with the amazing certainty that the decisions made here with regard to his person and message would be confirmed at the last judgment, nevertheless he did not give himself the title Son of man. Also we can hardly assume that the earthly Jesus saw himself as destined to be the heavenly judge of the world.[262]

Jeremias, on the other hand, states that "when Jesus speaks in the third person he makes a distinction not between two different figures, but between his present and the future state of exaltation."[263] Wilhelm Bousset notes:

> In all our considerations we have no wish to deny the possibility that an individual Son of Man saying could have come from the lips of Jesus. But one cannot escape the impression that in the majority of these sayings we have before us the product of the theology of the early Church. That is the sure starting point for our work.[264]

Todt quotes Matthew 12:32 and Luke 12:10 to show the developing theology of the early church.[265] R. H. Fuller calls attention to a fundamental change of emphasis in the Christological outlook which has taken place between the stage of development represented by Acts 3:20–21 and Acts 2:36. He attributes this theological development to "the delay of the parousia, and the increasing experience of the Spirit's working in the church."[266] Fuller further observes:

> Jesus had declared that his own eschatological word and deed would be vindicated by the Son of Man at the end. Now his word and deed has received preliminary yet uncertain vindication by the act of God in the resurrection. The earliest church expressed this newborn conviction by identifying Jesus with the Son of man who was to come.[267]

Norman Perrin goes further by observing that "Jesus had not referred to the Son of Man at all; all the Son of Man sayings stemmed from the early church."[268] He concludes that "every single Son of Man saying is a product of the theologizing of the early church."[269] J. Hick notes:

> There was the image of the son of man of Danielic prophecy, who was to come again in clouds of glory, and there was the image of the Messiah. However, it does not seem very probable that Jesus applied either of these images, or any other titles, to himself; rather, other people came to apply them to him.[270]

Branscomb observes: "I conclude, therefore, that the series of ideas which viewed Jesus as the Son of Man to come in glory on the clouds of heaven, with the holy angels, was the theological achievement of the Palestinian Church." He further observes that

> it never appears in the Gospels in the mouths of the disciples, probably for the following reason: It was known that this view of Jesus was not entertained by the disciples during Jesus' lifetime. In the tradition this fact took the form of the oft-repeated thought that the disciples did not understand until later what Jesus was endeavoring to teach them.[271]

Acceptance of this approach has significant implications upon our understanding of Christology.

Among all the Christological titles it is the Son of Man which is traced directly back to the Jesus of history. No other title, such as Son of God, Son of David, Christ, Lord etc., holds a modicum of the secure place in the early stratum of Christianity as does the Son of Man designation. Yet if this Son of Man title as well as Christology are a later Church invention then what are we left with in Christology in terms of relating to the nature, person and role of Christ? R. Augstein candidly begs the question: "If Jesus was neither the Messiah nor the son of man nor the son of God, and if he did not even think he was any of those, what is left? ...what good could his death do?"[272]

Professor J. W. Bowker of the University of Lancaster, emphasizes on the other hand, that Jesus used this term as an alternative for the first pronoun "I" or "me" or to denote himself as a frail mortal. K. Armstrong observes that "the original Aramaic phrase (*bar nasha*) simply stressed the weakness and mortality of the human condition. If this is so, Jesus seems to have gone out of his way to emphasize that he was a frail human being who would one day suffer and die."[273] J. D. Crossan argues that

> if Jesus spoke about a son of man, his audience would not have taken the expression in either a titular or a circumlocutionary sense but, following normal and expected usage, in either a generic

> (everyone) or an indefinite (anyone) sense. He is talking, they would presume, about human beings, making claims or statements about humanity. An unchauvinistic English translation would be "the human one".[274]

This would entail that the designation Son of Man was merely a human one, not loaded with any divine or heavenly meanings but simply a reflection of the humble origins and feeble human nature of Jesus.

Such interpretation of this lofty title is too modest for some New Testament scholars, who maintain that Jesus used this term for himself in light of, and identifying himself with, the well-known Danielic Son of Man of the Old Testament and apocalyptic literature. C. F. D. Moule, for instance, states that the title Son of man "seems to have come through virtually unmodified from Jesus himself."[275] He further states that, "there is a strong case (or it seems to me) for the view that the phrase belonged originally among Jesus' own words as a reference to the vindicated human figure of Dan. 7 and as a symbol for the ultimate vindication of obedience to God's design."[276] J. Jeremias, Ben Witherington III and de Jonge also agree that the origin of this designation goes back to Jesus himself. The scholars who follow this trend differ widely over the true meanings of Daniel 7. Their views can be summarized into three main categories: (1) The figure mentioned in the Danielic vision refers to one or more angels. J. J. Collins persuasively argues this view.[277] (2) It stands for Israel, or at least for a faithful Israel, for those who endure persecution. To Casey it is a symbol of Israel's triumph.[278] (3) *Bar enash* does not represent Israel as much as it represents an individual figure who would represent Israel in the presence of Almighty God. This is the sense conveyed in the Similitude as well as in Daniel 7. B. Lindars states that the "figure of the Similitude, variously termed, as we have seen, the Righteous One, the Chosen One, or "that Son of man," is a leader of the righteous and chosen ones, i.e., the faithful Jews. Consequently he must be seen as a representative figure, embodying the expectation of the Jews that their righteousness before God will be vindicated, their enemies will be liquidated, and they will reign with God....It would be a mistake to suggest that he is in some way a corporate figure, i.e., identical with the faithful Jews. But he represents their aspirations and expectations, and so is the head of them as a group...."[279] What is true of the Similitudes is true of Daniel 7.

Hence, many scholars conclude that Jesus used the term "the Son of Man" for himself in conformity with the messianic figure envisioned in Daniel 7:13–14. B. Witherington observes:

> The proper matrix in which to interpret the Son of man material, that which provides the clues as to how Jesus himself viewed the material, is Dan. 7:13–14 and probably also the *Similitude of Enoch*. The evidence seems sufficient to conclude that because Jesus *bar enasha* implies a certain form of messianic self-understanding on his part, although it does not take the form of the popular Davidic expectation. Indeed, Mark 14:62 suggests that Jesus corrected such an interpretation of himself by referring to the Danielic Son of man. Only when he comes upon the clouds will he assume the role of world judge and, indeed, judge of the people of God.[280]

C. K. Barret believes that "the title Son of Man...does more than any other to cement the unity of the Gospel tradition. We have seen that in the background of this expression both suffering and glory play their part."[281] De Jonge concludes:

> There seems to be no reason to deny that Jesus himself did claim a particular authority, there and then and in the future; thought of himself in terms of suffering and vindication; and expressed this in the term "the Son of Man" – covertly referring to the destiny of the "one like a son of man" in Daniel.[282]

Even those scholars who disagree that the title originated with Jesus himself do agree with the thesis that its usage in the Gospels was meant to convey the aforementioned apocalyptic Danielic sense. N. Perrin, for instance writes,

> the evangelist Mark is a major figure in the creative use of Son of Man traditions in the New Testament period. To him we owe the

> general picture we have from the Gospels that "Son of Man" is Jesus' favorite self-designation and that Jesus used it to teach his disciples to understand both the true nature of his messiahship as including suffering and glory, and the true nature of Christian discipleship as the way to glory through suffering.[283]

There is one major difference between the approaches of evangelists, such as Ben Witherington, and the understanding of academicians such as Norman Perrin. Where academicians stop at the apocalyptic prophethood of Jesus, evangelists throw caution to the winds and make a huge jump, from the apocalyptic Son of Man to the divine nature and supra terrestrial being of Jesus. Their contention is that in using the Danielic Son of Man imagery Jesus was infact claiming to be God in the full sense of the term, that is, possessing everlasting dominion over his kingdom which would not pass away, and having all people, nations and men of every language serve him, a service due only to God Almighty. Thus for evangelists, Jesus by the Son of Man designation (Daniel 4:3) and the imagery of his coming on the clouds of heaven, enumerates all the characteristics of Yahweh.

Worth noting is the fact that all the Son of Man sayings in the New Testament occur in the third person, while in Revelation 1–3 we have the use of the first person for Jesus. This continuous use of the third person by Jesus indicates that these sayings were not meant "as him", that is Jesus, being the Son of Man but rather "about" the Son of Man. As it is too unnatural to view Jesus as continuously speaking about himself in the third person it would appear that the early Church retrojected its own understanding of Jesus as the Son of Man onto the lips of Jesus. We see an example of this early use of the third person in Acts 7:56 when Stephen sees the Son of Man standing on the right hand of God. Marcan sayings do not suggest that Jesus believed that he would become the Son of Man. The future sayings all refer to "coming" and not "becoming". It is quite possible that Jesus spoke of another individual as the future Son of Man but that later Church traditions identified Jesus himself to be that designation.

Assuming that Jesus is referring to a supra-terrestrial transcendent being, the apocalyptic "Son of Man" of Daniel 7:13, who has everlasting dominion over his own kingdom etc. then how can it be claimed that he was referring to himself in this figure given that these rights and predicates did not materialize in his own earthly life, which was one of suffering. The apocalyptic Son of Man is exclusively a triumphant figure while the earthly Jesus is a rejected one, and although some of the Son of Man sayings which depict a suffering figure could seem to refer to Jesus, these sayings do not refer to the Messianic figure mentioned in Daniel 7:13. Rather, the Son of Man seems least likely to refer to Jesus where it may seem to refer to the Daniel 7:13 figure. Further, any attempt to harmonize the two with recourse to a difference between Jesus' present and future role theory, between a suffering and a triumphant figure, etc. holds no water for no kingdom was given to Jesus, as promised in Daniel 7:13, in spite of evangelistic claims that it would take place in the life span of Jesus' disciples (Matthew 16:27–28; Mark 8:38, 9:1).

Daniel 7:13 is a political text probably referring to the Jewish Messiah, a fact made abundantly clear in Daniel 7:16–18:

> I came near to one of those who stood by, and asked him the truth of all this. So he told me, and made known to me the interpretation of the things. These great beasts, which are four, are four kings, which shall arise out of the earth. But the holy ones of the most High shall take the kingdom, and possess the kingdom for ever, for ever and ever.

It is the *holy ones* and not *a holy one* who will *possess the kingdom*. Jews have always understood this text to point to a political Messiah who will establish the kingdom for the community, the holy ones of Daniel. They also argue that none of these Messianic prophecies were ever fulfilled by Jesus. It seems that evangelists read too much into the text which in itself is historically questionable. Not many biblical scholars accept the Book of Daniel as an authentic compilation of the historical Daniel.

Additionally, there is no sense of pre-existence or godhead implied in the Son of Man sayings even if their authenticity is granted. All that these sayings could possibly refer to is the future Messianic role of the Son of Man and not a pre-existent being like God existing before His earthly manifestation. The Son of Man is "given" the dominion so does not own the dominion. What is the status of the Son of Man before receiving the dominion? Can the giver of the dominion and the recipient of the favor be equals? What was Jesus' status before becoming the Son of Man or the Messiah? Even an inspired prophet would be able to see into the future or could be aware of God's plans for the future. Indeed, there is no notion of deity or godhead in these Messianic sayings. Moreover, the Son of Man is commonly used in rabbinic literature to denote a frail and mortal human being. The title is void of any absolute divine tone.

Our prime interest in the title lies in the fact that in classical Christian theology, as will be discussed later, the Son of Man has often been contrasted with the other significant title accorded to Christ, the Son of God, to designate a dogma "true God–true Man" crucial for our study of anthropomorphism and corporealism. For the time being it is sufficient to quote Morton S. Enslin who notes:

> The term "Son of man," whether Jesus did or did not employ it for himself, indicated a supernatural figure of cosmic importance, an angel far removed from common clay, and quite apart from "flesh and blood." Thus for preachers to persist in using the term as an antithesis to "Son of God": "He was both 'Son of God' and 'Son of man'," is unqualifiedly wrong and misleading. The term did not connote participation in the common lot of men, either by humble birth or amazing condescension. It was a unique and – to adopt a modern phrase – an "altogether other" figure. There were many "sons of God"; there was, could be, but *one* "Son of man."[284]

The Son of God Christology

The Gospels frequently call Jesus the Son of God. It is such a pervasive designation in the Gospels as well as in subsequent Christian thought and dogma that its simple utterance alone somehow ushers in the notion of divinity. The Gospel of Mark starts with this highly significant title, "The beginning of the gospel of Jesus Christ, the Son of God" (Mark 1:1). In fact, few passages in the Gospels put this title into the mouth of Jesus himself: (Mark 13:32; Matthew 11:27; Luke 10:22). In large part it is either the Spirit of God (Matthew 3:16–17; Mark 1:11) or a voice from the clouds (Matthew 17:5; Luke 9:35) or unclean spirits (Mark1:23–24, 3:11, 5:7) or the high priest (Matthew 26:63) or the Centurion (Mark 15:39) who address Jesus with this title. It is in Matthew 16:15–17 where Jesus reportedly seems to have approved this title, "He saith unto them, but whom say ye that I am? And Simon Peter answered and said, Thou art the Christ, the Son of the living God. And Jesus answered and said unto him, Blessed art thou, Simon Barjona: for flesh and blood hath not revealed it unto thee, but my father which is in heaven." In John 10:36 Jesus is reported to have used the title for himself when he says to the Jews, "Say ye of him, whom the Father hath sanctified, and sent into the world, Thou blasphemest; because I said, I am the Son of God?" (See also Matthew 26:63–64; Mark 14:61–62; Luke 22:70; John 5:25, 11:4).

On the other hand Jesus is reported to have used the title "My Father" more frequently. For instance Matthew 11:27 reads, "All things are delivered unto me of my father: and no man knoweth the Son, but the Father; neither knoweth any man the father, save the Son, and he to whomsoever the Son will reveal him" (see also Mark 13:32). In Matthew 26 Jesus prays two times with the words "O my Father" (Matthew 26:39–42) and in Mark 14:36 he addresses God with the most intimate word "*Abba*".

The title, Son of God, in mainstream Christianity, is used to denote Jesus' divinity as the Second Person of the Trinity. It is maintained that Jesus was the only begotten Son of God for he did not have a human father. Consequently he is declared perfect God and perfect man. Wayne Grudem argues that the title Son of God "*when applied to Christ* strongly affirms his deity as the eternal Son in the Trinity, one equal to God the Father in all his attributes."[285] Another acceptable view is that the Synoptic Gospels use this title for Jesus to denote his intimacy and closeness to God Almighty.

It is the Gospel of John that gives this title its theological climax. John declares the Son to be the Pre-existent Word, Lamb of God, the only begotten Son of God (John 1:1–18). Martin Luther, commenting on the beginning verses of John, observes that:

> From the very beginning the evangelist teaches and documents most convincingly the sublime article of our holy Christian faith according to which we believe and confess one true, almighty, and eternal God. But he states expressly the three distinct Persons dwell in that same single divine essence, namely God the Father, God the Son, and God the Holy Spirit. The Father begets the Son from eternity, and the Holy Spirit proceeds from the Father and the Son, etc. Therefore there are three distinct Persons, equal in glory and majesty; yet there is only one divine essence.[286]

He further illustrates the birth of the Son of God:

> As a human son derives his flesh, blood, and being from his father, so the Son of God, born of the Father, received his divine essence and nature from the Father from eternity. But this illustration, as well as any other, is far from adequate; it fails to portray fully the impartation of the divine majesty. The Father bestows His entire divine nature on the Son. But [a] human father cannot impart his entire nature to his son; he can give only a part of it. This is where the analogy breaks down.[287]

Thus, the thinking goes that the Son became flesh to mediate and redeem humanity from its sinful nature. The Gospel of John makes this point very clear: "For God so loved the world, that he gave his only begotten Son, that whosoever believeth in him should not perish, but have everlasting life" (John 3:16). According to the Gospel of John, the Son of God is God in his self-revelation.

The Epistle of Hebrews 1:1–10 makes the point even clearer:

> In the past God spoke to our forefathers through the prophets at many times and in various ways, but in these last days he has spoken to us by his Son, whom he appointed heir of all things, and through whom he made the universe. The Son is the radiance of God's glory and the exact representation of his being, sustaining all things by his powerful word. (Hebrews 1:1–3)

Many conservative theologians contend that in Hebrews this title is used to equate Jesus with God or to point to his absolute deity and participation in God. "But about the Son he says, 'Your throne, O God, will last for ever and ever, and righteousness will be the scepter of your kingdom'" (Hebrews 1:8). This interpretation of the Son of God quickly dominated early Christian thought with reference to Jesus and it is this Christology which permeated early Christian literature. Jesus' deification became more imminent in the minds of early Christians as they heard stories of his resurrection. The risen Lord somehow conveyed to them the knowledge which could not have been revealed by "flesh and blood" (Matthew 16:17) and they felt obliged to proclaim it to everyone that Jesus was the only Son of God. "Jesus is the 'Son of God'" is therefore certainly one of the most ancient cradle statements of the early Church.

The phrase "son of God" however was also current in Greek as well as Jewish traditions though with a wide range of implications. It was applied both to human and superhuman beings. Grant observes that:

> We are so accustomed to the traditional language of the Christian Church that we think it is perfectly natural to find Jesus called "Son of God" and "Son of Man" in the early Christian books, and to have these titles explained as referring to his divine nature (Son of God) and his human nature (Son of Man). These titles are not as simple as they look. In the Jewish literature of the first century, the title "Son of God" is actually used of human beings. A fragment from the Dead Sea Scrolls speaks of the Messiah, a man chosen by God, as "Son of God"; and in the apocalyptic book of Enoch there is a supernatural, heavenly figure who is called "Son of Man."[288]

The title son of God was *metaphorically* used for kings, pharaohs, religious leaders, emperors, wise men and many other leading figures who were thought to be in the spirit of God or close to God. The designation was used to highlight their servitude to God and in no way or form insinuated their participation in the divinity or Godhead. The ancient Hebrew kings were anointed in this metaphorical sense as the instruments of God's plan on earth and called sons of God. Likewise in Exodus 4:22 Israel is mentioned as the son of God, "Israel is my Son, My first born." In Psalms 2:7 David says that, "The Lord had said unto me, 'Thou art my Son, this day have I begotten thee.'" In 1 Chronicles 22:10 Solomon is told to be the Son of God. Even in the New Testament the title is used for human beings other than Jesus. Luke 3:38 ends the genealogy of Jesus by writing "...son of Adam, which was the son of God." Matthew 5:44 declares those who love their enemies and 5:9 declares the peacemakers as the children of God. Moreover Jesus is shown to have used phrases like "My Father", "Your Father" and "Our Father" frequently. Grant observes that examples like these should "warn us against thinking that we can have some kind of "instant understanding" of what the titles assigned to Jesus by the early church really meant. They are more strange and complicated than we assume they are."[289]

Now, in the historical person of Jesus, these variety of implications were woven together to create a mysterious and awe inspiring figure. The Jesus figure then became a crystallization of the multiple elements already in existence.

When we turn to the Gospels we see a variety of Son of God sayings as already alluded to. The New Testament scholars differ widely over the construction, authenticity, historicity and meanings of these statements. There are two passages in the Synoptic Gospels which attribute the title directly to Jesus himself. These are Mark 13:32 and Matthew 11:27 with the same in Luke 10:22. Geza Vermes and C. K. Barret have discussed these passages at length reaching the conclusion that "on the basis of his surviving teachings, it turns out that it is impossible to prove, and unwise to suppose, that Jesus defined himself as the *son of God*."[290] Vermes also shows that Messiah statements such as "You are the Messiah, the son of the living God" (Matthew 16:16) are not meant to express divinity. They

> simply expressed the symbolism inherent in Psalm 2:7: 'You are *my son*, today I have begotten you.' No significance should in consequence be ascribed to it beyond that of divine appointment and adoption...It must follow that if...Jesus declined the status of

> Messiah, he must also have rejected the title, 'Messiah *son of God*'.[291]

Scholars like B. M. F. van Iersel, C. K. Barret, H. Conzelmann and Geza Vermes are convinced that Jesus never alluded to himself as *son of God* let alone *the Son of God* of the Christian tradition. Bultmann and Ferdinand Hahn expound how the title evolved in the early Christian community. For instance, Bultmann has suggested three stages in the evolution of this concept. The first and initial stage took place in the Palestinian community where Jesus was described as the King Messiah and given the ancient formula of royal divine adoption. The second took place in the Gentile Hellenistic Church where the Jewish concept of son of God was metamorphosed to denote Jesus' nature rather than his office or mission. The third stage, the half divine, half man classical mythology of kings and emperors was brought into play to highlight the redemptive acts of Jesus. The result was the Jesus of incarnation, the God Man Savior of the world.

But there is a distinctive element in Jesus' use of the term "*Abba*". It is a very intimate, personal and unusual term for a Jew of the first century CE to use. Michael Goulder observes, "Although there are a number of examples in Jewish literature of rabbis and other holy men being spoken of as God's sons, there is no serious parallel for the use of *Abba* in address to God, the term being normal for a human child to his father."[292] Many New Testament scholars have diligently researched the term and concluded its extraordinary significance in connection with Jesus' close affinity with God. Hans Kung notes:

> Hitherto only one explanation has been found: *abba* – like our "Daddy" – is originally a child's word, used however in Jesus' time also as a form [of] address to their father by grown-up sons and daughters and as an expression of politeness generally to older persons deserving of respect. But to use this not particularly manly expression of tenderness, drawn from the child's vocabulary, this commonplace term of politeness, to use this as a form of addressing God, must have struck Jesus' contemporaries as irreverent and offensively familiar, very much as if we were to address God today as "Dad."[293]

Some scholars argue that the frequent use of this term by the historical Jesus makes Jesus' exclusive sonship a reality. No Jewish contemporary of Jesus would dare to use the term *Abba* in the prayer language of Judaism. Jeremias maintains that:

> All this confronts us with a fact of fundamental importance. *We do not have a single example* of God being addressed as *'Abba* in Judaism, but Jesus *always* addressed God in this way in his prayers. The only exception is the cry from the cross (Mark 15:34 par. Matt. 27:46), and the reason for that is its character as a quotation.[294]

Oscar Cullmann and others argue that the use of the title "the Son of God" for Jesus by others and Jesus' own use of intimate terms like my Father and *Abba*, "point to Christ's coming from the Father and his deity but not in the sense of later discussions about 'substance' and 'natures'."[295] Grillmeier sees in this title germs of the later Christological developments. He sees in it a unique relationship of the Son who is the mediator between God and his elects and God the Father. It denotes more than a prophet, a king or an obedient servant. He observes that the "Son of God" is a title

> which, while affording a special insight into the primitive church's understanding of Jesus (cf. Mark 1:1,11, 9:7, 14:61; Luke 1:35, 22:70; Matt. 2:15, 14:33, 16:16, 27:40, 43), nevertheless has its basis in the unique consciousness of divine Sonship in Jesus himself. The consciousness (Mark 12:6, 13:32, 14:6), together with Jesus' claim to be the only saving way to the Father (Matt. 11:25–27), is the decisive starting point not only for the confessions of primitive Christianity and the early church, but also for the christology which developed from them and led up to Chalcedon.[296]

It seems that Cullmann and others have taken this title and the term *Abba* to its extent. Although it denotes intimacy and propinquity, *Abba* does not symbolize Jesus' exclusive divine sonship or ontological proximity to God. Furthermore, there are instances of its use in the ancient Jewish Hasidic piety tradition. Geza Vermes has shown that *Abba* was part of the Hasidic piety tradition[297] as the Talmud clearly states:

> Hanan ha-Nehba was the son of the daughter of Honi the Circle-Drawer. When the world was in need of rain the Rabbis would send to him school children and they would take hold of the hem of his garment and say to him, Father, Father, give us rain. Thereupon he would plead with the Holy One, Blessed be He, [thus], Master of the Universe, do it for the sake of these who are unable to distinguish between the Father who gives rain and the father who does not.[298]

The term used for God and for the Rabbi is the same *Abba*. Vermes finds interesting corroboration between this Talmudic use of the term *Abba* and its employment in Matthew 23:9 where Jesus has reportedly said, "Call no man your father on earth, for you have one Father who is in heaven."

Therefore, deriving a divinity for Jesus equal with God Almighty, based upon titles such as the Son of God or *Abba* is unwarranted. The wide ontological gulf between God and the son of God cannot be bridged by mere suppositions. Vermes comments that none of the Synoptic Gospels have tried to mitigate or eliminate this wide gulf:

> Indeed, it is no exaggeration to contend that the identification of a contemporary historical figure with God would have been inconceivable to a first-century AD Palestinian Jew. It could certainly not have been expressed in public, in the presence of men conditioned by centuries of biblical monotheistic religion.[299]

Even Paul who was quite comfortable with the Greco Roman worldview, could not and would not eliminate these boundaries. The theologizing writer of the Gospel of John shied away from this full merger of God into the so-called Son of God. Some of the New Testament epistles which seemingly blur this gap, never exceed the "notion of exalted Lord and revelation incarnate."[300] This hesitation disappeared only when the Gospels were Hellenized to attract the Roman population. This is why Jeremias warns that

> the fact that the address 'Abba expresses a consciousness of sonship should not mislead us into ascribing to Jesus himself in detail the 'Son of God' Christology, e.g. the idea of pre-existence, which developed very early in the primitive church. This over interpretation of the address 'Abba is prohibited by the everyday sound of the word.[301]

Later Christian creeds and doctrines all the way to the Council of Chalceaderi were not inspired by the language or teachings of Jesus of Nazareth, nor even by Paul, the Diaspora Jew. They were and are the product of Gentile Christianity's interpretations of the Gospels adapted to satisfy the pagan Hellenistic mentality quite alien to Jesus and his surroundings.

Kyrios Christology

Paul's favorite title and a central Christological concept is *Kyrios* a Greek work meaning God, Lord, master (Romans 1:3, 7, 5:1–11, 10:9, 16:24; 1 Corinthians 1:2, 3, 7, 8, 9, 10). Paul, as discussed earlier, introduced the idea of pre-existence and the worship of Christ as *Kyrios*. Even though the notion of pre-existence is more supposed and less taught, Paul girds it to a concept of universal salvation and provides it with a broader historical and spiritual framework. The title '*Kyrios*' had been common amongst Judaic as well as Greek circles to denote reverence, lordship, mastership, ownership and authority. Paul seemingly gave it a theological twist by broadening and deepening its implications and adapting it to the Hellenistic worldview. Consequently his use of the word became unique in the sense that it contained more than just the postulate of lordship or exaltation. In the later New Testament books it clearly took a definite form and absolute use, meaning "the Lord", "for he is Lord of lords and King of kings" (Revelation 17:14).

In the Synoptic Gospels the title is used for Jesus, as well as by Jesus for himself but without any absolute tone. Passages like Mark 11:3, Matthew 7:21, even John 13:13, can be interpreted as meaning "teacher" or "master". The designation Rabbi, Master or Lord Jesus and the title '*Kyrios*' received its full or absolute meaning only in Pauline Christology and only after Jesus' supposed death, resurrection and exaltation. "But to us there is but one God, the Father, of whom are all things, and we in him; and one Lord Jesus Christ, by whom are all things, and we by him" (1 Corinthians 8:6). "Therefore let all the house of Israel know assuredly, that God hath made that same Jesus, whom you have crucified, both Lord and Christ" (Acts 2:36, see also Acts 2:13–14). The pre-existent Word who was with God before the creation is now exalted to the right hand of God "to be a Prince and Saviour..." (Acts 5:31, see also Acts 7:55–56). The designation *Kyrios* or Lord, argues Cullmann,

> expresses as does no other thought that Christ is exalted to God's right hand, glorified and now intercedes for men before the Father. In designating Jesus as the Kyrios the first Christians declared that he is not only a part of divine Heilsgeschichte in the past, nor just the object of future hope, but a living reality in the present – so alive that he can enter into fellowship with us now, so alive that the believer prays to him, and the Church appeals to him in worship, to bring their prayers before God the Father and make them effective.[302]

Jesus' being a living reality, an object of worship, and his cosmic lordship, are the aspects which give this title such a vitality and significance not equally present in the other titles discussed earlier. This makes it the center and base of other Christological developments. The early Christians worshipped Jesus saying, "Come Lord Jesus" (Revelation 22:20) and could credit to him all the passages and hence works and attributes which the Old Testament attributes to God the Father. For instance, Isaiah 45:23 is quoted by Paul in Philippians 2:10 in the following words: "That at the name of Jesus every knee should bow, of things in heaven, and things in earth, and things under the earth, and that every tongue should confess that Jesus Christ is Lord, the glory of

God the Father." Commenting on this C. F. D. Moule states:

> At least, it represents Paul himself, or, at earliest, a pre-Pauline formula; and it boldly transfers to Jesus a great monotheistic passage from Isa. 45:23, in which God is represented as declaring that he must have no rivals: it is now to *Kurios lesous Christos* that every knee shall bow, and it is he whom every tongue shall confess. Professor M. Black is inclined to think that the same passage is intended in the name of the Lord Jesus even in Rom. 14:11. Certainly in Heb. 1:10ff. (though this may, of course, be later), a great, monotheistic passage in Ps. 102, manifestly intended in the original to be addressed to God the Creator, is boldly assumed to be addressed to Christ.[303]

The designation *Kyrios* served as the springboard for all the other high Christologies. Thus it was used in early hymns, worship formulas and Church services. Most of the New Testament's highest Christological affirmations and formulation owe their origins and substance to this title. Hans Kung notes:

> This is a Christocentrism working out to the advantage of man, based on and culminating in a theocentrism: "God through Jesus Christ" – "through Jesus Christ to God." As the Holy Spirit came to be inserted in such binitarian formulas – as the one in whom God and Jesus Christ are present and active both in the individual and the community – they were turned by Paul at this early stage into trinitarian formulas, the basis for the later development of the doctrine of the Trinity, of the triune God who is Father, Son and Holy Spirit.[304]

The Epistle of Philippians 2:5–11, especially verses 5 & 6, is extremely significant regarding this discussion: "Let this mind be in you, which was also in Christ Jesus: Who, being in the form of God, thought it not robbery to be equal with God." O. C. Quick argues that "St. Paul here affirms that Christ was originally that is, before he was born on earth, "in the form of God"....The Christ therefore was from the beginning a divine person."[305] He further argues that

> whereas before his self-humiliation Christ had the *nature* of Godhead, in the exaltation which followed the humiliation he received also the *name* of Godhead, so that all may worship him as they worship the Father. That St. Paul did definitely, if one may be allowed the expression, rank Jesus with God, is abundantly clear from evidence which extends all through his epistles.[306]

Modern Evangelists contend that the word *Kyrios* was used to translate the name of the Lord almost 6,814 times in the Greek Old Testament. Therefore any Greek speaking reader of the Greek Old Testament would have instantaneously recognized the fact that the use of *Kyrios* for Jesus meant nothing short of Jesus' divinity as the creator of the universe. Therefore, Paul and others had pinpointed the same fact by implying *Kyrios* to describe Jesus. This radical trend has dominated traditional Christianity since then. To popular Christianity Jesus is nothing short of God Almighty, the Omnipotent and Omniscient creator of all. Therefore we can conclude that the title *Kyrios* is the most significant among all the other Christological titles for our study of anthropomorphism and corporealism, for it eliminated all boundaries between God and man. By allowing itself to be the vehicle of transportation (divine qualities and attributes of Yahweh to the Jesus of history), the *Kyrios* managed to bring the transcendent God of developed Judaism to the spatio-temporal existence of man. It provided God with a historical context and sacrificed Him and His transcendence to assure man's salvation. This was too much of a sacrifice and Paul the Jew could not have done it. This is why many New Testament scholars do not subscribe to the aforementioned and sketched traditional interpretations of the title *Kyrios* and its context within some very early Christian hymns. For instance, K. Armstrong, argues that the earlier mentioned

> hymn seems to reflect a belief among the first Christians that Jesus had enjoyed some kind of prior existence "with God" before becoming a man in the act of "self-emptying" (*kenosis*) by which, like a *bodhisattva*, he had decided to share the suffering of the human condition. Paul was too Jewish to accept the idea of Christ existing as a second divine being beside YHWH from all eternity.

> The hymn shows that after his exaltation he is still distinct from and inferior to God, who raises him and confers the title *Kyrios* upon him. He cannot assume it himself but is given this title only "to the glory of God the Father."[307]

Armstrong further stresses:

> Paul never called Jesus "God". He called him "the Son of God" in its Jewish sense: he had simply possessed God's "powers" and "Spirit," which manifested God's activity on earth and were not to be identified with the inaccessible divine essence. Not surprisingly, in the Gentile world the new Christians did not always retain the sense of these subtle distinctions, so that eventually a man who had stressed his weak, mortal humanity was believed to have been divine.[308]

Long before Armstrong, A. Harnack emphasized the same point:

> Under the influence of the Messianic dogmas, and led by the impression which Christ made, Paul became the author of the speculative idea that not only was God in Christ, but that Christ himself was possessed of a peculiar nature of a heavenly kind. With the Jews, this was not a notion that necessarily shattered the framework of the Messianic idea; but with the Greeks it inevitably set an entirely new theory in motion. Christ's *appearance* in itself, the entrance of a divine being into the world, came of necessity to rank as the chief fact, as itself *the real redemption*. Paul did not, indeed, himself look upon it in this light; for him the crucial facts are the death on the cross and the resurrection, and he regards Christ's entrance into the world from an ethical point of view and as an example for us to follow: "For our sake he became poor"; he humbled himself and renounced the world. But this state of things could not last.[309]

How could this radical change of direction and perspective have possibly occurred in the minds of the early Christians who after all had inherited the Jewish Bible from Jesus, containing passages that leave no room for any partner, equal, or rival for God. There was, as is commonly held, "no sign of any difference between their (Christians) ideas of God and the ideas of their countrymen. They too worshipped the one and only God, creator and ruler of the world, the God of Abraham, of Isaac and of Jacob...."[310] Why then do some of the New Testament books attribute the creation and universal cosmic lordship, omnipotence, omnipresence, omniscience and eternity of God to Jesus? And why do Christians worship and pray to him with absolute terms like *Kyrios*?

In his classic work *Kyrios Christo*, Bousset and following him R. Bultmann in his *Theology of the New Testament*, maintained that this radical change was an outcome of the cultic veneration which had existed. When Jesus, the Rabbi or Master, became the object of cultic veneration titles assigned to him like Lord changed into absolute tones of glory, power and authority, and he became "the one Lord". This radical change took place when Christianity moved from Palestine to Antioch, from the Jewish to the Hellenistic environment. Christ worship first begins here and the titles attributed to Jesus became used in an ever more absolute sense in the early Christian writings that belong to this environment. Following this thesis McGiffert argues that, "In passing from Jews to Gentiles the faith of the original disciples was thus transformed and instead of a Jewish Messianic sect there came into existence a new religion, one of the many religions of personal salvation in the Roman Empire."[311]

Others, like Cullmann and Moule for instance, disagree with this thesis. Cullmann argues that it was not the Hellenistic Church of Antioch which initially implied the term *Kyrios*, but the very earliest original Church in Jerusalem. He discusses at length the philology of the ancient Aramaic prayer *Maranatha* which occurs in various New Testament passages like 1 Corinthians 22–24 and concludes that the Aramaic word '*Mar*' "Lord" constitutes the clue that determines how the Hellenistic word *Kyrios* became applied to Jesus in its absolute sense:

> The non-Christian use of the Kyrios name in the Hellenistic world, its relation to emperor worship, and above all its use as the name

> of God in Septuagint – all this certainly contributed to making *Kyrios* an actual *title* for Christ. But this development would not have been possible had not the original Church already called upon Christ as the Lord. Bouusset is right in saying that the *Kyrios* title goes back to the experience of the Church's worship; but it is the experience of worship in the *original* Church.[312]

Moule maintains the same when he argues:

> I am not for a moment denying that developed language about cosmic dimensions might be the fruit of long speculation and cogitation; but I am inclined to believe that a good case could be made for the ingredients for such conclusions being present immediately in the experience of the risen Christ.[313]

F.V. Filson emphasizes that "from the first days of the Apostolic Church an explicit and high Christology was an integral part of its message, and that this Christology was basically no Hellenistic product, but had its chief ties with the Old Testament and found expression in the earliest Apostolic preaching."[314]

Filson and others fail to prove the point from the Old Testament itself. It seems likely that the process of treating Jesus as a Deity equal to God in attributes and works was the result of non-Judaic influences external to the environment of Jesus himself and his immediate disciples as is clear from Harnack and others. It is not the Old Testament but adaptation to the mythological concepts prevalent in the Hellenistic milieu that makes Paul use this title in the absolute tones he did.

Logos or *Theos* Christology

This Christology is found only in the Gospel of John. The beginning and end chapter of John's Gospel contain references to Jesus which are traditionally translated as "God". This designation is highly critical for our study of anthropomorphism because if Jesus is adorned with all the majestic attributes of God (divinity, eternity, absolute cosmic Lordship), and is considered equal with God, worshipped and finally designated with the actual title 'God', then it becomes impossible to say that the

New Testament concept of the deity/Jesus is not anthropomorphic. Jesus never called himself God, nor did the first three evangelists, authors of the Synoptic Gospels. It is, as Cullmann observes, "the Gospel of John and Hebrews (that) provide the clearest and least ambiguous evidence of the attribution of *Oeos* to Jesus."[315] In John 1:1 it is stated: "In the beginning was the Word, and the Word was with God, and *the Word was God.*" In John 20 we have:

> And after eight days again his disciples were within, and Thomas with them: then came Jesus, the doors being shut, and stood in the midst, and said, peace be unto you. Then saith he to Thomas, Reach hither thy finger, and behold my hands; and reach hither thy hand, and thrust it into my side: and be not faithless, but believing. And Thomas answered and said unto him, *My Lord and my God.* (John 20:26–28)

To this designation, that is the absolute title 'God', the fourth evangelist presents Jesus as not responding negatively. Rather Jesus seems to have approved it when he is quoted to have said: "Thomas, because thou hast seen me, thou hast believed: blessed are they that have not seen, and yet have believed" (John 20:29). If therefore, according to Cullmann, the

> whole Gospel culminates in this confession, and, on the other hand, the author writes in the first verse of the first chapter, "And the Logos was God", then there can be no doubt that for him all the other titles for Jesus which are prominent in his work ('Son of Man', 'Son of God', 'Lord', and in the prologue, 'Logos') ultimately point toward this final expression of his Christological faith.[316]

Following Harnack's lead, scholars such as Bart Ehrman maintain that the theos Christology was not original to the Gospel of John. It was interpolated into it either by a later author or the original author/authors after an earlier edition of the book had already been published. They contend that the highly poetic style of John 1:1 is missing in the rest of the Gospel. Jesus is never called the "Word" elsewhere in the Gospel. Ehrman concludes that "this opening passage came from a different source than the rest of the account..."[317]

There are additionally problems with the translation. The popular translation "and the Word was God" is disputed by many leading translators. For instance James Moffat, Hugh J. Schonfield and Edgar Goodspeed translate the phrase as "and the Word was divine." There also exist multiple other translations and interpretations such as "the Word was a god", and "godlike sort was the Logos" and "so the Word was divine." The source of the problem lies in the original Greek manuscripts of the Gospels, which importantly are all in upper case script, that is in capital letters only, meaning that for instance there is no distinction, and no way to distinguish, between "God" and "god". The original word used in the manuscript is *theos* and cannot have the definite article in accordance with grammatical rules. Furthermore, the word God had a broader application and could refer to generally people of rank, leadership and authority. John 10:35 for instance uses it for human rulers as "gods". Origen of Alexandria, third century Church Father and a specialist in Greek grammar, noticed the difference by stating that John uses "the article, when the name of God refers to the uncreated cause of all things, and omits it when the Logos is named God... The true God, then, is The God."[318] The Greek term used is "*ho theos*" and not just "*theos*", *ho* meaning 'the' and *theos* meaning 'god'. This observation alludes to the fact that when the anarthrous (meaning occurring without an article) noun "*theos*" is applied to the Word it is not a definite but an indefinite noun.

These grammatical challenges are quite often used to manipulate meanings and to substantiate specific theological positions. Hence mainstream Christianity prefers the popular rendition as it vindicates its own "Jesus is God" theology. Opposing groups favor the other translations to prove Jesus' subordination to God the Father. Even some evangelical scholars such as Murry J. Harris, who otherwise support the Johanian *theos* Christology, do not deny the fact that "from the point of view of grammar alone, [QEOS HN ho LOGOS] could be rendered "the Word was a god...""[319] After a detailed study of *theos* in the Septuagint, extra biblical literature and the New Testament,

Harris argues that the main reason *theos* in John 1:1 is anarthrous is that it emphasizes nature rather than personal identity. Had John written "*ho theos*", that is with a definite article, it would have eliminated the distinction between the person of God the Father and the person of God the Son. John uses the qualitative rather than the definite article to avoid "Modalism". This explanation is sufficient to show how theological rather than grammatical reasons come into play when translating John 1:1.

The other important term, the Greek word *Logos,* on the other hand, carries multiple and varying meanings. In addition to the popular translation "Word" it can also mean thought, speech, reason, principle, logic, meaning, account etc. It also has varying connotations in different time periods and fields of religious and philosophical studies. Middle Platonism was the prevalent philosophical worldview of the pre and post Jesus era. Neoplatonism succeeded it down the centuries to the Reformation period. The emanation theory of Platonism was used by transcendental Jews like Philo of Alexandria to protect the perfect God's absolute transcendence and purity beyond this material existence, an existence marked by evil and immorality. Philo contended that the pure God had brought this defective cosmos into being not because of a direct act of creation but through a pure act of intellectual will. The result of this pure intellectual will was *Logos, the Word.* The material cosmos was brought forth through the intermediary agency of the Logos and other Intellects, the Logos here comparable to Plato's World Soul. The One and the Infinite source of existence was not, and is not, equal to derivative and secondary existences such as the Logos. One can easily see this ideology at work in the early Church Fathers' treatment of Jesus as the Logos. For instance Origen states:

> God on the one hand is Very God (Autotheos, God of Himself); and so the Saviour says in His prayer to the Father, John 17:3 That they may know You the only true God; but that all beyond the Very God is made God by participation in His divinity, and is not to be called simply God (with the article), but rather God (without article). And thus the first-born of all creation, who is the first to be with God, and to attract to Himself divinity, is a being of more

> exalted rank than the other gods beside Him, of whom God is the God, as it is written, The God of gods, the Lord, has spoken and called the earth. It was by the offices of the first-born that they became gods, for He drew from God in generous measure that they should be made gods, and He communicated it to them according to His own bounty. The true God, then, is The God, and those who are formed after Him are gods, images, as it were, of Him the prototype. But the archetypal image, again, of all these images is the Word of God, who was in the beginning, and who by being with God is at all times God, not possessing that of Himself, but by His being with the Father, and not continuing to be God, if we should think of this, except by remaining always in uninterrupted contemplation of the depths of the Father.[320]

How different is this monistic divinity to the mainstream popular concept of Jesus' hard divinity?

It seems that once the Church had decided that Jesus was God, especially in light of the Easter experience, the *theos* of John, which might have been used by John just as a communicative tool, was loaded with the absolute tones of *ho theos*. The transition highlights the historical fact that the high Christology and hard divinity of Jesus was not the original idea of Jesus or his immediate disciples, but rather owes its origins and substance to the later Christian understandings of Jesus in light of the Easter experience. Its later absolute overtures and gambits being purely theologically motivated.

Like the Prologue, there are numerous issues with John 20:28. Mainstream Christianity has always used this climactic confession of Thomas ("And Thomas answered and said unto him, *My Lord and my God*") as the supreme Christological pronouncement of faith in Jesus as Lord and God. Many scholars such as C. K. Barrett have also observed that the Gospel of John culminates in the Confession of Thomas:

> With this confession the evangelist has bracketed the entire gospel between two affirmations that Jesus is God (cf. 1:1...). John's Christology, for all of its explorations of various motifs, stands

> finally on the radical claim that Jesus is none other than the divine ultimate reality...Jesus is to be fully identified with God.[321]

Cyril of Alexandria long ago contended that John in the confession used the definitive article *o* (the) before the words Lord and God (*o Kyrios mou kai o Theos mou*), which gives to the statement a characteristic of absoluteness. James F. McGrath has argued that "it seems certain that the risen Christ is called 'God' in 20.28; that Jesus is understood as the incarnation of the Logos who is God is also clear."[322]

Despite this broader consensus, opinions seem to diverge over the true meanings and implications of this absolute designation. Mainstream Christianity subscribes to the idea that this designation is meant to denote Jesus' unqualified categorical hard divinity, that is his being God the Father, as the title My God and My Lord is clearly used for God Almighty in the Old Testament. Some non-traditional scholars contend that this designation was applied to Jesus in a broader sense current in contemporary Judaism. John who did not equate God with Logos in the Prologue could not have then obliterated all distinctions between God and Logos at the end of his Gospel. Scholars like Meeks, Lierman and McGrath quote evidence from Jewish sources for the belief

> that Moses was exalted to the position of 'God' and 'king', and that Adam, as the image of God, was regarded as functioning as God's agent and thus 'as God' over the earth... It is interesting to note that, in the only instance where John hints that the application of the designation 'God' to Christ may have been an issue (10.33–5), an appeal is made to this broader use of the term 'God'.[323]

John 10:33–35 states:

> "We are not stoning you for any of these," replied the Jews, "but for blasphemy, because you, a mere man, claim to be God." Jesus answered them, "Is it not written in your Law, 'I have said you are gods'? If he called them 'gods,' to whom the word of God came—and the Scripture cannot be broken."

Meek quotes Exodus 7:1: "Then the LORD said to Moses, 'See, I have made you like God to Pharaoh, and your brother Aaron will be your prophet.'" From passages such as Exodus 7:1 and Midrash Deuteronomy Rab. 11:4, Meeks concludes that in the Jewish traditions of the first century BC, Moses was described as somehow imbued with the fiery substance of God and divinity.[324] After a detailed analysis of a late second century BC Jewish book, *The Exagoge of Ezekiel the Tragedian*, John Lierman concludes that "it would indeed be difficult to resist the implication that Moses has indeed been deified."[325] They conclude that John 20:28 designated Jesus with the title God in this broader Jewish sense.

Bart Ehrman, on the other hand, insinuates that the absolute article *ho* (the) does not exist in the fifth century codex Bezae and other earlier church manuscripts.[326] This means that Thomas did not address Jesus with an absolute divine tone but called him "My divine lord". Long ago Theodore of Mopsuestia (c.350–428), the Bishop of Mopsuestia, understood this verse as directed to God the Father and not to Jesus. Following this lead some modern Christians especially the Jehovah's Witnesses argue that Thomas' words are nothing but exclamations of surprise "My God!" or "My Lord!" They are expressions of disbelief and outbursts of surprise rather than affirmations of Jesus' hard divinity as God Almighty. Additionally, the God designation never occurs in any of the Synoptic Gospels. Thomas the doubter is not a recognized disciple either. Even in the Gospel of John this designation is used for the risen lord, the heavenly Christ and not for the earthly Jesus.

Outside the Johannine corpus it is only Hebrews that unequivocally applies the title 'God' to Jesus. However, Hebrews 1:6–8, like the earlier passages discussed, has been translated in more than one way, and one of its translations reads:

> And again, when God brings his firstborn into the world, he says, "Let all God's angels worship him." In speaking of the angels he says, "He makes his angels winds, his servants flames of fire." But about the Son he says, "Your throne, O God, will last for ever and ever, and righteousness will be the scepter of your kingdom." (Hebrews 1:6–8).

Luther derives a true Godhead for Jesus from these verses stating:

> Although we read that the angels were worshipped by Moses, by Lot and Abraham, and by Joshua and other prophets...yet nowhere do we read that angels worshipped any angel or man. Therefore there is firm proof that the man Christ is true God, because it is recorded that He is worshipped by the angels, not only by some but by every one of them.[327]

In sum, material which was neither authored nor authorized by the historical Jesus, was implied to conclude his absolute divinity, and this process was gradual like the canonization process itself. The Church had decided that Jesus was divine in light of the heavenly Jesus' Easter experience and carefully selected those Gospels and other material which were thought to support the Church's various positions. The otherwise mutually exclusive Christologies of Jesus as a prophet, angel, Messiah and Lord, were metamorphosed to describe a human being with divine attributes and qualities, and ultimately godhead. Hence humanity and divinity became somehow merged in the historical human figure of Jesus of Nazareth, crystallizing into the ultimate climax and supreme illustration of anthropomorphism and corporealism. In this development, the Pauline and Johannine corpus proved to be handy, providing the context, terminology and conceptual framework for the later Christians to take the hazardous leap of identifying Christ with God. Meaning that it was perhaps due to the influence of Pauline and Johannine Christology that the Apostolic Fathers felt no hesitation to confess Jesus' divinity and deity. For instance Ignatius had no misgivings in calling Jesus "God" although not in the absolute sense of God the Creator, his argument being that, "There is only one physician of flesh and of spirit, generate and ungenerate, God in man."[328]

It seems clear from the preceding discussion that some New Testament books, especially if understood in the light of later theological developments, probably exalted Jesus Christ to the status of actual divinity, making him in certain passages, equal to God. Though various interpretations are given to these passages, the derivation of the later Christological claims of absolute divinity (such as that of the Father in all respects) is questionable, especially given the existence of explicitly monotheistic passages in the New Testament which cannot be ignored. For instance, there are several passages, particularly in the Synoptic Gospels, that emphasize the Transcendent God's absolute unity and uniqueness (see Mark 12:29–32). In fact, it is both the Pauline and Johannine passages which can be treated as having led to some of the later claims concerning the absolute divinity of Christ, aided by the artificial efforts of the interpreter. There are furthermore, other passages that point to Jesus' subordination to God the Father and his adoption at baptism (Luke 6:12, 10:22; Matthew 19:17, 11:27; John 7:29–33, for adoption see Matthew 3:16–17; Luke 3:22). Pelikan observes that the aforementioned "divinity" passages along with the "subordination or adoption" passages, when studied in light of the four sets of Old Testament passages, ultimately speak of "Christ as divine". The four sets of Old Testament passages being:

> Passages of adoption, which, by identifying a point in time at which he became divine, implied that the status of God was conferred on the man Jesus Christ at his baptism or at his resurrection; passages of identity, which, by speaking of Yahweh as "the Lord," posited a simple identification of Christ with God; passages of distinction, which, by speaking of one "Lord" and of another "Lord," drew some difference between them; and passages of derivation, which, by referring to the Father as "the greater" or using such titles as angel, Spirit, Logos, and Son, suggested that he "came from" God and was in some sense less than God.[329]

It must be noted that none of the aforementioned passages prove the absolute divinity of Jesus as believed by a great many traditional Christians. Derivative, finite or subordination divinity is not the same as absolute divinity. Additionally whilst these passages could be interpreted as giving a divine status to Jesus, nevertheless they leave a number of important issues unresolved regarding Jesus' relationship with God and with human beings, as will be seen in this chapter.

CHURCH FATHERS AND LATER DEVELOPMENTS

The early Church had no hesitation, or misgivings, in assigning to Jesus full-scale divinity, equating Jesus with God, including the designation of absolute divine titles, actions, attributes and functions; and this ascription of divinity did not cause many problems as long as the faith remained confined to Christians interested solely in the salvation. It was God and God alone, and nobody less than He, who could have brought salvation to a humanity engulfed in sin. And this is the implication we get from reading the oldest surviving sermon of the Christian Church after the New Testament writings: "Brethren, we ought so to think of Jesus Christ as of God, as of the judge of living and dead. And we ought not to belittle our salvation; for when we belittle him, we expect also to receive little."[330]

Problems surfaced when the Church had to face the external world having to prove to it the significance and wisdom of Christian teachings. For the one whom Christians had called God was also one who had lived a fully human life, having been born, lived for around thirty years, eaten, drunk, suffered and been relentlessly crucified, all realities which the Church itself had witnessed. The Alexandrian pagan philosopher Celsus' observations identified the problem accurately:

> Everyone saw his suffering, but only a disciple and a half crazed woman saw him risen. His followers then made a God of him, like Antinous... The idea of the coming down of God is senseless. Why did God come down for justification of all things? Does not this make God changeable?[331]

The pagan Celsus vehemently attacked the Christian concept of the Deity and dubbed it as thoroughly corporeal and anthropomorphic. He concluded that

> Christianity is not merely a religious revolution with profound social and political consequences; it is essentially hostile to all positive human values. The Christians say... 'Do not ask questions,

> only believe'. They say, 'Wisdom is foolishness with God'... they will flee to the last refuge of the intellectually destitute, 'Anything is possible to God'.[332]

Clement and Origen's statements regarding the difficulties of biblical anthropomorphisms and their insistence upon the utter transcendence of God, as discussed above, were responses to such penetrating attacks. In the words of Grillmeier:

> The hour had come for the birth of speculative theology, of theological reflection, of *theoligie savante*. The confession of Jesus Christ as the Son of God, the *novum* of Christian faith... demanded of Christian theology a twofold demonstration, first that it was compatible with Jewish monotheism, and secondly that it was different from pagan polytheism.[333]

There was pressure from within too. In the first place this confusion called forth some of the earliest doctrinal controversies in the Church and then forced the Church to become more precise. The inner pressure demanded logical defense and intelligible explanations of the contradictory positions especially to avert the fierce attacks of both the Jews and pagans. Within early Christianity, voices declaring ideas such as "his suffering was but a make believe" were raised by Marcion, Ptolemy and the Gnostics. Marcion, for instance, absolutely denied Jesus' humanity. His Jesus was too lofty to be confined within the prison of the flesh. This was clear "Docetism" (a belief that states that Jesus only *seemed* to have a physical body and to physically die, but in reality he was incorporeal, a pure spirit, and hence could not die).

The Church while trying to defend Christs' humanity could not itself escape from the very problem it was trying to solve, the problem of 'Docetism'. The Church itself had been emphasizing the divinity of Jesus to such a degree that the demarcation line between his humanity and divinity had become prematurely blurred. Church Father Clement of Alexandria, according to Bigg, was "near to the confines of Docetism".[334] The more the Church emphasized the absolute divinity of Christ using the God concept the more difficult it became to prove that Jesus of Nazareth was also the Son of God and of the same substance of God. The Church had no escape from mild Docetism and Moltmann confesses as much, "a mild docetism runs through the christology of the ancient church."[335]

Christianity, to prove its intellectual worth and avert the cerebral attacks of paganism, Greek philosophy and Judaism, had no choice but to be a little more precise in its teachings with regards to the relationship between God the Father and Jesus the Christ. It was difficult for both non-Christian Jews and pagans simultaneously to understand the assertions of strict monotheism on the one hand and the divinity of Jesus Christ including his suffering and crucifixion as God on the other. Christian apologists such as Justin Martyr, Theophilus, Tatian, Aristides and Athenagoras responded to this rather embarrassing situation with philosophical suppositions to vindicate the truth of Christianity, trying to draw a rather clear line between God and Jesus using the then available philosophical concepts.

Justin, the most renowned of them, for instance insisted that though Jesus had come from God he was not identical with God. "The ineffable Father and Lord of all," he says, "neither comes anywhere nor walks nor sleeps nor rises up, but remains in his own place wherever that may be, quick to behold, quick to hear, not with eyes or ears but with indescribable power." Justine's God was a transcendent being who could have not come into contact with the utilitarian sphere of man and things. To Justin, it seemed altogether absurd that such a transcendent God could be born of a woman, eat, drink and eventually be mercilessly crucified. However, strict belief in God's transcendence did not stop Justin from thinking of Jesus as divine, and to defend Christ's relationship with God he made use of the then current Christian phraseology calling Jesus the Son of God, Logos and also the Angel. Indeed according to him, Christ was worthy of these titles on account of his wisdom, virgin birth and because he was God's first begotten Logos: "Thou art my son; this day have I begotten thee." Jesus, the Son of God, was not like other men. He was generated in a very special way. As a fire is kindled by fire or as a light is produced from the light of the Sun, Jesus was God born of God. He was divine but not in the original sense. His divinity was derivative. In the words of Norris, Jesus' divinity

> was derivative, and for that reason inferior to the one God.... In Justin's system there truly was, in the last resort, only one ultimate God. The Logos represented a slightly lower level of divinity, something between the pure divinity of God and the nondivinity of creatures. Justin had made sense of the incarnational picture of Jesus by adopting a hierarchical picture of the world-order in which the Logos stands as a kind of bumper state between God and the world, and it is this fact that makes Justin's Christology problematic.[336]

He was a pre-existent Logos, God's agent in creation, through whom all creatures were created. Therefore, he could be called Lord and worshipped as divine but in terms of being of second rank. As Justin in one of his confessions put it:

> Thus we are not atheists, since we worship the creator of this universe...and that we with good reason honour Him Who has taught us these things and was born for this purpose, Jesus Christ, Who was crucified under Pontius Pilate...having learned that He is the Son of the true God and holding Him in the second rank, and the prophetic Spirit third in order, we shall proceed to demonstrate.[337]

Justin could not have convinced his Jewish counterparts with this kind of hierarchical interpretation of the Godhead and derivative nature of divinity. Monotheism stood in his way as an insurmountable hurdle. So he adopted another approach, to try and prove that the Jewish Scriptures had borne witness to two Gods: first the transcendent, supreme, unbegotten, ingenerate God, the ineffable Father, who never appeared on the earth; and second, the God of theophanies, who came down to earth on several occasions and finally became incarnate in Christ. In his Dialogue with the Jewish Trypho, he argued the matter at length:

> I will give you, my friends, another testimony from the Scriptures that as a beginning before all creatures God begat from himself a

> certain rational power which is called by the Holy Spirit now Glory of the Lord, again Wisdom, again Angel, again God, again Lord, and Logos. Also he called himself Captain of the host when he appeared to Jesus the Son of Nave in the form of a man. For he can be called by all these names since he serves the Father's will and was begotten of the Father by will.[338]

And

> when my God says 'God went up from Abraham,' or 'the Lord spake unto Moses,' and 'the Lord came down to see the tower which the sons of men had built,'... you must not imagine that the unbegotten God himself came down or went up anywhere.... Therefore not Abraham nor Isaac nor Jacob nor any other man saw the Father and ineffable Lord of all and of Christ himself as well, but they saw him who according to his will was at once God, his Son, and the angel who ministered to his will, and who it pleased him should be born man by the Virgin; who also was fire when he spake with Moses from the bush.[339]

As the passage quoted indicates, to Justin Christ was the Logos, the divine reason, the second God of the Old Testament theophanies, begotten before the creation of the world, who became incarnate in the historical person of Jesus of Nazareth. Justin also called the Logos the servant, the angel, the apostle. Grillmeier observes:

> In calling the Logos the servant, the apostle, the angel of the absolutely transcendent Father, Justin gives him a diminished transcendence, even if he does not make him a creature. He compares the Logos with Herms, the Logos-interpreter of Zeus... There is a *deus inferior* subordinate to the *theos hypsistos*.[340]

Other apologists such as Tatian and Hippolytus followed Justin in his ideas of God's transcendence, ineffability, immutability and otherness while maintaining his Logos Christology.

J. N. D. Kelly underlines the two most important points that were common among all the Apologists:

> (a) that for all of them the description 'God the Father' connoted, not the first Person of the Holy Trinity, but the one Godhead considered as author of whatever exists; and (b) that they all, Athenagoras included, dated the generation of the Logos, and His eligibility for the title 'Son', not from His origination within the being of the Godhead, but from His emission or putting forth for the purposes of creation, revelation and redemption. Unless these points are firmly grasped, and their significance appreciated, a completely distorted view of the Apologists' theology is liable to result.[341]

The Apologists clearly portrayed the Logos as required for the work of creation in subordination to God the Father. They also manifestly limited the Logos as compared to God Himself to safeguard the indispensable idea of monotheism. There were residuals of Middle Platonism in this Logos interpretation of the Apologists. The Logos was understood in relation to the cosmos and the world to stress God's absolute transcendence, invisibility and unknowableness. Almighty God was too transcendent to directly deal with men and the world. The Logos, a product of God's creative will, was a subordinate mediator, a derivative god. The idea of subordination was fortified by the close linking of the creation of the world with the procession of the Logos and then by the scheme of salvation or man's redemption through his intermediate agency.

Church Fathers like Tertullian (160–220) and Origen (185–254) clearly maintained the Apologists' position in regards to Christ's relationship with God. Tertulian, accepting Justin's mediatorial idea of the Logos, differentiated between God and Jesus, the Word, by arguing that "by him who is invisible, we must understand the Father in the fullness of his majesty, while we recognize the Son as visible by reason of dispensation of his derived existence."[342] Tertullian in his treatise *Against Praxeas* explained that the Logos first existed in God as his Reason and then was "made a second" to God, or "uttered" as the Word through whom all things were made. In Tertullian we see a crystal clear line of demarcation between God the Father and the Logos, emphasizing the mediatorial and secondary character of the Logos and his "derivation and portion", to use his terms, from the father's divine substance. He observes that, "With regard to him (the Logos), we are taught he is derived from God and begotten by derivation so that he is Son of God and called God because of the unity of substance."[343]

God's transcendence and *monarchia* is preserved as the Son uses the powers and rule given to him by the Father. The Son will return this to the Father when the world comes to an end. The Father is the guarantee of the *monarchia,* the Son comes in at second place whilst the Spirit is assigned third place. Tertullian's trinity is not metaphysical but economic or dynamic in nature. Only the Father remains the eternal transcendent God while the other two entities proceed from the *unitas substantiae* because they have a task to fulfill. His concept of unity is also not mathematical. There is no subdivision within the Godhead. Rather, it is more philosophical, more organic, as there is a constructive integration within the Godhead of the will and the persons. It is Tertullian who introduced the concept of 'person' in Christology. He argued that the triune God was one in substance and different in person: "You have two (Father-Son), one commanding a thing to be made, another making it. But how you must understand "another" I have already professed, in the sense of person, not of substance."[344]

Origen also emphasized the derivative, intermediary and secondary role of Jesus. He equated the procession of the Logos from the Father with the procession of the will from the mind. The act of will neither cuts anything from the mind nor causes division within it. Origen differed from Justin and Tertullian in saying that the Logos was the eternal self-expression of God and was of the same substance as God: "The Father did not beget the Son once for all, and let him go after he was begotten but he is always begetting him."[345] Origen's idea of the eternal generation of the Logos did not mean that he had made the Logos equal with God. In his treatise *Against Celsus* he clearly differentiated between the Logos and God by making the Logos subordinate to God and thereby declaring him in some sense less than God and a "second God". McGiffert commenting on Origen's Logos Christology observes that there exists a marked subordinationism in Origen because he was "always more interested in the subordination of the Son to the Father than his oneness with him."[346] All in all,

Origen's Trinitarian scheme is thoroughly Platonistic Subordinationism. Kelly observes:

> The unity between Father and Son corresponds to that between light and its brightness, water and the steam which rises from it. Different in form, both share the same essential nature; and if, in the strictest sense, the Father alone is God, that is not because the Son is not also God or does not possess the Godhead, but because, as Son, He possesses it by participation or derivatively.[347]

Bigg observes that:

> We shall however wrong Origen, if we attempt to derive his subordinationism from metaphysical considerations. It is purely Scriptural, and rests wholly and entirely upon the words of Jesus, 'My Father is greater than I', 'That they may know Thee the only true God', 'None is Good save One'.[348]

The Logos then is of secondary rank and merits secondary honor. This being the case, Origen does not permit the worship of any generate being such as Christ, but only sanctions worship of God the Father to Whom even Christ prayed. The prayers offered to Christ are meant to be conveyed to the Father through the intermediary agency of Christ. God transcends both Christ and the Spirit as they transcend the realm of inferior beings. The Son and Spirit are God as related to creatures but

> from the viewpoint of the ineffable Godhead He is the first in the chain of emanations. This conception of a descending hierarchy, itself the product of his Platonizing background, is epitomized in the statement that, whereas the Father's action extends to all reality, the Son's is limited to rational beings, and the Spirit's to those who are being sanctified.[349]

Irenaeus (202) and Clement of Alexandria (150–215) were perhaps more traditionalists than philosophers. They did not look for intellectual interpretations to denote the relationship between the

Father, the Son and the Holy Spirit, preferring instead to rely on traditional terminology over philosophical concepts. On multiple occasions they widely differed to the Apologists with regards to their understanding of the Logos Christology, and for both, the Logos who had become incarnate in Jesus Christ, was no less than God himself. In his famous treatise *Against Heresies* Irenaeus argued that the Logos existed eternally with God; did not begin to be God's Son at any particular point in history; and that the salvation and redemption of a sinful humanity could not have been attained except through God in the flesh humbling himself to the point of death. Lord Jesus Christ, the Logos of God, adopted human conditions so that humanity might become what he himself was. "How can they be saved unless it be God who wrought out their salvation on earth? And how shall man be changed into God unless God has been changed into man?"[350] In other words the Son of God was made Son of Man so that humans could become sons of God. This guaranteed man's immortality like that of the Logos so that the "corruptible might be swallowed up by incorruption and the mortal by immortality" (1 Corinthians 15:53–54).

For Irenaeus to think of the Logos in derivative terms and to subordinate him to God or to think of him as another being as the Apologists did, was detrimental to his saving work and hence impossible. He identified the Logos or the Son with the Father completely. "For the Father is the invisible of the Son, but the Son is the visible of the Father."[351] In short the Logos is God but God revealed and not God unapproachable, inaccessible and apart from the world.

Clement of Alexandria, like Irenaeus, was a moralist rather than a systematic theologian. He adopted an almost identical course in determining Jesus' relationship with God. In his view Jesus was neither derived nor a secondary or subordinate divine being to God, rather he was fully divine, God in his own right. In the tenth chapter of his *Protrepticus* Clement calls Jesus "the truly most manifest God."[352] Bigg observes that "Clement's mode of statement is such as to involve necessarily the Unity, Equality, and Eternity of the First and Second Persons. It has been asserted, that he hardly leaves sufficient room for a true distinction of Hypostasis."[353] Like his predecessors – such as Justin – Clement transfers the peculiar and absolute divine titles referring to God in the Bible, to the Son, by implying the Old Testament passages for the Son. Consequently Clement's Logos, the Second Person of divinity, is equally God Almighty as is his God the Father Almighty. Like Ireneaus he designates the Logos as God in revelation. Additionally, Clement insists that somehow Jesus' "Flesh was not wholly like ours..." Scholars differ as to whether or not Clement believed in Jesus' human soul but they do not differ over the fact that to Clement Jesus alone was both God and man. On the other hand, some contemporary theologians strive hard to depict him as an early Christian intellectual thinker who insisted upon the sheer transcendence of the Deity by allegorically interpreting the Hebrew Bible's anthropomorphic passages. Yet how could Clement possibly be considered a hero of the Christian transcendental God Paradigm when he himself was among the early traditionalists who obliterated the true boundaries between man and God? Although Clement maintained a kind of graded hierarchy within the Godhead, a common feature of the Platonic conception, nevertheless his union of the three persons was apparently so complete that it obscured the distinction between them. Call it what you will, whether a lack of adequate vocabulary or a spiritualizing tendency, what is clearly apparent is that Clement's divine Logos is so dominant in the person of the historical Jesus that Jesus' human soul or nature is effectively eliminated or at least inactivated. Not only does this definitely border on Docetism but also on Modalism.

We conclude this part of the discussion by noting that until the second century CE, both the Christian God Paradigm in general and the doctrine of Christ's Person were not fixed views but rather flexible, fluid and confusing concepts. The ideas of subordination, and the derivative and secondary rank of Christ, were common among thoughtful Christians such as Justin and Origin. However, traditionalists as well as the orthodox Church, if we can possibly use this term for purposes of convenience, inclined more towards the Unity, Equality and Eternity of Christ, and that on a par with God the Father. The latter was not without its inherent confusions and problems, and was moreover a form of possible Docetism. As such those holding this view were accused of corporealism, anthropomorphism, as well as irrationalism by their opponents, such as the pagan Greek philosopher Celsus.

The Monarchians

From the start, the belief that Christ was a god was common among many Christians, especially the Gentiles. There were many who felt it degrading to assign to Jesus a secondary or subordinate position and thought it deeply offensive to place another God alongside with or over him assuming that this would diminish their salvation. So, they contended that Jesus was the same and only God who had created the universe and that he had become flesh to die for their sins. There exist traces of such tendencies among Christians during Justin's times and he makes explicit references to groups such as these in his *Apology*. Writing in the early third century Hippolytus of Rome observed, "Cleomenes and his followers declare that he (Christ) is the God and Father of the universe."[354] They were later called "Modalist Monarchians".

J. N. D. Kelly summarizes 'Modalistic Monarchianism' well as follows:

> This was a fairly widespread, popular trend of thought which could reckon on, at any rate, a measure of sympathy in official circles; and the driving-force behind it was the twofold conviction, passionately held, of the oneness of God and the full deity of Christ. What forced it into the open was the mounting suspicion that the former of these truths was being endangered by the new Logos doctrine and by the efforts of theologians to represent the Godhead as having revealed Itself in the economy as tri-personal. Any suggestion that the Word or Son was other than, or a distinct Person from, the Father seemed to the modalists (we recall that the ancient view that 'Father' signified the Godhead Itself was still prevalent) to lead inescapably to blasphemy of two Gods.[355]

It was Praxeas (c. 210) and then Noetus, both of Asia Minor, who gave this belief a regular theological touch around c. 200. They argued that the whole of God was present in Jesus. It was Sabellius (c. 215) who became the most vocal and important theologian of the movement. Their position was quite simple. There is no God but the one creator and sustainer of the world as stated in the Scriptures. Christ was God.

Then he is that creator whom people call Father. They made use of passages of Identity such as "I and the Father are one" and stressed the absolute likeness and identity of Jesus with God. Hippolytus quotes them as saying,

> there exists one and same Being, called Father and Son, not one derived from the other, but himself from himself, nominally called Father and Son according to changing of times; and that this One is that appeared [to the patriarchs], and submitted to birth from a virgin, and conversed as man among men. On account of his birth that has taken place he confessed himself to be the Son to those who saw him, while to those who could receive it he did not hide the fact that he was the Father.[356]

Epiphanius quotes Sabellians as saying: "Do we have one God or three?"[357] If God is One, then the words of Isaiah 44:6 applied also to Christ: "Thus says the Lord, the King of Israel and his Redeemer, the Lord of hosts: I am the first and I am the last; beside me there is no God."

It is hard to verify details concerning the exact position and terminology of Sabellius. Most of the surviving documents date to over a century later. It seems that Sabellians, as they were called, were interested in monotheism. They accused orthodox Christians, as Tertullian reports, of polytheism, "they accuse us of preaching two and three Gods while they claim that they are worshippers of one God."[358] As a result, Tertullian gave them the name "Monarchians" which has clung to them to this day. Historically they are called the 'Modalist Monarchians'.

This extreme position as well as preciseness with regards to Jesus' relationship with God may have been an offshoot of orthodox teachings and underlying ambiguity. As Harnack notes, "many facts observed in reference to the earliest bodies of Monarchians that come clearly before us, seem to prove that they bore features which must be characterized as pre-Catholic, but not un-Catholic."[359] Worshipping Jesus with absolute titles like Lord and explicitly calling him God could have led anybody to eradicate the distinction between Jesus and God. We are told that phrases such as "God is born," "the suffering God," or "the dead God" were so widespread among Christians that even Tertullian, for all his hostility to the Modolist Monarchians, could not escape using them. The main difference between the two parties is that of precision and systematization. The Modalist Monarchians systematized the popular Christian belief in Christ in a clear and precise manner. It was a bold step towards giving a precise theological color to the rather ambiguous Christian devotional language. The Church could not accept it because of its dangerous implications. It was nothing but naive corporealism and patripassianism. Though it safeguarded Jesus' deity as well as monotheism, the objective for which the Church had been aspiring, the Church could not approve of it in such bold terms because of its subtle implications. Linwood Urban observes: "If the whole of God is present in the historic Jesus, the *transcendence* of God is nullified. The Pre-Nicene solution asserts that there is part of God which is not incarnate, and so allows for God to transcend his presence in Jesus."[360]

In his work *Against Praxeas* Tertullian explains the reason arguing:

> How is it that the omnipotent, invisible God, whom no man hath seen or can see, who inhabiteth light inaccessible...how is it, I say, that the Most High should have walked at evening in paradise seeking Adam,...unless these things were an image and a type and an allegory? These things indeed could not have been believed even of the Son of God, had they not been written; perhaps they could have not been believed of the Father even had they been written. For these persons bring him down into Mary's womb, place him at Pilot's tribunal, and shut him in the tomb of Joseph. Hence their error becomes evident....Thus they believe that it was always one God, the Father, who did the things which were really done through the Son.[361]

Turtullian's passage is enough to pinpoint the underlying theological complexities. The anthropomorphic and corporeal passages of the Old Testament had played an important role towards the triune interpretation of divinity. God was also known to be transcendent for

Greek philosophy would have made mockery of an anthropomorphic or any other conception of God as rudimentary or paganistic. The secondary, derivative divine being of the Platonism scheme was initially helpful to preserve God's absolute transcendence and to avoid accusations of being pagan. On the other hand, this kind of notion of divinity was not adequate for the purposes of salvation. Common believers preferring their own salvation over and beyond God's transcendence sacrificed Him at the altar of their sins. This tension is intrinsic to the entire history of Christology, as will be seen in forthcoming discussions.

Given that God's transcendence and ineffability was at stake, the defenders of orthodoxy, except Zephyrinus, the Bishop of Rome, condemned this group of Monarchians as heretics. Then formally, in the sixth-century Synod of Braga, orthodoxy decreed that:

> If anyone does not confess that the Father and the Son and the Holy Spirit are three persons of one essence and virtue and power, as the catholic apostolic church teaches, but says that [they are] a single and solitary person, in such a way that the Father is the same as the Son and this One is also the Paraclete Spirit, as Sabellius and Priscillian have said, let him be anathema.[362]

In order to preserve God's transcendence and stability, observes Urban, "Trinitarians were ready to give up the divine simplicity. Trinitarians assert that, although God is one and simple in most respects, there are some in which he is Triune."[363] The Monarchian anthropomorphic position has continued to surface even after its condemnation, for throughout Christian history "men have been frequently condemned for denying the deity of Christ but rarely for denying the distinction between the Father and the Son. To deny the former has generally seemed unchristian; to deny the latter only unintelligent."[364] In spite of strong opposition, Modalism, or the crystal clear anthropomorphic concept of God, remained widespread, especially among the simpleminded and ordinary Christians. It was shared, as observes McGiffert, "by the majority of the common people and was in harmony with the dominant piety of the age. "What harm am I doing in glorifying Christ?" was the question of Noetus and in it he voiced the sentiment of multitudes."[365]

Dynamic Monarchianism

Meanwhile, another kind of Monarchianism became current both in the East and the West, and it took the question of Jesus' relationship with God to the other extreme. In the West, Theodotus (c. 190), a leather-worker, taught that Jesus was a man. Jesus was born of a virgin as a result of God's special decree through the agency of the Holy Spirit. His virgin birth did not make him a god or a divine being. God tested his piety for a period of Jesus' earthly life and then let the Holy Ghost descend upon him at the time of baptism. God had a purpose for him and equipped him for that vocation. Jesus became the Christ at the time of his baptism and as a result of his vocation and not due to his heavenly nature or divinity. Additionally, Jesus excelled all humanity in virtues and became an authority over them. His adoption in no way or form diluted his humanity or made him God. He always remained an obedient servant of God. Theodotus was afterwards characterized as the founder of the God-denying revolt, adoptionism. The adoptionists made use of the biblical monotheistic passages, the Gospel passages of distinction and subordination, and finally the crystal clear Gospel passages that emphasize Jesus' feeble humanity and earthly nature. They were also able to strike a balance between the transcendence of God and human salvation through Christ's redeeming death. Their solution was not adequate for the Orthodoxy though. Such an understanding of Jesus, observes Urban, "preserved the simplicity of God, but at the price of unfaithfulness to the tradition."[366]

In the East this movement was significantly revived under the leadership of Paul of Samosata, the Bishop of Antioch, the capital of Queen Zenobia of Palmyra's kingdom. Bishop Paul enjoyed authority almost like a viceroy and used his political influence to expound his theological views concerning Christ. He observed that Jesus did not have an essential divine nature. His nature was pure human as he was a man from beneath and not from above having divine substance. Jesus had a normal human birth and grew into knowledge and wisdom. The Logos of God inspired him from above and dwelt in him as an inner man. Jesus did neither lose his humanity nor his human nature. It always remained the dominant nature in Jesus. It was polished, civilized and guided by the Logos. The union of the Logos and Jesus was not a union of substance or merger or diffusion of natures but rather that of will and quality. Mary neither bore nor delivered the divine Logos, but the human Jesus, just as other humans. Moreover, Jesus the man was anointed at baptism with the Spirit from above and not the Logos. Jesus was special in the sense that he lived under the constant divine grace of a very special degree. His uniqueness lay in his union of disposition and will and not in the unity of his substance or nature with God. As Jesus advanced in the manifestation of goodness and submission to the will of God, he became the

> Redeemer and Savior of the human race, and at the same time entered into an eternally indissoluble union with God, because his love can never cease. Now he has obtained from God, as the reward of his love, the name which is above every name; God has committed to him the Judgment, and invested him with divine dignity, so that now we can call him "God" [born] of the virgin.[367]

Likewise we are allowed to talk of his preexistence in connection with his goodness and in the sense of the prior degree of God. It is clear that bishop Paul did not believe in the divine nature of Jesus. On the other hand, in addition to his adoptionism, he sought to prove that the assumption that Jesus had the divine nature or was by nature the Son of God was detrimental to monotheism as it led to duality in the Godhead. He became God but somehow, as says, Paul Tillich, "he had to deserve to become God."[368] Bishop Paul banished from divine service all Church psalms that expressed in any sense the essential divinity of Christ. Consequently, Paul was condemned at a Synod of Antioch held in 268, two earlier synods having failed to take action in the matter. He was declared as heretical because he denied Jesus' pre-existence and his unity of substance with God or in other words his proper divinity.

Though both types of Monarchianisms were condemned as heretical, in different ways they challenged and pushed the orthodoxy to look into the immense difficulties involved in their understanding of the transcendence and unity of God and attempts to clarify it in intelligible terms. The orthodox Fathers insisted upon their concept of the relative unity of God by holding on to their Logos Christology. By the end of the third century Logos Christology had become generally accepted in all parts of the Church and found its place in most of the creeds framed in that period, especially in the East.

Arianism

Though the official Logos Christology, or belief in the divine nature of Jesus, disposed of the divine-human doctrine of Dynamic Monarchianism, the doctrine did not pass without leaving a trace. Lucian and Arius were inspired by the interpretations and logic of Bishop Paul. Arius, a presbyter from Alexandria, was a man of mark. He brought the debate regarding Christ's nature and his relationship to God, to the public and caused vehement excitement. Dorothy Sayers has neatly paraphrased the impact of Arius' views:

> "If you want the logos doctrine, I can serve it hot and hot:
> God beget him and before he was begotten he was not."[369]

Arius maintained that God is one both in substance and in person. He is the only eternal and unoriginated being. The Logos, the pre-existent being, is merely a creature. There was a time when he was not and then was created by the Father out of nothing. What is true of the filial relationship is true of Jesus the Son and God the Father. The Father existed before the Son. The Son Jesus was created by the Father from a substance which was non-existent prior to Jesus' creation. Arius, observes Norris,

> was a firm believer not only in the unity of God but also in a doctrine of divine transcendence which saw God's way of being as inconsistent with that of the created order. Logically enough, therefore, his doctrine of the Logos was so formulated as to express two convictions: first, that the Logos cannot be God in the proper sense; second, that the Logos performs an essential mediatorial role in the relation of God to [the] world. He taught,

> accordingly, that the Logos belongs to the created order but at the same time that he is quite superior creature, ranking above all others because he was brought into being by God "before the ages" to act as the agent of God in creation.[370]

Arius used scriptural evidence such as John 14:28 where Jesus categorically states that the Father is "greater than I" and John 17:20–26 where Jesus encouraged the disciples to become "one as we are one." Arius contended that the disciples could not have been one with God or Jesus in terms of embodying the divine nature or substance, but in will. Likewise, the unity of the Son with the Father was that of will and not of divinity or substance. Additionally 1 Corinthian 8:5–6 was quoted to differentiate between God and Christ. In Arius' words:

> The Father alone is God, and the Son is so called only in a lower and improper sense. He is not the essence of the Father, but a creature essentially like other creatures...or unique among them. His uniqueness may imply high prerogatives, but no creature can be a Son of God in the primary sense of full divinity.[371]

Arius, states Hilaire Belloc, "was willing to grant our Lord every kind of honour and majesty short of the full nature of the Godhead...He was granted one might say (paradoxically) all the divine attributes – except divinity."[372]

God is perfect but the Son of God advances in wisdom and knowledge and hence is changeable. The Son can be called Logos but is to be sharply distinguished from the eternal impersonal logos or reason of God. The essence of the Son is identical neither with that of God nor with that of human beings. The Son, who became incarnate in Jesus, is the first of all creatures and hence higher in order than any other being whether angels or men. Jesus did not have a human soul. "The soul of Christ was the Logos; only his body was human. As a consequence all that he did and suffered was done and suffered by the Logos."[373] Because of what he did during his earthly life, maintaining unswerving devotion to the divine will, the Son was given glory and lordship and would even be called "God" and worshipped. But to identify him with God's essence is to commit blasphemy. "So stark a monotheism", observes Pelikan, "implied an equally uncompromising view of divine transcendence."[374] Arius then was, we can conclude with Bright, "speaking of Him as, after all, only the eldest and highest of creatures; not denying to him the title of God, but by limitations and glosses abating its real power."[375] In spite of the fact that Arius had a high view of Jesus' humanity so much so that he denied his human nature and emphasized a mild incarnation even allowing him the title "God", his position was rejected by the Church because he denied Jesus' full divinity. The Church felt that Arius had at once affirmed and then nullified both the divinity and humanity of Christ. H. M. Gwatkin argues that Arius' "doctrine was a mass of presumptuous theorizing, supported by alternate scraps of obsolete traditionalism and uncritical text-mongering, on the other it was a lifeless system of unspiritual pride and hard unlovingness."[376] T. E. Pollard argues that Arius transformed the "living God of the Bible" into the "absolute of the philosophical schools."[377]

This "half-god", to use Tillich's term, theology of Arius was rejected by the champions of the orthodox Logos Christology and finally defeated as heresy. Harnack notes that

> the defeated party had right on its side, but had not succeeded in making its Christology agree with its conception of the object and result of the Christian religion. This was the very reason of its defeat. A religion which promised its adherents that their nature would be rendered divine, could only be satisfied by a redeemer who in his own person had deified human nature.[378]

This inherent tension between the transcendental views of Godhead and redemption through the sacrificial death of God was the source of both parties' concerns. The Arians somehow preferred the transcendence of God over their own divinization and presumed redemption. The official party could live with this tension and make sense of it by artificial bandages and irrational presuppositions. That is what was achieved by Athanasius in the Council of Nicea – arguing against Arius and his doctrine of the distinct Christ – and the Logos Christology was rendered victorious over its opponents once and for all. In 325 CE Emporer Constantine convened and presided over the Council of Nicaea in order to develop a statement of faith to unify the church. The Nicene Creed was written, declaring that "the Father and the Son are of the same substance" (homoousios). And "when the Logos Christology obtained a complete victory, the traditional view of the Supreme deity as one person, and, along with this, every thought of the real and complete human personality of the Redeemer was condemned as being intolerable in the Church."[379] Even though Arius was condemned as an arch heretic and treated as such for centuries, his sincere concerns for Christianity and his genuine insights into scriptural passages and monotheistic transcendental history could not be denied.

New estimates of Arius' contributions to Christological discussions have been made by modern scholars. Out of these new reconstructions a different picture of Arius is evolving. Francis Young, for instance, comments that "Arius was not himself the arch-heretic of tradition, nor even much of an inquirer; rather he was a reactionary, a rather literal-minded conservative who appealed to scripture and tradition as the basis of his faith."[380] Many of the earlier Alexandrians had also held most of the views propagated by Arius. His transcendental conception of God had close affinities with Athenagoras and his subordinationism belonged to the Origenist tradition. He was not as much interested to demote the Son as much as to exalt the Father. Further, Lucian of Antioch, a canonized Saint of the Catholic Church, held Christological views very similar to Arius, the main difference being that earlier Christian leaders had not resorted to the use of vicious witch hunters like Athanasius. Arius' Trinitarian scheme was as hierarchical as that of Origen. Athanasius' accusation was that Arius had brought the Logos down from heights of lofty divinity to the level of creatures whilst Arius had constantly emphasized that the transcendence of God had been compromised by the attribution of physical processes to Him such as generation and emanation. In reality Arius had done nothing new aside from synchronizing and systematizing earlier transcendental concerns in an open and coherent form. Moreover, he had forced the orthodoxy out of their comfort zone to make them face realities they were neither pleased nor ready to encounter.

The reaction of the orthodoxy was proportionately damaging. They accused Arius of violating Scripture yet failed to notice they had done the same. Further, they were forced to adopt the non-scriptural, and utterly philosophical as well as paradoxical term, *homoousios* (of the same substance) to exclude Arius' views. We may conclude with F. Young that:

> Indeed, the popularity of his biblical solution to the tension between monotheism and faith in Christ is beyond dispute; and there is no reason to doubt Arius' sincerity or genuine Christian intention. Though his opponents attributed his popularity to deception, it is more likely that it was a response to one who was enthusiastic in his pursuit of [the] true meaning of the Christian confession.[381]

Traditional Christianity has been evading real and searching questions regarding its notions of transcendental monotheism and its understanding of the person of Christ. In the name of mysteries and paradoxes, it has long confused many rationally oriented believers. Arius brought these genuine concerns into the public sphere and in doing so echoed the anxieties of the masses. This was the real source of his popularity. He might still have many followers today, even among contemporary Christian believers, laypersons and the clergy alike. C. S. Lewis speaks of Arianism as "one of those 'sensible' synthetic religions which are so strongly recommended today and which, then as now, included among their devotees many highly cultivated clergymen."[382] In short, Arius was one of those adventurous yet cultivated souls who had tried to locate and find a solution to the unsolved problem of Christ's relationship with Almighty God using precise exposition and clarity of thought; factors which to the Church, would destroy the 'mystery' of incarnation. This mystery was maintained by the Council of Nicea, explored next in a little more detail.

The Council of Nicea

The Arian controversy caused division in the Church. It was feared by the Emperor that this rift would split the Roman Empire whose favored religion was Christianity. In June of 325 CE Emperor Constantine summoned the general assembly of bishops from all parts of the empire to meet at Nicea (present-day Iznik in Turkey). There are extant several lists of the bishops who responded to the Emperor's call. The first of the five lists printed by C. H. Turner contains different countings: the first, 218 names; the second, 210; the third, 223; the fourth, 221; and the fifth, 195 names. A Syriac list gives 220 names and two Latin lists given by Mansi give 227 and 204 names. Constantine's own letter to the Alexandrian Church leaders speaks of more than 300 bishops while Athanasius, the stalwart opponent of the Arian controversy, writing soon after 350 CE, fixes the figure at 318, the number generally accepted in the eastern as well as the western Church.

As mentioned, St. Athanasius was the most prominent figure in the Arian controversy. He spent over forty years of his life defending the equality of Jesus Christ with God Almighty against the half god theology of the Christian Arians and the Jesus-is-not-God notions of the non-Christians. St. Athanasius has been highly regarded by the early Church as the Father of Orthodoxy. Frances Young gives a different view of the Saint observing that, "The enhanced role of Athanasius at Nicaea is one feature of the 'legend of Athanasius' which rapidly developed. This 'good tradition' has affected all the main sources, for Athanasius' own apologetic works were a primary source for the historians."[383] She further argues that:

> Alongside this 'good tradition' however, there are traces of a less favourable estimate of Athanasius current among his contemporaries. Certainly he must have been a politician capable of subtle maneuvers; the first seems to have been in his own election, which was definitely contested, may have been illegal, and looks as though it was enforced. There seems to have been a pitiless streak in his character – that he resorted to violence to achieve his own ends is implied by a good deal of evidence.[384]

As a comprehensive discussion of the person is beyond the scope of this study, we will restrict ourselves to exploring only his Christology.

For Athanasius the central objective of the Christian religion was "Redemption" and he subordinated every other thing to this objective. Archibald Robertson finds Athanasius' greatness in this all-pervasive view of Christ's redemption:

> Athanasius was not a systematic theologian; that is, he produced no many-sided theology like that of Origen or Augustine. He had no interest in theological speculation, none of the instincts of a schoolman or philosopher. His theological greatness lies in his firm grasp of soteriological principles, in his resolute subordination of every thing else, even the formula *homoousia* [identical in nature, consubstantial], to the central fact of Redemption, and to what the fact implied as to the Person of the Redeemer.[385]

According to Athanasius 'Salvation' or 'Redemption' demands incarnation, "the salvation was possible only on one condition, namely, that the Son of God was made in Jesus so that we might become God." In his *De Incarnatione et Contra Arianos* he discussed the matter at length:

> For in speaking of the appearance of the Savior amongst us, we must need speak also of the origin of men, that you may know that the reason of his coming down was because of us, and that our transgression called forth the loving-kindness of the Word, that the Lord should both make haste to help us and appear among men. For of his becoming incarnate we were the object, and for our salvation he dealt so lovingly as to appear and be born even in a human body. Thus, then, God was made man, and willed that he should abide in incorruption...[386]

Hence the

> Son of God became the Son of man in order that the sons of men, the sons of Adam, might be made sons of God. The Word, who was begotten of the Father in Heaven in an ineffable, inexplicable, incomprehensible and eternal manner, came to this earth to be

> born in time of the Virgin Mary, Mother of God, in order that they who were born of earth might be born again of God, in Heaven.[387]

The Son does not have any beginning; eternally the Father had the Son, "the beginning of the Son is the Father, and as the Father is without beginning therefore the Son as the Father's...is without beginning as well."[388] It seems that Athanasius was not much concerned with the philosophical implications of what he was saying. He was just a preacher. His concept of the Son's origin in the Father does imply the Son's beginning and in a way subordination which he emphatically denied. Athanasius presumed more and rationalized less. He assumed that the Son was of the same substance of the Father and was exactly like the Father. The Father was the light and the Son was His brightness.

Jesus, then, is the Logos, the Son of God from eternity, uncreated, ungenerated, of the very nature and substance of the Father. McGiffert notes that it was

> not necessary according to Athanasius that Christ should be personally identical with God, that he and God should be the same individual, but it was necessary that he and God should be of one substance or essence. To be equal with God or at one with him in will and purpose was not enough. He must actually possess the very nature of God himself.[389]

It is interesting to note here that Athanasius like all the other Fathers insisted upon the ineffable, invisible nature of God the Father. To him God was not apprehensible to anybody in His ontological or expressive nature but apprehensible only in his works and manifestation through Christ.

This idea of Christ being God and that in the Son we have the Father was not new or original with Athanasius. He was sincerely following the age old tradition of Orthodoxy. Athanasius did differ, however, with Origen and the Apologists in completely denying subordination, adoptionism, and any significant distinction between the Son and the Father. In doing so, he landed in Modalism and was accused of Sabellianism by his opponents. It is difficult to defend Athanasius of this accusation. If in the Son we have the full and proper Godhead, the true and proper nature and substance of God, and in the Virgin Mary the "Mother of God" then what in the world could be more corporeal and anthropomorphic (Sabellianism) than this conception of the deity? F. Young observes:

> On many occasions, Athanasius's exegesis is virtually docetic and seems to us forced and unnatural. All is subordinated to the purpose of showing that the Logos in himself had all the attributes of divinity, e.g. impassability, omniscience, etc. The texts implying weakness or ignorance he explains as merely referring to the incarnation-situation. At one point, Athanasius even goes so far as to say... he imitated our characteristics.[390]

Seemingly Athanasius maintained that Jesus had withheld his divine omniscience and acted as if he were a man due to our human limitations. This Docetic tendency encouraged him to describe Jesus in terms which clearly limited his humanity. It was faith and salvation which led Athanasius to this point in asserting Christ's proper and complete divinity but he, as Harnack puts it, "in making use of these presuppositions in order to express his faith in the Godhead of Christ, *i.e.*, in the essential unity of the Godhead in itself with the Godhead manifested in Christ, fell into an abyss of contradictions."[391] It simply was, to use Harnack's term, "an absurdity". But,

> Athanasius put up with absurdity; without knowing it he made a still greater sacrifice to his faith – the historical Christ. It was at such a price that he saved the religious conviction that Christianity is the religion of perfect fellowship with God, from being displaced by a doctrine which possessed many lofty qualities, but which had no understanding of the inner essence of religion, which sought in religion nothing but "instruction," and finally found satisfaction in an empty dialectic.[392]

Such a lengthy discussion of Athanasius' Christology is justified by the impact it had on later generations. Indeed the history of Christian dogma following Athanasius is the history of his concept of faith in a God-man. The posterity followed him in defining Christianity as a faith centered around the redemptive works of Jesus, the God-man, and both eastern and western Christianity have loyally stuck to the broader framework of Athanasius' Christology even though small differences have been introduced here and there.

Appraisals of Athanasius vary, and in the same vein evaluations of the theological outcome of the Council are also divergent. Traditional scholars frequently portray a rosy picture of the Council and present it as the natural culmination of Apostolic Christianity. For instance Bright contends that over three hundred learned bishops did the following,

> after a thoughtful survey of the subject, in harmony with the Churchly spirit, and in fidelity to transmitted belief and worship, the great Creed was written out, and doubtless read aloud in full Council, in the Emperor's presence, apparently by Hermogenes, afterwards bishop of Cappadocian Caesarea.[393]

Bright's account of the Council is very traditional. The real situation however was a lot more complex, more political, personal and confusing than the staid "thoughtful" or theological event Bright would have us believe took place. Its theological impact upon posterity is however undeniable.

In the Council the creed originally presented by Eusebius of Caesarea, a supporter of the Logos Christology and a foe of every form of Sabellianism, was accepted with certain additions. The will of the Emperor was the decisive factor. Constantine was not so much interested in establishing the truth of theology as he was in political harmony and power. In pursuit of this he was willing to accommodate any creed or theological position which ensured political stability and tolerance. Kelly is correct in observing that there is thus "a sense in which it is unrealistic to speak of the theology of the council."[394] Constantine was so influential that R. L. Fox could write of him that, "Among his other innovations, it was Constantine who first mastered the art of holding, and corrupting, an international conference."[395] Constantine himself, his relationship to Christianity and his conversion, are controversial subjects to this day. It is tempting to agree with Kelly that

> the status of the Nicene creed was very different in the generation or so following the council from what we many have been brought up to believe. One is perhaps tempted to sympathize with the somewhat radical solution of the problem provided by that school of historians which treat the Nicene symbol as purely political formula representative of no strain of thought in the Church but imposed on the various wrangling groups as a badge of union.[396]

It was neither the Holy Spirit nor the ecumenical synod of three hundred or so bishops who steered the Council proceedings. It was the emperor and his iron fist rule. This was the decisive factor, though lip service and occasional reverence was shown to them.

Unfortunately, later traditional Christianity gave a great deal of significance and authority to the Council's decisions and terms whose religious nature seemed more inclined to political fervor and to combat Arianism than anything else. The Nicene Creed begins:

> We believe in One God, the Father Almighty, Maker of all things both visible and invisible: And in one Lord Jesus Christ, the Son of God, Begotten of the Father, Only-begotten, *That is, from the Essence of the Father*, God from God, Light from Light, Very God from Very God, Begotten, not made, *of one essence with the Father*; by whom all things, both in heaven and earth, were made; Who for us men and for our salvation came down, and was incarnate, and became man, suffered, and rose again the third day; ascended into heavens; cometh to judge the quick and dead. And in the Holy Spirit.[397]

Then it goes on to say:

> But those who say, once He was not, and – before He was begotten, He was not, and – He came into existence out of what was not,' or – That the Son of God was a different "hypostasis"

or "ousia" or – that He was made,' or – is (was) changeable or mutable are anathematized by the Catholic and Apostolic Church of God.[398]

The central phrase of this fundamental Christian confession is *homoousios* meaning of one substance with the Father. Though obviously a theological term, it was not exactly an adequate theological solution. It was a layman's solution to pin down a pure and stark divinity for Christ without much precision, explanation and rationality. It neither preserved the boundaries between the transcendent God and Christ by an emanative scheme of a hierarchal emanative Trinity, as affected by the early Platonist Fathers, nor kept the mystery of its secret locked in its box. Rather, it brought the redemptive Monarchian scheme into the public sphere and in confidently touted clear terms. Consequently it was accused of being Sabellianism along with its defenders, Athanasius and Marcellus.

Disputing it vigorously Arians argued that such an analogy and identity was absolutely inappropriate to the relationship between God and the Logos, putting forward three reasons to substantiate their position: (1) God the Father was self-existent, unoriginated, eternal while the Son was produced by the Father. Therefore the Father and the Son could not be fully equal. (2) The Father was neither begotten nor was begettable while the Son was begotten and begettable. (3) The Father had begotten the Son, the God, while the Son had not begotten another Son. How could the unoriginated Father and the originated Son be equal? Arian reasoning was logical, rational and systematic. That of the traditional Apostolic Fathers such as Athanasius on the other hand was illogical and confusing, and their answers moreover, self-contradictory. Their doctrine made the Son both unbegotten and begotten, unbegotten as part of the whole of Deity, yet begotten of the Father as a relationship within the Trinity. Harnack rightly argues that there is "in fact, no philosophy in existence possessed of formulae which could present in an intelligible shape the propositions of Athanasius."[399] The same can be said of subsequent Christian Trinitarian thought at large.

The Council decided to favor the unintelligible, self-contradictory doctrine of Christology at the expense of clear precision and logic. All bishops present subscribed to this formula with the exception of two, Theonas of Marmarika and Secundus of Ptolemais, alongside Arius. Arians were condemned and called "Porphyrians", and their works ordered to be burned because, in the words of Julius of Rome, "For theirs was no ordinary offense, nor had they sinned against man, but against our Lord Jesus Christ Himself, the Son of the Living God."[400] The Emperor gave his final approval asserting that, "what satisfied the three hundred bishops is nothing else than the judgment of God, but most of all where Holy Spirit being present in the thought of men such as these and so ripe in years, made known the Divine will."[401] A majority of modern traditional Christian scholars view these historical dogmatic developments as an illustration of "how the Holy Spirit brings about a gradual increase in the Church's actual consciousness of the mysteries revealed by Jesus Christ."[402] A. Harnack, on the other hand, views them as an outcome of a lack of understanding and education:

> As regards the composition of the Council, the view expressed by the Macedonian Sabinus of Heraclea (Socr. I. 8), that the majority of the bishops were uneducated, is confirmed by the astonishing results. The general acceptance of the resolution come to by the Council is intelligible only if we presuppose that the question in dispute was above most of the bishops.[403]

Whatever the composition of the Council, the impact it had and the high position its creed and confession enjoys to this day in traditional Christianity is overwhelming. It is called "the greatest of all Synods" and is generally described with great praise and lofty terms:

> The Council of Nicaea is what it is to us quite apart from all doubtful or apocryphal traditions: it holds a pre-eminent place of honour, because it established for all ages of the Church that august and inestimable confession, which may be to unbelief, or to anti-dogmatic spirit, a mere stumbling block, a mere incubus, because it is looked at *ab extra*, in a temper which cannot sympathize with the faith which it enshrines, or the adoration which it stimulates; but to those who genuinely and definitely

> believe in the true divinity of the Redeemer, the doctrine of Nicaea, in the expanded form which Christendom has adopted, is prime treasure of their religious life, the expression of a faith coherent in itself, and capable of overcoming the world in the power of the Incarnation who is the "Co-essential," that is, as St. Athanasius was careful to explain it, the "real" Son of God.[404]

Surprisingly, theological coherence is absent from the Christological solutions and creeds adopted by the Council. It seems that lofty aspirations and gracious ideas were the intended goals, as well as the elimination of competition, with the truth of scripture paying homage to the needs of the State, rather than the achievement of a coherent theology. The outcome of this great comprise in effect created and entrenched the Jesus of today and one wonders whether or not it did service or disservice to the Christian God paradigm. If disservice then theological truth had been thoughtlessly sacrificed in the interests of unity, and the price paid a terrible one, leaving the Church and Christianity in an apalling state of affairs. To claim a pure, hard-core divinity for the Son, forgetting the true essence and transcendence of God the Father and ignoring the terrible inconsistencies of this approach is mind-boggling. This approach looked upon the Father not as the Father but as the Father of the Son, Jesus Christ. The ethical gospel of Jesus was completely lost in the metaphysical contortions of the Trinity giving rise to the labyrinthine discussions of the divine substance and persons which have endlessly followed, tragically to the detriment of the Church and the loss of souls. Fairbairn rightly laments that the

> Church, when it thought of the Father, thought more of the First Person in relation to the Second than of God in relation to man; when it thought of the Son, it thought more of the Second Person in relation to the First than of humanity in relation to God.... The Nicene theology failed here because it interpreted God and articulated its doctrine in the terms of the schools rather than in the terms of the consciousness of Christ.[405]

He concludes observing:

> The division of the Persons within Godhead had as its necessary result the division of God from man, and the exaltation of miraculous and unethical agencies as the means of bridging over the gulf. The inadequacy in these cardinal respects of the Nicene theology would be inexplicable were we to regard it as a creation of supernatural wisdom or the result of special Divine enlightenment; but it is altogether normal when conceived as a stage in the development of Christian thought.[406]

The Aftermath of the Nicene Council

Christianity had entered the halls of power but the political authority achieved was no real solution to the unresolved theological complexities which dogged it. These profound theological convolutions continued haunting the Church leadership as well as the common believers.

It is obvious that a clear doctrine of the "Trinity" is incorporated in the Nicene Creed even though only one indefinite statement is made with regards to the Holy Spirit, the Third Person of the Holy Trinity. The deity of Christ (the central problem for our study of anthropomorphism in Christianity) was fully conserved and rendered immune to the theological as well as philosophical criticism that had previously discredited Modalism. All avenues leading to the Godhead of Christ, the Savior, and impulses leading to his exaltation to the highest possible place and worship, that of God Himself, were given free play without his worshippers being convicted of polytheism, obscurantism or anthropomorphism. No such emphasis was laid upon the equal divinity of the Holy Spirit. The Nicene Creed's newly added Holy Spirit clause was left vague and ambiguous.

On the other hand, as the Creed was carried in the Council under pressure of Constantine against the inclinations of a great majority of the bishops in attendence, it did not settle the theological dispute concerning the divinity of the Holy Spirit. The nature of Jesus had been decided but the Council failed to elaborate upon the role or nature of the Holy Spirit, the supposed equal and eternal member of the divine Trinity. The Council in reality provided political or diplomatic solutions to the inherent theological problems. The Council's arbitrary decisions temporarily succeeded in passifying prevailing conflicting emotions and interpretations without much long-term theological impact or satisfaction. The original claims that the Council's decisions were directed by the Providence of the Holy Spirit were soon exposed and proven wrong. It needed only a change of mind in Constantine himself (in 336), especially on his death in 337, to change the so-called Holy Spirit stamped Council decisions and exposition of the divine will. This turned everything upside down. The Saints of the Council were turned into culprits by the emperial decree and the culprits were made into Saints. Arias along with his previously regarded heretical views was honored and Athanasius exiled. Jerome's words are not wholly exaggeration when he writes, "the whole world groaned in astonishment to find itself Arian."[407] It was once again imperial power first in the figure of Valentinian (364) and then Theodosius (380) which came to the rescue of the Nicene Creed with some alterations and additions at the Council of Constantinople in 381. The Nicaeno-Constantinopolitan Creed reads:

> We believe in one God Father Almighty, Maker of heaven and earth and all things visible and invisible; and in one Lord Jesus Christ, the only-begotten Son of God, who was begotten of the Father before all ages, light from light, true God from True God, begotten not made, of one substance with the father, through whom all things were made; who for us men and for our salvation came down from heaven and was incarnate of the Holy Spirit and Mary the Virgin, and was made man, and was crucified on our behalf under Pontius Pilate, and suffered and was buried, and rose on the third day according to the Scriptures, and ascended into heaven, and sitteth at the right hand of the Father, and cometh again with glory to judge quick and dead, of whose kingdom there shall not be an end; and in the Holy Spirit, the Lord, the life-giver, who proceedeth from the Father, who with Father and Son is worshipped and glorified, who spoke through the prophets; in one holy Catholic and Apostolic Church. We confess one baptism for remission of sins; we accept a resurrection of the dead and the life of age to come.[408]

This Creed whose origination at the Council of Constantinople is questioned by F. J. A. Hort and A. Harnack as well as by established scholars like Eduard Schwartz, Badcock and Kelly was dispersed everywhere throughout the East and the West in the sixth century under the name of the Nicene Creed. The Creed represents more nearly the position of the Cappadocians than that of the Athanasians. It represents the *homoiousionoi*, who accepted *homoiousios* (meaning "similar") but not *homoousios*. This explains why it omits the words "from the same substance (*homoousios*) of the Father" which was the most important phrase to Athanasius. Though more moderate than the earlier original Creed, it aims at achieving the same goal, the proper divinity and deity of Jesus Christ, hence conserving the results achieved at the Nicene Council.

It is worth mentioning at this point that the Cappadocian Fathers, Basil the Great (330–379), Gregory of Nazianzuz (329–389) and Basil's brother, Gregory of Nyssa (329–394), were all known for their adherence to the Trinitarian formula. Although they agreed completely with Athanasius in attributing a real and proper divinity to Jesus Christ, accepting him as being from the same substance and nature as the Father, they disagreed with him with regard to the question of persons. According to Athanasius, the Father, the Son and the Holy Spirit were the same being living in a threefold relationship. As a man can be a father, a son and a brother, the being of God can be the Father, the Son or the Holy Spirit. The Cappadocians disagreed. They contended that the Father, the Son and the Spirit were three equally alike beings, insisting on their unity, but were also independent persons. This is what Basil described when he discussed the matter at length:

> Many, not distinguishing in theology the common substance from the hypostases, fall into the same fancies and imagine that it make no difference whether substance (*ousis*) or hypostasis be spoken of. Whence it has pleased some to admit without examination that if one substance then also one hypostasis should be affirmed. And on the other hand those who accept three hypostases think themselves compelled to confess an equal number of substances. I have therefore, that you may not fall into a similar error, written

> you a brief discourse concerning the matter. This then, to put it briefly, is the meaning of the word: Some nouns which are used to cover many and various objects have a more general sense like man.... When we imply this word we designate the common nature... not some particular man to whom the name especially belongs. For Peter is no more man than Andrew or John or James. Hence, as the word embraces all that are included under the same name, there is need of some mark of distinction by which we may recognize not man in general but Peter or John. There are other nouns which stand for a particular object and denote not the one nature but a separate thing having nothing in common, so far as its individuality goes, with others of the same kind, like Paul or Timothy....Thus when two or more are taken together, such as Paul and Silvanus and Timothy, and inquiry is made concerning their substance, we do not use one word for the substance of Paul, another for that of Silvanus, and other for that of Timothy....If then you transfer to theology the distinction you have drawn in human affairs between substance and hypostasis you will not go wrong.[409]

Gregory of Nazianzuz explained the formula using the following example:

> What was Adam? A creature of God. What, then, was Eve? A fragment of the creature. And what was Seth? The begotten of both. Does it, then, seem to you that creature and fragment and begotten are the same being? Of course it does not. But were not these persons consubstantial? Of course they were. Well, then, here it is an acknowledged fact that different persons may have the same substance.[410]

He further argues:

> For the Father is not Son, and yet this is not due to either deficiency or subjection of essence; but the very fact of being unbegotten or begotten, or proceeding, has given the name of Father to the first,

> of the Son to the second, and to the third, him of whom we are speaking, of the Holy Ghost, that the distinction of three persons may be preserved in the one nature and dignity of the Godhead. For neither is the Son Father, for the Father is one, but he is what the Father is; nor is the Spirit Son because he is of God, for the only-begotten is one, but he is what the Son is. The three are one in Godhead, and the one three in properties; so that neither is the unity a Sabellian one, nor does the Trinity countenance the present evil distinction.[411]

Gregory of Nyssa gives the example of gold observing that "there may be many golden staters, but gold is one, so we may be confronted with many who individually share in human nature, such as Peter, James, and John, yet the "man" [the human nature] in them is one."[412] There is a complete operational harmony between these three distinct Persons:

> We do not learn that the Father does something on his own, in which the Son does not co-operate. Or again, that the Son acts on his own without the Spirit. Rather does every operation which extends from God to creation and is designated according to our differing conceptions of it have its origin in the Father, proceed through the Son, and reach its completion by the Holy Spirit. It is for this reason that the word for the operation is not divided among the persons involved. For the action of each in any matter is not separate and individualized. But whatever occurs, whether in reference to God's providence for us or to the government and constitution of the universe, occurs through the three Persons, and is not three separate things.[413]

He distinguishes between Persons on the basis of causality:

> the only way by which we distinguish one Person from the other, by believing, that is, that one is the cause and the other depends on the cause. Again, we recognize another distinction with regard to that which depends on the cause. There is that which depends

> on the first cause and that which is derived from what immediately depends on the first cause. Thus the attribute of being only-begotten without doubt remains with the Son, and we do not question that the Spirit is derived from the Father.[414]

How the uncaused first cause and that which is caused or derived from the Father can be considered the same, equal in all properties and respects, is a valid question not satisfactorily answered by any of the Cappadocians. The Father did not grow in knowledge and wisdom, as did the Son. The Father did not pray to the Son, as did the Son to the Father. The Father never stated that the Son was greater than He, as did the Son. The Father never suffered death nor cried out to the Son from the cross for the Son's help, as did the Son, etc. It requires no intelligence to grasp this, and the Gospels are crystal clear about these facts. The Cappadocians needed rationale to substantiate their claims of the absolute equality of the Son with the Father. What they ended up with however, were mere suppositions and sheer presumptions, forcing them to hide behind a smoke screen of mystery phraseology, both unintelligible and woolly.

This Cappadocian Trinitarian analogy is one of the two chief types of analogy that has been used throughout the course of Christian history to explain notions of the Trinity. The Cappadocians begin with a consideration of three persons, as we have just seen, while Augustinian analogy emphasizes a co-equal Trinity by distinguishing the persons in terms of their internal relations within a person (e.g., memory, will, and intelligence or love, the lover – *amans* – and the object loved, *quod amatur*). Both are unsatisfactory and contain several flaws. The former, for instance, could lead to tritheism while the latter could lead to Sabellianism or Unitarianism. Francis Young rightly remarks concerning Gregory of Nyssa's analogy that, "No matter how much he protests their common eternity, common activity and common will, it is difficult to call a theology based on such a definition of their common nature, monotheistic."[415] Others like Harnack, F. Loofs, F. W. Green etc., have observed that this Cappadocian position was really a kind of Homoean view, or to use Harnack's words, "the community of substance in the sense of likeness (or equality) of substance, not in that of unity of substance."[416] To E. R. Hardy this observation is misleading and far from fair: "The *ousia* in the Godhead is identical in each Person: the common humanity in men is only *generic*."[417]

Hardy's explanation is attractive but seems a little forced and artificial. The Cappadocians seem to have used the terms in their generic forms without much specifications. It would be too much to say that the Cappadocian Fathers intended tritheism but it seems quite fair to observe that their distinction between three Persons of the Trinity and their usage of the analogy of Peter, James, and John could easily lead to tritheism, as was observed even during their own life time. Our present understanding of the human person leaves very little room to doubt the validity of this objection. Undoubtedly to the Cappadocians, as to almost all Fathers, God is incomprehensible, ineffable, one and infinite. It is also true that Basil and others roundly denied any suffering by, or human weakness in, the Godhead itself. On the other hand, it is equally true that the understanding of God the Cappadocians aspired to and propagated by their writings did not and cannot remove them from a number of problems and confusions which have been found in almost all the orthodox Fathers, such as the relationship of Christ to God. Grillmeier correctly notes that the "Cappadocians have seen something, but neither their path nor their goal is stated clearly. As a result, the solution of christological problems is made much more difficult, as will be evident in the case of Nestorius."[418]

Gregory of Nazianzuz in opposition to Gregory of Nyssa takes over Origen's notion of the soul as mediator between Godhead and flesh. He clearly uses the orthodox problematic terminology and also declares Christ's divine nature to be dominant over his inferior human nature. "In this the stronger part (sc. the Godhead) prevailed in order that I too might be made God so far as he is made man."[419] Yet, if his human nature became God, then any claim of denial of suffering and weaknesses in the Godhead loses ground. This is in fact pure corporealism and faces the very same problems which beset the solutions propagated by the Church Fathers before them. It also brings us to the heart of the issue. How could the suffering Son be equal to the non-suffering Father if their substance and divinity are said to be the same? Consequently like their predecessors, the Cappadocians sought refuge in unexplainable "mystery" terminology, a convenient sanctuary when under scrutiny of logic. In the end, their dogmatic theology fell by the wayside and collapsed in mystery, however some of their bold phrases remained to haunt them with the labels of Sabellianism or Modalism. Gregory's famous simile of the absorption of the flesh in the Godhead 'like a drop of vinegar in the sea' is just one such example.

Though the Cappadocian's Trinitarian formula of the divinity – one substance in three persons *(personae)*, or three independent realities – is called "the scientific" formula, it failed to provide any intelligible solution to the problem it was formulated to solve, i.e. the nature of the historical Jesus and his relationship to God. The words used to distinguish the persons in the eternal trinity are, as observes Tillich, "empty." "And what do such words mean? They are words without content, because there is no perception of any kind which can confirm their meaning."[420] The formula may not lead to Docetism, Sabellianism, or the Modalism of Athanasius, but it could lead to something more disastrous, namely "tritheism".

It will be apparent by now that the orthodox Fathers insisted upon the true, perfect, full divinity and Godhead of Jesus Christ. They aspired to maintain two mutually contradictory principles i.e., the transcendence and ineffability of God in the figure of God the Father, and the full incarnation of God in the human figure of Christ. All the explanations given to elucidate this, whether as modes, or persons, or any other interpretation, betray unquestionable corporealism and anthropomorphism. It is impossible to maintain that a human being who lived a true, historical and full human life was in fact the full incarnation of God and then aspire to avoid or deny charges of corporealism and anthropomorphism. This becomes even more evident when we turn to discussions concerning the will and nature of the person of Jesus Christ which were at the center of later controversies.

THE PERSON OF JESUS CHRIST

It was, and always has been, the Christian desire to attain redemption that has led the Christian faith to proclaim and maintain the deity of

Jesus Christ. From the earlier Fathers to the Council of Constantinople a common thread or concern has woven Christian doctrine together, and this has been the need to safeguard the proper divinity of Christ along with attempts to maintain the transcendence of God. At the same time, there has always remained the question of Christ's humanity. It was impossible to deny this humanity for according to the Gospels, Jesus had been a historical reality. Once the Church, over various gradual attempts, had finally arrived at the conclusion that Jesus was God and fully divine, they were faced with the issue of how to in some way reconcile this divine / human unity, to strike a balance between and interpret the relationship. The difficulty of regarding Christ as both divine and simultaneously human led some to Docetism and others to Adoptionism. The recognition of an absolute, pure divinity for Jesus made the problem more acute and insistent. Just a few decades after the Council of Nicea the pendulum swung completely in the other direction. Focus now was no longer on the pre-existence of the Son or the relationship of God the Son to the Father, but rather the relation of God to man in the person of the historical Jesus. The God incarnate formula of the Council was considered too metaphysical to be an intelligible part of real human history. If Jesus was indeed God incarnate then what was his real nature, human or divine? Human history had no parallel to explain this incarnational paradigm so how to understand it in logical human terms?

It was Apollinarius (d. 390), bishop of Laodicea and a close friend of Athanasius, who proposed a somewhat rational solution to this complex problem. Apollinarius made a subtle and rigorous attempt to propound a formula of Christ's nature and internal formulations of relationships within Christ's Person. He took the long accepted Alexandrian Christology of the Word-flesh to its logical limits. As mentioned earlier, to Athanasius and the Nicene Creed the absolute divinity of Christ was considered essential to ensure redemption, and it was strongly held that only the true Son of God could reveal God to man. Adhering to this Word-flesh Christology, Apollinarius argued that this act of redemption could not be possible without the deification of the man Jesus Christ. Therefore, he contended that Jesus had only one theo-anthropic or divine-human nature. At the point of incarnation the

Logos, a divine spirit or mind, was united with the human body and soul of Christ to become thence onwards the active personal element in Jesus' being while relegating the human element, comprised of the body and soul, to a secondary or passive level. The frankly acknowledged presupposition of this argument is that the divine Word was substituted for the normal human soul in Christ. Apollinarius believed that if the divine was separated from the human in Christ, salvation would be imperiled so he emphasized the deity of Christ and the unity of his person through a merger of the human with the Logos making the human element glorified. How he reasoned could humans be baptized in Jesus' name and be redeemed by his atoning death if he were just an ordinary man?

In his confession Apollinarius summarized this theme: "We declare that the Logos of God became man for the purpose of our salvation, so that we might receive the likeness of the heavenly One and be made God after the likeness of the true Son of God according to nature and the Son of man according to flesh, our Lord Jesus Christ."[421] In this process of complete fusion or union the human, historical Jesus, and his humanity, was replaced by divinity and completely transformed by the divine Logos. Apollinarius used to delight in speaking of Christ as "God incarnate", "flesh-bearing God", or "God born of a woman". He concluded saying:

> One and the same is the body and the God, of whom it is the body, not that the flesh has been changed into that which is incorporeal, but that it has a property which is from us..., in accordance with the generation from the Virgin, and that which is above us..., in accordance with the mixture or union with God the Logos.[422]

He affirmed that Christ's flesh was "divine flesh" or "the flesh of God" and was the proper object of worship. It was virtually a clear Docetic tendency implying that Christ was not a real man but only appeared as a man. This was a culmination of the all out corporeal tendency which had all along been a part of Church thinking but often concealed. It meant that Christ in his incarnation had retained his divine soul, nature or *ousia*, and had not adopted a human rational soul or nature. It was because of this denial of a human rational soul in Christ that Apollinaris had to deny the two natures and two persons in Christ. Kelly recognizes that, "The brilliance and thoroughgoing logic of Apollinarius' synthesis are undeniable."[423]

Apollinarian thought or "Monophysitism" as it was later called, was another expression of Monarchianism. Pelikan observes that Apollinaris was expressing a common opinion when he spoke of "innumerable teachings supplied everywhere throughout the divine Scripture, all of them together bearing witness to the apostolic and ecclesiastical faith."[424] In Harnack's words, Apollinarius

> merely completed the work of Athanasius inasmuch as he added to it the Chriostology which was demanded by the Homousia of the Logos. They both made a supreme sacrifice to their faith in that they took from the complicated and contradictory tradition regarding Christ those elements only which were in harmony with the belief that He was the Redeemer from sin and death.[425]

But it was widely felt that Apollinarius had safeguarded the divinity of Jesus on account of his humanity. The Cappadocian Fathers, the two Gregories and other churchmen, opposed him by criticizing that his Christology failed to meet the essential condition of salvation and atonement, i.e. the unity of the human rational soul, the seat of sin, with the Logos. In his famous phrase Gregory Nazianzen argued that, "What has not been assumed cannot be restored; it is what is united with God that is saved."[426] Apollinarius was condemned as heretical at the second council of Constantinople in 381.

On the other hand, the representatives of the Antiochian school challenged 'Monophysitism' or Apollinarianism with their scientific Christological dogma. In general, the Antiochian's interest in Jesus was more ethical than redemptive. They viewed in him a perfect ethical and moral example. Jesus could have not been a perfect ethical model had he not been a complete human being with free will and a genuine human personality. The Antiochian school, argues Kelly, "deserves credit for bringing back the historical Jesus."[427] Diodorus of Tarsus and then Theodore of Mopsuestia, like Paul of Samosata, advocated a moral union 'unity of grace and will' rather than unity of substance and nature. Their Christology conformed to the "Word-man" scheme rather than the Alexandrian "Word-flesh" scheme.

Theodore emphasized the perfect humanity of Christ: "A complete man, in his nature, is Christ, consisting of a rational soul and human flesh; complete is the human person; complete also the person of the divinity in him. It is wrong to call one of them impersonal."[428] Opposing Monophysitism, he argued: "One should not say that the Logos became flesh but one should say "He took on humanity.""[429] To conform his views to that of the Logos Christology and Nicene doctrine of Christ's proper divinity, he had no choice but to assert Christ's two natures: one of a complete human, the other complete divine, each with a full personality and all qualities and faculties that go therewith. None of these persons or natures mixed with the other: "The Logos dwelt in man but did not become man; the human was associated and united with the divine but was not deified."[430] Their association and closeness was essential for salvation but not so close as to render it irrelevant to man as man or to involve the unchangeable, immutable Logos in the suffering of the cross. In Theodore's formula,

> the Godhead was separated from the one who was suffering in the trial of death, because it was impossible for him to taste the trial of death if [the Godhead] were not cautiously remote from him, but also near enough to do the needful and necessary things for the [human] nature that was assumed by it.[431]

He further argued that while the scripture distinguishes the natures, it at the same time stresses the unity between them. Therefore, he contended, "we point to difference of natures, but to unity of Person" or in other words "the two natures are, through their connection, apprehended to be one reality."[432]

As we see, Theodore emphatically denies the transformation or transmutation of the Logos into flesh. He also held that the divine nature did not change the human nature. Jesus, having human nature, by grace and free will could follow the divine nature. Therefore, one could say that Mary gave birth to God. This clearly was a metaphorical rather than substance designation.

Theodore's opponents rejected this theory as leading to a "monster with two heads", a being with two personal centers and a combination of two sons.[433] Theodore denied this as mere accusation but, to McGiffert, "to all intents and purpose he was doing so."[434] Cyril of Alexandria singled him out for attack and since the Fifth General Council of Constantinople in 533 he has been labeled as a Nestorian before Nestorius. Modern scholarship vindicates him of this accusation as Kelly observes:

> In modern times, especially since the rediscovery of the relatively innocuous *Catechetical Homilies*, there has been a decided reaction against this verdict. It has been emphasized, for example, that he was deeply concerned, so far as his categories of thought allowed, to establish the oneness of subject in the God-man....He can write, for example, 'Thus there results neither any confusion of the natures nor any untenable division of the Person; for our account of the natures must remain unfocused, and the Person must be recognized as indivisible'; and again, 'We display a distinction of natures, but unity of Person'. For these and similar reasons the traditional estimate has been replaced by a more appreciative one which views him primarily as a theologian who championed the reality of the Lord's manhood against Apollinarianism and strove to do justice to His human experience.[435]

F. Young observes that, "If Theodore stresses the duality, it is because for him the unity is obvious."[436]

Theodore's is another reflection of the contradictory nature of the New Testament writings. On the one hand they emphasize transcendental monotheism, and Jesus' feeble humanity and subordination to God Almighty, whilst on other occasions they seemingly attribute a kind of divine status to Jesus especially in the Pauline and Johannine writings. The traditionalists bent on attaining salvation through the redemptive death of Jesus and their own union with divinity have inclined towards the Johannine interpretations and pushed them to their limits. The rational believers have always been worried about the danger this approach poses to transcendental monotheism and ethical piety.

Christianity is the name and product of these antithetical and diametrically opposed tendencies as well as concerns. Many innocent and sincere believers have had to pay for the contradictory nature of their scriptural writings. Nestorius is a good example of this theological nightmare.

The controversy regarding the person of Christ came to a head on collision in the fifth century when Nestorius, a younger member of the Antiochian school, became bishop of Constantinople (428). He protested against the tendency very common among the masses, especially among the monks in the neighborhood of the capital, to exalt the Virgin Mary as "Mother of God" or *theotokos*.

> God cannot have a mother, he argued, and no creature could have engendered the Godhead; Mary bore a man, the vehicle of divinity but not God. The Godhead cannot have been carried for nine months in a woman's womb, or have been wrapped in baby-clothes, or have suffered, died and been buried.[437]

H. Chadwick notes that, "Nothing caused so much scandal as a remark of Nestorius that 'God is not a baby two or three months old.'"[438] Nestorius held that she should either be called 'mother of the man Jesus' or 'mother of Christ'. His objection was to the transference of human attributes to the divine Logos. He emphatically denied that the Logos participated in the sufferings of the human nature of Christ.

Nestorius believed that Jesus had two natures. He maintained that before the union of the man and the Logos in Jesus, the man was a person distinct from the Logos. Then "He who is the similitude of God has taken the person of the flesh."[439] After the union these two separate persons retained their identity: "There the persons exist not without ousia, nor here again does the ousia exist without the person, nor also the nature without person, nor yet the person without ousia."[440] His watchword was that, "I hold the natures apart, but unite the worship".[441] He, following Theodore of Mopsuestia in his two nature Christology, held that, "When we distinguish the natures, we say that the nature of the Divine Logos is complete that His person also is complete...[likewise we say] that man's nature is complete and his person also is complete. But when we consider the union, we say there is one person only".[442] Nestorius argued that after incarnation there resulted a new person, namely the person of Jesus, of which the Logos and man were two component parts. He believed that for true redemption, the second Adam must have been a real man. Kelly comments:

> It was all-important in his eyes that the impassability of 'the God' should be preserved, and that 'the man' for his part should retain his spontaneity and freedom of action. Hence, though speaking on occasion of a 'union'..., the term he preferred was 'conjunction'..., which seem to avoid all suspicion of a confusion or mixing of the natures.[443]

To Nestorius it was a "perfect", "exact" and "continuous" union. Unlike the Alexandrian Christological view that upheld "hypostatic or natural" union, his view of union was "voluntary". By this he meant "the drawing together of the divine and human by gracious condescension on the one hand, and love and obedience on the other. As a result of their mutual adhesion, Christ was a single being, with a single will and intelligence, inseparable and indivisible."[444] Addressing Cyril of Alexandria he states: "I said and affirmed that the union is in the one person of the Messiah... but thou [actest] in the reverse way, because thou wishest that in the two natures God the Word should be the person of the union."[445] Nestorius was anathematized by the Fifth Ecumenical Council at Constantinople (533) for his supposed heresy of the two natures and two persons concept.

Cyril in his letter of 430, which was used as one of the sources in the Council, had already written 12 anathemas which were specifically pointed towards Nestorius. The main three points directed to Nestorius were:

> (1) If anyone does not confess that Emmanuel is God in truth, and therefore the holy Virgin is *theotokos* – for she bore in the flesh the Word of God became flesh – let him be anathema. (2) If anyone does not confess that the Word of God the Father was

> united by hypostases to the flesh and is one Christ with his own flesh, that is, the same both God and man together, let him be anathema. (3) If any one divides the hypostases in the one Christ after his union, joining them only by conjunction in dignity, or authority or power, and not rather by coming together in a union by nature, let him be anathema.[446]

Cyril's position emphasized a physical or a metaphysical unity of the divine and human nature in Christ. It paid lip service to human nature and considered the incarnate nature of God as the real one in the historical Jesus. His formula, "out of two natures, one" left no room to doubt that the Logos God had assumed humanity. Hence, it can be said that 'God is born', that 'God suffered', if only it be added, 'according to the flesh'. He also insisted that, "Since the holy Virgin gave birth after the flesh to God who was united by *hypostasis* with flesh, therefore we say that she is *theotokos*..."[447] Cyril championed the popular theological position and won the wide support of the masses. This was a victory of the worship of Mary as the mother of God quite widespread in Christian circles of his time. Cyril used his popularity and political clout to mercilessly suppress all opposition to his position. He not only deified the human Jesus but also brought God to the womb of the very human Mary thus obliterating all possibilities, confusions and mysteries, so far vaguely maintained by the Church, between the transcendent God and the human Jesus. It was not his theology or spiritualism but his skill at political maneuvering that won him support against an otherwise more spiritual and sincere Nestorius. In Campenhausen's view Cyril, "was not greatly concerned with the truth; outwardly, however, he continued to play the part of the anxious, thoughtful leader who refuses to take action for reasons of purely personal spite, leaving the first steps to his best friends and go-between."[448] It was due to Cyril's efforts and political genius that Nestorius was made guilty of heresy and deposed in the general Council of Ephesus (431) but, the final settlement was reached at the Council of Chalcedon.

It was views about the person of Jesus held by Theodore and which were at bottom not much different from the orthodox Fathers which caused Nestorius to suffer the stigma of heresy. Some modern scholars like J. F. Bathune-Baker, F. Loofs and M. V. Anastos have tried to rehabilitate Nestorius' orthodoxy. Anastos, for instance, observes:

> If Nestorius and Cyril could have been compelled to discuss their differences calmly and to define their terms with precision, under the supervision of a strict and impartial arbiter who could have kept them under control until they had explained themselves clearly, there is little doubt that they would have found themselves in substantial agreement theologically, though separated *toto caelo* as far as their respective archiepiscopal sees was concerned.[449]

Kelly notes that, "When we try to assess the character of Nestorius's teaching, one thing which is absolutely clear is that he was not a Nestorian in the classic sense of the word."[450] Grillmeier observes that "we can recognize just as clearly that he need not have been condemned had attention been paid to his care for tradition and to the new problem which he posed, despite his speculative 'impotence' (G. L. Prestige) to solve it."[451] F. Young writes:

> Nestorius was the victim. He has become the symbol of one type of christological position taken to extremes. And for that he suffered. He could legitimately complain that his condemnation had been unfair: Cyril had plotted his downfall; Cyril chaired the synod; Cyril was his accuser and his judge; Cyril represented Pope and Emperor. Cyril was everything! Nestorius had no chance of a hearing. There can be few who would defend the proceedings at Ephesus.[452]

P. Tillich remarks: "If we say that Nestorius became a heretic, we could say that he was the most innocent of all heretics. Actually he was a victim of the struggle between Byzantium and Alexandria."[453]

When looked at from the perspective of our study, it becomes evident that traditional Christianity for the sake of salvation and redemption, has always intended to crucify God and has denied all efforts to make the cruxifiction the suffering of a mere human being.

This is crystal clear corporealism and could not have been maintained on the basis of speculative theology or any logical effort alone. It required the backing of the state, and exploitive and political power to suppress all rational and curious inquiries, made available to several traditional Logos-flesh theologians. Further, this act of blaspheming God, to use Nestorius' term, could not have been done by the Holy Spirit as always claimed by so-called Orthodoxy but rather by the political powers of secular and at times pagan emperors.

In conclusion it is worth quoting the following famous passage from Nestorius, who wrote:

> It is my earnest desire that even by anathematizing me they may escape from blaspheming God [and that those who so escape may confess God, holy, almighty and immortal, and not change the image of the incorruptible God for the image of corruptible man, and mingle heathenism with Christianity... but that Christ may be confessed to be in truth and in nature God and Man, being by nature immortal and impassable as God, and mortal and passable by nature as Man – not God in both natures, nor again Man in both natures. The goal of my earnest wish is that God may be blessed on earth as in heaven]; but for Nestorius, let him be anathema; only let men speak of God as I pray for them that they may speak. For I am with those who are for God, and not with those who are against God, who with an outward show of religion reproach God and cause him to cease from being God.[454]

The words of Nestorius speak for themselves. How in the world can anyone who considers Mary to be the mother of God, and as such accepts that the Logos God spent nine months in the womb of a woman, grew like a baby, harbored complete human needs, and died on the cross, deny accusations of heathenism? This is the true challenge and struggle of popular Christianity. F. Young pays homage to Nestorius in the following words:

> It was a great Christian who wrote those words. There have been many who were prepared to die as martyrs for what they believed

> to be the truth, but Nestorius was prepared to live cursed and consigned to oblivion, as long as God was not dishonored... In tribulation he showed a greater generosity of spirit than many who have received the name saint rather than heretic.[455]

The Council of Chalcedon

The decisions of the general Council of Ephesus did not settle the issue of the person of Christ. Just fifteen years after the agreement patched up in 433, quarrel broke out again in 448 when Eutyches, Archimandrite of a monastery in the neighborhood of Constantinople, vehemently opposed Nestorianism or the Antiochian party's "inspired man" Christology in favor of Cyrillianism or the Alexandrian God-man Christology. It is hard to determine Eutyches' original doctrine due to lack of proper historical documentation. It is clear though that he maintained the absolute unity and merger of the divine nature into the human nature of Jesus at his birth. He vehemently repudiated the two natures tenet in the incarnate Son and declared them non-scriptural. Although he never claimed that Jesus' flesh was from heaven, he nevertheless refused to accept that it was consubstantial with humanity. Flavian, successor to Proclus, condemned him as Apollinarian. Many modern historians argue that Eutyches was not a theologian but a confused thinker obsessed with salvation through Christ. To guarantee salvation he ended up upsetting the tenuous balance required in connection with Christology. R. V. Sellers argues that

> if we are to understand Eutyches aright, we must not think of him as the instructed theologian, prepared to discuss the doctrine of the Incarnation. Rather does he appear as the simple monk who, having renounced the world, had also renounced all theological inquiry, and considered that it behoved him obediently to follow what had been said by the orthodox Fathers, since these were the experts in matters concerning the faith.[456]

Eutyches however, appealed his condemnation. Dioscorus of Alexandria accused Flavian of requiring a test of orthodoxy other than the Nicene Creed. The Emperor Theodosius II summoned a council to meet at Ephesus in August of 449 to decide the matter. Pope Leo of Rome declined to participate in person but dispatched on June 13, 449 his famous Dogmatic Letter, or *Tome*, to Flavian, and clearly condemned the 'One Nature after the Union' doctrine of Eutyches. Leo stated in his letter that the properties of each nature and substance were combined together to form one person, "the distinctness of both natures and substance is preserved, and both meet in one Person..."[457] He wrote that

> when Eutyches, on being questioned in our examination of him, answered, "I confess that our Lord was of two natures before the union, but after the union I confess one nature," I am astonished that so absurd and perverse a profession as this of his was not rebuked by a censure on the part of any of his judges, and that an utterance extremely foolish and extremely blasphemous was passed over....[458]

He also directly attacked the reluctance Eutyches had shown in accepting Christ's consubstantiality with humans. He concluded that denying Jesus' body and flesh the human element was tantamount to denying his bodily sufferings.

This letter was carefully phrased to shun Nestorianism on the one hand and Eutychianism on the other. But Nestorius, writes Chadwick, "reading the Tome in his lonely exile, felt that the truth had been vindicated at last, and that he could die in peace."[459] Leo's *Tome* was never read to the synod. Under imperial power Eutyches was immediately rehabilitated and his orthodoxy vindicated. The confession of two natures was anathematized. The letter of Leo, which was suppressed in this so-called "Robber Synod" or "Latrocinium" (Brigandage) of Ephesus, was approved at Chalcedon. In fact the letter became decisive for the outcome at Chalcedon. The opportunity for this was provided by the death of Theodosius on July 28, 450. Marcian succeeded to the throne and cemented his position by marrying the late emperor's sister Plucheria. Marcian and Plucheria both were sympathizers of the Two Nature doctrine. The Pope persuaded them to summon the council to annul the theological work of the Robber Synod. Originally planned for Nicaea, the council was transferred to Chalcedon. The proceedings of this important Council opened on October 8, 451.

The Fourth Ecumenical Council, which was actually the most largely attended synod of antiquity, solemnly approved the Nicene Creed as the standard of orthodoxy, canonized Cyril's two letters and Leo's *Tome*, and finally, under imperial pressure, approved the following formula:

> Following the Holy Fathers we all with one consent teach men to confess one and the same Son, our Lord Jesus Christ, the same perfect in deity and perfect in humanity, God truly and man truly, of a reasonable soul and body, of one substance with the Father in his deity, and of one substance with us in his humanity, in all things like unto us without sin; begotten before the ages of the Father in his deity, in the last days for us and for our salvation born of Mary the Virgin, the mother of God, in his humanity; one and the same Christ, Son, Lord, only begotten, acknowledged in two natures, without confusion, without change, without division, without separation; the distinction of the natures being by no means taken away because of the union, but rather the property of each nature being preserved, and concurring in one person and one hypostasis, not divided or separated into two persons but one and the same Son and only begotten God Logos, Lord Jesus Christ; as from the beginning the prophets and the Lord Jesus Christ himself taught us concerning him, and the creed of the Fathers handed down to us.[460]

By this formula the Council asserted against Nestorianism the unipersonality of Christ and asserted against Eutychianism Christ's possession of two natures, divine and human, each perfect and unchanged. As mentioned earlier, the victory was political rather than theological. Grillmeier observes that, "It was only under constant pressure from the emperor Marcian that the Fathers of Chalcedon agreed to draw up a new formula of belief."[461] Kelly notes, "the imperial commissioners, in their desire to avoid a split, had to exert considerable pressure before agreement could be reached."[462] W. A.

Wigram writes that the Council

> failed to command respect, because it was imposed for political reasons, by a government that, as was too often the case, was making a fetish of uniformity. The verdict was, and was felt to be, a "government job," and not a free decision of the fathers of the Church. Had Theodosius lived longer, the Council would not have been held at all, and its decision was given, as things were, largely through the votes of Bishops who had gone with Dioscurus at Ephesus, and who shifted round readily to the opposite side, as soon as it was clear what line the Emperor was going to take.[463]

He further observes that

> in large districts, the Council was rejected at once, and in none, save only in Rome, was there any enthusiasm for its doctrine. For more than a century, however, the antagonism felt for it was admitted to be that of a party in the Church, and not that of a separatist body. The word "heretic" was not applied to those who rejected Chalcedon, even by the Bishops who persecuted them. They were called "Distinguisher," or one may say "Non-conformists."[464]

The critics of Chalcedon like Timothy (surnamed Aelurus, 477) and Philoxenus, on the other hand, honestly believed that "in their ignorance the so-called Fathers who had assembled to define the faith 'had ordained nothing other than that the impure doctrines of Nestorius should be received and preached in all the Churches of God.'"[465] To them the Council "so separates, and personalizes, what is divine and what is human in Christ that the hypostatic union is dissolved, and its place taken by a mere conjunction of the divine Logos and a Man."[466] Likening themselves to the tribe of Judah they parted company with the orthodoxy: "For how could they, who alone were worthy of the title 'orthodox', offer obedience to a Council which had caused Israel to sin? Nay, a curse lay upon that Council, and upon all who agreed with it, for ever."[467] Therefore, with the passage of time the old theological controversies surfaced again and again. Monophysites once again asserted their old claim of Jesus having one nature and one theanthropic will or monothelitism. Orthodoxy opposed this trend and in 680 at the third council of Constantinople (the sixth ecumenical council) was able to get its doctrine of 'dyothelitism' approved. By this doctrine the idea that Christ had two wills, one divine and one human, was officialized and has remained the orthodox position ever since, both in the East and the West.

At Chalcedon and later at Constantinople the human element of the picture of Christ was saved. Grillmeier contends that:

> If the person of Christ is the highest mode of conjunction between God and man, God and the world, the Chalcedonian 'without confusion' and 'without separation' show the right mean between monism and dualism, the two extremes between which the history of christology also swings. The Chalcedonian unity of person in the distinction of the natures provides the dogmatic basis for the preservation of the divine transcendence, which must always be a feature of the Christian concept of God. But it also shows possibility of a complete immanence of God in our history, an immanence on which the biblical doctrine of the economy of salvation rests.[468]

The Chalcedonian formula had attempted to solve a long standing Christological problem but in no way, shape or form did it provide logical or intelligible categories to satisfactorily answer the questions of Jesus' person or inner relational difficulties. In point of fact it was more presumed than explained that Christ was at once a complete God and a complete man. What type of man he was when he did not have the sinful nature was neither addressed nor resolved. His humanity was neither a complete humanity like that of ordinary human beings, nor his divinity like that of the Father. The whole thing was in fact a hodgepodge of presumptuous confusion rather than rational theology. Commenting on the significance of Chalcedon Paul Tillich writes:

> To understand the steps in the christological doctrine, always keep in mind two pictures: (1) The being with two heads, God and man,

> where there is no unity; (2) The being in which one head has disappeared, but also humanity has disappeared. The one remaining head is the head of the Logos, of God himself, so that when Jesus acts, it is not the unity of something divine and something human, but it is the Logos who is acting. Thus all the struggles, all the uncertainties, the despair and loneliness, which the Gospels present, were only seemingly experienced by Jesus, but not really. They are inconsequential. This was the danger in the Eastern Development. The fact that this danger was overcome is due to the decision of Chalcedon.[469]

The figure of two heads with no unity is as strange as both the other discourses mentioned by Tillich. It is more unintelligible and exposed to more subtle questions and curiosities than even the Docetic or Monarchian positions. It is impossible to logically determine the demarcation line between God and Man while insisting upon their unity, as the traditional dogma asserts. For intance, who determines when God in Jesus is acting and when the man in Jesus is steering his actions? There is neither proper guidance nor any specific formula given by the Scriptures. The Holy Spirit has been so often suppressed or evaded by emperors and Church politicians alike that claims of his abstract providence are of no real meaning in this regard. Is the figure dying on the cross the human Jesus or Jesus as God? If God than which God other than himself was he crying out to? If the figure dying was Jesus the man, then salvation is not complete. The Chalcedonian formula is full of theological contradictions.

Nevertheless despite its inherent weaknesses the Chalcedonian concept of a unified being with two heads or natures (human and divine) has remained the official doctrine of Christian Orthodoxy to the present times. The contemporary theologian E. Brunner writes:

> The Jesus Christ shown to us in the Scriptures accredits Himself to us as the God-Man. One who meets Him with that openness to truth which the Bible calls "faith", meets in Him One who, in the unity of His Person, is both true God and true Man. It would be good for the Church to be content with this, and not wish to know

> more than they can know, or more than we need, if we are to trust Him and obey Him as we should.[470]

If you can't resolve the problem, simply accept it at face value. This is faith at the expense of human logic and intellectual precision.

It is pertinent to mention that the Council of Chalcedon was a kind of victory of Antiochene theology over the Alexandrian Logos theology. Although it addressed the old unresolved issue, and finally drew a line between God the Son and Jesus the human by emphasizing Christ's humanity, in reality it did not, and could not, resolve the issue at all. The historical human Jesus, was declared to have two distinct natures, both perfect human and perfect divine, unified in one theanthropic person the Logos, the Son of God. Moreover he was unlike ordinary human beings because he was sinlessness. Brunner rightly expresses the implications

> when we agree with the verdict "He is a man like ourselves", we are also obliged to come to the exactly opposite view and say: He is *not* a man like ourselves....We know of no other man in whose life sin plays no part, whose life is pure and unstained, reflecting the holy love of God; who therefore, without hypocrisy or self-assertion could come forth to meet man as One coming from God.[471]

The contradiction is mind-boggling! Jesus is a man but not like men. Furthermore, this fully man and fully God doctrine of one Person and two natures as understood in traditional circles, leads us in reality back to the old Alexandrian Cyrillian Christology and does not help much in an understanding of the humanity of Christ. Mascall's view of the person or human knowledge of Christ suffices to elaborate the point:

> In Christ, however, the person is really distinct from the human nature; the nature with which the Person is really identical is not the human but the divine, and in this it shares in the omniscience which is the inalienable possession of Godhead. Is it therefore unreasonable to suppose that the contents of Christ's human mind

> will include not only that experimental knowledge which is acquired by him in the course of his development from infancy to manhood in a way substantially the same as, though immeasurably more consistent and unimpeded than, the way in which we acquire ours, but also an infused knowledge which is directly communicated to his human nature from the divine Person who is its subject, and which is a participation in the divine omniscience and is limited only by the receptive capacity of human nature as such?[472]

Now, if the person of Christ consists of two natures, two wills, but in reality is identical with the divine nature and knowledge rather than the human nature, then one is fully justified in querying as Maurice Wiles does as to how genuine this humanity is and "How genuinely human is so qualified a human will?"[473] Moreover, this doctrine of the absolute unity of the person and two natures, or unipersonality, faces a number of other crucial challenges. Most are logically obvious. For instance, who is actually doing the speaking and to whom? The narratives of Jesus praying to God, calling upon him with words such as "My God, My God" etc. make no sense. Is he appealing to himself? Even if we accept that it was Jesus' human nature that was engaged in acts of prayer such as these, was it the Person of Jesus calling the Person of Christ? Surely the idea of one calling out to the other indicates at the very least a split in the unified personality? As a unity both would have the power to alleviate the suffering so why cry out in agony? Further, being unified surely the Godhead would have also suffered the agonies of Crucifixion. At which point we have to ask ourselves who actually died on the Cross? If it is claimed that the human element of Christ suffered on the Cross, then how in the world can salvation, redemption, and atonement be achieved, for the divine element would have to be present, the raison d'etre for the whole Christological myth and for which it has been brought into existence?

The world has yet to see a theologian or a philosopher who can resolve these contradictions and explain in intelligible terms the Chalcedonian doctrine of Christ's person. Brunner contends that, "The aim of this doctrine is not that it may solve the mystery of Jesus. We know that when we confess Him as God-Man, and must so confess

Him, we are saying something which goes far beyond anything we can understand."[474] W. Bright, after strongly defending the outcome of the Council of Chalcedon, finally admits, "After all, if Christ is believed in as One, yet as both truly God and truly Man – however little we can comprehend the relation thus created – that belief is all that the Chalcedonian terminology implies: to hold it is to be at one with the Fourth Council."[475] J. S. Whale reaches the same conclusion:

> Of course, an explanation of Christ's person must always be beyond our reach if by 'explain' we mean 'put into a class'. Jesus is inexplicable just because he cannot be put into a class. His uniqueness constitutes the problem to be explained. It is impossible to describe him without becoming entangled in paradoxes. The great merit of Creeds is that they left the paradox as such.[476]

The illogical, the impossible, the contradictory cannot be justified in the name of paradox, this is an insult to human intelligence; Faith is the exposition of Truth, and must be substantiated by facts, it cannot create them. To hide behind the smoke screens of mystery, blind faith, mysticism, spirituality and/or the Spirit's providence etc. is to make nonsense of scripture and simply create awe for that which pays homage to a primitive, superstitious mentality. Furthermore, it is the prerogative of faith that it is made available to all and not just a select few, able to understand the intellectual contortions of mystery based doctrines. In reality, the history of the Trinitarian dogma is so saturated with political intrigue, the overriding needs of the State, exploitative elements moving through the corridors of power and so on, that actual scripture seems to have paid second fiddle to political expediency. And the monolithic impress of the doctrine has existed for so long that the whole is now taken for granted. The fact of the matter is that in the Trinity we have either the exposition of illogical truth or, what dare not be comprehended, heresy and theological scandal of the greatest magnitude. There is no inbetween. We conclude here with the remarks of McGiffert:

> The problem is metaphysical and purely speculative. Except by those interested to trace the formation of the particular dogmas involved, the whole Trinitarian and Christological development

> might be dismissed as unworthy of notice were it not for the profound religious difference that underlay it....[477]

Contemporary Christian Standpoint

Throughout history Christian dogma has continuously wrestled over the varying concepts and pictures that have emerged of Jesus down the centuries. As this chapter has discussed and illustrated, the origin of these differences can easily be traced back to the differing and mostly contradicting accounts of Christ as presented by the authors of the New Testament books, especially the four Gospels. Crossan rightly notes that if one reads

> those four texts vertically, as it were, from start to finish and one after another, you get generally persuasive impression of unity, harmony, and agreement. But if you read them horizontally, focusing on this or that unit and comparing it across two, three, or four versions, it is disagreement rather than agreement that strikes one most forcibly. By even the middle of the second century, pagan opponents, like Celsus, and Christian apologists, like Justin, Tatian and Marcion were well aware of those discrepancies, even if only between, say, Matthew and Luke.[478]

The Church has over the centuries been selective when it comes to scripture, using only those documents validating its own theological position and credentials. In other words, the documents chosen were mainly those which allowed the Church to prove what it wanted to have proven. Yet ironically, even these carefully selected documents contain no one single uniform picture of the person around whom the entire material is supposed to revolve. Following the New Testament, Christianity has always grappled with the question of Jesus' identity, forever trying to understand who he really is and what he represented. D. Cupitt rightly observes that, "More than any other religion Christianity has revolved obsessively around one particular man: it has loved him, worshipped him, mediated upon him, portrayed him, and sought to imitate him – but he slips away."[479] There is no single preached Christ:

> An immense variety of ideals of character have been based upon the example of Jesus: an historical man who lived only one life has been made the exemplar of a great range of different forms of life. Jesus has been declared to be a model for hermits, peasants, gentlemen, revolutionaries, pacifists, feudal lords, soldiers and others. If we restrict attention to the religious life of men in the Latin West alone, the diversity is great among the ideals of Benedict, Francis, Bruno, and Ignatius Loyola.[480]

Even contemporary scholarship is polarized over which picture or image of Jesus is to be accepted as authentic. In a presidential address to the Catholic Biblical Association at Georgetown University on 6 August 1986, Daniel J. Harrington categorized this variety into seven different images of Jesus currently prevailing in contemporary scholarship. We have Jesus the political revolutionary (S. G. F. Brandon), the magician (Morton Smith), Galilean charismatic (Geza Vermes), Galilean rabbi (Bruce Chilton), Hillelite or proto-Pharisee or an essene (Harvey Falk), and eschatological prophet (E. P. Sanders). To Crossan this "stunning diversity is an academic embarrassment."[481]

This "embarrassing" diversity of pictures, ideals, concepts and interpretations of Jesus Christ has led some to conclude that "everyone who writes a life of Jesus sees his own face at the bottom of a deep well."[482] To compound matters there exists only a very limited number of reliable narrations concerning Jesus, which even if combined fail to give us access to the man himself. One is left with no choice but to conclude with R. H. Lightfoot that, "the form of the earthly no less than of the heavenly Christ is for the most part hidden from us."[483]

This perhaps is the reason that Christians throughout their history have not been able to universally agree upon one single, logical and uniform doctrine concerning the person of Christ and have always remained perplexed by Christology. Almost all New Testament books as well as the subsequent history of dogma are witness to this fact. The same too is exactly the situation with regards to contemporary Christian thought. On the other hand, a great majority of Christians, while differing over ideas of Christ's person and relationship with God, seem to agree upon the idea of his cross and the significance of his redemptive work. In other words, the concept of 'Incarnation' is so pervasive in most contemporary Christian circles and in Christian tradition as a whole, that Christianity is often described as an incarnational faith. If there is any difference, and there are many as mentioned earlier, it is only because of the different understandings of 'incarnation' that prevail.

The Traditional Orthodox Standpoint

The Orthodox follow the theology of the Church Fathers as enshrined in the Creeds of Nicea and Chalcedon, which, in sum, fully recognized an entire and proper divinity/Godhead for Christ, his co-existentiality and equality with the Father, and a two nature unified-in-one-Person personality for his being, as well as belief in the redemption. Orthodox understanding of the doctrine of incarnation is that God's incarnation took place in the particular individual Jesus of Nazareth.

This is the old 'Modalistic Monarchianism' theology which claimed that the trinity was of three modes, of God manifesting Himself as the Father, the Son, and the Holy Spirit, outlined earlier. It has been hugely influential, at work at the bottom of orthodox theology in the past and still prevalent in orthodox circles today. In fact, as McGiffert observes, "the orthodox Christology was built not on the life of the historic figure Jesus Christ, as reflected in the gospels, but on a theory of redemption framed in large part independently of him and translated into the terms of prevailing philosophy of the age."[484] Throughout our discussion of the development of Christology we have seen that for the sake of salvation, Christ has always been deified, worshipped, and exalted to the level of complete equality and eternity with God. His humanity, though asserted superficially, has only been paid lip service by the orthodoxy. "It is true", writes Paul Badham, "that all orthodox writers pay lip service to Christ's humanity and describe him as "consubstantial with us" in his human nature. But all meaning seems evacuated from these claims when Christ is denied any human individuality or subjectivity."[485] In addition, certain Fathers such as Irenaeus and Gregory of Nyssa, as well as certain ordinary Christian believers have been deified through Jesus the Christ. It may not be inappropriate to quote Harnack here who remarks:

> There is an old story of a man who was in a condition of ignorance, dirt, and wretchedness and who was one day told by God that he might wish for anything he liked and that his wish would be granted. And he began to wish for more and more and to get higher and higher, and he got all he wanted. At last he got presumptuous and wished he might become like God Himself, when at once he was back again in his dirt and wretchedness. The history of religion is such a story; but it is in the history of the religion of Greeks and Easterns that it came true in the strictest sense....They became Christians and desired perfect knowledge and a supra-moral life. Finally they wished even in this world to be as God in knowledge, bliss, and life, and then they fell down, not all at once, but with a fall that could not be stopped, to the lowest stage in ignorance, dirt, and barbarity.[486]

The notion of incarnation in its developed sense, as we have discussed, is not clearly spelled out in the New Testament. "Incarnation", observes Maurice Wiles, "in its full and proper sense, is not something directly presented in scripture. It is a construction built on the variegated evidence to be found there."[487] But to ensure salvation, the Greek and Alexandrian Fathers made it the sole theme of their understanding of the person of Christ from the divergent New Testament pictures of him. They brought the person of the transcendent God *of* the universe *into* the universe itself, in the material world of flesh and body and crucified him on the cross. And though they have always denied doing this, crucifying God, in reality this is exactly what they have done and intended to do for the sake of salvation. St. Gregory Nazaianzus was honest enough to admit this plainly: "We needed an incarnate God, a God put to death that we might live."[488] Salvation would not have been possible if the entity crucified was not God. Athanasius also said this clearly when he confessed that the body crucified was God's body: "The Word bore the weakness of the flesh as His own, for it was His own flesh, and the flesh was serviceable to the working of the Godhead, for it was in the Godhead, it was God's body."[489] Whether one accepts this analogically or metaphorically, the language is too corporeal and anthropomorphic. Therefore, as Tillich notes, "Salvation is the problem of Christology."[490] If according to their own definition Jesus the historical human being was a unified God-Man Person, one in substance with God, whose flesh was God's own flesh, and who was co-eternal, pre-existent, a proper God, Omnipotent, Omniscient, sinless, the Lord of Glory and Majesty, the worshipped and adored one, in whom the One divine Person was at work, then whatever method orthodox Christianity adopts to stop the divine from being seen as crucified, is in vain for according to their own witness it was the body of God, Jesus Christ who was crucified. Some of them had the courage to assert this. Others tried to hide it behind the garb, or to use Paul Badham's term, the "smoke-screen"[491] of paradox and mystery. According to Dorothy Sayers, "All this was not very creditable to us, even if He was (as many people thought and think) only a harmless crazy preacher. But if the Church is right about Him, it was more discreditable still; for the man we hanged was God Almighty."[492]

Incarnation in the literal sense of salvation does not in any way solve the problem of Jesus' relationship to God. The whole issue becomes submerged in contradiction and paradox whichever way one tries to interpret it. Moreover, its terminology as well as development owes a great deal to Greek philosophy and imperial politics. John Hick is right in insisting that:

> There are strong reasons then for seeing the patristic development and interpretation of incarnational belief, not as gradual dawning of the truth inspired by the Holy Spirit, but as historically determined development which led to the blind alley of paradox, illogicality and docetism. It is not satisfactory to assert that nevertheless it was in the providence of God that philosophical system was available and made possible the resultant true formulations. Appeals to providence are too easily invalidated by subsequent history.[493]

Moreover, whatever the intention, the incarnational language itself is so anthropomorphic, corporeal and mythological, that one can easily conclude with Richard Jeffery, who in reference to Christ's crucifixion notes, "If God had been there, he would not have let them do it."[494] On the other hand, the real problem is that the traditional Christian religion or in the words of Whale, "the whole of Christian religion rests on the fact that God was there."[495]

Once 'Incarnation' was declared as the central doctrine of Christianity, observes Harnack, "The one God, whom the people have never understood, threatened to disappear, even in the views of refined theologians...."[496] If in Jesus the fullness of God is incarnate then Jesus without hesitation can be worshipped independently of God the Father. This is exactly what happened. Jesus was invoked directly in the Liturgy, distinctly from God the Father, by the so-called Orthodox opponents of Arianism. There is no reason then to deny the fact that incarnation in the Christian traditional sense does lead some believers to naive polytheism. This has been the case with a great majority of Christian believers, the Christianity, to use Harnack's term, of "second rank":

> There existed in Christendom,...from the end of the second century, a kind of subsidiary religion, one of the second rank, as was subterranean, different among different peoples, but every where alike in its crass superstition, naive doketism, dualism, and polytheism. Whenever religions change, it is as if mountains open. Among the great magic snakes, golden dragons and crystal spirits of the human soul, which ascend to the light, there come forth all sorts of hideous reptiles and a host of rats and mice....There probably never was an age in which Christendom was free from this "Christianity", just as there never will be one in which it shall have been overcome.[497]

And let us not forget that Jesus Christ, God incarnate, was also the son of Mary; and this incarnation and relationship led to the early Church Fathers' usage of terms like 'the Bearer of God', '*Theotoka* or Mother of God' to describe it, which in turn promoted the worship of Mary, a mere human being. Nestorius cried in vain to Cyril and to the Church in general, "Do not make the Virgin into a goddess." It was an outrageous innovation. But, as Don Cupitt notes, "It brings out an odd feature of Christianity, its mutability and the speed with which innovations come to be vested with religious solemnity to such an extent that anyone who questions them [is] *himself* regarded as the dangerous innovator and heretic."[498] Nestorius was declared a heretic and Mary was exalted above all creatures, above Cherubim and Seraphim, elevated no less to a position at the right hand of the Son. The reason, clear from the statement of John of Damascus, is that the "name 'Bearer of God' represents the whole mystery of the Incarnation. The Holy Spirit purified Mary with a view to the conception."[499] Not surprisingly, she was worshipped, called upon in prayers for support and venerated through Christian iconography. Images of her abounded and were worshipped. Commenting on this development Harnack points out:

> Pictures of Christ, Mary and the saints, had been already worshipped from the fifth (fourth) century with greetings, prostration, a renewal of ancient pagan practices. In the naive and confident conviction that Christians no longer ran any risk of idolatry, the Church not only tolerated, but promoted, the entrance of paganism. It was certainly the intention to worship the divine in the material; for the incarnation of deity had deified nature (ousia).[500]

In addition to these problems, the doctrine of Incarnation taken literally could lead to God's depiction in concrete corporeal human images. Don Cupitt correctly explains:

> If it is the case that in the incarnation God himself has permanently assumed human nature, and can legitimately be depicted as God in human form, then eventually the ultimate mystery of deity will be conceived anthropomorphically, and the pagan notion of a deity as a superhuman person with gender will be restored. In due course this happened, aided by the traditional Father-Son imagery.[501]

In the East the Church showed reservation on this matter permitting only the depiction of the Deity in human form different from the human form of Christ such as i.e. the standard iconography of scenes like the

Baptism, where a hand emerges from the cloud to release the dove upon Jesus' head. After the sixteenth century, under the influence of the West, images of God appeared in the East also. The West has been less conservative in this regard. Anthropomorphic images of God became very common in the West after about 1100.[502] Don Cupitt is correct to protest against these developments:

> It is my contention that the doctrine of Christ as God's divine Son has here humanized deity to an intolerable degree. The strangeness of it is seldom noticed even to this day. A sensitive theologian like Austin Farrer can dwell eloquently upon a medieval icon of the Trinity, and a philosopher as gifted as Wittgenstein can discuss Michelangelo's painting of God in the Sistene Chapel, and in neither case is it noticed there *could* be people to whom such pagan anthropomorphism is abhorrent, because it signifies a 'decline of religion' in the only sense that really matters, namely, a serious corruption of faith in God.[503]

In view of what has been said, it becomes evident that the traditional Christian concept of deity is anthropomorphic and corporeal, especially in terms of the language that has been used throughout Christian history to describe these concepts. Further, it is not only paradoxical, it is contradictory. It does not solve the problem of Jesus' relationship with God, the problem for which it was invented, neither does it explain or achieve salvation. D. Sayers writes: "What are we to make of that? ...if He was God and nothing else, His immortality means nothing to us; if He was man and no more, his death is no more important than yours or mine."[504] It is also notoriously difficult to understand the two natures (simultaneously true human and true God) in one person doctrine and the mode of union between them. The whole is little more than mere speculation and conjecture, having very little impact on the practical understanding of the person of Jesus, or God for that matter. They render, observes Sayers, "The Father incomprehensible, the Son incomprehensible, and the whole thing incomprehensible. Something put in by theologians to make it more difficult – nothing to do with daily life or ethics."[505] These kinds of contradictions or mysteries, hard though it is to imagine, might have been of some sense in their time, that is the era of the early Church Fathers in the light of Platonism, Stoicism, Neo-Platonism, or other trends, schools or philosophies in fashion, but look strange, and intellectually childish if not foolish today. Our present day knowledge and thought patterns make it impossible for anyone to understand literally the doctrine of "Incarnation" without landing into crude anthropomorphism and polytheism, especially the crucifixtion part. "That God should play the tyrant over man is a dismal story of unrelieved oppression; that man should play the tyrant over man is the usual dreary record of human futility; but that man should play the tyrant over God and find Him a better man than himself is an astonishing drama indeed."[506]

These difficulties are recognized by a number of modern Christian theologians. R. Bultmann, for instance, discussing the traditional doctrine of 'atonement' and 'salvation' argues:

> How can the guilt of one man be expiated by the death of another who is sinless – if indeed one may speak of a sinless man at all? What primitive notions of guilt and righteousness does this imply? And what primitive idea of God? The rational of sacrifice in general may of course throw some light on the theory of atonement, but even so, what a primitive mythology it is, that a divine Being should become incarnate, and atone for the sins of men through his own blood!...Moreover, if the Christ who died such a death was the pre-existent Son of God, what could death mean to him? Obviously very little, if he knew that he would rise again in three days.[507]

Becoming more emphatic with regards to salvation theory, and describing the doctrine of God-man as Gnostic, he continues stating that

> gnostic influence suggests that this Christ who died and rose again, was not a mere human being but a God-man....It is only with effort that modern man can think himself back into such an intellectual atmosphere, and even then he could never accept it himself, because it regards man's essential being as nature and redemption as a process of nature.

He further argues that

> as for the pre-existence of Christ, with its corollary of man's translation into a celestial realm of light, and the clothing of the human personality in heavenly robes and a spiritual body – all this is not only irrational but utterly meaningless. Why should salvation take this particular form?[508]

He declares this a 'myth' and calls upon the Church to reinterpret this myth in the light of modern knowledge and Kerygma. Though "Little we know of his life and personality" claims Bultmann, "we know enough of his *message* to make for ourselves a consistent picture."[509] Without understanding the New Testament mythology in the light of Kerygma the Christian message would be unintelligible to modern man. "The danger both for theological scholarship and for the Church is that this uncritical resuscitation of the New Testament mythology may make the Gospel message unintelligible to the modern world."[510] Paula Fredriksen asserts:

> After the introduction of Galileo's map of the universe, the technological advances of the Scientific Revolution, and the social and cultural revolutions that followed in its wake, modern culture no longer looks to Plato. More current systems of thought – anthropology, psychology, psychoanalysis, phenomenology, existentialism, evolutionary science, medicine – now provide the meaningful constructs that in turn effect theological ideas of personhood. Modern Christianity, in consequence, must search for new ways to express its ancient faith in Jesus Christ as true God and true man.[511]

It is John Hick, whose revolutionary and controversial book *The Myth of God Incarnate*, has taken great strides in the direction of recognition and then reconstruction of the incarnation issue. In this work Hick attempts to bring the old theological controversies back to the Christian intelligentsia, theologians and philosophers, with a view to making Jesus intelligible and acceptable to people of the modern world. He starts his article "Jesus and the World Religions" with a recognition of the problem stating:

> If we start from where we are, as Christians of our own day, we begin amidst the confusion and uncertainty which assail us when we try to speak about Jesus, the historical individual who lived in Galilee in the first third of the first century of the Christian era. For New Testament scholarship has shown how fragmentary and ambiguous are data available to us as we try to look back across nineteen and a half centuries, and at the same time how large and how variable is the contribution of the imagination to our 'pictures' of Jesus. In one sense it is true to say that he has been worshipped by millions; and yet in another sense, in terms of subjective 'intentionality', a number of different beings, describable in partly similar and partly different ways, have been worshipped under the name of Jesus or under the title of Christ.[512]

Hick believes that the traditional or 'Incarnational' interpretation of Jesus is mostly the work of the Greco-Roman world which produced this unique Christ-Figure to meet its spiritual needs. Here in this strange environment, he argues, the Christian theology "made the very significant transition from 'Son of God' to 'God the Son', the Second Person of Trinity."[513] In his *God and the Universe of Faiths* he observes:

> What seems to have happened during the hundred years or so following Jesus' death was that the language of divine sonship floated loose from the original ground of Jewish thought and developed a new meaning as it took root in Graeco-Roman culture....Thus the meaning of the Christ-event was first expressed by saying that Jesus was a Messiah, to whom in the Old Testament God has said, 'Thou art my beloved Son'; and then this divine sonship was later understood as his being of one substance with God the Father.[514]

The Christian understanding of Jesus might have been quite different had it expanded eastward. Hence incarnational theology is not part and parcel of Christian revelatory history but a progressive and evolutionary cultural development. The Church used the context and intellectual categories of the existing Hellenistic culture to define and interpret the Jesus event. As it is historically and culturally bound, Christianity has been and will keep on changing further to remain relevant to the societies of its existence. Consequently adherence to any specific doctrine and imposition of any dogma as intrinsically Christian will impede Christianity's ongoing development and relevance. Insistence upon incarnational theology has already rendered Christianity irrelevant to modern man. According to Hick:

> The Christian's faith in the deity of Christ is an interpretation of a human life and personality as being more than human, as being continuous with the life of God. This interpretation both involves and transcends an ethical valuation of his personality. The deity of Christ was mediated first through his moral character.[515]

Jesus' deity was neither part of his own consciousness nor intended by his disciples in a metaphysical sense. How could the early disciples, whose background was Jewish, ontologically equate Jesus with God? They used the spiritual terms of their times to express Jesus' closeness to God:

> it seems pretty clear that Jesus did not present himself as being God incarnate. He did not present himself as the second person of a divine trinity leading a human life. If in his lifetime he was called "son of God," as is entirely possible, it would be in the metaphorical sense that was familiar in the ancient world.[516]

This spiritual experience of the disciples and their mystical expressions were later twisted theologically to focus on the person of Christ and his incarnation rather than on his message. To Hick, the problem lies in the Church Fathers' literal interpretation of the New Testament's metaphorical as well as mythological language concerning Christ:

> [The] fateful development that created what was to become orthodox Christian belief for many centuries occurred when this

> poetry hardened into prose and the metaphorical son of God, with a small s, was transmuted into the metaphysical God the Son, with a capital S. The philosophers then developed the explanatory theory that Jesus had two complete natures, one human and the other divine, and that in his divine nature he was of the same substance as God the Father, while [in] his human nature he was of the same substance as humanity.[517]

He contends that this traditional two-nature Christology of Nicea and Chalcedon was a literal understanding of Incarnation:

> If we distinguish between, on one hand, a literal statement (whether it be empirical or metaphysical), and on the other hand metaphorical, poetic, symbolic and mythological statements, the Nicene formula was undoubtedly intended to be understood literally. It asserts that Jesus was literally (not mere metaphorically) divine and also literally (and not mere metaphorically) man. As divine he was not analogous to God, or poetically-speaking God, or as-if God; he was, actually and literally God-incarnate. And again, as human he was really, truly and literally a man.[518]

The Church made the transition from the metaphorical to the literal in an effort to intensify the religious experience. The exercise backfired. It deprived the faith of all meaning and content:

> orthodoxy has never been able to give this idea any content. It remains a form of words without assignable meaning. For to say, without explanation, that the historical Jesus of Nazareth was also God is as devoid of meaning as to say that this circle drawn with a pencil on paper is also a square. Such a locution has to be given semantic content: and in the case of the language of incarnation every content thus far suggested has had to be repudiated.[519]

The problem with traditional Christian belief is that it is irrational and contradictory to the core. It uses impossible and mutually antithetical categories to explain the logic and rationality of its dogmas. According to V. A. Harvey, "in contrast to all other texts, it sets aside our present critically interpreted experience when it comes to interpreting the New Testament. It assumes that in this case alone what our critically interpreted experience tells us is "impossible" is not only possible but probable and certain."[520]

According to Hick's understanding, the doctrine of 'Incarnation' is a mythological idea and literally not true at all. No Christian should be asked to accept the outmoded theological and philosophical theories of the third and fourth centuries. Like every other myth, incarnation was introduced to "evoke an attitude." The real significance of Jesus does not lie in his divinity or incarnation but in his example and model. It is through his model that humanity can find God in their lives. Jesus to Hick is the "sufficient model of true humanity in a perfect relationship to God."[521]

Unfortunately, the view of Jesus, or Christology, which looks upon him as the perfect "example", and thereby draws a clear-cut line between God and Jesus, saving Christianity from crude anthropomorphism and the shadow of paganism, and making Christian faith in line with and meaningful to other universal faith groups, is rejected for it does not comply with the set rules of traditional Christianity. As Brunner observes:

> The view of Jesus as the perfect Ideal of ethical or religious truth would then correspond to one part of the Christian creed, namely, the statement that Jesus is not only a true man, but that He is *the* true Man. But the exceptional position assigned to Jesus – an absolute and not a relative one – which is implied in the Christian doctrine of Real Humanity of Jesus, presupposes that Jesus, True Man, the Sinless One, could only be True Man because He was more than man; because He was also-God.[522]

The 'Traditionalists' reject this interpretation because in this solution "the Person of Jesus has no constitutive significance."[523]

Traditional Christianity wants to have God. But how is this possible? Paul Tillich answers, "Because of the incarnation, for in the incarnation God became something which we can have, whom we can see, with whom we can talk etc."[524]

CONCLUSION

Throughout history Christians have been trying to make sense of God, accepting anthropomorphic images of Him, yet disagreeing as to what these mean, whilst at the same time trying to save the transcendent God from corporeality and anthropomorphism. However, their desire for salvation has very often resulted in the opposite, a view of God as an anthropomorphous triune-person entity, based not only on weak and unconvincing arguments at an exegetical level, but also preconceived bias, absorption of Greek philosophy and faith in corporeal gods, and political accommodation. How much is this notion of a corporeal triune-God the Bible's and/or Jesus' teaching and how much the result of supplemental additions by the Church Fathers of later centuries?

Regardless of the weight of various Church council decrees, complex exegeses, and emperor approval, this confusing version of God was not entirely to the satisfaction of everyone. Not surprisingly, and according to Karen Armstrong, it was probably among one of the key factors that led to the crystal clear Islamic version of transcendence and monotheism (as enshrined in the Qur'an) to

> spread with astonishing rapidity throughout the Middle East and North Africa. Many of its enthusiastic converts in these lands (where Hellenism was not at home ground) turned with relief from Greek Trinitarianism, which expressed the mystery of God in an idiom that was alien to them, and adopted a more Semitic notion of the divine reality.[525]

NOTES

[1] Bigg, *The Christian Platonists of Alexandria*, pp.92–93.

[2] Greer, *Origen*, p.127.

[3] Bigg, *The Christian Platonists of Alexandria*, p.195.

[4] Greer, *Origen*, p.127.

[5] Ibid., p.128.

[6] See ibid., p.30.

[7] Northrop Frye, "The Religious Vision of William Blake," *Toward a New Christianity*, Thomas J. J. Altizer, ed. (New York: Harcourt, Brace & World Inc., 1967), p.40.
[8] Ian R. Netton, *Text and Trauma: An East-West Primer* (Richmond: Curzon Press, 1996), p.91.
[9] Philip Schaff, *History of the Christian Church* (Michigan: W. B. Eerdmans, 1976), vol.2, p.570.
[10] Joachim Jeremias, *New Testament Theology*, John Bowden, trans. (New York: Charles Scribner's Sons, 1971), p.1.
[11] Grant, *The Formation of The New Testament*, p.8.
[12] C. P. S. Clarke, *Short History of The Christian Church* (London: Longman, 1966), p.28.
[13] John N. D. Kelly, *Early Christian Doctrines* (New York: Harper and Brothers, 1958), p.53.
[14] Philip Schaff, Henry Wace, eds., *The Nicene and Post-Nicene Fathers* (Michigan: W B. Eerdmans, 1978), vol.4, pp.551–52; also see Harnack, *History of Dogma*, vol.3, p.196.
[15] Alexander Souter, *Text and Canon of the New Testament* (New York: Scribners', 1925), p.215.
[16] Harris, *Inspiration and Canonicity of the Bible*, p.202.
[17] Schaff, *History of the Christian Church*, p.571.
[18] Harris, *Inspiration and Canonicity of the Bible*, pp.234–35.
[19] Henry T. Fowler, *The History and Literature of the New Testament* (New York: Macmillan, 1934), p.429.
[20] Norman L. Geisler, William E. Nix, *A General Introduction to the Bible* (Chicago: Moody Press, 1969), p.179.
[21] Harris, *Inspiration and Canonicity of the Bible*, p.249.
[22] Brooke F. Westcott, *A General Survey of the History of the Canon of the New Testament* (New York: Macmillan, 1896), p.500.
[23] Hans Conzelmann, *History of Primitive Christianity*, John E. Steely, trans. (New York: Abingdon Press, 1973), p.23.
[24] Fox, *The Unauthorized Version: Truth and Fiction in the Bible*, p.120.
[25] John D. Crossan, *The Historical Jesus: The Life of a Mediterranean Jewish Peasant* (San Francisco: Harper Collins, 1991), p. XXXI.
[26] R. Joseph Hoffmann, ed., *The Origins of Christianity, A Critical Introduction* (New York: Prometheus Books, 1985), p.182; for more details see Dennis E. Nineham, *Saint Mark* (London: Pelican Books, 1969), pp.1–25.

[27] Frederic R. Crownfield, *A Historical Approach to the New Testament* (New York: Harper & Brothers, 1960), p.4.

[28] Jeremias, *New Testament Theology*, p.2.

[29] Ibid., pp.2–3.

[30] Hans Kung, *On Being a Christian*, E. Quinn, trans. (New York: Doubleday & Co., 1976), p.152.

[31] Ibid., pp.151–52.

[32] John Hick, *The Metaphor of God Incarnate* (London: S.C.M. Press, 1993), p.16.

[33] Ibid., p.18.

[34] Howard Kee, *What Can We Know About Jesus?* (Cambridge: Cambridge University Press, 1990), p.90.

[35] Paula Fredriksen, *From Jesus to Christ: The Origin of the New Testament Images of Jesus* (New Haven: Yale University Press, 1988), p.80.

[36] Hoffmann, *The Origins of Christianity*, pp.193–94; for more details see Ernst Kasemann, *Essays on New Testament Themes* (London: S.C.M. Press, 1964), pp.59–61.

[37] Hick, *The Metaphor of God Incarnate*, p.15.

[38] Stephen Neill, *The Interpretation of the New Testament 1861–1961* (New York: Oxford University Press, 1966), pp.77–78.

[39] Rudolf K. Bultmann, *The History of the Synoptic Tradition*, J. Marsh, trans. (Oxford: Basil Blackwell, 1963), pp.122–28.

[40] M. Eugene Boring, "How May we Identify Oracles of Christian Prophets in the Synoptic Tradition? Mark 3:28–29 as a Test Case," *Journal of Biblical Literature* (1972), vol.91, pp.501–21; and also see his *Sayings of the Risen Jesus: Christian Prophecy in the Synoptic Tradition* (Cambridge: Cambridge University Press, 1982).

[41] Hendrikus Boers, *Who Was Jesus? The Historical Jesus and the Synoptic Gospels* (San Francisco: Harper & Row, 1989), p.94.

[42] Hans Conzelmann, *Jesus: The Classic Article From RGG Expanded and Updated*, J. R. Lord, trans., J. Reumann, ed. (Philadelphia: Fortress Press, 1973), p.5.

[43] I. Howard Marshall, *The Gospel of Luke: A Commentary on the Greek Text, New International Commentary on the New Testament* (Exeter: Paternoster Press, 1978), p.33.

[44] Richard A. Burridge, *What Are the Gospels? A Comparison with Graeco-Roman Biography* (New York: Cambridge University Press, 1992), p.257.

[45] Gilbert G. Bilezikian, *The Liberated Gospel: A Comparison of the Gospel of Mark and Greek Tragedy* (Michigan: Baker, 1977), p.140.

[46] Jeremias, *New Testament Theology*, p.37.

[47] Birger Gerhardsson, *The Origins of the Gospel Traditions* (Philadelphia: Fortress Press, 1979), p.19.

[48] Ibid., p.73.

[49] Ibid., p.77.

[50] E. P. Sanders, *The Tendencies of the Synoptic Tradition* (Cambridge: Cambridge University Press, 1969), p.296.

[51] Ben Witherington, III, *The Christology of Jesus* (Minneapolis: Fortress Press, 1990), p.15.

[52] Hoffmann, *The Origins of Christianity*, p.199.

[53] Gerhardsson, *The Origins of the Gospel Traditions*, p.33.

[54] S. W. Sykes, J. P. Clayton, eds., *Christ Faith and History* (Cambridge: Cambridge University Press, 1972), pp.203–04.

[55] Howard C. Kee, *Jesus in History: An Approach to the Study of the Gospels* (New York: Harcourt, Brace & World Inc., 1970), p.269.

[56] E. P. Sanders, *The Historical Figure of Jesus* (New York: Penguin, 1993), p.10.

[57] Ibid., p. XIII.

[58] Paul Badham in his "Introduction" to Leslie Badham's, *Verdict on Jesus: A New Statement of Evidence* (New Delhi: IKON, 1995), p. X.

[59] Hick, *The Metaphor of God Incarnate*, p.18.

[60] Kung, *On Being a Christian*, p.154.

[61] Crossan, *The Historical Jesus*, p. XXX.

[62] Neill, *The Interpretation of the New Testament*, p.250.

[63] Ibid.

[64] Helmut Koester, "The Text of the Synoptic Gospels in the Second Century," *Gospel Traditions in the Second Century: Origins, Recensions, Text, and Transmission*, William L. Petersen, ed. (Notre Dame, Indiana: University of Notre Dame Press, 1989), p.19.

[65] Bigg, *The Christian Platonists of Alexandria*, p.160.

[66] Fox, *The Unauthorized Version*, p.154.

[67] Ibid., p.143.

[68] Grant, *The Formation of The New Testament*, p.82.

[69] Fox, *The Unauthorized Version*, p.147.

[70] Geisler, Nix, *A General Introduction to the Bible*, p.348.

[71] John Ferguson, *Clement of Alexandria* (New York: Twayne Publishers Inc., 1974), p.58.

[72] Gunther Bornkamm, *The New Testament: A Guide to Its Writings*, R. H. Fuller, Ilse Fuller, trans. (Philadelphia: Fortress Press, 1973), pp.80–81.
[73] Albert Schweitzer, *The Mysticism of Paul the Apostle*, W. Montgomery, trans. (New York: The Seabury Press, 1968), p.47.
[74] Hugh Anderson, *Jesus and Christian Origins* (New York: Oxford University Press, 1964), p.267.
[75] Victor P. Furnish, *Jesus According to Paul* (Cambridge: Cambridge University Press, 1993), p.40.
[76] Hick, *The Metaphor of God Incarnate*, p.31.
[77] Burridge, *What Are the Gospels?*, p.257.
[78] Quoted from George A. Wells, *Did Jesus Exist?* (London: Pemberton, 1968), p.56.
[79] Francois Bovon, "The Synoptic Gospels and the Noncanonical Acts of the Apostles," *Harvard Theological Review* (1988), vol.81, p.20.
[80] Maurice Wiles, *The Making of Christian Doctrine* (Cambridge: Cambridge University Press, 1967), p.43.
[81] Harris, *Inspiration and Canonicity of the Bible*, p.238.
[82] Eliade, *The Encyclopedia of Religion*, vol.2, p.186.
[83] Richard A. Burridge, *Four Gospels, One Jesus? A Symbolic Reading* (Grand Rapids: W. B. Eerdmans, 2005), p.10.
[84] Neill, *The Interpretation of the New Testament*, p.123.
[85] Hoffmann, *The Origins of Christianity*, p.191.
[86] Burridge, *Four Gospels, One Jesus?*, p.10.
[87] Kung, *On Being a Christian*, pp.152–53.
[88] Crossan, *The Historical Jesus*, p.432.
[89] Ibid., p. XXXI.
[90] Fox, *The Unauthorized Version*, p.151.
[91] Bruce M. Metzger, *The New Testament, Its Background, Growth and Content* (New York: Abingdon Press, 1965), p.276.
[92] Kelly, *Early Christian Doctrines*, pp.57–58.
[93] W. J. McDonnell, et al., eds., *New Catholic Encyclopedia* (New York: McGraw-Hill, 1967), vol.2, p.394.
[94] Metzger, *The New Testament*, p.276.
[95] Kelly, *Early Christian Doctrines*, pp.59–60.
[96] Fox, *The Unauthorized Version*, p.153.
[97] Ibid., pp.152–53.

[98] Neill, *The Interpretation of the New Testament*, p.63.
[99] Ibid., p.79.
[100] Matthew Arnold, *Literature and Dogma* (New York: AMS Press, 1970), p. XXIV.
[101] Ibid., p. XXV.
[102] Benjamin B. Warfield, *Revelation and Inspiration* (New York: Oxford University Press, 1927), p.71.
[103] Ibid., p.399.
[104] Norman L. Geisler, ed., *Inerrancy* (Michigan: Zondervan, 1979), p. IX.
[105] Glearson L. Archer, "Alleged Errors and Discrepancies in the Original Manuscripts of the Bible," *Inerrancy*, Geisler, p.59.
[106] Oliver B. Greene, *The Second Coming of Jesus* (Greenville: Gospel Hour, 1971), p.314.
[107] Francis A. Schaeffer, *No Final Conflict: The Bible Without Error in All That It Affirms* (Illinois: InterVarsity Press, 1975), pp.33–34.
[108] James I. Packer, *"Fundamentalism" and The Word of God: Some Evangelical Principles* (Michigan: W. B. Eerdmans, 1974), p.61.
[109] Quoted from Stevick, *Beyond Fundamentalism*, p.86.
[110] Kelly, *Early Christian Doctrines*, pp.61–62.
[111] Ibid., p.64.
[112] Charles Smyth, *Church and Parish: Studies in Church Problems* (London: SPCK, 1950), p.159.
[113] Quoted from Dennis E. Nineham, *The Use and Abuse of The Bible* (New York: Macmillan, 1981), p.48.
[114] Kelly, *Early Christian Doctrines*, p.64.
[115] St. Augustine, *Concerning the City of God Against the Pagans*, H. Bettenson, trans., David Knowles, ed. (Baltimore: Penguin Books, 1972), p.534.
[116] Ibid., p.535.
[117] Hans W. Bartsch, ed., *Kerygma and Myth* (New York: Harper & Row, 1961), p.1.
[118] Ibid., pp.3–4.
[119] Ibid., p.4.
[120] Ibid., p.10.
[121] Ibid., p.11.
[122] Ibid., p.16.
[123] Brunner, *The Christian Doctrine of God*, p.25.

[124] Ibid., p.34.
[125] Paul Tillich, *Biblical Religion and the Search for Ultimate Reality* (Chicago: University of Chicago Press, 1955), p.4.
[126] Nineham, *The Use and Abuse of The Bible*, pp.140–41.
[127] Ibid., p.71.
[128] Ibid., p.187.
[129] Quoted from ibid., p.45.
[130] Ibid., p.177.
[131] Ibid., p.210.
[132] Ibid., p.196.
[133] Ibid., p.229.
[134] Ibid., p.230.
[135] Richard Swinburne, *Revelation: From Metaphor to Analogy* (Oxford: Clarendon Press, 1992), p.208.
[136] Ibid., pp.208–09.
[137] Bigg, *The Christian Platonists of Alexandria*, p.195.
[138] Ronald J. Teske, *To Know God and the Soul: Essays on the Thought of St. Augustine* (Washington: The Catholic University of America Press, 2008), p.31.
[139] See for details Burridge, *What are the Gospels?*, pp.271–74.
[140] Charles Gore, *The Incarnation of the Son of God* (New York: Scribner's Sons, 1960), p.1.
[141] Shirley C. Guthrie, Jr., *Christian Doctrine* (Richmond: CLC Press, 1968), p.223.
[142] Wayne Grudem, *Systematic Theology: An Introduction to Biblical Doctrine* (Michigan: Zondervan, 1994), p.545.
[143] Richard Bauckham, *God Crucified: Monotheism and Christology in the New Testament* (Michigan: W. B. Eerdmans, 1999), p.55.
[144] Robert M. Bowman, J. Ed Komoszewski, Darrell L. Bock, *Putting Jesus in His Place: The Case for the Deity of Christ* (Michigan: Kregal, 2007), p.244.
[145] Ibid., p.245.
[146] Gary R. Habermas, Michael R. Licona, *The Case for the Resurrection of Jesus* (Michigan: Kregal, 2004).
[147] Gary Habermas, "The Case for Christ's Resurrection," *To Everyone an Answer: A Case for the Christian World View*, Francis J. Beckwith, William Lane Craig, J. P. Moreland, eds. (Downers Grove: InterVarsity Press, 2004), p.190.
[148] Raymond Brown, "Did Jesus Know He was God?," *Biblical Theology Bulletin* (1985), vol.15, pp.77–78.

[149] Witherington, *The Christology of Jesus*, p.276.
[150] Ibid., p.277.
[151] Donald M. Baillie, *God was in Christ: An Essay on Incarnation and Atonement* (New York: Scribner's Sons, 1948), p.82.
[152] Grudem, *Systematic Theology*, p.543; See Donald Guthrie, *New Testament Theology* (Downers Grove: InterVarsity Press, 1981), pp.235–365; Murray J. Harris, *Jesus as God: The New Testament Use of Theos in Reference to Jesus* (Grand Rapids: Baker Publishing Group, 1992).
[153] Michael Ramsey, *Jesus and the Living Past* (Oxford: Oxford University Press, 1980), p.39.
[154] Charles F. D. Moule, *The Origin of Christology* (Cambridge: Cambridge University Press, 1977), p.136.
[155] Brian Hebblethwaite, *The Incarnation: Collected Essays in Christology* (Cambridge: Cambridge University Press, 1987), p.74.
[156] David Brown, *The Divine Trinity* (London: Duckworth, 1985), p.108.
[157] John Knox, *The Humanity and Divinity of Jesus* (Cambridge: Cambridge University Press, 1967), pp.66–67.
[158] John N. D. Kelly, *Early Christian Creeds* (New York: David McKay Co., 1972), pp.12–13.
[159] Hick, *The Metaphor of God Incarnate*, p.34.
[160] Ibid., p.36.
[161] Ibid., p.30.
[162] Adolf V. Harnack, *What is Christianity?*, Thomas B. Saunders, trans. (London: G. P. Putnan's Son's, 1901), p.154.
[163] Ibid., p.157.
[164] Arthur S. Peake, "The Messiah and the Son of Man", *Bulletin of the John Rylands Library* (1942), vol.8, pp.3–32.
[165] Harnack, *What is Christianity?*, p.154.
[166] Ibid., p.155.
[167] Ibid., p.198.
[168] Ibid.
[169] John Hick, *God and the Universe of Faiths* (London: Macmillan, 1973), p.114.
[170] Hick, *The Metaphor of God Incarnate*, p.33.
[171] John Hick, "A Remonstrance in Concluding," *Jesus in History and Myth*, R. J. Hoffmann, G. A. Larue, eds. (Buffalo: Prometheus Books, 1986), p.213.
[172] Hick, *The Metaphor of God Incarnate*, p.40.

[173] Ibid., p.27.

[174] Ibid., p.5.

[175] Wayne A. Meeks, *The Writings of St. Paul: A Norton Critical Edition* (New York: W. W. Norton & Co., 1972), p.278.

[176] Ibid., p.279.

[177] Ibid., p.278.

[178] Ibid., pp.288–89.

[179] Ibid., p.294.

[180] Ibid., p.291.

[181] Ibid., p.299.

[182] Ibid.

[183] Ibid., p.300.

[184] Gunther Bornkamm, *Paul, Paulus*, D. M. G. Stalker, trans. (New York: Harper & Row, 1969), p.230.

[185] Ibid., pp.229–30.

[186] Martin Buber, *Two Types of Faith*, Norman P. Goldhawk, trans. (New York: Macmillan, 1951).

[187] Leo Baeck, "Romantic Religion," *Judaism and Christianity*, W. Kaufmann, trans. (Philadelphia: Jewish Publication Society of America, 1960).

[188] Hans-Joachim Schoeps, *Paul, The Theology of the Apostle in the Light of Jewish Religious History*, Harold Knight, trans. (Philadelphia: The Westminster Press, 1961).

[189] Schweitzer, *The Mysticism of Paul*, p. VIII.

[190] Ibid., p.40.

[191] Rudolf K. Bultmann, "New Testament and Mythology," *Kerygma and Myth*, Hans W. Bartsch, ed., R. H. Fuller, trans., 2nd edn. (London: Oxford University Press, 1964), p.1.

[192] Meeks, *The Writings of St. Paul*, p.417.

[193] Ibid., pp.414–15.

[194] John K. Riches, *A Century of New Testament* (Pennsylvania: Trinity Press International, 1993), p.125.

[195] Ibid., p.153.

[196] Robert H. Lightfoot, *History and Interpretation in the Gospels* (London: Hodder & Stoughton, 1935), p.22.

[197] Ibid., p.39.

[198] Ibid., p.37.

[199] Alois Grillmeier, *Christ in Christian Tradition*, John Bowden, trans. (Atlanta: John Knox Press, 1975), vol.1, p.3.
[200] Quoted from ibid., p.4.
[201] Michael Ramsey, *The Resurrection of Christ: An Essay in Biblical Theology* (London: Geoffery Bles, 1962), p.33.
[202] Ibid., p.7,
[203] Kung, *On Being a Christian*, pp.402–03.
[204] Ibid., p.403.
[205] Armstrong, *A History of God*, p.81.
[206] Ibid., p.83.
[207] Ibid., p.81.
[208] Richard A. Norris, Jr., ed. and trans., *The Christological Controversy* (Philadelphia: Fortress Press, 1980), p.2.
[209] Thomas S. Kepler, ed., *Contemporary Thinking About Jesus: An Anthology* (New York: Abingdon-Cokesbury Press, 1944), p.223.
[210] Ibid.
[211] Baillie, *God was in Christ*, p.86.
[212] Ibid.
[213] Kepler, *Contemporary Thinking About Jesus*, p.223.
[214] Nicholas T. Wright, *The Challenge of Jesus: Rediscovering Who Jesus Was and Is* (Downers Grove: InterVarsity Press, 1999), p.96.
[215] Ibid., p.123.
[216] Ibid., p.124.
[217] Gore, *The Incarnation of the Son of God*, p.10.
[218] Martin E. Marty, *A Short History of Christianity* (Minneapolis: Fortress Press, 1987), p.3.
[219] Richard Sturch, *The Word and the Christ: An Essay in Analytic Christology* (Oxford: Clarendon Press, 1991), p.8.
[220] Karl Barth, *The Doctrine of the Word of God* (Edinburgh: T & T Clark, 1956), p.420.
[221] Baillie, *God was in Christ*, p.136.
[222] Clement C. J. Webb, *God and Personality* (London: Allen & Unwin, 1918), p.54.
[223] Ibid., p.55.
[224] Leonard Hodgson, *The Doctrine of the Trinity* (London: Nisbet, 1943); Jurgen Moltmann, *The Trinity and the Kingdom: The Doctrine of God* (San Francisco: Harper & Row, 1981).

[225] Gerald O'Collins, Mario Farrugia, *Catholicism: The Story of Catholic Christianity* (Oxford: Oxford University Press, 2003), p.142.
[226] Bart D. Ehrman, *Jesus, Apocalyptic Prophet of the New Millennium* (Oxford: Oxford University Press, 1999), p.245.
[227] Ibid.
[228] Morton S. Enslin, *The Prophet From Nazareth* (New York: McGraw-Hill, 1961), p.60.
[229] Jeremias, *New Testament Theology*, p.77.
[230] Ibid., pp.79–80.
[231] Geza Vermes, *Jesus the Jew: A Historian's Reading of the Gospels* (Minneapolis: Fortress Press, 1981), p.99.
[232] Ibid., pp.98–99.
[233] Ibid., p.86.
[234] Ibid., p.88.
[235] Ibid., p.90.
[236] E. P. Sanders, *Jesus and Judaism* (London: S.C.M. Press, 1985), p.319.
[237] Hick, *The Metaphor of God Incarnate*, p.19.
[238] Gore, *The Incarnation of the Son of God*, p.18.
[239] Vincent Taylor, *The Names of Jesus* (London: Macmillan, 1953), pp.16–17.
[240] Grillmeier, *Christ in Christian Tradition*, vol.1, p.10.
[241] Ibid., p.46.
[242] Martin Werner, *The Formation of Christian Doctrine*, S. F. G. Brandon, trans. (San Francisco: Harper & Brothers, 1957), p.120.
[243] Ibid., p.131.
[244] Grillmeier, *Christ in Christian Tradition*, p.48.
[245] B. Harvie Branscomb, *The Gospel of Mark* (New York: Harper & Brothers, n.d.), pp.145–52.
[246] Gunther Bornkamm, *Jesus of Nazareth* (New York: Harper & Row, 1960), p.172.
[247] William Wrede, *The Messianic Secret* (Greenwood: Attic Press, 1971).
[248] Hendrika N. Roskam, *The Purpose of the Gospel of Mark in Its Historical and Social Context* (Boston: Brill, 2004), p.175.
[249] Ibid., pp.187–88.
[250] John Hick, ed., *The Myth of God Incarnate* (Philadelphia: The Westminster Press, 1977), p.18.
[251] Rudolf Augstein, *Jesus Son of Man*, H. Young, trans. (New York: Urizen Books, 1977), p.54.

[252] Bornkamm, *Jesus of Nazareth*, p.172.

[253] Ibid., p.173.

[254] Ben Witherington III, *The Gospel of Mark: A Socio-Rhetorical Commentary* (Grand Rapids: W. B. Eerdmans, 2001), p.40.

[255] Ibid., p.41.

[256] Edwyn C. Hoskyns, Francis N. Davey, *The Riddle of the New Testament* (London: Faber & Faber, 1985), p.145.

[257] Quoted from Witherington, *The Gospel of Mark*, p.265.

[258] Ibid., p.270.

[259] H. E. Todt, *The Son of Man in the Synoptic Tradition*, D. M. Barton, trans. (London: S.C.M. Press, 1965), pp.114–25.

[260] Moule, *The Origin of Christology*, p.12.

[261] See Bultmann, *The History of the Synoptic Tradition*, p.152.

[262] Bornkamm, *Jesus of Nazareth*, p.177.

[263] Jeremias, *New Testament Theology*, p.276.

[264] Quoted from Norman Perrin, *A Modern Pilgrimage in New Testament Christology* (Philadelphia: Fortress Press, 1972), p.43; Wilhelm Bousset's *Kyrios Christos* has been published by Abingdon Press, Nashville in 1970.

[265] Todt, *The Son of Man*, pp.114–25.

[266] Reginald H. Fuller, *The Foundations of New Testament Christology* (New York: Charles Scribner's Sons, 1965), p.186.

[267] Ibid., pp.143–44.

[268] Perrin, *A Modern Pilgrimage*, p.5.

[269] Ibid., p.45.

[270] R. Joseph Hoffmann, Gerald A. Larue, eds., *Jesus in History and Myth* (New York: Prometheus Books, 1986), p.213.

[271] Kepler, *Contemporary Thinking About Jesus*, p.358.

[272] Augstein, *Jesus Son of Man*, p.65.

[273] Armstrong, *A History of God*, p.82.

[274] Crossan, *The Historical Jesus*, p.243.

[275] Moule, *The Origin of Christology*, p.12.

[276] Ibid., p.17.

[277] See J. J. Collins, "The Son of Man and the Saints of the Most High in the Book of Daniel," *Journal of Biblical Literature* (1974), vol.93, pp.50–66; also see his *The Apocalyptic Imagination* (New York: Crossroad, 1984), pp.68–92.

[278] Delbert Burkett, *The Son of Man Debate: A History and Evaluation* (Cambridge: Cambridge University Press, 2000), p.116.

[279] Witherington, *The Christology of Jesus*, p.241.
[280] Ibid., pp.261–62.
[281] Charles K. Barrett, *Jesus and the Gospel Tradition* (Philadelphia: Fortress Press, 1968), p.67.
[282] Marinus de Jonge, *Christology in Context: The Earliest Christian Response to Jesus* (Louisville: Westminster John Knox Press, 1988), p.172.
[283] Perrin, *A Modern Pilgrimage*, p.84.
[284] Enslin, *The Prophet From Nazareth*, p.148.
[285] Grudem, *Systematic Theology*, p.547.
[286] Jaroslav Pelikan, ed., *Luther's Works* (St. Louis: Concordia Publishing House, 1959), vol.22, pp.5–6.
[287] Ibid., p.6.
[288] Robert McQueen Grant, *The Early Christian Doctrine of God* (Charlottesville: University Press of Virginia, 1966), p.37.
[289] Ibid., p.38.
[290] Vermes, *Jesus the Jew*, p.201.
[291] Ibid., pp.201–02.
[292] Hick, *The Myth of God Incarnate*, p.53.
[293] Kung, *On Being a Christian*, p.315.
[294] Jeremias, *New Testament Theology*, p.66.
[295] Oscar Cullmann, *The Christology of The New Testament*, Shirley C. Guthrie, Charles A. M. Hall, trans. (Philadelphia: The Westminster Press, 1963), p.270.
[296] Grillmeier, *Christ in Christian Tradition*, p.11.
[297] Vermes, *Jesus the Jew*, pp.210–11.
[298] Talmud – Mas. Ta'anith 23b.
[299] Vermes, *Jesus the Jew*, p.212.
[300] Ibid., p.213.
[301] Jeremias, *New Testament Theology*, pp.67–68.
[302] Cullmann, *The Christology of The New Testament*, p.195.
[303] Moule, *The Origin of Christology*, pp.41–42.
[304] Kung, *On Being a Christian*, p.403.
[305] Oliver C. Quick, *Doctrines of the Creed, Their Basis in Scripture and Their Meaning Today* (New York: Scribner's Sons, 1938), p.81.
[306] Ibid., p.83.
[307] Armstrong, *History of God*, pp.88–89.
[308] Ibid., p.83.

[309] Harnack, *What is Christianity?*, p.199.
[310] Arthur C. McGiffert, *A History of Christian Thought* (New York: Charles Scribner's Sons, 1960), vol.1, p.14.
[311] Ibid., p.19.
[312] Cullmann, *The Christology of The New Testament*, p.215.
[313] Moule, *The Origin of Christology*, p.44; also see his "A Reconsideration of the Context of *Maranatha*," *New Testament Studies* (1960), vol.6, pp.307–10.
[314] Floyd V. Filson, *The New Testament Against Its Environment* (London: S.C.M. Press, 1963), p.41.
[315] Cullmann, *The Christology of The New Testament*, p.308.
[316] Ibid.
[317] Bart D. Ehrman, *Misquoting Jesus* (San Francisco: Harper, 2005), p.61.
[318] *Commentary on the Gospel of John* (Book II), ch.2, http://www.newadvent.org/fathers/101502.htm.
[319] Harris, *Jesus as God*, p.60.
[320] *Commentary on the Gospel of John* (Book II), ch.2, http://www.newadvent.org/fathers/101502.htm.
[321] Charles K. Barrett, *The Gospel According to St. John: An Introduction with Commentary and Notes on the Greek Text*, 2nd edn. (Philadelphia: The Westminster Press, 1978), p.573.
[322] James F. McGrath, *John's Apologetic Christology: Legitimation and Development in Johannine Christology* (New York: Cambridge University Press, 2001), p.130.
[323] Ibid., p.66.
[324] Wayne A. Meeks, "Moses as God and King," *Religions in Antiquity: Essays in Memory of Erwin Ramsdell Goodenough*, J. Nuesner, ed. (Leiden: E. J. Brill, 1970), pp.354–71.
[325] John Lierman, *The New Testament Moses: Christian Perceptions of Moses and Israel in the Setting of Jewish Religion* (Tubingen: Mohr Siebeck, 2004), p.99.
[326] Bart D. Ehrman, *The Orthodox Corruption of Scriptures* (New York: Oxford University Press, 1993), p.266.
[327] Pelikan, *Luther's Works*, vol.29, p.115.
[328] Quoted from Fisher, *History of Christian Doctrine*, p.45.
[329] Jaroslav Pelikan, *The Christian Tradition: A History of the Development of Doctrine* (Chicago; London: University of Chicago Press, 1971), vol.1, p.175.
[330] Quoted from ibid., p.173.

[331] Quoted from Jurgan Moltmann, *The Crucified God* (New York: Harper & Row, 1974), p.89.
[332] Henry Chadwick, *Early Christian Thought and the Classical Tradition* (New York: Dorset Press, 1967), p.25.
[333] Grillmeier, *Christ in Christian Tradition*, p.106.
[334] Bigg, *The Christian Platonists of Alexandria*, p.102.
[335] Moltmann, *The Crucified God*, p.89.
[336] Norris, *The Christological Controversy*, p.7.
[337] Kelly, *Early Christian Creeds*, p.72.
[338] Quoted from McGiffert, *A History of Christian Thought*, vol.1, p.113.
[339] Quoted from ibid., p.114.
[340] Grillmeier, *Christ in Christian Tradition*, p.110.
[341] Kelly, *Early Christian Doctrines*, pp.100–01.
[342] Quoted from Norris, *The Christological Controversy*, p.114.
[343] Grillmeier, *Christ in Christian Tradition*, p.119.
[344] Ibid., p.125.
[345] McGiffert, *A History of Christian Thought*, vol.1, p.219.
[346] Ibid., p.223.
[347] Kelly, *Early Christian Doctrines*, p.130.
[348] Bigg, *The Christian Platonists of Alexandria*, pp.223–24.
[349] Ibid., p.132.
[350] McGiffert, *A History of Christian Thought*, vol.1, p.143.
[351] Ibid., p.144.
[352] Ibid., p.205.
[353] Bigg, *The Christian Platonists of Alexandria*, p.97.
[354] McGiffert, *A History of Christian Thought*, vol.1, p.233.
[355] Kelly, *Early Christian Doctrines*, p.119.
[356] Pelikan, *The Christian Tradition*, vol.1, p.178.
[357] Ibid., p.179.
[358] McGiffert, *A History of Christian Thought*, vol.1, p.234.
[359] Harnack, *History of Dogma*, vol.3, p.12.
[360] Linwood Urban, *A Short History of Christian Thought* (New York: Oxford University Press, 1995), p.58.
[361] Quoted from McGiffert, *A History of Christian Thought*, vol.1, pp.235–36.
[362] Pelikan, *The Christian Tradition*, vol.1, pp.181–82.
[363] Urban, *A Short History of Christian Thought*, p.59.

[364] McGiffert, *A History of Christian Thought*, vol.1, p.275.
[365] Ibid., p.239.
[366] Urban, *A Short History of Christian Thought*, p.57.
[367] Harnack, *History of Dogma*, vol.3, pp.41–42.
[368] Paul Tillich, *A History of Christian Thought*, Carl E. Braaten, ed. (New York: Simon & Schuster, 1968), p.65.
[369] Dorothy L. Sayers, *The Emperor Constantine* (New York: Harper & Brothers, 1951), p.119.
[370] Norris, *The Christological Controversy*, pp.17–18.
[371] Henry M. Gwatkin, *Studies of Arianism* (New York: AMS Press, 1978), p.24.
[372] Hilaire Belloc, *The Great Heresies* (New York: Sheed & Ward, n.d.), p.33.
[373] McGiffert, *A History of Christian Thought*, vol.1, p.248.
[374] Pelikan, *The Christian Tradition*, vol.1, p.194.
[375] William Bright, *The Age of Fathers* (New York: AMS Press, 1970), vol.1, p.57.
[376] Gwatkin, *Studies of Arianism*, p.26.
[377] T. E. Pollard, "The Origins of Arianism," *Journal of Theological Studies* (1958), vol.9, p.104.
[378] Harnack, *History of Dogma*, vol.3, p.10.
[379] Ibid.
[380] Frances M. Young, *From Nicaea to Chalcedon* (London: S.C.M. Press, 1983), p.64.
[381] Ibid.
[382] C.S. Lewis, in his Introduction to *The Incarnation of the Word of God, Being the Treatise of St. Athanasius*, Geoffrey Bles, trans. (London: The Centenary Press, 1944), p.11.
[383] Young, *From Nicaea to Chalcedon*, p.65.
[384] Ibid., p.67.
[385] Archibald Robertson in his Introduction "St. Athanasius: Select Works and Letters," *A Select Library of Nicene and Post-Nicene Fathers of the Christian Church* (Grand Rapids: W. B. Eerdmans, 1957), vol. IV, p. IXXII.
[386] Edward R. Hardy, C. C. Richardson, eds., *Christology of the Later Fathers*, The Library of Christian Classics (Philadelphia: The Westminster Press, n.d.), vol. III, pp.58–59.
[387] Ibid., p.60.
[388] Quoted from Eginhard P. Meijering, *God Being History: Studies in Patristic Philosophy* (Amsterdam: North-Holland Publishing Company, 1975), p.93.

[389] McGiffert, *A History of Christian Thought*, vol.1, pp.253–54.
[390] Young, *From Nicaea to Chalcedon*, p.74.
[391] Harnack, *History of Dogma*, vol.4, p.46.
[392] Ibid., p.49.
[393] Bright, *The Age of Fathers*, vol.1, p.95.
[394] Kelly, *Early Christian Doctrines*, pp.236–37.
[395] Robin L. Fox, *Pagans and Christians* (New York: Alfred & Knopf Inc., 1987), p.655.
[396] Kelly, *Early Christian Creeds*, p.255.
[397] Ibid., pp.215–16.
[398] Bright, *The Age of Fathers*, vol.1, p.96.
[399] Harnack, *History of Dogma*, vol.4, p.47.
[400] Bright, *The Age of Fathers*, vol.1, p.98.
[401] Harnack, *History of Dogma*, vol.4, pp.58–59.
[402] George S. J. Meloney, *The Cosmic Christ, From Paul to Teilhard* (New York: Sheed & Ward, 1968), vol.1, p.99.
[403] Harnack, *History of Dogma*, vol.4, p.51.
[404] Meloney, *The Cosmic Christ*, vol.1, p.110.
[405] Andrew M. Fairbairn, *The Place of Christ in Modern Theology* (New York: Scribner's Sons, 1911), pp.90–91.
[406] Ibid., p.91.
[407] W. H. C. Frend, *The Early Church* (Philadelphia: Fortress Press, 1985), p.157.
[408] J. N. D. Kelly, *Early Christian Creeds* (London, Continuum International Publishing Group, 2006), pp.297–98
[409] Basil, Epistle 38 to his brother Gregory of Nyssa, quoted from McGiffert, *A History of Christian Thought*, vol.1, pp.268–69.
[410] Hardy, Richardson, *Christology of the Later Fathers*, p.200.
[411] Ibid., p.199.
[412] Ibid., p.265.
[413] Ibid., pp.261–62.
[414] Ibid., p.266.
[415] Young, *From Nicaea to Chalcedon*, p.112.
[416] Harnack, *History of Dogma*, vol.4, p.97.
[417] Hardy, Richardson, *Christology of the Later Fathers*, p.243.
[418] Grillmeier, *Christ in Christian Tradition*, p.368.
[419] Ibid., p.370.

[420] Tillich, *A History of Christian Thought*, p.78.

[421] Quoted from Pelikan, *The Christian Tradition*, vol.1, p.233.

[422] Quoted from Harry A. Wolfson, *The Philosophy of the Church Fathers*, 3rd edn. (Cambridge, MA: Harvard University Press, 1970), vol.1, p.437.

[423] Kelly, *Early Christian Doctrines*, p.295.

[424] Pelikan, *The Christian Tradition*, vol.1, p.243.

[425] Harnack, *History of Dogma*, vol.4, p.162.

[426] Kelly, *Early Christian Doctrines*, p.297.

[427] Ibid., p.302.

[428] Tillich, *A History of Christian Thought*, p.82.

[429] Ibid.

[430] McGiffert, *A History of Christian Thought*, vol.1, p.279.

[431] Quoted from Pelikan, *The Christian Tradition*, vol.1, p.254.

[432] Kelly, *Early Christian Doctrines*, p.306.

[433] See Tillich, *A History of Christian Thought*, p.82; see for details Francis A. Sullivan, *The Christology of Theodore of Möpsuestia* (Rome: University Gregorian, 1956), pp.219 ff.

[434] McGiffert, *A History of Christian Thought*, vol.1, p.280.

[435] Kelly, *Early Christian Doctrines*, p.307.

[436] Young, *From Nicaea to Chalcedon*, p.210.

[437] Kelly, *Early Christian Doctrines*, p.311.

[438] Henry Chadwick, *The Early Church* (New York: Dorset Press, 1967), p.198.

[439] Quoted from Wolfson, *The Philosophy of the Church Fathers*, vol.1, p.452.

[440] Ibid., p.455.

[441] Kelly, *Early Christian Doctrines*, p.312.

[442] Quoted from Wolfson, *The Philosophy of the Church Fathers*, vol.1, p.456.

[443] Kelly, *Early Christian Doctrines*, p.314.

[444] Ibid., p.315.

[445] Wolfson, *The Philosophy of the Church Fathers*, vol.1, p.457.

[446] Hardy, Richardson, *Christology of the Later Fathers*, p.353.

[447] Ibid., p.352.

[448] Ibid., p.351.

[449] Milton V. Anastos, "Nestorius was Orthodox," *Dumbarton Oaks Papers* (Cambridge, MA, 1962), vol.16, p.120.

[450] Kelly, *Early Christian Doctrines*, p.316.

[451] Grillmeier, *Christ in Christian Tradition*, p.463.

[452] Young, *From Nicaea to Chalcedon*, p.239.
[453] Tillich, *A History of Christian Thought*, p.84.
[454] G. R. Driver, L. Hodgson, eds. and trans., *The Bazar of Heraclides Nestorius* (Oxford; New York: Clarendon Press, 1925), p.370.
[455] Young, *From Nicaea to Chalcedon*, p.229.
[456] Robert V. Sellers, *The Council of Chalcedon: A Historical and Doctrinal Survey* (London: SPCK, 1961), p.59.
[457] Hardy, Richardson, *Christology of the Later Fathers*, p.363.
[458] Ibid., p.368.
[459] Chadwick, *The Early Church*, p.202.
[460] Kelly, *Early Christian Doctrines*, pp.339–40.
[461] Grillmeier, *Christ in Christian Tradition*, p.543.
[462] Kelly, *Early Christian Doctrines*, p.340.
[463] William A. Wigram, *The Separation of the Monophysites* (London: The Faith Press, 1923), p.13.
[464] Ibid., p.16.
[465] Sellers, *The Council of Chalcedon*, p.255.
[466] Ibid., p.266.
[467] Ibid., p.301.
[468] Grillmeier, *Christ in Christian Tradition*, p.553.
[469] Tillich, *A History of Christian Thought*, p.90.
[470] Brunner, *The Christian Doctrine of God*, vol.2, pp.324–25.
[471] Ibid.
[472] Eric L. Mascall, *Christ, The Christian and The Church* (London: Longman, 1946), pp.56–57.
[473] Hick, *The Myth of God Incarnate*, p.5.
[474] Brunner, *The Christian Doctrine of God*, vol.2, p.349.
[475] Bright, *The Age of Fathers*, vol.2, p.550.
[476] John S. Whale, *Christian Doctrine* (Cambridge: Cambridge University Press, 1961), p.110.
[477] McGiffert, *A History of Christian Thought*, vol.1, p.289.
[478] Crossan, *The Historical Jesus*, p. XXX.
[479] Don Cupitt, *Christ, Faith and History: Cambridge Studies in Christology*, S. W. Sykes, J. P. Clayton, eds. (Cambridge: Cambridge University Press, 1972), p.134.
[480] Ibid., p.137.
[481] Crossan, *The Historical Jesus*, p. XXVIII.

[482] Ibid., p.132.

[483] Lightfoot, *History and Interpretation in the Gospels*, p.22.

[484] McGiffert, *A History of Christian Thought*, vol.1, p.320.

[485] Frank K. Flinn, ed., *Christology, The Center and the Periphery* (New York: Paragon House, 1989), pp.87–88.

[486] Harnack, *History of Dogma*, vol.4, p.268.

[487] Hick, *The Myth of God Incarnate*, p.3.

[488] Vladimir Lossky, *The Mystical Theology of the Eastern Church* (London: J. Clarke, 1957), p.153.

[489] Quoted from Brunner, *The Christian Doctrine of God*, vol.2, p.361.

[490] Tillich, *A History of Christian Thought*, p.73.

[491] Flinn, *Christology*, p.90.

[492] Dorothy L. Sayers, *Creed or Chaos* (New York: Harcourt, Brace & Company, 1949), p.5.

[493] Hick, *The Myth of God Incarnate*, p.29.

[494] Quoted from Whale, *Christian Doctrine*, p.98.

[495] Ibid.

[496] Harnack, *History of Dogma*, vol.4, p.307.

[497] Ibid., p.304.

[498] Hick, *The Myth of God Incarnate*, p.133.

[499] Quoted from Harnack, *History of Dogma*, vol.4, p.316.

[500] Ibid., pp.316–17.

[501] Hick, *The Myth of God Incarnate*, p.143.

[502] See for more details Margaret Rickett, *Painting in Britain, The Middle Ages* (New York: Penguin Books, 1954), plates 92, 102, 178.

[503] Hick, *The Myth of God Incarnate*, p.144.

[504] Sayers, *Creed or Chaos*, p.6.

[505] Ibid., p.22.

[506] Ibid., p.7.

[507] Bartsch, *Kerygma and Myth*, p.8.

[508] Ibid.

[509] Rudolf K. Bultmann, *Jesus and the Word*, L. P. Smith, E. H. Lantero, trans. (New York: Charles Scribner's Sons, 1958), p.11.

[510] Ibid., p.12.

[511] Fredriksen, *From Jesus to Christ*, p.214.

[512] Hick, *The Myth of God Incarnate*, p.167.

[513] Ibid., p.175.

[514] Hick, *God and the Universe of Faiths*, p.116.

[515] John Hick, *Faith and Knowledge* (New York: Cornell University Press, 1966), p.223.

[516] Hoffman, Larue, *Jesus in History and Myth*, p.213.

[517] Ibid., p.214.

[518] Hick, *The Myth of God Incarnate*, p.177.

[519] Ibid., p.178.

[520] Hoffmann, Larue, *Jesus in History and Myth*, p.200.

[521] Hick, *The Myth of God Incarnate*, p.179.

[522] Brunner, *The Christian Doctrine of God*, vol.2, p.331.

[523] Ibid., p.330.

[524] Tillich, *A History of Christian Thought*, p.85.

[525] Armstrong, *History of God*, p.131.

CHAPTER 4

Anthropomorphism, Transcendence and the Qur'an

IN ISLAM GOD STANDS ALONE: Transcendent and Majestic. The faith is marked by a strict and uncompromising ethical monotheism, signifying the absolute Oneness, Unity, Uniqueness and Transcendence of God, in its highest and purest sense, and which formally and unequivocally eliminates all notions of polytheism, pantheism, dualism, monolatry, henotheism, tritheism, trinitarianism, and indeed any postulation or conception of the participation of persons in the divinity of God. Thus, it is a universal truth that mainstream Islam has always emphasized the absolute transcendence and unity of God, avoiding corporeal notions and anthropomorphic images of His being.

However, this understanding of transcendence is not abstract in the philosophical sense of the term, for many poetical expressions are used in the Qur'an to establish a kind of divine yet vague modality with regards to God, so as to make the transcendent Deity immanent and live, and to allow for the provision of ample opportunities to develop a meaningful relationship with Him. There are few Qur'anic expressions, which if taken absolutely literally, could lead to mildly anthropomorphic perceptions of the Deity, and these seemingly anthropomorphic expressions have been the center of debate for Muslim theologians for centuries. Hence, phrases referring to the 'hand,' 'face,' 'eyes,' of God, though very few in number, are taken as mysteries by the majority of Muslim scholars and are either often accepted as they stand with the pronouncement *bilā kayf* (literally, "without how" but figuratively as "in a manner that suits His majesty and transcendence") or interpreted metaphorically. The acceptance *bilā kayf* of these phrases is always accompanied with the absolute denial of any similarity between God and His creatures (anthropomorphism) and with repeated emphasis upon the divine otherness and transcendence of God. The total submission to the moral will of this transcendent and unique God is Islam.

The word "Islam" means submission and peace: submission to the moral will of the One and Transcendent God, and peace with the Creator and His creatures. Islam claims to be in unison with the original messages of the prophets Moses and Jesus, but finds fault with the historical Judaic and Christian notions of the deity. The Hebrew Bible's anthropomorphic conceptions of Yahweh (God) and Christianity's belief in a triune God, are both unacceptable to Islam for they are viewed as having compromised God's transcendence and unity. The Islamic Scripture, the Qur'an, on one level, is believed to have been revealed as a corrective measure, to rectify not only the polytheistic conceptions of God but also to clarify and amend Jewish and Christian compromises with regards to God's transcendence. Islam identifies the source of this compromise in the historical adulteration of the previous revelations (both intentional and unintentional) and claims to have fixed the problem through the revelation of the Qur'an, returning to original purity the message that had been undermined and corrupted.

Islam also claims to have avoided the historical mistakes which led to the intermixing or interjection of the words of man with the word of God. Indeed, the faith deems historical authenticity, textual purity and solemn preservation of the original scripture, as key safeguards to guarantee and preserve the transcendence of God and humanity's correct perception of Him.

To demonstrate that the Qur'an has been historically and authentically preserved, and that transcendental monotheism is the essence of the Islamic faith, we discuss initially the Qur'an, the central document of the Islamic faith, to Muslims the very word of God Almighty, and the concept of *al-Tawḥīd*, the Islamic doctrine of God's unity and the foremost Muslim profession and affirmation that Allah is the One, the absolute, transcendent Creator, the Lord of all that is, independent entirely of creation and of everything.

THE QUR'AN: AN INTRODUCTION

The Qur'an is the "Holy Scripture" of the Muslims. It is one of the most widely and seriously read books in the world and one of the leading sources of Arabic learning. To Philip K. Hitti, "the Koran is the most widely read book ever written. For besides its use in worship it is the textbook from which practically every young Moslem learns to read Arabic."[1] The Qur'an is at once the most memorized and the most influential book in the daily life of Muslims and arguably the most influential book in the history of mankind. Held as deeply sacred, Muslims all over the world read it, reflect upon it, and take it as the original, authentic, divine revelation given by God to man. It is universally accepted as the first determining principle and the primary source of the Islamic system of beliefs, laws, ethics, behavior and even emotions and attitudes. It has been the dynamic force behind the rise of Islamic culture and civilization for the last fourteen centuries and regarded by Muslims as the very word of God Almighty, therefore normative and binding in nature. It is neither simple prose nor poetry yet has the ability to arouse its hearers to heights of spiritual ecstasy. The Qur'an's combination of practical daily instruction and dedication to the One and only God makes it the most uniquely treated book in the world.

It could be argued of course that all religious scriptures are of deep significance to their followers and thus held as sacred. Nonetheless, few would contend that the Qur'an is 'something else,' for want of a better phrase, and exits on a very special plane. It refers to itself for instance within its own verses and is aware of its existence. But far more than this, where it is very often the case that people do not live their lives on a daily basis according to the scriptural dictums of their chosen faith, with the Qur'an the opposite is true. God and His revelation fill the consciousness of Muslims with a presence that is rarely witnessed elsewhere and certainly not in the numbers that exist in the Islamic faith. Quite often the dualistic dichotomy of the sacred and the profane plays a key role in the life of man, dividing his existence into two realms, the secular and the religious. By this is meant that religious scriptures are limited to application in terms of spiritual or so-called religious aspects, while the mundane everyday aspects of life are governed by mostly non-scriptural and culturally conditioned secular laws. The Qur'an is unique in the sense that it is the alpha and omega of the Islamic religion tackling this dualistic dichotomy to allow the sacred to dissolve and overcome the profane, merging life into a God-centered whole, suffusing every aspect with a consciousness of the divine. In this way, the otherwise most mundane dimensions of life, such as politics, and the most mysterious such as sexuality, are elevated to great and sacred realms. Boundaries such as those that exist between Church and State are effectively eliminated by the Qur'anic principle of *al-Tawḥīd i.e.,* Oneness of God and oneness of the existence, meaning that both Church and State must reflect divine unity by following the divine axioms of universal justice and human equality. In short, it will be found that each and every aspect of Muslim existence and Islamic society, whether Islamic law, culture, civilization, spiritual or ethical teachings, education, social and political systems etc. is rooted in the explicit or implicit teachings of the Qur'anic text. As the Muslim newborn enters the world the first thing he/she hears is the Qur'an, specifically the *adhān* (the Muslim call to prayer containing the *shahādah* a Qur'anic verse), recited into the baby's ear immediately at birth. As the child grows he/she lives his entire life surrounded by the sound of the Qur'an, particularly in traditional Islamic societies where recitations permeate the day. Finally, at death, the Qur'an is recited to facilitate the transition from this material existence to the life hereafter. In a sense, all Muslims whether male or female, are enveloped in the psalmody of the Qur'an from the cradle to the grave; and this has been the situation since the inception of Islam in the seventh century CE.

The word *qur'ān* is an Arabic word. It is an infinitive verbal noun derived from the root *qara'a* which means "to read", "to recite", "to combine things together". Therefore, the word *qur'ān* literally would mean "reading, recitation, collection, revelation, a book recited or read". The literal meanings of the term correspond to the nature of the Book. It is read, recited, and in reading and recitation the letters and words are joined together to convey the message. On the other hand Imam al-Shāfiʿī (d.204 AH), founder of one of the four schools of thought in Islamic jurisprudence, held that *qur'ān* is not a derivative noun but a proper noun denoting the divinely revealed book.

The Qur'an

The "Qur'an", as a technical term, refers to the Book which is commonly defined by Muslim scholars and theologians as the inimitable word of God revealed to the Prophet Muhammad, transmitted from Prophet Muhammad successively without any break, and whose recitation is an act of devotion. Ismail R. al-Faruqi 1921–1986, a Palestinian-American philosopher and scholar, defines it as the final revelation of God's will to the Prophet Muhammad, "conveyed in Arabic and relayed to his companions, memorized verbatim and publicly and continuously recited by them and their descendants to the present time."[2] Hamilton Alexander Rosskeen Gibb (1895–1971), a Scottish orientalist, introduces the Qur'an in the following words:

> The Koran is the record of those formal utterances and discourses which Mohammad and his followers accepted as directly inspired. Muslim orthodoxy therefore regards them as the literal Word of God mediated through the angel Gabriel. They are quoted with the prefix 'God has said'; the phrase 'The Prophet said' is applied only to the sayings of Mohammad preserved in the Traditions. Mohammad's own belief, which is still held without question by his followers, was that these discourses were portions of a 'Heavenly Book' sent down to or upon him in Arabic version, not as a whole, but in sections of manageable length and in relation to the circumstances of the moment.[3]

The organization of the Qur'an: The Qur'an consists of a text of 114 chapters (*suwar* sing. *sūrah*) of very unequal length, 6,616 verses (*āyāt*), 77,934 words, and 323,671 letters. The 114 chapters are divided into *makkī* chapters (those revealed in the city of Makkah) and *madanī* chapters (those revealed in the city of Madinah), after the names of the two cities in Arabia where the Prophet Muhammad lived, received and delivered the revelation. The *madanī* chapters are usually longer than the *makkī* chapters. The present order of the chapters is not chronological. The period of revelation spanned 22 years, 2 months and 22 days. Qur'anic verses were revealed in stages, bit by bit, over this time in varying contexts addressing different issues. Therefore, Muslims universally acknowledge that an accurate and complete chronological arrangement of the Qur'an is not possible. To facilitate public or private recitations, the Qur'an has been further divided into thirty parts (*ajzā'* sing. *juz'*) and 60 *aḥzāb* or sections.

The language of the Qur'an is Arabic. Yet Arabic in a uniquely other and higher plane, for it differs from other Arabic literary compositions and treatises in a number of ways. The Qur'an is also held as a miracle. This follows from not only its own declarations of itself as such,[4] but also due to its contents, linguistic and literary nature, as well as other factors. There is, and always has been, a consensus among Muslim scholars and theologians that the Qur'an is miraculous in character and the miracle of Allah, although views concerning what constitutes this miraculous nature (*iʿjāz*) differ amongst different scholars.

With the exception of a few skeptics like Abū al-Ḥusayn Aḥmad ibn Yaḥyā ibn al-Rawandī (827–911), an early Muslim heretic and a critic of religion in general, Muslim writers have unanimously held the Qur'an to be *muʿjiz* "inimitable". Helmut Gatje observes that, "Although opinions concerning the validity and significance of these views, and concerning particulars, may vary, the fundamental existence of the miraculous nature of the Qur'an has not been doubted by Muslim exegetes."[5]

So what constitutes the miraculous nature of the Qur'an? As mentioned a great majority of Muslim scholars both historically and today, hold the language, style, beauty and ideas of the Qur'an to be inimitable and miraculous. As well as the language of the Qur'an itself, which is held as divine, perfect, eternal, unchangeable and unsurpassable, several other factors point to its miraculous nature and these include, the presence of correct scientific data, accurate predictions of future events, reports concerning the past, historical facts unknown at the time, a great variety of ideas, concepts and the timeless nature of its principles etc.

Abū Sulaymān Ḥamd ibn Muḥammad al-Khaṭṭābī (319–388/931–998), the famous Shāfiʿī jurist, observes that the key to the Qur'an's miraculous nature and inimitability or *iʿjāz*, is its eloquence: "The Qur'an is inimitable", he writes, "in that it employs the most eloquent words in ideal forms of composition (*aḥsan nuẓum al-taʿlīl*), embodying the truest meanings."[6] Abū Bakr al-Bāqillānī (338–403/950–1013), an

Ashaʿrite Islamic scholar and Mālikī jurist, argues that the Qur'anic inimitability is connected with the *nuẓum* and *badīʿ*. The *badīʿ* denotes that branch of eloquence that deals with the use of literary devices such as the *mumāthalah* (similarity), *mubālaghah* (emphatic statement), *muṭābaqah* (contrasting pairs), *tajnīs* (paronomasia), *istiʿārah* (metaphor) etc. Bāqillānī discusses these literary devices in detail[7] and argues that the Qur'an has made use of these devices in such an eloquent manner (without effecting proper communication) that noone can imitate such a usage and eloquence. Though the *iʿjāz* is not confined to these aspects only, the greater part of it, to Bāqillānī, lies in the Qur'anic *naẓm* as a whole i.e. the unique relationship between the words and meanings. Abū Bakr al-Jurjānī (d.471/1078), renowned Persian grammarian of the Arabic language, also discusses at great length in his book *Dalā'il al-Iʿjāz*, the many literary devices and subtleties of the Arabic language as employed by the Qur'an.[8] Like Bāqillānī, he too connects the Qur'anic *iʿjāz* with the *naẓm*, arguing that the Qur'an relates words in such a fashion as to establish a natural connection between them. The Qur'an miraculously maintains this *naẓm* while fully adhering to *mʿānī al-naḥw* (grammatical rules or meanings). Abū al-Qāsim al-Zamakhsharī also wrote extensively concerning the *iʿjāz* (inimitability) of the Qur'an. In the beginning of his famous commentary on the Qur'an, he thanks God for revealing "*kalaman mu'allafan munaẓẓaman*" meaning "a well-composed and well-knit discourse".[9] His concept of the Qur'anic *naẓm*, in essence, is similar to the views of Bāqillānī and Jurjānī. All these scholars regard the Qur'anic language as inimitable.

Contemporary Muslim scholars and literary specialists also consider the language of the Qur'an to be beautiful, its style inimitable and its composition unrivaled and unmatchable. For instance, according to famous Egyptian poet Mustafa Sadiq al-Rafʿi (1880–1937), the Qur'an's *iʿjāz* (in addition to those aspects of it's inimitability just discussed) is most fully revealed in what he terms its *al-nuẓum al-mūsīqī* that is, its musical form.[10] Sayyid Qutb (1906–1966), renowned Egyptian author, poet and ideologue, emphasizes the Qur'an's "*al-taṣwīr al-fannī*" as the most revealing aspect of it's inimitability, meaning it's artistic, imaginative, and vivid representations and depiction of thoughts, ideas, incidents, and scenes.[11] This would be an interesting aspect of the Qur'an to study in light of modern educational or learning psychology,[12] for modern psychology has shown that mental images, as well as vivid and imaginative representations and depictions play a vital role in the encoding, storing, and retrieval of information. Allan U. Paivio (b.1925), emeritus professor of psychology at the University of Western Ontario for instance conducts research on memory and encoding through imagery and verbal forms. His findings if applied to some of the techniques employed in the Qur'an would be illuminating.[13]

Al-Faruqi observes that:

> Without a doubt, the Qur'an is beautiful, indeed, the most beautiful literary composition the Arabic language has ever known. Its beauty, however, is not the consequence of faith but its very cause. The esthetic judgment – that the Qur'an is beautiful, nay, sublime – is not a pronouncement of faith. It is a critical judgment, reached through literary analysis. Hence, its beauty is not only held by Muslims but also by non-Muslims conversant with the literary esthetics of the Arabic language. Instead of beauty depending upon the divine origin and flowing out of faith in that origin, the divine origin of the Qur'an is the reasoned consequence of its literary beauty. Beauty is the cause and evidence for its divine origin.[14]

Fazlur Rahman (1919–1988), a liberal Muslim scholar, notes:

> There is a consensus among those who know Arabic well, and who appreciate the genius of the language, that in the beauty of its language and the style and power of its expression the Qur'an is a superb document. The linguistic nuances simply defy translation. Although all inspired language is untranslatable, this is even more the case with the Qur'an.[15]

John L. Esposito (b.1940), renowned contemporary Christian scholar of Islam, agrees with this conclusion: "Indeed, throughout history, many Arab Christians as well have regarded it as the perfection of Arabic language and literature."[16] Long before Esposito, Philip K. Hitti (1886–1978), a Maronite Christian scholar of Islam, observed: "No small measure of its force lies in its rhyme and rhetoric and in its cadence and sweep, which cannot be reproduced when the book is translated."[17]

As one historical proof of the inimitable nature of the Qur'an, its *iʿjāz*, traditional theologians cite an incident which took place between the polytheists of Makkah and the Prophet. The former harbored great animosity to the new faith and wanted to defeat the Prophet at any cost. As they considered themselves at the pinnacle of literary skill, eloquence and poetry (a fact not untrue) the Qur'an challenged them to produce a book similar to it (Qur'an 2:23 52:34), even ten chapters or *suwar* (11:13) or even one chapter. As the shortest chapter of the Qur'an consists of less than thirty words they were in effect being shown that Allah was not making the challenge difficult for them but giving them great scope to meet it, which of course they were told they could not, thereby proving categorically that the Qur'an was not of human, but divine, origin. Whilst we read of the incident rather glibly, through the spectacles of time, we should be aware that the challenge in fact was a tremendous one, and the stakes were high; for producing even one small verse or chapter equivalent to that of the Qur'an would have granted the Makkans decisive victory over the Prophet sparing them the terrible struggle they would wage, and the great financial, human, social and political cost this would entail. Despite multiple attempts the Makkans failed and could not surpass the Qur'an in eloquence or literary beauty.

Non-Muslim scholars of Islam also agree to this historical evaluation. Professor Gibb writes:

> But the Meccans still demanded of him a miracle, and with remarkable boldness and self-confidence Mohammed appealed as the supreme confirmation of his mission to the Koran itself. Like all Arabs they were connoisseurs of language and rhetoric. Well then, if the Koran were his own composition other men could rival it. Let them produce ten verses like it. If they could not (and it is obvious that they could not), then let them accept the Koran as an outstanding evidential miracle.[18]

Issa J. Boullata, professor of Islam at McGill University, points out, "The fact that the qur'anic challenge [*taḥaddī*] has never been taken up successfully, either in Muhammad's lifetime or later on, gave Muslim thinkers cause to consider this as a divine authentication of the Qur'an and proof of the veracity of his prophethood."[19] From these historical as well as internal factors, al-Faruqi concludes, that the Qur'an is "so beautiful that it is inimitable; it is so inimitable that it is miraculous. It is therefore not the work of humans but of God."[20]

In opposition to this view stands the view of Abū Isḥāq Ibrāhīm al-Naẓẓām (d. 232/846), a Muʿtazilite theologian. Al-Naẓẓām argued that the Qur'an was not miraculous in its language or style but simply scripture, like other scriptures, containing rules and regulations pertaining to religious matters. Its miracle, he stated, lay in its reports of the past. And its inimitability lay in "*ṣarafa*" meaning that God averted the attention of the opponents from producing anything like the Qur'an though they had the ability to do so. This notion was accepted by a few Muslim scholars such as Hishām al-Fuwāṭī (d. 218/833), ʿIbbād ibn Sulaymān (3rd/9th century) and al-Rummānī (d. 386/996). Some contemporary Shiʿites like Ali Dashti (1894–1982), Iranian rationalist and contemporary Iranian statesman, also argued that neither Qur'anic Arabic nor the Qur'an's style was miraculous. He wrote:

> The Qor'an contains sentences which are incomplete and not fully intelligible without the aid of commentaries; foreign words, unfamiliar Arabic words, and words used with other than the normal meaning; adjectives and verbs inflected without observance of the concords of gender and number; illogically and ungrammatically applied pronouns which some times have no referent; and predicates which in rhymed passages are often remote from the subjects. These and other such aberrations in the language have given scope to critics who deny the Qor'an's eloquence.[21]

This view is highly disputed for a great many scholars have roundly rejected the presence in the Qur'an of any such linguistic aberrations.[22] On the other hand, Dashti himself observes that:

> In all fairness the Qor'an is a wonder. Its short *suras* of the Meccan period are charged with expressive force and persuasive power. Its style has no precedent in the Arabic language. Its effusion from the tongue of an illiterate man with no education, let alone literary training, is a phenomenon which, in this respect, can justifiably be described as a miracle.[23]

He concludes contending that, "The Qor'an is miraculous because it enabled Mohammad, single-handedly and despite poverty and illiteracy, to overcome his people's resistance and found a lasting religion; because it moved wild men to obedience and imposed its bringer's will on them."[24]

Though scholars, like al-Naẓẓām and Dashti, do not deny the divine and miraculous nature of the Qur'an, they do deny the fact that the miracle lies in its language, beauty or style. Their views were debated and rejected by their own followers. For instance, al-Naẓẓām's own student al-Jāḥiẓ and other known Muᶜtazilites like al-Qāḍī ᶜAbd al-Jabbār, rejected his views *viz-à-viz* the Qur'anic *iᶜjāz*. Even a modernist like Fazlur Rahman observes that

> the question of ideas and doctrines apart, it appears certain that the claim of the miraculous nature of the Qur'an is connected with its linguistic style and expression. Unfortunately, non-Arab Muslims do not realize this enough; while they correctly assume that the Qur'an is a book of guidance and hence may be understood in any language, they yet not only deprive themselves of the real taste and appreciation for the Qur'anic expression but – since even a full understanding of the meaning depends upon the linguistic nuances – also cannot do full justice to the content of the Qur'an.[25]

In the West, several views have existed concerning the origin, nature, style, language and composition of the Qur'an. Unfortunately, since the advent of Islam and until today, there have always been individuals who have looked upon the Qur'an as the work of an impostor and a collection of fabricated stories and absurdities. But what has fuelled this seemingly entrenched antipathy? Islam rose in seventh century Arabia (a peninsula comprised of mostly desert and barren land), achieving territorial expansion with unprecedented speed, and within a few short years following the death of its founder, overrunning much of the Middle East Christian world, as well as crucial parts of the Church of North Africa. This brilliant success was enormously threatening. As a result, the initial seeds of hostility were sown as opposition to and propaganda against Islam and the Prophet mushroomed, becoming harsh and vociferous. And, from the time of Rudolph de Ludheim (620) until the present, this antipathy has remained. For example, Nichlas de Cuse (1401–1464), German philosopher and bishop, Juan Luis Vives (1493–1540), Valencian Spanish scholar and humanist, Louis Maracci (1612–1700), an Italian Catholic priest who translated the Qur'an into Latin in 1698 in Padua, Johann Jakob Hottinger (1652–1735), Zurich theologian, Theodore Bibliander (1506–1564), Swiss orientalist, Humphrey Prideaux (1648–1724), Oxford theologian, and many other reputed figures have down the centuries presented the Prophet as an impostor, Islam as a cluster of all heresies, the Muslims as brutes, and the Qur'an as a tissue of absurdities. With the onset of the Crusades, the tone and words chosen to present the Prophet Muhammad as well as the Qur'an and its message, became increasingly bitter. Such was the state of affairs that in the Middle Ages a preposterous story of a "dove" and "bull" became the almost standard interpretation of the Islamic revelation. "One tale", writes K. Armstrong,

> spoke of a white bull which had terrorized the population and which finally appeared with the Qur'an the scripture which Muhammad had brought to the Arabs, floating miraculously between its horns. Muhammad was also said to have trained a dove to peck peas from his ears so that it looked as though the Holy Spirit were whispering into them.[26]

In 1697, at the very beginning of the Enlightenment, two influential books appeared on Islam. Barthelmy d'Herbelot de Molainville (1625–1695), a French orientalist, was author of the first, *Bibliotèque Orientale*. In it, he describes Prophet Muhammad with the words: "This is the famous impostor Mahomet, Author and Founder of a heresy, which has taken on the name of religion, which we call Mohammadan."[27] Author of the second was Humphry Prideaux, a Doctor of Divinity, who in his *The History of The Life of The Great Impostor Mahomet* writes about the Prophet:

> For the first Part of his Life he led a very wicked and licentious Course, much delighting in Rapine, Plunder, and Blood-shed...His two predominant Passions were *Ambition* and *Lust*. The Course which he took to gain Empire, abundantly shews the former; and the multitude of Women which he had to do with, proves the latter. And indeed these two run through the whole Frame of his *Religion*, there being scarce a Chapter in his *Alcoran*, which doth not lay down some Law of war and Blood-shed for the promoting of the one; or else give some Liberty for use of Women here, or some Promise for the enjoyment of them hereafter, to the gratifying of the other.[28]

Ironically despite the 'age of reason' in which these books were written, an age marked by its supposed belief in rationality liberating thinking from dogmatism and crippling religious biases, both books revert to the worst anti-intellectualism of the past, reiterating the same irrational propaganda against the Prophet Muhammad which had prevailed in the Middle Ages.

It is a trend we find continuing even into the eighteenth century with writers such as Simon Ockley, George Sale, and Voltaire, as well as historians such as Gibbon etc., accusing Muhammad of insincerity, ambition and lust. Simon Ockley, for instance, describes Muhammad as a "very subtle and crafty man, who put on the appearance only of those good qualities, while the principles of his soul were ambition and lust."[29]

In 1841, renowned Scottish historian Thomas Carlyle (1795–1881), took a stand against this vicious and centuries old hostility, considering Muhammad to be neither an impostor nor ambitious but:

> A silent great soul; he was one of those who cannot but be in earnest; whom Nature herself had appointed to be sincere.... Such

> sincerity, as we named it, has in very truth something of divine. The word of such a man is a Voice direct from Nature's own Heart.... To be Sheik of Mecca or Arabia, and have a bit of gilt-wood put into your hand, ... will that be one's salvation? I decidedly think not. We leave it altogether, this impostor hypothesis, as not credible; not very tolerable even, worthy chiefly of dismissal by us.[30]

Many writers followed Carlyle in this regard. French philosopher Ernest Renan (1823–1892), described Muhammad as "a man gentle, sensible, faithful, and free from hatred. His affections were sincere; his character in general bent to benevolence... All his conduct gives the lie to the enterprising audacious character which has been commonly attributed to him."[31] James William Hampson Stobart, Principal of La Martiniere College, Lucknow, India, argued that

> the impostor pictured by some writers is refuted alike by his unswerving belief in the truth of his own mission, by the loyalty and unshaken confidence of his companions, who had ample opportunities of forming a right estimate of his sincerity, and, finally, by the magnitude of the task which he brought to so successful an issue. No impostor, it may safely be said, could have accomplished so mighty a work. No one unsupported by a living faith in the reality of his mission, in the goodness of his cause, could have maintained the same consistent attitude through long years of adverse fortune, alike in the day of victory and the hour of defeat, in the plenitude of his power and at the moment of death.[32]

Despite this drastic change in attitude towards Muhammad, most Westerners persisted in maintaining the centuries-old maxims concerning Islam. Hence the Qur'an was condemned as inconsistent, disjointed, the most boring book in the world in fact, and viewed as the word of Muhammad and not of God.

Thomas Carlyle himself described the Qur'an "as toilsome reading as I ever undertook, a wearisome, confused jumble, crude, incondite.

Nothing but a sense of duty could carry any European through the Koran."[33] Tor Julius Efraim Andrae (1885–1947), a Swedish scholar of comparative religion and bishop of Linköping, well summarized the European attitude toward the Qur'an, noting:

> The eloquence of the Koran has made even less impression on the Occident. Voltaire called it "an incomprehensible book which violates our common sense upon every page", and since Voltaire most European readers have found that the Koran is most boresome reading that can be imagined.[34]

Although both François-Marie Arouet Voltaire (1694–1778) and Carlyle are reported to have later changed their views on the Qur'an, their first dictum has frequently been echoed in many western writings. English historian Edward Gibbon (1737–1794), for instance describes the Qur'an as "the endless incoherent rhapsody of fable, and precept, and declamation, which seldom excites a sentiment or an idea, which sometimes crawls in the dust, and is sometimes lost in the clouds."[35] Hartwig Hirschfeld (1854–1934), lecturer on Judaeo-Arabic studies at Jews College, London, observes that there are "manifold difficulties" in the Qur'an and these difficulties, "repel rather than encourage the study of the Qur'an." [36]

The old biases and stereotypes of the medieval age still surface occasionally in some Evangelical circles. William St. Clair Tisdall (1859–1928), British historian, philologist and missionary, contends:

> The Qur'an breathes the air of the desert, it enables us to hear the battle-cries of the Prophet's followers as they rushed to onset, it reveals the working of Muhammad's own mind, and shows the gradual declension of his character as he passed from the earnest and sincere though visionary enthusiast into the conscious impostor and open sensualist.[37]

Salomon Reinach (1858–1932), French archaeologist, claims:

> From the literary point of view, the Koran has little merit. Declamation, repetition, puerility, a lack of logic and coherence

> strike the unprepared reader at every turn. It is humiliating to the human intellect to think that this mediocre literature has been the subject of innumerable commentaries, and that millions of men are still wasting time in absorbing it.[38]

There are several views commonly held about the Qur'an and its first recipient in contemporary western academic circles. William Montgomery Watt (1909–2006), Professor of Islamic Studies at the University of Edinburgh, and influential scholar in his field, like many other contemporary western writers, believed in the utmost sincerity of Muhammad[39] and his capacity to distinguish between divine revelation and the product of his own consciousness.[40] He also professes that the Qur'an contains many divine truths, "I am not a Muslim in the usual sense, though I hope I am a *muslim* as 'one surrendered to God'; but I believe that embedded in the Qur'an and other expressions of the Islamic vision are vast stores of divine truth from which I and other occidentals have still much to learn."[41] Watt also recognized the originality and individuality of the Qur'anic literary nature: "Not merely was it in Arabic language, but in many respects it is typically Arab in its literary form, even though there is no other Arabic literature quite like it."[42]

In spite of all these factors, Watt drew the conclusion, as other orientalists have done, that the Qur'an was a product of Muhammad's creative imagination and that he may have been mistaken in his belief that it was a divine message. "What seems to a man to come from outside himself may actually come from his unconscious."[43] He also felt that the Qur'an's arrangement was "unsystematic", declaring "disjointedness" as a characteristic of the Qur'an and observing that the scripture lacked "sustained composition at any great length".[44] Sir James Norman Anderson (1908–1994), English missionary and academic Arabist, looked upon the Qur'an as "the result of wishful thinking."[45] Edinburgh based Arabist, Richard Bell (1876–1952), propounded a "written-document" hypothesis to explain what he felt was Qur'anic inconsistency, speculating that the Prophet wrote his revelations on certain bits of paper whilst writing certain other chapters (surahs) on the back of these sheets, explaining why heterogeneous matters, according to him, appear mixed up in the surahs, and drawing the conclusion that verses of the Qur'an became disjointed because they were "wrongly assembled, interrupted or detached."[46] Tor Andrae concludes: "However, although certain passages are characterized by genuine beauty of style, it must be admitted that as a whole the Koran can hardly be regarded as fascinating reading."[47] Arthur Stanley Tritton, (1881–1973), a British historian and scholar of Islam, wrote: "Those, who are not Muslims, cannot endorse these high praises."[48] Patricia Crone (b.1945), a Danish historian of Islam, and Michael Allan Cook (b.1940), a Scottish historian and scholar of Islamic history, write of the Qur'an in their controversial book *Hagarism*, that it is "strikingly lacking in overall structure, frequently obscure and inconsequential in both language and content, perfunctory in its linking of disparate materials, and given to the repetition of whole passages in variant versions."[49] Andrew Rippin, dean of humanities at the University of Victoria, British Columbia, Canada, observes that, "The text of the Qur'an presents many ambiguities, difficult words whose precise readings are unsure, problems of textual division and apparently incompatible statements."[50]

In contrast, Arthur John Arberry (1905–1969), a prolific and widely respected scholar of Arabic, Persian, and Islamic studies, voiced his protest against such crude treatment of the Qur'an contending that the disciples of the Higher Criticism had enthusiastically tried to demolish the Qur'an by artificial and arbitrary methodologies of their own. They had cut into pieces the main body of the Qur'anic revelation but in doing so the

> erudite sleuths have found themselves with a corpse on their hands, the spirit meanwhile eluding their preoccupied attention. So they have been apt to resort to the device of explaining away what they could not explain; crushed between their fumbling fingers, the gossamer wings of soaring inspiration have dissolved into powder. The most extreme representative of this school of thought, which once tyrannized over Koran studies in the West was no doubt the late Dr. Richard Bell.[51]

After explaining Bell's hypothesis, Arberry goes on to criticize it, contending that both Bell and other champions of the Higher Criticism of the Qur'an had committed violence against it:

> It is against this excess of anatomical mincing that I argue the unity of the sura and the Koran; instead of offering the perplexed reader *disjecta membra* scattered indifferently over the dissecting table, I ask him to look again at the *cadaver* before it was carved up, and to imagine how it might appear when the lifeblood of inspiration flowed through its being. I urge the view that an eternal composition, such as the Koran is, cannot be well understood if it is submitted to the test of only temporal criticism. It is simply irrelevant to expect that the themes treated in the individual sura will be marshaled after some mathematical precision to form a rationally ordered pattern; the logic of revelation is not the logic of the schoolmen. There is no 'before' or 'after' in the prophetic message, when the message is true, everlasting truth is not held within the confines of time and space but every moment reveals itself wholly and completely.[52]

Many modern Muslim scholars also defend the Qur'an against allegations of disjointedness, lack of overall structure, and ambiguity. Abul A'la Mawdudi (1903–1979), Pakistani scholar and ideologue, argues that the Qur'an is a unique book of revelation. It will defy any preconceived notions of an ordinary book because the Qur'an is "unique in the manner of its composition, in its theme and in its contents and arrangement."[53] He argued that the Qur'anic unity lay in its subject, purpose, and central thesis; the subject of the book was man and the purpose, man's salvation. The central concepts of the book are related to God, man and the universe in their mutual relationship to human salvation. The book is neither a book of history nor science: "The real object of the Book is to call people to this 'right way' and to illuminate God's true guidance, which has often been lost either through man's negligence and heedlessness or distorted by his wicked perversity."[54] The Qur'an in its entirety is geared towards this central theme of ethical monotheism and salvation through submission to the moral will of God and peace with man and his surroundings. Mawdudi concludes that:

> If we study the Qur'an with these facts in mind it is bound to strike us that the Qur'an does not deviate one iota from its main subject, its central theme and its basic objective. All the various themes occurring in the Qur'an are related to the central theme; just as beads of different sizes and colors may be strung together to form a necklace.[55]

M. Mahmud Hijazi, a contemporary Egyptian Qur'anic studies scholar, emphasizes "topical unity" in the Qur'an.[56] He observes that the coherence of the Qur'an becomes evident when all the Qur'anic verses on a given subject are brought together and studied in the light of each other. Fazlur Rahman emphasizes the Qur'anic "cohesive outlook on the universe and life"[57] arguing that Qur'anic teaching has "no inner contradictions" but coheres as a whole.[58] Indian Islamic scholar, Hamiduddin Farahi (1863–1930), notes that each chapter of the Qur'an revolves around a central theme which he calls "*ᶜAmūd*" meaning pillar or column or hub of the chapter.[59] Amin Ahsan Islahi (1904–1997), a Pakistani exegete, argues that there is a structural as well as thematic coherence in the Qur'an.[60] He elaborates upon the concept of "*ᶜAmūd*" as one of the methods of showing unity and coherence in the Qur'an. Farahi, Islahi, Tabatabai and Sayyid Qutb, all of them try to show that the Qur'an is not inconsistent or disjointed by emphasizing that "each sura is a thematically complete discourse that has been presented in a coherent structural framework."[61] Mustansir Mir, a Youngstown University scholar of Islamic studies, has discussed many of these responses and approaches in detail. After discussing Islahi's work at great length, he concludes:

> Islahi has convincingly shown – although it is not necessary to agree with all of his conclusions – that the Qur'an has design and method. He has shown that individual qur'anic surahs revolve around specific central themes, that an essential complementarity exists between the members of surah pairs, and that larger sets of

> surahs, which he calls surah groups, display identifiable patterns of nazm. A study of *Tadabbur-i Qur'an* is bound to leave one with the impression that, contrary to the usually held view, the Qur'an is a well-ordered book.[62]

As the Qur'an to certain degrees is pedagogically oriented (*hudā* guidance and *nūr* light), the findings of modern scholars such as these, can possibly be studied and grasped more fully in light of the findings of educational or learning psychology. For instance, it has been observed by a number of psychologists that breaking down topical units into smaller subunits (multiple discrimination) and presenting these subunits over specific intervals and by a variety of methods, greatly facilitates understanding, assimilation, and retention of the material.[63] The Qur'an's supposed disjointedness, seen in this light, transforms into something to be understood and appreciated in this sense. Similarly, the repetitive material of the Qur'an can now be interpreted in light of what psychologists call the process of "*shaping*" through the "*schedules of reinforcement*".[64] "The behavior is shaped through a series of successive approximations to the desired behavior, each made possible by selectively reinforcing certain responses and not others. Thus behavior gradually is brought closer and closer to the desired pattern."[65] The Qur'an, it can be argued, uses a kind of *fixed* as well as *variable interval schedules of reinforcement*, the intention being to bring the reader closer and closer to the desired pattern and goal through constant reinforcement or repetition.

To fully appreciate the repetitions and topical variety found in the Qur'an, an understanding of the Qur'an's discourse on the universe and reality may be required. There is a unity of purpose in the diversity of topics and themes. Sachiko Murata (b. 1943) and William C. Chittick, two Stony Brook University professors of religion, argue that:

> For Westerners, the Koran is an extremely difficult text to appreciate, especially in translation. Even for those who have spent enough years studying the Arabic language to read the original, the Koran may appear as disorderly, inaccurate, and illogical. However, there is enough evidence provided by Islamic civilization

> itself, and by the great philosophers, theologians, and poets who have commented on the text, to be sure that the problem lies on the side of the reader, not the book. The text is undoubtedly one of the most extraordinary ever put down on paper. Precisely because it is extraordinary, it does not follow people's expectations as to what a book should be.[66]

They further contend that our cultural milieu is dominated by mass media, internet and educational institutions, meaning that our thought patterns are not shaped by the church, synagogue or other centers of religious learning but predominantly by the media and educational institutions. So, even though the Qur'anic worldview bears close affinity with that of Judaism and Christianity, this has little bearing, for most people whether consciously or unconsciously have little understanding of the biblical world view either:

> We may like to think that our education is scientific and unbiased, but this is a highly biased judgment, as many contemporary thinkers and social critics have told us. As a rule, it seems, when people with no grounding in the Islamic world view pick up a translation of the Koran, they have their prejudices confirmed, whatever these may be. No real entrance into the Koranic view of things is possible without some idea of the type of thinking that infuses the text. And that thinking is foreign to the way that we are taught to think in our own culture and modern education in general.[67]

There is a third group of western writers and thinkers, whose views on the language, composition and impact of the Qur'an, come very close to those of Muslims regarding these issues. Johann Wolfgang von Goethe (1749–1832), famous German writer and polymath, for example famously commented on the Qur'anic style, "As often as we approach it, it always proves repulsive anew, gradually, however, it attracts, it astonishes and in the end it forces admiration."[68] H. A. R. Gibb, commenting on Carlyle's statement that the Qur'an is "as toilsome reading as I ever undertook," writes:

> But years of close study confirm his further judgment that in it 'there is a merit quite other than the literary one. If a book come from the heart, it will contrive to reach other hearts; all art and authorcraft are of small account to that.' Though, to be sure, the question of literary merit is one not to be judged on *a priori* grounds but in relation to the genius of the Arabic language; and no man in fifteen hundred years has ever played on that deep-toned instrument with such power, such boldness, and such range of emotional effect as Mohammed did.[69]

Emil Derenghem observes that, "Its literary beauty, its irradiation, an enigma even today, have the power of putting those who recite it into a state of fervor, even if they are the least pious."[70] George Sale (1697–1736), the English orientalist, stated that the Qur'an is of

> ... the utmost elegance and purity of language, ... to its miracle did Mohammad chiefly appeal for the confirmation of his mission, publicly challenging the most eloquent men in Arabia – which was at that time stocked with thousands whose sole study and ambition was to excel in elegance of style and composition – to produce a single chapter that might be compared with it.

He further observes that, "The Style of the Qur'an is beautiful, it is adorned with bold figures after the Eastern taste, enlivened with florid and sententious expressions and in many places where the majesty and attributes of God are described, sublime and magnificent."[71] John Alden Williams, the William R. Kenan Jr. Professor of Humanities at the College of William and Mary in Virginia, observes that, "the Arabic of the Qur'an is by turns striking, soaring, vivid, terrible, tender and breathtaking.... It is meaningless to apply adjectives such as "beautiful" or "persuasive" to the Qur'an; its flashing images and inexorable measures go directly to the brain and intoxicate it."[72]

The real problem for those in the West, including orientalists, is that of the Qur'an's translation. It is extremely difficult to convey real poetry in a foreign idiom without loss of profundity and beauty, and this to an enormous degree is the case with the Qur'an. If some of the most beautiful and eloquent lines of Rumi or Shakespeare are rendered banal when expressed in another language, is it any wonder that given the beauty and literary power of the Arabic language, its true nature and rich erudition become lost in translation? We see this in the many masterpieces of Arabic prose and poetry which have become unrecognizable when translated into other tongues. And if this is the case with the latter, then how much more so for the Qur'an? Renowned scholar of comparative religions, Karen Armstrong (b.1944), has this to say:

> There is something about Arabic which is incommunicable in another idiom: even the speeches of Arab politicians sound stilted, artificial and alien in an English translation. If this is true of ordinary Arabic, of mundane utterance or conventional literature, it is doubly true of the Qur'an which is written in highly complex, dense and allusive language. Even Arabs who speak English fluently have said that when they read the Qur'an in an English translation, they feel that they are reading an entirely different book.[73]

Oxford scholar John Naish comments, "The Qur'an in its original Arabic dress has a seductive beauty and charm of its own. Couched in concise and exalted style, its brief pregnant sentences, often rhymed, possess an expressive force and explosive energy which it is extremely difficult to convey by literal word by word translation."[74] Prolific English writer, Ronald Victor Courtenay Bodley, after having spent years with the nomadic Arab tribes of the western Sahara, stated of the Qur'an that, "In addition to its delivery and its subject, it depends a great deal on its phraseology.... the Koran lose its inspiring rhythm when taken out of Arabic."[75] This would explain the frustrations that those in the West as well as orientalists claim to experience on encountering the Qur'an. More importantly it would also call into question the worth of their assessment, for in point of fact so much is lost in translation that one is forced to question the value of any assessment that uses as its basis a translated edition. In other words, being so far removed from the language of the original they may not be in a position to appreciate the literary composition, beauty and erudition of this deep and complex text.

The Qur'an's composition is unique in the sense that it is neither complete prose nor poetry. It is neither full history nor biography. Unlike Jesus' Sermon on the Mount, it is not an anthology. Unlike the Buddhist Sutras, it shuns metaphysical dialects. It also defies abstract philosophical homiletics such as Plato's conferences of the wise and foolish teachers. It is a Semitic cry focused upon morality, social transformation, peace, justice and eternal salvation. It eliminates the dualistic dichotomy of the sacred and profane realms. It unifies material life with the spiritual realm and gives conceptual framework and meanings to this worldly life so much so that the transformation of time and space becomes an urgent matter, of great concern to man here and now. The Qur'an is egalitarian and moral through and through. This is why it transformed, as Bodley explains, "the simple shepherds, the merchants and nomads of Arabia into warriors and empire builders."[76] It is worthwhile quoting Philip Hitti here who observes that:

> Its length is four-fifths that of the New Testament in Arabic. The religious influence it exercises as the basis of Islam and the final authority in matters spiritual and ethical are only part of the story. Theology, jurisprudence and science being considered by Moslems as different aspects of one and the same thing, the Koran becomes the scientific manual, the textbook, for acquiring a liberal education.... Its literary influence may be appreciated when we realize that it was due to it alone that the various dialects of the Arabic-speaking peoples have not developed into distinct languages. While today an Iraqi may find it a little difficult fully to understand the speech of a Moroccan, he would have no difficulty in understanding his written language, since in both Iraq and Morocco – as well as in Syria, Arabia, Egypt – the classical language modeled by the Koran is followed closely everywhere. At the time of Muhammad there was no work of the first order in Arabic prose. The Koran was therefore the earliest, and has ever since remained the model prose work. Its language is rhythmical and rhetorical, but not poetical. Its rhymed prose has set the

> standard which almost every conservative Arabic writer today consciously strives to imitate.[77]

Observations such as these, when joined with others – like that of Alphonse Marie Louis de Prat de Lamartine (1790–1869), a French writer, poet and politician,[78] Arnold Joseph Toynbee (1889–1975) a British historian,[79] Hans Küng (b.1928), a Swiss Catholic priest, controversial theologian, and prolific author,[80] John Louis Esposito (b.1940), a Georgetown University Professor of Islamic Studies, and many others[81] – come very close to traditional Islamic views and impressions held of the nature of the Qur'an. It must be borne in mind that the Qur'an was revealed to seventh century Arabs, steeped in literary tradition, to be read, recited, and practiced. What this means, in the first instance, is that an extensive knowledge of classical Arabic is essential to appreciate its style, beauty and composition; a critical factor which Mohammad Asad, European Jewish convert to Islam (born Leopold Weiss 1900–1992), acclaimed translator and modern scholar of the Qur'an, recognized.[82] Asad asserted that "familiarity with the Bedouin speech of Central and Eastern Arabia – in addition, of course, to academic knowledge of classical Arabic – is the only way for a non-Arab of our time to achieve an intimate understanding of the diction of the Qur'an."[83]

This does not mean, however, that one needs to be proficient in the various subtleties of the Arabic language to understand the message of the Qur'an. Even if translated into any other language the message itself is simple and easy to grasp. However, in terms of deeper literary / linguistic appreciation of the text, meaning apprehension of the Qur'an's literary style, beauty, and composition, a thorough grasp of the intricacies of classical Arabic is essential. Once a person becomes acquainted with the latter, and combines this with a good working knowledge of other related Islamic sciences, it may become easy for him to appreciate the aesthetic and rhetorical features of the Qur'an. He may then conclude with Arthur J. Arberry that the richly varied rhythms of the Qur'an and its message constitute its "undeniable claim to rank amongst the greatest literary masterpieces of mankind."[84]

Therefore, the remarks and claims of non-Muslim readers that the Qur'an is "crude", "toilsome", and "incoherent rambling" can be understood and explained in light of these observations and realities. It may not be inappropriate here to conclude with Charles J. Adams that, "The study of the Qur'an for its own sake as the basic document of the Islamic community must now be fostered and encouraged, and study of this kind stands in the first rank of importance for the deepened understanding of Islam as a religion."[85] Attempts along these lines have been made by various scholars like Toshihiko Izutsu (1914–1993), McGill University Professor of Islam,[86] Bishop Kenneth Cragg (b.1913), renowned Anglican scholar of Islam,[87] Fazlur Rahman,[88] and especially Angelika Neuwirth,[89] a contemporary German expert on the Qur'an, and Pierre Crapon de Caprona, French scholar of the Qur'an. A. Neuwirth, after studying oath clusters (kinds of oaths implied to emphasize points) in the Makkan surahs, concluded:

> 'The book' is thus the only relic from among a complex ensemble of manifold 'accessories of revelation', originally comprising cosmic, vegetative, topographic, cultic and social elements. The book as the symbol of revelation *par excellence* thus acquires even in early Makkan times the dignity which it has preserved until the present day: to represent the noblest emblem of Islamic religion.[90]

It is only after attempts such as these and the application of genuine fresh approaches can the Muslim idea of Qur'anic *iʿjāz* be better apprehended and more fully appreciated.

In terms of compilation, the Qur'an is very unlike the present day Bible. For one thing the Qur'an was sanctified, recorded, carefully preserved, and canonized from the very moment of its revelation, i.e. its very inception. Harvard Professor William A. Graham rightly observes that the Christian and Jewish concept of scriptural canonization over time is foreign to Muslims. Muslims view the Qur'an as God's last and final revelation to mankind:

> in the course of one prophetic career during which and immediately afterward it was collected into book form. The collected text, as God's direct Speech, has been explicitly recognized as scripture since the actual time in which it "came

> down." Of a process of canonization Muslims know nothing analogous to that of Jewish and Christian scripture.[91]

Muslim sources agree that the Qur'anic text was fully memorized and put into some written forms during the lifetime of the Prophet. At the end of his life, writes al-Faruqi, "Muhammad had about 30,000 contemporaries who had heard and memorized the Qur'an in whole or in part. Several of them could read and write and had committed the Qur'an to writing in part or in toto."[92] The fact that Prophet Muhammad was conscious of the divine nature and otherness of the Qur'an from the very beginning of his mission, is something well attested by historical facts and recognized by western scholars.[93] A. Guillaume, a London University Professor of Arabic states, "It is beyond doubt that his hearers recognized the symptoms of revelation, otherwise his *obiter dicta* which the literature of tradition purports to record would be included in the Qur'an."[94] Western scholars of Islam also agree that the Prophet's followers committed the text of the Qur'an to memory, as was the case with most literary works in Arabia.[95] German Professor of Islam, Helmut Gatje observes that "Muhammad seems to have begun quite early the practice of reciting passages from the Qur'an to his followers for as long as necessary until they knew them by heart. This type of transmission had its model in the propagation of ancient Arabic poetry."[96] It is pertinent to quote at this point Sir William Muir, a resolute Christian missionary:

> The divine revelation was the cornerstone of Islam. The recital of a passage from it formed an essential part of daily prayer public and private; and its perusal and repetition were enforced as a duty and a privilege fraught with religious merit. This is the universal voice of early tradition, and may be gathered also from the revelation itself. The Coran was accordingly committed to memory more or less by every adherent of Islam, and the extent to which it could be recited was one of the chief distinctions of nobility in the early Muslim empire. The custom of Arabia favored the task... The recollective faculty was thus cultivated to the highest pitch; and it was applied, with all the ardor of an awakened spirit, to the

> Coran. Such was the tenacity of their memory, and so great their power of application, that several of Mahomet's followers, according to early tradition, could, during his life-time, repeat with scrupulous accuracy the entire revelation.[97]

It is also recognized by orientalists that writing skill was common in the metropolitan town of Makkah due to its mercantile atmosphere. According to Watt, "The Meccan merchants must have kept some record of their transactions, and it may be assumed that writing was well enough known there."[98]

That Muhammad used secretaries to write down the Revelation, is also a fact widely affirmed historically and recognized by western scholarship.[99] Gatje observes that "Muhammad also probably dictated connected sections of the revelation to be written down even before his departure for Medinah."[100] Watt quotes several traditional stories to conclude: "it shows that some revelation had been written down by the middle of the Meccan period."[101]

W. Muir observes:

> Besides the reference in the Coran to its own existence in a written form, we have express mention made in the authentic traditions of Omar's conversion, of a copy of the 20th Sura being used by his sister's family for social and private devotional reading. This refers to a period preceding, by three or four years, the emigration to Medina. If transcripts of the revelations were made, and in common use, at that early time when the followers of Islam were few and oppressed, it is certain that they must have multiplied exceedingly when the Prophet came to power, and his Book formed the law of the greater part of Arabia.[102]

It is true, observes Watt, that "After Muhammad went to Medina his employment of secretaries is well attested. Among those used for the writing down of revelations were ʿUthman, Muʿawiya, Ubayy ibn-Kaʿb, Zayd ibn-Thabit and ʿAbd-Allah ibn-Abi-Sarh."[103]

From these facts and other related authentic traditions, Muslim scholars conclude that the entire text of the Qur'an was written down in some shape or form in the lifetime of the Prophet. They also unanimously hold that Prophet Muhammad himself was responsible for the arrangement of the verses into surahs.

Many western scholars, like Muir, Burton and Smith agree with these conclusions. Muir, for instance, writes:

> there is good reason for believing that many fragmentary copies, embracing amongst them the whole Coran, or nearly the whole, were made by Mahomet's followers during his life. Writing was without doubt generally known at Mecca long before Mahomet assumed the prophetical office. Many of his followers are expressly mentioned as employed by the Prophet at Medina in writing his letters or dispatches... The ability thus existing, it may be safely inferred that the verses which were so indefatigably committed to memory, would be likewise committed carefully to writing.[104]

Burton also concludes that the present text of the Qur'an was organized by the Prophet himself, observing that the present text, "is none other than the unique text of the revelations...the text which has come down to us in the form in which it was organized and approved by the Prophet."[105] K. Cragg notes that "there is no place for serious misgiving that what is here was substantially what the Prophet said or that what he said under conditions of qur'anic inspiration is not here."[106]

Other orientalists, like Watt, Tritton, Gibb, hold that the Qur'an was partially and not entirely written down in the lifetime of the Prophet. Watt states that "much of the Qur'an was written down in some form during Muhammad's lifetime."[107] A. Guillaume observes that, "There is no doubt that at the death of Muhammad a good deal of the Qur'an was already written down, though not all of it, for while he was alive new suras or chapters were constantly being added."[108] A. S. Tritton concludes:

> The Koran contains the revelations given to Muhammad. These had not been collected during his lifetime though partial collections had been made. A definitive collection was begun

> during the reign of his successor and this was revised during the reign of Uthman; there is no reason to doubt the authenticity of the result.[109]

It is pertinent to mention here that Abū Bakr (632–634), who succeeded Prophet Muhammad (who died in 632), ordered the collection of the written material in one volume after ʿUmar urged him to do so. The massacre of Yamāmah had claimed the lives of many of the memorizers (*ḥuffāẓ*) and reciters of the Qur'an and as such a written volume became essential. Scholars like Gibb, Watt, and Burton, have critically examined various traditions *vis-à-vis* who started the work of collection in the first place, and believe, as Watt has expressed, that the traditions are "open to criticism on a number of grounds."[110] Still they reach the same conclusion that it was a careful, sincere and scholarly collection of what was recorded in the lifetime of the Prophet. Burton, for instance, observes that, "The task, whoever first accomplished it, was merely one of assembling the Qur'an which already in the lifetime of the Prophet was recorded in writing. Abū Bakr's contribution was to arrange for the transfer of these sheets, then scattered about Medina, into a single volume."[111] It was Zayd ibn Thābit, the secretary of the Prophet, who headed the commission and did the job for Abū Bakr. He collected the written texts of the Qur'an, verified them against his own memory (he was a *ḥāfiẓ)*, used other safeguards, and produced the single volume. "The original copy", observes Sir W. Muir:

> prepared by Zeid was probably kept by Abu Bakr during the short remainder of his reign. It then came into the possession of Omar who... committed it to the custody of his daughter Haphsa, the Prophet's widow. The compilation of Zeid, as embodied in this exemplar, continued during Omar's ten years' Caliphate to be the standard and authoritative text.[112]

ʿUthmān (644–656), who succeeded ʿUmar, ordered the same Zayd to produce in written form a single transcript, meaning text, in accordance with the standard Makkan dialect. The reason being that Islam had spread far and the conversion of many non-Peninsular Arabs as well as non-Arab peoples was causing a variety of expression in the modes of recitation of the Qur'anic text to enter, which itself did allow various variant readings since the time of the Prophet, as we will see in the coming pages. Alarmed by the diversity, ʿUthmān ordered recension of the Qur'anic text to one standard transcript and ordered others to be burnt. These burnt pre-ʿUthmānic codices of, for instance, ʿAbd Allāh ibn Masʿūd (d. circa 653), Ubayy ibn Kaʿb (d. circa 639 or later), Abū Mūsā al-Ashʿarī (d. circa 662 or later), and Miqdād ibn ʿAmr (d. 653), with the exception of a few variant readings, observes Gatje, "had the same suras as the Uthmanic Qur'an, although in somewhat different orders."[113] After critically examining the traditions concerning these codices, Professor Watt concludes that:

> on the whole the information which has reached us about the pre-Uthmanic codices suggests that there was no great variation in the actual contents of the Qur'an in the period immediately after the Prophet's death. The order of the suras was apparently not fixed, and there were many slight variations in reading; but of other differences there is no evidence.[114]

We may kind of agree here with Muir who observes that, "We may then safely conclude that Othman's recension was, what it professed to be, namely, the reproduction of the text of Zeid, with a more perfect conformity to the dialect of Mecca, and possibly a more uniform arrangement of the component parts – but still a faithful reproduction."[115] Here we may add a word of caution that ʿUthmān did neither edit nor add anything to the existing text of the Qur'an. He faithfully reproduced the already existent text. This ʿUthmānic text, observes Burton:

> had been arrived at only after the most rigorous inquiries by the commission appointed for the purpose by the Head of State. We have seen something of the scholarly caution with which the commission had approached its sacred task, including in the completed draft only what it had no human reason to doubt had come down from the direct instruction of the Prophet via the most veracious witnesses.[116]

Gibb concludes that "it seems reasonably well established that no material changes were introduced and that the original form and contents of Mohammed's discourses were preserved with scrupulous precision."[117] K. Cragg notes, "the consensus of view – Shi'ahs excepted – is that the Qur'an as it stood in ʿUthman's recension omits no significant and includes no extraneous material. The Prophet's death had decisively closed the Book."[118] Therefore, within a short span of 12 years after the departure of the Prophet as al-Faruqi contends,[119] or about 18 years as Watt argues,[120] a standard, complete, written codice of the Qur'an was officially published and made available along with expert teachers to the metropolitan cities of the empire. Al-Faruqi points out that

> several copies were made and distributed...Except for the diacritical marks and some improvements of orthography and calligraphy, the Qur'an extant in every Muslim home around the world today, or kept and recited from memory by the millions, is identical to the material that was recited and conveyed by the Prophet to his companions fourteen centuries ago.[121]

John Wansbrough, a Reader in Arabic at the School of Oriental and African Studies, University of London, who passed away in 2002, authored two controversial books in an effort to critique the Qur'an, denying its existence in the life of the Prophet Muhammad or even before the end of the second/eighth century. Of course much is pure speculation, ignoring as Charles Adam rightly points out with regards to Wansbrough's views, the fact that, "Such matters as the formation of the Qur'an text, the chronology of the materials assembled in the text, the history of the text, variant readings, the relationship of the Qur'an to prior literature, and a host of other issues of this kind have been investigated thoroughly."[122] Nevertheless, refuting all conclusions drawn by conventional Islamic as well as western scholars, Wansbrough in the opinion of Andrew Rippin "has made it clear that we have really only scratched the surface of these studies."[123]

Wansbrough, applied the 'literary' method of biblical criticism to the Qur'an (following Geza Vermes[124] and Raphael Loewe's treatment of the Bible), undertaking a form-critical analysis of the Qur'anic text to reach a very unusual conclusion. He isolated four major features of the Qur'anic message – divine retribution, sign, exile, and covenant – all taken from the traditional stock of monotheistic imagery,[125] to observe that these motifs are repeatedly signaled but seldom developed in the Qur'an. From here he discerned that the Qur'an has a "referential" style,[126] a significant insight, and to elaborate his point that the Qur'an presumes its audience to fill in the missing details of the narratives[127] refers as example the story of prophet Joseph and his brothers, narrated in surah 12:59. Wansbrough goes on to maintain that this referential character of the Qur'an is a key to understanding that it is not an exclusively Arabian book and that it should not be detached from its Judeo-Christian background.[128] The Qur'an, he argued was produced in an atmosphere of intense Judeo-Christian sectarian debate and was a composite work of "variant traditions."[129]

This emphasis upon the Judeo-Christian background of the Qur'an is an old hypothesis and has been repeatedly mentioned by many western writers. J. Wellhausen, R. Bell, Tor Andrae, S. Zwemer,[130] Gardner,[131] Margoliouth,[132] Torrey,[133] Goitein,[134] W. Ahrens, Anderson, Rodinson, and Jeffery are just a few examples. Wellhausen, Bell, Andrae and Ahrens advocated a Christian Aramaic background to the Qur'anic text, whilst H. Hirschfeld, D. Kuenstlinger, R. Lesczynsky, H. Speyer, Anderson, C. Torrey, A. Geiger, and Katsh, asserted the Judaic foundations of Islam. Anderson, for instance, claimed that, "The long rambling accounts of Jewish patriarchs and prophets [in the Qur'an] correspond in so much detail with the Talmud that of their essentially Jewish origin there can be no doubt."[135] Gieger concluded that, "Muhammad had appropriated much from Jewish sources by means of oral communication, frequently without being aware of the differences between sacred text and later embellishments or exegetical comment, between primary biblical and post-biblical materials."[136]

On the other hand, Bell himself recognized that, "Of any intimate knowledge for the Prophet of either [of] these two religions or the Bible itself there is no convincing evidence."[137] Additionally two thirds of the Qur'an was revealed in Makkah. J. Fueck observes that, "There is no evidence for the existence of a strong Jewish colony with a living tradition at Mecca, nor does [the] Qur'an give evidence of that intimate knowledge of Jewish matters which we would expect if Muhammad had actually been dependent on Judaism."[138] Ahrens argued that Muhammad "during the greater part of the Meccan period...was predominantly dependent upon Christians in the formulation of his doctrines."[139] He also claimed that Muhammad compromised the best of those principles that had been drawn from Christianity because of political opportunism. Johann W. Fück (Fueck) (1894–1974), a German orientalist, refuting these allegations, argues:

> How, we ask, is it possible for a gang leader who supposedly had no scruples against using whatever means were available to achieve his goals, who carried out "general massacre," and who "took delight in enemies slain," to exert such influence on world history that 1300 years after his death over three hundred million persons confess their faith in him? The witness of many centuries of history and the witness today of an Islam that is still vigorous refute more conclusively than any other argument the judgments that Ahrens expressed on the basis of a flawed interpretation.[140]

Fueck further asserts that the concept of cyclical revelation is intrinsic to Muhammad's prophetic consciousness:

> This cyclical theory of revelation cannot be derived either from Judaism or from Christianity. The idea ... seems to be Muhammad's own creation. It reflects his philosophy of history and indicates how he understood his relationship to other peoples who had previously received a divine revelation. It is convincing evidence that Muhammad could not have received the decisive stimulus to prophetic action from either Jews or Christians.[141]

The presence in the Qur'an of many biblical stories is often cited as proof of Muhammad's dependence upon Christian and Jewish sources. Yet this is false logic and there is no rational justification for this, for a number of reasons. First, the Qur'an itself has come to affirm the truth of previous scriptures and to correct that which has been corrupted.

Second, and as any student of the Qur'an and the Bible would easily notice, the Qur'anic accounts contain many detailed and important differences as well as focusing on points of emphasis. In fact, the Qur'an focuses largely upon the lessons to be drawn, the glad tidings and warnings that are to be understood, explanation of Islamic doctrines, and consolation of the Prophet through these stories: "All that We relate to thee of the stories of the messengers, with it We make firm thy heart: in them there cometh to thee the Truth, as well as an exhortation and a message of remembrance to those who believe" (11:120). Further, the Qur'an does not give a detailed account of all the previous prophets sent to mankind: "Of some messengers We have already told thee the story; of others we have not" (4:164), and of those prophets whose stories are mentioned, little historical detail is given concerning them. The Qur'an's emphasis is upon the moral and spiritual lessons to be gained from these stories. One important point of difference is that the Qur'an makes no mention of the immoral behavior which the Bible attributes to a number of prophets including Lot (Genesis 19:30–38), David (II Samuel 11:1–27), and Solomon (I Kings 11:1–10). Rather, it vindicates them, purging their personality and character of the indecencies, obscenities, and myriad of moral and spiritual defects ascribed to them.[142] In the Qur'an they are not only presented as God's prophets and messengers but as men of great character, infallible human beings who lived their lives as walking embodiments of submission to God's will and commandments. Watt observes that "there is something original in the Qur'an's use of the stories and in its selection of points for emphasis,"[143] and to him "[i]ts originality consists in that it gave them greater precision and detail, presented them more forcefully and by its varying emphasis, made more or less coherent synthesis of them; above all, it gave them a focus in the person of Muhammad and his special vocation as messenger of God."[144] Additionally biblical stories are used in the Qur'an as illustrative material, playing a subordinate role, to substantiate Qur'anic themes. Fueck observes:

> it was the discovery of a substantive correspondence between his own preaching and what Christians and Jews found in their sacred books that first motivated him to concern himself more directly

> with their tradition, for it is the second Meccan period that first reflects an extensive knowledge of biblical stories.[145]

Watt observes that, "There is no great difficulty in claiming that the precise form, the point and the ulterior significance of the stories came to Muhammad by revelation and not from the communications of his alleged informant."[146] In addition to this, if Muhammad had borrowed material from the Christians or Jews he could never have preached a faith so radically different from Christianity and Judaism. Moreover, given the hostile climate and antagonism that existed between Muhammad and his adversaries, and given that he lived in the full light of history with his life an open book and the subject of detailed and prolific research, the name of an alleged informant could scarcely have remained unknown to his enemies and contemporaries or non-existent down the centuries.

The Qur'an informs us that similar accusations of Muhammad having borrowed and learnt from others were also leveled by the Makkan elite:

> But the misbelievers say: "Naught is this but a lie which he has forged, and others have helped him at it." In truth it is they who have put forward an iniquity and a falsehood. And they say: "Tales of the ancients, which he has caused to be written: and they are dictated to him morning and evening." (25:4–5)

The Makkans would also mention certain individuals as Muhammad's teachers, as the Qur'an states: "And we know well that they say: Only a man teaches him. The speech of him at whom they falsely hint is outlandish and this is manifest Arabic speech" (16:103).

Several reports concerning the alleged teachers of the Prophet exist. One of them names the person as Jabr, a Roman slave of ʿĀmir ibn al-Ḥaḍramī, another mentions ʿĀ'ish or Yaʿīsh, a slave of Huwaytib ibn ʿAbd al-ʿUzzā, and yet another points to Yasār, a Jew, whose agnomen (*kunyah*) was Abū Fukayḥah, and who was the slave of a Makkan woman. Still another report mentions someone by the name of Balʿān or Balʿām, a Roman slave. In fact rather like grasping at straws any acquaintance of Muhammad who had the slightest knowledge of the Torah or Gospels was touted as the alleged teacher of the Prophet. The Qur'an refuted these allegations by arguing that the individuals being pointed to were non-native Arabs with minimal language skills while the Qur'an was an Arabic composition of the highest linguistic standards. The evidence therefore spoke for itself.

Today little has changed, with the same accusations still being leveled by writers such as Gardner and others, in this instance naming Salmān, a Persian convert, as the chief aid of the Prophet in composing the Qur'an.[147] However, in reality Salmān only met the Prophet in Madinah, and as mentioned earlier, the greater part of the Qur'an was revealed in Makkah with most of the stories in question revealed in the later part of the Makkan period. So, given historical facts, the Prophet could not in fact have learned the stories from Salmān. Moreover, Salmān was a devoted follower of the Prophet, a reality that would categorically not have been the case were either he or any other person for that matter, to have been teaching Muhammad behind the scenes. Consequently, any attempt to prove Muhammad's dependence upon Jewish or Christian sources, argues Fueck, "leads inevitably to insoluble difficulties and contradictions."[148] Muslim explanation of the similarities that exist between the biblical and Qur'anic accounts is clear: a) the source of both scriptures is one, Almighty God, b) the Qur'an came to affirm the truth of previous scriptures c) it came as a corrective force to realign mankind to the straight path where deviation had occurred through tampering with earlier revelation and biblical narrations (whether through changes, insertions or deletions). So Muslims consider similarities neither unusual nor impossible for they form a universal norm that stands for all time.

Then we have Wansbrough, who in addition to emphasizing the Judeo-Christian background of the Qur'an, contends it to be post-Muhammad:

> It is, however, worth recalling that those sources which may with some assurance be dated before the end of the second /eighth century (and thus before Ibn Ishaq) contain no reference to Muslim scripture. A possible exception might be the much cited

> and recently disputed chapter of John Damascene's De Haeresibus. I am myself disposed to accept Abel's arguments for later compilation and pseudepigraphy, but were the document authentic it could anyway not be adduced as evidence for a canonical text of Muslim scripture.[149]

Connecting the canonization and stabilization of the Qur'anic text with the formation of the community,[150] he argues that:

> Upon the vexed question of a Vorlag for Ghevond text of the alleged correspondence between Leo III and ʿUmar b. ʿAbd al-ʿAziz I am unable to offer an opinion, though it is of some interest to note that connection of a composition/redaction of the Qur'an with the figure of Hajjaj b. Yusuf, included in both the Risala of ʿAbd al-Masih Kindi and the 'Jerusalem dispute' ascribed to one Ibrahim Taberani, is also found there. That motif, as well as several others in the same correspondence, was characteristic of polemical literature not in the first/seventh but in the third/ninth century. Its point would seem to be [a] quarrel about the authenticity of a Muslim scripture, in the sense of valid suppression of the Biblical dispensations. On the other hand, the witness of both the Patriarch Timotheos and of the Christian tract contained in Heidelberg Papyrus 438, possibly contemporary with the author of sira (d.151/768), might reflect the circumstances obtaining within the Muslim community.[151]

Hence, we have Wansbrough's conclusion of the text of the Qur'an being post-Muhammad – and not the outcome of Muhammad's discourses – supposedly a result of the stabilization of political power by the end of the second/eighth century.[152]

Patricia Crone and Michael Cook espouse the same theory in their controversial work *Hagarism*. Without any further inquiry or questioning of premises they confess their indebtedness to Wansbrough for their views on the Qur'an concluding that, "There is no hard evidence for the existence of the Koran in any way before the last decade of the seventh century, and the tradition which places this rather opaque revelation in its historical context is not attested before the middle of the eighth."[153] Apparently they would seem to deny the historical existence of Muhammad even, taking both the Qur'an and the entire corpus of Islamic teachings to be simply a conspiracy and fabrication of mysterious "Hagarenes" who supposedly invented their prophet:

> Where the Hagarenes had to fend for themselves was in composing an actual sacred book for their prophet, less alien than that of Moses and more real than that of Abraham. No early source sheds any direct light on the questions how and when this was accomplished. With regard to the manner of composition, there is some reason to suppose that the Qur'an was put together out of plurality of earlier Hagarene religious works. In the first place, this early plurality is attested in a number of ways. On the Islamic side, the Koran itself gives obscure indications that the integrity of the scripture was problematic, and with this we may compare the allegation against ʿUthman that the Koran had many books of which he had left only one. On the Christian side, the monk of Bet Hale distinguishes pointedly between the Koran and the surat al-baqara as source of law, while Levond has the emperor Leo describe how Hajjaj destroyed the old Hagarene 'writings'.[154]

Crone and Cook further assert that the literary character of the Koran, its obscurity of meanings, lack of structure and repetition of whole passages leads one plausibly to argue that "the book is the product of the belated and imperfect editing of materials from a plurality of traditions. At the same time the imperfection of the editing suggests that the emergence of the Koran must have been a sudden, not to say hurried, event."[155] And they go on to conclude that this conspiracy took place at the time of Ḥajjāj (by the end of the seventh century): "It is thus not unlikely that we have here the historical context in which the Koran was first put together as Muhammad's scripture."[156]

This theory is so nonsensical and historically unsubstantiated that Christian, Jewish and Islamic scholars have rejected it altogether. In his review of Wansbrough's *Qur'anic Studies*, Serjeant dismissively states that, "An historical circumstance so public [as the emergence of the

Qur'an] cannot have been invented."[157] He further observes that John Burton "argues vastly more cogently than Wansbrough's unsubstantiable assertions, that the consonantal text of the Qur'an before us is the Prophet's own recension."[158] N. Daniel reviewing *Hagarism*, writes: "The notion that a "conspiracy" is involved in such a historical reconstruction becomes a rallying point for many objections."[159] Rippin, on the other hand, defends the theory, arguing:

> one hundred years is a long time, especially when one is dealing not with newspaper headlines and printing presses but the gradual emergence of a text at first within a select circle, then into ever widening circles. One could point to similar instances of "conspiracies" in the canonization of the other scriptures, for example the identification of John the disciple with the Gospel of John is well less than a century after the emergence of the text.[160]

Rippin still has to substantiate his claim that the same "conspiracy" took place in connection with the Qur'an.

Fazlur Rahman observes that there are a number of problems with Wansbrough's thesis. Consider first Wansbrough's second thesis, that the Qur'an is a composite of several traditions and hence post-Prophetic: "I feel that there is a distinct lack of historical data on the origin, character, evaluation, and personalities involved in these "traditions." Moreover, on a number of key issues the Qur'an can be understood only in terms of chronological and developmental unfolding within a single document."[161] He further argues that, "Wansbrough's method makes nonsense of the Qur'an, and he washes his hands of the responsibility of explaining how that "nonsense" came about."[162] Fazlur Rahman declares these methods as "so inherently arbitrary that they sink into the marsh of utter subjectivity."[163] We conclude the discussion with R. W. Bulliet's statement in his recent work *Islam, The View from the Edge*:

> I cannot imagine how so abundant and cohesive a religious tradition as that of the first century of Islam could have come into being without a substantial base in actual historical event.

> Concocting, coordinating, and sustaining a fantasy, to wit, that Muhammad either did not exist or lived an entirely different sort of life than that traditionally depicted, and inculcating it consistently and without demur among a largely illiterate community of Muslims dispersed from the Pyrenees to the Indus River would have required a conspiracy of monumental proportion. It would have required universal agreement among believers who came to differ violently on issues of far less import.[164]

The question of the integrity of the Qur'anic text so easily raised out of thin air by the authors of *Hagarism* is not surprisingly unsubstantiated. What we are in fact left with is simple repetition of earlier medieval stereotypes which should have been laid to rest a long time ago as products of an age of ignorance. I refer specifically to the "dove" and "bull" stories and claims of Pedro de Alfonso as well as others who alleged that the existing Qur'an did not really represent what the Prophet originally claimed. It is a universally recognized, historical fact that the unity, integrity, and absolute textual uniformity of the Qur'an has been maintained since its compilation into a single volume and text, and to challenge this fact is to leap into the realm of the absurd. Wild theorizing has no place where facts are indisputable. There has only ever been one same Qur'anic text in the entire world. W. Muir, recognizing the purity of the ʿUthmānic text, asserted:

> The recension of Uthman had been handed down to us unaltered. So carefully, indeed, has it been preserved, that there are no variations of importance – we might almost say no variations at all – among the innumerable copies of the Coran scattered throughout the vast bounds of the empire of Islam. Contending and embittered factions, taking their rise in the murder of Uthman himself within a quarter of a century from the death of Mahomet, have ever since rent the Mahometan world. Yet but ONE CORAN has been current amongst them; and the consentaneous use by them all in every age up to the present day of the same scripture, is an irrefragable proof that we have now before us the very text prepared by command of the unfortunate Caliph. There is

> probably in the world no other work which has remained twelve centuries with so pure a text.[165]

Burton concludes his book with the following words: "only one text of the Qur'an has ever existed. This is the universally acknowledged text on the basis of which alone the prayer of the Muslim can be valid. A single text has thus already always united the Muslims....What we have today in our hands is the mushaf of Muhammad."[166] H. Lammen's suggests:

> The Qoran, as it has come down to us, should be considered as the authentic and personal work of Muhammad. This attribution cannot be seriously questioned and is practically admitted, even by those Muhammaden sects who obstinately dispute the integrity of the text; for all the dissidents, without exception, use only the text accepted by the orthodox.[167]

The dissident sects he refers to are those of certain extreme Shiites who claimed that two chapters of the Qur'an regarding the merits of the Prophet's family (*Ahl al-bayt*) as well as their right to rule in general and ʿAlī's privileges in particular, were omitted by the first three caliphs who succeeded Muhammad to power. Some of these sects also maintained that ʿAlī's collection of the Qur'anic text was different to that of Abū Bakr and ʿUthmān's. Nevertheless, these reckless, clearly politically motivated, claims of falsification in the Qur'anic text have been roundly rejected by both Sunnis as well as mainstream Shiite scholars. Reaching the same conclusions as mainstream Muslims they have also been dismissed by a number of oriental scholars having thoroughly examined the issue. Gatje writes that, "Such accusations, which are tantamount to alleging a conscious falsification to the determent of ʿAli and his successors, do not stand up under investigation. On the contrary, a so-called 'Sura of Light', which has been handed down outside the Qur'an, represents with certainty a Shiʿite falsification."[168] Burton argues that, "Ali succeeded ʿUthman and if he had any reservation about the Qur'an text, he could easily have reinstated what he regarded as the authentic revelation."[169] Muir denounces these accusations as "incredible". Giving a number of reasons to reject these accusations he writes:

> At the time of the recension, there were still multitudes alive who had the Coran, as originally delivered, by heart; and of the supposed passages favoring Ali – had any ever existed – there would have been numerous transcripts in the hands of his family and followers. Both of these sources must have proved an effectual check upon any attempt at suppression.

He further argues:

> The party of Ali shortly after assumed an independent attitude, and he himself succeeded to the Caliphate. Is it conceivable that either Ali, or his party, when thus arrived at power, would have tolerated a mutilated Coran – mutilated expressly to destroy his claims? Yet we find that they used the same Coran as their opponents, and raised no shadow of an objection against it.

Muir concludes that, "Such a supposition, palpably absurd at the time, is altogether an after-thought of the modern Sheeas."[170]

According to orthodox Muslims, the preservation of the Qur'anic text in such a fashion is no less than a miracle of Allah, a lasting miracle in fact. Indeed, the Qur'an itself in its very early Makkan period cites Allah's promise to protect it: "We have, without doubt, sent down the Message and We will assuredly guard it [from corruption]" (15:9). And it is due to this divine promise and the Qur'an's wondrous nature and inimitability (*ʿijāz*), that nobody, including the extreme Shiite sects mentioned, have been able to introduce anything into its text. This meticulous preservation is a historically attested and universally recognized fact. So much so that the Shiites, observes Lammens, have "not dared to introduce these restitutions into Qorans which the sect uses for liturgical ceremonies and which agree with the edition transmitted by the Sunni channel."[171] Consequently, there has only ever been one text of the Qur'an in the hands of both Sunni and Shiite Muslims, this universally recognized text enjoying normative authority for both. David Pinault a modern scholar on Shiism observes:

> In Sunnism and Shiism alike the Qur'an enjoys an authority not fully comparable with that of the Bible in Judaism and Christianity. The latter religions ascribe the Bible to human authors (albeit divinely inspired) and consider the component texts comprising Scripture to be the product of human history, the records of the Creator's interaction with His people. From a Muslim perspective the author of the Qur'an is not Muhammad nor any other human but rather God Himself...[172]

S. Hossein Nasr, who himself happens to be a Shiite, puts the point in a nutshell: "There is only one text accepted by all Muslims, Sunnis and Shi'ites and other branches of Islam alike, and it is this definitive book which stands as the central source of truth, guidance and of inspiration for all Muslims."[173]

The Qur'an is held to be revealed in seven variants of recitation or *qirā'ah*. These variants of recitation were approved and tolerated by the Prophet himself because they were congenial to the reciters' tribal or local linguistic traditions, in other words the purpose was to facilitate recitation for Muslims. These variants do not cause much change either in the meaning or the structure or format of the verses. However, some orientalists have misunderstood and overemphasized these various modes of recitation to insinuate a sort of disunity and nonconformity in the Qur'anic text failing to understand that the text of the Qur'an has allowed several equally valid ways of recitation without affecting as mentioned meaning or structure. Other orientalists have concurred with Muslim scholars, and have concluded over the years that these variants are just different ways of reciting the text which does not make much difference either to the Qur'an's meaning or the overall sense of the text. As A. S. Tritton observes:

> There are seven or ten different 'readings' of the Koran; these are for the most part what the English word implies, different ways of pronouncing the text, elision or assimilation of certain letters. Many variants in vocalization are recorded but they are so slight as to be negligible, except for specialists: they make no vital difference to the sense.[174]

Sir W. Muir writes: "The various readings are wonderfully few in number, and are chiefly confined to differences in the vowel points and diacritical signs."[175] Willaim A. Graham remarks:

> Accordingly, seven, ten, or fourteen traditions of *qira'at* are sometimes cited as "authentic" in the Muslim literature, and even these traditions have branched to form subtraditions. As a result, the panoply of variant *riwayat* that the expert must master is quite large, even though the actual textual variations they represent are relatively minor and do not involve crucial differences in the literal meaning of the sacred text.[176]

These conclusions drawn by orientalists are almost identical to the views of Muslims regarding the issue at hand. Muslims maintain that these variant readings were authorized by the Prophet himself, and the disciples kept them as exegetical footnotes in their commentaries and passed them on from generation to generation as *qirā'ah* or "recitation tradition." These variant readings affect neither the form nor the substance nor the meaning of the Qur'an.

These facts led contemporary Harvard scholar H. P. Smith to reach conclusions fairly close to those of traditional Muslim views *viz-à-viz* the authenticity and integrity of the Qur'an. He observes with regards to the Qur'an that

> there is no reason to suspect either its integrity or its authenticity. The assurances we have on this point are very complete. The prime fact is that the revelations were committed to memory by a large body of converts during the life of Mohammad....There can be no reasonable doubt that the copies in our hands correspond very closely with this original, and that this original does not vary in any important particular from the text recited by Mohammad himself.[177]

R. V. C. Bodley observes that

> today there is no possible doubt that the Koran which is read wherever there are Moslems, is the same version as that translated

> from Hafsa's master copy.... What is important is that the Koran is the only work which has survived for over twelve hundred years with an unadulterated text. Neither in the Jewish religion nor in the Christian is there anything which faintly compares to this.[178]

In addition Arabic, the original language of the Qur'an and the Prophet, is one of the most widely spoken languages in the world today, actively used by millions as their first language. In fact, it is the only Semitic tongue which has remained uninterruptedly alive for thousands of years, and moreover is the only living language which has remained largely unchanged for the last fourteen centuries. We have already quoted Hitti who argued that it was the Qur'an that "kept the language uniform. So that whereas today a Moroccan uses a dialect different from that used by an Arabian or an Iraqi, all write in the same style."[179] In fact it was the Qur'an which, according to Esposito, was "central to the development of Arabic linguistics and provided the basis for the development of Arabic grammar, vocabulary, and syntax."[180]

Moreover, unlike the Bible, the followers of the Qur'an believe it to be the divine word of God, the revelation verbatim. It is authoritative and normative to the very definition of the word, and although Muslims may differ, and have differed, over the interpretations and meanings of Qur'anic words, they have never questioned the authenticity, truthfulness and authoritative nature of its text. It is interesting to note that Muslims throughout their history and without exception, have unanimously accepted every part of the Qur'an – the entire Qur'anic text – as the verbatim word of God. They have revered it as the first determining principle of their religious beliefs, the fundamental source of their Law, and the unequivocal authority regarding matters of faith and religion by no way superseded by any other authority. A. Rippin notes that

> whatever the case, one thing remains quite clear. The Qur'an is, and has been from the beginning of the emergence of Islam as a religion, the primary source and reference point. Indeed, the Qur'an in its function as that source of authority is the defining point of Islamic identity. The emergence of the Muslim community

> is intimately connected with the emergence of the Qur'an as an authoritative text in making decisions on matters of law and theology.[181]

Josef van Ess also observes that "the Muslims are not cut off from the word of God, for the Qur'an not only interprets what God has said but contains God's ipsissima verba. Each and every denomination of Islam believes in Muhammad's verbal inspiration. This was a logical result of the Islamic notion of prophecy, and we have already seen it taken for granted at every point when God turns to Muhammad with the imperative "Say." Islamic theology is thus spared the trouble of searching the Qur'an for the authentic sayings of Muhammad; and only an unbelieving student of Islamics could claim that the utterances of the Qur'an reflect the faith of the earliest Muslim community."[182] This is in contrast to the Christian scriptures where theologians struggle to differentiate the genuine words of Jesus from the words and sayings of his disciples. Therefore, the entire text of the Qur'an carries equal and indisputable religious authority.

There has been a tendency among several contemporary Muslim scholars to conceive of a human aspect with regards to Qur'anic revelation by emphasizing the part played by the person of the Prophet in receiving it. These are modernists some of whom have also emphasized the need to apply historical, philological, and literary methods to the text of the Qur'an.[183] For instance, Fazlur Rahman contends that, "The Qur'an is thus pure Divine Word, but, of course, it is equally intimately related to the inmost personality of the Prophet Muhammad whose relationship to it cannot be mechanically conceived like that of a record. The Divine Word flowed through the Prophet's heart."[184]

Rahman, furthermore, distinguishes between the moral regulations of the Qur'an and the legal regulations. To him, "The moral law is immutable: it is God's "Command", Man cannot make or unmake the Moral Law: he must submit himself to it..."[185] Legal regulations, on the other hand, are contingent. Quoting the Qur'anic injunctions regarding polygamy and the institution of slavery as examples, Rahman concludes:

> These examples, therefore, make it abundantly clear that whereas the spirit of the qur'anic legislation exhibits an obvious direction towards the progressive embodiment of the fundamental human values of freedom and responsibility in fresh legislation, nevertheless the actual legislation of the Qur'an had partly to accept the then existing society as a term of reference. This clearly means that the actual legislation of the Qur'an cannot have been meant to be literally eternal by the Qur'an itself. This fact has no reference to the doctrine of the eternity of the Qur'an or to the allied doctrine of the verbal revelation of the Qur'an.[186]

Rahman forgets that the institutions of polygamy and slavery were not original to the Qur'an. Polygamy existed centuries before the revelation of the Qur'an. As a guidance to mankind, the Qur'an had to address these issues. The Qur'an's condoning of polygamy was not as a piece of pure male chauvinism. It was meant to be a piece of social legislation. The Qur'an merely regularized the then unlimited choice (spousal number) of men to four wives, connecting this choice closely to the then pressing practical problem of the Muslim community namely, the heavy losses incurred at the battle of Uhud and the resulting surplus number of orphans. The Qur'an also connected this social responsibility with the stern condition of absolute justice, "But if ye fear that ye shall not be able to deal justly (with them), then only one or which your right hands possess" (4:3). It also warned men from the outset that, "Ye are never able to do justice between wives even if it is your ardent desire..." (4:129). Therefore it can be argued, that there is nothing in the Qur'anic understanding of the institution of polygamy that is specific or related only to the society of seventh century Arabia. Polygamy, for the Qur'an, is not a privilege; it is a social responsibility. In the presence of pressing situations and circumstances such as those prevailing in Madinah after the battle of Uhud, the Qur'anic institution of polygamy with its qualifying principles, may serve as an alternative, better than promiscuity or serial polygamy, even in current times.

Similarly, the institution of slavery was an ancient custom, not only a feature of Arabian society at the time, but also intrinsic to most societies of the day. Unlike prevailing practice however, the Qur'an condoned neither maltreatment of slaves, nor the institution of slavery to a great extent. Rather, the Qur'an took practical and revolutionary steps to gradually eliminate the vast gulf that lay between slaves and their masters: (a) the Qur'an legislated for the freeing of slaves (*al-ᶜItq*) as atonement for many intentional and non-intentional religious violations (4:92; 5:89; 58:3), (b) it promised great rewards for the freeing of slaves or the buying of their freedom (90:13), (c) it frequently emphasized the absolute equality and brotherhood of slaves and masters calling for mutual respect (49:13), (d) it encouraged masters to marry or free slave-girls, (e) it promulgated the institution of *mukātabah* i.e., allowing a slave to purchase his/her freedom in installments paid over a period of time (24:33), (f) it assigned a special portion of zakah for the freeing of slaves and other related areas such as helping a *mukātab* etc. (9:60) etc. The latter are just a few of the ways by which the Qur'an dealt with the issue of slavery and its dilution as a force in society, eliminating its ancient hold. Moreover, the stern attitude of the Prophet regarding the rights, equality, and respect of slaves as brothers in humanity and faith, worked as an additional element factor enforcing the Qur'anic spirit of equality and kindness towards them. Islam could not have unilaterally abolished slavery so long as the world did not agree to put an end to one of its primary sources, war, through enslavement of prisoners-of-war. But when the anti-slavery concord was reached by the international community, Islam welcomed it.

Such a sharp difference of focus and perspective on the part of the Qur'an regarding the issues of polygamy and slavery, alone refutes Rahman's claims that the Qur'an accepted the then existing society as a point of reference. Rather, it is the other way around. Moreover, such a legislation of the Qur'an cannot be interpreted as temporal or connected with a specific society or region. The existence and public practice of the institution of slavery until our modern times, nullifies such a supposition. Therefore, these examples do not prove the point Rahman has raised i.e., that the Qur'anic legal regulations are contingent. In addition, mainstream Islam has always accepted all Qur'anic regulations as eternal and authoritative. What the bases for Rahman's differentiation between the moral and legal legislations of the Qur'an are, is unknown.

Rahman however only goes so far, and interpretations and views such as his have been taken to astonishing extremes by others. To Rippin, for instance, these interpretations of Rahman mean that the Qur'an is not "revealed literally but... installed in Muhammad's heart and then spoken through the human faculties of the prophet. The language, therefore, is Muhammad's, although it is still possible to hold that this is ultimately God's word also."[187]

Rahman has made it very clear through his works that the words of the Revelation were also from God, arguing that, "Whatever the agency of Revelation, however, the true revealing subject always remains God, for it is He Who always speaks in the first person..."[188] He further observes, the fact that

> the Prophet actually mentally "heard" words is clear from 75:16–19: "Do not hasten your tongue with it [the Revelation] in order to anticipate it. It is our task to collect it and recite it. So *when we recite it, follow its recital*, and then it is also our task to explain it" (see also 20:114). It is also clear that, in his anxiety to retain it or to "anticipate" it in a direction different from that of his Revealing Spirit, the Prophet moved his tongue of his own ordinary human volition, the intrusion of which was repudiated by God. This necessarily implies the total "otherness" of the agent of Revelation from the conscious personality of Muhammad in the act of Revelation.[189]

We may possibly interpret Rahman's views as more fully related to the interpretations given to the Qur'anic text over the centuries by Muslim orthodoxy, rather than with the Qur'anic text itself. I would probably have the same observations about Rahman as Ian Richard Netton (b. 1948), Head of the Department of Arabic and Middle Eastern Studies, University of Leeds, did with regards to the blind Syrian poet, Abū al-ʿAlā' al-Maʿarrī (973–1057), whose *Risālat al-Ghufrān* (The Epistle of Pardon) and "skeptical attitudes towards religion aroused considerable suspicions."[190] Netton observed that al-Maʿarrī, "was probably not anti-religion *per se* but against its organization and ritualized aspects. He sought truth but objected strongly to the truth being encapsulated in rigid formulae."[191] Likewise, Rahman seems to be critical of so-called orthodoxy and its claims to sole authority in interpreting the Qur'an. To Rahman, the text of the Qur'an is the word of God and normative; however, he seems somewhat dissatisfied with the method by which this text has been understood by some Muslims in the past. Like other neo-modernists (i.e. Muhammad Ahmad Khalaf Allah, Nasr Hamid Abu Zayd, Mohammad Arkoun, to name a few), Rahman seems to be looking for such interpretations of the Qur'anic text that, to him, are appropriate or essential in connection with the developing circumstances of modern day life. He wants to do this without denying the divine origin of the Qur'an. Therefore, neo-modernists like Rahman cannot be quoted as an example within Islam of the trend common to modern biblical scholars of viewing scriptures as the word of God mixed with the word of man or emphasizing the human aspect in revelation. The Qur'an, to all Muslims without exception, is the word of God.

In contrast, the firm Muslim belief in the divine composition of the Qur'an is a factor / stance persistently denied by western writers down the years. The overwhelming majority of these have categorically rejected the claims of the Qur'an, the Prophet Muhammad, as well as Muslims of all ages and times, that God Almighty Himself directly revealed the text of the Qur'an to Muhammad and that Muhammad's sole function was to receive and convey the Qur'an to mankind with absolute sincerity and precision. A great majority of western scholars claim that the Qur'an was composed by Muhammad, with or without the help of others. For instance, Sale asserts, "That Muhammad was really the author and chief contriver of the Qur'an is beyond dispute; though it be highly probable that he had no small assistance in his design from others."[192] Sir William Muir in the 19th century,[193] Wollaston in 1905, Menezes in 1911, Draycott in 1916,[194] Lammens in 1926, Champion and Short in 1959,[195] Glubb in 1970, and Rodinson as late as 1977, advocated the same view, with Menezes writing that the Qur'an is "nothing else but a pure creation and concoction of Mohammed and of his accomplice."[196]

Muslim scholars on the other hand analyze linguistic and stylistic differences between the Qur'an and hadith to highlight the Qur'an's divine origins. They also contend that the depth, variety and infinite range of the Qur'anic ideas were beyond Muhammad's mortal mind. They quote many Qur'anic verses bearing true and exact scientific information to argue that the subject matter of these verses was far beyond Muhammad's finite knowledge and mortal creative imagination. Maurice Bucaille,[197] Seyyed Hossein Nasr,[198] Imad-ad-Dean Ahmad,[199] ʿAbd al-Majid A. al-Zindani,[200] and many other Muslim writers have taken this route to argue for the divine origin and composition of the Qur'an; the intention being to prove the absolute divine nature of the Qur'an from the scientific data available within it.

Finally, it will be pertinent to mention here that the Qur'an divides its verses into *muḥkam* and *mutashābih*. The word *muḥkam* means "solid, firm, accurate, precise, exact, tight etc." Therefore, the *muḥkam* are those verses that convey the precise and exact meanings without rendering different or conflicting interpretations. The *mutashābih*, on the other hand, are those verses which render more than one apparently similar meanings or interpretations. These kinds of verses i.e., the *mutashābih*, are very few in number and are to be understood in the light of the precise verses. The *muḥkam* verses, according to the Qur'an, are "the mother" and the foundation of the Qur'an. This does not mean the denial of the text or the meanings of such (*mutashābih*) verses or their complete hijacking through devices of allegorism. Rather, it implies a selection or the choosing of one of the philological meanings of the *mutashābih* phrases as their metaphorical interpretation and as appropriate or intended meanings. Such a selection has to take place in light of the clear and precise passages of the Qur'an. The very few Qur'anic verses that express God in seemingly anthropomorphic terms are, for instance, placed under this category. Followers of various Islamic sects differ over the meanings and interpretations of these Qur'anic phrases without denying the canonization or authority of the text or the passages containing such phrases. The Qur'an, to all mainstream Muslims, is *the* holy Scripture, the very word of God verbatim, and cannot be altered or superseded by any other authority. It will be useful to quote Graham once more, who observes:

> The specific understanding of their own scripture is also different among Muslims from that among either Jews or Christians. While

> all three traditions have been characterized by the centrality of scripture in worship, piety, devotion, and faith, the Qur'an stands more clearly alone as the transcendent focus of Muslim faith than does the Christian or even the Jewish Bible in its tradition of faith. It is of course true that the Torah in its most basic sense as the Law revealed at Sinai plays a role for Jews akin in significance to that of the Qur'an for Muslims, and further that Christians, especially Protestant Christian's, attachment to the scriptural Word of God has been overwhelmingly important. Nevertheless, the character of the Qur'an as the verbatim speech of God sets it apart. Whereas the divine presence is manifest for Jews in the Law and for Christians in the Person of Christ, it is in the Qur'an that Muslims directly encounter God.[201]

TRANSCENDENCE OF GOD AND THE QUR'AN

Divine transcendence is the essence of the Qur'anic message. The Qur'anic worldview divides reality into two generic realms: God and non-God. God is the Eternal Creator and nothing is like unto Him. He remains forever the transcendental Other devoid of any resemblance, similarity, partnership and association. He is that unique Being who can only be called the Reality and the Being as everything other than Him derives its reality, existence and being from Him. Allah, the Arabic word for God, is semantically the highest focused word of the Qur'an. The Qur'anic worldview is theocentric to the core. Ontologically nothing can stand equal or opposed to God. He always remains the transcendental Other who presides over the entire system of existence as its Master and Creator. Everything other than Him is His creature and stands inferior to Him in the hierarchy of being.

The second realm consists of everything other than God. It is the order of time-space, creation and of experience. Ontologically these two orders always remain disparate. The Creator neither descends to the realm of space-time and experience to be united, incarnated, diffused or confused with creatures, nor can creatures ascend to be ontologically united or diffused with the Creator. He always remains the utterly sublime transcendental Other. This is the Qur'anic concept of divine Unity. That is the thread which runs through the entire Qur'anic corpus as the core of the Qur'anic message. All Qur'anic concepts, ideas, and ideologies are woven together to pinpoint, elaborate, and describe this very doctrine of the Oneness, Unity, and Transcendence of God, and to encourage mankind to establish a meaningful and right relationship with Him. There is so much emphasis placed in the Qur'an upon the Oneness, Unity and Uniqueness of Almighty God that no stone seems to be left unturned to make this concept crystal clear even to a cursory reader. Moreover, the Qur'anic concept of "Monotheism" is neither progressive nor ambiguous. It is neither confusing nor contradictory. It is monotheistic and theocentric to the very definition of the word. It is negative, affirmative, rational, normative and self-explanatory.

Qur'anic monotheism does not start with monolatry or with affirmations of the existence or Oneness of the Deity. It starts by absolutely negating all concepts, kinds, ideas, understandings, and illusions of divinity or godhead other then the One and the only Divine. It starts with the Credo of Islam *Lā ilāha illa Allāh*, the *shahādah* or confession, which is derived from the Qur'an itself. The whole Qur'an, observes Charles Eaton, is "a commentary on these four words, or as an amplification of them."[202] The first part of this declaration, *Lā ilāha*, negates the existence of each and any false god, and condemns false devotion, worship, and ideas of dependence upon such gods. The profession of faith (*shahādah*) is a commitment to radical transcendental monotheism.

The Arabic word *ilāh* is a comprehensive word. It stands for a number of mutually interconnected meanings. The root of this word consists of three letters i.e., *alif, lām* and *hā'*. Rāghib al-Iṣfahānī and Mawdudi have shown the connotations of various derivatives of this word, as found in the lexicons, as follows:

1. Became confused or perplexed;
2. Achieved peace and mental calm by seeking refuge with someone or establishing relations with him;
3. Became frightened of some impending mishap or disaster, and someone gave him the necessary shelter;

4. Turned to another eagerly, due to the intensity of his feelings for him;
5. The lost offspring of the she-camel rushing to snuggle up to its mother on finding her;
6. Became hidden, or concealed, or elevated;
7. Adored, offered worship to.[203]

These literal meanings of the word make it clear that the word *ilāh* stands for any thing awfully mysterious, concealed, frightening, extremely attractive, absorbing one's whole being, demanding absolute love, adoration, dependence, and worship. Whatever and whosoever possesses these qualities, and makes human beings adore, worship, or take refuge in it or him, can be called *ilāh*. Therefore, the word can refer to any being, person, matter, or concept which attracts people's full attention and is taken as an object of worship and absolute adoration whether out of love or fear. This is why the Qur'an uses the word in both positive and negative senses meaning that it may denote the true God or a false god. It may be added that the Qur'an frequently uses the term for the true God. There are some verses where it uses the same term for false gods also (see for instance see 28:38; 15:96; 17:22, 17:39; 25:43; 45:23).

By means of the first part of the *shahādah,* the existence as well as the reality of any and every god and object of worship is absolutely negated. With an explosive "No" all allusions of multiplicity, self-sufficience, godhead and divinity are at once shattered. The third word of the confession *illā* is the link and isthmus between what is negated and what is affirmed. All that is denied is finally restored by the fourth word Allah. It means that there is no reality, no god, none self-sufficient except Allah, the true Reality.

The second part of the *shahādah* contains an immediate corollary on the mission and prophethood of Muhammad. It says, *Muḥammadun Rasūl Allāh*, "and Muhammad is the Messenger of God." The true Reality is historically revealed through the mission and prophethood of Muhammad. Prophet Muhammad is the embodiment of the divine message and not a reflection of the divine Person.

The pronouncement of this confession is the pronouncement of God's Oneness, Uniqueness and Transcendence. Perhaps this is the reason why it has been mentioned both in the Qur'an and the Prophetic traditions (Sunnah) more frequently than any other phrase. It has been referred to as *kalimah ṭayyibah* (sacred utterance) (14:24), *al-qawl al-thābit* (the firm word) (14:27), *kalimah al-taqwā* (utterance of piety) (48:26), *maqālīd al-samawāti wa al-arḍ* (key to the heavens and the earth) etc. As this confession is the essence of the Islamic faith and the only token of entry into it, it can safely be asserted that the Oneness, Unity and Unicity of God forms the essence of the Islamic religion. This is why the *shahādah* stands as the supreme religious act in Islam and its mere recitation brings one within the fold of the "community of believers". Prophet Muhammad is reported to have said that one who recites with sincerity that there is no god but God will enter Paradise. In another report he said that he who bears testimony to that fact, that there is no god but Allah and that Muhammad is the Messenger of Allah, Allah makes him immune from Hell-Fire. According to Muslim traditions, prophet Moses' request for a special formula of remembrance was responded to by God in the following words: "If the seven heavens and the seven earths were placed in one pan of the Balance, and the Kalimah *La ilaha illa Allah* in the other, the latter will outweigh the former."[204] Therefore, this confession is a Muslims' sublime obsession. It occupies Muslim thought and action and polarizes the thought of Islam into real and non-real.

In the Qur'an, the Islamic unitarian formula with its *Lā ilāha* form occurs 41 times. This is in addition to the numerous other forms (23 different formulas) that the Qur'an uses to negate godhead or divinity. The Qur'an states: "And your God is One God: there is no god but He, Most Gracious, Most Merciful" (2:163).[205] In another place it states: "Allah! There is no god but He, the Living, the Self-Subsisting, the Supporter of all" (3:2). The reality of divine unity and transcendence is witnessed by God and by all of His righteous creatures: "There is no god but He: that is the witness of Allah, His angels, and those endowed with knowledge, standing firm on justice. There is no god but He the Exalted in Power, the Wise" (3:18). The famous "Verse of the Throne" (*Āyat al-Kursī*) also starts with the same confession:

> Allah! There is no god but He, the Living, the Self-subsisting, Supporter of all, no slumber can seize Him nor sleep. His are all things in the heavens and on earth. Who is there who can intercede in His presence except as He permitteth? He knoweth what (appeareth to His creatures as) Before or After or Behind them. Nor shall they compass aught of His knowledge except as He willeth. His Throne doth extend over the heavens and the earth, and He feeleth no fatigue in guarding and preserving them for He is the Most High, the Supreme (in glory)."(2:255)

Al-Qurṭubī relates that one day the Messenger of Allah asked Ubayy ibn Kaᶜb, (one of the Companions of the Prophet):

> "O Abū al-Mundhir! Do you know which of the verses of the Book of God in your possession is the greatest?" Ubayy said, "God and His Apostle know best." The Prophet repeated the question, and Ubayy answered, "God! There is no god but He, the Everlasting, the Eternal Sovereign." The Prophet struck Ubayy in the chest and exclaimed, "You possess true knowledge...."[206]

Ibn Kathīr relates on the authority of Abū Umāmah that the Prophet said: "Whoever recites the Throne Verse after every prescribed prayer, nothing will stand between him and the *Jannah* (Paradise) except death."[207] Al-Bukhārī narrates on the authority of Ibn Masᶜūd that the Prophet said: "When you go to your bed, recite *Āyat al-Kursī*, for then there will be a guard from Allah who will protect you all night long, and Satan will not be able to come near you till dawn."[208] There are many other virtues mentioned in the books of *tafsīr* and hadith regarding the *Āyat al-Kursī*.

The point of emphasis in the verse is clear. It is one of the countless Qur'anic verses that leave no room for any confusion or ambiguity *vis-à-vis* the absolute Oneness, Uniqueness, Omnipotence, Omnipresence, Omniscience and Transcendence of God. Mawdudi explains the first part of the verse:

> Irrespective of the number of gods or objects of worship set up by ignorant people, the fact remains that godhead in its entirety

belongs exclusively to the Eternal Being, Who is indebted to no one for His existence. In fact, He is not only self-existent, but upon Him rests the entire order of the universe. None shares either His attributes or His power and might, and no one has the same claims against creatures as He. Hence, if anywhere in the heavens or the earth someone sets up anything or anybody as an object of worship and service (*ilah*) either instead of or in addition to the One True God, this amounts to declaring war on reality.[209]

With regards to the *shahādah*'s significance, L. Gardet observes that "Even if monotheism cannot thus be considered the exclusive prerogative of Islam, the affirmation of the divine unicity in and by the Shahadah remains its characteristic heritage, the central fact structures its religious universe."[210] Al-Faruqi observes:

This seemingly negative statement, brief to the utmost limits of brevity, carries the greatest and richest meanings in the whole of Islam. Sometimes a whole culture, a whole civilization, or a whole history lies compressed in one sentence. This certainly is the case of *al-kalimah* (pronouncement) or *al-shahadah* of Islam. All the diversity, wealth and history, culture and learning, wisdom and civilization of Islam is compressed in this shortest of sentences – *la ilaha illa Allah* (There is no god but God).[211]

In addition to the *shahādah*, the Qur'an uses many other formulas to highlight the Unity and Oneness of God. "Allah has said: 'Take not (for worship) two gods: for He is just One God: then fear me (and Me alone).' To Him belongs whatever is in the heavens and on earth, and to Him is the religion always: then will ye fear other than Allah?" (16:51–52). "But your God is One God: so submit then your will to Him..." (22:34). Prophet Muhammad is ordained to declare: "Say: 'What has come to me by inspiration is that Your God is One God: will ye therefore bow to His Will (in Islam)?'" (21:108). "Say: 'I am but a man like yourselves, (but) the inspiration has come to me, that your God is One God: whoever expects to meet his Lord, let him work righteousness, and in the worship of his Lord, admit no one as partner'"

(18:110; see also 13:30; 13:36; 6:56; 6:71; 6:162; 6:163; 10:104; 13:16; 17:42, 17:53; 39:11; 39:14; 39:38; 39:64; 40:66; 41:6; 72:20).

In the famed surah, *al-Kāfirūn* "the disbelievers" (109), the Prophet is ordered to absolutely and completely disavow himself from the unbelievers and what they worship other than the One God. But it is in surah 112 *al-Ikhlāṣ*, literally "sincerity", in which the Prophet is given such a comprehensive lesson of the Oneness, Uniqueness, Unicity and Transcendence of God that if one read nothing of the Qur'an other than this short surah and properly apprehended its meaning, then one could not admit any doubt or confusion concerning the pure Qur'anic concept of transcendence and strict monotheism. T. B. Irving translates *Sūrāh al-Ikhlāṣ* as follows:

> Say: "God is **Unique**! God is the Source [for everything]; He has not fathered anyone nor was He fathered, and there is nothing comparable to Him."

Al-Ikhlāṣ consists of four Makkan verses only. Yet, this brief construction heralds monumental implications: it emphasizes God's divine Unity, Uniqueness, Self-Sufficiency, Transcendence and Purity; stands as a powerful statement against the Christian concept of a triune God – the trinity of divine Persons; acts as a profound declaration against the Son of God Christology; and demands sincere and sole worship of the One and Only God eliminating possibilities of any partnership or association with Him. It is also equal to one third of the Qur'an (hadith reported by Bukhārī, 4628) since it explains *al-tawḥīd* one of the three most essential doctrines of Islam, the other two being Prophethood/Revelation and the Day of Judgement.

The pagans of Makkah queried the Prophet about the lineage (origin) of Allah. As a response Allah revealed this verse "Say: 'Allah is Unique.'" The Arabic term *Aḥad* is used in this surah to indicate the Unicity of God instead of the frequently used Qur'anic term *wāḥid*.[212] The term *Aḥad* is much more precise than the much more frequently used term *wāḥid* which means "one". *Aḥad* has the added connotations of absolute and continuous unity and the absence of equals. Al-Alusi explains that the root of the word *aḥad* is *wāḥid*. The difference being that *aḥad* cannot be divided, distributed or analyzed while *wāḥid* could be.[213] Al-Bayhaqī states that *al-aḥad* is the

> One who does not have any similar, like or an equivalent or match while *al-wahid* means the one who has no associate or partner. That is why God Almighty gave this name to Himself... As if the verse "He begets not neither is He begotten" is a kind of explanation of the verse "He is One"... and Almighty God can never be divided nor come to an end...[214]

L. Gardet observes:

> The qur'anic teaching does not limit itself to the affirmation of a strict monotheism. It is also clearly stated that the unique (*wahid*) God is one (*ahad*) in himself, one in his nature as deity.... Juxtaposed with the striking initial profession of faith ("Allahu ahad") is the final correlative, "not any one," no one ("Lam yakun ahad"). This affirmation-negation is the decisive confrontation between the creator and the created. It displays, like a diamond in its setting, the unfathomable and incommunicable mystery of the deity.[215]

The second verse of the chapter contains the word *al-Ṣamad* that has been used nowhere else in the Qur'an except in this surah. The word itself is so comprehensive that it has been translated differently by different translators. *Al-Ṣamad* is one of the "most beautiful names" of God, and its root has the primary meaning of "without hollow" or "without cleft". Allah is without mixture of any sort, without any possibility of division into parts, because in Him there is no 'hollow'. Louis Massignon would translate it as "dense to the absolute degree", whilst L. Gardet as "impenetrable."[216] *Al-Ṣamad* denotes that God is unknowable, enjoying intrinsic self-sufficiency and unicity without cleft or internal division. There are others who have explained the word *al-Ṣamad* as meaning, "The Master who is depended upon in all matters."[217] Abū Hurayrah, Companion of the Prophet Muhammad, stated that *Al-Ṣamad* is the "One who is free from want and does not need anything from anybody, while everything other than Him needs Him in everything." Ibn Jubayr stated that it refers to the "One who is perfect in His attributes as well as actions." Ibn al-Anbārī said that *Al-Ṣamad* is the "Master above whom there is no master, and upon whom all the people rely for their needs and affairs"[218] M. Asad translates it as "God the Eternal, the Uncaused Cause of All Being." He further observes:

> This rendering gives no more than an approximate meaning of the term as-samad, which occurs in the Qur'an only once, and is applied to God alone. It comprises the concept of Primary Cause and eternal, independent Being, combined with the idea that everything existing or conceivable goes back to Him as its source and is, therefore, dependent on Him for its beginning as well as for its continued existence.[219]

The third verse of *Sūrah al-Ikhlāṣ*, "He begets not, and neither is He begotten" reaffirms this unicity by categorically rejecting any multiplicity within the divine unity. It also simultaneously shatters the "daughters of God" concept, held by the polytheists of Makkah, as well as the Christian concept of the Holy Trinity. Muslims were put on their guard during the very early stages of revelation against any association and multiplicity within the godhead, and it didn't take long for the supposed mystery of the Trinity or incarnation to be declared a betrayal of the divine transcendence, unity and uniqueness of God and a "cleft" in the godhead. It was unequivocally understood that Allah is everlasting while creatures are temporal; that no changeable circumstances effect the divine existence, ever, while creatures are changeable; that Allah is perfect while creatures are imperfect; and that birth, multiplication and development are an absurdity with regards to Allah while intrinsic to His creatures. In sum, so wholly strict and pristine was this stipulated quality of "One" that it included total refutation of utterly human and creaturely limitations including any notion of familial relations (father, son, daughter).

It will be apparent that the Qur'an categorically rejects the Christian concept of the Trinity, its categorization of Jesus as the son of God, and the two central doctrines of Christianity discussed in the previous chapter. The categorical rejection of the Christian doctrine of Incarnation is not only found in this chapter but also in many other chapters and passages of the Qur'an. After giving a detailed description of the virgin birth of prophet Jesus the Qur'an states: "It is not befitting to (the majesty of) Allah that He should beget a son. Glory be to Him! When He determines a matter, He only says to it, 'Be', and it is" (19:35). There are in addition many other Qur'anic passages which address the issue of divine sonship at length: "They say: 'Allah hath begotten a son': Glory be to Him. – Nay, to Him belongs all that is in the heavens and on earth: everything renders worship to Him. The Originator of the heavens and the earth: when He decreeth a matter, He saith to it: 'Be,' and it is" (2:116–17). The Qur'an argues the same point from a different perspective:

> No son did Allah beget, nor is there any god along with Him: (if there were many gods), behold, each god would have taken away what he had created, and some would have lorded it over others! Glory to Allah! (He transcends) the (sort of) things they attribute to Him! He knows what is hidden and what is open: too high is He for the partners they attribute to Him. (23:91–92)

> Wonderful Originator of the heavens and the earth: how can He have a son when He hath no consort? He created all things, and He hath full knowledge of all things. That is Allah, your Lord! There is no god but He, The Creator of all things: then worship ye Him: and He hath power to dispose of all affairs. (6:101–2)

The Qur'an addresses the "People of the Book" directly:

> O People of the Book! Commit no excesses in your religion: nor say of Allah aught but the truth. The Messiah Jesus the son of Mary was (no more than) a Messenger of Allah, and His Word, which He bestowed on Mary, and a Spirit proceeding from Him: so believe in Allah and His Messengers. Say not "Three": desist: it will be better for you: for Allah is One God: Glory be Him: (for Exalted is He) above having a son. To Him belong all things in

> the heavens and on earth. And enough is Allah as a Disposer of affairs. Christ disdaineth not to serve and worship Allah, nor do the angels, those nearest (to Allah): those who disdain His worship and are arrogant, He will gather them all together unto Himself to (answer). (4:171–72)

The Qur'an came as a rectifier of Jewish and Christian excesses against God. The Christian tradition claimed to have believed in monotheism, but, to the Qur'an, the Christian dogma of the Trinity and incarnation was a clear violation of the divine unity and transcendence. Hence Allah revealed the Book (al-Qur'an) to His servant (Muhammad), "that He may warn those who say, 'Allah hath begotten a son': no knowledge have they of such a thing, nor had their fathers. It is a grievous thing that issues from their mouths as a saying. What they say is nothing but falsehood" (18:4–5). The Prophet was asked to employ different arguments to bring the point across: "Say: 'Praise be to Allah, Who begets no son, and has no partner in (His) dominion: nor (needs) He any to protect Him from humiliation: yea, magnify Him for His greatness and glory!'" (17:111). "Say: 'If the Most Gracious had a son, I would be the first to worship.' Glory to the Lord of the heavens and the earth, the Lord of the Throne! He transcends the things they attribute (to Him)!" (43:81–2). To the Qur'an, the most serious sin one can commit is the claim that God has begotten a son.

> They say: "The Most Gracious has begotten a son!" Indeed ye have put forth a thing most monstrous! At it the skies are about to burst, the earth to split asunder, and the mountains to fall down in utter ruin, that they should invoke a son for The Most Gracious. For it is not consonant with the majesty of The Most Gracious that He should beget a son. Not one of the beings in the heavens and the earth but must come to The Most Gracious as a servant. (19:88–93).

According to the Qur'an:

> Certainly they disbelieve who say: "(Allah) is Christ the son of Mary." But said Christ: "O Children of Israel! Worship Allah, my

> Lord and your Lord." Whoever joins other gods with Allah, Allah will forbid him the Garden, and the Fire will be his abode. There will for the wrong-doers be no one to help. They disbelieve who say: Allah is one of three (in a Trinity): for there is no god except One God. If they desist not from their word (of blasphemy), verily a grievous chastisement will befall the disbelievers among them. Why turn they not to Allah and seek His forgiveness? For Allah is Oft-Forgiving, Most Merciful. Christ the son of Mary was no more than a Messenger; many were the messengers that passed away before him. His mother was a woman of truth. They had both to eat their (daily) food. See how Allah doth make His Signs clear to them; yet see in what ways they are deluded away from the truth! (5:72–76)

It is worth noting that these Qur'anic statements roundly reject both interpretations of the Trinity. The first verse refutes Christian docetistic tendencies whilst the second rejects Trinitarian claims, both Augustinian as well as Cappadocian. The Qur'an blames Christian dogma of blurring the transcendental realm with the utilitarian sphere of want and need.

It becomes evident then that the third verse of *al-Ikhlāṣ* is refuting Christian understanding of the Holy Trinity whilst the next verse roundly rejects Christ's or the Holy Spirit's equality with God – in essence, glory, or majesty, as authorized by the Council of Niceae.

The last verse of *al-Ikhlāṣ* dispels all possibilities of a crude anthropomorphism, corporealism and incarnation existing in relation to God. The verse is unequivocal in stating that nothing resembles God either in His being or in His actions and attributes. In fact, God is the only effective power in existence. He is the absolute reality with absolute qualities and attributes. Everything other than Him is relative and dependent upon His transcendental being for its existence, sustenance and continuity. The claims of God's absolute unity and uniqueness made in the previous verses are hereby sealed, confirmed and elaborated by this final verse "there is nothing like unto Him". M. Asad writes:

> The fact that God is one and unique in every respect, without beginning and without end, has its logical correlate in the statement that "there is nothing that could be compared with

> Him"– thus precluding any possibility of describing or defining Him....Consequently, the *quality* of His being is beyond the range of human comprehension or imagination: which also explains why any attempt at "depicting" God by means of figurative representations or even abstract symbols must be qualified as a blasphemous denial of the truth.[220]

Al-Bukhārī, interpreting this surah, narrates on the authority of Abū Hurayrah that the Prophet said:

> Allah said: "The son of Adam tells a lie against Me, though he hasn't the right to do so. He abuses me though he hasn't the right to do so. As for his telling a lie against Me, it is his saying that I will not recreate him as I created him for the first time. In fact, to repeat or to recreate a thing is easier for the One Who has created it first (so it is easier for Me to repeat or recreate a creation which I created first). As for his abusing Me, it is his saying that Allah has begotten a son, while I am the One, As-Samad (self-sufficient Master Whom all creatures need, I neither eat, nor drink). I beget not, nor was I begotten, and there is none equal or comparable unto Me."[221]

He also narrates from Muᶜādh ibn Jabal that the Prophet said:

> "O Mu'adh! Do you know what Allah's Right upon His slave is?" I said, "Allah and His Messenger know best." The Prophet (peace be upon him) said, "To worship Him (Allah) Alone and to join none in worship with Him (Allah). Do you know what their right upon Him is?" I replied, "Allah and His Messenger know best." The Prophet (peace be upon him) said, "Not to punish them (if they do so)."[222]

We conclude this part of the discussion with Murata and Chittick's observation that the brief Islamic confession "there is no god but God" excludes any worship and sincere service in the absolute sense to anybody or anything other than God Almighty since everybody or everything other than God can only be a false god. The Bible as well as Judaeo/Christianity's comprehension of God had left many problems unsolved (as detailed in previous chapters) and the Qur'anic account came to purge the confused, adulterated, even mystical understanding of the Divine contained in i.e. ideas such as the incarnation, corporealism and physical anthropomorphism of God, that had come to prevail. Monotheistic theology is nothing new in the history of western religious traditions. Nevertheless, the radical monotheism of Islam offers distinctive solutions to the difficult and thorny problems of the nature of God, freewill and predestination, the relationship of good to evil, and of reason to revelation. Islamic insistence upon God's absolute transcendence and perfect unity is quite distinctive among the Semitic traditions. Therefore the distinctive feature of Islam, as Richard C. Martin rightly observes, is that, "Among the Western religious traditions, Islam has most insistently asserted the unity and oneness of God."[223]

In addition to insisting upon the unity, unicity, and transcendence of God, affirming this time and time again, the Qur'an aggressively attacks all forms of idolatry, monolatry and polytheism. *Shirk*, the act of associating anything or anybody with God, is according to the Qur'an, the only unforgivable sin: "Allah forgiveth not that partners should be set up with Him; but He forgiveth anything else, to whom He pleaseth; to set up partners with Allah is to devise a sin most heinous indeed" (4:48). Verse 4:116 reiterating the same message contains an additional line: "one who joins other gods with Allah, hath strayed far, far away (from the right path)." In verse 31:13, *shirk* is declared the "the highest wrong-doing". "Being true in faith to Allah, and never assigning partners to Him: if anyone assigns partners to Allah [he] is as if he had fallen from heaven and been snatched up by birds, or the wind had swooped (like a bird on its prey) and thrown him into a far-distant place" (22:31). Mawdudi notes that in this parable, heaven

> means the original human nature. Man by nature is the servant of none else but Allah and inherently accepts the Doctrine of *Tawḥīd*. That is why the one who follows the guidance of the Prophets becomes firm in these dictates of his nature and soars higher and

> higher. On the other hand, the one who rejects Allah or associates a partner with Him falls down from the "heaven" of his nature. Then he either becomes a victim of Satans and evil leaders like the birds of the parable, which snatch away the fallen man, or he becomes a slave of his lusts, passions, whims, etc., which have been likened to the wind in the parable. They lower him down from one wrong position to the other till he falls into the deepest abyss of degradation.[224]

In addition to these appalling warnings, the Qur'an has vehemently denied the existence of gods as divinities other than the Almighty:

> Whatever ye worship apart from Him is nothing but names which ye have named, ye and your fathers, for which Allah hath sent down no authority: the Command is for none but Allah: He hath commanded that ye worship none but Him: that is the right religion, but most men understand not. (12:40)

Therefore gods are nothing but human inventions having no independent reality of their own. In *Sūrah al-Najm* it states:

> Have ye seen Lat, and ʿUzza, and another, the third (goddess), Manat? What! For you the male sex, and for Him, the female? Behold, such would be indeed a division most unfair! These are nothing but names which ye have devised, – ye and your fathers, – for which Allah has sent down no authority (whatever). They follow nothing but conjecture and what the souls desire! – Even though there has already come to them Guidance from their Lord! (53:19–23)

There is an incident narrated in the historical writings of Ṭabarī and Ibn Saʿd relating to the *Sabab al-Nuzūl* (context of revelation) of these verses.[225] Interestingly, the incident narrated received almost universal publicity with the publication of Salman Rushdie's controversial novel *The Satanic Verses* in 1988.[226] It has also long been seized upon by a great many scholars in the West to argue that there was a time during Muhammad's mission when he accepted the existence and validity of the Makkan gods, and did so in an effort to reconcile with the Makkan opposition, as well as consolidate his political position. For instance, Watt quotes from Ṭabarī's account to argue that while seeing the Makkans turning away from his message, Muhammad had a great desire to make it easier for them to accept it. At this juncture *Sūrah al-Najm* was revealed, but when Muhammad came to the verses, "Have ye considered *al-Lāt* and *al-ʿUzzā*, and *Manāt*, the third, the other?" the following, according to the tradition, occurred: "as he was saying it to himself, eager to bring it to his people, Satan threw upon his tongue (the verses), 'these are the swans exalted, Whose intercession is to be hoped for'". On hearing this, the Makkans became delighted, and at the end when Muhammad prostrated himself, they all did likewise. News of this event reached the Muslims in Abyssinia who had migrated there due to Makkan persecution. Watt concludes that subsequently Gabriel came to Muhammad and showed him his error, and God revealed verse 22:51 to comfort the Prophet, abrogating the 'satanic verses' in question by revealing the true continuation of the surah. The Quraysh naturally stated that Muhammad had changed his mind about the position of the goddesses, but in the meantime the satanic verses had been eagerly seized upon by the idolaters.[227]

Narrating a number of other versions and how they differ from the above account, Watt argues that if we compare the different versions and try to distinguish between the external facts in which they agree and the motives which the various historians ascribe in order to explain the facts, we find

> at least two facts about which we may be certain. Firstly, at one time Muhammad must have publicly recited the satanic verses as part of the Qur'an; it is unthinkable that the story could have been invented later by Muslims or foisted upon them by non-Muslims. Secondly, at some later time Muhammad announced that these verses were not really part of the Qur'an and should be replaced by others of a vastly different import. The earliest versions do not specify how long afterwards this happened; the probability is that it was weeks or even months.[228]

Elsewhere, Watt argues that, "The story is so strange that it must be true in essentials."[229] Maxime Rodinson also argues that the tradition "may reasonably be accepted as true because the makers of Muslim tradition would never have invented a story with such damaging implications for the revelation as a whole."[230]

The conclusion Watt reaches is desperate. He argues:

> The Muslim scholars, not possessing the modern Western concept of gradual development, considered Muhammad from the very first to have been explicitly aware of the full range of orthodox dogma. Consequently it was difficult for them to explain how he failed to notice the heterodoxy of the satanic verses. The truth rather is that his monotheism was originally, like that of his more enlightened contemporaries, somewhat vague, and in particular was not so strict that the recognition of inferior divine beings was felt to be incompatible with it. He probably regarded al-Lat, al-ʿUzza, and Manat as celestial beings of a lower grade than God, in much the same way as Judaism and Christianity have recognized the existence of angels. The Qur'an in the later...Meccan period speaks of them as jinn, although in the Medinan period they are said to be merely names. This being so, it is perhaps hardly necessary to find any special occasion for the satanic verses. They would not mark any conscious retreat from monotheism, but would simply be an expression of views which Muhammad always held.[231]

Watt emphatically asserts that, "Indeed there is little about idols through the whole Meccan period."[232] M. Rodinson argues along the same lines observing:

> Muhammad's unconscious had suggested to him a formula which provided a practical road to unanimity. It did not appear to conflict with his henotheism, since these 'great birds' were, like angels or jinns, conceived of as subordinate to Allah. Elsewhere they were called the 'daughters of Allah'. On the other hand this provided a clear indication that the new teaching was in no way

> revolutionary, and that the new sect honored the city's divinities, respected their shrines and recognized their cult as legitimate one.[233]

Watt explains the motive behind these verses by claiming that the leading Quraysh made some sort of offer to Muhammad; he was to receive certain worldly advantages, and in return make some acknowledgment of their deities. The promulgation of the satanic verses was doubtless linked to this bargain, and their abrogation simply a result of the failure of compromise. Watt further claims that Muhammad

> came to realize that acknowledgment of the Banat Allah, as the three idols (and others) were called, meant reducing God to their level. His worship at the Kaʿbah was outwardly not very different from theirs at Nakhlah, at-Ta'if, and Qudayd. And that would mean that God's messenger was not greatly different from their priests and not likely to have much more influence; hence the reform on which Muhammad had set his heart would not come about.[234]

In other words, it was not the strict monotheistic conception of God which alerted Muhammad to this awful mistake and prompted him to change his position but rather the desire for political advantage. Rodinson argues that Muhammad changed his mind because such an acknowledgment

> meant that the sect renounced all claim to originality. Jews and Christians pointed out maliciously that Muhammad was reverting to his pagan beginnings. Besides, what force had the threat of the Last Judgment if the daughters of Allah, propitiated by traditional offerings and sacrifices, would intercede on behalf of sinners and save them from eternal damnation? Above all, what authority was left to the herald sent by Allah if any little priest of al-ʿUzza or Manat could pronounce oracles contradicting his message?[235]

By drawing these conclusions both Watt and Rodinson touch upon several sensitive issues crucial to the very core of the Islamic faith. It is important therefore, to analyze their assumption and reasoning respectively and in detail.

First is the issue of the certainty with which Watt attests to the authenticity of this tradition, particularly the part claiming that the words quoted with regards to the goddesses were pronounced by the Prophet himself. No doubt al-Ṭabarī, and following him, many historians and Qur'anic exegetes have repeated the tradition. All the more strange is that even Ibn Ḥajar al-ᶜAsqalānī observes that, "Even though all the links by which this Tradition has been related are either weak or "broken", except in one case that of Saᶜīd ibn Jubayr, the very fact that it has been related through so many "links" is a proof that there is some truth about it."[236] He also observes that "there are two more chains of narrators (in addition to the one mentioned above) that satisfy the conditions of Bukhārī and Muslim (*al-Saḥīḥayn*) requisite for an authentic report."[237] At the same time, he observes that, "These reports are however, all "*mursal*" traditions, and those who believe the "*mursal*" traditions may argue on their basis."[238] *Mursal* is hadith terminology used to denote a disconnection between the Prophet and the original reporter of a tradition.

The authenticity of the "links", however, does not necessarily mean that all contents of the narration are historically correct or based on facts that cannot be denied. Such a supposition is clearly reflected from the observations of Ibn Ḥajar himself. He notes that although there is enough proof to conclude that the story has some truth in it, nevertheless parts are so atrocious that they must be rejected and interpreted in the light of other facts. One of these consists of the assertion that Satan put the words "they are exalted swans and their intercessions are to be hoped" into the mouth of the Prophet. He argues that:

> This cannot be accepted due to the fact that the Prophet was infallible. It is impossible for the Prophet to intentionally add something to the Qur'an that does not belong to it, or forgetfully say something contradictory to what he had brought about "*Tawḥīd*" (Oneness and Unity of God). That is why the scholars had given the tradition various interpretations....[239]

The best among these interpretations, contends Ibn Ḥajar, is the one which states:

> The Prophet (peace be upon him) was reciting the Qur'an. Satan kept an eye out waiting to insert something into his recitation. Satan found this opportunity during one of the pauses of the Prophet's recitation and uttered these words in a tone resembling that of the Prophet. The people close to the Prophet heard it, took it as his words and publicized it.... Therefore, these words are the words of Satan and in no way the words uttered by the Prophet himself....[240]

It is evident, as apparent in the case of Ibn Ḥajar, that even those few scholars who discussed the historical authenticity of the tradition, equally argued against the truthfulness of the assertion that the Prophet uttered any such words, praising or accepting the Makkan gods. Therefore, to claim that the tradition is authentic by a) implying that Muhammad uttered these words himself, or b) without qualifying it with the qualifiers used by the aforementioned scholars, is misleading.

Moreover, the tradition is a *mursal* one, meaning that the one narrating it (as is the case with all chains of narrations of this type), is not someone directly narrating it from the Prophet or from a Companion or disciple of the Prophet even. Rather such reports issue from a Successor i.e., *Tābiʿī* (of the Successor – *Ṣaḥābī* – of the Prophet), using the formula that "the Prophet said so and so". *Mursal* narrations are therefore regarded as weak by Islamic scholars, because they are not direct Prophetic reports, missing as they do the original link in the chain – that is, the Prophet's disciple/Companion (*Ṣaḥābī*). Consequently, it is difficult to accept a weak narration and give it authority and certainty, and it certainly cannot be considered as evidence especially when it contradicts the very essence of the Qur'anic message. That the Oneness of God is the very essence of the Qur'an's message is a fact beyond dispute, authenticated by all historical and scriptural proofs as discussed.

On the other hand, there have been many eminent historians and exegetes who have declared the story as utterly baseless. M. M. Ahsan has provided a detailed list of distinguished Muslim scholars who have categorically "rejected the story as preposterous and without foundation."[241] For instance, the renowned exegete Ibn Kathīr observed that, "Many exegetes have mentioned the story of swans..., but through links all of them are inauthentic. I have not found a correct version of this story with continuous links."[242] Muḥammad ibn Isḥāq, the writer of *Sīrah* declared the story as "the work of *Zanādiqah* (atheists)".[243] Imam Abū Manṣūr al-Māturīdī argued, that the story was "what the Devil inspired to his atheist followers so as to cause doubts about the authenticity of the religion (Islam) in the minds of the weak. The majesty of the Prophet is absolved from such a narration or act."[244] According to Ibn Khuzaymah, "This story had been invented by the heretics." Al-Qāḍī ʿIyāḍ gave a detailed refutation of it arguing:

> The very fact that this narration has neither been narrated by any of the authentic collections of the hadith nor by any creditable narrator with continuous and authentic links, is a proof of its baselessness. It has been narrated frequently only by those exegetes and historians who are fond of going after all kinds of odd and obscure narration, and who seize upon any thing that comes their way without looking into its nature or truthfulness.[245]

The entire account is riddled with doubt. Detailing the variety of links involved and how they differ and contradict each other over the content, place and context of the story, ʿIyāḍ declares such contextual variety enough to prove the story demonstrably false with no footing to stand on. He further points to the Muslim consensus that the Prophet was infallible, and so transcended the commitment of any such abhorrent act. Muhammad was sent as a mercy to mankind and his name is linked to Allah in the Qur'an, so for Muslims it is as much blasphemous to accept that the Prophet wished to be given verses praising gods besides Allah, as it is to accept that Satan was somehow able to dominate and so confuse him into projecting something non-Qur'anic as Qur'anic. It is also an act of profanity to accept the claim that the Prophet did not know of this alleged confusion until Gabriel warned him of it or to allege that the Prophet happened to pronounce these words intentionally or forgetfully. Those chosen by God as His prophets and messengers do not succumb to Satan in any way, shape or form, neither are they duped by him. Lapses of this or in fact any kind would be impossible for a prophet let alone Muhammad the greatest of them all. Further it is inconceivable that the alleged incident would not have been mentioned either in the Qur'an, or the Hadith or indeed in any of the authentic sources. In fact the whole fabrication is so absurd, so sensationally riven with internal inconsistencies, so fully rejected, based on non-evidence, by scholars, that it's invention speaks for itself.

Al-Qāḍī also rightly observes that had the incident actually taken place, both the pagans of Makkah and the Jewish tribes would have made it a point to use it zealously against Muhammad disputing his truthfulness; further, the incident would also have resulted in some of the weaker Muslims apostatizing from the Faith (as was the case after *al-Isrā'*, the night journey of the Prophet to Jerusalem and ascension into Heaven), or at least to expressions of such a tendency as occurred in the incident of the *Ḥudaybiyyah Treaty*. So, why was the episode not publicized, discussed, and used to vilify Muhammad? The event had it occurred would have been a monumental scandal with every minute detail finding its way into the Hadith. The fact that no Muslim ever abandoned Islam as a result of this enormously damaging conciliatory act, and that none of the Prophet's foes incredulously ever made an issue of it even, (there is no historical report that they even discussed it), is sufficient to prove that the entire story was a later invention with no historical basis.[246]

Qāḍī Abū Bakr ibn al-ʿArabī puts forward ten separate arguments to refute the claim that the Prophet ever pronounced these alleged words which supposedly acknowledged the Makkan's pagan deities. As he concludes:

> The Qur'an very eloquently, and both explicitly and implicitly explains the infallibility of the Prophet... So we advise you to place the Qur'an in front of your eyes and read the words carefully, so as not to attribute to the Qur'an what does not belong there, or to connect to it meanings utterly unacceptable.[247]

In addition to the scholars discussed, Imam Fakhar al-Dīn al-Rāzī,[248] Muḥammad ibn Aḥmad al-Qurṭubī,[249] Muḥammad ibn Yūsuf al-Kirmānī,[250] Maḥmūd ibn Aḥmad Badr al-Dīn al-ʿAynī,[251] and al-Alusi have all rejected the account as baseless and absurd.[252]

Among modern Muslim scholars, Shibli Numani observes that "this story is evidently an absurd myth that deserves no comment."[253] Mawdudi furnishes a detailed refutation by focusing upon its internal and external evidence. For example, the story alleges that the incident took place after the first migration to Ḥabashah (Abyssinia), referring to some of the migrants returning to Makkah after hearing of the event. The Abyssinian migration took place in the month of Rajab (the seventh month of the Islamic calendar) during the fifth year of Prophethood, with some of the migrants returning to Makkah three months later, i.e. in Shawwal of the same year. Verses 73–75 in Chapter 17 of the Qur'an in which the Prophet was supposedly "reproved" for the incident in question were revealed in the eleventh or twelfth year of Prophethood. Does it make sense that Allah would admonish him five or six years after the supposed incident took place? "[V]erse (52) in which the interpolation by Satan was abrogated was sent down in the first year of Hijrah, i.e. about two years after the reproof. Can a person in his senses believe that the Holy Prophet was reproved for the interpolation after six years, and it was abrogated after nine years?"[254]

After discussing the context of the verses, Mawdudi declares that even a casual reader would detect an obvious contradiction in the passage. The fabricated insertion of "[These are the high-flying ones, whose intercession is to be hoped for!]" is so clearly apparent and such a clumsy attempt at fabrication that no sensible person could accept it other than invention.

> Have ye seen Lat and ʿUzza, And another, the third (goddess), Manat? [**These are the high-flying ones, whose intercession is to be hoped for!**] What! for you the male sex, and for Him, the female? Behold, such would be indeed a division most unfair! These are nothing but names which ye have devised, – ye and your fathers, – for which Allah has sent down no authority (whatever). They follow nothing but conjecture and what their own souls

desire! – Even though there has already come to them Guidance from their Lord! [Qur'an 53:19–23]

Looking at the insertion (in bold) the internal incongruity pointing to fabrication is glaringly obvious. Are we supposed to accept that immediately after supposedly praising the goddesses, Lāt, ʿUzzā and Manāt, Allah then in complete contradiction hits their worshippers hard, as if to say: "O foolish people! How is it that you have ascribed daughters to Allah and sons to yourself? All this is your own invention which has no authority from Allah."[255] Thus the internal evidence alone is enough to discredit the story as utterly absurd and meaningless.

Mawdudi also argues, that the revelation of these verses as asserted in the story does not "fit in with the chronological order of the Qur'an."[256] In connection with the relevant context of the passages he observes:

> We reiterate that no Tradition, however strong links it might have, can be accepted when the Text itself is a clear evidence against it, and when it does not fit with the wording, the context, the order etc. of the Qur'an. When the incident is considered in this background, even a skeptical research scholar would be convinced that the Tradition is absolutely wrong.[257]

The majority of Muslim exegetes such as Qutb, Mufti M. Shafi and Islahi view the story as theatrical nonsense, so baseless and contradictory to the fundamental principles of the Islamic religion and such an affront to the intelligence, that to discuss it in any way, shape or form is not appropriate,[258] in other words a complete waste of time.

Among modern historians, M. H. Haykal regards all arguments forming the basis for the veracity of the story as "false, incapable of standing any scrutiny or analysis."[259] For Haykal, "It is a story whose incoherence is evident upon the least scrutiny"[260] with the multiplicity of the tradition being proof of its lack of authenticity. Haykal claims that there were two motives for the Muslims to return from Ethiopia: (a) The conversion of ʿUmar ibn al-Khaṭṭāb to Islam, and (b) The breaking out of a revolution against the Negus "in which his personal faith as well as his protection of the Muslims were under attack."[261] He further argues against the story from the inverted evidence of the Qur'anic text:

> Another proof of the falsity of the story, stronger and more conclusive than the foregoing, is the fact that the contextual flow of *sura* "al-Najm" does not allow at all the inclusion of such verses as the story claims.... The contextual background in which the addition is supposed to have been made furnishes unquestionable and final evidence that the story of goddesses was a forgery.[262]

Haykal, like Shaykh Muhammad Abduh, rightly points out that nowhere did the Arabs ever describe their gods or goddesses in terms such as *al-gharānīq*, neither in their poetry, speeches or traditions, and that the word *al-gharānīq* (or *al-gharnīq*) was in fact the name of a black or white water bird, sometimes used figuratively to refer to a handsome blond youth. The fact is irrefutable that the Arabs never looked upon their gods in this manner. Arguing that the story contradicts Muhammad's candidness, he concludes:

> The forgers must have been extremely bold to have attempted their forgery in the most essential principal of Islam as a whole: namely, in the principle of *tawhid*, where Muhammad had been sent right from the very beginning to make proclamations to all mankind in which he has never accepted any compromise whatever; he was never swayed by anything the Quraysh had offered him whether by way of wealth or royal power.[263]

Muhammad never compromised the unity and transcendence of God even at the most difficult junctures of his prophetic mission. He did not entertain substantial offers of wealth, power and prestige at the most vulnerable stages of his life as they included compromise of the divine unity and otherness. So to impudently suggest that he would sacrifice *tawḥīd* to gain the approval of his adversaries is to fly in the face of historical fact.

Many Muslim scholars in addition to Haykal, have written extensively on the issue, M. Nasr al-Albani[264] and Zafar Ali Qureshi[265] are just two examples.

If the story is an obvious forgery it could well be asked why not simply dismiss it and avoid any detailed discussion? One of the reasons is that this particular forgery strikes at the heart of the Islamic faith, specifically the fundamental dogma of the Unity (Oneness) of God and the infallibility of the Prophet, implying that to accept the authenticity of the tradition without proper qualification, as Watt has done, would mean the demolition of the very foundation of the Islamic religion and the debasing of its revelation from all kinds of claims to divine origin. It is, furthermore, all the more degrading to link the story as Watt has done with the bargain offers made to Muhammad. History is witness to the fact that bargains of such kind were repeatedly made to Muhammad, yet he never accepted these offers or compromised on the issue of the absolute Unity, Oneness, and Transcendence of God even during times of crushing opposition and absolute lack of resources.

Even the critic Rodinson is forced to quote the famous story of the offer made by the Makkan pagans to Muhammad, and its rejection, just before mentioning the story of the satanic verses. In response to Abū al-Walīd ʿUtbah ibn Rabīʿah's offers of business, prestige, and sovereignty, Muhammad's answer was, and I quote Rodinson:

> to recite some verses from the Koran. ʿUtba listened carefully and went back to his companions with this advice: 'Leave him alone. By God, his words will have vast consequences. If the Arabs [that is, the Beduin] kill him, then you will be delivered from him by others. But if he triumphs over the Arabs, his sovereignty will be your sovereignty and his glory will be your glory, and through him you will be the most prosperous of men.'[266]

This incident of the bargain, in Rodinson's opinion, "had some foundation in fact"[267] and "had an element of truth in it".[268] Many other examples exist of the Prophet being offered enticing worldly bargains in return for compromise on the fundamental issue of God's Unity and Transcendence. All of which he resolutely refused. Even in response to ʿUtbah's offer the Prophet recited, as Ibn Hishām narrates, the verses of surah 41 (*Fuṣṣilat*), containing the essential monotheistic message, "Say thou: 'I am but a man like you: it is revealed to me by inspiration, that your God is One God: so take the straight path unto Him and ask for His forgiveness.' And woe to those who joined gods with Allah..." (41:6). In certain other incidents Muhammad's response was even sterner. For instance, his reply to his uncle Abū Ṭālib's plea was: "By God if they keep the sun in my right hand and the moon in my left hand to abandon this matter (call to the sincere worship of One God) I would not do so."[269] Therefore, it is extremely misleading and all the more unjust to attribute to this great Prophet an instance of such abject compromise – particularly in this fashion too of viewing him as supposedly attempting to appease the pagans for worldly benefit – given his absolute loyalty to God in the face of the most acute persecution. The history of the Prophet's early mission is filled with incidents of insult, intimidation, verbal and physical abuse, social, financial and political setbacks and impending dangers to his life. Neither were his handful of early Companions of much help to him being themselves the victims of these abuses. It would seem awkward and antithetical to the demeanor, disposition, nature and aptitude of Muhammad to accept the intercession of false gods simply to obtain the approval of his enemies at a later stage of his mission.

In conclusion to this part of the discussion it is enough to firstly end with the observations of two orientalists with regards to the story. According to John Burton, "those *hadiths* have no historical basis"[270] and as he further argues, "this story must be decisively rejected once and for all."[271] According to K. Armstrong:

> this story is in conflict with other traditions and with the Qur'an itself. We must remember that a Muslim historian like Tabari does not necessarily endorse all the traditions he records: he expects the reader to compare them with others and to make up his or her own mind about their validity. At this very early stage of his prophetic career, Muhammad was not interested in political power. So the story, as told by Abu al-Aliyah, is not very likely. The Qur'an... denies that Muhammad should have a political

> function in Mecca at this point, and later the Prophet would turn down similar deals with leading Quraysh without a second's thought.[272]

Secondly, according to Islamic doctrine, Satan is a more manageable reality then usually perceived by some other faith groups, meaning that he has no authority over God's conscious people. The Qur'an explains: "For over my servants no authority shalt thou have, except such as put themselves in the wrong and follow thee" (15:42). Hence, if this is the case with God's righteous servants then how much more so for the Prophet. In other words, Satan would not at any level have been able to affect, play with or to confuse Muhammad. And this is worth repeating. If even common Muslims become immune from satanic impulses and temptations while reciting the Qur'an, then how impossible for the Prophet to be deceived, the original recipient of the revelation! This is an established principle within the Qur'anic conceptual framework.

Thirdly, we come to the more serious issue of Muhammad's monotheism. Rodinson has dubbed it as "henotheism". To Watt, "his monotheism was originally, like that of his more enlightened contemporaries, somewhat vague, and in particular was not so strict that the recognition of inferior divine beings was felt to be incompatible with it."[273] Neither in the Qur'anic text nor in the authentic traditions of Muhammad is anything found of henotheism or vague monotheism, no room whatsoever is allowed for inferior divine beings. The Qur'anic text is vociferous against such claims. The strict monotheism peculiar to the later Islamic tradition had been propagated by Muhammad from the very beginning of his mission in Makkah. Most of the Qur'an (about two thirds) had been revealed in Makkah. The earliest surahs of the Qur'an emphatically asserted the Oneness of Almighty God and declared worship of others besides Him as blasphemous and heretical. According to Stanley Lane-Poole:

> During the years of struggle and persecution of Mekka.... ninety out of the 114 chapters of the Koran were revealed, amounting to about two-third of the whole book. All these chapters are inspired with but one great design, and are in strong contrast with the

> complicated character of the later chapters issued at Medina. In the Mekka chapters Mohammed appears in the unalloyed character of prophet; he has not yet assumed the functions of a statesman and law-giver. His object is not to give men a code or a constitution. *But call them to the worship of the One God. This is the only aim of Mekkan speeches.... Every chapter is directed simply to the grand design of the Prophet's life to convince men of the unutterable majesty of the One God, who brooks no rivals...*[274] [italics mine].

It is surprising that a scholar like Watt would have the audacity to claim that there is little concerning idols mentioned throughout the whole Makkan period and that acceptance of the Makkan goddesses as lower divine angelic beings capable of intercession on behalf of their admirers was something not incompatible with Muhammad's "vague monotheism".[275] This is akin to calling black, white, and vice versa. To attempt to establish a theory whilst ignoring every fact on the ground, beggars belief. It is illogical to even think that out of the two-thirds of the Qur'an revealed at Makkah, there is little concerning idols or idol worship. There is for instance, surah 112 *al-Ikhlāṣ*, discussed earlier, which not only forms the cornerstone of strict Islamic monotheism and God's transcendence, but is also a measuring rod against all kinds of polytheism, henotheism and paganism. Noldeke places this surah in the very first Makkan period.[276] H. Hirschfeld writes, "I feel inclined to place it among the first revelations."[277] Muir argues that it was the 20th chapter revealed in Makkah hence putting it in the very early phase of Muhammad's mission.[278] The same is said by Muir and Noldeke with regard to *Sūrah al-Kāfirūn* (109), the mere recitation of which disavows Muhammad from all kinds of *shirk* (polytheism).

There is a consensus among Muslim scholars that *Sūrah Yūsuf* (chapter 12) is without doubt a Makkan chapter. Muir, Noldeke, and Grimme also agree that it was revealed in Makkah.[279] We have had the opportunity of quoting verse 40 of *Sūrah Yūsuf* wherein it clearly says:

> Whatever ye worship apart from Him is nothing but names which ye have named, ye and your fathers, – for which Allah hath sent

> down no authority; the Command is for none but Allah: He hath commanded that ye worship none but Him: that is the right religion, but most men understand not... (12:40)

How else could the Qur'an have possibly stated its position with regards to idolatry and polytheism? There is no "vague monotheism" either in this verse or the entire Qur'an. Conversely, what there is in point of fact is a strict monotheism to the very definition of the term. In addition to those mentioned, there exist many other Makkan chapters which address the issue aggressively and comprehensively.[280] The case against those who would indicate otherwise is irrefutable.

Furthermore, what on earth was Muhammad being persecuted, tortured, and opposed for, by the Makkan pagans, if not for his strict monotheism and stern opposition to polytheism? The Prophet was constantly being ordered by the Makkans to stop opposing their gods and respect the religion of their forefathers.[281] It was undoubtedly his strict monotheism and stern opposition to worship of any person or object besides God that caused him such opposition in Makkah and such brutal, inhumane retaliation. Muhammad never compromised on the issue of the Oneness, Uniqueness and Transcendence of God, neither in Makkah nor in Madinah. T. Noldeke observes:

> Muhammad's single aim in the Meccan suras is to convert the people, by means of persuasion, from their false gods to the one God. To whatever point the discourse is directed this always remains the ground thought; but instead of seeking to convince the reason of his hearers by logical proofs, he employs the art of rhetoric to work upon their minds through the imagination. Thus he glorifies God, describes His working in Nature and History, and ridicules on the other hand the impotence of the idols. Especially important are the descriptions of the everlasting bliss of the pious and the torment of the wicked: these, particularly the latter, must be regarded as one of the mightiest factors in the propagation of Islam...[282]

According to Julian Obermann:

> In early Surahs we have to do with oracle-like pronouncements of a prophet and visionary.... In contents, his early message is of extreme simplicity, it is marked by complete absence of either ritual or legal elements of any kind. What it offers is an outline, the barest rudiments of monotheistic theology. God is One, He has no equal; He is the creator of the universe and His care provides bountiful sustenance for man and beast (argument from creation): in the past He had punished people for their wrongdoing (argument from history); in the future He will judge man according to his deeds, rewarding obedience with the delights of paradise and requiting disobedience with the scourge of Hellfire.[283]

Reuben Levy:

> The earliest divine manifestations commanded him to "recite" what he heard. It was followed by others which bade him denounce the idolatrous beliefs and practices of his fellow townsmen, to whom he was to reveal a higher faith and a purer system of life. The central point of the new faith was that there is no God but Allah, a deity which was already known in the Arabian pantheon but who was henceforth to be not supreme, but unique.[284]

Francesco Gabrieli:

> ...In this, the earliest, and the following short, ecstatic revelations... are expressed in an enthusiastic and lyrical rather than a logical form the fundamental outlines of Muhammad's vision: one single omnipotent God (for whom the name Allah was the natural choice, not a new one to the pagan Arabs but filled with a new content and raised far above any polytheistic conception), author and ruler of creation, lord of the life of man, giver of blessing and chastisement, stern judge of the day of doom...[285]

Charles J. Adams:

> Muhammad's preaching in Mecca centered upon the one sovereign deity, Allah, who controlled the destiny of mankind. In place of the numerous powers recognized by the pagan Arabs, Muhammad proclaimed a unique God who created the universe, established its order, and encompassed its fate in his hand.[286]

Even Richard Bell, upon whom Watt depended heavily in his treatment of the Qur'an, did not deny the fact that the strict monotheism and refutation of paganism was the cardinal element of Muhammad's mission during the Makkan period. He wrote: "Muhammad claimed to be the Messenger of God to his people. He began by advocating monotheism, the worship of one God upon whose power and bounty man was dependent..."[287] going on to state that:

> More characteristic of the Qur'an is the reaction from pagan ideas. It was Muhammad's life-mission to overthrow the polytheism of his people... The fundamental doctrine of the Qur'an is that there is only one God. From that doctrine Muhammad *never wavered from start to finish of his mission*.... For the most part it is directed against the polytheism of his own Arab people.[288] [italics mine].

Rodwell,[289] Grimme,[290] W. Irving,[291] P. de Lacy Johnstone,[292] E. Gibbon,[293] Hitti,[294] J. J. Saunders,[295] A. Schimmel,[296] Helmer Ringgren and A. V. Storm[297] and K. Cragg,[298] are also among those scholars who fully recognize the fact that Muhammad's monotheism and understanding of God's uniqueness and transcendence was never vague and that he never compromised the issue from the very beginning through to the very end of his prophetic mission. For instance H. Ringgern and A. V. Storm maintain:

> In a systematic summary of the contents of the Koran, the doctrine of the absolute oneness of God would undoubtedly come out as its principal tenet. 'There is no God but Allah, and Mohammad is his prophet'... so runs the Islamic creed, and it is, indeed, an apt

> synopsis of the teaching of the Koran. God is one, and has no one by his side. Polytheism is fiercely attacked....[299]

It must by now be evident that Watt's hopeless allegations of Muhammad's vague monotheism are nothing more than a desperate attempt to portray a progressive element in the Qur'anic concept of the divine unity and uniqueness of God. Equipped and influenced by biblical historical criticism, Watt has no right to draw arbitrary, and one might add audacious, parallels between the biblical and Islamic monotheistic consciousness, attempting to divest Islam of its crowning element, transcendental monotheism, based on nothing more than a single flimsy fairy tale of dubious content and dubious origins.

Coming back to our original discussion, it must be emphasized that the Qur'an is not satisfied in merely attacking all kinds of polytheism but repeatedly emphasizes the point that false gods have no existence of their own, being nothing more than a product of their worshippers' imagination: "Behold! verily to Allah belong all creatures, in the heavens and on earth. What do they follow who worship as His "partners" other than Allah? They follow nothing but conjecture, and they do nothing but lie"(10:66).

> Say (O Muhammad): "Of your partners', can any originate creation and repeat it?" Say: "It is Allah who originates creation and repeats it: then how are you deluded away (from the truth)?" Say: "Of your 'partners' is there any that can give any guidance towards Truth?" Say: "It is Allah who gives guidance towards Truth. Is then He who gives guidance to Truth more worthy to be followed, or he who finds not guidance (himself) unless he is guided? What then is the matter with you? How judge ye? But most of them follow nothing but conjecture: truly conjecture can be of no avail against Truth. Verily Allah is well aware of all that they do." (10:34–36)[300]

Contrary to this, Henry P. Smith strangely claims:

> The proposition that Allah is the only God does not necessarily mean that the other so-called gods have absolutely no existence.

> This was too radical a step to take all at once. Mohammad conceded the existence of spirits or demons who had seduced men to their worship. The Arabic word for these beings is *Jinn* (collective)...[301]

Claims such as these, especially in the face of crystal clear Qur'anic passages such as those above, are not only unjustified but misleading.

Is there willful ignorance here? One wonders. It must be said at the outset that the Qur'an has never denied the existence of those who are worshipped by pagans, either human beings or the jinn, as realities that exist or have existed in the past, a good example being the person of Jesus, the son of Mary, worshiped as a triune God. So, the existence of God's creation being worshipped by certain people is not in question. What the Qur'an categorically denies is the fact of their existence as divinities capable of benefit or harm independently of God. When the Qur'an confirms the existence of spirit beings such as the jinn, devils, and angels it makes it categorically clear, leaving no stone unturned, that they are powerless creatures of God, under the supreme authority of God, owing all that they have to the power of God, without any power of their own, exercising only whatever is permitted to them by God and hence having no share in the divinity at all. For instance, concerning the jinn[302] the Qur'an states: "And the Jinn race, We had created before, from the fire of a scorching wind" (15:27). "And He created Jinns from fire free of smoke" (55:15). The jinn have been granted astonishing physical capabilities (27:39; 34:12–13; 21:82; 38:37) that differentiate them from ordinary human beings. On the other hand, just like human beings, they are created for the purpose of worshipping God. "I have only created the jinns and men, that they may serve Me" (51:56). There are among them who believe (46:29–32), and others who reject the truth (6:112; 7:38; 7:179; 41:29).[303] Likewise, the jinn will be held answerable (for their deeds) on the Day of Judgement (6:128; 11:119; 72:15).

The angels are also God's creation and His servants: "And they make into females angels who themselves are servants of the Most Gracious..." (43:19). In contrast to jinn and mankind, angels are obedient to God's commands, programmed to be so by their very nature: "They are (but) servants raised to honor. They speak not before

He speaks, and they act (in all things) by His command. He knows what is before them, and what is behind them, and they offer no intercession except for those with whom He is well-pleased and they stand in awe and reverence of His (glory)" (21:26–28). The difference between the jinn and the angels is the same as that between mankind and the angels, the jinn like man, are created with free will while the angels are otherwise. The Devil (Iblīs) was "one of the Jinns, and he broke the Command of his Lord..." (18:50). Like the jinn, Satan was created out of fire (7:12). Due to acts of submission he was allowed to worship God in the company of the angels. Satan never possessed, neither before his rejection nor after his expulsion, any divine powers or abilities. The only power Iblīs is allowed to exercise and that for a specified time only is the power of persuasion.

> (Iblis) said: "O my Lord! give me then respite till the Day the (dead) are raised." (Allah) said: "Respite is granted thee till the day of the Time Appointed." (Iblis) said: "O my Lord! because Thou hast thrown me out of the way, I will make (wrong) fair-seeming to them on the earth, and I will put them all in the wrong, except Thy chosen servants among them..." (15:36–40; also see 7:14–17)

God made it clear to Iblīs that, "For over My servants no authority shalt thou have, except such as put themselves in the wrong and follow thee" (15:42). "No authority has he over those who believe and put their trust in their Lord. His authority is over those only, who take him as patron and who join partners with Allah" (16:99–100). In *Sūrah Ibrāhīm,* the Qur'an depicts a dialogue that will take place on the Day of Judgment between Satan and his followers:

> Satan will say, once the matter has been settled: "God has given you a true promise, while I have both promised you and then broken my word with you. I had no authority over you except that I appealed to you, and you responded to me. Do not blame me but blame yourself! I have no claim on you nor have you any claim on me..." (14:22)

It is evident that although the Qur'an does not deny the existence of angels and jinn, as creatures of God, subject to His power, discipline, and justice, it categorically rejects their claim to any power or ability as divine beings. Nothing is divine except the One Almighty God, Transcendent and Majestic (6:100–102). On the other hand, for those who worship these beings in the false belief that they possess divine powers and abilities, or have the least share in them, we are informed by the Qur'an that this act of worship is mere conjecture on the part of the worshippers. So Smith's other statement that, "Mohammad admitted that the false gods have a real existence. What he denied was not their reality but their divinity – their power to help or harm",[304] although is closer to the reality, is nevertheless still misleading. The statement must be qualified by the proper qualifier that the existence of such beings *as gods* is rejected, while their existence as God's creatures, worshipped wittingly or unwittingly by others, is affirmed. (See 5:116–118; 6:22; 10:28; 25:17; 34:40; 46:6).

The Qur'an modified the Arab conception of angels as superior jinn worthy of worship and veneration, allotting to angels a specific place in the hierarchy of supernatural beings. In the new Islamic theocentric system of reality the angels played a vital role but as created agents of God. The Qur'an classifies angels into several categories in accordance with their assigned duties and functions. Therefore within the universal hierarchy of created beings a specific angelic hierarchy was formed. The angels were still accepted as invisible, celestial beings belonging to a higher ontological order than man and jinn, but without any shade of divinity or adoration ascribed to them. They were the humble obedient servants of God. The source of their respect and veneration lay in their absolute servitude and obedience to God and not in their being divine in any way, shape or form.

It is evident by now that the Qur'an neither affirms nor allows any room to proclaim the existence of any god or divinity besides God. All that is other than God is His creation. No one possesses any iota of power or ability to benefit or harm human beings except by the permission of God. Those worshiped by humans other than God are mere creations of their followers' imagination. We conclude this part of the discussion with Izutsu who puts the matter succinctly:

> In the Koranic system, too, there is the concept of aliha. We must not confuse the ontological order of things with the semantic one. In other words, the fact that the Koranic world is essentially monotheistic should not lead us into thinking erroneously that *semantically* as well as ontologically, Allah stands alone without any peers. On the contrary, there *are* concepts of "gods" and "idols" in the Koranic system. Only, all these stand in negative relation to Allah; they are there simply as something the existence of which must be denied most emphatically. Speaking in more semantical terms, they are there in the Koran to be connected with the concept of "falsehood" *batil*, while the concept of Allah is to be connected with that of "truth" *haqq*.[305]

In the realm of supernatural beings Allah stands alone as the "Real" depriving all other so called gods of all possible reality. These were now "mere names", not corresponding to any real entities existing outside of language. "In the terminology of modern semantics, we should say that in this conception the term *ilah* (pl. *alihah*), when applied to anything other than Allah Himself is nothing but a word having connotation but no denotation."[306]

Furthermore, the Qur'an brings the point home using various arguments from creation to establish the fact. Almighty God is the Creator. He has created the heavens and the earth and all that is in the universe. He is the sole Sustainer: "He it is Who has created for you all that is on earth, and has applied His design to the heavens and fashioned them into seven heavens; and He alone has full knowledge of everything" (2:29).

> Praise be to Allah, Who created the heavens and the earth, and made the Darkness and the Light. Yet those who reject Faith hold (others) as equal with their Guardian Lord. He it is Who created you from clay, and then decreed a stated term (for you). And there is with Him another determined term; yet ye doubt within yourself! And He is Allah in the heavens and in earth, He knoweth what you hide, and what ye reveal, and He knoweth the (recompense) which ye earn (by your deeds). (6:1–3)

> It is Allah Who hath created the heavens and the earth and sendeth down rain from the skies, and with it bringeth our fruits wherewith to feed you; it He Who hath made the ships subject to you, that you may sail through the sea by His Command; and the rivers (also) hath He made subject to you. And He hath made subject to you the sun and the moon, both diligently pursuing their courses; and the Night and the Day hath He (also) made subject to you. And He giveth you of all that ye ask for. But if ye count the favors of Allah, never will ye be able to number them. Verily, man is given up to injustice and ingratitude. (14:32–34)

"He has created the heavens and the earth with truth; far is He above having the partners they ascribe to Him" (16:3; also see 7:54; 7:185; 9:36; 10:3, 10:5; 10:6; 14:19; 25:2, 25:59; 30:8; 31:10).

The Qur'an then inquires "...*Such is the Creation of Allah: now show Me what is there that others besides Him have created: nay, but the transgressors are in manifest error*" (31:11).

> Say: "Have ye seen (these) 'partners' of yours whom ye call upon besides Allah? *Show me what it is thay have created in the (wide) earth. Or have they a share in the heavens?* Or have We given them a Book from which they (can derive) clear (evidence)?- Nay, the wrong-doers promise each other nothing but delusions." (35:40)

> Say: "Do ye see what it is ye invoke besides Allah? *Show me what it is they have created on earth, or have they a share in the heavens?* Bring me a Book (revealed) before this, or any remnant of knowledge (ye may have), if ye are telling the truth! And who is more astray than one who invokes, besides Allah, such as will not answer him to the Day of Judgment, and who (in fact) are unconscious of their call (to them)? And when mankind are gathered together (at the Resurrection), they will be hostile to them and deny that (men) had worshipped them." (46:4–6)

"Those whom they invoke besides Allah create nothing and are themselves created. (They are things) dead, lifeless: nor do they know when they will be raised up" (16:20–21). This verse undoubtedly refers to human beings such as saints, prophets, emperors, and kings who having enjoyed political or spiritual powers in the past are ultimately consigned to the earth, to graves, after their death. This excludes Satan and the angels who are thought to be alive.

In *Sūrah al-Ḥajj*, the Qur'an makes the point succinctly:

> O Men! A parable is set forth [herewith]; hearken, then, to it! Behold, those beings whom you invoke instead of God cannot create [as much as] a fly, even were they to join all their forces to that end! And if a fly robs them of anything, they cannot [even] rescue it from him! Weak indeed is the seeker, and [weak] the sought! No true understanding of God have they [who err in this way]: for, verily, God is most Powerful, Almighty! (22:73–74)

The conclusion the Qur'an wants people to derive from this is simple and straightforward: "Is then He Who creates like one that creates not? Will ye not receive admonition?" (16:17).

Another contrast is that of response to prayers. The true and only God guides, listens and responds to prayers. He is the only one who helps those in need: "Our Lord is the One Who has given everything its own constitution; then guided it" (20:50; also see 2:143; 2:213; 6:90; 6:149; 7:43; 7:178; 16:9; 63:11; 35:8 etc.).[307] "When My servants ask thee concerning Me, I am indeed close (to them): I respond to the prayer of every suppliant when he calleth on Me: Let them also, with a will, listen to My call, and believe in Me: That they may walk in the right way" (2:186). Al-Ṭabarī relates on the authority of Ḥasan al-Baṣarī, that a man asked the Prophet, "Is our Lord near that we can pray to Him in private or is He far that we cannot cry out to Him?" The verse was therefore revealed.[308] Ibn Kathīr relates, that some of the Prophet's Companions asked him, "Where is our Lord?" This verse was revealed in response to that question.[309] Al-Bukhārī relates from Abū Masʿūd:

> We were in the company of the Prophet (peace be upon him) on a journey, and whenever we ascended a high place, we used to say Takbir (*Allahu Akbar* meaning God is the Most Great) (in a loud

> voice). The Prophet (peace be upon him) said, "O people! Be kind to yourself, for you are not calling upon a deaf or an absent one, but you are calling an All-Hearer, and an All-Seer...."[310]

Ibn ʿArabī gives this verse a great mystical significance *vis-à-vis* the man-God relationship and man's quest for Him:

> If my servants who are journeying toward me 'ask you concerning' knowledge of 'me,' 'certainly I am near' and manifest. 'I answer the prayers of the suppliant when he calls upon me' with the tongue of his state and potential by granting him what his state and potential require. 'Let them therefore answer my call' by purifying their potential with asceticism and acts of worship. For to myself do I call them in order that I may teach them how to journey to me. Let them behold me when they are in the state of purity so that I may manifest myself in the mirrors of their hearts. This, in order that they may be well guided in rectitude and achieve goodness in themselves.[311]

In *Sūrah Ghāfir,* it is written: "And your Lord says: 'Call on Me; I will answer your prayer...'" (40:60). Abū Hurayrah narrates a *ḥadīth qudsī* (the sayings of the Prophet Muhammad as revealed to him by the Almighty)[312] from the Prophet, that Almighty Allah says:

> I am as My servant thinks I am (another possible rendering of the Arabic is: "I am as My servant expects Me to be"). I am with him when he makes mention of Me. If he makes mention of Me to himself, I make mention of him to Myself: and if he makes mention of Me in an assembly, I make mention of him in an assembly better than it. And if he draws near to Me a hand's span, I draw near to him an arm's length, and if he draws near to Me an arm's length, I draw near to him a fathom's length. And if he comes to Me walking, I go to him at speed.[313]

Therefore, narrates Anas ibn Mālik, "To call upon God is the essence of worship." Unlike other gods, narrates Abū Hurayrah,

"Almighty God gets angry with the one Who does not call upon Him."[314] In contrast, false gods neither guide nor listen. They do not and cannot respond to prayers:

> To Him alone should all prayer be addressed, *for those to whom they do address their prayers besides Him are altogether powerless to respond to them. The example of praying to any other than Allah is that of a man who stretches out his hands to water, asking it to reach his mouth, although water has no power to reach his mouth. The prayers of the unbelievers are a sheer waste.* (13:14)[315] [italics mine]

> *And those whom you invoke besides Him own not a straw. If you invoke them they will not listen to your call, and if they were to listen, they cannot answer your (prayer). On the Day of Judgment they will reject your "Partnership". And none, (O Man!) can inform you like Him who is All-Aware.* (35:14) [italics mine]

"And who is more astray than one who invokes, beside Allah, such as will not answer him to the Day of Judgment, and who (in fact) are unconscious of their call (to them)" (46:5). Izutsu observes that:

> The Divine response to the human *duʿa* is signified in the Koran by the word *istijabah* meaning literally "answering" being ready in response. Semantically we may describe this by saying that the concept of *duʿa* stands in correlation with that of *istijabah*. Unlike *duʿa*, which is essentially verbal, *istijabah* is non-verbal. In the Koran, God Himself declares positively that He is always ready to "answer" if only men call upon Him sincerely.... Moreover, the Koran attaches the highest importance to the concept of *istijabah*, as is evident from the fact that it makes the incapacity for *istijabah* one of the most salient marks of a false god. The gods whom the Kafirs worship apart from Allah *cannot* respond to their *duʿa*, however much the worshippers call upon them. They do not hear the Kafirs prayer, and even if they did, they would not able to answer anything.[316]

The true God is the true sovereign. He helps whomsoever He pleases, benefits whomsoever He wants, and causes harm to whosoever deserves so. "There is no victory except from Allah, the Exalted, the Wise" (3:126). "If Allah helps you, none can overcome you: if He forsakes you, who is there, after that, that can help you? In Allah, then, let Believers put their trust" (3:160). "If Allah touch thee with affliction, none can remove it but He; if He touch thee with happiness, He hath power over all things. He is Irresistibly Supreme over His servants. And He is the Wise, Acquainted with all things" (6:17–18). "If Allah afflicts you with any hardship, none other than He can remove it; and if He will any good for you, none can avert His bounty. He bestows good upon whomsoever of His servants He will. He is All-Forgiving, All-Merciful" (10:107). "What Allah out of His Mercy doth bestow on mankind none can withhold: what He doth withhold, none can grant apart from Him: And He is Exalted in Power, Full of Wisdom" (35:2). The Prophet said:

> Be mindful of Allah, and you will find Him in front of you. If you ask, ask of Allah; if you seek help, seek help of Allah. Know that if the Nations were to gather together to benefit you with anything, it would benefit you only with something that Allah had already prescribed for you, and that if they gather together to harm you with anything, they would harm you only with something Allah had already prescribed for you. The pens have been lifted and the pages have dried.[317]

In contrast, false gods can neither benefit nor cause harm: "They call upon such deities, besides Allah, as can neither hurt nor profit them: that is straying far indeed (from the Way)! They call on one whose hurt is nearer than his profit: evil, indeed, is the patron, and evil the companion (for help)!" (22:12–13). "Say: 'Call on those – besides Him – whom ye fancy: they have neither the power to remove your troubles from you nor to change them'" (17:56) "Say: 'Call upon other (gods) whom you fancy, besides Allah: they have no power, – not the weight of an atom, – in the heavens or on earth: no (sort of) share have they therein, nor is any of them a helper to Allah.'" (34:22) "They serve, besides Allah, what can hurt them not nor profit them, and they say: 'These are our intercessors with Allah.' Say: 'Do ye indeed inform Allah of something He knows not, in the heavens or on earth? – Glory to Him! and far is He above the partners they ascribe (to Him!)'" (10:18). "And those whom they invoke besides Allah have no power of intercession; – only he who bears witness to the Truth, and with full knowledge" (43:86; also see 10:106; 25:55; 21:66; 6:71; 5:76). Actually false gods do not possess the power to benefit or harm themselves:

> Say: "Do ye then take (for worship) protectors other than Him, such as have no power either for good or for harm to themselves?" Say: "Are the blind equal with those who see? Or the depths of darkness equal with Light?" Or do they assign to Allah partners who have created (anything) as He has created, so that the creation seemed to them similar? Say: "Allah is the Creator of all things: He is the One, the Supreme and Irresistible." (13:16)

"Yet have they taken, besides Him, gods that can create nothing but are themselves created: that have no control of hurt or good to themselves; nor can they control Death nor Life nor Resurrection" (25:3). If they are unable to help themselves, how could they help anybody else?

> Do they indeed ascribe to Him as partners things that can create nothing, but are themselves created? No aid can they give them, nor can they aid themselves....Verily those whom ye call upon besides Allah are servants like unto you: call upon them, and let them listen to your prayer, if you are (indeed) truthful!... But those ye call upon besides Him, are unable to help you, and indeed to help themselves. (7:191–197; also see 21:42; 36:75)

From the above discussion it becomes evident that the Qur'an has categorically refuted all kinds of polytheism, henotheism and associationism, in addition to vigorously affirming the transcendental otherness and Godhead of the One God. In the Qur'an just as the concept of *tawḥīd* is presented with strong and convincing arguments, likewise that of polytheism, henotheism and associationism is rejected with strong and irrefutable evidence. The Qur'an does not confine itself to mere assertions of God's Oneness, Unity, and absolute Sovereignty. It uses various arguments both logical and cosmological to substantiate such claims. The Qur'an implies a variety of methods, processes, techniques, thought processes and cognitive categories to drive home the point of the transcendental uniqueness of God Almighty. It safeguards an already self-explaining and convincing concept with additional measures and parameters so as to allow no doubt or confusion to enter concerning it. As belief in a strict monotheism is the primordial act needed for the salvation of humanity in its entirety, the Qur'an presents this belief in a very simple, straightforward and logical way. The countless Qur'anic passages which delineate this belief are so simple and clear that no external help is needed to elaborate the point of their emphasis. They are self-explanatory and self-sufficient in this regard. They are also coherent, systematic and methodical. Unlike the Old Testament, there exist no layers of progressive or evolutionary revelation or conflicting tendencies in the Qur'an. Qur'anic monotheism is thorough, transcendental, unique and systematic to the core.

The Qur'anic Concept of Monotheism: *Al-Tawḥīd*

The external as well as internal unity of God is described in Islam by the word *al-tawḥīd*. *Tawḥīd* is the verbal noun of the second form of the root *w-ḥ-d*. It indicates the action of unifying and of conferring unity. Etymologically it designates the knowledge one has of the unity of a thing. Although the word *tawḥīd* is non-Qur'anic, it does appear in the authentic sayings of the Prophet Muhammad.[318]

When the religious sciences later came to be developed in the Islamic community, the particular science of *ʿIlm al-Kalām* (meaning the science of the word of God or about God, to be discussed later in the chapter) was also called *ʿIlm al-Tawḥīd* (the science of divine unicity). However, when the term *tawḥīd* is used in reference to God Almighty it means realization of the divine unity and transcendence in all of man's actions directly or indirectly related to God. It is the belief that Allah is One and Unique, without partner in His dominion and His actions (*rubūbiyyah*), One without similitude in His essence and attributes (*asmā' wa ṣifāt*), and One without rival in His divinity and in worship (*ulūhiyyah/ʿibādah*). The science of *Tawḥīd* revolves around these three constituent elements so much so that omission of any of these at times overlapping categories will nullify the essence and mission of the science as well as the creed.

These three categories of *tawḥīd,* are sometimes referred to as *Tawḥīd al-Dhāt* (unity of the Being), *Tawḥīd al-Ṣifāt* (Unity of the Attributes) and *Tawḥīd al-Afʿāl* (Unity of the Actions). The Unity of God, according to the Qur'an, implies that God is the Absolute One in His person (*dhāt*), Absolute One in His attributes (*ṣifāt*) and Absolute One in His works (*afʿāl*). The Oneness of His person means that there is neither plurality of gods, nor plurality of persons in the Godhead; the Oneness of attributes implies that no other being possesses one or more of the Divine attributes in the absolute sense; His Oneness in works implies that none can do the works which God has done, or which God may do. It may be added here, that this tripartite division of *tawḥīd* owes its origin to the Qur'an, as its material is wholly Qur'anic, though the specific names mentioned above have resulted from later theological expositions.[319]

We have already discussed several passages of the Qur'an that give detailed description of the concept of *tawḥīd* in Islamic Scripture without alluding to the aforementioned categories. Here we will expand upon these three aspects of *tawḥīd* and what they imply to demonstrate how meticulously the Qur'an has explained and safeguarded the absolute monotheism and divine transcendence of God, and how such an elaborated and transcendental concept of the Deity differs from other faith traditions.

1: ***Tawḥīd al-Rubūbiyyah*** or Oneness of Lordship: This kind of *tawḥīd* means to accept Almighty God as the only *Rabb*. The word *Rabb* combines two senses; that of fostering, bringing up, or nourishing, and that of regulating, completing, and accomplishing. The word *Rabb* signifies fostering of a thing in various stages and conditions until it attains perfection. Mawdudi quotes many examples from Arabic literature to conclude that the word *Rabb* entails the following meanings:

1. One who brings up, rears, fosters or nourishes, or is responsible for doing all or one or more than one of these;
2. Guardian, patron; one who supervises or is responsible for carrying out improvements;
3. One who occupies a central or focal position, who himself gathers people round himself of his own or round whom people gather of themselves;
4. Leader, head, chief, or lord; one whose word is obeyed, and whose supremacy or lordship acknowledged, and who has authority to dispose of men or things;
5. Owner; master.[320]

The Qur'an has used the word *Rabb* in all these five senses.

Tawḥīd al-Rubūbiyyah, then, means to accept Almighty God not only as the Creator but also the only Sustainer, the Nourisher, the Lord, the Master, the Sovereign, the Supreme authority. Therefore, when a Muslim is asked to affirm that, "There is no Deity but One God", he is being asked to state that there is no other Creator and Sustainer of the universe, no other Ruler nor Law-Giver, no other Reality that can harm or benefit, give or withhold, cause life or death, except with the permission of God Almighty. He creates and sustains creation out of His mercy, without any need for it. Nobody can challenge His sovereignty. He is an exalted Lord who is not accountable to anyone, while everybody else is accountable to Him, "He cannot be questioned for His acts, but they will be questioned (for theirs)" (21:23).

The passages expressing *Tawḥīd al-Rubūbiyyah* prevail throughout the Qur'an with the first Qur'anic revelation itself containing the very core of *Tawḥīd al-Rubūbiyyah*: "Read in the name of thy Lord and Cherisher, Who created, created man, out of a clot: Proclaim! and thy Lord is Most Bountiful, He Who taught (the use of) the Pen, taught man that which he knew not" (96:1–5). The first chapter of the Qur'an, called *al-Fātiḥah,* starts with the same message: "Praise be to Allah the Cherisher and Sustainer of the Worlds: Most Gracious, Most Merciful" (1:2–3). The formula "Lord and Cherisher of the Worlds", occurs 41 times in the Qur'an in addition to its mention in *Sūrah al-Fātiḥah*:

> Say: "Truly, my prayer and my service of sacrifice, my life and my death, are (all) for Allah, the Cherisher of the Worlds: No partner hath He: this am I commanded, and I am the first of those who submit to His Will. Say: "Shall I seek for (my) Lord other than Allah. When He is the Cherisher of all things (that exist)?" (6:162–64)

> Your Guardian Lord is Allah, Who created the heavens and the earth in six Days, then He settled Himself on the Throne: He draweth the night as a veil over the day, each seeking the other in rapid succession: and the sun, the moon, and the stars, (all) are subservient by His Command. Verily His are the creation and the Command, Blessed be Allah, the Cherisher and Sustainer of the Worlds! (7:54)

Ibn Kathīr narrates from Ibn ʿAbbās, Mujāhid, and Aḥmad ibn Ḥanbal, and al-Shawkānī narrates from Ibn Abī Ḥātim, that the six days mentioned in verse 7:54 are not days of the week as known to man but rather "days" in accordance with God's scale where each day is equal to a thousand years. As the Qur'an itself informs us, "A Day in the sight of thy Lord is like a thousand years of your reckoning" (22:47).[321] For Ibn Kathīr and al-Shawkānī the verse denotes that the absolute rule, supreme authority, sovereignty, and unrestricted right of disposal belongs to Almighty God alone.[322]

The main thrust of the verse is that God after creating the universe did not detach Himself from nor become indifferent to His creation. He effectively rules over the universe as a whole as well as every part of it. All power and sovereignty rest with Him. The universe is not on autopilot as some scientists seem to suggest. It is actively governed and administered by God Almighty. The verse dispels misconceptions of absolute human or cosmic autonomy. Two suppositions come into play when God is divorced from the cosmos. Firstly, beings other than God are considered to have the power to make or mar man's destiny. Man is bound to turn to these beings in devotion and subservience. The second possibility is for man to consider himself the master of his own destiny. In this case man considers himself independent of and indifferent to any higher being. The vocabulary employed in the verse denotes divine kingship, dominion and sovereignty to dispel these suppositions. The absolute unity and transcendence of God is maintained with regards to authority and sovereignty.

So prevalent is the concept of God's absolute Sovereignty and Lordship in the Qur'an, so much the focal point, that no reader of the Qur'an can possibly miss it:

> Whatever is in the heavens and on earth, declares the Praises and Glory of Allah: for He is the Exalted in Might, the Wise. *To Him belongs the dominion of the heavens and the earth*: it is He Who gives Life and Death; and He has Power over all things. He is the First and the Last, the Evident and the Hidden: and Has full knowledge of all things. He it is Who created the heavens and the earth in six Days, then He established Himself on the Throne. He knows what enters within the earth and what comes forth out of it, what comes down from heaven and what mounts up to it. And He is with you wheresoever ye may be. And Allah sees well all that ye do. *To Him belongs the dominion of the heavens and the earth: and all affairs go back to Allah.* He merges Night into Day, and He merges Day into Night; and He has full knowledge of the secrets of (all) hearts. (57:1–6) [italics mine]

> He created the heavens and the earth in true (proportions): He makes the Night overlap the Day, and the Day overlap the Night: He has subjected the sun and the moon (to His law): each one follows a course for a time appointed. Is not He the Exalted in Power- He Who forgives again and again? He created you (all) from a single Person: then created, of like nature, his mate; and He sent down eight head of cattle in pairs: He creates you, in the wombs of your mothers, in stages, one after another, in three veils of darkness. *Such is Allah, your Lord and Cherisher: to Him belongs (all) dominion.* There is no god but He: then how are ye turned away (from your true Lord)? (39:5–6; see also 2:107; 3:26; 3:189; 5:17; 5:18; 5:40; 5:120; 9:116; 17:111; 24:42; 42:49; 43:85; 45:27; 48:14; 64:1; 67:1; 85:9). [italics mine]

The same point is reinforced, underscored, and made perfectly clear with other examples:

> It is Allah Who causeth the seed-grain and the date-stone to split and sprout. He causeth the living to issue from the dead. And He is the One to cause the dead to issue from the living. That is Allah: then how are ye deluded away from the truth? He it is that cleaveth the day-break (from the dark): He makes the night for rest and tranquillity, and the sun and moon for the reckoning (of time): such is the judgment and ordering of (Him), the Exalted in Power, the Omniscient. It is He Who maketh the stars (as beacons) for you, that ye may guide yourselves, with their help, through the dark spaces of land and sea: We detail Our Signs for people who know. It is He Who hath produced you from a single soul: then there is a resting place and a repository: We detail Our Signs for people who understand. It is He Who sendeth down rain from the skies: with it We produce vegetation of all kinds: from some We produce green (crops), out of which We produce, close-compounded grain out of the date-palm and its sheaths (or spathes) (come) clusters of dates hanging low and near: and (then there are) gardens of grapes, and olives, and pomegranates, each similar (in kind) yet different (in variety): when they begin to bear fruit, feast your eyes with the fruit and the ripeness thereof. Behold! in these things there are Signs for people who believe. (6:95–99; also see 13:2–4).[323]

Almighty God is the Creator of mankind as He is the Creator of everything else in the universe:

> O mankind! if ye have a doubt about the Resurrection, (consider) that We created you out of dust, then out of sperm, then out of a clot, then out of morsel of flesh, partly formed and partly unformed, in order that We may manifest (our power) to you; and We cause whom We will to rest in the wombs for an appointed term, then do We bring you out as babes, then (foster you) that you may reach your age of full strength; and some of you are called

> to die, and some are sent back to the feeblest old age, so that they know nothing after having known (much).... (22:5; also see 2:21; 6:2; 16:4; 16:70; 30:20; 30:40; 35:11; 37:96; 40:67; 55:14 etc).

K. L. Moore, Professor of Anatomy at the University of Toronto, was "amazed at the scientific accuracy of these statements which were made in the 7th century AC"[324] Moore has discussed various verses from the Qur'an demonstrating their scientific accuracy. According to him, the stages of human embryos delineated by this Qur'anic verse in the 7th century were "not proposed until the 1940's (Streeter, 1942), and the stages used nowadays...were not adopted worldwide until a few years ago..."[325] He concludes: "The agreement I have found between statements in the Koran and sayings in the Hadith may help to close the gap between science and religion which has existed for so many years."[326]

Moreover, human beings are not left to the mercy of nature or any other agency. The Qur'an insists that after their creation, it is God and He alone Who provides for them: "It is Allah Who has created you; further, He has provided for you your sustenance..." (30:40), "For Allah is He Who gives (all) Sustenance, – Lord of Power, – Steadfast (for ever)" (51:58), "Allah enlarges the sustenance (which He gives) to whichever of His servants He pleases; and He (similarly) grants by (strict) measure, (as He pleases): for Allah has full knowledge of all things" (29:62). Also see 13:26; 16:71; 17:30; 28:82; 30:37; 34:36; 34:39; 39:52; 42:12. In His hand is power and honor:

> Say: "O Allah! Lord of Power (and Rule), thou givest Power to whom Thou pleasest, and Thou strippest off Power from whom Thou pleasest: Thou enduest with honor whom Thou pleasest, and Thou bringest low whom Thou pleasest: in Thy hand is all good. Verily, over all things Thou hast power. Thou causest the Night to gain on the day, and Thou causest the day to gain on the Night; Thou bringest the Living out of the Dead, and Thou bringest the Dead out of the Living; and Thou givest sustenance to whom Thou pleasest, without measure." (3:26–27)

> He is the Irresistible, Supreme over His servants, and He sets guardians over you.... (6:61)

In short, to God belongs the creation, the dominion (*al-mulk*), the Command (*al-amr*) and the rule (*al-ḥukm* 6:57; 6:62; 12:40; 12:67; 13:41; 28:70; 28:88; 40:12). Nobody shared in the creation, "I called them not to witness the creation of the heavens and the earth, not (even) their own creation: nor is it for Me to take as helpers such as lead (men) astray!" (18:51). No one can share His dominion and actions, "Say: 'Praise be to Allah, Who begets no son, and has no partner in (His) dominion: nor (needs) He any to protect Him from humiliation: yea, magnify Him for His greatness and glory'"(17:111).

Furthermore, the Qur'an insists that the idea of the Oneness of the Divine Lordship is ingrained in human nature, due to a covenant which human beings had made with God prior to their coming to this existence: "When thy Lord drew forth from the Children of Adam – from their loins – their descendants, and made them testify concerning themselves, (saying): 'Am I not your Lord (who cherishes and sustains you)?' – They said: 'Yea! We do testify!' (This), lest ye should say on the Day of Judgment: 'Of this we were never mindful'"(7:172). The best interpretation of this event is found in a statement made by Ubayy ibn Kaᶜb, who has probably given the substance of what he heard from the Prophet himself. Ubayy's reports that:

> God gathered all human beings, divided them into different groups, granted them human form and the faculty of speech, made them enter into a covenant, and then making them witnesses against themselves He asked them: 'Am I not your Lord?' they replied: 'Assuredly you are Our Lord.' Then God told them: 'I call upon the sky and the earth and your own progenitor, Adam, to be witness against you lest you should say on the Day of Judgment that you were ignorant of this....' [327]

This covenant is the "*fiṭrah*" (nature), which the Qur'an refers to in verse 30:30 of *Sūrah al-Rūm:* "The nature in which Allah has made mankind: no change (there is) in the work (wrought) by Allah: that is the true Religion: but most among mankind know not." The Prophet emphasized the same when he said: "Every child is born with the nature (*ʿalā al-fiṭrah*)...."[328] M. Asad observes:

> According to the Qur'an, the ability to perceive the existence of the Supreme Power is inborn in human nature (*fitrah*); and it is this instinctive cognition – which may or may not be subsequently blurred by self-indulgence or adverse environmental influences – that makes every sane human being "bear witness about himself" before God. As so often in the Qur'an, God's "speaking" and man's "answering" is metonym for the creative act of God and of man's existential response to it.[329]

Al-Shawkānī interprets the event as allegorical,[330] and Ibn Kathīr narrates from al-Ḥasan al-Baṣarī a report that amounts to the same.[331]

In short, the Qur'anic sense of the Oneness of Divine Lordship means to accept Almighty God as the only Creator, and the Sustainer who after creating everything other than Him is continuously sustaining creation by active involvement in its affairs, including the world of men. All that exists or takes place is the expression of His power and will, from the behavior of each individual atom to the large-scale occurrences of human history to events of cosmic proportion. His is the creation and His is the rule and sovereignty. Nobody has any share in any of these acts of "Lordship". Izutsu rightly points out:

> In the Islamic system, on the contrary, creation marks just the beginning of the Divine rule over the created things. All human affairs even the minutest and apparently most insignificant details of life are put under the strict supervision of Allah. And the most important point about this is that this God, according to the Koran, is the God of Justice, who never does any wrong (*zulm*) to anybody.[332]

Therefore, it can be stated that the *tawḥīd* of Divine Lordship places God over and above this universe of man and matter, as its Creator, Sustainer, and Master, and not as someone bound to any of the limitations of this utilitarian sphere of here and now.

2: ***Tawḥīd al-Ulūhiyyah*** (The Unity of Worship or *ʿibādah*): To accept and believe that there is no *Ilāh* (deity) other than God Almighty and to *worship Him alone* is the core of ***Tawḥīd al-Ulūhiyyah***. As mentioned earlier, the word *al-Ilāh* in the Arabic language means the one who is *al-ma'lūh* meaning *al-maʿbūd* (worshipped.) Worship or *al-ʿibādah* means utmost humbleness, extreme self-abasement, humility, submission, obedience, compliance and service to God. Ibn al-Qayyim defines it as, "the perfect love accompanied with total submission."[333] Therefore, *Tawḥīd al-Ulūhiyyah* denotes sincere and unadulterated inner as well as external worship of God, an absolute sense of dependence upon and devotion to Him alone with the exclusion of everything other than Him. This second kind of *al-tawḥīd* eliminates all possibilities of associationism, trinitarianism and saintly worship. In spite of the wide range of implications contained in the first category *of al-tawḥīd,* firm belief in the Oneness of the Divine Lordship is not sufficient to fulfill the requirements of the Qur'anic concept of *tawḥīd* or monotheism. It must be accompanied with a strong faith in the Oneness of Divine worship, devotion, and obedience in order for *tawḥīd* to be completed. This aspect of the Qur'anic monotheism is unique to Islam and distinguishes it from the Christian understanding of monotheism. Christianity in its various forms has historically allowed worship of Jesus, Mary and other saintly figures. Islam denounces such worship as an act of *shirk* or associationism.

To fulfil the transcendental monotheism of Islam one has to confess the divine lordship of God as well as one's worship in submission. This point is substantiated by the fact that the Qur'an vehemently attacked the Makkan belief system as one of associationism dubbing its followers as *Mushrikūn* (polytheists) in spite of their confirming many aspects of the oneness of divine lordship. The Qur'an reports of the polytheists of Makkah that:

> If thou ask them, who it is that created the heavens and the earth. *They will certainly say, "(Allah)"*. Say: "Praise be to Allah." But most of them understand not. To Allah belong all things in heaven and earth: verily Allah is He (that is) free of all wants, worthy of all praise. (31:25–26)[334] [italics mine]

Now it is interesting to note that the polytheists of Makkah did believe that God was Exalted in Power, full of Knowledge (43:9). Further, they also believed that other natural phenomena like the sun and moon were also the creation of God Almighty, "If indeed thou ask them who created the heavens and the earth and subjected the sun and moon (to His Law), *they will certainly reply, 'Allah'*. How are they then deluded away (from the truth)?" (29:61). They also confessed that God was the only source of rain and cultivation, "And if indeed thou ask them who it is that sends down rain from the sky, and gives life therewith to the earth after its death, *they will certainly reply, 'Allah'*! Say, 'Praise be to Allah!' But most of them understand not." (29:63). They also recognized the fact that they owed their own creation to God Almighty, "If thou ask them, *Who created them, they will certainly say, Allah:* how then are they deluded away (from Truth)?" (43:87). They understood that both sustenance, life, death, and the keys of affairs were all in the hands of God:

> Say: "Who is it that sustains you (in life) from the sky and from the earth? Or who is it that has power over hearing and sight? And who is it that brings out the living from the dead and the dead from the living? And who is it that rules and regulates all affairs?" They will soon say, "Allah". Say, "Will ye not then show piety (to Him)?" (10:31)

They also confessed God to be the Absolute Lord of the heavens and the earth:

> Say: "To whom belong the earth and all beings therein? (Say) if ye know!" *They will say, "To Allah!"* Say: "Yet will ye not receive admonition?" Say: "Who is the Lord of the seven heavens, and the Lord of the Mighty Throne?" *They will say, "(They belong) to Allah."* Say: "Will ye not then fear?" Say: "Who is it in whose hands is the sovereignty of all things, – Who protects (all), but is not protected (of any)? (Say) if ye know." *They will say, "(It belongs) to Allah."* Say: "Then how are ye deluded?" (23:84–89) [italics mine]

So, given all this acknowledgement of the Creator why were the Makkans polytheists? Izutsu observes that though the Makkans believed in Allah as the Creator of the universe, this belief did not play a vital role in their daily life. The occurrence of

> words like *khalq* "creation", *khaliq* "creator", *bari* "originator" etc. in pre-Islamic literature should not mislead us into thinking that the concept of Divine Creation was playing a decisive role in the Jahili Weltanschauung... Unlike the Koranic system in which Allah the Creator governs the entire Weltanshauung Jahiliyyah did not attach great importance to this semantic field... This is tantamount to saying that the idea of Allah's being the very "source" of human existence, if it was there, meant very little to the minds of the pre-Islamic Arabs. And this is why the Koran tries so hard to bring home to them the very significance of this idea and to awaken them to the grave implication of it.[335]

Although Allah was conceived of as the divine lord, this fact didn't really amount to an awful lot for he was very much regarded as a distant God, put aside, relegated to the back burner as it were, in matters of daily life including society's social, financial and political dealings. God did not interfere in man's affairs. Thus there existed a clear distinction between what was thought to be religious and what was perceived to be mundane. The dualistic dichotomy of this strange mixture of the sacred and profane was so complete that Allah, as stated, despite being Lord, in fact was not given much of a role to play in the mundane affairs of day to day life. Hence, remote and really preferred out of the way He was relegated to the detached realms of heaven and abstract religious metaphysics. Izutsu elaborates:

> In the jahili system, the creative activity of Allah is both the beginning and the end of His intervention in human affairs. He does not as a rule take care of what He has brought into existence just like an irresponsible father who never cares for his children; the task is taken over...by another Being called Dahr. In the Islamic system, on the contrary, creation marks just the beginning of the Divine rule over the created things.[336]

Interestingly, this ancient Makkan conception of the Divine coincides closely with many modern secular trends. Much like the Makkans, God The Creator is perceived today as divorced from the world and the cosmos, with the universe and all that it contains somehow thought to run on autopilot. Ergo, the modern concept of "Nature" comes very close to the Makkans' understanding of the being, or force, they termed *dahr*. The *Tawḥīd al-Ulūhiyyah* aimed at purging God of any and every element of associationism, or multiplicity, in man's conception of the Divine Being, as well as establishing with full and clear force God's absolute control and running of the universe and His creation. Notions of God's practical divorce from nature and man were eradicated, putting God back in the driving seat as Ruler and Lawgiver, fully in control of man's daily affairs and surroundings.

Despite their view of God as a distant force, the pagans of Makkah used nevertheless to call upon Him in times of distress: "Now, if they embark on a boat, *they call on Allah, making their devotion sincerely (and exclusively) to Him;* but when He has delivered them safely to (dry) land, behold, they give a share (of their worship to others)!" (29:65). "When a wave covers them like the canopy (of clouds), *they call upon Allah, offering Him sincere devotion.* But when He has delivered them safely to land, there are among them those that falter between (right and wrong)..." (31:32). Izutsu calls this attitude a "temporary monotheism."[337] The Qur'an has elaborated upon this point in several passages:

> He it is who enableth you to traverse through land and sea; till when ye even board ships; – they sail with them with a favorable wind, and they rejoice thereat; then comes a stormy wind and the waves come to them from all sides, and they think they are being overwhelmed: *they pray unto Allah, sincerely offering (their) duty unto Him, saying, "If Thou dost deliver us from this, we shall truly show our gratitude!"* But when He delivereth them, behold! they transgress insolently through the earth in defiance of right! (10:22–23)

In the time of difficulty "*Lo, it is to Him alone that you cry* and then, if He so will, He removes the distress for which you had cried to Him.

Then you forget the partners you had set up with Allah" (6:41). ʿIkrimah, the son of Abū Jahl was a disbeliever at the time of Makkah's conquest, a vehement opponent of the Prophet and the Muslims. He fled to Jeddah and sailed from there towards Abyssinia. During the voyage the boat ran into a threatening storm. As a result, people began calling on their gods and goddesses to save them. Later, when the storm grew even worse and the passengers were convinced that the boat would sink, they began to feel it was time to call on God alone, for He alone could save them. This occurrence opened ʿIkrimah's eyes, and his heart cried out that calling upon Allah alone was precisely what the Prophet had constantly told people. This experience proved to be a turning point in ʿIkrimah's life and he accepted Islam.

Furthermore, the Makkans used to fear and worship Allah in many ways. They honored the sanctity of the Kaʿbah, the Sanctuary in Makkah, faithfully devoted various types of worship to God, performed Hajj (pilgrimage), recited a kind of "*talbiyah*" (the monotheistic formula Muslims recite during days of Hajj),[338] served visiting pilgrims (9:19), offered a kind of prayer,[339] fasted certain days of the year,[340] offered charity in God's name (6:136), started their writings with the name of Allah,[341] and sacrificed animals using His name etc. Yet, in spite of all these seemingly monotheistic beliefs and actions, the Qur'an dubbed them as disbelievers (*kuffār*) and polytheists (*mushrikūn*). The reason being their practice of associationism, which opened the door to multiplicity and compromise of the divine unity. In other words, they associated others as gods with God, invoking them, worshiping them and taking them as mediators and intercessors between God and His creation. "Instead of God they serve what neither harms nor benefits them, and they say: '*These are our intercessors with God*'" (10:18).

> Is it not to Allah that sincere devotion is due? But those who take for protectors others than Allah (say): "*We only serve them in order that they may bring us nearer to Allah.*" Truly Allah will judge between them in that wherein they differ. But Allah guides not such as are false and ungrateful. Had Allah wished to take to Himself a son, He could have chosen whom He pleased out of those whom He doth create: but Glory be to Him! (He transcends such things.) He is Allah, the One, the Overpowering. (39:3–4)

The Makkans lacked purity of worship. To the Qur'an this was paganism. That such a kind of religiosity prevailed in the Arabian Peninsula at the time of Muhammad is confirmed by historical research and by modern scholarship. Joseph Henninger concludes his famous work *Pre-Islamic Bedouin Religion* with the observation that:

> Here then are the elements of this religion: Allah, creator of the world, supreme and undisputed lord, but relegated to the background in the cultic and practical life of the people; next, manifesting the rudiments of a polytheism, several *astral divinities* (at least that of the planet Venus) and *atmospheric divinities* (perhaps the attributes of a creator god which have been hypostatized); finally, ancestors and *jinn*, these last having more importance in the belief system than in the cult. All of this, moreover, is somewhat vague and far from being organized into a real pantheon or hierarchical system.[342]

Discussing the pre-Islamic formulas of *talbiyah* at length, M. J. Kister concludes that the formulas provide a clue towards a better understanding of the religious ideas of the tribes during the period of *jāhiliyyah*. The tribes of course had their gods, and the places of worship of these gods were usually shared by other tribes allied with them or living in their neighborhood. "They believed however in a supreme God, who had His House in Mecca. On their pilgrimage to Mecca they directed themselves to this God, who held supremacy over their tribal gods." Kister further observes that when intending to perform the pilgrimage to the Sanctuary at Makkah, every tribe would come to (the abode of) their idol and pray there; then they would set out uttering the *talbiyah*...until they reached Makkah:

> This report demonstrates to what extent there prevailed harmonious co-existence and co-operation between the tribal deities and the supreme God of Mecca. The Jahiliyyah tribes cannot be said to have been straightforward polytheists; they were *mushrikun*, i.e. while accepting and admitting the existence and supreme authority of God, they associated other deities with Him.[343]

F. E. Peters observes that Allah was unquestionably neither an unknown nor an unimportant deity to the Quraysh when Muhammad began preaching his exclusive worship at Makkah. What is equally certain is that Allah had what the Qur'an disdainfully calls "associates," other gods and goddesses who shared both His cult and His shrine. Peter writes:

> The processional chant of the pagans of the "Era of Ignorance" was, we are told, "Here I am, O Allah, here I am; you have no partners except such a partner as you have; you possess him and all that is his." The last clause may reflect what was an emerging tendency toward henotheism, the recognition of Allah as the "High God" of Mecca... the Quraysh are relentlessly chastised for "partnering God," and from what we otherwise know of Muhammad's Mecca, the charge is not an unjust one.[344]

David Waines gives more details of the Makkans' belief system; for instance he explains that for the pagans Allah was the "High God"; neither the sole object of worship nor indeed the sole existent god. For Makkans Allah merely stood above, or apart from, all other tribal divinities. Despite this marginalization He nevertheless played a particular role in pagan life: first, as the giver of rain, to ensure the sustenance of life for the inhabitants of the arid desert. Second, as the guarantor of oaths, and therefore regarded as crucial to the binding nature of agreements, tribal or individual, sworn in His name. Indeed violation of such an oath was deemed a grave offense, as it involved serious consequences for social peace and order. Waines writes:

> In a somewhat vague way, too, Allah was viewed as the creator of the heavens and the earth, although in general no moral conclusions seem to have been drawn from this regarding an individual's behavior and future well-being.... Thus in matters of daily concern, Allah occupied a particular place, but alongside other gods in the Arab's pantheon.[345]

The other gods (*Lāt, Manāt, ʿUzzā, Hubal* etc.) were consulted on various matters of domestic and other concerns. For instance the setting of a date for marriage, confirmation of a child's parentage, the settlement of a quarrel etc. as well as the most propitious moment to embark upon a journey. Matters such as these all fell within the purview of the partner gods whose advice would subsequently be sought. In addition their help, as mentioned earlier, would also be sought whether for rain or assistance in battle against a rival tribe and so on. K. Armstrong notes that the "shrine [Kaʿbah] was also surrounded by 360 idols, or effigies of the gods, that may have been the totems of all different tribes that came to worship there during the appointed month."[346] It was not only in Makkah and around the Kaʿbah that other gods were being worshipped. They were celebrated all over the Arabian Peninsula.

What becomes quickly apparent is that modern western scholarship differs little from the Qur'anic depiction of the pre-Islamic Arab religion. The former also substantiates the claim made earlier that the Qur'anic concept of monotheism neither legitimizes nor allows worship, devotion and obedience to and of other gods besides Allah. The act of sole worship, absolute devotion, and utmost submission to the One God is more fundamental and intrinsic to the Qur'anic concept of the Deity than belief in Him as the sole Creator, Sustainer, and Master of the universe. For the Qur'an, *Tawḥīd al-Rubūbiyyah* without *Tawḥīd al-Ulūhiyyah* is mere polytheism. Perhaps there would not have been much opposition to Muhammad's message had it not been for his uncompromising stance against any and every kind of associationism with Allah. The Qur'anic concept of the Deity was intensely stringent, approving nothing except the absolute pure worship of and total devotion to the One and Only God. This was the primordial issue and the demarcation line between the Qur'anic understanding of the Deity and that of the pagans' conception of God. And it is this that the Makkans recognized and disputed: "Has he made gods (all) into One? Truly this is a strange thing!" (Qur'an 38:5).

M. Watt, theorizes that the pre-Islamic pagan religion was the result of a long development. Prominent among the objects originally worshipped were stones and trees. These were sometimes regarded not as divinities but as divine houses or dwellings. The nomads appear to have had little serious belief in them, perhaps because they were originally the gods of agricultural communities. In view of the opposition to

Muhammad at Makkah it is conceivable that certain small groups there, especially those concerned with particular religious ceremonies, had a slightly higher degree of belief. Watt portrays the pre-Islamic Arabs as faithless heathens in an effort to emphasize the politico-economic nature of the conflict between the Makkans and the Prophet, and to insinuate that Muhammad's opposition to the Makkans was not primarily due to their associationism but mostly due to their faithlessness.

Perhaps it is too much to assume that the nomadic Arab tribes had little serious belief in their gods because they were originally the gods of agricultural communities. Rather, and a fact which even Watt recognizes, is their obvious commitment to these gods, evident not only from the intense animosity they displayed toward the Qur'anic message but also in the type of sacrifices they made to preserve the ways of their forefathers with regards to the worship of these deities. It was not only the Makkans who fiercely opposed the Qur'anic message fighting it with every means possible. In fact, the entire Arabic community, with very few exceptions, sided with them in their struggle against Prophet Muhammad and his religion. The issue of the gods always seemed to be the major concern continuously brought up in their dialogue with the Prophet or his aides. Even prior to the coming of Islam, what is clearly apparent is the majority of the Arabs' commitment to their various gods and goddesses in many aspects of their lives. K. Armstrong quotes a revealing incident in which Zayd ibn ᶜAmr is expelled from Makkah by his very own brother Khaṭṭāb for merely criticizing the Makkan goddesses. She expounds:

> The story is instructive. It eloquently expresses the questing spirit of some of the Arabs at this time. But it also shows the opposition that anybody who threatened the pagan religion could expect to face. There were many Quraysh like Khattab ibn Nufayl who were devoted to the faith of their fathers and could not bear to hear a word against the old gods and goddesses.[347]

However, this observation does not imply high and lofty claims about a developed intellectual system of belief regarding these deities on the part of the pre-Islamic Arabs. And the same was further not the case everywhere in Arabia. Not all of the Arabs were such staunch supporters of, and unwavering believers in, these deities or their abilities to help or harm them, that they never violated their worship of them. Quite the reverse. There are several incidents where as a result of a failure or disaster, some of the gods are abandoned, disrespected, and even broken into pieces. Imru'ū al-Qays is a typical example of this attitude. Hitti informs us that:

> Having set out to avenge the murder of his father he stopped at the temple of dhul-al-Khalasah to consult the oracle by means of drawing arrows. Upon drawing 'abandon' thrice, he hurled the broken arrows at the idol exclaiming, 'Accursed One! had it been thy father who was murdered thou wouldst not have forbidden my avenging him.'[348]

This sort of disbelief was not due to the fact of the gods being originally gods of agricultural communities or not taken seriously at all times. In reality, the reaction seems to have been due to the greater importance given to the respect and veneration of one's honor, tribe, and tribal ties, denoted by what was called *murū'ah* or "tribal humanism". Watt himself has observed that this was the effective religion of the Arabs of Muhammad's day.

In the presence of this pervasive attitude of status pride, it is easy to discern that the archaic religion or the gods would sometimes be abandoned or left unattended if the act of worship stood in the way of *ʿirḍ* or personal honor, or the realization of some tribal goal or interest. Therefore, Hitti's observation seems to be more accurate than Watt's claims of the Arabs' faithlessness. Hitti notes that, "To spiritual impulses he (the pagan Arab) was luke-warm, even indifferent. His conformity to religious practice followed tribal inertia and was dictated by his conservative respect for tradition."[349] To Armstrong this was the reason that,"Muhammad is constantly accused by his enemies of being a danger to society, of neglecting the religion of the fathers and of atheism..."[350]

We can therefore infer that the pre-Islamic Arabs were "religious" in their own way yet different from modern connotations of the term "religious". Their religiosity owed much to their enthusiasm for continuity with the past or traditionalism rather than the outcome of an intellectually thought out and developed system of belief. As such, this enthusiasm would fade if in conflict with their craze for tribal honor and pride, *murū'ah*. We can also infer that they worshipped idols made of wood and stone, angels, jinn, saints and other lesser deities as intercessors and intermediaries between themselves and Allah, regarding these deities as absolute, independent gods, autonomous from Allah, the supreme Deity, that is other than Him.

It was against such notions of divinity, and not mere faithlessness, that the Qur'an preached its exclusive transcendental monotheism, the strict monotheism which excluded the worship, mediation, intercession and help of anyone other than Allah in the absolute religious sense, regarding any such act as detrimental to the very core of monotheism. "And they have been commanded no more than this: *To worship Allah, offering Him sincere devotion*, being true (in faith)..." (98:5). "Say: '*I have been ordered to serve God sincerely, [making] religion exclusively His. I have been ordered to be the first of those who submit their will to Him.*' Say: "I fear the torment of an awful day if I should disobey my Lord.' Say: '*God do I worship sincerely; my religion belongs to Him...*'" (39:11–14).

To the Qur'an both categories of the doctrine of *al-tawḥīd* discussed thus far, are mutually inter-connected; two sides of the same coin. The Qur'an leads us from the Oneness of Lordship to the Oneness of worship and devotion: "O Men! Remember the grace of Allah unto you! Is there a Creator, other than Allah, to give you sustenance from heaven or earth? There is no god but He: how then are ye perverted?" (35:3):

> Or, who has created the heavens and the earth, and who sends you down rain from the sky? Yea, with it We cause to grow well-planted orchards full of beauty and delight: it is not in your power to cause the growth of the trees in them. (Can there be another) god besides Allah? Nay, they are a people who swerve from justice. Or, who has made the earth firm to live in; made rivers in its midst; set thereon mountains immovable; and made a separating bar

> between the two seas (can there be another) god besides Allah? Nay, most of them know not. Or, who listens to the distressed when he calls on Him, and Who relieves his suffering, and makes you (mankind) inheritors of the earth? (Can there be another) god besides Allah? Little it is that ye heed! Or, who guides you through the depths of darkness on land and sea, and who sends the winds as heralds of glad tidings, going before His Mercy? (Can there be another) god besides Allah?- High is Allah above what they associate with Him! Or, who originates Creation, then repeats it, and who gives you sustenance from heaven and earth? (Can there be another) god besides Allah? Say, "Bring forth your argument, if ye are telling the truth!" (27:60–64; also see 44:7–9)

"It is He Who is God in heaven and God on earth... And those whom they invoke besides Allah have no power of intercession; – only he who bears witness to the Truth, and with full knowledge" (43:84–86).

The conclusion the Qur'an draws from these elaborations is that nobody should worship, devote themselves to, call upon, depend upon, humble themselves or submit to (in the absolute sense of the words) anyone other than Almighty God i.e., not to take any *ilāh* for worship except *the Ilāh* (God): "Take not with Allah another god: or thou (O man!) wilt sit in disgrace and destitution"(17:22). "Take not, with Allah, another object of worship, lest thou shouldst be thrown into Hell, blameworthy and rejected" (17:39). This emphatic concentration upon the purity of worship and devotion to God Almighty, in Izutsu's opinion, is "undoubtedly the most 'dramatic' moment of the whole Koranic Divina Commedia."[351] Islamic transcendental monotheism leaves no stone unturned to drive home the fact that it is only Almighty God who is the Ultimate Reality and the ultimate concern of man and his actions. Absolute submission to the moral will of this God and peace with Him and with His creatures is the essence of the Islamic message. This, in short, *is* "Islam".

3: ***Tawḥīd al-Asmā' wa al-Ṣifāt:*** As Almighty God is One, Unique, and incomparable in His lordship, sovereignty, and worship, He is also

One and Unique in His names and attributes. In Judaism and Christianity, the conception of God is to a greater or lesser extent bound to the limitations of His creatures as seen in previous chapters. Islam emphatically proclaims that Almighty God, the Transcendent and Exalted Lord and Sustainer of all that exists, is far above possessing any of the creaturely attributes which have been ascribed to Him by man. He is not bound to any of the limitations of human beings or any other of His creatures. He has neither form nor body, nor corporeal or physical attributes, features, or characteristics. Rather His attributes are infinite and absolute. They are far above any sort of limitations, defects, and deficiencies, such as his having a beginning or an end, begetting or being begotten, having physical dimensions, or having needs such as requiring food, rest, or procreation etc. He is the One Who gives such dimensions and characteristics to His creations, while not sharing them in the slightest degree.

This third dimension of *al-tawḥīd* is specifically directed towards Judaic and Christian compromises of the divine transcendence. Judaism, Christianity, and Islam constitute successive moments of Semitic consciousness in their long march through history as carriers of a divine mission on earth. Identifying itself with the original pristine message sent by God to mankind, Islam as the final Revelation, notably protected from scriptural corruption, stands as a corrective element, finding fault with the Jewish and Christian conception and portrayal of God as delineated in the historical documents accepted by the two faiths as scriptures. Islam holds these documents accountable for compromising the divine transcendence and hence committing the most grievous error against the Semitic consciousness, polluting its once pure essence. As detailed in previous chapters, the biblical conception of God is anthropomorphic and corporeal. After criticizing a number of biblical passages portraying God in anthropomorphic terms, al-Faruqi asserts:

> Islam also charged that the relation Judaism claimed to bind God to "His People" straight-jacketed Him into granting them favors despite their immorality, their hardship and stiffneckedness (Deuteronomy 9:5–6). A "bound" god, bound in any sense or degree, is not the transcendent God of Semitic consciousness.[352]

Likewise, Christianity gravely misconceived the divine unity by reformulating it as a triune Godhead, using the incarnational gambit as justification to commit excesses against God and place countless limitations upon Him. According to al-Faruqi the "Christians have committed themselves to divine non-transcendence so resolutely that it had become with them an *idee fixe*, enabling Paul Tillich to declare *sub specie eternitatis* that the transcendent God is unknown and unknowable unless He is concretized in an object of nature and history."[353]

Equally improper has been God talk in Christianity including the language and terminology used to express creedal prepositions. Although Christianity has never ceased to claim that God is transcendent, nevertheless it has always spoken of Him as a real man, living in this earthly domain, walking and doing all the things men do, including suffering the agonies of death. So, to Christians, Jesus has always been both man and God. As discussed in chapter 3, this man-God statement is inherently flawed, more of a claim than a logical preposition substantiated by rational arguments or reasonable facts. This being so, Christianity has never been able to systematically articulate the God-man dogma in intelligible terms or take a consistent position on Jesus' humanity or divinity; and not surprisingly its turbulent history has been fraught with accusations of apostasy and heresy hurled back and forth. This also explains why Christian God language has always been confusing, at best, for confusion sows confusion. When pinned down, every Christian has to admit that the God he/she worships is both transcendent and incarnate. Yet this claim of transcendence to al-Faruqi is "*ipso facto* devoid of grounds. To maintain the contrary, one has to give up the laws of logic."[354] In sum, a wide gulf of conceptual differences regarding the doctrine of divine transcendence exists and separates Islam from both Judaism and Christianity.

Islam emphasizes that God by very definition of His reality cannot simply be a sort of supernatural or superhuman personality/being, directing worldly affairs from the heavens/soaring clouds whilst simultaneously sharing in creaturely attributes, needs, and qualities. For God is nothing less than the Creator, Originator, and Fashioner of this vast universe, the One Who keeps it functioning in accordance with His infinite wisdom, knowledge and master plans. God infinitely transcends anything which the human mind can possibly perceive or comprehend, or the senses grasp, imagine, or explain. God is far, far above any similarity or comparability with any of His creatures. This special emphasis upon the Divine transcendence is what the third category of *al-tawḥīd* is designated for. God is One in His Names and Attributes. His Names, Actions and Attributes surpass human names, actions and attributes as much as His Being surpasses their beings. The Absolute Creator utterly transcends the relative actions and attributes of His creatures. This is implied in the first assertion of the Islamic creed that "There is no god but God". In addition to being a denial of any associates to God in His worship, rule and judgeship of the universe, it also contains a denial of the possibility of any creature representing, personifying, or in any way or form expressing the divine Being. The Qur'an says of God: "To Him is due the primal origin of the heavens and the earth: When He decreeth a matter, He saith to it: "Be," and it is" (2:117; 2:163). "There is no God but He, Ever-Living, Ever-Active" (3:2). "May He be glorified beyond any description!" (6:100). "... No sense may perceive Him" (6:103). "... Praised be He, the Transcendent Who greatly transcends all claims and reports about Him" (17:43). As a result of this stringent emphasis upon the divine transcendence, Muslims have been supremely careful never to associate, in any manner possible, any image or thing with the presence of the divine or with their consciousness of the divine. This fact is well reflected in Muslim discourse, speech, and writings concerning the divine. Indeed, Muslims have only ever employed the language of the Qur'an, and its terms and expressions, to present or describe God – the transcendental language and terminology chosen by God Himself in fact to depict Himself in the verses of the Qur'an.

The Qur'an prescribes the fundamental transcendental criterion in the following verses: "There is nothing whatever like unto Him" (42:11). "And there is none like unto Him" (112:4, which we have already had the opportunity to quote and explain in this chapter), and "knowest thou of any who is worthy of the same Name as He?" (19:65). After having established this criterion, the Qur'an represents God as having "the Most Beautiful Names":

> Allah is He, than Whom there is no other god:-Who knows (all things) both secret and open; He, Most Gracious, Most Merciful. Allah is He, than Whom there is no other god;- the Sovereign, the Holy One, the Source of Peace (and Perfection), the Guardian of Faith, the Preserver of Safety, the Exalted in Might, the Irresistible, the justly Proud, Glory to Allah! (High is He) above the partners they attribute to Him. He is Allah, the Creator, the Originator, the Fashioner to Him belong the Most Beautiful Names: whatever is in the heavens and on earth, doth declare His Praises and Glory: and He is the Exalted in Might, the Wise. (59:22–24)

This is a passage of great sublimity. It sums up the generic attributes and names of Allah. While establishing the fundamental principle of divine otherness by the words "nothing is like unto Him", the passage institutes the basis of a possible divine modality. The One and Unique God is the most Merciful, the Compassionate. His knowledge extends to everything seen and unseen, present and future, near and far, in being and not in being; in fact these relative contrasts do not even apply to the Absolute God. He is unknowable in His being yet knowable through His names and attributes. These beautiful names and attributes are the only source and basis of a possible divine modality. This is perhaps the reason why the Qur'an and Hadith have taken upon themselves to fix the boundaries of this modality to avoid confusion and excesses.

Due to their sheer significance, these Qur'anic verses have been explained and reflected upon by a great many Qur'anic exegetes, mystics and theologians. Mere recitation of this passage is highly encouraged and said to carry great merits, the merits being connected with the beautiful names of God contained in the passage. The Prophet Muhammad is reported to have said that "Allah has ninety-nine names, one hundred less one; and he who memorized them all by heart will enter Paradise." To count something means to know it by heart.[355] Ibn al-Qayyim observes that a Muslim is "firstly, to count them and memorize their words; secondly, to understand their meanings and intent; and thirdly, to call upon God with them, as God has said in the Qur'an: (The most beautiful names belong to Allah: so call on Him by them.) (7:180)"[356]

Al-Tirmazī gives a count of these ninety-nine names in a report from Abū Hurayrah.[357] Ibn Ḥazm argues on the basis of such narration that there are only ninety-nine beautiful names of God and "it is not permissible to add any more name to it because the Prophet said hundred less one."[358] But the consensus of Muslim scholars is against such a view. They argue that the number ninety-nine should not be taken too literally. It is easy to find more than the ninety-nine names of God both from the Qur'an as well as from the authentic sayings of the Prophet. Ibn Ḥajar reports such a consensus from al-Nawawī.[359] Part three (chapter one) of al-Ghazālī's famous work *The Ninety-Nine Beautiful Names of God*, is titled: "On Explaining that the names of God most high are not limited to ninety-nine so far as divine instruction is concerned". In this chapter al-Ghazālī contends that the Qur'an and Hadith literature contain names other than the ninty-nine and several lists of divine names could be formulated by combining various hadith reports on the subject.[360] Al-Ghazālī, like Ibn Ḥajar, Ibn Taymiyyah and Ibn al-Qayyim,[361] argues that the Prophet said:

> Whatever distress or affliction that befalls a person, let him say: "O God, I am Your servant, and the son of Your servant, and the son of Your bondsmaid: my forelock is in Your hand, Your judgment concerning me is done. I implore You by every name which is Yours, by which You have named Yourself, or which You revealed in Your book, or which You taught to anyone from Your creation, or which You appropriated to Yourself in Your knowledge of hidden things, that You might make the Qur'an a renewal of my heart, a light for my inmost thoughts, a way through my affliction, and the unraveling of my distress"; and God – Great and Glorious – will remove his distress and affliction, and replace them with happiness.[362]

Al-Ghazālī argues that the Prophetic saying, "which You appropriated to Yourself in Your knowledge of hidden things" shows that the names are not limited to those mentioned in the well-known versions.[363]

Ibn al-ʿArabī has given a count of 146 names,[364] Ibn al-Wazīr 173, and Ibn Ḥajar has narrated a report from al-Rāzī that there are 4000 names for God, with the qualification that such a statement cannot be substantiated from the Qur'an or Sunnah.[365] Umar al-Ashqar has shown that 88 names are mentioned in the Qur'an itself and 22 more are mentioned in the Hadith.[366] These scholars argue that although to enumerate these ninety-nine names would suffice to grant a person entrance to paradise, in no way are the Divine names restricted to the number ninety-nine. It is, notes al-Ghazālī,

> like the king who has a thousand servants: one could say that the king has ninety-nine servants, and were one to seek their assistance, no enemy could oppose him. What is specified is the number required to obtain the assistance one needs from them, either because of the addition of their strength, or because that number would suffice to repel the enemy without needing any more; it does not specify that only they exist.[367]

The beautiful names of God can be classified into three main categories. Some of them can be called the "Names of God's essence (*Asmā' al-Dhāt*)", others as the "Names of God's attributes (*Asmā' al-Ṣifāt*)", and still others as the "Names of His acts (*Asmā' al-Afʿāl*)".[368] The essence *(dhāt)* of something is its reality, the innermost core that defines what it is. In the case of God, the question of *dhāt* means what is God's very self? What is His essence that makes Him God and differentiates Him fundamentally from everything other than Himself? The typical Qur'anic answer is that God is so unique and transcendent that "Nothing is like unto Him" (42:11). Therefore, God's essence is what He is and what everything else is not. That is what the first category of names intends to explain. Among commonly employed Qur'anic names, Allah is the most frequently used name. It occurs in the Qur'an 2602 times: 980 times in the *marfūʿan* (nominative) case, 592 in the *manṣūban* (accusative) case, 1125 in the *majrūran* (genitive) case and 5 times with the formula *Allāhumma*.[369] Many Muslim scholars and theologians argue that Allah is the proper name (*ism ʿalam*) that God has given to His (*dhāt*), to Himself. Al-Ghazālī observes:

> it is a name for the true existent, the one who unites the attributes of divinity, is subject of the attributes of lordship, and unique in true existence...It is most likely that in indicating *this* meaning (Allah) is analogous to proper names, so everything which has been said about its derivation and definition is arbitrary and artificial.[370]

Other theologians like Ibn al-Qayyim, and philologists like the renowned Sībawayh, prefer to derive it from *ilāh*, and hold that it means simply "the God".[371]

Among many others, al-Ghazālī argues that Allah is the greatest of the ninety-nine names of God because,

> it refers to the essence which unites all the attributes of divinity, so that none of them is left out, whereas each of the remaining names only refers to a single attribute: knowledge, power, agency, and the rest. It is also the most specific of the names, since no-one uses it for anyone other than Him, neither literally nor metaphorically, whereas the rest of the names may name things other than He, as in 'the Powerful', 'the Knowing', 'the Merciful', and the rest. So in these two respects it seems that this name is the greatest of these names.[372]

This is the reason that most Muslims prefer to use the name Allah instead of "God" while referring to the Supreme Being. This name transcends the sphere of time, space, and history, and is so specific that it is inconceivable that it could be shared, either metaphorically or literally.

The other names of essence are those that describe God's absolute transcendence and negate all kinds of imperfections. *Al-Quddūs* is one of the names of essence. It occurs in the Qur'an twice (59:23; 62:1) and means "*the Holy*". Al-Ghazālī observes that *Al-Quddūs* is the One

> who is free from every attribute which a sense might perceive, or imagination may conceive, or to which imagination may instinctively turn or by which the conscience may be moved, or which thinking demands. I do not say: free from defects and

> imperfections, for the mere mention of that borders on insult; it is bad form for one to say: the king of the country is neither a weaver nor a cupper, since denying something's existence could falsely imply its possibility, and there is imperfection in that false implication.[373]

Human beings can praise God by ascribing to Him attributes taken from their perfections i.e., knowledge, power, hearing, seeing etc., and denying to Him attributes taken from their imperfections, while God, argues al-Ghazālī,

> transcends attributes taken from their perfection as much as He does those reflecting their imperfections. Indeed God is free from every attribute of which the created can conceive; He transcends them and is above anything similar to them or like them. So if no authorization or permission had been given to use them, it would not be permissible to use most of them.[374]

Al-Salām is another name that describes God's transcendence in absolute terms. It means 'the Flawless'. Al-Ghazālī explains it as "the one whose essence is free from defect, whose attributes escape imperfection, and whose actions are untarnished by evil; and given that He is like that, there is nothing flawless in existence which is not attributed to Him, and originates from Him."[375] Al-Maydani defines it as "the one who is absolutely free from all kinds of defects in connection with His essence, His attributes and His actions. He is free from all that which are logically not befitting to the meanings of Godhead and Lordship, like resemblance or comparability with the contingent *(al-hadīth)*."[376]

Al-Subbūḥ, to al-Halimi, means the one "who transcends the defects and attributes that befall the contingent because of its contingency."[377] Al-Bayhaqī reports from the Prophet himself that "*al-Tasbīḥ*" or "*Subhān Allāh*" means, "God's absolute transcendence above and over all types of defects".[378] It means that God's glory, greatness, and transcendence is such that He is far beyond all creaturely understanding. *Al-ʿĀl* (the Most High),[379] *Al-Ghanī* (the Rich),[380] *Al-Ṣamad* (the Self-Sufficient, the Eternal),[381] *Al-Wāḥid* (the Unique),[382] *Al-Awwal* (the

First) and *Al-Ākhir* (the Last),[383] are also among the names that denote God's transcendence in absolute terms.

If the names of essence tell us what God is not, the names of attributes tell us what God is. It must be said at the outset that through these attributes one cannot fathom God's self. Therefore, there is no contradiction between God's unknowability and knowability. When we describe some of the attributes of a person and say of him that he is this or that, in no way can we exhaust that person's reality. Likewise, to say that God is Merciful, or All-Knowledgeable, or All-Hearing etc., is neither to describe God's essence nor exhaust His reality. He is far above being exhausted by finite knowledge, imagination, or perception. The limitations of human knowledge and comprehension for instance are obvious in the sphere of scientific knowledge. As for God, "Nothing is like unto Him" is the Qur'anic dictum that clearly tells us that in no way or form can we understand His Being or essence. "God is the infinitely and absolutely Real, about which the relatively real can know but little. We can understand reality to the extent that we are real. And that raises the question of how real we are. That is what *Tawhid* is all about."[384]

Allah is *Al-Raḥmān*[385] (which occurs 57 times in the Qur'an and 170 times in the *basmalah*), and *Al-Raḥīm* (occurring absolutely for God 114 times in the Qur'an), the Infinitely Good and the Merciful. Both the names are derived from the root "*Raḥmah*" meaning mercy. Mercy is one of the most frequently mentioned and discussed attributes of God in the Qur'an. "Thy Lord is Self-sufficient, full of Mercy" (6:133). "Your Lord is full of mercy all-embracing" (6:147). "He hath inscribed for Himself (the rule of) Mercy" (6:12). "Your Lord hath inscribed for Himself (the rule of) Mercy" (6:54; also see 7:156; 18:57; 40:7). God is in fact "the Most Merciful of those who show mercy" (12:64; 12:92; 21:83; 23:109; 23:118). In addition to these great many verses of the Qur'an, the *shahādah* itself is one of the great witnesses to this Divine attribute. The *shahādah* tells us that all mercy is the gift of the Merciful. "There is no god but the Merciful" which means that "There is no mercy but God's mercy," or "There is none merciful but the Merciful." God's mercy overshadows all the mercy in the universe. His mercy is the true and real mercy and others' mercy is relative. The Prophet expressed this idea in the following hadith:

> God created a hundred mercies on the day He created the heavens and the earth, each mercy of which would fill what is between the heaven and the earth. Of these He placed one mercy in the earth. Through it the mother inclines toward her child, and the birds and animals incline toward each other. When the day of resurrection comes, He will complete those mercies with this mercy.[386]

God's mercy is both inclusive and perfect. The act of mercy requires an object of mercy. No one requires mercy until and unless one is wanting. A compassionately merciful person may not be called truly merciful if he or she accomplishes mercy without volition, intention or sincere concern for the one in need. To al-Ghazālī, perfect mercy is

> pouring out benefaction to those in need, and directing it to them, for their care; and inclusive mercy is when it embraces deserving and undeserving alike. The mercy of God is both perfect and inclusive [*tāmmah wa ʿāmmah*]: perfect inasmuch as it wants to fulfill the needs of those in need and does meet them; and inclusive inasmuch as it embraces both deserving and undeserving, encompassing this world and the next, and includes bare necessities and needs, and special gifts over and above them. So He is utterly and truly merciful.[387]

Moreover, the mercy in our sense is accompanied with a painful empathy which effects the merciful and moves him to meet the needs of the one in need. Therefore, the one who is merciful out of such feelings of empathy and suffering comes close to intending to alleviate his own suffering and sensitivity by his actions. Human mercy is relative as well as a little selfish as humans by their acts of mercy look after themselves also. God's mercy is absolutely perfect. It is one way traffic as it is directed towards creatures and not vice versa. It does not relieve God of suffering or sensitivity, as these negative passions do not exist in God. He is the uniquely other. Hence, there are no anthropomorphic implications of this attribute in God. The name *Al-Raḥmān* is more specific than *Al-Raḥīm*. *Al-Raḥmān* is not used for anybody other than God while *Al-Raḥīm* can be used for others. Always preceeded by the definite article in the Qur'an the term *Al-Raḥmān* is considered a proper name of God because nothing is said of *Al-Raḥmān* that is not also said of Allah. Allah is then nothing but absolute Mercy. The term Allah focuses thought on the unfathomable unicity, while *Al-Raḥmān* focuses it on the depths of divine mercy and benevolence.

Many western scholars seem inclined to portray Allah as a fearful master, or tyrant, ever ready to mete out chastising punishments, a harsh God Who does what He feels like etc. Baillie, for instance considers that, "Islam is too moralistic.... Its God is too sheerly transcendent, the Lawgiver, but not the Gracegiver, not the indwelling source and author of the obedience which He demands."[388] Such a depiction of Allah seems quite arbitrary when reflected through the Qur'an's verses such as those regarding God's mercy and benevolence. The Qur'anic Deity is full of Grace. For instance, "Allah is Lord of abounding Grace", is a phrase which readers will frequently encounter even if flicking through the Qur'an (2:105; 3:74; 3:174; 8:29; 57:29; 62:4 etc.). "Allah is full of grace to mankind, but most of them are ungrateful" (2:243; 10:60; 40:61); "Allah is full of grace to all the worlds" (2:251); "Allah is full of grace to the believers" (3:152); His grace is manifest (27:16) and the highest (35:32; 42:22); He is Oft-Forgiving (*Ghafūr*). This name occurs in the Qur'an 71 times in the nominative case, and 20 times in the accusative case. God loves to forgive all sins for He is the Oft-Forgiving, is the message communicated throughout the Qur'an (5:39; 6:54; 7:153; 15:49; 16:119; 39:53); "Your Lord is Most Forgiving, Full of Mercy" (18:58). This is why He has given Himself the name *Al-Ghaffār*, which means, that not only does He love to forgive, but that He also conceals and covers sins so as not to humiliate or embarrass the sinners. So in what sense can God's mercy or grace or benevolence as stipulated in the Qur'an be disputed? Western scholars tend to cling tenaciously to the idea despite the wealth of Qur'anic verses in front of them.

Additionally, God is *Al-Laṭīf* (the Benevolent), *Al-Wadūd* (the Loving-kind), *Al-Ḥalīm* (the Mild), *Al-Ra'ūf* (the All-Pitying), *Al-ʿAfwū* (the Effacer of sins), *Al-Bārr* (the Doer of Good) and possesses many other such names to express His infinite Love, Mercy, Grace, and Kindness towards all of His creatures. Fazlur Rahman observes:

> The immediate impression from a cursory reading of the Qur'an is that of the infinite majesty of God and His equally infinite mercy, although many a Western scholar (through a combination of ignorance and prejudice) has depicted the Qur'anic God as a concentrate of pure power, even as brute power – indeed, as a capricious tyrant. The Qur'an, of course, speaks of God in so many different contexts and so frequently that unless all the statements are interiorized into a total mental picture – without, as far as possible, the interference of any subjective and wishful thinking – it would be extremely difficult, if not outright impossible, to do justice to the Qur'an concept of God.[389]

It is enough to simply quote the Qur'anic data to substantiate this claim. In the Qur'an the names referring to God's mercy are much more frequent than those describing him as a fearful master. In the Qur'an, God is called *Al-Qahhār* (the Fearsome) four times and once as *Al-Jabbār* (the irresistibly Terrible or the Awesome, 59:23). This is how he would appear to criminals, immoral hypocrites or impious disbelievers. In cases where the more stern names are used this is almost always with reference to an admonition against sinners, and yet despite the warning the admonition is generally followed by a salve, the wish that the sinner perhaps may return to God: "maybe he will return [unto God]"(48:43; 27:46) since God is both "Lord of majesty and of generosity" (55:78). For those who serve Him and are faithful He is the Most Indulgent One who never ceases to pardon, the continual Giver, the Dispenser of all that is good, the Generous, the Consenter, the Answerer, the Friend and Protector, the Pitying, the Guide and Leader, and the Most Patient who is slow to punish. All these are Qur'anic names that emphasize and clarify *Al-Raḥmān Al-Raḥīm*, the Merciful, the Compassionate. The attributes of mercy and omnipotence appear to be contradictory while in reality they are not. The Qur'anic dictum is that God's mercy is an expression of His omnipotence and hence inseparable from it. These two perfections represent the two poles of divine action and complement each other.

B. F. Skinner and many other leading psychologists and students of behaviorism have shown that, "When it is possible to arrange a situation so that punishment immediately follows the undesirable behavior, but does not occur at other times, it may be effective in suppressing undesirable behavior without producing harmful side effects."[390] Therefore the point can be made that the Qur'an's promises of severe punishment as an admonition to those who sin, could be a positive stimuli, suppressing the undesired behavior of sinners, without the harmful side effects of their despairing or losing sight of God's surpassing mercy. These two polar aspects (Omnipotence and Mercy) of the Divinity mutually strengthen each other, encouraging and fortifying the desired behavior. On the other hand, their correlativity is such a positive factor that it can be helpful in checking wrongful human attitudes or inclinations.

Unlike the Qur'an, the Muslim theological dispositions and treatises may not place enough emphasis upon God's mercy to strike a balance between the two correlative Divine aspects of omnipotence and mercy. However, the Qur'anic approach is quite balanced in this regard. The Qur'an indeed is very emphatic about the grace and mercy of God Almighty. Bishop K. Cragg rightly notes:

> Despite its uncompromising severity, however, it is throughout an understanding about mercy and compassion. Somehow these elements were less exposed to the issues which needed such vigilance from the theologians in respect of sovereignty and will. As befits its emphasis the classic theology of Islam is less concerned about the "comfort" of man than it is about the majesty and immunity of God, since these must be seen as, in every event, a prerequisite of the mercy. In its own urgent way, the Qur'an is warmer, kindlier, more compassionate than the theologians. While the Book of Islam underwrites and prompts the latter in many of their concerns and something of their temper, its vitality and fervor, its mission and movement, bring the reader into a different world from the aridity and calculation of the dogmatists.[391]

God's absolute Omniscience is expressed by the names *ʿĀlim al-Ghayb wa al-Shahādah* (the Knower of the hidden and the manifest), and by *Al-ʿAlīm* (the Omniscience). The name *ʿĀlim al-Ghayb* occurs in the Qur'an 13 times (10 times with the combination of both i.e., *ʿĀlim al-Ghayb wa al-Shahādah*), (6:73; 9:94; 9:105; 13:9; 23:92; 59:22). "Verily Allah knows (all) the hidden things of the heavens and the earth: verily He has full knowledge of all that is in (men's) hearts" (35:38; 3:119; 5:7; 8:43). "He knows what they conceal, and what they reveal: for He knoweth well the (inmost secrets) of the hearts" (11:5; 67:13). "Does not Allah know best all that is in the hearts of all creation?" (29:10). "He knows the treachery of the eyes, and all that the hearts (of men) conceal" (40:19). "And verily your Lord knoweth all that their hearts do hide, as well as all that they reveal" (27:74; 28:69). "He knows what is hidden and what is open: too high is He for the partners they attribute to Him"(23:92). This is why He is called the Omniscient *Al-ʿAlīm*. This name occurs 140 times (nominative case), 22 times (accusative case), and 4 times as *ʿAllām*. The perfection of this name lies in that Allah comprehends everything by knowledge – manifest and hidden, small and large, first and last, inception and outcome. His knowledge is the infinite as well as the perfect. Additionally, it is not derived from things known; rather things known are derived from it.

He is also *Al-Khabīr*, the All-Aware (33 times in the nominative and 12 times in the accusative case). *Al-Khabīr* is the one from whom no secret information is hidden, for nothing goes on in the realms of heaven or earth, no atom moves, and no soul is stirred or calmed, without His being aware of it. It has the same meaning as 'the Omniscient', yet when knowledge [*ʿilm*] is related to hidden secrets it is called 'awareness' [*khibrah*], and the One who possesses it is 'He who is aware of everything.' The Qur'an informs us that:

> With Him are the keys of the unseen, the treasures that none knoweth but He. He knoweth whatever there is on the earth and in the sea. Not a leaf doth fall but with His knowledge: there is not a grain in the darkness (or depths) of the earth, nor anything fresh or dry (green or withered), but is (inscribed) in a Record clear (to those who can read). (6:59)

Also, "... by Him who knows the unseen, from Whom is not hidden the least little atom in the heavens or on earth: nor is there anything less than that, or greater, but is in the Record Perspicuous" (34:3; 10:61).

He is also *Al-Samīʿ* (the All-Hearing). This name occurs in the Qur'an a total of 47 times (43 nominative and 4 accusative case). *Al-Samīʿ* is the One from whose perception nothing audible is removed, even if it be hidden. So He hears secrets as well as whispers, and what is subtler and more concealed than these. He hears the praise of those praising Him and rewards them, as well as the entreaties of those praying, and responds to them. Al-Ghazālī writes that,

> He hears without any auditory organs or ears, as He acts without limbs and speaks without a tongue; and His hearing is free from accidents which could befall it. When you elevate the All-Hearing above changes which happen to Him when audible sounds occur, and exalt Him above hearing by ears or by instruments and devices, you will realize that hearing, so far as He is concerned, is tantamount to an attribute by which the perfection of the qualities of things heard is dissolved. Whoever does not take care in considering this matter will inevitably fall into pure anthropomorphism. So be wary about it, and be precise when you consider it.[392]

The Qur'an requires the Prophet to witness this attribute of God with the following words: "Say: 'My Lord knoweth (every) word (spoken) in the heavens and on earth: He is the One that heareth and knoweth (all things)" (21:4).

He is also *Al-Baṣīr*, the All-Seeing (occurring 51 times, 36 nominative and 15 accusative case). God is the One who witnesses and sees in such a way that nothing is remote from Him, even what is under the earth. His seeing is also above having dependence on pupils and eyelids, and exalted beyond reference to the impression of images and colors on His essence, as they are impressed on men's pupils, for that is a form of change and influence which requires coming-into-existence. Since He is above this "seeing in His case is equivalent to an attribute through which the perfection of qualities of visible things is disclosed. And that is clearer and more evident than what may be grasped by perception on the part of a sight limited to the appearances of visible things."[393] The Qur'an states: "Verily Allah knows the Unseen of the heavens and the earth: and Allah sees well all that ye do" (49:18). This message is driven home by a great many Qur'anic verses (83 times as "He knows what you do '*taʿmalūn*'", and 56 times as "they do '*yaʿmalūn*'".) "He knows what enters within the earth and what comes forth out of it, what comes down from heaven and what mounts up to it. And He is with you wheresoever ye may be. And Allah sees well all that ye do" (57:4).

> Seest thou not that Allah doth know (all) that in the heavens and on earth? There is not a secret consultation between three, but He is the fourth of them,-nor between five but He is the sixth,- nor between fewer nor more, but He is with them, wheresoever they be: in the end will He tell them what they did on the Day of Judgment. For Allah has full knowledge of all things. (58:7)

"It was We Who created man, and We know what suggestions his soul makes to him: for We are nearer to him than (his) jugular vein" (50:16).

In short, God is Omniscient as much as He is Omnipresent. He is too exalted to be contained in any one place and too holy to be determined by time; for He created time and place. There is nothing like unto Him in His essence nor is there of His essence in any other besides Him. He changes not as He is far beyond contingencies. He abides through all generations with His glorious attributes, free from all imperfection. Therefore, the examples discussed of the Divine names and the related Qur'anic passages speak for themselves proving that the Qur'anic Deity is absolutely Omniscient and Omnipresent. God is absolutely free, in terms of His Omniscience and Omnipresence, of the limitations which we have seen are ascribed to Him in some biblical passages. Moreover, the Qur'anic representation of God's attributes of omniscience and omnipresence are abstract in the sense that they are not connected with any physical organs or corporeal qualities. His knowledge and power is felt but not imagined or represented in any way or form in human or material categories.

There are a number of names that denote God's absolute Omnipotence. *Al-Qādir* (the All-Powerful), *Al-Qawī* (the Strong), *Al-Matīn* (the Firm), *Al-Muqtadir* (the All-Determiner), *Al-Wājid* (the Resourceful), *Al-ʿAzīz* (the Eminent), *Al-Muqīt* (the Nourisher), *Mālik al-Mulk* (the King of Absolute Sovereignty), and *Al-Malik* (the King), are a just a few of them. The name *Al-Qādir* occurs in the Qur'an 7 times, *Qadīr* 45 times (39 nominative and 6 accusative case), and *Al-Muqtadir* 3 times. "To Allah belongeth the dominion of the heavens and the earth; and Allah hath power over all things" (3:189), is the thread which weaves through the Qur'anic fabric. The Divine omnipotence is extolled by frequent reference to the acts of creation, annihilation, sustenance, preservation, and unparalleled Lordship, "the Lord and Creator of all things" (6:164; 13:16). He is the absolute initiator (*Al-Badīʿ*) and creates whomsoever He wishes and causes death to whomsoever He wishes. When He wills something to be, it simply is: "When he decrees a thing, he but says to it 'Be' and it is" (2:117; 16:40; 19:35; 36:82: 40:68). Al-Ghazālī observes that the names All-Powerful and the All-Determiner,

> both mean 'one who possesses power', but 'the All-Determiner' is more emphatic. Power is equivalent to the intention by which a thing comes into existence according to determined plan of will and knowledge, and in conformity with both of them. The All-Powerful is one who does what he wills, or does not act if he so wills, and is not so conditioned as to will necessarily. So God is all-powerful in that He could bring about the resurrection now, and He would bring it about were He to will it. So if He does not bring it about, that is because He has not willed it, and He does not will it to happen now inasmuch as His knowledge had previously fixed its appointed time and moment according to plan, which hardly detracts from His power. The absolutely powerful is He who creates each existent individually without needing assistance from anyone else, and this is God most high.[394]

God cannot be dominated by anybody or anything from His creation as He is *Al-Qawī* and *Al-Matīn*, the Strong, the Firm. In God, strength indicates perfect power, while firmness indicates intensification of strength. He transcends creaturely weaknesses: "We created the heavens and the earth and all between them in Six Days, nor did any sense of weariness touch Us" (50:38). Hence, God could not have been dominated by Jacob or any other being, as depicted in the Hebrew Bible. He further did not require rest, needing to be refreshed, on the seventh day of creation as reported in the Bible. He is the Strong and the Firm.

All this emphasis upon God's Omnipotence is geared towards showing God's close proximity to His creatures. He is directly and intimately related with His finite creatures through His all comprehensive mercy, sustenance, guidance and knowledge.

Among this category of names, *Al-Malik* (the King), perhaps seems to give the most tangible impression about God. Just like the other divine names it is neither anthropomorphic nor pictured in concrete terms. It means that God's kingship is so absolute and real that nobody other than Him really deserves to be called a king. He is eternally King and His kingship never fades away. Humans gradually acquire kingship, work for it and then relinquish it at death. Real power, authority and sovereignty belong only to God while earthly rulers, presidents and kings at best represent pale reflections of God's kingly power. In reality the term is used in its metaphorical sense with regard to earthly rule while primarily denoting God's transcendental kingship. There is no king but the King. Likewise, any divine name can be placed in the sentence of *tawḥīd* "there is no god but God." Thus the Muslim confession can be utilized as a quick formula for stating the various implications of *divine unicity and transcendence*.

It is evident that the names of God's attributes maintain God's transcendence as vehemently as do the names of God's essence. The Qur'an has denied God all the limitations and imperfections of mortals (as well as all limitations and imperfections, period) while emphasizing His absolute attributes as the Ultimate Reality. The category of names discussed and the connected attributes perform another important function i.e., the immanence of God. They produce a kind of modality for human imagination, but soon the imagination is reminded of its limitations when clearly told that these names and attributes are not relative like the attributes of human beings or any of God's creatures. They are the attributes of the transcendent God who is absolute, hence His attributes know no bounds and transcend the utilitarian sphere of time and space as much as God Himself transcends His creatures. Furthermore, the relation of these predicates to their subject cannot be analyzed in the sense of the empirical world as all the human categories of expressions are finite while God and His attributes are infinite. Therefore, the pervasiveness of these names and attributes in the Qur'an and their commonly known and understood lexicographic meanings make the Qur'anic Deity very vivid, alive, and immanent, but at the same time infinitely mysterious, awesome, and transcendent. Such a presentation of the Deity gives enough opportunity for a kind of modality to exist allowing for a man-God communication, denying at the same time any similarity, comparison, and concrete image or images of the divine. Establishment of a meaningful, respectful and also a sort of demanding relationship is encouraged between God and man yet the limitations are always prescribed fervently so as to maintain the divine transcendence and otherness of God in all times and situations. The Qur'an very successfully establishes this immanence of God by bringing the beautiful names or related attributes of God as epilogues of a great majority of the Qur'anic passages. The use of these names and attributes is not arbitrary, it is wonderfully meaningful and closely contextual. The divine names are always connected with the subject matter of the passage under discussion. The names of mercy, love, and forgiveness, for instance, are brought as epilogues to those verses encouraging repentance or emphasizing God's love, mercy and grace.[395] "Say: 'O my Servants who have transgressed against their souls! Despair not of the Mercy of Allah: for Allah forgives all sins: for He **is Oft-Forgiving, Most Merciful**'" (39:53).

> Whatever is in the heavens and on earth, doth declare the Praises and Glory of Allah: to Him belongs Dominion, and to Him belongs Praise: and He has power over all things. (64:1)

> He knows what is in the heavens and on earth; and He knows what ye conceal and what ye reveal: yea, Allah **knows well** (*ʿAlīm*) the (secrets) of (all) hearts. (64:4) [emphasis mine]

> ...Allah is **Exalted in Power, full of Wisdom.** But if the thief repents after his crime, and amends his conduct, Allah turneth to him in forgiveness; for Allah is **Oft-Forgiving, Most Merciful.** Knowest thou not that to Allah (alone) belongeth the dominion of the heavens and the earth? He punisheth whom He pleaseth, and He forgiveth whom He pleaseth: And Allah **hath power over all things (*Qadīr*).** (5:38–40)[396] [emphasis mine]

The third category of the Divine Beautiful Names, denotes God's actions towards His creatures. The names of attributes do not need anybody or anything other than God Himself as they describe perfections of God. On the other hand, the names of acts are distinguished by the fact that they make sense only in terms of God's creatures, and that they have opposites that are also divine names. Examples are *Al-Muḥyī* (the Life-Giver) and *Al-Mumīt* (the Slayer), *Al-Muʿizz* (the Honourer) and *Al-Mudhil* (the One who humbles) etc. So God is *Al-Razzāq* (the Provider), *Al-Bārī'* (the Producer), *Al-Muṣawwir* (the Fashioner), *Al-Khāfiḍ* (the Abaser) and *Al-Rāfiʿ* (the Exalter), *Al-Mujīb* (the Answerer of prayers), *Al-Wakīl* (the Guardian), *Al-Māniʿ* (the Protector) and *Al-Ḍārr* (the Punisher) etc.

It is pertinent to reiterate that all of God's names are derived from the Qur'an and the Hadith; they are *tawqīfiyyah meaning that they are preconcertedly determined either by a Qur'anic text or an authentic prophetic report.* Nothing can be added to them or subtracted from them. The reason being to confess utter dependence upon God regarding the proper knowledge of and about His being. Such sheer dependence upon the revelatory knowledge is in fact a recognition of the impossibility of knowing God except through what He has decided to reveal to us. Another established criterion among all mainstream Muslim scholars is that God possesses all these perfections from eternity. God cannot be characterized by names insinuating that He acquired these perfections, or by blemish or bad names such as poor, cruel, cheat etc. He cannot be given any evil quality or attribute. The scholars also agree that diminutives of God's names are prohibited as are words alluding to dual meanings such as those conveying praise as well as condemnation. The other established criterion is that God's absolute transcendence and exalted majesty must be maintained at all costs. All ideas, concepts, imaginations, and even perceptions leading to resemblance, similarity, comparability, corporeality, and anthropomorphism must be denied of Him.

It is important to realize that the presence of some of these names and qualities in humanity is neither here nor there. Firstly because their presence does not make these attributes and qualities of God anthropomorphic or corporeal; and secondly because in God they are perfections and absolute, while in humanity they are imperfect and relative. God is the First and the Everlasting. These attributes are non-corporeal and are first present in Him and then in human beings. So, to describe God utilizing these non-physical attributes and absolute qualities in no way makes Him similar or comparable to man. They are simply expressions which pave the way for man to try to know God as much as human limitations allow. Al-Ghazālī rightly observes:

> So if God had an attribute or a specifying property, and there were nothing in us corresponding to it or sharing its name – even so much as the sweetness of sugar shares in the pleasure of intercourse – it would be inconceivable that we would ever understand [the attribute or property] at all. For each person only understands himself, and then compares his own attributes with those of God the most high. Yet His attributes are too exalted to be likened to ours! So this will be an inadequate knowledge in which imagining and resemblance are preponderant. So it needs to be complemented by the knowledge which denies any likeness, and which rejects any grounds for commensurability, even though the name be shared.[397]

Therefore, God is unknowable, as "knowing something is to know its reality and its quiddity, not the names derived from it."[398]

Consequently, all efforts should be directed towards reflecting upon the creatures of God instead of reflecting upon His essence, for there is no other way that one can comprehend it. "He knows what is before or after or behind them: but they shall comprehend Him not" (20:110). The Prophet pinpointed this fact by encouraging reflection upon God's creation and not upon God Himself.

In short, the Transcendent God has not the least resemblance to the limited, deficient, and imperfect creatures of His creation. Entirely out of the question is His resemblance to any and all other gods and of course their semi-human nature; deities fashioned by the minds of men, whose lack of knowledge and understanding, and need to supply the deficiencies of their own comprehension, caused such inane inventions. Contrary to this, God enjoys all attributes of perfection appropriate to His Divine Majesty and Exalted Power. Contemplation upon these and His beautiful names is the only recourse to grasp the barest glimpses of His Divine majesty.

In the light of what has been discussed so far, we can conclude that the Qur'anic concept of God is straightforward and self-explanatory. It consists of the absolute denial of the existence, authority, rule, sovereignty, and abilities to harm or benefit, of other gods (completely and utterly rejecting their worship and the representation of God in any way or form) whilst simultaneously restoring all these attributes and qualities in God Himself. Accordingly, God's attributes and qualities are absolute and are never connected with any physical object, body part or organ. For instance, God can speak through inanimate things such as a bush or a tree, as in the case of Moses (28:30) and in fact, "It is not fitting for a man that Allah should speak to him except by inspiration, or from behind a veil, or by sending of a Messenger to reveal, with Allah's permission, what Allah wills: for He is Most High, Most Wise" (42:51). God does not have a body. Nobody can see Him. Moses' request for a glimpse of God was answered in the following words:

> Allah said: "By no means canst thou see Me; But look upon the Mount; if it abides in its place, then shalt thou see Me." When his Lord manifested (revealed) Himself to the Mount, He made it as dust, and Moses fell down in a swoon. When he recovered his senses he said: "Glory be to Thee! To Thee I turn in repentance, and I am the first to believe." (7:143)

The reason being that, "No vision can grasp Him, but His grasp is over all vision; He is the Subtle, Well-Aware" (6:103). In short, the

Qur'an has explained its monotheism in simple, logical, and intelligible terms and categories, elaborated it with additional logical ways, methods and examples, and protected this concept well from possible violations. The Divine transcendence is an intrinsic part of the Qur'anic concept of the Deity. The transcendent God is immanent by dint of His countless absolute attributes expressed through His Beautiful Names and many other signs and manifestations throughout His creation. Moreover, the Qur'an makes special efforts to safeguard against all possible violations, confusions, and ambiguities, the immensely important concept of the Divine Unity, Uniqueness, and Transcendence of God. This original alertness, observes Bishop Cragg,

> against all false theologies accompanies the whole elaboration of Muslim religion. It is, as it were, a supreme "Protestantism" in its very genesis, a cry of heart and a mission of will against all that violated the Divine unity or distracted men from the single direction of their love, their loyalty, and their obedience.

Cragg continues that the

> ringing shout of praise that echoes through all Islamic ritual and dogma: *Allahu akbar*, "Greater is God," which, grammatically, is a comparative form made all the more striking by its refusal, indeed its inability, to enter any stated comparison. "God is greater" than all that could conceivably be set in any clause after "than." The idea of framing such a clause is itself unthinkable. Yet the superlative ("God is the greatest") is not preferred, for this could imply approximate equality and would, as such, be open to ambiguity, as the psalm is which declares: "He is a great king above all gods." Are we to understand that the gods exist, if only as underlings? Or do we mean that the Lord reigns in utter majesty alone? Islam has no truck with such double possibility of intention. It was not the existence of *Allah* that Muhammad proclaimed. The tribes knew Him by His name. It was His *sole* existence, negating all pluralism. God is exalted above all that might – though always impossibly – compare with Him.[399]

It is this notion of the absolute transcendence of God that has been reflected in Islamic art, language, and indeed so many other aspects of Islamic civilization and culture. Islam is, and always has been, unceasingly on guard, constantly on high alert against any corporeality, anthropomorphism or any form of comparability, injecting the divine with the non-divine. Unlike Christian art, Islamic art has always avoided sensory images, anthropomorphic depictions or corporeal portrayals of God in all times and places. No mosque has ever contained any object, depiction or statue even remotely connected with divinity. Students of religious art are amazed to see mosques devoid of any decorative pictures, depictions or iconography, aside from lace-like Qur'anic verses and abstract arabesques adorning walls and ceilings. The latter are in-themselves simply motifs, designs made of stylized stalk, leaf and flower, deliberately denaturalized and symmetrically repeated to dispel any suggestion of the creaturely natural being a vehicle of expression for the divine. Al-Faruqi writes that all the "arts in Islam developed in fulfillment of divine transcendence acting as supreme principle of esthetics..."[400]

The same strict precautions have been taken with regards to the Islamic language. Islamic theological discourse (God-talk) revolves strictly around Qur'anic terminology, despite the existence of, and in fact serving as an interface between, the tremendous geographical, linguistic, cultural and ethnic diversities that span the Muslim world. This is the objective of the Qur'anic dicta, "We (God) have revealed it as an Arabic Qur'an" (12:2; 20:113). So, any God-talk by Muslims is predominantly scriptural or Qur'an-talk, utilizing Arabic categories, terms, literary forms and expressions peculiar to the Qur'an. Muslims have always avoided the use of phrases such as father and son regarding the God-man relationship. Hence, phrases such as "God the Father", "Mother of God", "Son of God", "Crucified God" or "Sons of God" or their equivalent etc., will not be found in Islamic literature. They are utterly banished from the Islamic lexicon, and religious vocabulary, to eliminate and prevent the rise of any consciousness that could lead to pernicious confusion and difficulty with regard to the essence of God, as occurred with regard to Judaic and Christian conceptions of the Divine. The Qur'anic transcendental axiom is uncompromising in separating the divine realm from the non-divine creaturely one. For the sake of analogy, God stands on one side of the boundary, alone and unique, whilst everything other than He stands on the other, dividing the transcendent from the natural. This is the necessary criterion of Muslim God talk and a presupposition of God's axiological ultimacy. On the other hand, however, terms such as 'Lord', 'Master', the 'Most Merciful', the 'Compassionate', are frequently used to denote God, while phrases such as "servant" (*ʿabd*), "mankind" (*al-nās*), "human being" (*al-insān*), "creation" (*khalq*) etc., are used to denote man and creation.

Al-tawḥīd, with all its multiplex emphasis, is not meant merely to exalt God and chant His glories. It is also not meant to claim special privity with God, enjoy special privileges in His name or assert superiority over His creatures. None of these elements are implied in the Qur'anic understanding of monotheism. It is a responsibility rather than a privilege. It is meant to create the proper response in man, the response that is essential to encourage man to work towards transforming the human society of time and space in accordance with divine moral rules. The unity of God leads to the unity of His creation. No superiority is granted based upon origin, ethnicity, color, creed or financial or social status. The basic human rights of dignity, freedom, equality and justice are universally granted to all human beings because of their humanity. A right relationship with God is the sole guarantee of a just and right relationship between men. A loving connection between man and his God will assure a morally equipped caring human society. On the hand, any wrong understanding of who God is or a wrong relationship with Him will cause imbalance in man to man relationships. The Islamic transcendental monotheism if understood properly and applied in spirit, can warranty an ethically balanced and caring human society. It is grounded in human responsibility, socio-political and economic accountability and universal justice.

The essence of *al-tawḥīd* can be summarized in the following five terms:

(1) **Duality of reality** (God and non-God) and God as the moral normativeness: meaning the Being who commands (moral will of God) and whose commandments are ought-to-be.

(2) **Ideationality**: meaning that the relationship between the two orders of reality is ideational in nature. Man can understand this relationship and its demand easily through the faculty of understanding.
(3) **Teleology**: that the nature of the cosmos is teleological; that it is purposive, serving a purpose of its Creator, and doing so out of design. Man also has a purpose and that is to be God's vicegerent on earth.
(4) **Capacity of man and malleability of Nature**: since the nature of the cosmos is teleological, hence the actualization of the Divine purpose must be possible in space and time.
(5) **Responsibility and Judgment**: i.e., that man stands responsible to realize the moral will of God and change himself, his society, and environment so as to conform to the divine pattern. To do so is success and to disobey Him is to incur punishment and failure.

The forgoing five principles, argues al-Faruqi, are "self-evident truths. They constitute the core of *al-tawhid* and the quintessence of Islam."[401]

Therefore, the Qur'anic message is squarely aimed at man and his well-being. Indeed, it calls itself "guidance for mankind" (*hudan li al-nās* [2:185] and numerous equivalents elsewhere). Even though the divine names and attributes are the subject of countless Qur'anic verses, the Qur'an is not a treatise about God and His nature. The divine existence is functional. He is the Creator, Sustainer and Cherisher of man and his cosmos. He has created the universe to serve man. He is keen to guide man. He loves man and cares about his salvation. Finally He will judge man individually and collectively and mete out loving justice again for the sake of man. He has taken upon Himself that He will not forgive human violations until the man violated against is compensated for and satisfied. Izutsu presents the point in the following words:

> For among all these created things "man" is the one to which is attached so great an importance in the Koran that it attracts at least the same amount of our attention as God. Man, his nature,

> conduct, psychology, duties and destiny are, in fact, as much the central preoccupation of the Koranic thought as the problem of God Himself. What God is, says and does, becomes a problem chiefly, if not exclusively, in connection with the problem of how man reacts to it. The Koranic thought as a whole is concerned with the problem of salvation of human beings. If it were not for this problem, the Book would have not been "sent down", as the Koran itself explicitly and repeatedly emphasizes. And in this particular sense, the concept of man is important to such a degree that it forms the second major pole standing face to face with [the] principal pole, that is concept of Allah.[402]

Consequently, *tawḥīd* is directly connected with the moral sphere of human life. Its essence cannot be achieved without actualizing its demands of unity and universality of truth, unity, equality, and equity among the human race, and all that has to take place here and now i.e., practically in human society. Al-Faruqi expresses the point succinctly:

> Al-tawhid commits man to an ethic of action; that is, to an ethic where worth and unworth are measured by the degree of success the moral subject achieves in disturbing the flow of space-time, in his body as well as around him. It does not deny the ethic of intent where the same measurement is made by the level of personal values effecting the moral subject's state of consciousness alone, for the two are not incompatible....

He continues:

> Having acquiesced to God alone as his Master, having committed himself, his life and all energies to His service, and having recognized His Master's will as that which ought to be actualized in space-time, he must enter the rough and tumble of the market place and history and therein bring about the desired transformation. He cannot lead a monastic, isolationist existence unless it be as an exercise in self-discipline and self-mastery.[403]

This moral function of man, justifies his creation in God's moral image, in the best of form, as the vicegerent of God on earth. Therefore, Islamic understanding of monotheism is moralistic through and through.[404] This explains why the Qur'an almost always combines both faith (*īmān*) and good deeds (*ʿamal ṣāliḥ*) together, the one reflecting the other (2:25; 2:82; 2:277; 3:57; 4:57; 4:122; 4:173; 5:9; 5:93). The Qur'an also vehemently stigmatizes those who disobey God's moral will and follow their own desires, inclinations, and moods as gods. The word the Qur'an employs to denote this tendency is *hawā* (occurring 17 times), which can be translated as "caprice or whim." "Have you seen him who has taken his own caprice to be his god?" (25:43; 45:23). This moralistic understanding of *al-tawḥīd* along with its notion of the Day of Judgment is reflected in the very early Makkan chapters of the Qur'an. Such a concept of the Divinity is revolutionary and plays a vital role in Muslim life. The following early Makkan chapter (107 *al-Māʿūn* "Neighborly Needs"), is sufficient to give an example of the Qur'anic correlation of belief in God and the Day of Judgment and efforts to transform one's surroundings: "Seest thou one who denies the Day of Judgment. Then such is the one who repulses the orphan and encourages not the feeding of the indigent. So woe to the worshippers who are neglectful of their prayers, those who (want but) to be seen, but refuse (to supply even) neighborly needs."[405] It can therefore be claimed, clearly, loudly and unequivocally, that the Qur'an connects human salvation with morality, and not solely with family lineage or belief in or confession of a specific set of doctrines or dogmas. Our own actions in this earthly domain define and govern our existence in the Hereafter. The Qur'anic message of unity diametrically opposes tribalism, racism, nationalism, ethnic discrimination, human differentiation, cultic veneration, divine domestication, trinitarianism, superstitious dogmatism and secularism. Islam is less of an orthodoxy and more of an orthopraxy.

Furthermore, the Qur'anic concept of monotheism is not evolutionary. It is original and universal. The Qur'an gives this moralistic understanding of monotheism a universal dimension by claiming that this was the same message revealed to all the prophets and nations since the beginning of time: "For We assuredly sent amongst every People a

Messenger, (with the Command), 'Serve Allah, and eschew Evil'" (16:36; 35:24). The message is timeless, unchanged, and universal. So Noah for instance, one of the most ancient of prophets, was sent to his people with the message: "O my people! Worship Allah! Ye have no other god but Him..." (7:59). All subsequent prophets and messengers of God received and communicated the same message (7:65–93). This theme occurs very frequently in the Qur'an.[406] The Ten Commandments given to Moses were rehearsed by Jesus on the Mount and reiterated by Muhammad in the Qur'an. The *Shalome* of the original Hebrews is the *Salām* and Islam of the Qur'an. Jesus' original message of salvation was nothing but "follow the commandments". Love your God and love your neighbor we can therefore state is the essence of this universal monotheistic consciousness.

ANTHROPOMORPHISM: THE QUR'AN, HADITH AND SOME MUSLIM SECTS

In spite of its strong emphasis upon the transcendence, uniqueness, and inaccessibility of God, sometimes even to the point of jealousy, the Qur'an contains only *a few* verses whose somewhat picturesque style, if taken absolutely literally, could seem to ascribe certain human attributes or acts to God. This group of verses is often termed *mutashābih* meaning "ambiguous" verses, in contrast to the verses termed *muḥkam* whose meanings are firm and clearly established. The Qur'an says:

> He it is Who has sent down to thee the Book: in it are verses basic or fundamental clear (in meaning); they are the foundation of the Book: others are not entirely clear. But those in whose hearts is perversity follow the part thereof that is not entirely clear. Seeking discord, and searching for its interpretation, but no one knows its true meanings except Allah. And those who are firmly grounded in knowledge say: "We believe in it, the whole of it is from our Lord:" and none will grasp the Message except men of understanding. (3:7)[407]

This set of ambiguous verses has been the subject of much exegetical as well as theological dispute in later Islamic theological thought. Although mainstream Muslims have always denied and refuted any anthropomorphic conceptions of God, certain individuals and sects have fallen prey to an anthropomorphic conception of the Deity. And it is only because of this attempt at pernicious confusion that we are forced to give a detailed account of the responses *vis-à-vis* these Qur'anic verses and phrases.

It must be noted from the outset that the anthropomorphic tendency under discussion is neither crude nor graphic; nor is the problem, in addition, one of absolute corporealism or physical anthropomorphism (for the Muslim sects or individuals involved at least), which would have been dealt with rather summarily. What we have rather is a sort of relatively refined anthropomorphism, which crept into the thoughts of certain traditionalists such as Muqātil ibn Sulaymān and some early Shiite figures such as Hishām ibn al-Ḥakam (discussed later). In spite of his literal disposition Muqātil metaphorically interpreted many Qur'anic phrases that could have lead to corporeal depictions of God if taken literally. For Binyamin Abrahamov the case of Muqātil's alleged corporealism "needs further examination, because it demonstrates the unreliability of the sources where we learn about his views. His exegesis of the Qur'an which is now available presents him in a different way. Muqātil had different notions concerning anthropomorphic expressions in the Qur'an."[408] According to Hishām God had a body but one unlike other bodies, meaning that no resemblance or likeness exists between the divine body and non-divine ones. Proponents of this supposed anthropomorphism rationalized their speculation with the assumption that as all things existent have bodies, proof that God exists can be done through assigning Him a body, but one of course unlike other bodies.[409] We are hardly in the realms of marked anthropomorphism here, for in no way or form have these theorizers compared God with His creatures or completely blurred the line between the divine and non-divine realms. The only thing they are guilty of is to have seemingly slightly muddied the strict demarcation lines dividing the two realms, and this largely due to their literalism prone disposition and a sense of needing to prove God's existence. The result of this faulty speculation was severe chastisement by mainstream Muslims who dubbed them as corporealists, defending and underscoring with great fervor the well presented, guarded and uncompromising transcendental nature of the Qur'anic message.

It is significant and worth noting that the term "anthropomorphism" is used here as a rough equivalent for the Muslim use of the terms *tashbīh* and *tajsīm*. The two possibly interchangeable terms take material or sense perceptions as their point of reference, and can also be differentiated on a higher more refined level. The term *tashbīh* denotes the act of comparing God with non-God beings while *tajsīm* mainly focuses upon the object of the comparison. The Muslim concept of *tashbīh* and *tajsīm* is also at variance with the contemporary western use of the term "anthropomorphism". The western usage generally covers all attempts to conceive of God in human categories whether corporeal, emotional or rational. The Islamic terms focus more upon the sensual, material and corporeal aspects of the term though not completely ignoring the rational or emotional similarities. God's emotional or rational attributes are absolute while the same in humans are relative and finite. They are used regarding God for the sole purposes of existential confirmations, modality and a meaningful relationship between man and God. They are linguistic necessities, the result of human limitations, and must be taken as metaphorical expressions or figures of speech rather than reflections upon the divine essence.

An example of this category of Qur'anic passages and phrases is the Qur'anic usage of the word *wajh*, literally meaning "face," with regards to God, which occurs in a total of 11 verses (5 times as "the face of Allah" 2:115; 2:272; 30:38; 30:39; 76:9; once as "the face of their Lord" 13:22; once as "the face of your Lord" 55:27; once as "the face of his Lord" 92:20; and 3 times as "His face" 6:52; 18:28; 28:88). It is interesting to note the context in which the phrase occurs in several Qur'anic verses. For instance in 2:272 it says: "Whatever of good ye give benefits your own souls, and ye shall only do so seeking the 'Face' of Allah (*li wajhillāh*)." In 13:22 it says: "Those who patiently persevere (*li wajhi rabbihim*) 'for the face of their Lord'." From all these verses and others such as 30:30, 30:43 etc. it seems clear that the usage of the word "face" regarding God is more symbolic than literal, consequently leading many Muslim exegetes and scholars to interpret it as the *dhātillāh* that is, the being of Allah, or "for His sake".[410] This interpretation is substantiated by the other Qur'anic verses where it says: "And call not, besides Allah, on another god. There is no god but He. *Everything (that exists) will perish except His face.* To Him belongs the Command, and to Him will ye (all) be brought back" (28:88). In 55:26–7 we read: "All that is on earth will perish: but *will abide (for ever) the face of thy Lord,* – full of Majesty, Bounty and Honour." It is impossible to interpret this verse literally, and it will not make sense to state that everything will perish except God's face. Qur'anic exegetes agree that the word "*wajh*" (face) mentioned here refers to God Almighty Himself and not to any organ or body whatsoever.[411] The otherwise literalism prone Ibn Ḥazm observes that, "*wajhillāh* means Allah Himself."[412] Ibn Qayyim and Ibn al-Jawzī report a kind of consensus among the exegetes that this verse means: "your Lord will abide forever."[413]

Al-Bayhaqī observes that verse 28:88 stipulates that the "*wajh* means the being and not, in any way or form, denotes an attribute or an organ..."[414] Al-Bayhaqī discusses in detail the *aḥādīth* referring to God's face i.e. "pride and majesty as the cloak or mantle of His face",[415] or the supplication that "O Allah Grant me the bliss of a glance at Your face",[416] or that "the veil or cover of His face is light" [417] etc. to prove that the phrase *wajh* refers to God's being rather than any organ, body or body part belonging to Him.

This demonstrates that the Qur'an contains some phrases that cannot be given ostensibly literal meanings. The scripture clearly poses a hermeneutic challenge. Therefore rational faculties, and consideration of the overall scriptural scheme, and specific context and intention behind these expressions, must be employed properly to decipher the true meanings of these poetic expressions. The seemingly anthropomorphic expressions are used merely to emphasize the reality and existence of God especially to individuals such as the Makkan polytheists who had been immersed in the worship of idols and corporeal conceptions of divinity. A bare transcendental conception of the deity would have been irrelevant and incomprehensible to them. These expressions provide a vague departure point and a divine modality with the senses soon sharply reminded of the sheer limitations of human perception and understanding by the statement "nothing is like unto Him." A literalistic approach will merely accent the corporeal aspects of these scriptural phrases, as literalism is usually prone to taking sense experience as its frame of reference. Consequently, any face value literal interpretations of these anthropomorphic expressions only serves to reduce the Qur'anic God to the status of an idol, nullifying the Qur'anic intent of purging faith of idol worship. Phrases such as these have to be interpreted figuratively in light of the other Qur'anic verses and in accordance with the established rules of the Arabic language. Lack thereof would lead to a logical as well as a theological impasse.

Metaphorical delineation or *ta'wīl* is the mode of exegesis which transcends the elemental, literal and surface meaning of the text to replace it by a secondary and metaphorical sense. Human languages frequently admit of at least two levels of meaning i.e., the literal and the metaphorical. The Arabic language is heavily rich in these two levels of meanings i.e., the obvious (*ḥaqīqī*) and the metaphorical (*majāzī*). The need for a metaphorical meaning arises when a logical or theological impasse occurs such as when some few individuals decide to interpret as corporeal certain verses concerning the transcendental God. As reiterated earlier this fact was unknown to early Muslims because it was clearly obvious what was being referred to in the verses i.e. not literally the face of God but His Being and had never been an issue for the first generation of Muslims. Rather, Allah's Revelation was crystal clear, with *tawḥīd* so clearly spelled out that it could not be challenged on any level. The categories arose as a result of a few tending without any evidence to adopt a literalistic perspective, despite the context of the verses as well as the nuances of the Arabic language categorically demanding otherwise. So for instance Allah's throne or *ʿArsh* is referred to but He clearly does not "sit down" or have a "seat" to sit on. Islamically *ḥaqīqī* and *majāzī* are two polar tendencies and antithetical to each other.

The question arises as to why the Qur'an or Hadith would employ phrases such as these which could possibly create unnecessary tension with regard to meaning. The simple and straightforward answer is that linguistic and human limitations require this to be so. The Qur'an is a book of guidance for mankind and not a book of isolated metaphysics. To ensure human relevancy it has to employ phrases suitable to human understanding and imagery. This is perhaps a better option than a bare transcendental unity void of human imagination, relevancy and interaction. It must be kept in mind that the scripture does not always have multiple meanings. It is the context and the intention of the language that will determine, providing the clues, for a metaphorical or not interpretation. No violence to the established semantic, grammatical and philological nature of the text is permitted in the process of metaphorical interpretation, a tedious process of linguistic and textual analysis must be followed, conforming to the leads of lexicographers, grammarians, philologists, literary exegetes, poets and literary critics. Absolutely forbidden are arbitrary allegorical interpretations which do not follow a careful and thorough analysis, which lack scholarly tools or which render the text to arbitrary fanciful interpretations, without much linguistic or textual support. Human reason and rationale should follow the revelation and not supersede, supplant or nullify it.

It is clear from the examples quoted and ensuing discussion that the Qur'an and Hadith both contain poetical expressions which, if taken absolutely literally, could lead to anthropomorphism. In the words of I. R. Netton, "Islam too has had a problem of divine 'faces': not in the sense of a single deity divided up among, or represented by, many gods but simply in the fact that Muslims over the ages have regarded their one God in several widely differing ways."[418]

The Qur'anic expressions involved did not, as mentioned earlier, cause much problem to the first generation of Muslims. From a socio-phenomenological viewpoint it is apparent that the original sacred text of scripture is usually given a normative value in terms of religious thought with early believers very often hesitating to rationalize or free themselves from the explicit terms and phrases (terminology) of the message accepted as normative. And this was exactly the case with the first generation of Muslims. The ethico-practical nature of the Islamic faith, the simplicity and clarity of its basic creed, and the engagement of its followers in political solidification as well as territorial expansion from the very beginning did not leave much room for speculative and theoretical thinking among the generation of *Ṣaḥābah*, the Disciples or Companions of the Prophet. Although not discouraging logical thinking, the Prophet himself and his immediate successors are reported to have discouraged speculative inquiry into theoretical issues having little practical significance to the community. ʿUmar, the second Caliph, has been reported to have appropriated severe physical punishment upon individuals like ʿUbayd Allāh ibn Ṣabīgh, who vainly engaged themselves in inquiry about the *mutashābih* or ambiguous verses of the Qur'an. This is perhaps the reason why until the last years of the third Caliph ʿUthmān's reign, nobody discussed speculative or theological issues such as the attributes of God.[419] Due to the mass conversion of non-Muslims (some of them Christians and Jews), in addition to political unrest in the later part of ʿUthmān's government, and civil wars in the fourth Caliph ʿAlī's period, several theologically oriented and politically motivated attempts at theoretical speculation found their way into the Islamic community.[420]

Interestingly, anthropomorphism and corporealism were the first importees. Most Islamic historical and theological sources connect this development to ʿAbd Allāh ibn Saba', a Jew from Yemen, who, according to these sources, converted to Islam with a secret agenda to destabilize it.[421] Ibn Saba' was the first to exalt ʿAlī, the son-in-law of the Prophet and the fourth Caliph, to the level of divinity by addressing ʿAlī with phrases such as, "'Thou art Thou', that is, 'Thou art God'."[422] ʿAlī is reported to have deported Ibn Saba' to al-Madayn and punished many of his followers who attributed divinity to ʿAlī. Ibn Saba', on the other hand, continued exalting ʿAlī even after ʿAlī's death attributing to the Caliph several of the divine attributes and the second coming. Most of the extreme Shiite sects such as the *al-Bayāniyyah*, *al-Mughiyriyyah*, *al-Manṣūriyyah*, *al-Yūnusiyyah*, *al-Hishāmiyyah*, and many others assimilated Ibn Saba's corporeal thoughts travelling far on road of corporealism. Most Muslim historians count such extreme sects among the corporealists or *Mujassimah*.[423] A great majority of Muslim scholars also argue that the issue of anthropomorphism was introduced into Islam by Judaic influence for the latter were accustomed to such anthropomorphic tendencies with regards to God. Al-Shahrastānī, al-Rāzī, al-Isfrāyīnī, al-Ghurabī, al-Nashshar, Suhayr Mukhtar, Fathi M.

al-Zaghi and many others have emphatically argued that anthropomorphic and corporeal thought crept into Islamic circles through individuals such as Ibn Saba' and extreme Shiite sects in which they crystallized.[424] Goldziher attributes such a tendency to the Gnostic influences.[425] Some other Muslim scholars attribute this development to internal factors such as the literalism of Muslim literalists such as the *al-Hashawiyyah* and some traditionalists, and to their literal interpretations of the Qur'anic verses.

The fact is that literalists like Muqātil ibn Sulaymān, to whom most of the anthropomorphic interpretations of the Qur'anic expressions are attributed, died in 150 AH,[426] while Ibn Saba' propagated his corporealism in the late fifties and early sixties (AH of the Islamic century) as ʿAlī was killed in 61 AH. Matti Moosa observes that Ibn Saba' was the

> first [who] ascribed divinity to him. Ibn Saba preached that Ali would one day return in the clouds, with thunder as his voice, and lightning as the radiance of his whip... Ibn Saba and his followers never ceased to deify Ali, however. When Ali was assassinated in 661, they did not acknowledge his death but preached that he would return one day in the clouds.[427]

J. Wellhausen contends that "one is led to a Jewish origin of the sect. Certainly many things are called Jews and Jewish by the Muslims without any reason. But in fact the dogma of Shi'ism, the founder of which is considered to be Ibn Saba', seems to stem more from the Jews than from the Persians."[428] Al-Shahrastānī has long ago argued that:

> A strict form of anthropomorphism had existed amongst the Jews; not indeed all of them, but in a section of them...some of the Shiʿa also fell into one of two extremes: one was to make some of the Imams like God, the other to make God like a man. When the Muʿtazilites and scholastic theologians arose, some of the Shi'ites abandoned their extreme views and adopted Muʿtazilism; some of the early leaders, on the other hand, adopted a literal interpretation and became anthropomorphists.[429]

Contrary to Watt and Goldziher's viewpoint, the Muslims did not seem to have much contact and interaction with Gnostics by that time. On the other hand, contacts and interaction with the Jews, first in Madinah and then through mass conversion, were frequent and immanent. The influx of biblical stories and interpretations into Islamic circles and sciences through known Jewish converts to Islam such as Kaᶜb al-Aḥbār,[430] could easily have brought many Muslims face to face with the Qur'anic poetical expressions. It is highly likely that such encounter with Judaic material and thought could have resulted in anthropomorphic interpretations of the Qur'anic and hadith expressions under discussion. In sum, it would seem that external Jewish influence and internal literalism, pervasive in some early Muslim circles, appear to have played a major role in introducing and developing anthropomorphic thought in certain Muslim sects.

We now come to the issues of free will, predestination *(al-qaḍā' wa al-qadar)* and the divine attributes, which are connected with the other extreme, that is, the abstract transcendental tendency among Muslims. This was a reaction to the anthropomorphic tendency of some early Muslim groups. Discussion on these issues began in the Muslim community during the time of the later Companions such as ᶜAbd Allāh ibn ᶜUmar, ᶜAbd Allāh ibn ᶜAbbās, Anas ibn Mālik, Abū Hurayrah, and Jābir ibn ᶜAbd Allāh. Jaᶜad ibn Darham,[431] Jaham ibn Ṣafwān,[432] Maᶜbad al-Juhanī,[433] and Ghīlān al-Dimashqī were pioneers in this area of theological debate. Jaᶜad is reported to have initiated the issue of negating the attributes of God such as speech and others, in order to avoid anthropomorphism. Ibn Kathīr reports Jaᶜad to be the first to claim that "the Qur'an was created", to avoid the presence of two eternal and uncreated beings.[434] Ibn Taymiyyah, al-Dārimī, Ibn al-ᶜImād, and al-Kawtharī regard Jaᶜad as being the first to negate the divine attributes and actions, and to metaphorically interpret those Qur'anic verses which emphasized them.[435] He denied that God had talked with Moses or taken Abraham as a friend, as is commonly understood from the Qur'anic passages. Ali Sami al-Nashshar argues that Jaᶜad denied the eternal speech and not the contingent speech of God.[436] Madelung explains Jaᶜad's position as follows:

> God, in other words, does not speak in a literal sense. In order to communicate he creates the sound of speech which can be heard. This sound is figuratively called speech, although it is not genuine speech. It is easy to understand why the case of Moses is singled out for special mention. For Moses, according to Koranic doctrine, was the only prophet who heard God speaking directly, without an intermediary, to himself. The rule is, however, general. All "speech" of God, including the Koran, is created, not spoken, by God.[437]

It is evident that Jaᶜad did not intend to deny the Qur'anic passage concerning this incident, but the anthropomorphic implications of accepting God as talking directly to Moses. God, in Jaᶜad's view, was also exalted above being the friend of any creature. He interpreted the word *khalīl* in the Qur'anic verse 4:125: "God has taken Abraham as a *khalīl*", to mean needy, derived from *khalla*, need, rather than friend, derived from *khulla*, friendship. According to Madelung, Jaᶜad's emphatic stand on the issue of divine attributes "constituted an attack on the anthropomorphic, personifying concept of God of traditionalist Sunnism."[438] This fear of anthropomorphism and similarity between God and His creation led Jaᶜad also to emphasize predestination, in that the true creator of human actions was God and not human beings themselves.

It was Jaham ibn Ṣafwān (d.127/745) who treated the issue of divine attributes at length. He met Jaᶜad at Kufa and followed his theology. Like Jaᶜad, he emphasized the absolute transcendence of God by refuting all possibilities of anthropomorphism and metaphorically interpreted all the Qur'anic verses (*ta'wīl*) that could remotely lead to an anthropomorphic depiction of God. Al-Ashᶜarī reports that Jaham even denied that God was "a thing (*shay'*) because that is similarity with other things."[439] Aḥmad ibn Ḥanbal reports Jaham arguing that the Qur'anic verse "there is none like unto Him" meant that

> there is nothing from all the things which is like unto Him. He is under the seven earths as He is above the Throne. There is no place where He is not. He cannot be present at a specific place and

> absent from the other. He did not and does not speak. Nobody has seen Him in this world and nobody will see Him in the hereafter. He cannot be described or known by any attribute or action.... No mind can apprehend Him...[440]

Ibn Taymiyyah reports that Jaham even denied the Beautiful Names of God mentioned in the Qur'an and Hadith (discussed earlier) and, according to Ibn Taymiyyah, this was the reason that Jaham's followers were called "Extremists or absolute deniers".[441]

A detailed study of Jaham's position on the issue of divine attributes and names seems to indicate that he was not an absolute denier of the divine attributes as is usually asserted. Jaham absolutely denied only those attributes that could lead to any similarity or comparison between God and His creation. He divided the divine attributes into two categories: those specific to God only such as Powerful, Creator, the Giver of life and death; and those common to both God and man such as life, knowledge, intention etc. Al-Shahrastānī reports that Jaham,

> agreed with the Muʿtazila in denying the eternal attributes, but he also added other doctrines. These are as follows: (1) It is not lawful to apply to God an attribute which is also applicable to creatures, because this would imply likeness between God and creatures. He, therefore, denies that God is living and knowing, but maintains that he is powerful, an agent and a creator, because to no creature can be attributed power, action, and creation.[442]

The motivation of Jaham's doctrine is quite obvious. God cannot be described with any human attributes for He is ontologically other than creatures. Only the attributes which are exclusively God's can be ascribed to Him. Only God is *fāʿil*, truly acting, Giver of life and death and nothing else can be described by these terms. This is why Jaham argued that "man is determined in all actions by divine power, including the acts of faith and virtue or faithlessness and vice."[443] He further argued that

> a man does not have power over anything, nor can he be said to have capacity [to act]. Man is absolutely determined in his deeds.

> He has neither power, nor will, nor choice. God creates deeds in man just as he produces actions in all inanimate objects, and it is only in a metaphorical sense that, as with inanimate objects, deeds can be ascribed to man...[444]

Due to such emphasis upon the absolute divine transcendence to the exclusion of everything else, the followers of Jaham have been called *al-Jabariyyah* or determinists.

Consequently, to al-Nashshar, Jaham was not an absolute denier of God's attributes or their eternity, but just an adventurous soul emphasizing the need to "purge God of all shadows of similarity and anthropomorphism."[445] Jaham even went so far as to deny the everlasting nature of Paradise and Hell because presumably nothing is everlasting except God. He did so to maintain the absolute divine transcendence of God. Al-Shahrastānī reports Jaham as arguing that, "All motion in heaven and hell will come to an end. Paradise and hell will both pass away after those who have gone to paradise have enjoyed its bliss, and those who have gone to hell have suffered its torments."[446] Jaham argued that the time would come when everything other than God would perish. This transcendent God of Jaham's to the exclusion of everything else, argues Seale, "was closer to the Greek Absolute than to the God of the Qur'an."[447] Due to the later influence of Jaʿad and Jaham's theological positions over the Muʿtazilites as well as others, Madkur crowns them with the title of "the founders of philosophical theology in Islam."[448] Seale describes Jaham as the real founder of the Muʿtazilites instead of Wāṣil ibn ʿAṭā'.[449] Watt, on the other hand, argues against this accolade.[450]

Maʿbad ibn Khālid al-Juhanī (79/699) disagreed with Jaham over the issue of predestination, maintaining that man is free and capable to act. So, man was author of his deeds, whether good or evil. Even though Maʿbad and his follower Ghīlān diverged from Jaʿad and Jaham on the issue of predestination they converged with them in refuting anthropomorphisms. It was their contention that attributes pertaining to the divine person such as hand, sight, and hearing were to be taken figuratively, so that the transcendence of God could be preserved. "Predication of the attributes to God is unlike that of an accident or quality of the substance to which it adheres. For the attribute, they claimed, is another index for the divine self."[451]

There is a difference of opinion among scholars as to how abstract transcendental thought and the tendency to negate the divine attributes came to be introduced into *Jabariyyah* and *Qadariyyah* circles. A group of scholars attribute the development to Christian influences. For instance, De Boer argues that the Islamic

> doctrinal system has certainly been determined the most by Christian influences. In Damascus the formation of Muslim Dogmas was affected by Orthodox and Monophysite teachings, and in Basra and Baghdad rather perhaps by Nestorian and Gnostic theories. Little of the literature belonging to the earliest period of this movement has come down to us, but we cannot be wrong in assigning a considerable influence to personal intercourse and regular school-instruction. Not much was learned in the East at that time out of books, any more than it is today: more was learned from the lips of the teacher. The similarity between the oldest doctrinal teachings in Islam and the dogmas of Christianity is too great to permit any one to deny that they are directly connected.[452]

He further argues that the issue of divine attributes received the greatest prominence "under the influence assuredly of Christian dogmatics..."[453] D. B. Macdonald argues that

> in the development of the Murji'tes and Qadarites it is impossible to mistake the workings of the dialectic refinements of Greek theology as developed in the Byzantine and Syrian schools. It is worth notice, too, that, while the political heresies of the Shi'ites and Kharijites held sway mostly in Arabia, Mesopotamia, and Persia, these more religious heresies seem to have arisen in Syria first and especially at Damascus, the seat of the Umayyads.[454]

Emphasizing the significance of the polemic treatises of John of Damascus and his pupil Theodorus Abucara, Macdonald further argues:

> The close agreement of Murji'ites and Qadarite ideas with those formulated and defended by John of Damascus and by the Greek Church generally can only be so explained... In this case, also, we are not to think of the Muslim divines as studying the writings of the Greek fathers, but as picking up ideas from them in practical intercourse and controversy."[455]

Macdonald concludes that "so far it is clear that the influence of Greek theology on Islam can hardly be overestimated. The one outstanding fact of the enormous emphasis laid by both on the doctrine of the nature of God and His attributes is enough."[456] Seale,[457] Gibb and Kramers,[458] and Wolfson[459] are just a few more examples of this line of approach. Among Muslim scholars, al-Ashʿarī,[460] al-Shahrastānī,[461] and al-Taftazānī,[462] have emphasized the resemblance between Christian theology represented by the Greek Church Fathers and the Jahmites' and Qadarites' approach regarding the divine attributes.

A good number of Muslim scholars attribute the transcendental tendency (discussed above) to Judaic influences. Ibn al-Athīr,[463] al-Khaṭīb al-Baghdādī,[464] Ibn Kathīr, and Ibn Nubātah al-Maṣrī are just a few examples. Ibn Kathīr and Ibn Nubātah al-Maṣrī even pinpoint the names of Jewish individuals such as Abān ibn Samʿān and Ṭālūt ibn al-Aʿṣam who, according to them, taught Jaʿad ibn Darham doctrines such as that of the "created Qur'an", and hence the abstract approach regarding the divine attributes.[465]

A. J. Wensinck, on the other hand, contends that "neither orthodox Islam nor any of the sects merely took over the views of Christianity. There is no intellectual compulsion in any quarter, nor a special openness to foreign influence."[466] He also observes that "the history of Muslim dogmatics follows a logical course – that is to say, the sequence of the ideas is not of foreign origin, but is indigenous. At the same time, however, something must be attributed to the influence of Christianity."[467] Watt also argues that:

> The parallel, however, is not quite so close as it appears to be... Even if the similarity were to be closer than this, it does not necessarily follow that there was any direct influence. Islamic

> theology is now seen to have been brought about by inner tensions. It is thus not to be supposed that Muslim theologians copied Christian conceptions simply for the sake of copying. What is possible is that, having some awareness of Christian conceptions, they found among them items which were useful to them in maintaining their position against Islamic rivals.

Watt further observes:

> This awareness might come about in two ways. There were many Christians who had become Muslims without completely forgetting their Christian ideas; some may have become theologians, or at least talked with theologians. Also a number of religious discussions between Muslims and Christians are known to have taken place. It is only in this indirect way by providing suitable materials or lines of argument that Christian or any other extraneous thought can have influenced Islamic theology. What in the first place made men want to argue came entirely from within Islam.[468]

The views of Wensinck and Watt seem to be a more logical interpretation of the absolute transcendental tendency among some of the Muslim circles than the previous ones; therefore, the same views are held by many modern Muslim scholars such as Abd al-Halim Mahmud,[469] Irfan,[470] al-Nashshar,[471] and Madkur.[472]

It was the Muʿtazilite school which took over most of the Qadariyyah ideas such as free will, refutation of anthropomorphisms, negation of most of the divine attributes and the method of metaphorically interpreting the texts to meet their ends. So strongly, observes Wensinck, "was the likeness between the two sects felt, that their names are often used without discrimination. Yet the distinction between them is historically well documented."[473] Gibb and Kramers count Ghīlān, the founder of the Qadariyyah, as "among the fathers of the Muʿtazilah."[474] The recognized founder of the Muʿtazilites, Wāṣil ibn ʿAṭā', on the other hand, was a contemporary of Jaʿad and Jaham. Jaham's theology, argues Gibb,

> left distinct traces on that of the Muʿtazilah; the doctrine of the created Kur'an which was later to become a fundamental Muʿtazilah thesis was probably formulated by Djahm and in the doctrine of the divine attributes there are coincidences on both sides which cannot be accidental. On the other hand, there are many serious differences which are probably practical and political in their nature. Djahm professed in the most extreme form the doctrine of predestination (*djabr*). All the actions of man are involuntary. Wasil maintained the opposite thesis of free will.[475]

These historical realities tell us that the Muʿtazilites did not simply copy or blindly follow one person or a sect. They arrived at a time when rational inquiry and speculative argumentation as well as Greek philosophy and logic had already entered Islamic theological debate; picking and choosing from already existing religious ideas and theological expositions, they helped to create a systematic and speculative discourse among the Muslim community. This movement, observes Netton, "never produced a synthetic scheme of thought, nor even an eclectic system... but rather the interpretation of certain inherited doctrines in favor of a particular view of divine nature and human destiny..."[476]

It is commonly argued that the Muʿtazilites were liberals and free thinkers. Contrary to this view, Watt observes that their religious vigor, piety, missionary zeal, and commitment is proof, that they were "quite definite Muslims."[477] Gibb and Kramers contend:

> Nothing could then be less justifiable than to regard Muʿtazila as philosophers, free thinkers or liberals. On the contrary, they are theologians of the strict school; their ideal is dogmatic orthodoxy; philosophy for them is only an *ancilla fidei*; they are nothing less than tolerant. What they created was Muslim scholasticism.[478]

It must be noted that the Muʿtazilites utilized, in the first place, Greek logic and rationalism to support Islamic belief and revelation to convince non-Muslims of their vitality, but then later went to the extremist position of giving priority to reason (*al-ʿaql*) over revelation (*al-waḥy*), as Jarallah observes,[479] in effect subordinating the latter to the former. While the Qur'an, argues Rippin,

> had its place in the discussions, it was not so much a source, when used by Muʿtazila, as a testimony to the veracity of the claims which they were making. The basic assumptions of the Greek philosophical system (as understood and transmitted through Christian scholars) was the fundamental element underlying the whole position; it was argued that reason, and not only traditional sources, could be used as a source of reliable knowledge for human beings.[480]

This view of the role of reason, Rippin further argues, "is significant in terms of the ultimate fate of the Muʿtazila, for it implied that the legal scholars of Islam had, in fact, no particular claim to sole possession of the right interpretation of all Muslim dogma."[481] In addition, the Muʿtazilites became militant once given political authority. F. M. Denny states that the Muʿtazilites "far from being liberal intellectuals who wanted to accommodate the world to [a] vision of rationality and cooperation, were proponents of a strict and militant Islam which they sought to impose uniformly on their wayward coreligionists and to spread to the non-Muslims by means of propaganda."[482] This militant attitude along with many other factors brought about their downfall.[483]

The Muʿtazilite doctrine was founded on five axioms.[484] The first two i.e., *al-tawḥīd* (the unity of God) and *al-ʿadl* (the justice of God), were directly related to the nature of God and His actions. Like the *Qadariyyah*, the Muʿtazilite emphasized the uniqueness, transcendence, and unicity of God at all costs. If the Orthodoxy believed that the divine attributes were not God and were eternal, then, to the Muʿtazilites, transcendence could no longer be maintained. The Muʿtazilites asserted:

> Divine knowledge is either eternal or it is created. If eternal, it is either in God, outside of God, or nowhere. If in God, then God is a theater where change takes place. If outside of God, then God is not omniscient and someone else is. And knowledge cannot be nowhere. It is somewhere and eternal. But it cannot be outside of

> God for that involves polytheism. It must therefore be in God and intrinsic to Him.[485]

When Wāṣil ibn ʿAṭā', the founder of the Muʿtazilites, first negated the attributes, according to al-Shahrastānī,

> the doctrine was undeveloped and was explained by Wasil b. ʿAta in simple terms as follows: It is universally agreed that the existence of two eternal gods is impossible; so to assert the existence of an eternal entity, or an eternal attribute [in God], would be to say that there were two gods.[486]

Wāṣil, in Macdonald's view, "reduced God to a vague unity, a kind of eternal oneness."[487] The later Muʿtazilites, like Abu Hudhayl M. al-ʿAllāf (d. 226), made great advances regarding the issue of divine attributes utilizing the rational devices of the ancient philosophy. Al-ʿAllāf taught that

> the qualities were not *in* His essence, and thus separable from it, thinkable apart from it, but they *were* His essence. Thus, God was omnipotent by His omnipotence, but it *was* His essence and not *in* His essence. He was omniscient by His omniscience and it *was* His essence. Further, he held that these qualities must be either negations or relations. Nothing positive can be asserted of them, for that would mean that there was in God the complexity of subject and predicate, being and quality; and God is absolute unity... He endeavored – and in this he was followed by most of the Muʿtazilites – to cut down the number of God's attributes.[488]

Al-Shahrastānī reports al-ʿAllāf as arguing that, "the attributes they are not additional to his essence in the form of entities subsisting in it, but his essence itself. They may be regarded either negatively or as concomitants..."[489] Al-Ashʿarī reports that al-ʿAllāf observed:

> if you say: "God has knowledge" you affirmed knowledge of God which is He Himself and negated ignorance. When you said, "God

> is alive" you affirmed life which is Allah Himself and negated the death from Him. (Same is the case with all the attributes). He used to say that God has [a] face but His face is His ownself... He metaphorically interpreted the verses containing the word "*yad* [meaning hand]" as meaning His bounty, and interpreted the verse (made under my eye) [20:39] as meaning his [God] knowledge.[490]

Al-Ashʿarī also reports Ḍirār as arguing that "the statement 'God is knowledge' means that He is not ignorant... He is alive means He is not dead."[491]

Al-Naẓẓām (d. 231), according to Macdonald has the

> credit among later historians of having made use, to high degree, of the doctrines of the Greek philosophers. He was one of the Satans of the Qadarites, say they; he read the books of the philosophers and mingled their teachings with the doctrines of Muʿtazilites. He taught, in the most absolute way, that God could do nothing to a creature, either in this world or in the next, that was not for the creature's good and in accordance with strict justice. It was not only that God could not do it; He had not the power to do anything evil. Evidently the personality of God was fast vanishing behind an absolute law of right.[492]

Like Ḍirār, he argued that "the statement that 'God is knowledge' means affirming His essence and negating ignorance from Him...Same is the case with all attributes of His essence."[493] The difference between al-ʿAllāf and al-Naẓẓām was that al-ʿAllāf did not negate the attributes altogether. He affirmed them in the essence of God. Al-Naẓẓām, on the other hand, was closer to the philosophers in denying the attributes absolutely and replacing instead the essence of God itself. Al-Shahrastānī noted:

> The difference between saying that God is knowing with his essence and not by knowledge, and that he is knowing by knowledge which is his essence, is that the first proposition denies the attributes, while the second affirms either an essence which is

identical with his attributes, or an attribute which is identical with the essence.[494]

Abū Hāshim al-Jubbaʿī (850–915) did a "subtle refinement of the doctrine of the divine attributes"[495] by contending that these attributes were "*aḥwāl*" states "of the being of the entity of which they are attributes. In order to do that, he turned to the grammarians and grammatical theory."[496] He held that,

> God is knowing by his essence, is powerful, living and so on by his essence. The meaning of the expression 'by his essence' is that God does not need in his knowing either an attribute which is knowledge, or a 'mode' by which he is knowing. According to Abu Hashim, on the other hand, God is knowing by his essence in the sense that he has a mode, which is an attribute, recognizable over and above his being an existing essence. The attribute, however, can only be known along with the essence and not apart from it. Thus he maintained that there are modes which are attributes neither existing nor non-existing, neither known nor unknown; that is, in themselves they are not known as attributes, but are known only with the essence. Reason recognizes a necessary distinction between knowing a thing in itself and knowing it with an attribute. So one who knows the essence of God does not ipso facto know that he is knowing. Similarly, One who knows substance does not ipso facto know that it is in a place and is a substrate of accidents.[497]

Al-Qāḍī ʿAbd al-Jabbār reduced the attributes to only three i.e., knowledge (*al-ʿilm*), power (*al-qudrah*), and perception (*al-idrāk*). He insisted, like his predecessors, that these attributes were not other than God's essence.[498]

Al-Faruqi summarizes the Muʿtazilite's position on the issue of attributes as follows:

> all divine attributes must be declared either negative, denying that their opposites are predicable of God; or positive, affirming a facet

> of the divine self, not an accident or quality. The Islamic notion that the Qur'an was the eternal word of God invited the same kind of argument. The Muʿtazilah maintained that the Qur'an was created by God in time to fulfill a purpose He had for man and creation. The evidence they adduced was that the Qur'an was composed of language, of sound and meanings established by human custom, that it was kept in ink and paper and memorized completely by humans. It cannot be "in" or "of" God. On the other hand, to hold that the Qur'an is "outside" of God and eternal is to affirm the existence of another eternal being besides God.[499]

Rahman observes:

> with that of the Divine Attributes, the Muʿtazila went to extreme limits. Starting with a genuine anxiety to safeguard the idea of Divine transcendence, they explained away all expressions of Scripture and the Hadith that contained anthropomorphism in a rational spirit and ended up by negating all the Divine Attributes.[500]

The Muʿtazilite also refuted the orthodox dogma of the beatific vision of God in Paradise. God, they claimed, "cannot be beheld by the human eye, even in Paradise, for only material bodies can be seen. Hence, the Qur'anic verse affirming [the] same (75:22) must be interpreted to mean something else, such as consciousness of the divine presence."[501] They interpreted the Qur'anic verses related to this metaphorically and even rejected *aḥādīth* claiming the same by discrediting some of the narrators in their link. Al-Khayyāṭ reports Abū Mūsā al-Murdār as declaring that anybody claiming that, "Allah will be seen by the eyes without how (*bilā kayf*) is a disbeliever. Same is the one who doubts him being a disbeliever..."[502] This ultra strict position was taken by the Muʿtazilite to avoid any similarity between God and His creatures, and to avoid any anthropomorphic understanding of the Divine, which to them was equal to disbelief.

Finally, the Muʿtazilite metaphorically interpreted all verses of the Qur'an that refer to the face, hands, eye of God etc., and tried to impose such interpretations upon other Muslims. Despite "their several disagreements on points of doctrinal details", observes Netton, "most of the Muʿtazilites were agreed on a non-literal mode of interpretation of much of the anthropomorphic data about God in the Qur'an."[503] Thus, they interpreted the word "face" in the verse: "Everything (that exists) will perish except His own Face" (28:88) to mean the being of God Himself.[504] God's hand was interpreted as referring to His "favor or bounty"[505], God's eye as referring to His "knowledge", and God's settlement upon the Throne (*istiwā'*) as His "dominance", and His coming down in the later part of the night as meaning the closeness of His "mercy".[506] Watt observes that the Muʿtazilite dealt

> with the anthropomorphisms by the method of *ta'wil* or 'metaphorical interpretation'. More precisely this meant that they claimed they were justified in interpreting single words in the Qur'anic text according to a secondary or metaphorical meaning found elsewhere in the Qur'an or in pre-Islamic poetry. Thus, in the phrase (38:75) about God 'creating with his hands' they said that hands meant 'grace' (*niʿma*), and justified this by a usage roughly parallel to our colloquial phrase 'I'll give you a hand'. Similarly *wajh*, usually 'face', was said to mean 'essence'. Verses which spoke of God being seen in the world to come were interpreted in the light of other verses where 'see' did not mean physical sight. In some ways this method of interpretation is artificial; but at least it keeps thinkers at the 'grass roots' of religious experience and away from an abstract academic discussion of relations between attributes and essence.[507]

In a similar vein, Anawati observes, "hadith that go the wrong way will be rejected. It is necessary to maintain, at whatever cost, the absolute divine unity, strict monotheism."[508]

The central purpose and sole raison d'etre of the strict Muʿtazilite creed was to strictly stress and preserve the transcendence, uniqueness, and otherness of God, as well as His sheer incomparability with anything other than Himself. This is clearly evident from analysis of the vehemently upheld Muʿtazilite position with regard to God's divine attributes and interpretation of Qur'anic anthropomorphic expressions. God's absolute divine transcendence was for the Muʿtazilites the essence of the Islamic Faith, to be emphatically preserved at all costs. With this in mind it becomes easy to understand al-Ashʿarī's long account of the Muʿtazilite creed, each word and phrase of which seems to be an effort to affirm. Al-Ashʿarī declared:

> The Muʿtazila agree that God is one; there is nothing like him; he is hearing, seeing; he is not a body (*jism, shabah, juththa*), not a form, not flesh and blood, not an individual (*shakhs*), not substance nor attribute; he has no color, taste, smell, feel, no heat, cold, moisture nor dryness, no length, breadth nor depth, no joining together nor separation, no movement, rest nor division; he has no sections no parts, no limbs nor members; he is not subject to directions, left, right, in front of, behind, above, below; no place comprehends him, no time passes over him; inadmissible for him are contiguity, separatedness and inherence in places; he is neither characterized by any attribute of creatures indicating their originatedness, nor by finitude, nor extension, nor directional motion; he is not bounded; not begetting nor begotten, magnitudes do not comprehend him nor veils cover him; the senses do not attain him; he is not comparable with men and does not resemble creatures in any respect; infirmities and sufferings do not affect him; he is unlike whatever occurs to the mind or is pictured in the imagination...eyes do not see him, sight does not attain him, imagination does not comprehend him; he is heard by hearing; (he is) a thing, not as the things, knowing, powerful, living, not as (men are) knowing...[509]

According to Watt, "This passage expresses very well the otherness and transcendence of God which has always been [a] prominent strand in Islamic thought. This has, of course, a Qur'anic basis, and indeed some of the phrases in the passage...are from the Qur'an..."[510]

In spite of their great contributions to the intellectual life of Islam and despite being "founders of the discipline of speculative or philosophical theology",[511] the Muʿtazilite went far from the spirit of

Islamic revelation and hence from the outlook of the ordinary Muslim. "To insist on the bare unity of God", argues Watt, "was a tidy rational theory, but it did not do justice to the fullness of religious experience. The negative statements of Dirar and an-Nazzam are unsatisfactory to the ordinary worshipper..."[512] The Muᶜtazilite reduced the vivid and living God of Muhammad, as Macdonald puts it, to "a spirit, and a spirit, too, of the vaguest kind."[513] To Rahman they "denuded God of all content and rendered Him unsatisfactory for religious consciousness."[514] To Netton they "made God more unknowable rather than less, and dug a wider gulf between man and his Creator. A dry hermeneutic intellectualism restricted the former's mental image of his Deity..."[515] Their creed, observes Watt, "leads to an abstract, bare and featureless conception of God, which robs the religious consciousness of much that is precious to it."[516] Or in the words of Gibb turning God into "a vast old monument, beneath which the element of personal religious experience seemed to be crushed out of existence. Fortunately for Islam, it was not to be so."[517] According to Gibb, the simple and minor anthropomorphism of the Islamic faith, which speaks of God in terms of some of the categories and attributes of the human being, "was far less dangerous than anthroposophism which reasons about God in terms of human wisdom."[518] The Muᶜtazilite however,

> exercised an influence indirectly. An important role was played by al-Ashᶜari who, after being trained as a Muᶜtazilite, was 'converted' to a form of Hanbalite view. There were other channels, however, by which [the] Muᶜtazilite's ideas entered the main stream... It was then left to other men to sift these ideas so as to discover which were genuinely assimilable. In the end a great many ideas were retained, though seldom in precisely the form in which Muᶜtazilites had presented them.[519]

A good example of the assimilation process cited was the method of metaphorical interpretation, bequeathed by the Muᶜtazilite and later adopted by Sunni theologians such as al-Baghdādī, al-Juwaynī, and al-Ghazālī. Al-Rāzī noted that "all the Islamic sects affirm that metaphorical interpretation *(ta'wīl)* is a must with regards to the few (apparent words) of some Qur'anic verses and Prophetic reports."[520]

A further development came with religious philosophy and Islamic Hellenistic philosophers, as well as later with the Isma^cilites, who once again in the name of God's unity and transcendence, absolutely negated the attributes of God. Religious philosophers for instance like al-Fārābī (870–950), Ibn Sīnā (979–1037), and Ibn Rushd (1126–1198) in essence stripped God of all possible attributes ascribed to Him in the Qur'an.[521] Al-Fārābī's First Cause and necessarily existent One is indivisible in His substance and indefinable or ineffable.[522] He is simultaneously Intellect (*ᶜaql*) and the Discernment of the Intellect (*maᶜqūl*). He is eternally the All-Knowledge because He knows His Being (*yaᶜlamu dhātahu*).[523] Al-Ghazālī accuses both al-Fārābī and other philosophers of denying God's knowledge of the particulars and details of things. Ibn al-Jawzī accuses Ibn Sīnā of the same.[524] According to al-Ghazālī, who railed against Islamic Hellenistic philosophy, the philosopher philosophizing about God is more closer to ignorance than knowledge.[525] However, Ibn Rushd and many modern scholars such as Abu Raydah and A. Mahmud free al-Fārābī and Ibn Sīnā of this charge.[526] In point of fact, in his writings, al-Fārābī disagrees with Aristotle on the issue of God's knowledge with regards to the *juz'iyyāt* (details of things) pointing out that God's knowledge was eternal and therefore He knew everything. Al-Fārābī refers to the Beautiful Names of God recognizing them as pathways leading to a knowledge of His Exalted Majesty without adding or allowing anything additional or external to His being or essence.[527] For al-Fārābī, these Names merely denoted God's relationship with His creatures.[528] I. R. Netton observes that, "In his second mode al-Farabi emphasized among other things the different facets of perfection of the Deity, while underlining the fact that all His attributes were subsumed in, and not distinct from, His essence."[529] Madkur sees in al-Fārābī the origination of all the later theological debates regarding the divine attributes.[530] Al-Fārābī to a large degree defines God in negative propositions and statements to maintain His absolute transcendence. He renders God to a mere intellect or *ᶜaql*, as Netton observes, "The logic of al-Farabi's identification of attribute and essence means that God is intellect in action (*ᶜaql bi al-fiᶜl*) as well as wisdom, truth, and life themselves."[531] Unlike many others, Abd al-Halim Mahmud does not see in al-Fārābī's approach an un-Islamic, excessive or extravagant immersion in the divine transcendence, but rather his emphasis upon the divine transcendence as an off shoot of the Islamic concept of God's otherness.[532]

Ibn Sīnā's Necessary Being[533] is essentially one. According to Netton:

> Ibn Sina admits that it is possible for God to have a variety of characteristics (Persian: *sifat-ha*) without there being any kind of resultant multiplicity in His essence (*dhat*). But this admission implies no desire to indulge in a Muʿtazilite exercise of allegorizing the attributes out of all recognition into something else. The key is rather a very Neoplatonic urge towards negativity, similar to that which was previously encountered in the work of al-Farabi."[534]

Ibn Sīnā argues that:

> Since it is established that God is a Necessary Being, that He is One in every respect, that He is exalted above all causes... since it is further established that His Attributes do not augment His Essence, and that He is qualified by the Attributes of Praise and Perfection; it follows necessarily that we must state that He is Knowing, Living, Willing, Omnipotent, Speaking, Seeing, Hearing, and Possessed of all the other Loveliest Attributes. It is also necessary to recognize that His Attributes are to be classified as negative, positive, and a compound of the two: since His Attributes are of this order, it follows that their multiplicity does not destroy His Unity or contradict the necessary nature of His Being. Pre-eternity for instance is essentially the negation of not-being in the first place, and denial of causality and of primality in the second place; similarly the term One means that He is indivisible in every respect, both verbally and actually. When it is stated that He is a Necessary being, this means that He is a Being without cause, and that He is the Cause of other than Himself: this is a combination of the negative and the positive.[535]

All these attributes boil down to "... nothing but (1) union, where 'union' is an idea in the intelligence rather than in essence, or

(2) negation (*nafy*) and denial. In so doing they do not imply existence of many characteristics, but rather an omission of many characteristics."[536] To further emphasize the otherness of God, Ibn Sīnā insisted upon emanation of the First Intelligence, "Since the first thing to emanate from God was not a body, it follows that it was an abstract substance, namely, the First Intelligence."[537]

In short, the philosophers campaigned for an abstract and absolute divine transcendence which differed markedly to both Muᶜtazilite and Orthodox understanding of the deity, being very close, as Madkur observes, "to Aristotle's Metaphysics."[538] The Ismaᶜilites followed the philosophers in stripping God of all the attributes ascribed to Him, and then in ascribing all of the divine attributes to the First Intelligence.[539] And because the God of the Ismaᶜilites and philosophers was recast as a bare Reality and an absolute unknowable One, this First Intelligence thus rather than God Himself seemed to be the true Deity. God appeared to need the First Intelligence to create, sustain, protect, and love. In an effort to exalt God beyond all possible limitations and needs, the Muslim philosophers ended up binding Him too tight to their theory of emanation and hence with several of its inherent limitations. Netton differentiates between the Muᶜtazilite's deity and that of the Neoplatonic deity of the philosophers in the following words:

> The transcendent Deity of the Muᶜtazilites, whose several Qur'anic attributes were metamorphosed by allegory, was not bound up with ideas of emanation, nor with hypostases such as the Universal Intellect (*al-ᶜAql al-Kulli*) and the Universal Soul (*al-Nafs al-Kulliyya*). But the unknowable God of medieval Neoplatonic Islam was. The end result was the development of a transcendental theology in Islam, with the Ismaᶜili sect as its political and spiritual apotheosis, which was far more complex than anything of which the Muᶜtazila could have dreamed.[540]

There was nothing in the Qur'an allowing for the existence of this hierarchy of beings or hypostases as is required by emanation. The philosophers' emanation scheme, as Madkur observes, did not realize the goal assigned by the Qur'an to the creation. The philosophers' creation was not dependent upon God's will or power. Such a scheme was totally non-Qur'anic and closely related to the emanation theory of Neoplatonism. In this process, as Netton observes, "the simple monotheistic model or 'face' of the *Qur'anic* God was remolded to an image and likeness of which Plotinus might only sometimes have approved, and of which Muhammad would have assuredly despaired, even if he had understood it."[541] By this "alienation and Neoplatonism", the "old paradigm was transformed into another full and new paradigm, the 'Paradigm of Islamic Transcendence.'...And the transformation meant that all words used of 'God' were similarly transformed and could only be used as analogical signs, however inadequately."[542] Netton concludes his book by observing that, "For the stress on transcendence among some thinkers in medieval Islam, if pursued to its ultimate point, leads semiotically, logically, and inexorably to the 'death' of the word 'God,' though none, of course, articulated it like that."[543] Netton's conclusion may seem extreme, but in a sense it is true, for the philosophers so practically removed God from the day-to-day affairs of the world that He became a mere abstract idea. This concept of God was too abstract to generate the response intended by the Qur'an, especially with regard to common believers. On the other hand, it must be noted that this abstract transcendental tendency among many Muslim philosophers such as al-Fārābī and Ibn Sīnā, did not spring from apostasy or rebellion against the Qur'an or the Islamic concept of the Deity. It was perhaps their commitment and devotion to the divine transcendence that was the driving force behind their journey into deep abstraction. And as a consequence, their views regarding the divine transcendence as a whole cannot be dubbed as absolutely un-Islamic or non-Qur'anic. Although their ideas lacked the proper balance needed between the divine transcendence and immanence as stipulated in the Qur'an, still their concerns regarding God's absolute divine transcendence were an offshoot of the Qur'anic emphasis upon the divine otherness and hence a great sign of the philosophers' faith and trust in the Qur'an. Certainly they represented the utmost extreme of transcendental thought in Islam.

The *Al-Ḥashwiyyah*[544] followed a hugely controversial creed. So extreme was their interpretation of the nature of God that they were labelled *Mujassimah* or corporealists by their opponents, from the root word *jism* meaning body in the Arabic language. Seemingly anthropomorphic phrases of the Qur'an and hadith were given a highly literal interpretation to the extent of *sometimes* even comparing them to equivalent human counterparts. Although the trend was not confined to any specific sect or group, we can point to the following as examples, albeit a few, of its practice among the traditionalists: Maḍar ibn Muḥammad ibn Khālid ibn al-Walīd, Abū Muḥammad al-Asadī, Abū ʿAbd Allāh al-Baṣarī, Aḥmad ibn ʿAṭā', Kuhmus ibn al-Ḥasan al-Tamīmī (d. 139), and Muqātil ibn Sulaymān (d. 150). The latter opposed a metaphorical interpretation of the Revelation advocating a strict and literal following of the text to insist that revelation rather than reason was the only true source of religious understanding. Al-Shahrastānī notes:

> According to them God has a form and possesses limbs and parts which are either spiritual or physical. It is possible for him to move from place to place, to descend and ascend, to be stationary and to be firmly seated... Ashʿari has reported on the authority of Muhammad b. ʿIsa that Mudar, Kuhmus, and Ahmad al-Hujaimi allow the possibility of men touching God and shaking his hand; also that sincere Muslims may embrace him in this world as well as in the next, provided they attain in their spiritual endeavors to sufficient degree of purity of heart and genuine union with God.

He further observes:

> Kaʿbi reports of some of them that they say that God can be seen even in this life, and that God and men may visit one another. Dawud al-Jawaribi is reported to have said: 'Do not question me about the pudendum or the beard, but you may ask me about anything else'. He said: "God is body, flesh and blood. He has members and limbs, such as hands and feet, head and tongue, two eyes and two ears; nevertheless, he is a body unlike other bodies, with flesh unlike other flesh, and blood unlike other blood. This is true also of his other attributes: he does not resemble any creature, nor does any creature resemble him."[545]

In spite of their emphasis upon the incomparability and non-resemblance of God to creatures, these literalists nevertheless also ascribed to God the attributes and qualities of mortal bodies. Al-Shahrastānī reports that they took Qur'anic words such as *istiwā'* (settling down) and *wajh* (face) etc. literally,

> as they are understood when used of bodies. The same applies to words found in traditions, such as the word 'sura' (form) in the saying of the Prophet: 'Adam was created in the form of the Most Merciful'; or his other sayings: 'Till the Most Powerful puts his foot in the fire...' These and the like they understood in the same sense as would be understood of bodies. The Anthropomorphists have invented lies and added them to the traditions, attributing them to the Prophet; these were taken mostly from the Jews to whom anthropomorphism is natural... The Anthropomorphists also report that the Prophet said, 'God met me, shook hands with me, wrestled with me and put his hand between my shoulders, until I felt the coldness of his fingers.'[546]

It is entirely indisputable that the notion of God which the literalists had in mind was of a corporeal and anthropomorphic Deity, whatever the claims they would made as to His non-resemblance and incomparability. *Al-Karamiyyah*, the followers of Muḥammad ibn Karam (d. 255 AH), followed the corporeal concept of *al-Ḥashwiyyah* to such a degree that Ibn Karam came to be regarded as an "upholder of corporealism and anthropomorphism."[547] According to al-Shahrastānī, Ibn Karam declared that,

> God is firmly seated on the throne and that he is in person on the upper side of it. He uses the word 'corporeal' of God, and says in his book, *'Adhab al-Qabr*, that God is one in his essence and one in substance, and that he is in contact with the upper side of the throne. In his view, it is possible for God to move, change his position and descend. Some of the Karramites say that God occupies part of [the] throne, but others say that he occupies the whole of it.[548]

It was in response to these two extremist positions (the Muʿtazilite and their somewhat abstract interpretation, and the *al-Ḥashwiyyah* and their anthropomorphism), that the early Orthodox fathers or *Salaf* developed the formula *bilā kayf*. These early scholars were often called the People of Tradition (*Ahl al- Ḥadīth),* or *Salaf* and comprised *fuqahā'* such as Imam Abū Ḥanīfah (d. 767),[549] Imam Mālik (715–795),[550] Imam Shāfiʿī (767–820),[551] and Imam Aḥmad ibn Ḥanbal (d. 855).[552] They left the verses of the Qur'an in question as well as the related *aḥādīth* simply as they were, accepting the poetical statements just as they occurred, without applying much reason either to criticize or expand upon them. These conservatives observes Majid Fakhry, "tended to repudiate the use of any deductive method."[553] Their position was that these ambiguous verses must be understood in light of the Qur'anic dictum that, "there is nothing like unto Him" hence negating all possibilities of anthropomorphism. At the same time, they used and maintained the same phrases or terminology implied by the Qur'an with regards to God such as *wajh Allāh* without looking further into their meaning or exegesis. And this is what is being referred to by use of their phrase *bilā kayfa wa lā tashbīh*, meaning without inquiring how and without anthropomorphism or comparison. Binyamin Abrahamov observes that "on the one hand, this method manifests God's incorporeality (against *tashbih*) and the authority of the Qur'an (against *taʿṭīl*), and on the other hand, it attests to man's inability to know God's essence."[554] Abū Ḥanīfah puts the matter succinctly:

> All His qualities are different from those of creatures. He knoweth, but not in the way of our knowledge; He is mighty, but not in the way of our power; He seeth, but not in the way of our seeing; He speaketh, but not in the way of our speaking; He heareth, but not in the way of our hearing. We speak by means of organs and letters, Allah speaks without instruments and letters. Letters are created, but the speech of Allah is uncreated.[555]

He further declares that,

> Allah is [a] thing, not as other things but in the sense of positive existence; without body, without substance, without accidents. He

> has no limit, neither has He a counterpart, nor a partner, nor an equal. He has hand, face and soul, for He refers to these in the Kuran; and what He saith in the Kuran regarding face, hand and soul, this belongs to His qualities, without how (*bila kaifa*). It must not be said that His hand is His power or His bounty, for this would lead to the annihilation of the quality. This is the view of the Kadarites and the Muʿtazilah. No, His hand is His quality, without how. Likewise His wrath and His good pleasure are two of His qualities, without how.[556]

Both Mālik ibn Anas and al-Shāfiʿī's views were absolutely the same in this regard.

Very often this doctrine and formula of *bilā kayf* is connected with the name of Ibn Ḥanbal. But as just mentioned it was in fact Abū Ḥanīfah who initially used the phrase. Watt highlights this historic fact by stating that Ibn Ḥanbal "was doubtless building on the foundations of earlier men."[557] I. R. Netton observes the same of certain Muslim theologians who came later than Ibn Ḥanbal, noting that the seemingly anthropomorphic statements made of the face of God in the Qur'an were

> to be accepted as realities without further inquiry into their modality (bila kayf). It was sufficient to realize that the exact nature of such features as God's hand or eyes would be quite unlike any earthly hands or eyes. This was the classic stance of such theologians as Ahmad b. Hanbal (AD 780–855) and al-Ashʿari (AD 873/4–935/6). Both were concerned to stress the reality of the anthropomorphic descriptions found in the Qur'an. But logically, their attitude of *bila kayf*, or refusal to examine the mode of these descriptions, resulted in an intellectual cul-de-sac in which acceptance triumphed over analysis and incomprehension over reason.[558]

Was it 'acceptance' or 'incomprehension'? One could argue and in my opinion quite rightly, that it was in fact the triumph of wisdom over theorizing, for anything else would not have been 'analysis' but speculation and of a most dangerous sort in terms of its ramifications. Neither was it an absolute intellectual cul-de-sac, by which I mean that it allowed for a specific modality of the divine nature and reflection upon it, but with certain strict conditions and qualifications attached. James Pavlin observes:

> Thus using verses of the Qur'an and authentic Hadith, the traditional scholars maintained the reality of God's Names and Attributes without questioning how they exist in Him. In this way, a complete picture of the nature of God was formulated. For example, it is confirmed that God has an Essence (*Dhat*) and a Self (*Nafs*), that He has ninety-nine beautiful Names, that He interacts with His creation through actions and words, that He knows all things and wills all things into existence, and that He is beyond comprehension and is only known by the descriptions He has revealed. For the traditionalists, this was accepted based on the prohibition of asking how God's Attributes exist.[559]

This supposed cul-de-sac was moreover not the result of, or directed specifically to, any anti-intellectualism or use of reason, but the outcome of a specific religious rationale. Watt explains:

> Orthodoxy has been accused of making God similar to man. This charge they indignantly denied, and they inveighed against *tashbih* as vehemently as the Muʿtazila. They agreed that God was not corporeal and that He transcended and was different from all creatures; and in this they were quite genuine, for it was one side of the traditional Islamic outlook. At the same time, however, they clung to the text of the Qur'an, which they regarded as the very words of God. If the Qur'an spoke of God's hands and face, then God must have hands and face. How God Who is incorporeal has hands and a face may be difficult to understand, but this difficulty is not a valid reason for rejecting the phrases of Scripture or explaining them away by the method of *ta'wil*. One must maintain both the authority of Scripture and the incorporeality of God, even if one cannot reconcile them intellectually. In the doctrine of

> *balkayfiyya* this position was regularized and a formal acknowledgment made of the limits of the human intellect.[560]

To Oliver Leaman and Binyamin Abrahamov the *bilā kayfa* "doctrine is a moderate position, between that of the literalists (who hold that God really has a body) and that of the demythologizers (who think we need to interpret these verses allegorically)."[561]

That such a formula was intended to acknowledge sheer human dependence upon the Word of God, to maintain its authority over reason, and to block any attempt at anthropomorphism, is substantiated by the position taken by Aḥmad ibn Ḥanbal. Although Ibn Ḥanbal's opponents often accused him of literalism and corporealism with regard to the seemingly anthropomorphic Qur'anic expressions, he did not in fact take an absolute literal approach to them. Quite the reverse, Ibn Ḥanbal's strong opposition to any anthropomorphic interpretation of these Qur'anic phrases is evident of his stern and classical stance against anthropomorphic conceptions of God. Al-Shahrastānī reports that Ibn Ḥanbal stated:

> Whoever moved his hand while reading the Qur'an (xxxviii. 75), "I created with my hands," ought to have his hand cut off; and whosoever stretched forth his finger in repeating the saying of Muhammad, "The heart of the believer is between two fingers of the Merciful," deserved to have his fingers torn out.[562]

Watt rightly observes elsewhere that:

> There were naive anthropomorphists among the Traditionists, but he (Ibn Hanbal) opposed these as vigorously as he opposed the Muʿtazilites; he insisted that the anthropomorphic expressions of the Qur'an are to be understood "without stating the precise manner of their existence" (*bi-la kayf*, literally "without how"). The strength of Ibn Hanbal's feelings on this matter may be gauged by the fact that he broke off relations with a follower who attempted to refute the Muʿtazilites by their own methods of argument.[563]

This helps to show that, "the Hanbalites position was based on an awareness of the limitations of reason in this sphere, coupled with an understanding of the need to retain the concrete and "poetical" language of the Qur'an and the Traditions."[564] In the words of Armstrong, Ibn Ḥanbal was not anthropomorphist but was "stressing the essential ineffability of the divine, which lay beyond the reach of all logic and conceptual analysis."[565]

Consequently, it can certainly be claimed that the *Salaf's* insistence upon an understanding and acceptance of these Qur'anic expressions employing the caveat *without how* was neither literal nor anthropomorphic. They simply didn't want to traverse or trespass into territory specified for the Divine, which is why they confined themselves to the terms implied by the Qur'an and the Sunnah with proper qualification that no similarity or resemblance ever existed between God and His creatures. Al-Shahrastānī reports that one of the reasons the *Salaf* refrained from *al-ta'wīl* (metaphorical interpretation) was that an interpretation was "an opinion, and it is not lawful to give an opinion about the attributes of God; for we may sometimes interpret the verse in a way not intended by God, and thus we would fall into perversity."[566]

We need to differentiate between two later understandings of the *Salaf's* position which came into being. A group of Sunni, mostly Ḥanbalite, scholars apprehended it to mean that the ambiguous verses should be understood in light of the fixed rules of the language. Thus phrases like 'face of God' or 'hands of God' were to be understood in accordance with their common, daily, linguistic usages, as for instance we understand the meaning of the word 'face', without giving it a metaphorical interpretation. This comprehension, in their view, did not imply any comparison, corporeality, or anthropomorphism, for the level of these attributes in God is absolute while in His creation it is relative. God has already explained that none is like unto Him, but He is at the same time hearing and seeing. So if acceptance of His attributes such as those of hearing and seeing as well as many others, that are also shared by human beings, does not make Him similar to man, likewise acceptance of attributes like face and hand would not be anthropomorphic. For they would also be different from human hands and faces.[567] Therefore, when we say "God has a face or hands", it must be qualified with the qualifier "*not like our face or hands*" and *without how*. This is the position of Ibn Qudāmah (d. 620 / 1223),[568] Ibn Taymiyyah (d. 728 / 1328),[569] and many other traditional scholars. In their footsteps and following them come the "Salafi" groups of modern times such as the followers of Muḥammad ibn ʿAbd al-Wahhāb (1115–1201 / 1703–1787) who closely follow Ibn Taymiyyah's approach regarding the divine attributes.[570] In his discussion of God's attributes, Ibn Taymiyyah

> attempts to give greater depth of explanation to the traditionalist view of the nature of God. His main tool for this is the Arabic language. He sees Arabic as the unique vehicle of revelation, and thus all of its nuances must be understood properly and clearly. In addition to the Arabic language itself, one must read and understand the verses of the Qur'an within their natural setting, i.e., the Qur'an must be interpreted by the Qur'an. The examples, parables and linguistic usages of the Qur'an must be analyzed for their rules and principles, which in turn must be applied in a consistent and uniform manner. In this way, Ibn Taymiyyah does not reject the rational faculties of the mind (*ʿaql*), but uses them in submission to revelation in order to explain revelation.[571]

All this emphasis upon the linguistic meaning of the Qur'anic verses, argues Watt, "grew out of a realization that the concrete, "poetical" language of the Qur'an kept men closer to the deep springs of religious vitality than the abstractions of philosophical thinking."[572]

Ibn Taymiyyah argued that the *Salaf's* attitude towards the Names and Attributes of God was to "attest and confirm whatever has been affirmed by God for Himself in the Qur'an and the Sunnah of His Prophet, without alteration (*taḥrīf*) or suspension (*taʿṭīl* i.e., stripping God of those attributes) and without how (*takyīf*), or comparison (*tamthīl*)."[573] He contended that the words used by God for Himself in the Qur'an or those used by His Prophet to denote Him are realities carrying real meanings appropriate to God's Exalted Majesty. The meanings of these terms when used of God carry different realities to the meanings and corresponding realities they describe while used in the human context or sphere. Though the terms are the same, the corresponding realities are utterly different in accordance with the nature and essence of the two parties denoted and described by them. God is hearing, seeing, living, and some of His creatures are also hearing, seeing, and living. Such a concord of names does not "require resemblance of the Creator with the creation, but only denotes a kind of commonality or shared value between them both. The distinctive factors distinguishing one [God] from the other [creature] utterly outweigh and outnumber the factors common between them."[574] God was hearing and living long before the existence of creatures and He will be so eternally; therefore, the names and qualities ascribed to him were "realities about God without any of the creatures having any share of them, and without any doubt of resemblance or comparability."[575] Hence to accept the reality of these Qur'anic names, phrases, and attributes *vis-à-vis* God, is according to Ibn Taymiyyah, not to signify any corporeality, anthropomorphism, or resemblance existing between God and His creatures, for they denote realities utterly different and extremely disparate between the Sovereign God and His creation. The only condition that such an ascription can be allowed is that the names and the attributes so ascribed must be appropriate to the Divine Exalted Majesty and must have the stamp of revelation. And even then no one will ever be able to know the reality or how of these attributes.

Ibn Taymiyyah viewed any meaning of these phrases other than the literal to be alteration or *taḥrīf*; therefore, he vehemently opposed '*al-ta'wīl*', the method of metaphorical interpretation. For instance, according to Ibn Taymiyyah the term *yad*, cannot be interpreted as power or bounty because the power of God is one and cannot be denoted with a dual noun such as the Qur'anic *yad*.[576] Likewise the bounties of God are many and therefore cannot be denoted by a dual noun such as the Qur'anic *yadāhu* (two hands of God i.e. Qur'an 5:64) also used in the hadith. To Ibn Taymiyyah the Qur'anic phrase "*istawā ʿalā al-ʿArsh*", meant God "establishing Himself over and above the Throne":

> Although God's '*istawā ʿalā al-ʿArsh*' is so real as the reality of a man's [servant] *istawā* upon and over the boat, the *istawā* of the Creator is not like the *istawā* of the creatures. God does not depend upon or need anything; He is free from need of all the things [Self-sufficient]... If somebody argues that the acceptance of the reality of God's *istawā* necessitates that it be like the *istawā* of a man upon the boat, then let him claim that to accept the reality of God's knowledge, hearing, seeing, and speaking necessitates that such divine qualities be like [or resemble] the qualities of knowledge, hearing, seeing, and speaking among the creatures![577]

Ibn Taymiyyah further maintained that God's establishing of Himself upon the Throne did not require Him to touch it because He was not a body to occupy space:

> His establishing Himself over the Throne is confirmed by the revelation, while His exaltedness, highness, and otherness than everything other than Himself is confirmed by logic (*al-ʿaql*) as well as the revelation... All the arguments brought by the deniers... would come into effect if God were a body occupying space. But if He were above and over the Throne, and not a body or a space occupant, then none of these exigencies and anthropomorphic requirements or implications would come into effect.[578]

Ibn Taymiyyah insisted on confirming the revelation without anthropomorphic or corporeal implications. Moreover, he declared the metaphorical meanings of the term "*istawā*" such as "*istilā*'" meaning "appropriation, seizure, or taking possession", as tantamount to changing the intended meaning of the revelation. To say that God did not have hands or face was *taʿṭīl,* and to compare to, or give, the divine hands or face human or creaturely equivalence was *tamthīl.* Ibn Taymiyyah declared that the first part of the Qur'anic verse, "There is nothing like unto Him", automatically negated anthropomorphism and comparison; while the second part, "And He is the One that hears and sees" (42:11), was negation of heresy and suspension of the attributes.

He further stressed that the *Salaf* following the Qur'anic model confirmed the attributes in details, but confined themselves to a wholesale and comprehensive negation of any anthropomorphist element and comparison not appropriate to be attributed to God Almighty. In Ibn Taymiyyah's opinion, the *Salaf* believed in the commonly accepted meanings of these Qur'anic terms, in the way appropriate to the exalted majesty of God. Those meanings being absolutely different from their corresponding creaturely realities.

Unfortunately, despite all Ibn Taymiyyah's efforts to avoid anthropomorphism, and his categorical rejection of any resemblance between God and His creatures, and his genuine belief that God was not a corporeal or anthropomorphic being, it was his insistence upon giving literal meanings to Qur'anic anthropomorphic expressions, which became the focal point of simple minded fanatics allowing for the possible development of anthropomorphic shades of thought. There was no need for Ibn Taymiyyah to insist upon the literal sense of these expressions given that he was anti-anthropomorphism and categorically believed them not to denote their equivalent in the non-divine human realm, yet it was precisely this which led to the birth of certain suspicions and anecdotal narratives concerning him. The language, to use Netton's term, "is ruptured",[579] whether one calls it literal or metaphorical, it is a rupture of the language. In explaining the report of God's descent in the later part of the night Ibn Taymiyyah is supposedly reported to have said: "'God comes down from heaven to earth, just as I am coming down now,' and he (Ibn Taymiyyah) came down one of the steps of the pulpit staircase."[580] The same charge of corporealism incidentally was leveled at another Ḥanbalite, Abū ʿĀmir al-Qarashī, with similar anecdotal reports of his anthropomorphism circulating, such as his supposedly pointing to his leg and saying, "it is exactly the same as this [leg]" in explaining verse 68: 42 of the Qur'an. And it is in view of reports such as these, taking them at face value, that al-Nashshar,[581] Madkur, and Goldziher[582] have accused Ibn Taymiyyah of anthropomorphism and corporealism. Gibb and Kramers observe:

> An inveterate anthropomorphist, Ibn Taymiyyah interpreted literally all the passages in the Kur'an and tradition referring to

> the Deity. He was so imbued with this belief that, according to Ibn Battuta, he said one day from the pulpit in the mosque of Damascus: "God comes down from heaven to earth, just as I am coming down now", and he came down one of the steps of the pulpit staircase.[583]

As a result, Gibb counts Ibn Baṭūṭah, Ibn Ḥajar al-Ḥaytamī, Taqī al-Dīn al-Subkī, and Abū Ḥayyān al-Ẓāhirī among those who do not "agree on the orthodoxy of Ibn Taymiyyah."[584] Raghib al-Tabbakh, Muhammad Bahjah al-Baytar, and Muhammad Nasr al-Din al-Albani however have rejected these reports as mere fabrications and absurdities[585] defending Ibn Taymiyyah against all accusations of anthropomorphism and corporealism. Gibb observes: "However, those who praise are perhaps more numerous than his detractors..."[586]

It must be said that Ibn Taymiyyah, at least from his own writings, seems to be decidedly anti-anthropomorphic and anti-corporealist, as evidenced by his ceaseless emphasis upon the dissimilarity between God's attributes and man's attributes and his denunciation of any sort of resemblance existing between God and His creatures. Ibn Taymiyyah stresses that

> the statement about God's attributes is just like the statement about His essence (*Dhat*). There is absolutely none like unto Him either in His essence, or attributes, or actions... The knowledge of God, His coming down, and establishing Himself over the Throne, all [of these attributes and actions] are in a fashion appropriate to His essence, as the attributes of a servant [man] are suitable to him and appropriate to his human essence...; therefore, if anybody asks how God descends, or establishes Himself, knows, talks, measures, or creates, he should be replied: 'how is He in His being [essence]?' If the answer to this question is that, 'I do not know how of His being', then you should say: 'I do not know how of His attributes.' The knowledge of the how (*kayf*) of the attributes follows the knowledge of the how (*kayf*) of the one they are attributed to.[587]

Ibn Taymiyyah further argues that "the attributes of God are indeed different from and superior to the attributes of the creatures. Nobody knows the difference and the level of superiority except God Himself."[588] Even in explaining the reports of God's descent in the later part of the night, he is careful to point out that God's coming down did not consist of any movement or change of position that would make the Throne above God. For God is far beyond such creaturely attributes or propositions. Also, that "God descends to the heaven of the earth without the Throne being devoid of Him."[589] In short, according to Ibn Taymiyyah, God is God and not a creature. There is nothing like unto Him. Ibn Taymiyyah literally accepted God's reported attributes of face, hand, descent etc., but in a sense that was appropriate to His Exalted Majesty; and the nature of these attributes is unknown to humanity. This is the reason why many scholars including al-Dhahabī, Ibn Qudāmah, Ibn al-Wardī and ʿAlī al-Qārī (to name a few) and his own students including the renowned Ibn al-Qayyim al-Jawziyyah 1292/1350) refuted any accusations of anthropomorphism leveled against Ibn Taymiyyah, and moreover took him as a competent religious authority and a model to be followed in matters of faith and religion. Ibn al-Qayyim, for instance, followed his teacher literally with regards to the seemingly anthropomorphic expressions of the Qur'an and Sunnah. And there is no doubt that both by transmitting his teacher's works and faithfully publicizing his ideas in his own works, Ibn al-Qayyim did much to spread and perpetuate the influence of Ibn-Taymiyyah. Many other Ḥanbalites did the same with regards to Ibn Taymiyyah's teachings.

The debate raged on with the Ḥanbalites under fire. Despite their outward affinity with the Qur'anic expressions and claims to follow Ibn Ḥanbal's interpretive methodology, the literal position of many Ḥanbalites (discussed earlier) was severely attacked by other Muslim scholars who dubbed it as *Ḥashwiyyah* in the garb of *bilkafa*.[590] Ibn Ḥazm for instance declared literal understanding to be "an opening to the road ending in anthropomorphism."[591] Ḥanbalites such as ʿAlī ibn ʿUbayd Allāh al-Zaghunī, al-Qāḍī Abū Yaʿla, Abū ʿĀmir al-Qarashī, who followed a literal route to interpreting Qur'anic poetical expressions, were also severely censured. In contrast, other Ḥanbalites such as Ibn al-Jawzī al-Ḥanbalī and Ibn ʿAqīl vehemently opposed literalist interpretation, and seemed to have inclined towards a sort of rationalism closer to that of the Ashʿarites (discussed later in the chapter). They forbade discussion of ambiguous verses encouraging their acceptance without recourse to anthropomorphism or allegory.[592] Ibn al-Jawzī claims to have written his treatise *Dafaᶜ Shubhah al-Tashbīh* against those who "have fallen in the traps of anthropomorphism, but scorn its attribution to them. They claim to be from Sunnis but their statements are clear-cut anthropomorphisms."[593]

The second group of scholars argued that the *Salaf's* true position was not that of the ascription of a face or hands to God in their literal meaning *bilā kayf*, but rather the position of *al-tafwīḍ*. By *tafwīḍ* was meant acceptance of Qur'anic phrases without anthropomorphism, corporealism, or further inquiry into their meaning or realities, and to entrust true knowledge of this to God Himself. Al-Bayhaqī reports Sufyān ibn ᶜUyaynah as saying, "Whatever expressions God has employed in the Qur'an to describe His attributes, their elucidation (*tafsir*) is their reading. It is not permissible for anybody to explain them either in the Arabic or in the Persian language."[594] Ibn Ḥanbal is reported to have said, "We believe in these expressions and affirm them without how and without [further inquiry] into their meanings (*wa la kayf wa la maᶜnah*)." According to this understanding of the *Salaf*, Qur'anic expressions such as the 'face' or 'hands of God' did not carry a literal meaning comparable to their equivalent in human beings. That is, they did not literally mean the face or hands, or organs of God, as humans perceive them with regard to themselves, but rather attributes or qualities of God. There is no human being who knows the details or the how of these divine qualities just as nobody knows the essence of God's being. According to this group, the *Salaf* acknowledged their sheer ignorance of the divine realms, entrusting true knowledge of the meanings of these terms to God. Al-Rāzī, al-Shahrastānī, al-Ghazālī, Abd al-Halim Mahmud and M. Zahid al-Kawthari are just a few examples of the many who interpreted the standpoint of the *Salaf* in terms of *al-tafwīḍ*. Both Abū al-Ḥasan ᶜAlī al-Ashᶜarī (according to one dominant opinion) and Abū Manṣūr al-Māturīdī's (d. 331 AH) as well as al-Bāqillānī's (d. 403 AH)[595] position with regard to the Qur'anic expressions are quoted as examples of this *Salaf* line of approach.[596] For instance al-Rāzī observes that the *Salaf's* attitude to these ambiguous Qur'anic expressions was to "accept them without their literal meanings and to entrust the knowledge of their true meanings to God. Indulgence in their explanation (*tafsīr*) is not permissible."[597]

Al-Ashʿarī (873–935) studied the Muʿtazilite doctrines with al-Jubbaʿī, the head of the Basrian school of the Muʿtazilites, and converted to Sunnism or traditionalism as a result of a dream he had.[598] Watt observes that al-Ashʿarī "worked out his new theological position which may be described as the support of revelation by reason. This implies of course a subordination of reason."[599] In his early work *al-Ibānah*, al-Ashaʿrī declared that he was following in the footsteps of "Abū ʿAbd Allāh Aḥmad ibn Ḥanbal."[600] In this work, he sticks to the theological positions of Ibn Ḥanbal to such a degree that to Wensinck and Goldziher, he seems to be "the spiritual son of Ahmad ibn Hanbal."[601] In his later works such as *Maqālāt* and *al-Lumaʿ*, al-Ashaʿrī seems to have inclined more towards rational interpretations in support of revelation although Goldziher suspects his rationalism.[602] Watt remarks:

> The reader who now turns to translations of the works of al-Ashaʿri may at first find it difficult to discern any traces of "rational method" in them. They mostly consist of arguments from Qur'anic verses and Traditions. Yet even here a knowledge of the writings of men in the strict Hanbalite tradition shows that al-Ashaʿri really argues about these matters to a far greater extent. In addition other arguments are based on points of observation or of common knowledge, or on what the Muslims are agreed upon. Despite appearances, then, al-Ashʿari really introduced rational arguments; and this little piece of leaven quickly spread through the lump of Islamic theology.[603]

Al-Shahrastānī reports, that al-Ashʿarī "follows the early community in not attempting to interpret them [verses and ahadith], though according to one opinion reported of him he allows interpretation."[604]

Al-Ashʿarī attempted to straddle a middle position, between anthropomorphic literalism and Muʿtazilite neutralism, although Goldziher does not agree labelling al-Ashʿarī's position as "conciliatory".[605] Al-Ashʿarī argued:

> God is knowing with knowledge, powerful with power, living with life, willing with will, speaking with speech... These attributes...are eternal and subsist in the essence of God. It cannot be said that they are he or other than he; nor can it be said that they are not he, nor that they are not other than he.[606]

In *al-Ibānah,* al-Ashaʿrī dealt with the issue of both the Qur'an and the Sunnah's anthropomorphic expressions at length. There, he literally and faithfully followed the pattern set by the *Salaf.* He argued that God had a face, two eyes, two hands etc., but that these were "two hands not like hands."[607] He affirmed the reality[608] of these attributes with emphasis upon their dissimilarity with creatures and their acceptance under the clause of without how.[609] Watt notes that al-Ashʿarī "insisted that such Qur'anic phrases must simply be accepted "without specifying how.""[610] Wensinck states that in *al-Ibānah* al-Ashʿarī produces arguments in favor of the view that Allah has a face and two hands, knowledge, power and speech: "In all this there is scarcely a word that could not have been written by Ahmad ibn Hanbal."[611] Goldziher comments:

> Indeed, when he comes to speak of the anthropomorphist question, he heaps all his scorn on the rationalists who seek figurative explanations for the concrete terms of the holy scriptures. Not satisfied with the rigor of the orthodox theologian, he also shows himself a grammarian. God Himself says, after all, that He revealed the Qur'an in "clear Arabic"; it follows that the Qur'an can only be understood in the light of correct Arabic usage. But when in the world had any Arab ever used the word "hand" to mean "benevolence," and so on? What Arab has ever employed all those tricks of language that rationalist interpreters want to read into the clear text in order to despoil the idea of God of all content?[612]

Goldziher further argues:

> To escape crass anthropomorphism, he does, to be sure, insert into his creed the clause that by face, hand, foot, and so on, we are not

> to understand members of a human body, that all this is to be understood bila kayfa, without asking how... But to add this clause is not to be mediate; for traditional orthodoxy had held the same view. This was no mediation between Ibn Hanbal and the Muʿtazila; this was – as we could see from al-Ashʿari's prefatory declaration – the Muʿtazilite renegade's unconditional surrender to the standpoint of the traditionalists' inflexible *imam* and his followers. By his far-reaching concessions to popular belief, al-Ashʿari caused the loss to the Muslims of important Muʿtazilite achievements.[613]

This close similarity to and affinity with Ibn Ḥanbal has led many scholars (convinced that Ibn Ḥanbal was a literalist) to believe that al-Ashʿarī likewise took a literal position with regards to these anthropomorphic expressions, i.e., in Ibn Taymiyyah's opinion this was definitely the case.[614] However, M. Zahid al-Kawthari vehemently opposes this interpretation arguing that al-Ashʿarī never regarded the expressions in a literal sense and never once claimed that God had two hands, two eyes etc. and that all words denoting such anthropomorphic implications were later inventions and inserted into his writings.

Abū al-Maʿālī ibn ʿAbd al-Malik al-Juwaynī, Imam al-Ḥaramayn, argues that al-Ashʿarī admitted the existence of these divine qualities with the qualification of *tanzīh*: "Knowledge, but not like human knowledge... Hand and face are hand as a quality and face as a quality, just as hearing and sight. Concerning Allah's descending to the lowest Heaven, al-Ashʿari said that descending is a quality; likewise His sitting on the throne is a quality."[615] Al-Shahrastānī reports that al-Ashʿarī

> maintains that hearing and seeing are two eternal attributes of God. They are perceptions beyond knowledge, connected with their proper objects provided they exist. He holds also that hands and face are attributes that are reported of God; for, as he explains, revelation speaks of them, and, therefore, they must be accepted as they are revealed. He follows the early community in not attempting to interpret them, though according to one opinion reported of him he allows interpretation.[616]

M. Zahid al-Kawthari argues that al-Ashʿarī's *al-Ibānah* was according to the way of the *Salaf's 'tafwīḍ'* entrusting God with the meaning and "abstinence from fixation and specification of the intended meaning."[617] Therefore in Armstrong's opinion, al-Ashʿarī was different in that he

> opposed the literalists by pointing out that the Koran insisted that we could talk about God only in symbolic language. But he also opposed the Traditionist wholesale rejection of reason. He argued that Muhammad had not encountered these problems or he would have given the Muslims guidance; as it was, all Muslims had a duty to use such interpretive tools as analogy (*qiyas*) to retain a truly religious concept of God.[618]

Unlike the traditionalists, argues Watt:

> a thinker like al-Ashʿari who admitted a proper theological use of reason could not rest content in the acceptance of this disharmony in our theological conceptions. He, himself, though admitting *balkayfiyya*, never, as far as I am aware, went so far as Ibn Qutaybah in emphasizing the disharmony of the Scriptural conceptions; and the development of doctrine among his followers was largely guided by the ideal of finding harmony and system in the main conceptions of Scripture.[619]

Therefore, argues Armstrong, "Unlike Ibn Hanbal, Al-Ashʿari was prepared to ask questions and to explore these metaphysical problems, even though ultimately he concluded that it was wrong to try to contain the mysterious and ineffable reality that we call God in [a] tidy, rationalistic system."[620] Wensinck also observes the fact that "he adopted *kalam* as a method is certain."[621]

It must be added here that al-Ashaʿrī, at least from what is available of his writings, seems to have adopted a position very close to that of taking these terms literally without how and not metaphorically. He refutes metaphorical interpretations of terms such as *yad* and *wajh*[622] whilst confirming the "two hands of God in reality (*fī al-ḥaqīqah*)."[623] Rippin observes:

> God's attributes are real for al-Ashʿari because the Qur'an clearly states them and so it must be meaningful to speak of God's hand and God's face; de-anthropomorphization was one of the central elements of Muʿtazilites' thought which al-Ashʿari denounced, for he saw it as a symbol of rationalist excess and willful ignorance of the sense of the Qur'anic text. Still, he did not wish to deny that reason indicates that speaking of these attributes of God would seem problematic when put in conjunction with an infinite God. His solution was to speak of the reality of the attributes but that these are not attributes in the same way that humans have such: God does have a hand, but we just 'do not know how' this is to be conceived. The phrase *bila kayf*, 'without knowing how', became a key term in Ashʿarite theology, to be used whenever reason and the Qur'an or *hadith* met head-on in conflict.[624]

On the other hand, al-Ashaʿrī's somewhat deductive theological style differs to certain degrees from the traditionalists. His usage of terms such as "hands not like hands" as well as the existence of certain reports that he allowed metaphorical interpretation (*ta'wīl*), like that of al-Shahrastānī quoted above, all are factors combined to give the impression that he was what the later Ashaʿrites made him out to be. Otherwise, as far as his own writings are concerned, he was close to maintaining a literal understanding of these problematic expressions with the clause *bilā kayf* although he does not seem to have pushed for their literal meaning to the degree of Ibn Khuzaymah or Ibn Taymiyyah. In other words, a language rupture much more dense and intense can be granted to al-Ashaʿrī rather than the intensity of traditionalists like Ibn Khuzaymah and Ibn Taymiyyah. This was solely due to his background, training, and usage of *kalām* methodology and style, and not due to vocabulary employed in his books to explain these expressions. George C. Anawati observes that regarding Qur'anic anthropomorphism:

> al-Baqillani remains very close to al-Ashʿari': he affirms that God really has a face, and hands, that he is really on his throne. He refuses to interpret these expressions either in a realistic fashion (like the Hanabilah) or in an allegorical fashion (like the

> Muʿtazilah). Similarly, for the "vision of God" (pp.226–279), al-Baqillani insists on God's transcendence: there is no possible explanation for the way that vision will take place any more than there is for the way that divine speech is to be understood.[625]

Al-Bāqillānī argues that the ambiguous mention of God's attributes such as hand and face in certain Qur'anic verses should not be taken literally in terms of common human perception and usage. The eternal God cannot be assigned attributes or described in terms contingent on His creatures for He states in the Qur'an that, "There is none like unto Him" (42:11; 112:4). Therefore attributing to God transmutation, movement, staying at a place, standing, sitting and other items of this nature, is not permitted. Such attributes mark contingency and God transcends such attributes. To al-Bāqillānī, God's "*istawā ʿalā al-ʿArsh*" means "neither establishment upon the Throne nor any direction... because the Throne is contingent."[626] And, it does not mean "manner or mode or proximity because He is God in heavens as much as He is God on the earth."[627] God is eternal and everlasting while the Throne is not. Likewise God's hands are not "two hands i.e., organs and do not have any form, shape or appearance...,"[628] the same applying to other Qur'anic anthropomorphic expressions, underscored by the clause, we do not know the how of them.[629]

The third group, the "*Khalaf* or successors", most of them Ashʿarites, started with Ibn al-Furak al-Iṣbahānī (d. 406 AH) and ended with al-Shahrastānī (d. 548 AH). It was their contention that the metaphors were a reality recognized and used by the Qur'an and the Sunnah, and that there existed consensus among all mainstream Muslim scholars that the literal meaning of these phrases was not the intended meaning of the revelation because such meanings would lead to anthropomorphism. Hence, a metaphorical interpretation of Qur'anic anthropomorphic expressions substantiated by the fixed rules of the Arabic language and appropriate to the Exalted Majesty of God would be acceptable and immanent to avert any anthropomorphic implications.[630] Following this line of thought the *Khalaf* metaphorically interpreted anthropomorphic expressions by deriving or substantiating these interpretations with other Qur'anic verses or with the help of ancient pre-Islamic Arabic poetry or prose. Within a century of the death of al-Ashʿarī, observes Watt, "in 324/935 the school which took his name had abandoned the doctrine of *balkafiyya* on most of the points on which al-Ashʿari had contended for it and had adopted views similar to those of his opponents among the Muʿtazila."[631] Regarding the Divine Attributes, observes Gibb, "the scholastics maintained the doctrine of their eternity, but only by applying the Muʿtazilite principle of negation of anthropomorphic concepts."[632] Al-Baghdādī (d.429/1037),[633] al-Taftazānī,[634] al-Juwaynī (d.478/1085),[635] al-Ghazālī (505/1111),[636] al-Shahrastānī (548/1153),[637] and al-Rāzī (606/1209)[638] are just a few examples of this tendency.

These Ashʿarite theologians agreed that by the hands of God was meant His power, by His eyes was meant His seeing, and by his face was meant His essence or existence; and none of them took sitting on the throne literally or *bi-la kayf*. On the other hand, they held that God would be seen by the faithful on the day of resurrection, even considering that they could give a rational proof of the possibility of God's being seen; this alleged proof presupposed, of course, that God was not corporeal.[639]

The Ashʿarite theologians rendered all the divine attributes into seven major attributes: Power, Knowledge, Life, Will, Hearing, Seeing and Speech. In their rational or metaphorical interpretations of Qur'anic anthropomorphic expressions, these later Ashʿarites came closer to "Muʿtazilah and even closer to philosophers", as Madkur argues.[640] Watt observes that the *Mawāqif* of al-Ījī (d. 756/1355) as commented upon by al-Jurjānī (d. 816/1413), "perhaps comes back closer to the al-Ashʿari of the *Ibana*, but definitely does not return to the doctrine of *balkafiyya*."[641] Ashʿarism in its later manifestation along with its closest ally al-Maturidiyyah is still dominant in most parts of the Islamic world. Like al-Ashʿarī, observes Rippin, "al-Maturidi followed a middle path between Traditionalism and rationalism, forging an Islam which saw the written sources of the faith dominate but which found a place for the activities of the human mind."[642]

For instance, al-Ghazālī, the most known of the *Khalaf*, divides people into two categories: common people and scholars (*ʿulamā'*), advising the former (common folk) not to engage in interpretation of ambiguous Qur'anic expressions but,

> to eliminate from their belief system all that leads to anthropomorphism or contingency and to determine that God is such an existent there is none like unto Him and He is the hearing and the seeing. And if they happen to inquire about the meanings of the ambiguous Qur'anic verses, they should be warned about doing so.[643]

On the other hand,

> it is appropriate for the scholars to know and understand such verses. I do not say it is incumbent upon each individual scholar to know the true meanings of these expressions. The knowledge of their true interpretations is not required, it is voluntary. The obligation is confined to declaring God's transcendence above all that has any comparison or similarity...We do not agree with those who claim that such verses are ambiguous [*al-mutashābihāt*] like the words at the beginning of some Qur'anic chapters [*suwar*].[644]

Al-Ghazālī viewed the alleged anthropomorphic expressions of the Qur'an and Hadith as consisting of phrases commonly used and clearly understood by the Arabs, unlike those occurring as letters at the beginning of certain chapters of the Qur'an. And either the phrases carried literal meaning or they had to be understood in terms of their metaphorical set up and context. Now, as all parties were in agreement, argued al-Ghazālī, that God was neither a body nor a contingent and that the literal meanings of the anthropomorphic phrases could not and cannot be attributed to Him, the only option left would be to accept their metaphorical meanings.[645] Al-Juwaynī, the teacher of al-Ghazālī, points to the contradiction that lies between the conception that God is "with you whereinsoever you are" (57:4) and that "He established Himself upon the Throne" (57:4), reasoning that if God was on the Throne He could not be with all human beings. From this contradiction, as Watt observes,

> al-Juwayni draws the conclusion that the method of *ta'wil* cannot be avoided in some cases, and in particular that God's presence with the believers must mean His knowledge of their secrets. In

> this he is assuming that there must be harmonious rational interpretation of the Scriptural phrases, and apparently his opponents were not capable of defending the opposite view.[646]

What needs mentioning at this juncture is that the nature of these metaphorical interpretations differed markedly to the allegorical interpretations of certain Christian sects discussed in previous chapters lest comparison be made. The later Ashʿarites' metaphorical interpretations, unlike Christian allegorism, were bound by strictly fixed linguistic rules with regards to the language, to which they had to adhere, and their metaphorical interpretations were further limited by the fixed number of linguistic meanings governing each term. In other words interpretation was controlled by clearly defined linguistic parameters, forcing the Ashʿarites to employ one of the already existing linguistic meanings of the term under question as an appropriate or intended meaning, preventing the invention of far-fetched facts or speculative suppositions to fit or prove whatever was wanting proven from the text. Moreover, this fixation was further substantiated by the usage of the same meanings in established Arabic metaphors.[647] Although there was scope to arrive at a number of different yet mutually related interpretations with different scholars perhaps emphasizing different aspects or meanings out of the few commonly used meanings of a phrase, nevertheless this was a far fry cry from free and open speculation, closing the doors to fanciful and absurd interpretations. Watt rightly notes:

> We must be careful, however, not to exaggerate the liberty in interpretation claimed by men like al-Juwayni. The conceptions which they interpreted metaphorically were few in number, and even to these they applied the metaphorical interpretation only in order to bring them in harmony with principles which long discussion had convinced them were thoroughly in accordance with the sacred texts.[648]

Therefore, we see a kind of consensus existing among most of the interpreters over the meanings of several of these problematic Qur'anic expressions. Having said this, the method of metaphorical interpretation or *ta'wīl* employed by the Ashaʿrites was in contrast with that of other exponents of the method such as the Muʿtazilites or the *Jahmiyyah* in the sense that:

> It was not a rationalism in which reason was set above the revealed Scriptures, but one in which reason was assumed to be competent to understand and interpret the main truths contained in the Scriptures, and with these as basis to fathom the mystery of the Divine nature. That is to say, it was argued that, though the conceptions of religious intuition could not be reached by purely rational procedures yet, once they reached, they were thoroughly rational conceptions, forming [a] harmonious system.[649]

In light of these tendencies among Muslim theologians, let us go back to the Qur'anic verses and the *aḥādīth* themselves to see where they stand in terms of their anthropomorphism.

The word *ʿAyan* literally meaning "eye" occurs in a total of five Qur'anic verses in connection with God (once as my eye 20:39; and 4 times as our eyes 11:37; 23:27; 52:48; 54:14). After conferring favors upon Moses, God reminds him of these bounties by the following words:

> Behold! We sent to thy mother, by inspiration, the message: "Throw (the child) into the chest, and throw (the chest) into the river: The river will cast him up on the bank, and he will be taken up by one who is an enemy to Me and an enemy to him": but I endued thee with love from Me and (this) in order that thou mayest be reared *under Mine eye (wa li tuṣnaʿa ʿalā ʿaynī).* (20:38–39)

God is reported to have commanded Noah to "construct an Ark under *Our eyes* and Our inspiration, and address Me no (further) on behalf of those who are in sin: for they are about to be overwhelmed (in the Flood)" (11:37 also 23:27). In 52:48 Muhammad is told: "Now await in patience the command of thy Lord: for verily thou art in *Our eyes*" (or with Our eyes *bi 'aᶜyuninā*), and in 54:14 Noah's Ark is reported to float under God's eyes. The very non-anthropomorphic, non-corporeal, and in a sense metaphorical nature of the expression *ᶜAyan* in these Qur'anic verses is evident from their context. Al-Bayhaqī explains how the *aḥādīth* discussing the one-eye of the Anti-Christ and God having not been one-eyed, emphasizes God's attribute of omniscience.[650] Ibn Ḥajar explains that in this particular hadith the Prophet pointed to his eye not as a symbol of God's *ᶜAyan* but as a symbol of the Anti-Christ's eye.[651] Ibn Ḥazm argues that "it is not allowed for anybody to ascribe to God two eyes because the text does not prove so."[652]

The term *yad* literally meaning "hand" occurs in the Qur'an a total of nine times with regards to God Almighty. Out of these the phrase "hand of Allah" is conspicuous as it occurs in four verses out of the nine verses (3:73; 5:64; 48:10; 57:29). The non-anthropomorphic nature of this phrase becomes evident from its context. "Say: 'All bounties (grace) are in the *hand of Allah*. He granteth them to whom He pleaseth: and Allah careth for all, and He knoweth all things'" (3:73 also 57:29). In 5:64 both God's hands are mentioned: "And the Jews say, 'God's hand is shackled!' It is their own hands that are shackled; and rejected [by God] are they because of this their assertion. Nay, *both His hands* are widely outstretched: He giveth and spendeth (of His bounty) as He pleaseth..." The verse does not qualify for an absolute literalist interpretation, the metaphorical meaning of the phrase in terms of context is entirely self-evident conveying God's attribute of infinite generosity, giving, and grace to those who do good as well as to those who are evil.[653] Another reference occurs with regards to the treaty of Ḥudaybiyyah, and in connection with the incident of the pledge of Riḍwān (*Bayᶜah al-Riḍwān)*: "Verily those who plight their fealty to thee plight their fealty in truth to Allah: *The Hand of Allah* is over their hands: then any one who violates his oath, does so to the harm of his own soul, and any one who fulfills what he has covenanted with Allah, – Allah will soon grant him a great reward" (48:10). Here again context makes metaphorical interpretation self-evident, emphasis being upon the significance of the Muslims' plight and so God's hands referring to God's help. In verse 38:75 Allah questions Satan: "O Iblis! What prevents thee from prostrating thyself to one whom I have created with *My hands*?" If taken literally, at face value, the verse would seem to indicate a sort of anthropomorphism, because human beings create with their hands, and transposing this understanding onto the use of God's hands in the act of Adam's creation would seem a plausible inference. Regardless however, a literal meaning is out of the question, primarily because this is the only place in the Qur'an where the act of creation is connected with God's hands while in several other places the Qur'an connects the act directly to God Himself.[654] This perhaps explains why many scholars including Ibn Furak, Ibn al-ʿArabī, al-Ghazālī and others have interpreted the phrase "with My hands" to mean "with My power or authority or grace", i.e., without any other agent or any other means.[655]

Al-Ashʿarī argued against such metaphorical interpretation contending that, "It is not permissible to say (two hands) mean two bounties as it is not allowed by the language itself that someone can say "I did with my both hands" intending my bounty." After refuting both the other meanings, of physical hands as well as power, he argues that the only remaining possibility is that "these mean two hands not like (creatures') hands excluding all the above three possibilities."[656] He is not alone. Even scholars like al-Harawī, Ibn Taymiyyah, Ibn al-Qayyim, and al-Bayhaqī have avoided interpreting the term hands to mean power or grace whilst simultaneously rejecting any notion ascribing to them human equivalency, emphasizing that the two hands of God simply stand for the two divine attributes directly involved in Adam's creation and all the potential God bestowed upon him. It was their belief hence that the verse signified Adam's tremendous honor, dignity and distinction and not God having to physically create him making direct contact with Adam's anatomy. Ibn al-Jawzī al-Ḥanbalī observed that certain people believed that God had hands and so "wrongly argue that God touches. They go that far as claiming that God touched with His hand the clay from which Adam was created... This is a slander and a white lie regarding God..."[657] The Qur'an itself dispels any anthropomorphic implications of this verse by putting Jesus' virgin birth on a par with Adam's creation: "The similitude of Jesus before Allah is as that of Adam; He created him from dust, then said to him: 'Be': and he was."[658] In *Sūrah Āl ʿImrān* the Qur'an clearly states that the commandment "Be" was conveyed to Mary through an angel and not by any direct contact to or from God (3:45–47), see also *Maryam*, 19:17–21.

In addition to the phrase two hands, the Qur'an also mentions the term right hand in connection with God:

> No just estimate have they made of Allah, such as is due to Him: on the Day of Judgment the whole of the earth will be His handful (*qabḍatuhu* meaning grip, hold, handful), and the heavens will be rolled up in His right hand: Glory to Him! High is He above the partners they attribute to Him! (39:67)[659]

Al-Alusi and al-Bayhaqī point to several examples taken from Arabic literature to illustrate the metaphorical use of the phrase *qabḍah* to mean authority and the metaphorical use of the phrase *al-yamīn* to mean absolute power.[660] In several prophetic narrations it has been claimed that both God's hands are right. But as al-Bayhaqī and Ibn Furak establish, the Arabs used the phrase right hand as an idiom to express generosity and perfection. So the statement "both God's hands are right", according to them, denotes His absoluteness and perfection.[661]

It is in hadith literature that we find the use of more daring expressions which, if taken absolutely literally, would seem to depict God in somewhat anthropomorphic terms. For instance, God's fingers are mentioned: "Verily, the hearts of all the sons of Adam are between the *two fingers out of the fingers* of the Compassionate Lord as one heart. He turns them to any (direction) He likes. Then Allah's Messenger said: O Allah, the Turner of the hearts, turn our hearts to Thine obedience."[662] Ibn al-Athīr regards the fingers as symbolizing the swiftness with which God can transform and change hearts.[663] Ibn Ḥazm interprets fingers as denoting two of God's plans and bounties out of His countless divine plans and bounties.[664] Al-Nawawī observes that such Prophetic narration must be understood in light of the Qur'anic verse, "There is nothing like unto to Him" and that secondly, it can be interpreted metaphorically in accordance with the rules and regulations of language:

> When it is said "such and such is in my grip or in the palm of my hand" it does not mean that the person is literally in my palm or hand. It means I have power over him. In the same manner it is said "such and such is between my fingers I can change him the way I want to" it means that he is absolutely under my authority. Therefore the hadith means that God has absolute authority upon the hearts of His servants and can change them whatever way He wants...[665]

There are other reports indicating that on the Day of Judgment, "Allah will put all the heavens on one finger, and the earths on one finger, and the trees on one finger, and the water and the dust on one finger, and all the other created beings on one finger. Then He will say, 'I am the King'..."[666] Such reports can also be understood in light of al-Nawawī's interpretation.[667] Ibn Furak argues that

> the word "*al-iṣbaʿah*" is linguistically used for several mutually related meanings... It is also used for the organ, but is not specified for that purpose only. It is as much used to denote meanings other than organ as much as it is used to denote organ. And we have already explained and proved that God cannot be ascribed members, organs or other corporeal attributes. Therefore, the meanings other than organ or member must be the right meanings.[668]

Al-Ghazālī is also of the opinion that all these expressions are not meant to be taken literally. They must be interpreted metaphorically to deny any similarity to the corporeal or anthropomorphism.[669]

God's foot is mentioned in the following Prophetic report: "Narrated Anas: The Prophet said, 'The people will be thrown into the (Hell) Fire and it will say: "Are there any more (to come)?" (50:30) till Allah puts *His foot* over it and it will say, *Qati*! *Qati*! (Enough! Enough!)'".[670] This text, observes Goldziher, "was troublesome for a refined conception of God. Such versatility of ingenious thought went into its interpretation that it represents a complete sampler of the hermeneutical arts cherished by the Ashʿarite school."[671] Al-Bayhaqī interprets it metaphorically observing that by putting of the foot is meant a kind of reprimand to and pacification of Hell Fire as is said "I put such and such under my foot" meaning control, pacification, and extinction.[672] Al-Nawawī refers to the interpretation of al-Nadhīr ibn Shāmil that *al-qadam* means *al-mutaqaddim* [673] meaning preceding i.e. those whom God knew by His eternal knowledge would be the people of Hell Fire.[674] Ibn Furak al-Iṣbahānī gives many more explanations to conclude that "no explanation whatsoever can be accepted which would ascribe to God of members, organs, parts of body or any other corporeal attributes."[675] To Goldziher, on the other hand, such reports are evident examples of anthropomorphism and the interpretations given a mere "sampler of exegetical violence."[676]

The Qur'an uses the term "side of Allah" in a metaphorical sense when it says: "Turn ye to your Lord and submit to Him, before the Chastisement comes on you, after that ye shall not be helped... Lest the soul should (then) say: 'Ah! woe is me! in that I neglected (my duty) towards Allah (literally *in the side of Allah – janbillah*) and I was but among those who mocked'" (39:54–56). It seems clear that the phrase is not an anthropomorphic expression but stands, as argues al-Rāzī, for worship and obedience, which is why it has been translated as such.[677]

The coming of the Lord on the Day of Judgment is mentioned in the following verse: "Nay! When the earth is pounded to powder, and *thy Lord cometh*, and His angels, rank upon rank, and Hell, that Day, is brought, on that Day will man remember, but how will that remembrance profit him?" (89:21–23). It also says: "Are they waiting to see if the angels come to them, *thy Lord*, or certain of the Signs of thy Lord! The day that certain of the Signs of thy Lord do come, no good will it do to a soul to believe then..." (6:158). "Will they wait until *Allah comes to them* in canopies of clouds and angels and the matter is settled? But to Allah do all matters go back (for decision)" (2:210).

This coming of the Lord can be interpreted as the coming of His command and order in the shape of punishment as can be substantiated from other verses of the Qur'an which specifically state: "Will they wait until angels come to them or the Command (*amr*) of thy Lord comes?..." (16:33).[678] There is a famous saying of the Prophet that:

> Our Lord, the Blessed, the Superior, comes down (*yanzilu*) every night on the heaven of the world (*dunya* i.e. first Sky) during the last third of the night and He says: (Is there anyone) who invokes Me, so that I may respond to his invocation? Is there anyone who asks Me, so that I may grant him his request? (Is there anyone) who seeks My forgiveness, so that I may forgive him?[679]

Again this report can also be easily interpreted as a metaphor for, as al-Ghazālī explains,[680] *al-nuzūl* in the sense of movement or declining of position is impossible in connection with God, and therefore, it means His kindness, mercy and readiness to listen to and respond to the supplications of those who call upon Him at the later part of the night.[681] Badr al-Dīn al-ʿAynī and Ibn Furak argue that the word *nuzūl* in the Arabic language is used with five different meanings. (1) to mean change of location, position or station as in verse 25:48 of the Qur'an, (2) to mean notification, information, advice, as in verse 26:193, (3) to mean statement, utterance, speech as in verse 6:93, (4) to mean attention or responsiveness to and interest in, and (5) to mean arrival of a verdict, judgment, decision etc. as known from common usage of the term. They further argue that the only logical interpretation would be God's readiness and responsiveness to mankind as God is not a body that moves or changes location.[682] Gibb and Kramers also observe that the report of "the nightly descent of God to earth, [is] in itself really soteriological and edifying, in which the exact point actually lies in the hearing of prayer."[683] Goldziher, on the other hand, argues:

> In this case the anthropomorphism was removed by means of a grammatical trick, made available by the nature of the old Arabic script, which does not contain any graphic expression of the vowels. Instead of *yanzilu*, "he descends," they read the factitive form *yunzilu*, "he causes to descend," namely, the angels. Thus the text's statement about God's change of place vanishes; it is not God who descends, but He causes angels to descend, who sound these calls in God's name.[684]

The same metaphorical interpretations of mercy, grace, and generosity could also be applied to phrases used in other Prophetic reports to explain their correct meaning, i.e. the hadith which teaches that whosoever comes closer to God by the span of a hand, God comes closer to him by an arms-length; and whosoever comes to Him walking, He comes to him jogging/running (at quick pace).

Scholars like Ibn Taymiyyah, on the other hand, argue against such an interpretation of the report and contend that it is God Himself who descends to the heaven of the earth and not His command or mercy. This does not mean that we should rush to depict Ibn Taymiyyah as an anthropomorphist simply because he refuted a metaphorical interpretation of *al-nuzūl*. We know from his writings that he always claimed to follow the *Salaf* confirming attributes without anthropomorphism (comparison), depiction (portrayal), alteration (distortion), and suspension, arguing against an anthropomorphic understanding of such reports. Which is why he is careful, like other scholars, to often modify such reports with the qualifier that God descends in a mode appropriate to His Majesty, the mode of His descent being absolutely different from the mode of His creatures. After detailed discussion of the meaning of "*al-ḥarakah,* meaning *movement*" including its philosophical as well as scholarly definitions, Ibn Taymiyyah contends that '*al-ḥarakah*' is not confined to bodies only concluding that,

> the dictum to be definitely maintained is, that there is none whatsoever like Allah in all what He has attributed to Himself. So whosoever describes to Him anything of the creatures' attributes or qualities in any of the things or aspects, is absolutely wrong. Such is the one who says that God comes down i.e, moves or transmutes as a man comes from the roof to the lower part of the house or like the one who says [He comes down] and the Throne becomes devoid of Him. This makes His coming down mean emptying a place and occupying another which is absolutely absurd. Such understanding must be denied of God...[685]

He further argues that God is above everything, which does not mean that He is upon His Throne but that He is even above and over the Throne. Therefore, "the word '*al-nuzul*' and likewise are definitely interpreted because there is nothing there from where His coming down can be imagined."[686]

As explained it is clearly evident that Ibn Taymiyyah's insistence upon the literal meanings of these phrases is not due to any corporealism or anthropomorphism on his part but rather his insistence upon the superiority of revelation over logic and not otherwise. He vehemently refutes any similarity or comparison between God and His creatures by overwhelmingly emphasizing the fact that nobody knows the mode of God's coming, seeing or speaking for nobody knows the essence of God. Only one reality is known regarding God's *nuzūl* and other attributes and that is, that *all of them* are not anthropomorphic, but appropriate to His exalted majesty.[687] Given Ibn Taymiyyah's strident emphasis upon the impossibility of any comparison or resemblance between God and creation, we can only conclude that the claims of Ibn Baṭūṭah as well as the accusations of corporealism leveled by al-Nashshar, Goldziher and others against him, are biased.

The mention of God established/settled on/above His throne *(istawā ʿalā al-ʿArsh)* occurs in the Qur'an in seven verses: "Verily your Lord is Allah, who created the heavens and the earth in six days, and is firmly established on the throne (of authority), regulating and governing all things..." (10:3; also see 7:54; 13:2; 20:5; 25:59; 32:4; 57:4). This seemingly anthropomorphic Qur'anic expression has been the focus of many exegetical arguments and interpretations.[688] All mainstream scholars agree that *istawā* does not mean sitting or physically touching the Throne whether in this or in any other anthropomorphic or corporeal sense.[689] Imam Mālik, representing the *Salaf*, argued that "*al-istawā* is not unknown and how (*al-istawā* takes place) is unintelligible. To believe in this is essential and any inquiry into and question about it is innovation."[690] Rabīʿah ibn Abī ʿAbd al-Rahmān's (the teacher of Imam Mālik) reply in response to a question concerning the meaning of the verse was: "[The] [h]ow of that is unknown, and *al-istawa* is unintelligible, and it is essential for you and me to believe in it."[691] This was the classical stance adopted by the *Salaf*, as already discussed, to maintain the superiority of revelation over reason and to maintain a sort of mystery and ineffability with regards to God. Al-Ashʿarī remained very close to this position arguing that the Muʿtazilite's interpretation of the word *al-istawā* as power and dominance did not go with the fact of God's power and dominance extending to the whole of creation, the world and the universe. But no one

> from the Muslims [is] allow[ed] to describe Him as dominant over weeds and cells. Therefore it is not permissible to say that *al-istawa* means *al-istila'* (dominance) over the Throne as that is the case with everything else. So it is essential to accept it as meaning *istawa* specifically connected with the Throne with the exception of all other things.[692]

The phrase, to al-Ashʿarī, meant that God is even over and above His Throne which is the most magnificent and the highest of His creations. Many scholars like Mujāhid, Abū al-ʿĀliyah, and others followed the *Salaf* stance, taking *al-istawā* to mean "raised above the Throne" and not settled upon it i.e., rejecting any conveying of a sense of sitting as a physical body would do.[693] Ibn Taymiyyah also argued that *al-istawā* did not in any way or form convey a sense of God sitting upon or touching the Throne. Rather, it conveyed the attribute of "*ʿUlūw*" meaning highness and exaltedness over and above the Throne.[694]

The later Ashʿarites, on the other hand, preferred metaphorical interpretations to avoid anthropomorphismic implications. For instance al-Ghazālī argued that the literal meaning of the word *al-istawā* leads to corporealism (and could lead certain people to confusion or anthropomorphism) which is denied by all the parties concerned; therefore it is not appropriate to ascribe it to God Almighty who is neither a body nor contingent.[695] Therefore, he reasoned the metaphorical meaning of "*al-istiʿlā*' that is, dominance", is the only logical interpretation.[696] Al-Ghazālī even argued that Ibn Ḥanbal also knew that *al-istawā* did not mean God establishing Himself upon the Throne physically and that *al-nuzūl* did not mean God's physically descending, but he prohibited metaphorical interpretation anyway, so as not to open the door to exploitation of revelation and extremism.[697] The metaphorical, non-corporeal nature of the phrase has become so common among Muslims that Muslim scholarship is not hesitant to argue that nowhere does the Qur'an mention that God sits on an *ʿArsh*; it is always God's controlling power that is mentioned in connection with this.

Finally, we have a hadith in which the Prophet is reported to have said, "God created Adam in his form, his height being sixty ells."[698] This report bears close resemblance to Genesis 1:26 ("Then God said, 'Let us make mankind in our image, in our likeness...'") if taken to mean that God created Adam in God's form. However, it differs from Genesis in that it does not include that critical phrase "in his likeness" meaning the hadith excludes resemblance. Abū Muḥammad ibn Qutaybah took the hadith literally arguing that God has a "form but not like forms."[699] According to al-Qāḍī Abū Yaʿlā, "The term form may be applied to God although it is not a form like other forms; the same is true of the term essence (*dhat*) when applied to God."[700] Such literalism, in Ibn Furak's opinion, leads to clear anthropomorphism which is contradictory to the Qur'anic dictum that there is none like unto Him.[701] And to Ibn al-Jawzī al-Ḥanbalī such a literal interpretation was "repulsive and ugly,"[702] for it

> reflects serious confusion, for the term essence refers to the quintessential character (*ma'na*) of something whereas [the word] *form* (*sura*) implies a shape (*hay'a*) with limits (*takhatit*) and composition (*ta'lif*), and presupposes a fashioner or composer. Those who use the expression "a form not like other forms" face the same problem as those who say "a body not like other bodies" for [in both cases] they contradict themselves.[703]

In other words, if Adam was created in God's form (literally) then how in the world could someone simultaneously say God has a form unlike forms.[704] This is why traditionalists who stuck to a literal meaning of the Prophetic report were scolded by their colleagues as corporealists.

Trusted student of Imam Mālik, Ibn al-Qāsim reports that Mālik strictly prohibited any discussion of the "image" reports preferring complete silence over them.[705] Others had no reservation in discussing and interpreting them metaphorically arguing that God did not possess a form. Therefore a literal interpretation of the report would certainly not be acceptable. Badr al-Dīn al-ʿAynī and many others have interpreted it to meaning that God created Adam "in Adam's form. This is a better and the appropriate interpretation. It means that God created Adam as a full fledged man with full creation having a length of sixty ells unlike others who are first just a sperm, then a clot... go through stages."[706] This view was initially adopted by the famous hadith authority Abū Sulaymān al-Khaṭṭābī and followed by many theologians especially the later Ashʿarites such as al-Baghdādī, al-Juwaynī and al-Ghazālī.

Al-Bayhaqī contends that a form is a composition of various parts and as God defies all composition He cannot be ascribed any form (*ṣūrah*). Al-Bayhaqī quotes Abū Manṣūr Muḥammad ibn al-Ḥasan ibn Ayūb, the famous theologian, as stating that in this report "the Prophet wanted to explain that Adam's form did not change as happened to the Serpent when expelled from Paradise. He was created in his form which he had in Paradise without distortion or change in the creation."[707] Ibn Furak has given a detailed account of all of these interpretations[708] and Ibn al-Jawzī has discussed them at great length.[709] Watt observes that this metaphorical interpretation indeed could be

> construed as the denial of various views that were actually held, or might be held, within the Islamic world. It was a denial that Adam was changed, like the serpent or peacock, when he was expelled from the Garden; it was a denial that he came into being through natural process, whether physical or embryological, and had to undergo development in order to reach maturity. It could even be regarded as a denial that the form or conception of humanity was a mere abstraction of the human intellect. For the exponents of these views and for the more intellectual Muslims this might be a satisfactory way of dealing with what they felt to be objectionable in the assertion that God created Adam in his image or form; but such subtleties of interpretation could hardly have appealed to the ordinary man.[710]

Goldziher argues that "these examples demonstrate the very frequently applied method of using grammatical alterations to obviate theological difficulty."[711]

Other reports from the Prophet include: "Do not say, May God make foul his face and a face like his, for God created Adam in his form" and one that says: "If you are beating anyone, avoid his face, for God created Adam in his form".[712] These reports were also interpreted in such a manner as to avoid anthropomorphic implications. Here the pronoun 'his' was said to naturally refer to the man cursed or beaten.[713] Al-Ghazālī on the other hand argued that 'his form' can be taken to mean God's form. There are a few reports that attribute the "form" to *al-Raḥmān* (one of the beautiful names of God),[714] although not all of them are accepted as authentic.[715] But the form, to al-Ghazālī, was "not the external visible form, but "the 'inner form' (*ṣūrah bāṭinah*) belonging to the 'supernal world' (*ʿālam al-malakūt*)...""[716] He also argued that 'his form' meaning 'God's form' can be justified in two ways:

> Firstly, if God's form means a form in God's possession, then man may be regarded as a microcosm, a universe in little; this is a favorite conception with al-Ghazali. Secondly, if God's form means something characterizing him, then that might refer to the fact that just as God is living, knowing, willing, so man is living, knowing, willing; and the complex of these attributes might be held to constitute the 'inner form'... when attributes are said to belong to God and also to man, the correspondence is only verbal, and similarly in saying that God has a form and man has a form the correspondence is only verbal. To suppose that God's form is external and visible would of course be anthropomorphism (*tasbih*).[717]

Abū Bakr ibn al-ʿArabī emphatically prefers the second interpretation. He states that God created Adam with His attribute of being living, knowing, willing etc. God the Most Merciful does not have a specific form. This leaves no other option but to conclude that Adam was created in the spiritual (*maʿnawī*) image of God.[718] To him the term *ṣūrah* or *form* denotes a divine attribute (*ṣifah*) as it is sometimes said that "this is the form of the matter" (*hadhihi ṣūrat al-amr*). Ibn ʿAqīl and Ibn al-Jawzī, the two known Ḥanbalī scholars, also prefer this interpretation.[719]

In a detailed study of Imam Aḥmad ibn Ḥanbal's creed, Wesley Williams presents Aḥmad as scolding those who interpret the above reports metaphorically and render the report to mean that God created Adam in Adam's form. He, on the authority of al-Qāḍī Abū Yaʿlā, quotes Imam Aḥmad as stating that, "He who says that Allah created Adam according to the form of Adam, he is a *Jahmi* (disbeliever). Which form did Adam have before He created him?"[720] Williams concludes, "For Ibn Hanbal, to deny that God has a form is *kufr* (unbelief)."[721] He further quotes Aḥmad's presumed understanding of the *Ḥadīth al-Ru'yā*[722] (depicting God's sight on the Day of Judgment) and *Ḥadīth al-Shābb*[723] (the reported weak narration of Prophet Muhammad supposedly having claimed to have seen God probably in his dream as a young man), to conclude that Imam Aḥmad was a thorough corporealist and the "God of 9th–10th century Sunnism was Theophanous and Corporeal."[724] From here he reaches an even more provocative conclusion:

> Islam, apparently from its outset, played host to varying concepts of the divine, either of which – or, possibly, none of which – could claim true indigenousness. From a historical perspective, transcendentalism and anthropomorphism were two alternatives available to Muslim divines attempting to interpret the most important pillar of their faith, "There is no god but Allah," and there were times that anthropomorphism was the model preferred by Sunni Islam.[725]

All that Williams can point to are a few literal interpretations, challenged strongly in any case during their formulation, and even then the former strongly qualified with the there is none like unto Him statement, to draw a patently absurd conclusion based on scaling matters hugely out of proportion. It is astonishing that from these slim pickings he chooses to confidently assert dressed-up speculation as certainty, and ignoring facts on the ground as they historically existed. The strict non-anthropomorphic and monotheistic *tawḥīd* of Islam is unparalleled and indisputable. The most that can be said is that a certain blur, immediately qualified, surfaced, with debate really revolving around a controlled focus on a blurred understanding of a few phrases. Anthropomorphism was hardly "the model preferred by Sunni Islam", if anything Islamic understanding and debate has always been marked by anti-anthropomorphism. This chapter has carefully and in some detail demonstrated the originality of the Qur'anic transcendental monotheistic paradigm by comparing it with Judaic and Christian conceptions of God. It has shown that the preferred method for orthodox Muslim scholars has been "*Imra'ūhā ka mā jā'at*" meaning literally "pass them on just as they have come down" period. Hence, the Qur'anic passages and Prophetic reports in question were transmitted to posterity exactly as received in Scripture, intact, without metaphorical interpretation or literal explanation, or the asking 'how' of them. Their recital was taken as their interpretation.

The four known imams, as also discussed, subscribed to this doctrine of *Imrār* and *bilā kayf*, although some of their later followers were unable to maintain the mediate position blurring the line either by literal interpretation or metaphorical understanding. Those who metaphorically interpreted these poetical expressions contended that their literal meaning was not intended as this could lead to anthropomorphism, and further argued that the *Salaf* also did not accept or allow for their literal meaning otherwise they would have explained them using proper Arabic synonyms or allowed their translation into other languages.

In point of fact the literalists were quite a minority including the Ḥanbali school of thought. This minority sought approval for their views by subscribing the same to Imam Aḥmad while in fact slanting towards literal interpretations against and over Aḥmad's doctrine of *Imrār* and *bilā kayf*. They somehow took Aḥmad's fideism to extremes and, in their efforts to establish the supremacy of revelation over reason, ended up ascribing to revelation meanings which might not have been intended by Imam Aḥmad. They demystified the mysteries upheld by Aḥmad and others, and in this process of demystification blurred the demarcation line and lost the intended balance. These literalists were labeled by their colleagues as the "masses scholars" with clear lack of true scholarship. Their own fellow Ḥanbalīs took them to task by establishing the fact that the ascription of their literal views to Imam Aḥmad was wrong. A good example is Abū al-Faraj ʿAbd al-Raḥmān

ʿAlī ibn al-Jawzī's (510–597 / 1116–1201) rebuttal of al-Qāḍī Abū Yaʿlā Muḥammad ibn al-Ḥusayn al-Farrā' (380–458 / 990–1066), Abū ʿAbd Allāh al-Ḥasan ibn Ḥāmid al-Warrāq (d. 403 / 1012) and Abū al-Ḥasan ʿAlī ibn ʿUbayd Allāh al-Zaghūnī (d. 527 / 1132), the three influential Ḥanbalī scholars. He clearly stated in his book that, "I have come to the conclusion that a refutation of their views is essential if [the name of] Ahmad is not to be associated with such notions."[726] Al-Jawzī observed that:

> Imam Ahmad used to say: "Let the texts of scripture (*ahadith*) stand as they are." Some of his leading disciples followed this principle – men like Ibrahim al-Harbi, and Abu Dawud al-Ashram as well as some of the [latter] authorities of the school such as Abu'l-Hasan at-Tamimi, Abu Muhammad [at-Tamimi] Rizq Allah b.'Abd al-Wahhab, Abu al-Wafa b. 'Aqil.[727]

He blamed the likes of these three Ḥanbalī figures for jeopardizing Aḥmad's stance by taking "sense experience *('ala'l-hissiyat)* as its point of departure."[728]

The problem with Wesley Williams is the same. He has taken the literalism prone minority of Ḥanbalites such as al-Qāḍī Abū Yaʿlā as his point of reference. They seem to be his sole lenses through which to decode Aḥmad's inner feelings concerning these scriptural mysteries. There is a transmission problem involved also. Aḥmad reportedly did not compile his opinions in written form and prohibited his students from recording them. So very often two diverging opinions are attributed to Imam Aḥmad by the Ḥanbali authorities. This boils down to a matter of who to accept and who to reject when it comes to interpreting Imam Aḥmad's theological positions. There is nothing in the written creeds of Aḥmad which ostensibly substantiates Wesley Williams' controversial claims. Imam Aḥmad quotes the scriptural expressions exactly as they have been revealed without the slightest change in the scriptural order of the words or the substitution of Arabic words imagined to be synonyms. And he manifestly prohibited their translation into any other language. He also strictly forbade moving one's finger, hand, eyes or any other human organ while reciting or explaining the scriptural expressions which imply finger, hand or eyes for God.[729] His emphasis upon *Imrār bilā kayf wa lā maʿnā* is so vivid and authentic that binding any anthropomorphic or corporeal interpretations to his name would fly in the face of reality.

Consequently, guaging Imam Aḥmad's inner feelings through the narrow lense of those such as al-Qāḍī Abū Yaʿlā or even through that of Imam Aḥmad's own son ʿAbd Allāh ibn Aḥmad (d. 290 / 903 known for his weakness in hadith transmission as for example evidenced in his book *Kitāb al-Sunnah* which contained outright flimsy chains and was hence frowned upon by many scholars), and to guage the Sunni doctrine of God through the sole lense of Aḥmad ibn Ḥanbal whatever his influence may be, and then to declare the Islamic doctrine of God as Theophanous and corporeal based upon just Sunni interpretations to the exclusion of all other Muslims, is a far fetched, unwarranted and flawed scheme of argumentation. It is equally ludicrous to discard the entire Qur'an's absolute emphasis upon transcendental monotheism as well as ignore centuries of Muslim effort to either maintain the *bilā kayf* balance or explain it metaphorically, whilst wildly jumping to the conclusion not grounded in the facts of history, that the Islamic God paradigm is corporeal just like Judaism.

The hadith of *al-Ru'yā* mentioned earlier talks about God's beatific vision in the life to come. The thing to note is that the rules of the hereafter are altogether different from those of this temporal material existence. The Qur'an differentiates between the two totally disparate realms even by name, this worldly life being "*ʿĀlim al-Ghayb*" and the next life "*ʿĀlim al-Shahādah*". There is a consensus among Muslim scholars that nobody has ever seen God in this worldly life. Dreams are dismissed as imagination and theological discourses are not based upon imagination. Additionally the hadith of *Shābb* mentioned earlier is so weak that none of the authentic books of hadith have ever reported it. Even Imam Aḥmad who had a tendency to transmit some weak reports in his *Musnad*, categorically denied transmission of it in the *Musnad*. A clear repudiation of this hadith is also authentically reported from him. Therefore, Wesley Williams' controversial claims contain little if any merit. Orthodox Muslim scholars were neither anthropomorphists nor corporealists. Additionally, this clear tendency against accepting anthropomorphic interpretations of Prophetic reports did not spring merely from Muslim intellectualism. This proclivity has its origin in the Qur'an. Watt observes:

> What seems to have turned the scale against acceptance of the conception of man in God's form is the way in which the word sura and its cognates are used in the Qur'an. There are two main points to be noticed. Firstly, God is referred to in the Qur'an as *musawwir*, 'the form-giver', 'the one who forms'; and the activity of 'forming' is closely connected with that of creating, even of creating Adam in particular. Now, if creating and forming are similar or closely connected, the word 'form' would have the suggestion of something created and would therefore not be appropriate for God. Secondly, the word sura or 'form' tends to connote something composite because the one verse of the Qur'an where it is used runs: "in whatever form he willed he constituted thee" (or 'set thee together'). Though Westerners may consider form a principle of unity, the Arabs, perhaps under the influence of this verse, seem to have thought of sura as something complex. In this way also it was inappropriate that God should have a sura.[730]

As this chapter has shown the seemingly anthropomorphic expressions of the Qur'an and Hadith have been a source of controversy among many Muslim scholars and sects. Had they been accepted literally without proper qualification, these expressions would have led to an anthropomorphic conception of God otherwise vehemently denied by the Qur'an and the Sunnah. Therefore, two main tendencies have historically dominated the Muslim approach, either to accept them *bilā kayf* or to explain them with the help of genuinely accepted metaphors to avoid anthropomorphic implications. Abd al-Halim Mahmud views the first tendency as the true essence of Islam.[731] For most Muslims anthropomorphism is an unacceptable, unlawful, and mostly rejected doctrine. Some apparently literalist figures such as Ibn Taymiyyah also vigorously refuted accusations of anthropomorphism. Ibn Taymiyyah, who otherwise disagreed with later Ashʿarites in terms of their claim that the "*Salaf*" did not maintain the literal, commonly used meanings of these phrases under the clause 'without how', however agreed with them with regards to denying these expressions literal meaning if they paved the way to, or confused certain people into, anthropomorphism or corporeality. He only allowed such interpretation with the proviso "if the forbidden [anthropomorphic] meanings become evident or common with some people..."[732]

Moreover, extremists like Ḥishām ibn al-Ḥakam who otherwise are reported to have accepted these expressions literally and to have explained them corporeally, qualified their corporealism with phrases such as "not like bodies" or "things".[733] Even their understanding of God in a sense can be interpreted as non-anthropomorphic because their concept of 'body' or 'thing' is somewhat different to the literal meaning of the terms and their usages in the human sphere.

Al-Ashʿarī has reported from Ḥishām and Wilfred Madelung has observed that Ḥishām ibn al-Ḥakam "and probably the doctrine of his school also defined God as a body, in the meaning that he is existent (*muwjūd*)."[734] The reason for scholastic abhorrence of anthropomorphism and corporealism is rooted in the Qur'an, which emphasized in clear-cut and unambiguous terms, the absolute transcendence and uniqueness of God. Watt rightly observes that these issues introduce us

> to one of the deep tensions in Islamic thought – the tension between those who held God's absolute otherness and those who believed that there was an affinity between God and man. This study has also shown us... that the steady pressure through the centuries of the Qur'an had an important share in determining the final result.[735]

We can conclude with Gibb and Kramers who note:

> Yet when Muhammad speaks of Allah's two hands... or of his grasp... or of his eyes... or of his face... or describes him as settling himself upon his throne... we are not to regard that as due to an anthropomorphic theology but rather as the still plastic metaphor of a poet. To speak technically, we have here only *madjaz*; *tadjsim* and *tashbih* lay with the future exegetes.[736]

Therefore, it is safe to conclude that the presence of seemingly anthropomorphic expressions in the scripture have been problematic to a certain degree, but mainstream Islam has always emphasized the unconditional transcendence of God, His uniqueness and otherness. Moreover, this transcendence did not signify a bare unity or an abstract idea of God, but rather the opposite. The God of the Qur'an is a vivid, personal, and very loving Creator, as reflected throughout the Qur'an's verses, so as to make it easy for believers to reflect upon and relate to Him. Netton rightly observes that:

> The God portrayed in the Qur'an has both a transcendent and an immanent aspect. On the one hand 'like Him there is naught'; on the other hand, God announces in His revelation: 'We indeed created man; and We know what his soul whispers within him, and We are nearer to him than his jugular vein.'[737]

The immanent aspect was achieved by affirming the expressions and attributes of God discussed in this chapter under the clause of *bilā kayf*, as al-Faruqi argues:

> once the lexicographic meaning of the predicate is acknowledged and understood and then denied, it acts as a springboard for the mind to create a new modality for the predication in question, other than the empirical. But now no new modality is possible. Therefore, the mind perceives the impossibility of empirical predication while the understanding is still anchored to the lexicographic meaning of the term.[738]

Al-Faruqi continues:

> The imagination is thus compelled to produce the needed modality once the denial of empirical predication and transcendence both are upheld. In this suspense, an intuition of transcendence is obtained, not unlike that of infinity and sensory inexpressibility engendered by the arabesque. The lexicographic meaning of the term serves as anchor while the imagination soars in search of an

> applicable modality of the meaning in question, a modality that is impossible to reach. Indeed, the Qur'an likens the word of God to "a tree whose roots are firm in the earth, and whose branches are infinite and unreachable in the skies above" (14:24).[739]

Such a formula, according to Watt, was very much needed to maintain the divine mystery.[740]

We conclude this chapter with the claim that the Qur'anic Creator Paradigm does maintain a wonderful demarcation line between God and whatever is non-God by holding fast to the concept of His transcendence, uniqueness, and otherness. This concept is no bare unity or abstraction, but a vivid, alive, and demanding concept which makes God relevant to the 'here and now' by means of emphasizing His immanence through the modality it provides by the countless Qur'anic verses. The modality and the language are essentially structured in such a way so as to allow many possibilities of communication without making God resemble or disappear in the world He has created. This type of transcendental concept is pervasive throughout the Qur'an, the authentic Hadith literature, and also throughout the history of Islamic civilization. All mainstream Muslim thinkers, even the philosophers to an extent, seem to have followed the same line: the sense of and a belief in the transcendental Deity who is mysterious, ineffable, and unknowable in His essence, but at the same time very close to His creatures by dint of His knowledge, power, mercy, and love. Linguistically, observes Netton,

> such philosophers' employment of certain kinds of vocabulary to denote the transcendent marked a movement away from the familiar, almost cosy, language of the Qur'anic Creator Paradigm to [a] shifting evanescent area where language was often emptied of all normal meanings: the end result could be paradoxically and startlingly akin to that achieved by the theologies of al-Ashʿari and Ahmad b. Hanbal...[741]

This rupture of language, as discussed, was not meant to make God unknowable as Netton argues,[742] but quite the opposite. It was meant to admit the inadequacy and imperfection of the human language, the ineffable mystery of God, and humanity's utter dependence upon God and His revelation to achieve any authentic knowledge of His being.

NOTES

[1] Philip K. Hitti, *The Arabs: A Short History* (Washington: Regnery Gateway, 1993), p.42.

[2] Ismail R. al-Faruqi, *Towards Islamic English* (Virginia: International Institute of Islamic Thought, 1986), p.44.

[3] Hamilton A. R. Gibb, *Mohammedanism* (London: Oxford University Press, 1972), p.24.

[4] The Qur'an, 29:50–51. The Qur'an has expressed such a claim and a challenge in several places. In 17:88 it claims: "Say: 'If the whole of mankind and jinns were to gather together to produce the like of this Qur'an, they could not produce the like thereof, even if they backed up each other with help and support.'" In 11:13–14 it challenges them to produce ten chapters like those of the Qur'an: "Or they may say, 'He forged it.' Say, 'Bring ye then ten surahs forged, like unto it, and call (to your aid) whomsoever ye can, other than Allah – If ye speak the truth! If then they answer you not, know ye that this Revelation is sent down with the knowledge of Allah, there is no god but He! Will ye even then submit [to Islam]?" In 2:23–4, the challenge was reduced to one chapter: "And if you are in doubt as to what We have revealed from time to time to Our servant, then produce a surah like thereunto; and call your witnesses or helpers (if there are any) besides Allah, if you are truthful. But if you cannot – and of a surety you cannot – then fear the Fire whose fuel is men and stones, which is prepared for those who reject Faith."

[5] Helmut Gatje, *The Qur'ān and its Exegesis*, A. T. Welch, trans. (Los Angles: University of California Press, 1976), p.31.

[6] Muhammad Khalf Allah, Muhammad Zaghlul Sallam, eds., *Thalāth Rasā'il fī Iʿjāz al-Qur'ān li al-Rummānī wa al-Khaṭṭabī wa ʿAbd al-Qāhir al-Jurjāni*, 2nd edn. (Cairo: Dār al-Maʿārif, 1968), p.27.

[7] Abū Bakr Muḥammad ibn al-Ṭayyib al-Bāqillānī, *Iʿjāz al-Qur'ān*, M. A. Khifaji, ed. (Beirut: Dār al-Jīl, 1991), pp.120–58. For al-Bāqillānī's method of deducing Qur'anic *iʿjāz* from his empirical, stylistic analysis of *naẓm* and it's rhythm of *kalimāt* (structural rhetorical units) within the Qur'anic verses see Angelika Neuwirth, "*Ṭariqat al-Bāqillānī fī Iẓhār iʿjāz al-Qur'ān*," *Studia Arabica et Islamica*

[Arabic Section], Wadad al-Qadi, ed. (Beirut: American University, 1981), pp.281–96.

[8] See Abū Bakr al-Jurjānī, *Kitāb Dalā'il al-Iʿjāz*, Mahmud M. Shakir, ed. (Cairo: Maṭbaʿah al-Madanī, 1992), pp.43–370.

[9] Introduction of Abū al-Qāsim Maḥmūd ibn ʿUmar al-Zamakhsharī to his *Tafsīr al-Kashshāf ʿan Ḥaqā'iq Ghawāmiḍ al-Tanzīl wa ʿUyūn al-Aqāwīl fī Wujūh al-Ta'wīl* (Cairo: Muṣṭafā al-Bābī al-Ḥalabī, 1966).

[10] Mustafa Sadiq al-Rafi, *Tārīkh Ādāb al-ʿArab* (Beirut: Dār al-Kitāb al-ʿArabī, 1974), vol.2, pp.212 f.

[11] See Sayyid Qutb's, *al-Taṣwīr al-Fannī fī al-Qur'ān* (Cairo: Dār al-Shurūq, 2004), pp.33 ff; also his *Fī Ẓilāl al-Qur'ān* (Beirut: Dār al-Shurūq, 1994).

[12] See for instance R. L. Atkinson, et. al, eds., *Introduction to Psychology* (New York; London: Harcourt Brace Jovanovich Publishers, 1990), pp.306 ff; Norman E. Spear, *The Processing of Memories: Forgetting and Retention* (New York; London: John Wiley & Sons, 1978), ch.2, pp.47 ff; Burrhus F. Skinner, *The Technology of Teaching* (New York: Appleton-Century-Crofts, 1968).

[13] Allan Paivio, *Imagery and Verbal Processes* (New York: Holt, Rinehart & Winston, 1971).

[14] Ismail R. al-Faruqi, Lois L. al-Faruqi, *The Cultural Atlas of Islam* (New York: MacMillan Publishing Company, 1986), p.102.

[15] Fazlur Rahman, *Major Themes of the Qur'an* (Chicago: Bibliotheca Islamica, 1980), pp.104–05.

[16] John L. Esposito, *Islam the Straight Path* (New York: Oxford University Press, 1991), p.21.

[17] Hitti, *The Arabs*, p.46.

[18] Gibb, *Mohammedanism*, p.28.

[19] Issa J. Boullata, "The Rhetorical Interpretation of the Qur'an: Iʿjaz and Related Topics," *Approaches to the History of the Interpretation of the Qur'an*, Andrew Rippin, ed. (Oxford: Clarendon Press, 1988), pp.140–41. There were a few attempts made by some individuals to meet the Qur'anic challenge but in vain. See al-Bāqillānī, *Iʿjāz al-Qur'ān*, pp.238–40; see also Ignaz Goldziher, *Muslim Studies*, S. M. Stern, ed. (London: George Allen and Unwin, 1971), vol.2, pp.363–65.

[20] Al-Faruqi, *Cultural Atlas*, p.102.

[21] Ali Dashti, *Twenty Three Years, A Study of the Prophetic Career of Mohammad*, F. R. C. Bagley, trans. (London: George Allen & Unwin, 1985), pp.48–49.

[22] Al-Jurjānī's entire book is meant to prove the eloquence of the Qur'an through its grammatical structures and meanings.

[23] Dashti, *Twenty Three Years*, pp.52–53.
[24] Ibid., p.57.
[25] Rahman, *Major Themes of the Qur'an*, p.105.
[26] Karen Armstrong, *Muhammad: A Biography of the Prophet* (San Francisco: Harper Collins, 1992), p.11.
[27] Quoted in Edward W. Said, *Orientalism: Western Conceptions of the Orient* (New York: Crossroads, 1985), p.66.
[28] Humphry Prideaux, *The True Nature of Imposture, Fully Displayed in the Life of Mahomet* (London: E. Curll, 1723), p.80.
[29] Quoted in Norman Daniel, *Islam and the West: The Making of an Image* (Edinburgh: Edinburgh University Press, 1989), p.297.
[30] Thomas Carlyle, *The Best Known Works of Thomas Carlyle: Including Sartor Resartus, Heroes and Hero Worship and Characteristics* (Rockville, Maryland: Wildside Press, 2010), pp.191–192.
[31] Ernest T. Renan, *Studies in Religious History, History of the People of Israel and Religion of Antiquity* (London: Metheson & Co., 1886), p.132.
[32] James W. H. Stobart, *Islam and its Founder* (London: SPCK Press, 1901), p.231.
[33] Quoted from Gibb, *Mohammedanism*, p.25.
[34] Tor Andrae, *Mohammed: The Man and His Faith*, Theophil Menzel, trans. (New York: Books for Libraries Press, 1971), p.161.
[35] Edward Gibbon, *The Decline and Fall of the Roman Empire*, Dero E. Saunders, ed. (London: Penguin, 1980), pp.657–58.
[36] Hartwig Hirschfeld, "New Researches into Composition and Exegesis of the Quran," *Asiatic Monograph* (London: Royal Asiatic Society, 1902), vol. III, p.5.
[37] St. Clair-Tisdall, *The Original Sources of the Quran* (London: SPCK, 1905), p.27; for more details see Anis A. Shorrosh, *Islam Revealed* (Nashville: Thomas Nelson Publishers, 1988), pp.191–221. On p.198 the heading reads "Mistakes in the Arabic of the Quran" and on p.199 it reads "Poor Grammer". It is interesting to note that Anis finds fault with the Arabic of the Qur'an and doubts the grammatical structure of the Qur'anic text while other learned Christian scholars like Hitti and H. Lammens have concluded that the Qur'an is the masterpiece of the Arabic language and the standard of the national grammar. Father Lammens, a devout Christian missionary about whom E. Dermenghem writes: "Father Lammens, one of the most erudite of recent specialists, is unfortunately one of the most partial also." – Emile Dermenghem, *The Life of Mohamet*, A. Yorks, trans. (New York: Dial Press, n.d.), p. X. Even a partial writer like Father Lammens observes that the Qur'an "has served as the standard for fixing the rules of national grammer." – Henri Lammens,

Islam, Beliefs and Institutions, Sir E. D. Ross, trans. (London: Cass & Co., 1968), p.41. For Arabic sources about the issue see Abū Muḥammad ʿAbd Allāh ibn Muslim ibn Qutaybah, *Tafsīr Gharīb al-Qur'ān*, Ahmad Saqar, ed. (Beirut: Dār al-Kutub al-ʿIlmiyyah, 1978); and his *Ta'wīl Mushkal al-Qur'ān*, Ahmad Saqar, ed. (Cairo: Dār al-Turāth, 1973); Abū Ṭālib Muḥammad Makkī al-Qaysiyy, *al-ʿUmdah fī Gharīb al-Qur'ān*, Yusuf A. al-Marashili, ed. (Beirut: Mu'assasah al-Risālah, 1981).

[38] Salomon R. Orpheus, *A History of Religion* (New York: Livercraft Inc., 1932), p.176; and for a recent book see Robert Morey, *The Islamic Invasion: Confronting the World's Fastest Growing Religion* (Eugene: Harvest House Publishers, 1992), pp.108–09, 114–15.

[39] William M. Watt, *Muhammad at Mecca* (Karachi: Oxford University Press, 1979), p.52.

[40] William M. Watt, *What is Islam* (New York: Frederick Praeger Publishers, 1968), p.120.

[41] Watt, *Muhammad at Mecca*, p.21.

[42] Ibid., pp.80–85.

[43] William M. Watt, *Muhammad: Prophet and Stateman* (Oxford: Oxford University Press, 1961), p.15.

[44] Ibid., p.73.

[45] James N. Anderson, ed., *The World Religions* (London: Frank Cass, 1965), p.5.

[46] Richard Bell, *Introduction to the Qur'an* (Edinburgh: Edinburgh University Press, 1958), p.70; for refutation of this hypothesis and others see S. Vahiuddin, "Richard Bell's Dating of the Qur'an, A Critical Analysis," *Islamic Culture* (Hyderabad: Deccan, 1956), vol. XXXX, no.3, p.264.

[47] Andrae, *Mohammed*, p.116.

[48] Arthur S. Tritton, *Islam, Beliefs and Practices* (London: Hutchinson University Library, 1966), p.21.

[49] Patricia Crone, Michael Cook, *Hagarism, The Making of the Islamic World* (London: Cambridge Univeristy Press, 1977), p.18.

[50] Andrew Rippin, *Muslims: Their Religious Beliefs & Practices* (New York: Routledge, 1990), vol.1, p.27.

[51] Arthur J. Arberry, *The Koran Interpreted* (London: George Allen & Unwin, 1955), vol.2, pp.10–13.

[52] Ibid., pp.10–11.

[53] Sayyid Abul A'la Mawdudi, *Towards Understanding the Qur'an*, Zafar I. Ansari, trans. and ed., (Leicester: The Islamic Foundation, 1988), vol.1, p.9.

[54] Ibid., p.12.

[55] Ibid.

[56] See M. Mahmud Hijazi, *al-Waḥdah al-Mawḍuᶜiyyah fī al-Qur'ān al-Karīm* (Cairo: Dār al-Kutub al-Ḥadīthah, 1970). Since then many books have been written on the subject.

[57] Rahman, *Major Themes in the Qur'an*, p. XI.

[58] Fazlur Rahman, *Islam and Modernity: Transformation of an Intellectual Tradition* (Chicago; London: University of Chicago Press, 1982), p.6.

[59] See details in Mustansir Mir, "Coherence in the Qur'an: A Study of Islahi's Concept of Nazm," *Tadabbur-i Qur'an* (Indiana: American Trust Publications, 1986), pp.38 ff.

[60] See Amin A. Islahi, *Mabādi' Tadabbur al-Qur'ān* (Lahore: Dār al-Isha'at al-Islāmiyyah, 1971).

[61] Mir, "Coherence in the Qur'an," p.62.

[62] Ibid., p.100.

[63] This is reffered to as the process of "Organization". See Atkinson, et al., *Introduction to Psychology*, pp.309 ff. This approach is presently being used in many academic circles, especially in language studies. Cambridge University's *Elementary Modern Standard Arabic*, Peter F. Abboud, ed. (Cambridge: Cambridge University Press, 1996), is a good example of this approach.

[64] See a detailed study of the issue in Charles B. Ferster, Burrhus F. Skinner, *Schedules of Reinforcement* (New York: Appleton-Century-Crofts, 1957); Winfred F. Hill, *Learning, A Survey of Psychological Interpretations* (New York: Harper Collins, 1990), pp.75 ff.

[65] Hill, *Learning*, p.79.

[66] Sachiko Murata, William C. Chittick, *The Vision of Islam* (New York: Paragon House, 1994), p. XVIIII.

[67] Ibid., pp. XVIII-XIX.

[68] Quoted by Ronald V. C. Bodley, *The Messenger: The Life of Mohammed* (New York: Doubleday, 1946), p.237.

[69] Gibb, *Mohammedanism*, p.25.

[70] Dermenghem, *The Life of Mohamet*, p.249.

[71] George Sale, *The Koran, Commonly Called Al-Quran, with a Preliminary Discourse* (London: Fredrick Warne, 1899), p.47.

[72] John A. William, *Islam* (New York: G. Braziller, 1961), p.15.

[73] Armstrong, *Muhammad*, p.49.

[74] John Naish, *The Wisdom of the Qur'an* (Oxford: Oxford University Press, 1937), Preface, p. VIII.

[75] Bodley, *The Messenger*, p.237.

[76] Ibid., p.239.

[77] Hitti, *The Arabs*, pp.46–47.

[78] See Afzalul Rahman, ed., *Encyclopaedia of Seerah* (London: Seerah Foundation, 1981), vol.1, Book I, p.185.

[79] Arnold Joseph Toynbee, *A Study of History*, Edited by David Churchill Somervell (Oxford: Oxford University Press, 1987), v.2, p.31, 53.

[80] Hans Kung, et al., eds., *Christianity and the World Religions* (London: Harper Collins Publishers, 1992), pp.28–29.

[81] See Philip K. Hitti, *The Near East in History* (New York: D. Van Nostrand Co., 1961), p.194. Also, John L. Esposito, *What Everyone Needs to Know about Islam* (Oxford: Oxford University Press, 2002); *Islam: the Straight Path* (Oxford: Oxford University Press, 1998).

[82] Muhammad Asad, *The Message of the Qur'an* (Bristol: Book Foundation, 2003), pp. VI-VII.

[83] Ibid., p. X.

[84] Arberry, *The Koran Interpreted*, introduction, p. X.

[85] Charles J. Adams, "Islamic Religious Tradition," *The Study of the Middle East*, Leonard Binder, ed. (New York: John Wiley & Sons, 1976), p.65.

[86] Toshihiko Izutsu, *Ethico-religious Concepts in the Qur'an* (Montreal: McGill University Press, 1966).

[87] Kenneth Cragg, *The Mind of the Qur'an* (London: Allen & Unwin, 1973).

[88] Rahman, *Major Themes of the Qur'an*.

[89] Angelika Neuwirth, *Studien zur Komposition der mekkanischen Suren* (Berlin; New York: Walter de Gruyter, 1981). Hans Kung observes that "An apparently more solid and careful work than all the foregoing is Angelika Neuworth's *Studies on the Composition of the Meccan Suras* (1981). With her training in the form-critical approach to the Old Testament, Neuwirth can prove that, whatever the case with the rest of the Qur'an, the Meccan suras were put together by the Prophet himself for liturgical recitation, and that behind the text as we have it stands a single creative force, so that we are not reduced to postulating a mere editor who assembled variant readings with scissors and paste." Kung, et al., *Christianity and the World Religions*, p.34. Moreover, it is interesting to see how Neuwirth accepts the surahs as units and how she analyses the intricate patterns of rhythm, rhyme,

and assonance within each surah, and then structure of verses and their groupings within the surahs that lead to accept the surah as a unit.

[90] Angelika Neuwirth, "Images and Metaphors in the Introductory Sections of the Makkan Suras," *Approaches to the Qur'an,* G. R. Hawting, Abdul-Kader A. Shareef, eds. (New York; London: Routledge, 1993), pp.30–31.

[91] William A. Graham, "Qur'an as Spoken Word: An Islamic Contribution to the Understanding of Scripture," in *Approaches to Islam in Religious Studies*, Richard C. Martin, ed. (Tucson: University of Arizona Press, 1985), p.30.

[92] Al-Faruqi, *Cultural Atlas*, p.100.

[93] See Watt, *What is Islam*, pp.18–20.

[94] Alfred Guillaume, *Islam* (Baltimore: Penguin Books, 1969), p.56.

[95] See William Muir, Thomas H. Weir, *The Life of Mohammad* (Edinburgh: John Grant, 1912).

[96] Gatje, *The Qur'ān and its Exegesis*, p.24.

[97] Muir, Weir, *The Life of Mohammad*, p. XVI.

[98] William M. Watt, *Bell's Introduction to the Qur'an* (Edinburgh: Edinburgh University Press, 1970), p.31.

[99] See Gibb, Kramers, "Al-Kuran," *Shorter Encyclopaedia of Islam*, p.273.

[100] Gatje, *The Qur'ān and its Exegesis*, p.24.

[101] Watt, *Bell's Introduction*, p.37.

[102] Muir, Weir, *The Life of Mohammad*, p. XX.

[103] Watt, *Bell's Introduction*, p.37.

[104] Muir, Weir, *The Life of Mohammad*, p. XIX.

[105] John Burton, *The Collection of the Qur'an* (London: Cambridge University Press, 1977), p.239.

[106] Kenneth Cragg, *The Call of the Minaret* (New York: Oxford University Press, 1970), p.96.

[107] Watt, *Bell's Introduction*, p.37.

[108] Guillaume, *Islam*, p.56.

[109] Tritton, *Islam, Beliefs and Practices*, p.15.

[110] Watt, *Bell's Introduction*, pp.40–44.

[111] Burton, *The Collection of the Qur'an*, p.121.

[112] Muir, Weir, *The Life of Mohammad*, p. XXI.

[113] Gatje, *The Qur'ān and its Exegesis*, p.25.

[114] Watt, *Bell's Introduction*, p.46.

[115] Muir, Weir, *The Life of Mohammad*, p. XXV.

[116] Burton, *The Collection of the Qur'an*, p.157.

[117] Gibb, *Mohammedanism*, p.34.

[118] Cragg, *The Call of the Minaret*, p.97.

[119] Al-Faruqi, *Cultural Atlas*, p.100.

[120] Watt, *Bell's Introduction*, p.44.

[121] Al-Faruqi, *Cultural Atlas*, p.100.

[122] Adams, "Islamic Religious Tradition," p.61.

[123] Graham, "Qur'an as Spoken Word," p.158.

[124] See Geza Vermes' book *Scripture and Tradition in Judaism.*

[125] John Wansbrough, *Quranic Studies: Sources and Methods of Scriptural Interpretation* (Oxford: Oxford University Press, 1977), p.1.

[126] See ibid., pp.40 ff.

[127] See ibid., p.134.

[128] There have been previous efforts to show the Judeo-Christian background of the Qur'an. See Ricahard Bell, *The Origin of Islam in its Christian Environment* (London: Macmillan, 1926); and Charles C. Torrey, *The Jewish Foundation of Islam* (New York: KTAV Publishing House, 1967); Abraham Geiger, *Judaism and Islam*, [prolegomenon by Moshe Pearlman] (New York: KTAV Publishing House, 1970); Abraham I. Katsh, *Judaism and the Koran* (New York: A. S. Barnes & Co., 1962).

[129] Wansbrough, *Quranic Studies*, pp.20 ff.

[130] Samuel M. Zwemer, *The Muslim Christ Oliphant* (London: Anderson & Ferrier, 1912), p.12.

[131] James Gardner, *The Faiths of the World: An Account of All Religions and Religious Sects, Their Doctrines, Rites, Ceremonies, and Customs* (London: A. Fullarton, 1858), vol.2, p.279.

[132] See David S. Margoliouth, *The Early Development of Mohammedanism* (London: Williams and Norgate, 1914); and also his *Mohammedanism* (London: Butterworth, 1912).

[133] Torrey, *The Jewish Foundation of Islam.*

[134] See Shelomoh D. Goitein, "Mohammad's Inspiration by Judaism," *Journal of Jewish Studies* (1958), vol.9, pp.149–62; also his *Jews and Arabs: Their Contacts through the Ages* (New York: Schocken Books, 1955).

[135] Anderson, *The World Religions*, p.57.

[136] Geiger, *Judaism and Islam*, p. XX.

[137] Bell, *Introduction to the Qur'an*, p.70.

[138] Johann Fueck, "The Originality of the Arabian Prophet," *Studies on Islam*, M. L. Swartz, ed. (New York: Oxford University Press, 1981), p.88.
[139] Ibid.
[140] Ibid., p.89.
[141] Ibid., pp.92–93.
[142] For Lot see Qur'an 21:74–75, 26:160–173; for David and Solomon see 21:78–82, 27:15–44, 38:17–4.
[143] Watt, *Muhammad at Mecca*, p.85.
[144] Fueck, "The Originality of the Arabian Prophet," p.88.
[145] Ibid., pp.94–95.
[146] Watt, *Muhammad at Mecca*, p.160.
[147] Gardner, *The Faiths of the World*, vol.2, p.279.
[148] Fueck, "The Originality of the Arabian Prophet," p.89.
[149] John Wansbrough, *The Sectarian Milieu* (London: Oxford University Press, 1978), p.58.
[150] See Wansbrough's, *Qur'anic Studies*, p.49.
[151] Wansbrough, *The Sectarian Milieu*, pp.58–59.
[152] See Andrew Rippin, "Literary Analysis of Qur'an, Tafsir, and Sira: The Methodologies of John Wansbrough," *Approaches to Islam in Religious Studies,* Richard C. Martin, ed. (Tucson: University of Arizona Press, 1985), p.161.
[153] Crone, Cook, *Hagarism*, p.3.
[154] Ibid., pp.17–18.
[155] Ibid., p.18.
[156] Ibid.
[157] Robert B. Serjeant's, Review of "Qur'anic Studies," *Journal of the Royal Asiatic Society* (1987), p.76.
[158] Ibid., p.76.
[159] Norman Daniel's, Review of "Hagarism," *Journal of Semitic Studies* (1979), vol.24, p.296.
[160] Richard C. Martin, *Approaches to Islam in Religious Studies* (Tucson: University of Arizona Press, 1985), p.231.
[161] Rahman, *Major Themes of the Qur'an*, p. XIII.
[162] Ibid., p.201.
[163] Ibid., p.199.
[164] Richard W. Bulliet, *Islam, The View From the Edge* (New York: Columbia University Press, 1994), pp.23–24; also see Gustave E. von Grunebaum, *Islam,*

Essays on the Nature and Growth of a Cultural Tradition (Chicago: American Anthropological Association, 1955).

[165] Muir, Weir, *The Life of Mohammad*, p. XXII.

[166] Burton, *The Collection of the Qur'an*, pp.239–40.

[167] Lammens, *Islam, Beliefs and Institutions*, p.38.

[168] Gatje, *The Qur'ān and its Exegesis*, p.25.

[169] Burton, *The Collection of the Qur'an*, p.145.

[170] Muir, Weir, *The Life of Mohammad*, p. XXIV.

[171] Lammens, *Islam, Beliefs and Institutions*, p.44.

[172] David Pinault, *The Shiites* (New York: St. Martin's Press, 1992), p.27.

[173] Seyyed Hossein Nasr, *A Young Muslim's Guide to the Modern World* (Chicago: Kazi Publications Inc., 1994), p.10.

[174] Tritton, *Islam, Beliefs and Practices*, p.18. See also Ahmad Ali al-Imam, *Variant Readings of the Qur'an: A Critical Study of Their Historical and Linguistic Origins* (London: IIIT, 2006).

[175] Muir, Weir, *The Life of Mohammad*, p. XXIII.

[176] Graham, "Qur'an as Spoken Word," p.35.

[177] Henry P. Smith, *The Bible and Islam: Or, The Influence of the Old and New Testaments on the Religion of Mohammed* (New York: ARNO Press, 1973), p.25.

[178] Bodley, *The Messenger*, pp.234–35.

[179] Hitti, *The Near East in History*, p.194.

[180] Esposito, *Islam the Straight Path*, p.23.

[181] Rippin, *Muslims*, vol.1, p.24.

[182] Kung, et al., *Christianity and the World Religions*, pp.14–15.

[183] M. Arkoun is an example of such an approach to the Qur'an. It may be noticed here that the Qur'anic Science of the "*Asbāb al-Nuzūl*" i.e., the context of the revelation, is already a kind of historical approach to the text of the Qur'an. The traditional Muslim scholars should not be alarmed by such inferences. The Qur'anic text presents a different scenario and situation than the one discussed about the Bible in the previous chapters.

[184] Rahman, *Major Themes of the Qur'an*, p.33.

[185] Ibid., p.32.

[186] Ibid., p.39.

[187] Rippin, *Muslims*, vol.2, p.104.

[188] Rahman, *Major Themes of the Qur'an*, p.99.

[189] Ibid.

[190] Netton, *Text and Trauma*, p.79.
[191] Ibid.
[192] Sale, *The Koran*, p.84.
[193] See Muir, Weir, *The Life of Mohammad.*
[194] See G. M. Draycott, *Mahomet Founder of Islam* (London: Martin Secker, 1916), p.335.
[195] Selwyn G. Champion, Dorothy Short, *Reading from World Religions* (Greenwich, USA: Fawcett Publications, 1959), p.240.
[196] F. J. L. Menezes, *The Life and Religion of Mohammed, The Prophet of Arabia* (London: Sands & Co., 1911), p.158.
[197] See Maurice Bucaille, *The Bible, the Qur'an and Science* (Indiana: American Trust Publications, 1978); and also his *What is the Origin of Man?*, 9th edn. (Paris: Seghers, 1983).
[198] See Seyyed Hossein Nasr, *Islamic Science: An Illustrated Study* (London: World of Islam Festival Pub. Co., 1976); and also his *Science and Civilization in Islam* (Cambridge: Islamic Texts Society, 1987).
[199] See Imad-ad-Dean Ahmad, *Signs in the Heavens: A Muslim Astronomer's Perspective on Religion and Science* (Maryland: Writers' Inc. International, 1992).
[200] Abd al-Majid al-Zindani, *Kitāb Tawḥīd al-Khāliq* (Madinah: Maktabah Ṭayyibah, 1989); and his *Kitāb al-Tawḥīd* (Madinah: Maktabah Ṭayyibah, 1990).
[201] Graham, "Qur'an as Spoken Word," p.29.
[202] Charles Le Gai Eaton, *Islam and the Destiny of Man* (Albany: State University of New York Press, 1985), p.52.
[203] Sayyid Abul A'la Mawdudi, *Four Basic Qur'anic Terms*, Abu Asad, trans., 2nd edn. (Lahore: Islamic Publications Ltd., 1982), p.10.
[204] Muhammad Zakariyya Kandhalvi, *Faza'il-e-A'ama'l*, Abdul Rashid Arshad, trans. (Karachi: Darul Ishaat, n.d.), pp.111–12, there is a clear and very authentic hadith that declares the confession as the best of the formulas of remembrance of God. See Kandhalvi, *Faza'il*, p.109.
[205] The translation is from Abdullah Y. Ali, *The Holy Qur'an* (Madinah: King Fahd Holy Quran Printing Complex, 1989).
[206] Abū ʿAbd Allāh Muḥammad ibn Aḥmad al-Anṣārī al-Qurṭubī, *al-Jāmiʿ li Aḥkām al-Qur'ān* (Cairo: Dār al-Kitāb al-ʿArabī, 1967), vol.2, p.268; the translation is taken from Mahmoud M. Ayoub, *The Qur'an and its Interpreters* (Albany: SUNY, 1984), vol.1, pp.247–48.
[207] ʿImād al-Dīn Abū al-Fidā' Ismāʿīl ibn Kathīr, *Tafsīr al-Qur'ān al-ʿAẓīm* (Beirut: Dār al-Hilāl, 1990), vol.1, p.336.

[208] Abū ʿAbd Allāh Muḥammad al-Bukhārī, *Saḥīḥ al-Bukhārī*, Muhammad Zahir ibn Nasir, ed. (Beirut: Dār Ṭawq al-Najāt, 2001), vol.11, p.53, hadith no.3033.
[209] Mawdudi, *Towards Understanding the Qur'an*, vol.1, p.196; see more details about the verse Ayoub, *The Qur'an and its Interpreters*, pp.245 ff.
[210] L. Gardet, "God in Islam," *The Encyclopedia of Religion*, Mircea Eliade, ed. (New York: Macmillan, 1993), vol.6, p.27.
[211] Ismail R. al-Faruqi, *Al-Tawḥīd: Its Implications for Thought and Life*, 2nd edn. (Virginia: International Institute of Islamic Thought, 1992), pp.9–10.
[212] The terms "*Allāh al-Wāḥid*" and "*Ilāh Wāḥid*" have been used in the Qur'an 21 times.
[213] See S. Mahmud al-Alusi, *Rūḥ al-Maʿānī* (Multan: Maktabah Imdādiyyah, n.d.), vol.15, p.314.
[214] Abū Bakr Aḥmad ibn al-Ḥusayn ibn ʿAlī al-Bayhaqī, *Kitāb al-Asmā' wa al-Ṣifāt* (Beirut: Dār Iḥyā' al-Turāth al-ʿArabī, n.d.), p.32.
[215] Gardet, "God in Islam", p.28.
[216] Ibid.
[217] Al-Rāghib al-Iṣfahānī, *Muʿjam Mufradāt Alfāẓ al-Qur'ān* (Beirut: Dār al-Kitāb al-ʿArabī, 1972), p.294.
[218] Al-Alusi, *Rūḥ al-Maʿānī*, vol.15, p.314.
[219] Asad, *The Message of the Qur'an*, p.1124.
[220] Ibid.
[221] Al-Bukhārī, *Saḥīḥ*, vol.15, p.365, hadith no.4593.
[222] Al-Bukhārī, *Saḥīḥ*, vol.9, p.459, hadith no.2644.
[223] Richard C. Martin, *Islam, A Cultural Perspective* (New Jersey: Prentice-Hall, 1982), p.92.
[224] Sayyid Abul A'la Mawdudi, *The Meaning of the Qur'an*, Ch. M. Akbar, trans., A. A. Kamal, ed., 4th edn. (Lahore: Islamic Publications, 1983), vol.7, pp.201–02.
[225] The fact that the story has been recorded by historians like al-Ṭabarī and Ibn Saʿd does not make the story authentic by itself. See details in M. M. Ahsan, A. R. Kidwai, eds., *Sacrilege Versus Civility: Muslim Perspectives on The Satanic Verses Affair* (Leicester: The Islamic Foundation, 1991), pp.138–39.
[226] See Salman Rushdie, *The Satanic Verses* (London; New York: Viking Penguin, 1988).
[227] Watt, *Muhammad at Mecca*, pp.101–02.
[228] Ibid., p.103.
[229] Watt, *Muhammad: Prophet and Statesman*, p.61.

[230] Maxime Rodinson, *Muhammad*, Anne Carter, trans. (New York: Pantheon Books [Random House], 1971), p.104.

[231] Watt, *Muhammad: Prophet and Statesman*, p.104.

[232] Ibid., p.101.

[233] Rodinson, *Muhammad*, p.107.

[234] Watt, *Muhammad: Prophet and Statesman*, p.105.

[235] Rodinson, *Muhammad*, p.107.

[236] Aḥmad ibn ʿAlī ibn Ḥajar al-ʿAsqalānī, *Fatḥ al-Bārī bi Sharḥ Saḥīḥ al-Imām al-Bukhārī*, Muhibb al-Din al-Khatib, Muhammad F. Abd al-Baqi, Q. Muhibb al-Din al-Khatib, eds. (Cairo: Dār al-Diyān li al-Turāth, 1987), vol.8, p.293; also Mawdudi, *The Meaning of the Qur'an*, vol.7, p.216.

[237] Al-ʿAsqalānī, *Fatḥ al-Bārī*, vol.8, p.293.

[238] Ibid.; also Shibli Numani, *Sirat-un-Nabi*, M. T. B. Budayuni, trans. (Lahore: Kazi Publications, 1979), vol.1, p.214; Akram Diya al-Umri, *al-Sīrah al-Nabawiyyah al-Saḥīḥah* (Qatar: Dār al-Kutub al-Qaṭariyyah, 1991), vol.1, pp.171–72.

[239] Al-ʿAsqalānī, *Fatḥ al-Bārī*, vol.8, pp.293–94.

[240] Ibid., p.294.

[241] M. M. Ahsan, "The Muslim Arguement: The 'Satanic' Verses and the Orientalists," *Sacrilege Versus Civility*, p.132.

[242] Ibn Kathīr, *Tafsīr al-Qur'ān*, vol.4, pp.170–71.

[243] Al-Albani attributes the statement to Muḥammad ibn Isḥāq ibn Khuzaymah and not to Ibn Isḥāq, the writer of "*Sīrah*". See Muhammad Nasr al-Din al-Albani, *Naṣb al-Majānīq fī Nafs Qiṣṣah al-Gharānīq*, 2nd edn. (Beirut: al-Maktab al-Islāmī, 1989), p.25.

[244] Al-Alusī, *Rūḥ al-Maʿānī*, vol.9, p.177.

[245] Al-Qādī ʿIyāḍ ibn Mūsā ibn ʿIyāḍ, *al-Shifā' bī Taʿrīf Ḥuqūq al-Muṣṭafā*, Ali Muhammad al-Bajawi, ed. (Beirut: Dār al-Kitāb al-ʿArabī, 1977), vol.2, p.750.

[246] Ibid.

[247] Abū Bakr Muḥammad ibn Abd Allāh ibn Muḥammad [known as Ibn al-ʿArabī], *Aḥkām al-Qur'ān* (Beirut: Dār al-Kutub al-ʿIlmiyyah, n.d.), vol.5, pp.431 ff. For details see al-Albani, *Naṣb al-Majāniq*, pp.26 ff.

[248] See Fakhar al-Dīn al-Rāzī, *Tafsīr Mafātīḥ al-Ghayb* [known as *Tafsīr al-Kabīr*] (Beirut: Dār al-Fikr, 1978), vol.11, p.135.

[249] See al-Qurṭubī, *Aḥkām al-Qur'ān*, vol.12, pp.80–84.

[250] See al-ʿAsqalānī, *Fatḥ al-Bārī*, vol.8, p.498.

[251] Maḥmūd ibn Aḥmad Badr al-Dīn al-ʿAynī, *ʿUmdah al-Qārī' Sharḥ Saḥīḥ al-Bukhārī* (Beirut: Dār al-Fikr, n.d.), vol.9, p.47.
[252] Al-Alusī, *Rūḥ al-Maʿānī*, vol.9, pp.177–86.
[253] Numani, *Sirat-un-Nabi*, vol.1, p.214.
[254] Mawdudi, *The Meaning of the Qur'an*, vol.7, p.217.
[255] Ibid.
[256] Ibid., p.218.
[257] Ibid., pp.218–19.
[258] Mufti Muhammad Shafi, *Maʿārif al-Qur'ān* (Karachi: Idārah al-Maʿārif, 1990), vol.6, p.277; Islahi, *Mabādī' Tadabbur al-Qur'ān*, vol.5, p.271.
[259] Muhammad H. Haykal, *The Life of Muhammad,* I. R. al-Faruqi, trans. (Indianapolis: North Trust Publication, 1976), p.108; also see Antonie Wessels, *A Modern Arabic Biography of Muhammad: A Critical Study of Muhammad Husayn Haykal's Hayat Muhammad* (Leiden: E. J. Brill, 1972), pp.57–64.
[260] Haykal, *The Life of Muhammad*, p.107.
[261] Ibid., p.109; about the conversion of ʿUmar, Thomas W. Arnold observes: "While the result of the embassy to Abyssinia was being looked for in Mecca with the greatest expectancy, there occured the conversion of a man, who before had been one of the most bitter enemies of Muhammad, and had opposed him with the utmost persistence and fanaticism- a man whom the Muslims had every reason then to look upon as their most terrible and virulent enemy, though afterwards he shines as one of the noblest figures in the early history of Islam, *viz*, Umar b. al-Khattab.... The conversion of Umar is a turning-point in the history of Islam: the Muslims were now able to take up a bolder attitude. Muhammad left the house of al-Arqam and the believers publically performed their devotions together round the Kaʿbah...." Thomas W. Arnold, *The Preaching of Islam* (Lahore: Sh. Muhammad Ashraf, 1979), pp.16–17.
[262] Haykal, *The Life of Muhammad*, pp.111–12.
[263] Ibid., p.112.
[264] See al-Albani's, *Naṣb al-Majānīq*.
[265] Zafar A. Qureshi, *Prophet Muhammad and his Western Critics* (Lahore: Idārah Ma'ārif Islāmī, 1992), vol. II, pp.615 ff.
[266] Rodinson, *Muhammad*, pp.105–06.
[267] Ibid., p.105.
[268] Ibid., p.106.
[269] Abū Muḥammad ʿAbd al-Malik ibn Hishām ibn Ayyūb al-Ḥimyarī, *al-Sīrah*

al-Nabawiyyah [known as *Sīrah ibn Hishām*], 2nd edn. (Cairo: Maktabah Muṣṭafā al-Bābī al-Ḥalabī, 1955), vol.1, pp.265–66.

[270] J. Burton, "Those are the High-Flying Cranes," *Journal of Semitic Studies* (1970), vol.15, no.2, p.265.

[271] Ibid., p.248.

[272] Armstrong, *Muhammad*, p.113.

[273] Watt, *Muhammad at Mecca*, p.104.

[274] Stanley Lane-Poole, *Studies in a Mosque* (Beirut: Khayats, 1966), pp.127–88.

[275] Watt, *Muhammad at Mecca*, p.101.

[276] See Watt, *Bell's Introduction*, p.110.

[277] Hirschfeld, "New Researches into the Composition and Exegesis of the Qur'an," p.35.

[278] See Watt, *Bell's Introduction*, p.213.

[279] See ibid., pp.206–07.

[280] See for instance (35:3); (15:96); (38:5). Most of the Makkan chapters contain many verses denouncing polytheism, idolatry and emphasizing upon God's Unity and Transcendence.

[281] See Ibn Hishām, *al-Sīrah al-Nabawiyyah*, vol.1, pp.265, 293–94, 417–19.

[282] Reynold A. Nicholson, *A Literary History of the Arabs* (Cambridge: Cambridge University Press, 1953), p.160.

[283] Julian Obermann's article "Islamic Origins," *The Arab History*, Nabih Amin Faris, ed. (Princeton: Princeton University Press, 1944), pp.99 ff.

[284] Reuben Levy, *The Social Structure of Islam* (Cambridge: Cambridge University Press, 1959), introduction, p.1; also see Tritton, *Islam, Beliefs and Practices*, p.10.

[285] Francesco Gabrieli, *Muhammad and the Conquests of Islam*, Virginia Luling, Rosamund Linell, trans. (London: Weidenfeld & Nicholson, 1968), p.49.

[286] Charles J. Adams, "Islam," *Man and His Gods: Encyclopedia of World Religions*, Jeoffrey Parrinder, ed. (London: Hamlyn Publishing Co., 1971), p.394.

[287] Bell, *Introduction to the Qur'an*, p.22.

[288] Ibid., pp.139–40.

[289] See J. M. Rodwell, *The Koran*, (translated from the Arabic) with Introduction by Rev. G. Margoliouth, (New York: Everyman's Library, 1950), pp.3–4 of "Preface", pp.13–14.

[290] See Bell, *Introduction to the Qur'an*, p.102.

[291] See Washington Irving, *Life of Mahomet* (New York: Everyman's Library, 1949), p.46; also see Stobart, *Islam and its Founder*, p.65.

292 Pierce de Lacy Johnstone, *Muhammad and His Power* (Edinburgh: T & T Clark, 1901), p.58.

293 Gibbon, *The Decline and Fall of the Roman Empire*, vol.II, p.660.

294 See Philip K. Hitti, *History of the Arabs*, 9th edn. (London: Macmillan, 1968), p.113; and his *Capital Cities of Islam* (Minneapolis: University of Minnesota Press, 1973), pp.13–14.

295 John J. Saunders, *A History of Medieval Islam* (London: Routledge & Kegan Paul Ltd., 1965), p.24; also see Edward C. Hodgkin, *The Arabs* (Oxford: Oxford University Press, 1966), pp.26–28; Anthony Nutting, *The Arabs* (New York: C. N. Potter, 1964), p.19; F. R. J. Verhoeven, *Islam: Its Origin and Spread in Words, Maps and Pictures* (Amsterdam: Djambatan, 1962), p.23; Bernard Lewis, *The Arabs in History*, 3rd edn. (London: Hutchinson University Library, 1964), p.39; and also see George E. Kirk, *A Short History of the Middle East*, 2nd edn. (London: Methun, 1964), p.12.

296 See Jouco Bleeker, Geo Widengren, eds., *Historia Religionum* (Leiden: E. J. Brill, 1971), vol. II, p.12.

297 See J. C. G. Greig, ed., *Religions of Mankind Today and Yesterday*, Niele L. Jensen, trans. (Edinburgh; London: Oliver & Boyd, 1967), p.185.

298 Cragg, *The Call of the Minaret*, p.79; also his *The Event of the Qur'an* (London: Allen & Unwin, 1971), p.14; also see Erich W. Bethman, *Bridge to Islam* (London: Allen & Unwin, 1953), pp.23–24; Guillaume, *Islam*, p.29.

299 Greig, *Religions of Mankind*, p.185.

300 For more details see Mawdudi, *The Meaning of the Qur'an*, vol.4, pp.33–36.

301 Smith, *The Bible and Islam*, p.103.

302 The word "jinn" comes from the Arabic verb "*janna*" which means to hide. Therefore, the embryo hidden in the womb is called a *janīn* and the heart hidden in the chest is called the *janān*. As the jinns are invisible to human eyes in their normal original state, they are referred to as jinns or hidden ones.

303 Ibn Taymiyyah has given a detailed account of the Islamic concept of jinn in his *Risālah*. See Ibn Taymiyyah's *Essay on the Jinn*, abridged and translated by Abu Ameenah Bilal Philips (Riyadh: Tawheed Publications, 1989), pp.1–31; also see al-ʿAsqalānī, *Fatḥ al-Bārī*, vol.6, p.344, vol.8, p.675.

304 Smith, *The Bible and Islam*, p.104.

305 Toshihiko Izutsu, *God and Man in the Koran* (New Hampshire: Ayer Co. Publishers Inc., 1987), p.42.

306 Ibid., p.15.

307 Translation is from Thomas B. Irving, *The Qur'an*, 3rd edn. (Vermont: Amana Books, 1988).

308 Abū Jaʿfar Muḥammad ibn Jarīr al-Ṭabarī, *Jāmiʿ al-Bayān ʿan Ta'wīl Āy al-Qur'ān*, Mahmud Muhammad, Ahmad Muhammad Shakir, eds. (Cairo: Dār al-Maʿārif, 1954), vol.3, pp.480–82; also see Abū ʿAlī al-Faḍl ibn al-Ḥasan al-Ṭabarsī, *Majmaʿ al-Bayān fī Tafsīr al-Qur'ān* (Beirut: Dār Maktabah al-Ḥayāt, 1961), vol.2, p.225.

309 Ibn Kathīr, *Tafsīr al-Qur'ān*, vol.1, p.317.

310 Al-Bukhārī, *Saḥīḥ*, vol.10, p.169, hadith no.2770.

311 Muḥyī al-Dīn ibn al-ʿArabī, *Tafsīr al-Qur'ān al-Karīm*, Mustafa Ghalib, ed. (Beirut: Dār al-Andalus, 1978), vol.1, pp.114–15.

312 For definitions of Hadith, Sunnah and the difference between Hadith *qudsī* and ordinary Hadith see Manna al-Qattan, *Mabāḥith fī ʿUlūm al-Ḥadīth* (Cairo: Maktabah Wahabah, 1987), pp.10–13; Mahmud al-Tahhan, *Taysīr Muṣṭaliḥ al-Ḥadīth* (Riyadh: Maktabah al-Maʿārif, 1987), p.127; Abd al-Ghani Abd al-Khaliq, *Ḥujjiyyah al-Sunnah* (Virginia: International Institute of Islamic Thought, 1994), pp.43–70; also see Zain al-Dīn ʿAbd al-Raḥīm ibn al-Ḥusayn al-ʿIrāqī, *Al-Taqyīd wa al-'Īḍāḥ: Sharḥ Muqaddimah al-Salāḥ*, Abd al-Rahman Muhammad Uthman, ed. (Madinah: al-Maktabah al-Salafiyyah, 1969).

313 *Forty Hadith Qudsī*, 6th edn., selected and translated by Ezzeddin Ibrahim, Denys Johnson-Davies (Beirut: The Holy Koran Publishing House, 1990), p.78.

314 Muḥammad ibn ʿAlī al-Shawkānī, *Nayl al-Awtār* [known as *Tafsīr al-Shawkānī*] (Beirut: Dār al-Jīl, 1973), vol.4, p.499.

315 Translation from Mawdudi, *The Meaning of the Qur'an*, vol.4, p.230.

316 Izutsu, *God and Man in the Koran*, p.196.

317 Ibrahim, Johnson-Davies, *Forty Hadith Qudsī*, p.68.

318 The word *ahl al-tawḥīd* has ocurred in the hadith of Jābir ibn ʿAbd Allāh. See Imam Tirmazī, *Saḥīḥ Sunan al-Tirmazī*, M. N. al-Albani, ed., 1st edn. (Gulf States: Maktabah al-Tarbiyyah al-ʿArabī, 1988), vol.2, p.323; and Imam Tirmadhī, *Sunan al-Tirmadhī*, Ahmad Shakir, ed. (Beirut: Dār Iḥyā' al-Turāth al-ʿArabī, n.d.), hadith no.2737. When the Prophet sent Mu'ādh ibn Jabal as governer of Yemen in 9 AH, he told him, "You will be going to Christians and Jews (*ahl al-Kitāb*), so the first thing you should invite them to is the assertion of the oneness of Allah (*Yuwaḥḥidu Allāh*)." See al-Bukhārī, *Saḥīḥ*, vol.22, p.363, hadith no.6824.

319 Very often this division is attributed to Ibn Taymiyyah and his school of thought and many scholars do not take it as a standard. But we see it in its embryonic stage

in a number of earlier works. It is not that elaborate as is the case with later theological treatises but its seed is very much visible. See for instance Abū Muḥammad ʿAbd Allāh ibn Abū Zayd al-Qayrawānī (died 386 AH), *Kitāb al-Jāmiʿ fī al-Sunan wa al-Adab wa al-Maghāzī wa al-Tārīkh*, M. Abu al-Ajfan, Uthman Battikh, eds. (Beirut: Mu'assasah al-Risālah, 1983), pp.107–10; and also see Ibn Khuzaymah, *Kitāb al-Tawḥīd* (Cairo: Maktabah al-Kulliyyāt al-Azhariyyah, n.d.), Here we are adopting it to help us elaborate the point at discussion and not as the standard Islamic expression of the concept of *tawḥīd*.

[320] Mawdudi, *Four Basic Qur'anic Terms*, pp.31–32.

[321] Ibn Kathīr, *Tafsīr al-Qur'ān*, vol.2, p542.

[322] Ibid.

[323] For scientific implications and explanations of the verse see al-Zindani, *Kitāb Tawḥīd al-Khāliq*, pp.43–45.

[324] Keith L. Moore, "Highlights of Human Embryology in the Koran and the Hadith," presented at the Seventh Saudi Medical Meeting at King Faisal University on May 3–6, 1982 [published by Muslim Students Association of US and Canada, Ottawa, Quebec, n.d.], p.51.

[325] Ibid., pp.51–52.

[326] Ibid., p.58.

[327] Mawdudi, *Towards Understanding the Qur'an*, vol.3, p.97.

[328] Al-Bukhārī, *Saḥīḥ*, vol.5, p.182, hadith no.1296.

[329] Asad, *The Message of the Qur'an*, p.261.

[330] Al-Shawkānī, *Tafsīr*, vol.2, p.262.

[331] See Ibn Kathīr, *Tafsīr al-Qur'ān*, pp.605–06.

[332] Izutsu, *God and Man in the Koran*, p.129.

[333] Aḥmad ibn Ibrāhīm ibn ʿĪsā al-Sharqī, *Sharḥ Qaṣīdah ibn al-Qayyim*, 1st edn. (Beirut: al-Maktab al-Islāmī, 1962), vol.2, p.259; also see Abū ʿAbd Allāh Muḥammad ibn Abū Bakr al-Zarʿī al-Damashqī ibn al-Qayyim al-Jawziyyah, *Ighāthah al-Lahfan min Masayid al-Shaytān*, Muhammad S. Kaylani, ed. (Cairo: Maṭbaʿah Musṭafā al-Bābī al-Ḥalabī, 1961), vol.2, pp.128–29.

[334] The translation is from Irving, *The Qur'an*.

[335] Izutsu, *God and Man in the Koran*, p.123.

[336] Ibid., p.129.

[337] Ibid., p.103.

[338] Ibn al-Kalbī has narrated the formula of *talbiyyah* recited by the pagans of Makkah. It said: "*Labbayka Allāhumma labbayaka, lā sharīka laka illa sharīkun huwa laka, tamilkuhu wa-mā malaka*" ("Here I am, O God, here I am: Thou hast

no partner except such partner as Thou hast; Thou possesseth him and all that is his."). For a detailed study of this issue see M. J. Kister, *Society and Religion from Jahiliyyah to Islam* (London, UK: Variorum; Vermont, USA: Gower Publishing Group, 1990), ch.1 "*Labbaka, Allahumma, Labbayka...* On a monotheistic aspect of a Jahiliyyah practice", pp.33–57.

[339] Imam Muslim narrates Abū Dharr's words, "I used to observe prayer three years before my meeting with Allah's Messenger". See Imam Muslim, *Ṣaḥīḥ Muslim*: *al-Jāmiᶜ al-Ṣaḥīḥ*, Abdul Hamid Siddiqi, trans. (Lahore: Sh. Muhammad Ashraf, 1987), vol. IV, p.1316.

[340] Al-Bukhārī narrates from 'Ā'ishah that "Quraysh used to fast on the day of ᶜĀshūrā' in the Pre-Islamic period..." al-Bukhārī, *Saḥīḥ*, vol.6, p.7, hadith no.1489; also see Abū ᶜAbd Allāh Muḥammad ibn Abū Bakr al-Zarᶜī al-Damashqī ibn al-Qayyim al-Jawziyyah, *Zād al-Maᶜād*, Shuayb al-Arnut, Abd al-Qadir al-Arnut, eds. (Beirut: Muᶜassassah al-Risālah, 1982), vol.2, p.67.

[341] For instance the story of al-Maṭᶜam ibn ᶜAddī when he went to the Kaᶜbah to tear apart the social bycott contract paper that was hung on the door of the Kaᶜbah against Banu Hashim. He found it eaten away by insects except the word "*Bi-ismika Allāhumma*" (with your name O Allah). See Safi-ur-Rahman al-Mubarakpuri, *al-Raheeq al-Makhtum: The Sealed Nectar* (Makkah: Rabiṭah al-ᶜĀlam al-Islāmī, 1991), p.128.

[342] Joseph Henninger, "Pre-Islamic Bedouin Religion," *Studies on Islam*, Marlin L. Swartz, ed. (New York: Oxford University Press, 1981), p.15.

[343] Kister, *Society and Religion*, pp.47–48.

[344] Francis E. Peters, *A Reader on Classical Islam* (New Jersey: Princeton University Press, 1994), p.39.

[345] David Waines, *An Introduction to Islam* (New York: Cambridge University Press, 1995), pp.8–9.

[346] Armstrong, *Muhammad*, p.62.

[347] Ibid., p.71.

[348] Hitti, *History of the Arabs*, p.96.

[349] Ibid.

[350] Armstrong, *Muhammad*, p.110.

[351] Izutsu, *God and Man in the Koran*, p.203.

[352] Al-Faruqi, *al-Tawḥīd*, p.21.

[353] Ibid., pp.22–23; here he refers to Paul Tillich's, *Systematic Theology* (Chicago: Chicago University Press, 1957), vol.2, p.40.

[354] Al-Faruqi, *al-Tawḥīd*, p.23.

[355] Al-Bukhārī, *Saḥīḥ*, vol.22, p.393, hadith no.6843.

[356] Abū ʿAbd Allāh Muḥammad ibn Abū Bakr al-Zarʿī al-Damashqī ibn al-Qayyim al-Jawziyyah, *Badāiʿ al-Fawā'id* (Beirut: Dār al-Kitāb al-ʿArabī, n.d.), vol.1, p.164.

[357] See al-Tirmazī, *Sunan al-Tirmazī*, Ahmad Shakir, ed., vol.5, p.530, hadith no.3507.

[358] Abū Muḥammad ʿAlī ibn Aḥmad ibn Ḥazm al-Ẓāhirī, *al-Muḥallā: Kitāb al-Muḥallā bi al-Athār*, Ahmad Shakir, ed. (Beirut: al-Maktab al-Tijārī, n.d.), vol.1, p.30.

[359] Al-ʿAsqalānī, *Fatḥ al-Bārī*, vol.11, p.220.

[360] Abū Ḥāmid al-Ghazālī, *Al-Ghazālī on The Ninety-Nine Beautiful Names of God*, David B. Burrell, Nazih Daher, trans. (Cambridge: The Islamic Texts Society, 1992), p.167.

[361] See al-ʿAsqalānī, *Fatḥ al-Bārī*, vol.11, p.220.

[362] Abū ʿAbd Allāh Aḥmad ibn Ḥanbal, *Musnad al-Imām Aḥmad* (Cairo: Mu'assasah Qurṭubah, n.d.), vol.8, p.63, hadith no.3528.

[363] Al-Ghazālī, *Al-Ghazālī on The Ninety-Nine Beautiful Names of God*, p.169.

[364] Abū Bakr ibn al-ʿArabī, *Aḥkām al-Qur'ān* (Cairo: Maktabah ʿIsā al-Bābī, 1967), vol.2, p.805.

[365] See al-ʿAsqalānī, *Fatḥ al-Bārī*, vol.11, p.220.

[366] See a very good discussion in Umar S. al-Ashqar, *al-Asmā' wa al-Ṣifāt*, 1st edn. (Amman: Dār al-Nafā'is, 1993), pp.66–79.

[367] Al-Ghazālī, *Al-Ghazālī on The Ninety-Nine Beautiful Names of God*, p.171.

[368] This is only one of the ways to classify the names. There could be several ways to classify them. Al-Ṣanʿānī classified them into four kinds. The only difference between our classification and his classification is that he has further divided the names of essence into "Proper Name" which is Allah and "Negative Names" like *al-Quddūs*. (See Muḥammad ibn Ismāʿīl al-Amīr al-Sanʿanī, *Subul al-Salām fī Sharḥ Bulūgh al-Marām* (Cairo: Maktabah ʿIsā al-Bābī al-Ḥalabī, 1938), vol.4, p.209). We have modified it a little just for the purpose of convenience. Ibn al-Qayyim al-Jawziyyah divides them into six categories (see *Badā'iʿ al-Fawā'id*, vol.1, p.160), al-ʿAsqalānī into five (see *Fatḥ al-Bārī*, vol.11, p.223) and scholars of al-Kalām into four. See Abū Ḥāmid al-Ghazālī, *Kitāb al-Iqtiṣād fī al-Iʿtiqād* (Beirut: Dār al-Kutub al-ʿIlmiyyah, 1983), pp.19–83 for more details.

[369] See al-Ashqar, *al-Asmā' wa al-Ṣifāt*, p.89.

[370] Al-Ghazālī, *Al-Ghazālī on The Ninety-Nine Beautiful Names of God*, p.51; also see Abd al-Rahman Hasan H. al-Maydani, al-ʿ*Aqīdah al-Islamīyyah*, 3rd edn.

(Damascus: Dār al-Qalam, 1983), p.157; for details see Gibb, Kramers, *Shorter Encyclopaedia of Islam*, p.33.

[371] See Abd al-Rahman ibn Hasan Al al-Shaykh, *Fatḥ al-Mājīd Sharḥ Kitāb al-Tawḥīd* (Makkah: Maṭbaʿah al-Ḥukūmah, 1967), p.11; M. Yasin, *al-Imān* (Amman: Dār al-Furqān, 1985), p.35.

[372] Al-Ghazālī, *Al-Ghazālī on The Ninety-Nine Beautiful Names of God*, p.51.

[373] Ibid., p.59; also see al-Bayhaqī, *Kitāb al-Asmā'*, pp.37–38.

[374] Al-Ghazālī, *Al-Ghazālī on The Ninety-Nine Beautiful Names of God*, p.60.

[375] Ibid., p.61.

[376] Al-Maydani, *al-ʿAqīdah al-Islāmīyyah*, p.197.

[377] Al-Bayhaqī, *Kitāb al-Asmā'*, p.37.

[378] Ibid.

[379] See Al-Ghazālī, *Al-Ghazālī on The Ninety-Nine Beautiful Names of God*, pp.102–05.

[380] Ibid., p.143.

[381] See Ibid., pp.131.

[382] See Ibid., pp.130–31.

[383] See Ibid., pp.133–34.

[384] Murata, Chittick, *The Vision of Islam*, p.65.

[385] The fact the the name *al-Raḥmān* has been used as the proper name for God in several verses of the Qur'an has led some orientalists to conclude that "Muhammad derived the formula from South Arabia seems proved..." (Gibb, Kramer, *Shorter Encyclopaedia of Islam*, p.35). Andrew Rippin in his article "Rahman and the Hanifs" tries to prove the same. See Andrew Rippin, "Rahman and the Hanifs," *Islamic Studies Presented to Charles Adams*, W. B. Hallaq, D. P. Little, eds. (Leiden: E. J. Brill, 1991), pp.153–65. It may be added that the arguments presented in favor of this thesis are good guess works without much historical basis.

[386] Murata, Chittick, *The Vision of Islam*, p.66.

[387] Al-Ghazālī, *Al-Ghazālī on The Ninety-Nine Beautiful Names of God*, p.52.

[388] Baillie, *God was in Christ*, p.123.

[389] Rahman, *Major Themes of the Qur'an*, pp.1 ff.

[390] Hill, *Learning*, pp.72 ff.

[391] Kenneth Cragg, *The House of Islam* (California: Dickenson Publishing Co. Inc., 1969), p.7.

[392] Al-Ghazālī, *Al-Ghazālī on The Ninety-Nine Beautiful Names of God*, pp.83–84.

[393] Ibid.

[394] Ibid., pp.131–32.

[395] The books on *'Iʿjāz al-Qur'ān* give a detailed account of the relationship between these names and the subject matter of the passages.

[396] The verse 38 should not confuse the reader that the Islamic Law recommends such a severe punishment for small acts of theft. There are many strict prerequisites like proper investigation, enough eye witnesses, a big amount of the stolen commodity involved, etc. The books of fiqh in general and the books on *Fiqh al-Janā'ī* (Islamic Criminal Law) in particular give details of the requirements as well as the process. See Abd al-Qadir Aawdah, *al-Tashrīʿ al-Janā'ī al-Islāmī* (Beirut: Mu'assasah al-Risālah, 1986), vol.1 p.2; Abd al-Rahman al-Jazayri, *Kitāb al-Fiqh ʿalā al-Madhāhib al-Arbaʿah* (Beirut: Dār al-Irshād lī al-Ṭibāʿah wa al-Nashr, n.d.), vol.5, pp.124 ff; Abū al-Walīd Muḥammad ibn Aḥmad ibn Rushd, *Bidāyah al-Mujtahid wa Nihāyah al-Muqtaṣid* (Beirut: Dār al-Fikr, n.d.), vol.2, pp.372 ff. Due respect is given to the requirements of a fair and just trial. Moreover, the circumstances of the crime play a vital role in determining the punishment. The above mentioned capital punishment cannot be implemented if the individual was forced by his circumstances. For instance, ʿUmar refused to cut off the hands of those who stole during drought in Madinah in view of their circumstances. See Qutb, *Fī Ẓilāl al-Qur'ān*, vol.2, pp.882–86.

[397] Al-Ghazālī, *Al-Ghazālī on The Ninety-Nine Beautiful Names of God*, p.40.

[398] Ibid., p.37.

[399] Cragg, *The House of Islam*, p.7.

[400] Al-Faruqi, *al-Tawḥīd*, pp.24–25; also see his artical "Islam and Art," *Studia Islamica*, fasciculi XXXVII (1973), pp.81–109; and his "Misconceptions of the Nature of the Work of Art in Islam," *Islam and the Modern Age* (May, 1970), vol.1, no.1; and his "On the Nature of Art in Islam," *Islam and the Modern Age* (August, 1976), vol.1, no.2,; and his "Divine Transcendence and Its Expression," *World Faiths* (Spring, 1979), vol.17; Thomas W. Arnold, *Painting in Islam* (Oxford: Clarendon Press, 1928); Richard Ettinghausen, *The Characted of Islamic Art in the Arab Heritage*, N. A. Faris, ed. (Princeton: Princeton University Press, 1944).

[401] Al-Faruqi, *al-Tawḥīd*, p.14; I am heavily indebted to al-Faruqi in aspect of *al-Tawḥīd's* discussion. See for details ibid., pp.9–16.

[402] Izutsu, *God and Man in the Koran*, p.75.

[403] Al-Faruqi, *al-Tawḥīd*, p.33.

[404] See John E. Kelsay's doctoral thesis titled "Religion and Morality in Islam" (Chalottesville: University of Virginia, 1985); F. Carney, "Some Aspects of Islamic

Ethics," *Journal of Religion* (1983), vol.63, part.2, pp.159–74; Richard M. Frank, "Moral Obligation in Classical Muslim Theology," *Journal of Religious Ethics* (1983), vol.11, no.2, pp.204–23; for a general study Paul Helm, ed., *Divine Commands and Moral Requirements* (Oxford: Oxford University Press, 1981); Marshall G. S. Hodgson, *The Venture of Islam* (Chicago: Chicago University Press, 1974), vols.1–2; Janine M. Idziak, ed., *Divine Command Theory* (New York: Mellen Press, 1979); Wilferd Madelung, "Early Sunni Doctrine Concerning Faith," *Studia Islamica* (1970), vol.32, pp.233–54; Fazlur Rahman, "Some Key Ethical Concepts of the Qur'an," *Journal of Religious Ethics* (1983), vol.11, no.2, pp.170–85; and A. Kevin Reinhart, "Islamic Law as Islamic Ethics," *Journal of Religious Ethics* (1983), vol.11, no.2, pp.186–203; Majid Khadduri, *The Islamic Conception of Justice* (Baltimore: The John Hopkin University Press, 1984).

[405] See for details Fazlur Rahman, *Major Themes of the Qur'an*, chs.1–3.

[406] See for details Abū Isḥāq Ibrāhīm ibn Mūsā al-Shāṭibī, *al-Muwāfaqāt fī Uṣūl al-Sharīʿah*, 3rd edn. (Cairo: al-Maktabah al-Tijāriyyah al-Kubrā, 1975), vol.3, p.118; Mahmud Shaltut, *al-Islām ʿAqīdah wa Sharīʿah* (Cairo: Dār al-Qalam, 1966), p.29; M. Qutb, *Madhāhib Fikriyyah Muʿāṣarah*, 1st edn. (Beirut: Dār al-Sharq, 1983), p.13.

[407] This verse has been interpreted in two ways. Many scholars make a stop at "no one knows its true meanings except Allah" while, others, especially rationalists like Muʿtazilite, pause at "no one knows its true meanings except Allah and those who are firmly grounded in knowledge", implying permission for speculations about and allegorical interpretations of these verses. See Abu Muhammad Abd al-Haqq ibn Atiyya, *al-Muḥarrar al-Wajīz fī Tafsīr al-Kitāb al-ʿAzīz*, Abdullah ibn Ibrahim al-Ansari, al-Sayyid Abd al-Al, M. al-Shafi, eds. (Qatar: The Government of Qatar Edition, 1982), vol.3, p.24.

[408] Binyamin Abrahamov, *Anthropomorphism and Interpretation of the Qur'an in the Theology of al-Qasim ibn Ibrahim* (Boston: Brill, 1996), p.4.

[409] Ibid., p.3.

[410] See various books of tafsir in regards to this phrase. For instance see al-Alusi, *Rūḥ al-Maʿānī*, vol.2, p.46.

[411] See Ibn Kathīr, *Tafsīr al-Qur'ān*, vol.4, p.415; al-Alusi, *Rūḥ al-Maʿānī*, vol.11, pp.130–31.

[412] Ibn Ḥazm al-Ẓāhirī, *al-Faṣl*, vol.2, p.127.

[413] Merlin Swartz, *A Medieval Critique of Anthropomorphism: Ibn al-Jawzi's Kitab Akhbar as-Sifat* (Boston: Brill, 2002), p.139; Al-Bayhaqī, *Kitāb al-Asmā'*, p.301.

[414] Al-Bayhaqī, *Kitāb al-Asmā'*, p.301.

[415] Ibid., p.302.

[416] Ibid., p.305.

[417] Ibid., p.309.

[418] Netton, *Allah Transcendent*, p.2.

[419] Abd al-Halim Mahmud, *al-Tafkīr al-Falsafī fī al-Islām* (Cairo: Dār al-Maʿārif, 1984), pp.88–93; also see Ahmad ibn Ali al-Maqrayzi, *al-Khitāt wa al-Athar* (Cairo: Maṭbaʿah al-Nīl, 1907), vol.4, pp.180 ff.

[420] See ʿAlī ibn al-Ḥasan Abū al-Qāsim ibn ʿAsākir, *Tahzīb Tārīkh*, 1st edn. (Damascus: al-Maktabah al-ʿArabiyyah, n.d.), vol.1, p.299; Muḥammad ibn al-Murtaḍā al-Yamanī ibn al-Wazīr, *Īthār al-Ḥaq ʿalā al-Khalq* (Cairo: Maṭbaʿah al-Adab wa al-Mu'ayyid, 1900), p.97; Abū Naʿīm al-Iṣfahānī, *Ḥilyat al-'Awliyā' wa Ṭabaqāt al-Aṣfiyā'* (Cairo: Maṭbaʿah al-Saʿādah, 1932), pp.72–73.

[421] See Muḥammad ibn ʿAbd al-Karīm al-Shahrastānī, *Kitāb al-Milal wa al-Niḥal* (Cairo: al-Ḥalbī, 1968), vol.2, p.11. The Shiite scholar Murtada al-Askari doubts the historical existence of Ibn Saba'. He argues that most of the reports about him are narrated by Ṭabarī through Sayf ibn ʿUmar al-Tamīmī (d.170 AH). Sayf, to al-Askari, was not an authentic narrator. Therefore, to him, Ibn Saba' was a mythical figure created by later historians to blame Shiism of these developments. See Murtada al-Askari, *Abdullah ibn Saba' and Other Myths* (Qum: Sharif al-Rida Publishing Co., 1944). Among the non-Shiite, it is Taha Husayn who doubts Ibn Saba's existence. See his *al-Fitnah al-Kubrā, ʿAlī wa Banūh* (Cairo: Dār al-Maʿārif, 1961), p.90.

[422] A. K. Kazi, J. G. Flynn, trans., *Muslim Sects and Divisions: The Section on Muslim Sects in Kitab al-Milal wa al-Nihal by Shahrastani* (London: Kegan Paul International, 1984), p.150.

[423] See Abū al-Ḥasan ʿAlī al-Ashʿarī, *Maqālāt al-Islāmiyyīn wa Ikhtilāf al-Muṣallīn*, M. Abd al-Hamid, ed. (Beirut: al-Ḥikmah, 1994). It should be mentioned here that Hishām ibn al-Ḥakām argued that God is "a body but not like bodies." Al-Ashʿarī, *Maqālāt*, p.106; and Hishām al-Jawaliqi argued that God does not have "flesh and blood like us." Al-Ashʿarī, *Maqālāt*, p.108.

[424] Al-Shahrastānī, *Kitāb al-Milal*, vol.1, p.155.

[425] Ignaz Goldziher, *Introduction to Islamic Theology and Law* (Princeton: Princeton University Press, 1981), p.212.

[426] See Ibn Saʿd, *Ṭabaqāt*, E. Schau, ed. (Leiden: Brills, 1905), vol.7, p.105; M. Husayn al-Dhahabi argues that he died even before 150 AH. See *Mizān al-Iʿtadāl* (Cairo: Ṭabʿah ʿĪsā al-Bābī, 1907), vol.3, p.196.

[427] Matti Moosa, *Extremist Shiites, The Ghulat Sects* (New York: Syracuse University Press, 1988), pp.69–70.

[428] Julius Wellhausen, *The Religio-Political Factions in Early Islam*, R. C. Ostle, ed., R. C. Ostle, S. M. Walzer, trans. (New York: North-Holland / American Elsevier, 1975), p.151.

[429] Kazi, Flynn, *Muslim Sects and Divisions*, p.78.

[430] See for details M. Husayn al-Dhahabi, *al-Tafsīr wa al-Mufassirūn* (Beirut: Dār al-Kitāb al-ʿArabīyah, 1962).

[431] See for details Aḥmad ibn Yaḥya al-Balādhurī, *Ansāb al-Ashrāf*, Hamidullah, ed. (Cairo: Dār al-Maʿārif, n.d.), vol.2, p.241; ʿImād al-Dīn Abū al-Fida Ismā'īl ibn Kathīr, *al-Bidāyah wa al-Nihāyah* (Cairo: Maṭbaʿah al-Saʿādah, 1965), vol.9, p.350.

[432] See al-Dhahabi, *Mizān al-Iʿtadāl*, vol.1, p.426.

[433] See Ibid., vol.3, p.183; Tash Kubrizadah, *Miftaḥ al-Saʿādah* (Cairo: Dār al-Kutub al-ʿArabiyyah, n.d.), vol.2, p.32.

[434] Ibn Kathīr, *al-Bidāyah*, vol.9, p.350.

[435] See Abū Muḥammad ʿAbd Allāh al-Dārimī, *Kitāb al-Radd ʿalā al-Jahmiyyah* (Beirut: al-Maktab al-Islāmī, 1982), p.7.

[436] Ali Sami al-Nashshar, *Nash'at al-Tafkīr al-Falsafī fī al-Islām*, 3rd edn. (Cairo: Dār al-Maʿārif, 1965), vol.1, p.329.

[437] Welferd Madelung, *Religious Schools and Sects in Medieval Islam* (London: Variorum Reprints, 1985), p.506.

[438] Ibid., p.507.

[439] Al-Ashʿarī, *Maqālāt*, p.161.

[440] Al- Dārimī, *Kitāb al-Radd*, p.12.

[441] See Ibn Taymiyyah, *Majmūʿ al-Fatāwā*, Abd al-Rahman ibn Muhammad ibn Qasim, ed. (Rabat: Maktabah al-Maʿārif, n.d.), vol.5, p.39.

[442] Kazi, Flynn, *Muslim Sects and Divisions*, p.73.

[443] Al-Faruqi, *Cultural Atlas*, p.285.

[444] Kazi, Flynn, *Muslim Sects and Divisions*, p.73.

[445] Al-Nashshar, *Nash'at al-Tafkīr al-Falsafī fī al-Islām*, vol.1, p.337.

[446] Kazi, Flynn, *Muslim Sects and Divisions*, p.74.

[447] Quoted from Netton, *Allah Transcendent*, p.3; See Morris S. Seale, *Muslim Theology: A Study of Origins with Reference to the Church Fathers* (London: Luzac & Co., 1964), pp.58 ff.

[448] Ibrahim Madkur, *Fī al-Falsafah al-Islāmiyyah* (Cairo: Dār al-Maʿārif, 1976), p.29.

[449] Seale, *Muslim Theology*, p.48.

[450] William M. Watt, *The Formative Period of Islamic Thought* (Edinburgh: Edinburgh University Press, 1973), p.147.

[451] Al-Faruqi, *Cultural Atlas*, p.284.

[452] Tijitze J. De Boer, *History of Philosophy in Islam*, E. R. Jones B. D., trans. (London: Luzac & Co., 1970), pp.41–42.

[453] Ibid., p.47.

[454] Duncan B. Macdonald, *Development of Muslim Theology, Jurisprudence and Constitutional Theory* (Beirut: Khayats, 1965), p.131.

[455] Ibid., p.132.

[456] Ibid.

[457] Seale, *Muslim Theology*, pp.11–20, 50–74.

[458] Gibb, Kramers, *Shorter Encyclopaedia of Islam*, p.37.

[459] Harry A. Wolfson, *Philosophy of the Kalam* (London: Harvard University Press, 1976), p.62; also see his "Philosophical Implications of the Problems of Divine Attributes in the Kalam," *J.A.O.S.* (1959); and his *Repercussions of the Kalam in Jewish Philosophy* (Cambridge, Mass.: Harvard University Press, 1979).

[460] See Abū al-Ḥasan ʿAlī al-Ashʿarī, *al-Ibānah ʿan Uṣūl al-Diyānah*, Fawqiyyah H. Mahmud, ed. (Cairo: Dār al-Anṣār, 1977), p.53.

[461] See al-Shahrastānī, *Kitāb al-Milal*, vol.1, p.49.

[462] See Saʿd al-Dīn al-Taftazānī, *Sharḥ al-ʿAqā'id al-Nasafiyyah* (Cairo: Dār Iḥyā al-Kutub al-ʿArabiyyah, 1955), p.78.

[463] Ibn al-Athīr, *al-Kāmil fī al-Tārīkh* (Cairo: Dār al-ʿIlm li al-Malayīn, 1987), vol.7, p.49.

[464] Abu Bakr Ahmad ibn Ali Ahmad, *Tārīkh Baghdād* (Cairo: Dār al-Ma'ārif, 1931), vol.7, p.61.

[465] See Ibn Kathīr, *al-Bidāyah*, vol.9, p.350.

[466] Arent J. Wensinck, *The Muslim Creed: Its Genesis and Historical Development* (New York: Barnes & Noble Inc., 1965), p.70.

[467] Ibid., p.52.

[468] William M. Watt, *Islamic Philosophy and Theology* (Edinburgh: Edinburgh University Press, 1967), pp.65–66.

[469] Mahmud, *al-Tafkīr al-Falsafī fī al-Islām*, p.155.

[470] Irfan Abdul Hamid Fattah, *Dirāsāt fī al-Firaq wa al-ʿAqā'id al-Islāmiyyah* (Beirut: Mu'assasah al-Risālah, 1984), pp.231–32.

[471] Al-Nashshar, *Nash'at al-Tafkīr al-Falsafī fī al-Islām*, vol.1, pp.330–31.

[472] Madkur, *Fī al-Falsafah al-Islāmiyyah*, vol.2, p.29.

[473] Wensinck, *The Muslim Creed*, p.52.

[474] Gibb, Kramers, *Shorter Encyclopaedia of Islam*, p.423.

[475] Ibid.

[476] Netton, *Allah Transcendent*, p.4.

[477] Watt, *Islamic Philosophy and Theology*, p.46.

[478] Gibb, Kramers, *Shorter Encyclopaedia of Islam*, p.424.

[479] See Zahdi Hasan Jarallah, *al-Muʿtazilah* (Cairo: al-Mu'assasah al-ʿArabiyyah li al-Dirāsāt wa al-Nashr, 1947), pp.33, 256; Watt, *The Formative Period of Islamic Thought*, pp.249–50.

[480] Rippin, *Muslims*, vol.1, p.65.

[481] Ibid., p.69.

[482] Frederick M. Denny, *An Introduction to Islam* (New York: Macmillan, 1985), p.180.

[483] See Watt, *Islamic Philosophy and Theology*, pp.58–63; for a detailed study see Walter M. Patton, *Ahmad b. Hanbal and the Mihna* (Leiden: E. J. Brill, 1897).

[484] See Qāḍī ʿAbd al-Jabbār, *Sharḥ al-Uṣūl al-Khamsah*, Abd al-Karim Uthman, ed., 1st edn. (Cairo: Maktabah Wahabah, 1965); Al-Faruqi, *Cultural Atlas*, pp.287–91.

[485] Al-Faruqi, *Cultural Atlas*, p.287.

[486] Kazi, Flynn, *Muslim Sects and Divisions*, p.43.

[487] Macdonald, *Development of Muslim Theology*, p.136.

[488] Ibid., pp.136–37.

[489] Kazi, Flynn, *Muslim Sects and Divisions*, p.46.

[490] Al-Ashʿarī, *Maqālāt*, p.74. (Translation is mine).

[491] Ibid., p.75.

[492] Macdonald, *Development of Muslim Theology*, pp.140–41.

[493] Al-Ashʿarī, *Maqālāt*, p.76.

[494] Kazi, Flynn, *Muslim Sects and Divisions*, p.46; see for details, Wolfson, "Philosophical Implications of the Problems of Divine Attributes in the Kalam," p.73.

[495] Watt, *Islamic Philosophy and Theology*, p.70.

[496] Richard M. Frank, *Beings and Their Attributes, The Teaching of the Basrian School of Muʿtazila in the Classical Period* (Albany: SUNY Press, 1978), p.19.

[497] Kazi, Flynn, *Muslim Sects and Divisions*, p.67.

[498] ʿAbd al-Jabbār, *Sharḥ al-Uṣūl al-Khamsah*, pp.151–75.

[499] Al-Faruqi, *Cultural Atlas*, p.288.

[500] Rahman, *Islam and Modernity*, p.89.

[501] Al-Faruqi, *Cultural Atlas*, p.288; al-Jabbār, *Sharḥ al-Uṣūl al-Khamsah*, p.248; al-Zamakhsharī, *Tafsīr al-Kashshāf*, vol.2, p.54.

[502] Abu al-Husayn Abd al-Rahim al-Khayyat, *Kitāb al-Intiṣār* (Cairo: Dār al-Nahḍah al-ʿArabiyyah, 1925), pp.67–68.

[503] Netton, *Allah Transcendent*, pp.4–5.

[504] See al-Ashaʿrī, *Maqālāt*, p.74.

[505] Ibid.

[506] See a detailed discussion of these interpretations in J. M. S. Baljon, "Qur'anic Anthropomorphism," *Islamic Studies* (Islamabad: Islamic Research Institute, 1988), vol.27; also al-Ashʿarī, *al-Ibānah*, pp.36–45; al-Jabbār, *Sharḥ Uṣūl al-Khamsah*, pp.227 ff.

[507] Watt, *The Formative Period of Islamic Thought*, pp.248–49.

[508] George C. Anawati, "Attributes of God: Islamic Concepts," *Encyclopedia of Religion* (1987), vol.1, p.514.

[509] Translation taken from Watt, *Islamic Philosophy*, pp.246–47; see original in al-Ashaʿrī, *Maqālāt*, pp.65–66.

[510] Watt, *Islamic Philosophy*, p.70.

[511] Ibid.

[512] Watt, *The Formative Period of Islamic Thought*, p.246.

[513] Macdonald, *Development of Muslim Theology*, p.145.

[514] Fazlur Rahman, *Islam* (Chicago: University of Chicago Press, 1979), p.89.

[515] Netton, *Allah Transcendent*, p.5.

[516] William M. Watt, "Early Discussions about the Qur'an," *Muslim World* (1950), vol. XL, p.31.

[517] Hamilton A. R. Gibb, *Modern Trends in Islam* (New York: Otagon Books, 1972), pp.19–20.

[518] Ibid., p.19.

[519] Watt, *The Formative Period of Islamic Thought*, p.250.

[520] Fakhar al-Dīn al-Rāzī, *Asās al-Taqdīs* (Cairo: Maṭbaʿah Muṣṭafā al-Bābī, 1935), p.180.

[521] See details of their philosophical positions in Seyyed H. Nasr, Oliver Leaman, eds., *History of Islamic Philosophy* (London; New York: Routledge, 1996), vol.1, pp.178–97.

[522] See for a detailed study Netton, *Allah Transcendent*, pp.106 ff.

[523] Abū Naṣr al-Fārābī, *al-Thamarat al-Mardiyah* (Leiden: Brills, 1895), pp.57 f.

[524] Jamāl al-Dīn Abū al-Faraj ʿAbd al-Raḥmān ibn ʿAlī ibn al-Jawzī, *Talbīs Iblīs* (Beirut: Dār al-Kutub al-ʿIlmiyyah, n.d.), p.48.

[525] Abū Ḥāmid al-Ghazālī, *Tahāfut al-Falāsifah*, Sulayman Dunya, ed. (Cairo: Dār al-Maʿārif, 1947), pp.179 ff.

[526] See Mahmud, *al-Tafkīr al-Falsafī fī al-Islām*, pp.255 f.

[527] See details in ibid.

[528] Abū Naṣr al-Fārābī, *Mabadi' Ara' Ahl al-Madina al-Fadila* (Leiden: Brills, 1890), pp.17–18; Richard Walzer has translated it into English. See *Al-Farabi on the Perfect State* (Oxford: Clarendon, 1985). See more details in al-Fārābī's, *Kitāb al-Millah wa Nuṣūṣ Ukhrā*, Muhsin Mahdi, ed. (Beirut: Dār al-Mashriq, 1968).

[529] Netton, *Allah Transcendent*, p.104.

[530] Madkur, *Fī al-Falsafah al-Islāmiyyah*, vol.2, p.82.

[531] Netton, *Allah Transcendent*, p.109.

[532] Mahmud, *al-Tafkīr al-Falsafī fī al-Islām*, pp.252–54.

[533] See Arthur J. Arberry, *Avicenna on Theology* (Connecticut: Hyperion Press, 1979), p.25; Netton, *Allah Transcendent*, pp.150–53.

[534] Netton, *Allah Transcendent*, p.154.

[535] Arberry, *Avicenna on Theology*, p.32.

[536] Quoted from Netton, *Allah Transcendent*, p.154.

[537] Arberry, *Avicenna on Theology*, p.36; also see Netton, *Allah Transcendent*, pp.162 f.

[538] Madkur, *Fī al-Falsafah al-Islāmiyyah*, vol.2, p.82.

[539] See Ḥāmid al-Dīn al-Kirmānī, *Rāḥat al-ʿAql* (Cairo: Dār al-Fikr al-ʿArabī, 1952), p.46; also Arif Tamir, *Khams Rasāil Ismāʿīliyyah* (Damascus: Dār al-Inṣāf, 1956); Adil al-Awa, *Muntakhabāt Ismāʿīliyyah* (Damascus: Maṭbaʿah al-Jāmiʿah al-Sūriyyah, 1957); Netton, *Allah Transcendent*, pp.203–09.

[540] Netton, *Allah Transcendent*, p.6.

[541] Ibid., p.16.

[542] Ibid., p.326.

[543] Ibid., p.332.

[544] See al-Ashʿarī, *Maqālāt*, pp.106–08; see also Abraham S. Halkin, "The Hashwiyya," *Journal of the American Oriental Society* (December, 1934), vol.54, no.4, pp.1–28.

[545] Kazi, Flynn, *Muslim Sects and Divisions*, pp.89–90.

[546] Ibid., p.92.

[547] Ibid.

[548] Ibid.

[549] Nuʿmān Abū Ḥanīfah, *al-Fiqh al-Akbar*, Mulla Ali al-Qari, ed. (Cairo: ʿĪsā al-Bābī, 1955). For English translation and commentary see Wensinck, *The Muslim Creed*. Some scholars like Watt attribute this book to some later (between 900–950 CE) Hanafi sources.

[550] See Shams al-Dīn Abū ʿAbd Allāh Muḥammad ibn Aḥmad al-Dhahabī, *Mukhtaṣar al-ʿUlūw li al-ʿAlīyy al-Ghaffār*, M. Nasr al-Din al-Albani, ed., 1st edn. (Beirut: al-Maktab al-Islāmī, 1981), pp.140–41.

[551] See Jalāl al-Dīn al-Suyūṭī, *Ṣawn al-Manṭaq wa al-Kalām*, Ali Sami al-Nashshar, Suad Ali Abd al-Razzaq, eds. (Cairo: Silsilah Iḥyā' al-Turāth, Dār al-Naṣr, 1970), vol.1, pp.47–49.

[552] See Aḥmad ibn Ḥanbal, *al-Radd ʿalā al-Zanādiqah wa al-Jahmiyyah* ʿAbd al-Rahman Umayrah, ed. (Riyad: Dār al-Liwā', 1982).

[553] Fakhry, *A History of Islamic Philosophy* (New York: Columbia University Press, 2004) p.xix; also see Muḥammad ibn ʿAlī al-Shawkānī, *al-Tuḥaf fī Madhāhib al-Salaf* (Cairo: Maṭbaʿah al-Imām, n.d.).

[554] Abrahamov, *Anthropomorphism and Interpretation of the Qur'an*, p.6.

[555] Wensinck, *The Muslim Creed*, p.189.

[556] Ibid., p.190.

[557] William M. Watt, *Early Islam: Collected Articles* (Edinburgh: Edinburgh University Press, 1990), p.88. Wesley Williams goes against the scholarly consensus and argues that Ibn Ḥanbal never implied the *bilā kayf* formula in his writings. See his "Aspects of the Creed of Imam Ahmad Ibn Hanbal: A Study of Anthropomorphism in Early Islamic Discourse," *International Journal of Middle East Studies* (2002), vol.34, pp.448–49.

[558] Netton, *Allah Transcendent*, p.4.

[559] Nasr, Leaman, *History of Islamic Philosophy*, p.107.

[560] Watt, *Early Islam*, pp.88–89.

[561] Oliver Leaman, *A Brief Introduction to Islamic Philosophy* (Cambridge: Polity Press, 1999), p.49; Binyamin Abrahamov, "The *Bi-lā Kayfa* Doctrine and its Foundations in Islamic Theology," *Arabica* (November, 1995), vol.42, pp.365–79.

[562] Muḥammad ibn ʿAbd al-Karīm al-Shahrastānī, *Kitāb al-Milal wa al-Niḥal: Book of Religious and Philosophical Sects: Part 1*, William Cureton ed. (London: Society for the Publication of Oriental Texts, 1842), p.76.

[563] Watt, *Islamic Philosophy and Theology*, p.80.

[564] Ibid.

[565] Armstrong, *A History of God*, p.165. Wesley Williams, a University of Michigan graduate, argues against an established scholarly consensus and declares Ibn Ḥanbal as "an anthropomorphist. He affirmed for the divine a human form, including a face, eyes, curly hair, mouth, voice, breath, chest and two elbows, back, arms, hands with a palm, five fingers and fingertips, legs, shin, feet, soul, physical beauty, a limit, and even, shockingly, loins. He affirmed the external meanings of these attributes and refused to qualify them with bilkafa." Williams, "Aspects of the Creed of Imam Ahmad Ibn Hanbal," p.449.

[566] Kazi, Flynn, *Muslim Sects and Divisions*, p89.

[567] See details in Ibn Taymiyyah, *al-Fatāwā,* vol.5, pp.323 ff.

[568] See Muwaffaq al-Dīn ʿAbd Allāh ibn Aḥmad ibn Qudāmah al-Maqdisī, *Censure of Speculative Theology. An Edition and Translation of Ibn Qudāma's Taḥrīm an-Naẓar fī Kutub Ahl al-Kalām*, George Makdisi, trans. (London: Luzac, 1962).

[569] See Ibn Taymiyyah, *Minhāj al-Sunnah fī Naqd Kalām al-Shīʿah wa al-Qadariyyah*, Muhammad ibn Rashad Salim, ed. (Riyadh: Islamic University of al-Imam Muhammad bin Saud, 1985); *Naqd al-Manṭiq*, 1st edn. (Cairo: Maṭbaʿah al-Sunnah al-Muḥammadiyyah, 1951).

[570] See for instance Umar S. al-Ashqar, *Aṣal al-Iʿtiqād*, 1st edn. (Kuwait: Dār al-Nafā'is, 1990); and his *al-ʿAqīdah fī Allāh* (Amman: Dār al-Nafā'is, 1995); also see Muhammad Nasr al-Din al-Albani, *Sharḥ al-ʿAqīdah al-Ṭaḥāwiyyah* (Beirut: al-Maktab al-Islāmī, 1984).

[571] Nasr, Leaman, *History of Islamic Philosophy*, vol.1, pp.116–17.

[572] Watt, *Islamic Philosophy and Theology*, p.162.

[573] Mohammad ibn Salih al-Uthaymin, *al-ʿAqīdah al-Wasaṭiyyah lī Ibn Taymiyyah* (Virginia: Institute of Islamic and Arabic Sciences, 1991), p.6; Ibn Taymiyyah, *al-Fatāwā*, vol.1, p.324.

[574] Ibn Taymiyyah, *al-Fatāwā*, vol.5, p.202.

[575] Ibid., p.207.

[576] See details of the arguement in Ibn Taymiyyah, *al-Risālah al-Madaniyyah fī Taḥqīq al-Majāz wa al-Ḥaqīqah fī Ṣifāt Allāh Taʿālā*, 2nd edn. (Makkah: al-Maṭbaʿah al-Salafiyyah, 1932), pp.7–10.

[577] Ibid., p.199. (Translation is mine).

[578] Ibid., pp.284–85.

[579] Netton, *Allah Transcendent*, p.325.

[580] Arthur J. Arberry, *Revelation and Reason in Islam* (London: George Allen & Unwin Ltd., 1965), p.22.

[581] Al-Nashshar, *Nash'at al-Tafkīr al-Falsafī fī al-Islām*, vol.1, p.641.

[582] Madkur, *Fī al-Falsafah al-Islāmiyyah*, vol.2, p.34; George Makdisi, "Hanbalite Islam," *Studies on Islam*, M. L. Swartz, ed. (New York: Oxford University Press, 1981), pp.216–74, see especially, pp.226, 253.

[583] Gibb, Kramers, *Shorter Encyclopaedia of Islam*, p.152.

[584] Ibid.

[585] See details in al-Dhahabī, *Mukhtaṣar al-ᶜUlūw*, p.74.

[586] Gibb, *Mohammedanism*, p.152.

[587] Ibn Taymiyyah, *al-Fatāwā*, vol.5, p.330.

[588] Ibid., p.349.

[589] Ibid., p.243.

[590] See Abū Bakr Taqī al-Dīn al-Huṣnī, *Dafᶜu Shubah Man Shabbaha wa Tamarrada wa Naṣaba dhālik ilā al-Imām Aḥmad* (Cairo: al-Ḥalbī, 1931), p.16.

[591] Ibn Ḥazm al-Ẓāhirī, *al-Faṣl*, vol.1, p.166.

[592] See Jamāl al-Dīn Abū al-Faraj ᶜAbd al-Raḥmān ibn ᶜAlī ibn al-Jawzī, *Dafaᶜ Shubhah al-Tashbīh*, al-Kawthari, ed. (Cairo: al-Maktabah al-Tawfīqiyyah, n.d.), p.8; also his *Talbīs Iblīs* (Cairo: al-Maṭbaᶜah al-Munīriyyah, n.d.).

[593] Al-Jawzī, *Dafaᶜ Shubhah al-Tashbīh*, p.8.

[594] Al-Bayhaqī, *Kitāb al-Asmā'*, p.397.

[595] Abū Bakr Muḥammad ibn al-Ṭayyib al-Bāqillānī, *Kitāb al-Tamhīd*, Yusuf al-Yasui, ed. (Beirut: al-Maktabah al-Sharqiyyah, 1957), see chapter on *tawḥīd*, chapter on *al-ism wa al-musammā*.

[596] See al-Ashᶜarī, *al-Ibānah*; and his *Maqālāt*; for the English translation, see *The Theology of al-Ashᶜari: The Arabic Texts of al-Ashᶜari's "Kitab al-Lumaᶜ" and "Risalat Istihsan al-Khawd fi ᶜIlm al-Kalam,"* with briefly annotated translations and appendices by Richard J. McCarthy (Beirut: Imprimerie Catholique, 1953).

[597] Al-Rāzī, *Asās al-Taqdīs*, p.223.

[598] See details in Watt, *Islamic Philosophy*, pp.84 ff.

[599] Ibid., p.85.

[600] Al-Ashᶜarī, *al-Ibānah*, pp.8–9.

[601] Wensinck, *The Muslim Creed*, p.90; Goldziher, *Introduction to Islamic Theology and Law*, p.105.

[602] Goldziher, *Introduction to Islamic Theology and Law*, pp.104–05.

[603] Watt, *Islamic Philosophy*, p.85.

[604] Kazi, Flynn, *Muslim Sects and Divisions*, p.85.

[605] Goldziher, *Introduction to Islamic Theology and Law*, pp.104 f.

[606] Ibid., p.80; al-Shahrastānī, *Kitāb al-Milal*, vol.1, p.95.

[607] Al-Ashʿarī, *al-Ibānah*, p.43.

[608] See ibid., p.45.

[609] See al-Ashʿarī, *Maqālāt*, pp.109–10.

[610] Watt, *Islamic Philosophy*, p.86.

[611] Wensinck, *The Muslim Creed*, p.92.

[612] Goldziher, *Introduction to Islamic Theology and Law*, p.105.

[613] Ibid., pp.105–06.

[614] Ibn Taymiyyah, *al-Fatāwā*, vol.5, pp.90 ff.

[615] Wensinck, *The Muslim Creed*, pp.92–93.

[616] Kazi, Flynn, *Muslim Sects and Divisions*, p.85.

[617] See M. Zahid al-Kawthari's commentary on *Ibn ʿAsākir's Tabyīn Kadhb al-Muftrā* (Damascus: Maṭbaʿah al-Tawfīq, 1954), p.28.

[618] Armstrong, *History of God*, pp.166–67.

[619] Watt, *Early Islam*, pp.89–90.

[620] Armstrong, *History of God*, p.167.

[621] Wensinck, *The Muslim Creed*, p.93.

[622] See al-Ashʿarī, *al-Ibānah*, pp.40 f.

[623] Ibid., p.45.

[624] Rippin, *Muslims*, vol.1, p.70.

[625] Anawati, "Attributes of God: Islamic Concept," p.516.

[626] Abū Bakr Muḥammad ibn Ṭayyib al-Bāqillānī, *al-Inṣāf fī mā Yajibu I'tiqāduh wa lā Yajūz al-Jahal bih* (Damascus: Izzat al-Husayni Publishers, 1950), pp.41–42.

[627] Ibid., p.25.

[628] Ibid., p.24.

[629] See another contemporary of al-Bāqillānī who was likewise an Ashʿarī: Abū al-Muẓaffar al-Isfrāyīnī, *al-Tabṣīr fī al-Dīn* (Cairo: Maktabah al-Khanjī, 1955).

[630] For a contrasting view of *ta'wīl* see Umar S. al-Ashqar, *al-Ta'wīl: Khuṭūratuhu wa Atharuh* (Amman: Dār al-Nafā'is, 1992).

[631] Watt, *Early Islam*, p.90.

[632] Gibb, *Mohammedanism*, p.79.

[633] ʿAbd al-Qāhir al-Baghdādī, *al-Farq Bayn al-Firaq* (Damascus: Ṭabʿah al-Sayyid ʿIzzat al-ʿAṭṭār al-Ḥusaynī, 1948).

[634] Al-Taftazānī, *Sharḥ al-ʿAqā'id al-Nasafiyyah*.

[635] See Abū al-Maʿālī ibn ʿAbd al-Malik al-Juwaynī, Imam al-Ḥaramayn, *Kitāb al-Irshād ilā Qawāṭiʿ al-Adillah fī Uṣūl al-Iʿtiqād*, Jean Dominique Luciani, ed. and trans. (Paris: E. Leroux, 1938).

[636] Al-Ghazālī, *Kitāb al-Iqtiṣād fī al-Iʿtiqād*; *Kitāb Iljām al-ʿAwām ʿan ʿIlm al-Kalām* (Cairo: Maktabah al-Munīriyyah, 1933); *al-Munqadh min al-Ḍalāl* (Beirut: Dār al-Kutub al-ʿIlmiyyah, 1988).

[637] Al-Shahrastānī, *Kitāb al-Milal wa al-Niḥal*; and *Nihāyah al-Aqdām fī ʿIlm al-Kalām* (Beirut: Dār al-Kutub al-ʿIlmiyyah, 2004).

[638] al-Rāzī, *Tafsīr Mafātīḥ al-Ghayb*; *Asās al-Taqdīs*; *Iʿtiqādāt Firāq al-Muslimīn wa al-Mushrikīn* (Cairo: Maktabah al-Nahḍah, 1938).

[639] Watt, *Early Islam*, p.90.

[640] Madkur, *Fī al-Falsafah al-Islāmiyyah*, vol.2, pp.55–56.

[641] Watt, *Early Islam*, p.90.

[642] Rippin, *Muslims*, vol.1, p.71.

[643] Al-Ghazālī, *Kitāb al-Iqtiṣād fī al-Iʿtiqād*, p.36; also see his *Kitāb Iljām al-ʿAwām* which was specifically written for this purpose.

[644] Al-Ghazālī, *Kitāb al-Iqtiṣād fī al-Iʿtiqād*, p.36.

[645] Al-Ghazālī, *Kitāb al-Iqtiṣād fī al-Iʿtiqād*, pp.36–41; also see *Kitāb Iljām al-ʿAwām*, p.7 where he gives example of "Surah" in connection with God.

[646] Watt, *Early Islam*, p.91.

[647] See for definition of '*ta'wīl*' in ibn Rushd, *Faṣl al-Maqāl*, pp.32–33; al-Rāzī, *Asās al-Taqdīs*, p.182.

[648] Watt, *Early Islam*, pp.91–92.

[649] Ibid., p.93.

[650] Al-Bayhaqī, *Kitāb al-Asmā'*, pp.312–14.

[651] Ibid., p.395.

[652] Ibn Ḥazm al-Ẓāhirī, *al-Faṣl*, vol.2, pp.127–28.

[653] That is what is attributed to Ibn ʿAbbās. See Nasir Khusraw, *Tanwīr al-Miqbās Min Tafsīr Ibn ʿAbbās*, 1st edn. (Tehran: Intisharat Istiqlal, n.d.), p.97; also see Jalāl al-Dīn Muḥammad ibn Aḥmad al-Maḥallī, Jalāl al-Dīn ʿAbd al-Raḥmān ibn Abī Bakr al-Suyuṭī, *Tafsīr al-Jalālayn* (Beirut: Dār al-Fikr, 1993), p.97.

[654] See for instance (7:11); (15:28–29).

[655] See al-Alusi, *Rūḥ al-Maʿānī*, vol.12, pp.225–26.

[656] Al-Ashʿarī, *al-Ibānah*, p.43.

[657] Al-Bayhaqī, *Kitāb al-Asmā'*, p.401.

[658] Ibn al-Qayyim al-Jawziyyah and al-Bayhaqī refute the hadith narrated by ʿUrwah ibn Rawīm specifying that Adam's creation was different from the rest of creation with the commandment "Be". They argue that this ʿUrwah, who narrates this report from Jābir ibn ʿAbd Allāh al-Anṣārī, never had the opportunity to see or learn from

Jābir as he died before him. This is in addition to a number of other inauthentic reporters in the chain like ʿAbd Rabbih ibn Sāliḥ and Ḥishām ibn ʿAmmār. See al-Bayhaqī, *Kitāb al-Asmā'*, p.317.

[659] Also see Qur'an 69:44–47.

[660] See al-Bayhaqī, *Kitāb al-Asmā'*, p.331; al-Alusi, *Rūḥ al-Maʿānī*, vol.13, p.26.

[661] See al-Bayhaqī, *Kitāb al-Asmā'*, pp.331–32.

[662] Abū al-Ḥasan Muslim ibn al-Ḥajjāj, *Saḥīḥ Muslim* (Beirut: Dār Iḥyā' al-Turāth al-ʿArabī, n.d.), vol.13, p.119; al-Bayhaqī, *Kitāb al-Asmā'*, p.340; al-Ḥāfiẓ ʿAlī ibn ʿUmar al-Dāraquṭnī has colleted most of the *aḥādīth* in connection with attributes of God in his book *Kitāb al-Ṣifāt*, Abdullah al-Ghunayman, ed., 1st edn. (Madinah: Maktabah al-Dār, 1981).

[663] See al-Bayhaqī, *Kitāb al-Asmā'*, p.340.

[664] Ibn Ḥazm al-Ẓāhirī, *al-Faṣl*, vol.2, p.128.

[665] Abū Zakariyyā Yaḥyā ibn Sharaf al-Nawawī, *Sharḥ Ṣaḥīḥ Muslim* (Riyad: Maktabah al-Riyāḍ al-Ḥadīthah, n.d.), vol.15, p.204.

[666] Al-Bukhārī, *Saḥīḥ*, vol.22, pp.420, hadith no.6863.

[667] See for more details al-Bayhaqī, *Kitāb al-Asmā'*, pp.333–34.

[668] Abū Bakr Muḥammad ibn al-Furak al-Iṣbahānī, *Mushkal al-Ḥadīth wa Bayanuh*, Musa Muhammad Ali, ed., 2nd edn. (Beirut: ʿĀlam al-Kutub, 1985), p.240.

[669] See al-Ghazālī, *Kitāb al-Iqtiṣād*, pp.36–37.

[670] Al-Bukhārī, *Saḥīḥ*, vol.15, p.85, hadith no.4470.

[671] Goldziher, *Introduction to Islamic Theology and Law*, p.108.

[672] See al-Bayhaqī, *Kitāb al-Asmā'*, p.352.

[673] Al-Nawawī, *Sharḥ Saḥīḥ Muslim*, vol.18, p.183.

[674] For more discussion of this and other reports especially the one discussing "the Chair (*Kursī*) being the place of His two feet", see al-Bayhaqī, *Kitāb al-Asmā'*, pp.352–61. Al-Bayhaqī discusses the inauthentic nature of that report on page p.354.

[675] Al-Iṣbahānī, *Mushkal al-Ḥadīth*, p.131.

[676] Goldziher, *Introduction to Islamic Theology and Law*, p.109.

[677] See al-Bayhaqī, *Kitāb al-Asmā'*, p.361.

[678] See ibid., p.448.

[679] Al-Ḥajjāj, *Saḥīḥ Muslim*, vol.4, p.139, hadith no.1262.

[680] See al-Ghazālī, *Kitāb al-Iqtiṣād*, pp.39–40.

[681] Ibid., p.40.

[682] See al-Iṣbahānī, *Mushkal al-Ḥadīth*, pp.199–211; and al-Bayhaqī, *Kitāb al-Asmā'*, pp.450 ff.

[683] Gibb, Kramers, "Tashbih," *Shorter Encyclopaedia of Islam*, p.583.

[684] Goldziher, *Introduction to Islamic Theology and Law*, pp.107–08.

[685] Ibn Taymiyyah, *al-Fatāwā*, vol.5, p.578.

[686] Ibid., p.579.

[687] See more details in al-Dhahabī, *Mukhtaṣar al-ᶜUlūw*, pp.191 f.

[688] See details in al-Alusi, *Rūḥ al-Maᶜānī*, vol.9, pp.153–61.

[689] See details of reports about the issue in Muḥammad ibn ᶜUthmān ibn Abī Shaybah (d. 297 AH), *Kitāb al-ᶜArsh wa mā Ruwiya Fīhā*, Muhammad ibn Hamd al-Humud, ed. (Beirut: Dār al-Jīl, 1991); and Muwaffaq al-Dīn ᶜAbd Allāh ibn Aḥmad ibn Qudāmah al-Maqdisī, *Ithbāt al-ᶜUlūw*, Badar ibn Abdullah al-Badar, ed., 1st edn. (Kuwait: al-Dār al-Salafiyyah, 1986).

[690] Al-Bayhaqī, *Kitāb al-Asmā'*, p.408.

[691] Ibid., pp.408–09.

[692] Al-Ashᶜarī, *al-Ibānah*, p.37.

[693] Al-Dhahabī, *Mukhtaṣar al-ᶜUlūw*, pp.49 ff.

[694] See Ibn Taymiyyah, *al-Fatāwā*, vol.5, pp.578 ff; see Abdullah al-Sabat, *al-Raḥmān ᶜalā al-ᶜArsh Istawā* (Kuwait: al-Dār al-Salafiyyah, 1978), pp.37–38.

[695] Al-Ghazālī, *Kitāb al-Iqtiṣād*, p.35; *Iḥyā' ᶜUlūm al-Dīn* (Damascus: ᶜĀlam al-Kutub, n.d.), p.95.

[696] Al-Ghazālī, *Kitāb al-Iqtiṣād*, p.35, 38; for more details see al-Bayhaqī, *Kitāb al-Asmā'*, pp.405–15; Gatje, *The Qur'ān and its Exegesis*, p.149.

[697] Al-Ghazālī, *Iḥyā' ᶜUlūm al-Dīn*, p.92.

[698] Al-Bukhārī, *Saḥīḥ*, vol.11, p.107, hadith no.3079. Al-Iṣbahānī has brought all the other narrations of this report and interpreted them metaphorically. See his *Mushkal al-Ḥadīth*, pp.45–65.

[699] See al-Iṣbahānī, *Mushkal al-Ḥadīth*, p.67; Swartz, *A Medieval Critique of Anthropomorphism*, pp.174–75.

[700] Swartz, *A Medieval Critique of Anthropomorphism*, p.175.

[701] Al-Iṣbahānī, *Mushkal al-Ḥadīth*, p.67.

[702] See Ibn al-Jawzī, *Dafa' Shubah al-Tashbīh*, p.60; Al-Iṣbahānī, *Mushkal al-Ḥadīth*, pp.67–68.

[703] Swartz, *A Medieval Critique of Anthropomorphism*, pp.175–76.

[704] George Makdisi, *Ibn 'Iqil: Religion and Culture in Classical Islam* (Edinburgh: Edinburgh University Press, 1997), pp.103 ff.

[705] See Ibn Taymiyyah, *Daqā'iq al-Tafsīr al-Jāmiᶜ lī Tafsīr Ibn Taymiyyah* (Damascus: Mu'assasah ᶜUlūm al-Qur'ān, 1983), vol.2, p.171.

[706] Al-ʿAynī, *ʿUmdah al-Qārī'*, vol.18, p.284; al-Bayhaqī, *Kitāb al-Asmā'*, p.290; see Watt, "Created in His Image: A Study in Islamic Theology," *Early Islam*, pp.94–95.

[707] Al-Bayhaqī, *Kitāb al-Asmā'*, p.290; Watt, *Early Islam*, p.95.

[708] Al-Iṣbahānī, *Mushkal al-Ḥadīth*, pp.50 ff.

[709] Swartz, *A Medieval Critique of Anthropomorphism*, pp.170 ff.

[710] Watt, *Early Islam*, p.95.

[711] Goldziher, *Introduction to Islamic Theology and Law*, p.108.

[712] Al-Bayhaqī, *Kitāb al-Asmā'*, p.291; Watt, *Early Islam*, p.96.

[713] Al-ʿAynī, *ʿUmdah al-Qārī'*, vol.18, p.284; Al-Bayhaqī, *Kitāb al-Asmā'*, p.291; Watt, *Early Islam*, p.96.

[714] See for details, al-Iṣbahānī, *Mushkal al-Ḥadīth*, pp.62 ff.

[715] See Swartz, *A Medieval Critique of Anthropomorphism*, pp.173 ff.

[716] Watt, *Early Islam*, p.99.

[717] Ibid.; al-ʿAynī, *ʿUmdah al-Qārī'*, vol.18, p.284.

[718] Ibn al-ʿArabī, *Aḥkām al-Qur'ān*, vol.8, p.82; Al-Qurṭubī also prefers this interpretation. See his *Aḥkām al-Qur'ān*, vol.20, p.114.

[719] Swartz, *A Medieval Critique of Anthropomorphism*, pp.174 ff.

[720] Williams, "Aspects of the Creed of Imam Ahmad," p.443.

[721] Ibid.

[722] Ibid., pp.443 ff.

[723] Ibid., pp.445 ff.

[724] Ibid., p.454.

[725] Ibid., p.455.

[726] Swartz, *A Medieval Critique of Anthropomorphism*, p.137.

[727] Ibid., pp.134–35.

[728] Ibid., p.137.

[729] Ibn al-Qayyim al-Jawziyyah reports the same about the Shāfiʿī jurist Abū al-ʿAbbās Aḥmad ibn ʿUmar ibn al-Surayj. See Abū ʿAbd Allāh Muḥammad ibn Abū Bakr al-Zarʿī al-Damashqī ibn al-Qayyim al-Jawziyyah, *Ijtimāʿ al-Juyūsh al-Islāmiyyah ʿalā Ghazwī al-Muʿaṭṭalah wa al-Jahmiyyah* (Beirut: Dār al-Kutub al-ʿIlmiyyah, 1984), vol.1, p.101.

[730] Watt, *Early Islam*, p.100; for more details of the argument see al-Bayhaqī, *Kitāb al-Asmā'*, p.289.

[731] Mahmud, *al-Tafkīr al-Falsafī fī al-Islām*, pp.98–106; and his *al-Islām wa al-ʿAql* (Cairo: Dār al-Maʿārif, 1988), pp.128 ff.

[732] Ibn Taymiyyah, *al-Fatāwā*, vol.5, p.108.

[733] See al-Ashʿarī, *Maqālāt*, p.106.

[734] Madelung, *Religious Schools and Sects in Medieval Islam*, p.122.

[735] Watt, *Early Islam*, p.100.

[736] Gibb, Kramers, *Shorter Encyclopaedia of Islam*, p.34.

[737] Netton, *Allah Transcendent*, p.22.

[738] Al-Faruqi, *al-Tawḥīd*, p.27.

[739] Ibid.

[740] Watt, *Early Islam*, p.93.

[741] Netton, *Allah Transcendent*, pp.27–28.

[742] Ibid., pp.331–32; unless Netton meant from the term that our language about God is always inadequate and imperfect.

Conclusion

This study has attempted to demonstrate how humanity has managed to envision God in human terms bending religion to the service of this cause, and the various strange dimensions this has led to with regards to perceptions of the Divine. The great defence has always been resort to scripture, highly questionable as I have shown, and theological debate as to whether the language used to illuminate God should be interpreted metaphorically or literally.

There are three main reasons for a strong objection to an anthropomorphized understanding of God: 1) With regards to scripture itself it is an indefensible position belying the message of the prophets 2) It is not a rational perspective, hence most writings and theological discussions take on an apologetic and/or controversial form, and a reasoned understanding of faith is conspicuous by its absence 3) The response particularly since the rise of literacy and the age of the enlightenment, has been one of growing alienation, if not outright skepticism and/or vacant understanding, as to who God actually is, rather than intellectual conviction and clarity of thought of the highest order.

Whatever the case, there seems to be a direct and inverse relationship between anthropomorphism, the ascription to God of human characteristics and emotions, the visualisation of God whether in verbal imagery or physical form, and strict monotheism. Meaning that notions of a transcendent and unique God together with an internalized consciousness of His Unity, become ever more diluted, to the point of non-existence, the more corporeal aspects are introduced and legitimized.

And the more the attempt to "reveal" God is made, the more elusive "hidden" He becomes, accounting for the endless theological studies, and oftentimes heated debates, that have historically proliferated as to His nature, essence, and outward form. This inverse relationship is significant by its existence and should be noted.

Because ambiguity begets ambiguity, and dangers of a diffused understanding of God's unity and transcendence become amplified once ideas of anthropomorphism are introduced, the Qur'an adopted a clear, highly contained approach. So explicit are the Qur'anic verses that one of Islam's deepest fears has been to violate in any way, shape, or form the principles of *tawḥīd* as enshrined in the Qur'an and Hadith. Thus in Islam God stands alone, unique and majestic, and Muslims remain ever vigilant against weakening or adulterating their understanding of His Oneness and His transcendence.

It is my contention that in an age of intellect and scientific inquiry, an anthropomorphized God spells in fact, and as the opening lines of this study indicate, the death of God. Although couched in dramatic terms the statement is rather a matter of fact one, and fortunately not entirely true. For it is the anthropomorphasized God who has died but certainly not the monotheistic one. In my opinion the success of the secularist worldview largely resides in its apparent intellectual appeal when juxtaposed against a non-intellectual version of God, a God controlled by our five senses and one who constantly in the words of Nietzsche deserves our "pity". For any solution to the problem we have to admit that secularism is not the triumph of intellect over superstition but rather an indication of humanity's global alienation, its loss of the purpose and meaning of life, and its need for a transcendent God, something greater than man and the cosmos he lives in.

God created Man in His *moral image* meaning that He wished humanity to live a life marked by justice, equality, fair dealing, mutual respect, sympathy, love, compassion, and charity etc. Humanity on the other hand chose to violate even the most basic moral commandments of God and returned the favor by creating God in *Man's own image* rather crudely bringing the ineffable transcendental Other into the realms of structure and space, to serve nothing but hidden agendas and selfish desires. Indeed, the children of Abraham (by this is meant the

Semitic consciousness) so personalized, nationalized and anthropomorphized the transcendental Deity that He in effect became just a larger, more powerful and lethal version of themselves. As such humanity did not hesitate to impart onto God its varied individual, communal and national agendas, practices, ideas, likes and dislikes etc., to thereby create an absolute out of finite ideas of nationhood, ethnicity, race, polity, ideology and even theology.

Elevating to the highest levels of significance limited historical phenomena such as land, race, a historical person or a particular notion of divinity or law, what humanity ultimately managed to do was to replace the One and Only absolute with infinitely inferior erected multiple absolutes of an inherently finite nature and value beside Him. It was inevitable that this idolatrous venture, this man-made idea of a national or personalized God, would lead to heated response, violent resistance and eventually degenerate into nothingness. Enlightenment "Deism" followed by scientific agnosticism and finally atheism would be the fated outcome. As science inexorably developed, and a philosophy of secular humanism and materialism replaced ideas of religion and God, becoming the new cultural ethos, bold assertions such as those of Karl Marx that religion was the opium of the people, came to hold a deeper grip on imagination. The key to human happiness now lay in maximizing ones material needs in this life and not deferring gratification to some sort of paradise after death. Forgetting of course that the raison d'etre of religion was to solve the problem of meaning in life and prepare for life after death and not to satisfy man's immediate needs.

Meanwhile, that which could not be measured, quantified, or simply observed, was rendered obsolete. Hence, the transcendental Other Who stood against and beyond the utilitarian sphere and did not render Himself to an empirically demonstrable scientific fact was in turn rendered useless, with religion simply dismissed as the product of infantile fears and experiences. The result has been a tremendous and tragic loss of faith such that even American theologian Harvey Cox is able to declare in his bestseller, *The Secular City*, the death of God and the deification of humanity rather than a transcendent deity.

Yet statistics speak louder than statements. The brave new world of Western orthodoxy embodied in scientific rationalism and secular humanism may have succeeded to some extent in eliminating both God, spirituality and religion from our immediate conscious, but it has not succeeded in eliminating human suffering, inequity and violence. Indeed some of the worst wars in human history have been fought under the banner of secular ideologies and dictators such as Hitler and Mussolini. Some would argue that the hopes of the Enlightenment died in Auschwitz, the romance of socialism and communism during the 1917 Bolshevik Revolution and the glamour of capitalism and science during the two world wars. Furthermore, atheistic ideas of the past few centuries are themselves becoming irrelevant to 21st century man or in the words of John D. Caputo, mere "perspectives... constructions, and fictions of grammar,"[1] just " one more story told by people with historically limited imaginations, with contingent conceptions of reason and history, of economics with labor, of nature and human nature, of desires, sexuality, and women, and of God, and faith."[2] Jean-Paul Sartre (1905–80) once spoke of a God-shaped hole in the human consciousness by which he meant living in a universe devoid of meaning and purpose. The quest for God is intrinsic to human nature because it is the quest for meaning, for the purpose of our existence. A deified humanity is no solution to this universal longing. The true solution lies in the mysterious, ineffable and transcendent Other Who is the source of existence and the ultimate answer to humanity's craving for meaning. In the words of Caputo, "Whatever it is you say God is, God is more... the very formula that describes God is that there is no formula with which God can be described."[3] This is so true because "there is no God but One God" as the Islamic affirmation stipulates.

The true solution to humanity's suffering, anxiety and longing lies in a proper response to this transcendental source of being rather than worrying about His essence or just believing in His existence. Religion is a deeply subjective experience, and so God is known not through measurement but inner communication. This type of response requires involvement of the totality of our being, a set of spiritual exercises and a pious, dedicated, disciplined and moral lifestyle. And it is this compassionate lifestyle that will enable humanity to break free of the shackles of selfhood, greed, ego, and narrow identity to reflect the true unity of God Almighty by furthering the unity of humanity, existence and the cosmos.

Conclusion

In sum it is the opinion of this author that the postmodern and post-secular longing for God will not be quenched by pre modern anthropomorphic and corporeal concepts of the Divine which have simply brought God down to this cosmos, with a precise historical function and a specified location, reducing Him to a lowercase god, and causing the soul to detract from the great sense of awe and reverence that it should and has been created to feel at mention of Him.

The primary assertions, findings and conclusions of this study are summarized below:

(1) THE GOD PARADIGM presented by the data of the Hebrew Bible is not consistent. Polar tendencies are quite visible. Although transcendental monotheism is present it is very much scattered throughout the books of the Hebrew Bible and not systematically presented, clearly elaborated or completely safeguarded against possible misconceptions, exploitation and violence. In practice this means that to derive a concept of the absolute otherness and transcendence of God from the text of the Hebrew Bible one has to sift through a great many contradictory statements and assertions, plough through an inordinate amount of information, and face certain thorny problems in order to generate some level of understanding. And this cannot be done satisfactorily without external help.

In contrast an anthropomorphic conception of the Deity is strikingly evident. Crude and overt anthropomorphic descriptions, attributes, qualities, and portrayals abound and are so pervasive throughout the text that even a cursory read will leave the impression of the God of the Hebrew Bible as being undoubtedly anthropomorphic. Many of the biblical anthropomorphisms are naive, and at times powerfully concrete and corporeal. Yet, such graphic depictions are not essentially needed for the sort of modality intrinsic to proper religious communication except for the type of religious understanding which holds God as absolutely corporeal. God is presented as a body, walking, talking, searching after somebody, weeping and crying, resting, wrestling, repenting, lamenting etc. In certain incidents He is further shown lacking power, knowledge, mercy, justice, impartiality, universality and so on, the basic traits in other words of a transcendent God. On the other hand, many human limitations, qualities and categories are ascribed to God such that He often appears like a human being albeit of a higher rank and/or gigantic in proportion. Many of these passages can be interpreted metaphorically but a great majority of them would not render to such an interpretation without violence to the text. At times it would ironically appear that what we have in front of us is man creating God in his own image, likeness and form rather than the other way around. Consequently, that image quite often suffers the finitude of its creator. In sum the God of the Hebrew Bible as painted by the scripture is not a Being one would deem to be the "Transcendent Perfect" Deity but one rather Who is weak suffering the many imperfections of human beings and really a supernatural mirror of themselves.

(2) THE HEBREW BIBLE'S God paradigm seems to be progressive and evolutionary. The conception of God of the later prophets, especially those after 8th century BC, is more elaborate, systematic and unified than the earlier writings though not necessarily non-corporeal or non-anthropomorphic. This prophetic conception, as outlined in the scripture at least, is as much anthropomorphic as the earlier writings but in a different way. The anthropomorphic expressions utilized are, to certain degrees, refined and at times convey a sense of mystical experience or spiritual reflection. Many of them render to metaphorical interpretation more easily than their counterparts in the so-called books of Moses and other earlier writings. Nevertheless, they still ultimately convey nothing less than the concept and imagery of an anthropomorphic and imperfect deity.

(3) THE TRADITIONAL RABBINIC mind is very close to the God paradigm of the Hebrew Bible. Indeed, there are times when the Rabbinic God seems more anthropomorphic, corporeal, familiar and bound than the God of the Hebrew Bible.

(4) PHILOSOPHICAL AND TRANSCENDENTAL thinking, in the sense of non-corporealism or non-anthropomorphism, had been looked upon (by religious Jewry at large) as non-biblical. Such an understanding of God had not been very popular in Judaic tradition over the centuries

following the Rabbinic period. The few rational souls such as Philo and Maimonides, who attempted to incorporate philosophical transcendence into the Hebrew conception of the divine (mostly under foreign influence) failed unfortunately to convince the orthodoxy of their transcendental ideas. Their views were regarded as not in conformity with the written texts and the Hebrew legacy.

(5) IT IS NOT VERY HARD to determine the origins of anthropomorphic biblical passages and human nature. Human creativity seems to have played a vital role in the creation of these anthropomorphically oriented, corporeally constructed, and at times immorally tuned, passages of the Hebrew Bible. This human element, origin and nature of the Hebrew Bible, ignored over the centuries, has been highlighted by many biblical scholars since the 19th century. It has almost become a standard explanation, particularly in academic circles, of the many theological, moral and religious difficulties presented by the text of the Hebrew Bible.

(6) IT HAS BECOME IMPOSSIBLE to logically prove or rationally substantiate the traditional claims of the Hebrew Bible as being the inerrant word of God verbatim. Modern critical scholarship looks upon it as the word of man or at best an indirect inspiration with the word of God mixed up with the words of man. The presence of a labyrinthine maze of centuries old allegorical interpretations and polar and contradictory tendencies with regards to the Deity are not proofs of the depths and infinite mysteries of these problematic passages but rather the other way around, evidence of the sheer limitations and imperfections of their human writers and a descendency in thinking. The existence of all these problems, wittingly or unwittingly confessed by almost all biblical scholars, prove the point that the Hebrew Bible in its present shape and form cannot be taken as the inerrant word of God.

(7) THE NEW TESTAMENT seems to be far removed from the Hebraic universe of discourse and very close to Hellenistic thought patterns and world view. Furthermore, it is not theocentric but Christocentric. A greater variety of theologies (Christologies) is presented in the New

Testament than the variety one notices in the Old Testament and not all of them are mutually congruent. These theological models are more problematic, divergent and mutually dissonant.

(8) THE NEW TESTAMENT is not what Jesus said and wrote about himself, and probably not even what he understood about himself. It is what the Church and later Christians understood and interpreted that he was or should have been.

(9) TRADITIONAL CHRISTIAN INCARNATIONAL THEOLOGY is a result of centuries of later reflections, controversies and developments. It is neither a necessary reflection of what the text of the New Testament presents nor a sole product of pure theological curiosity. In fact cultural realities, political motivations and personal agendas and vendettas have played a significant role in formulating its shape and content. Neither is incarnational theology clearly charted out in the New Testament in its developed, traditional, and literal sense. No one can prove it to be the essence of New Testament writings as a whole without external intrusions and arbitrary interpretations. It could possibly be construed from some New Testament writings but not without superficial efforts and violence to the text on the part of the one who intends to do so.

(10) CHRISTIAN INCARNATIONAL THEOLOGY, especially in its literal sense, is absolutely corporeal and anthropomorphic and involves the fevered veneration of a triune Godhead. In point of fact it forms the epitome of corporeal thought in the religious consciousness of some Semites. In Incarnation, the practical separation between the divine and human becomes impossible. In reality it is the divine, the Logos, which is dominant, visible and worshipped, whilst the human Jesus is conceded and concealed somewhere in the shadows. Yet, God is often claimed but seldom given a true and natural existence of His own. In reality, God the Father, the supposed first person of the holy Trinity and the original source of all, seems to play second fiddle to Lord Jesus Christ, the supposed second person of the Trinity, who often is shown to be taking over in such a fashion that God the Father often becomes invisible. Christianity, in its traditional popular sense, is really what the

word "Christianity" literally means. It is a faith about Jesus Christ, and a deification of his person. Exalting this historical human figure to the status of full divinity represents a degeneration in Christian development. Incarnation is truly anthropomorphic and thoroughly corporeal and what Christianity has ultimately done is to bring down the "Sacred Transcendent Perfect", the holy Other, God of the universe to the realms of imperfection and profanity. It has bound Him to the chains of imperfection and in effect crucified Him twice, once physically and once conceptually, devaluing Jesus' message and fashioning it anew. This is the utmost violence against God and against Semitic monotheistic consciousness that has ever been conceived.

(11) INCARNATIONAL THEOLOGY is not paradoxical. It is thoroughly and utterly contradictory. Centuries of theological debate, difficulties, developments, controversies and political interferences attempting to pin down the true nature of Christ and his relationship to God are manifest indicators and clear proofs of the contradictory nature of this Christian doctrine, all inevitable and unavoidable given that Incarnational theology poses serious challenges to the human intellect and rational thinking. One has to violate all logical categories and rational axioms to accommodate Incarnational claims and to present them in intelligible forms and categories. These logical impasses can only be averted if one accepts the dictum that the Gospel of Jesus has more to do with God the Father and our relation to our neighbors than to the person of Jesus himself. The Gospel dictum of love your God and love your neighbor is the only way out of these theological nightmares. Without such frank and honest confession even the metaphorical interpretations of the Incarnation in its traditional garb would be misleading and incomprehensible.

(12) THE COMPILATION AND CANONIZATION process of the New Testament was a long and convoluted affair. Spread out over centuries, covering many regions, persons and intentions etc., it naturally left a great many questions and impossibilities unresolved, calling into question the New Testament text being the inerrant word of God. Perjuries, insertions, textual violence and many other factors (as outlined in this

study) raise serious questions as to the textual purity and historical authenticity of the New Testament. All these difficulties are currently well recognized by a majority of New Testament scholars. Given this as well as the lengthy canonization process (in itself a major proof of human intervention, manipulation and exploitation of the New Testament text) it is time to accept and highlight the human origins and nature of the New Testament writings.

(13) UNLIKE THE BIBLE, THE QUR'AN was canonized from its inception. Its compilation process was not spread out over centuries but the small span of a few years and within the lifetime of its original recipients. The authenticity, purity and universality of its text is a historical fact admitted by both Muslim as well as non-Muslim scholars and sources. Many questions and objections concerning various aspects of the Qur'an have been raised by many non-Muslim scholars over the centuries. Currently, there seems to be a sort of consensus among those who are actively involved in the field of Qur'anic studies that the unity, universality and purity of the Qur'anic text is indisputable – a historical fact beyond doubt. Moreover, the Qur'anic challenge of producing a rival verse like that of the Qur'an still stands unmet after fourteen centuries, though efforts have been made. On the other hand, its claim of divine protection, preservation and purity of text, also made fourteen centuries ago, has not been violated. The textual purity, unity, integrity and universality of its text over these long centuries is witness to the fact of its divine status as the word of God.

(14) THE QUR'ANIC GOD PARADIGM is transcendental. Its monotheism is pure, strict and absolute. The Qur'an has a systematically well explained conception of God's transcendence, otherness, uniqueness and perfection. This is supported by countless Qur'anic verses and substantiated by a variety of methods and arguments. Unlike the Bible, this absolute transcendence and unity of God is safeguarded against any possible violation or corruption (such as the existence of other gods as true gods, their ability to harm or benefit without the leave of God, division of power, knowledge, or person or any other division within the Godhead etc.). Moreover, it is not a bare and

abstract notion of transcendence but a balanced, vivid and live concept of God. The transcendent God is immanent by dint of His infinite knowledge, power, love, mercy and other positive attributes spelled out in the text of the Qur'an. Unlike the Bible, the Qur'anic paradigm is consistent. There is only one transcendent God who is absolutely perfect in His names and attributes. Though unknown in His essence, He is known through His signs, attributes, qualities and actions. The idea of this magnificently transcendent God is consistently conveyed throughout the text of the Qur'an. Its strong ethical nature and egalitarian tone is also evident from the Qur'anic text itself. The Qur'an's ethical transcendental monotheism is systematic and self sufficient. The Qur'an does not need external help or arbitrary explanations to present, explain and safeguard its God paradigm from possible violation, infiltration or corruption.

(15) THE QUR'ANIC GOD PARADIGM is neither corporeal nor anthropomorphic. The few seemingly anthropomorphic expressions of the Qur'an readily render themselves to metaphorical interpretations, without invention of facts or metaphors not existent in the text itself. Such non-anthropomorphic explanations can be derived either from the context (or from within the Qur'anic text) or through metaphors commonly used in the language. This fact has been established by a great many Muslim scholars and theologians over the centuries. Additionally, these seemingly anthropomorphic phrases, if kept within Qur'anic parameters, help create a needed modality in the communication process between God and man. The Qur'anic paradigm is able to create this modality without recourse to graphic anthropomorphism or corporealism. Consequently Islam has been known for its strong anti-anthropomorphic stance, and except for the absolute literalists, mainstream Islamic thought has always shunned and rebuked corporeal and anthropomorphic depictions of God. This delicate balance is maintained by the well preserved text of the Qur'an itself.

This is perhaps the reason why the Islamic faith has not been secularized or shaken to the extent that certain other traditions have been over the past centuries. Ernest Gellner, a British Sociologist, observes that:

> At the end of the Middle Ages, the Old World contained four major civilizations. Of these, three are now, in one measure or another, secularized. Christian doctrine is bowdlerized by its own theologians, and deep, literal conviction is not conspicuous by its presence. In the Sinic World, a secular faith has become formally established and its religious predecessors disavowed. In the Indian World, a state and the elite are neutral *vis-a-vis* what is a pervasive folk religion, even if practices such as astrology continue to be widespread. But in one of the four civilizations, the Islamic, the situation is altogether different.[4]

He further argues that "there is one very real, dramatic and conspicuous exception to all this: Islam. To say that secularization prevails in Islam is not contentious. It is simply false. Islam is as strong now as it was a century ago. In some ways, it is probably much stronger."[5] He attributes this stability and resisting power to its "emphatic and severe monotheism, the view that the Message received by the Prophet is so to speak terminal, and that it contains both faith and morals – or, in other words, it is both doctrine and law, and that no genuine further augmentation is to be countenanced."[6] Therefore, it can easily be contended that the Qur'anic God paradigm has the potential to stand the ground against modern atheistic challenges and avert the dangers that have shaken other civilizations to the very core of their essence.

The Qur'anic God paradigm is systematic, moral and transcendental. It is logical as well as simple to the core. It focuses more upon human salvation, piety, and socio, political and economic reformation than on the person of Muhammad, the Prophet of Islam or even God Himself. It is homocentric rather than being theo-centric. It is also truly universal in its nature and moral implications and does away with all possibilities of racial bias, notions of chosen race, promised lands and other possible narrow identities. Its intrinsic Divine unity guarantees a universal human unity.

(16) MODERN MAN IS BECOMING further and further removed from God and seemingly ever more entrenched in faithlessness. One of the major reasons for this alienation is the existence of an exceedingly

anthropomorphic and corporeal concept of God along with insistence upon the Bible being the inerrant word of God verbatim. The irony of the fact is that instead of discarding the human aspects and interpretation of the Scriptures, modern man seems to be rejecting the Deity Himself, and this in favour of a nihilist philosophy that focuses on the physical world alone, with all else meaningless. People do not want to subscribe to the idea of guilt, redemption, suffering, denial of the world, the strange elevation of a man to God, the illogicality of a triune Godhead etc. Religion is not perceived as an intellectual exercise and becomes a depressing affair. Yet, all this death of God perception can be avoided by emphasizing the transcendent God, Who is beyond all shortcomings, imperfections, human qualifications, and does not seem to be created by man but is the Creator and Master of everything existing in the universe.

Such a notion of God has been aspired to by all three Semitic traditions though the text of the Bible is not consistent concerning it. By emphasizing the non-corporeal and non-anthropomorphic elements in the Deity one would not do terrible injustice to these traditions. Quite the reverse, one would very much be within the aspired goals of these faith traditions. With the help of this simple yet magnificent conception of the Deity, the wide gulf between alienated man and God can be narrowed and science and faith can be brought closer if not together. This is not fanciful for modern science and philosophy seem to be opening up to belief in God.[7] For instance Paul Charles William Davies (b. 1946), a physicist, cosmologist and astrobiologist working at Arizona State University, strongly argues against notions of the purposelessness and meaninglessness of the universe:

> Through my scientific work I have come to believe more and more strongly that the physical universe is put together with an ingenuity so astonishing that I cannot accept it merely as a brute fact. There must, it seems to me, be a deeper level of explanation. Whether one wishes to call that deeper level "God" is a matter of taste and definition.[8]

Davies further observes that, "Although many metaphysical and theistic theories seem contrived and childish, they are not obviously more absurd than the belief that the universe exists, and exists in the form it does, reasonlessly... We are truly meant to be here."[9] He believes that science offers a surer path than religion in search of God, and at the same time wants to distance himself from the "organizational-manipulative God" of theology. Davies does not believe in the anthropomorphically personal God of religion. His God is not a person in any simple sense. He emphasizes the need to think of God in less anthropomorphic ways and not to have a naive image of God but perhaps think of God as transcendent "universal mind", "supreme holistic concept" "Being-itself" or a "Creative Force" or as a "mathematician". He argues that only a God that transcends space-time and is above human manipulations can have any real meaning and relevance for the natural activity taking place all around us.

Sir John Leslie (1766–1832), a Scottish mathematician and physicist best remembered for his research into heat, wrote: "If God is real then his reality seems to me most likely to be as described in the Neoplatonist theological tradition. He is then not an almighty person but an abstract Creative force which is "personal" through being concerned with creating persons and acting as a benevolent person would."[10]

I am not saying that religion should follow the scientist's concept of God or subordinate revelation to science. Rather, what I want to emphasize is that a crude, anthropomorphic or corporeal notion of God is a great hurdle, standing resolute between modern intellectual thought and belief in God. It has at best weakened the authority of religion and God and at worst annihilated it. Human intellect is truly at a loss to digest or reconcile the idea of a man-God or a human looking God for what we worship cannot be within our purview but greater than the universe itself. Anthropomorphically corporeal concepts of the Divine are perhaps among the leading factors of modern atheism. This gulf between religious consciousness and intellectual thinking can be narrowed considerably by emphasizing and insisting upon the moral transcendent God. The difficulty in believing today is not due to belief as such but rather a concept of God that is anthropomorphic and corporeal, which does not appeal to the intellect and which appears at once weak, without strength, vigour or transcendence. Yet there is a solution. The Qur'an provides the authority, God, that people are looking for and can accept, couched in a language and underscored by a logic that allows for an immediate, complete and intelligent understanding of the Divine. As such it is the Qur'an which can contribute more than the Bible to a revival of global belief in a transcendent Deity and religion itself. Its focused stress on the absolute Oneness, Unity, Uniqueness and Transcendence of God, in its highest and purest sense, and its unequivocal rejection of anthropomorphic imagery and depictions of God averting the dangers of corporeal notions, is unparallelled, and speaks to the highest intellect as well as the most average mentality. It is also testament to the vigour of the Islamic faith which has indisputably withstood the twin onslaught of complex atheistic philosophy and widespread disbelief in the fundamentals of religion. Nothing less will do than the reinstatement of God as majestic, unique, alone, and one, the Creator and Ruler of the cosmos and all that it contains.

NOTES

[1] John D. Caputo, *On Religion; Thinking in Action* (London: Psychology Press, 2001), p.59.

[2] Ibid, pp.59–60.

[3] John D. Caputo, Gianni Vattimo, Jeffrey W. Robbins, *After the Death of God, Insurrections: Critical Studies in Religion, Politics and Culture*, edited by Jeffrey W. Robbins (New York: Columbia University Press, 2009), p.147.

[4] Earnest Gellner, *Postmodernism, Reason and Religion* (London; New York: Routledge, 1993), pp.5–6.

[5] Ibid., p.5.

[6] Ibid., p.6; see also Earnest Gellner, *Muslim Society* (Cambridge: Cambridge University Press, 1981).

[7] See details in Paul Badham's "Introduction" to *Verdict on Jesus*, p. XIXFF; see also Paul Johnson, "Peaceful Co-Existence," *Prospect London* (April, 1996), no.7, pp.34–38; Terry Miethe, Antony Flew, *Does God Exist?: A Believer and an Atheist Debate* (New York: Harper, 1991).

[8] Paul Davies, *The Mind of God: The Scientific Basis for a Rational World* (London: Simon & Schuster, 1992), pp.16 ff; see also his *God and the New Physics* (New

York: Simon & Schuster, 1983), pp.25 ff, 214 ff and his *The Edge of Infinity* (New York: Simon & Schuster, 1982), pp.171 ff.

[9] Davies, *The Mind of God*, pp.231–32.

[10] John Leslie, *Universe* (London: Routledge, 1996), p.2.

Bibliography

Selected Arabic Sources

Aawdah, Abd al-Qadir, *al-Tashrīʿ al-Janā'ī al-Islāmī* (Beirut: Mu'assasah al-Risālah, 1986).

Ahmad, Abu Bakr Ahmad ibn Ali, *Tārīkh Baghdād* (Cairo: Dār al-Maʿārif, 1931).

al-Albani, Muhammad Nasr al-Din, *Sharḥ al-ʿAqīdah al-Ṭaḥāwiyyah* (Beirut: al-Maktab al-Islāmī, 1984).

_____, *Naṣb al-Majānīq fī Nafs Qiṣṣah al-Gharānīq*, 2nd edn. (Beirut: al-Maktab al-Islamī, 1989).

Allah, Muhammad Khalf, Zaghlul Sallam, Muhammad, eds., *Thalāth Rasā'il fī Iʿjāz al-Qur'ān li al-Rummānī wa al-Khaṭṭābī wa ʿAbd al-Qāhir al-Jurjānī*, 2nd edn. (Cairo: Dār al-Maʿārif, 1968).

al-Alusi, S. Mahmud, *Rūḥ al-Maʿānī* (Multan: Maktabah Imdādiyyah, n.d.).

al-ʿArabī, Abū Bakr ibn, *Aḥkām al-Qur'ān* (Cairo: Maktabah ʿĪsā al-Bābī, 1967).

al-ʿArabī, Muḥyī al-Dīn ibn, *Tafsīr al-Qur'ān al-Karīm*, Mustafa Ghalib, ed. (Beirut: Dār al-Andalus, 1978).

ʿAsākir, ʿAlī ibn al-Ḥasan Abū al-Qāsim ibn, *Tahdhīb al-Tārīkh*, 1st edn. (Damascus: al-Maktabah al-ʿArabiyyah, n.d.).

al-Isfrāyīnī, Abū al-Muẓaffar, *al-Tabṣīr fī al-Dīn* (Cairo: Maktabah al-Khānjī, 1955).

al-Ashʿarī, Abū al-Ḥasan ʿAlī, *Kitāb al-Lumaʿ*, Father McCarthy, ed. (Beirut: 1953). *Risālah fī Istiḥsān al-Khawḍ fī al-Kalām*, see for English translation *The Theology of al-Ashʿarī: The Arabic Texts of al-Ashʿarī's "Kitāb al-Lumaʿ" and "Risālat Istiḥsān al-Khawḍ fī ʿIlm al-Kalām,"* with briefly annotated translations and appendices by Richard J. McCarthy (Beirut: Imprimerie Catholique, 1953).

_____, *Maqālāt al-Islāmiyyīn wa Ikhtilāf al-Muṣallīn*, M. Abd al-Hamid, ed. (Beirut: Al-Ḥikmah, 1994).

______, *al-Ibānah ʿan Uṣūl al-Diyānah*, Fawqiyyah H. Mahmud, ed. (Cairo: Dār al-Anṣār, 1977).

al-Ashqar, Umar S., *Aṣl al-Iʿtiqād*, 1st edn. (Kuwait: Dār al-Nafā'is, 1990).

______, *al-ʿAqīdah fī Allāh* (Amman: Dār al-Nafā'is, 1995).

______, *al-Asmā' wa al-Ṣifāt*, 1st edn. (Amman: Dār al-Nafā'is, 1993).

______, *al-Ta'wīl: Khuṭūratuhu wa Atharuh* (Amman: Dār al-Nafā'is, 1992).

al-Askari, Murtada, *Abdullah Ibn Saba' and Other Myths* (Qum: Sharif al-Rida Publishing Co., 1944).

al-ʿAsqalānī, Aḥmad ibn ʿAlī ibn Ḥajar, *Fatḥ al-Bārī bi Sharḥ Saḥīḥ al-Imām al-Bukhārī*, Muhibb al-Din al-Khatib, Muhammad F. Abd al-Baqi, Q., eds. (Cairo: Dār al-Diyān li al-Turāth, 1987).

al-Athīr, Ibn, *al-Kāmil fī al-Tārīkh* (Cairo: Dār al-ʿIlm li al-Malayīn, 1987).

Atiyya, Abu Muhammad Abd al-Haqq ibn, *al-Muḥarrar al-Wajīz fī Tafsīr al-Kitāb al-ʿAzīz*, Abdullah ibn Ibrahim al-Ansari, al-Sayyid Abd al-Al, M. al-Shafi, eds. (Qatar: The Government of Qatar Edition, 1982).

al-Awa, Adil, *Muntakhabāt Ismāʿīliyyah* (Damascus: Maṭbaʿah al-Jāmiʿah al-Sūriyyah, 1957).

al-ʿAynī, Maḥmūd ibn Aḥmad Badr al-Dīn, *ʿUmdah al-Qārī Sharḥ Ṣaḥīḥ al-Bukhārī* (Dār al-Fikr, n.d.).

al-Baghdādī, ʿAbd al-Qāhir, *al-Farq Bayn al-Firaq* (Damascus: Ṭabʿah al-Sayyid ʿIzzah al-ʿAṭṭār al-Ḥusaynī, 1948).

al-Balādhurī, Aḥmad ibn Yaḥya, *Ansāb al-Ashrāf*, Hamidullah, ed. (Cairo: Dār al-Maʿārif, n.d.).

al-Bāqillānī, Abū Bakr Muḥammad ibn al-Ṭayyib, *al-Inṣāf fī mā Yajibu Iʿtiqāduh wa lā Yajūz al-Jahal bih* (Damascus: ʿIzzat al-Ḥusaynī Publishers, 1950).

______, *Kitāb al-Tamhīd*, Yusuf al-Yasui, ed. (Beirut: al-Maktabah al-Sharqiyyah, 1957).

______, *Iʿjāz al-Qur'ān*, M. A. Khifaji, ed. (Beirut: Dār al-Jīl, 1991).

al-Bayhaqī, Abū Bakr Aḥmad ibn al-Ḥusayn ibn ʿAlī, *Kitāb al-Asmā' wa al-Ṣifāt* (Beirut: Dār Iḥyā' al-Turāth al-ʿArabī, n.d.).

al-Bukhārī, Abū ʿAbd Allāh Muḥammad, *Saḥīḥ al-Bukhārī*, Muhammad Zahir ibn Nasir, ed. (Beirut: Dār Ṭawq al-Najāt, 2001).

al-Dāraquṭnī, al-Ḥāfiẓ ʿAlī ibn ʿUmar, *Kitāb al-Ṣifāt*, Abdullah al-Ghunayman, ed., 1st edn. (Madinah: Maktabah al-Dār, 1981).

al-Dhahabi, M. Husayn, *al-Tafsīr wa al-Mufassirūn* (Beirut: Dār al-Kutub al-ʿArabī, 1962).

______, *Mizān al-Iʿtadāl* (Cairo: Ṭabʿah ʿĪsā al-Bābī, 1907).

al-Dhahabī, Shams al-Dīn Abū ʿAbd Allāh Muḥammad ibn Aḥmad,

Mukhtaṣar al-ʿUlūw li al-ʿAlīyy al-Ghaffār, M. Nasr al-Din al-Albani, ed., 1st edn. (Beirut: al-Maktab al-Islāmī, 1981).
al-Fārābī, Abū Naṣr, *al-Thamarat al-Mardiyah* (Leiden: Brills, 1895).
______, *Mabadi' Ara' Ahl al-Madina al-Fadila* (Leiden: Brills, 1890).
______, *Kitāb al-Millah wa Nuṣūṣ Ukhrā*, Muhsin Mahdi, ed. (Beirut: Dār al-Mashriq, 1968).
Fattah, Irfan Abdul Hamid, *Dirāsāt fī al-Firaq wa al-ʿAqā'id al-Islāmiyyah* (Beirut: Mu'assasah al-Risālah, 1984).
al-Ghazālī, Abū Ḥāmid, *Iḥyā' ʿUlūm al-Dīn* (Damascus: ʿĀlam al-Kutub, n.d.).
______, *Kitāb Iljām al-ʿAwām ʿan ʿIlm al-Kalām* (Cairo: Maktabah al-Munīriyyah, 1933).
______, *Tahāfut al-Falāsifah*, Sulayman Dunya, ed. (Cairo: Dār al-Maʿārif, 1947).
______, *al-Munqidh min al-Ḍalāl* (Beirut: Dār al-Kutub al-ʿIlmiyyah, 1988).
______, *Kitāb al-Iqtiṣād fī al-Iʿtiqād* (Beirut: Dār al-Kutub al-ʿIlmiyyah, 1983).
al-Ḥajjāj, Abū al-Ḥasan Muslim ibn, *Saḥīḥ Muslim* (Beirut: Dār Iḥyā' al-Turāth al-ʿArabī, n.d.).
Ḥanbal, Abū ʿAbd Allāh Aḥmad ibn, *Musnad al-Imām Aḥmad* (Cairo: Mu'assasah Qurṭubah, n.d.).
Ḥanbal, Aḥmad ibn, *al-Radd ʿalā al-Zanādiqah wa al-Jahmiyyah*, Abd al-Rahman Umayrah, ed. (Riyad: Dār al-Liwā', 1982).
Ḥanīfah, Nuʿmān Abū, *al-Fiqh al-Akbar*, Mulla Ali al-Qari, ed. (Cairo: ʿĪsā al-Bābī, 1955).
Hijazi, M. Mahmud, *al-Waḥdah al-Mawḍūʿiyyah fī al-Qur'ān al-Karīm* (Cairo: Dār al-Kutub al-Ḥadīthah, 1970).
Hishām, Abū Muḥammad ʿAbd al-Malik ibn Hishām ibn Ayyūb al-Ḥimyarī ibn, *al-Sīrah al-Nabawiyyah* [known as *Sīrah ibn Hishām*], 2nd edn. (Cairo: Maktabah Muṣṭafā al-Bābī al-Ḥalabī, 1955).
Husayn, Taha, *al-Fitnah al-Kubrā, ʿAlī wa Banūh* (Cairo: Dār al-Maʿārif, 1961).
al-Huṣnī, Abū Bakr Taqī al-Dīn, *Dafʿu Shubah Man Shabbaha wa Tamarrada wa Naṣaba dhālik ilā al-Imām Aḥmad* (Cairo: al-Ḥalbī, 1931).
al-ʿIrāqī, Zain al-Dīn ʿAbd al-Raḥīm ibn Ḥusayn, *Al-Taqyīd wa al-Īḍāḥ: Sharḥ Muqaddimah al-Ṣalāḥ*, Abd al-Rahman Muhammad Uthman, ed. (Madinah: al-Maktabah al-Salafiyyah, 1969).
al-Iṣbahānī, Abū Bakr Muḥammad ibn al-Furak, *Mushkal al-Ḥadīth wa Bayānuh*, Musa Muhammad Ali, ed., 2nd edn. (Beirut: ʿĀlam al-Kutub, 1985).

al-Iṣfahānī, Abū Naᶜīm, *Ḥilyat al-Awliyā' wa Ṭabaqāt al-Aṣfiyā'* (Cairo: Maṭbaᶜah al-Saᶜādah, 1932).

al-Iṣfahānī, al-Rāgib, *Muᶜjam Mufradāt Alfāẓ al-Qur'ān* (Beirut: Dār al-Kitāb al-ᶜArabī, 1972).

Islahi, Amin A., *Mabādi' Tadabbur al-Qur'ān* (Lahore: Dār al-Isha'at al-Islāmiyyah, 1971).

ᶜIyād, al-Qāḍī ᶜIyād ibn Mūsā ibn, *al-Shifā' bī Taᶜrīf Ḥuqūq al-Musṭafā*, Ali Muhammad al-Bajawi, ed. (Beirut: Dār al-Kitāb al-ᶜArabī, 1977).

al-Jabbār, Qāḍī ᶜAbd, *Sharḥ al-Uṣūl al-Khamsah*, Abd al-Karim Uthman, ed., 1st edn. (Cairo: Maktabah Wahabah, 1965).

Jarallah, Zahdi Hasan, *al-Muᶜtazilah* (Cairo: al-Mu'assasah al-ᶜArabiyyah li al-Dirāsāt wa al-Nashr, 1947).

al-Jawzī, Jamāl al-Dīn Abū al-Faraj ᶜAbd al-Raḥmān ibn ᶜAlī ibn, *Dafᶜ Shubhah al-Tashbīh*, al-Kawthari, ed.(Cairo: al-Maktabah al-Tawfīqiyyah, n.d.).

_____, *Talbīs Iblīs* (Cairo: al-Maṭbaᶜah al-Munīriyyah, n.d.).

_____, *Talbīs Iblīs* (Beirut: Dār al-Kutub al-ᶜIlmiyyah, n.d.).

al-Jawziyyah, Abū ᶜAbd Allāh Muḥammad ibn Abū Bakr al-Zarᶜī al-Damashqī ibn al-Qayyim, *Ighāthah al-Lahfān min Maṣāyid al-Shayṭān*, Muhammad S. Kaylani, ed. (Cairo: Maṭbaᶜah Musṭafā al-Bābī al-Ḥalabī, 1961).

_____, *Zād al-Maᶜād*, Shuayb al-Arnut, Abd al-Qadir al-Arnut, eds. (Beirut: Mu'assassah al-Risālah, 1982).

_____, *Badā'iᶜ al-Fawā'id* (Beirut: Dār al-Kitāb al-ᶜArabī, n.d.)

_____, *Ijtimāᶜ al-Juyūsh al-Islāmiyyah ᶜalā Ghazwi al-Muᶜaṭṭalah wa al-Jahmiyyah* (Beirut: Dār al-Kutub al-ᶜIlmiyyah, 1984).

al-Jazayri, Abd al-Rahman, *Kitāb al-Fiqh ᶜalā al-Madhāhib al-Arbaᶜah* (Beirut: Dār al-Irshād li al-Ṭibāᶜah wa al-Nashr, n.d.).

al-Jurjānī, Abū Bakr, *Kitāb Dalā'il al-Iᶜjāz*, Mahmud M. Shakir, ed. (Cairo: Maṭbaᶜah al-Madanī, 1992).

al-Juwaynī, Abū al-Maᶜālī ibn ᶜAbd al-Mālik, Imam al-Ḥaramayn, *Kitāb al-Irshād ilā Qawāṭiᶜ al-Adillah fī Uṣūl al-Iᶜtiqād*, Jean Dominique, ed. and trans. (Paris: E. Leroux, 1938).

Kathīr, ᶜImād al-Dīn Abū al-Fidā' Ismāᶜīl ibn, *al-Bidāyah wa al-Nihāyah* (Cairo: Maṭbaᶜah al-Saᶜādah, 1965).

_____, *Tafsīr al-Qur'ān al-ᶜAẓīm* (Beirut: Dār al-Hilāl, 1990).

al-Kawthari, M. Zahid, *Ibn ᶜAsākir Tabyīn Kadhb al-Muftrā* (Damascus: Maṭbaᶜah al-Tawfīq, 1954).

al-Khaliq, Abd al-Ghani Abd, *Ḥujjiyyah al-Sunnah* (Virginia: International Institute of Islamic Thought, 1994).

al-Khayyat, Abu al-Husayn Abd al-Rahim, *Kitāb al-Intiṣār* (Cairo: Dār al-Nahḍah al-ʿArabiyyah, 1925).
Khusraw, Nasir, *Tanwīr al-Miqbās Min Tafsīr Ibn ʿAbbās*, 1st edn. (Tehran: Intisharat Istiqlal, n.d.).
Khuzaymah, Ibn, *Kitāb al-Tawḥīd* (Cairo: Maktabah al-Kulliyyāt al-Azhariyyah, n.d.).
al-Kirmānī, Ḥāmid al-Dīn, *Rāḥat al-ʿAql* (Cairo: Dār al-Fikr al-ʿArabī, 1952).
Kubrizadah, Tash, *Miftāḥ al-Saʿādah* (Cairo: Dār al-Kutub al-ʿArabiyyah, n.d.).
Madkur, Ibrahim, *Fī al-Falsafah al-Islāmiyyah* (Cairo: Dār al-Maʿārif, 1976).
al-Maḥallī, Jalāl al-Dīn Muḥammad ibn Aḥmad, al-Suyuṭī, Jalāl al-Dīn ʿAbd al-Raḥmān ibn Abī Bakr, *Tafsīr al-Jalālayn* (Beirut: Dār al-Fikr, 1993).
Mahmud, Abd al-Halim, *al-Tafkīr al-Falsafī fī al-Islām* (Cairo: Dār al-Maʿārif, 1984).
_____, *al-Islām wa al-ʿAql* (Cairo: Dār al-Maʿārif, 1988).
al-Maqdisī, Muwaffaq al-Dīn ʿAbd Allāh ibn Aḥmad ibn Qudāmah, *Ithbāt al-ʿUlūw*, Badar ibn Abdullah al-Badar, ed., 1st edn. (Kuwait: al-Dār al-Salafiyyah, 1986).
al-Maqrayzi, Ahmad ibn Ali, *al-Khitāt wa al-Athar* (Cairo: Maṭbaʿah al-Nīl, 1907).
al-Maydani, Abd al-Rahman Hasan H., *al-ʿAqīdah al-Islāmīyyah*, 3rd edn. (Damascus: Dār al-Qalam, 1983).
Mubarakpuri, Safi-ur-Rahman, *al-Raheeq al-Makhtum* [The Sealed Nectar] (Makkah: Rabiṭah al-ʿĀlam al-Islāmī, 1991).
Muḥammad, Abū Bakr Muḥammad ibn ʿAbd Allāh ibn, [known as Ibn al-ʿArabī], *Aḥkām al-Qur'ān* (Beirut: Dār al-Kutub al-ʿIlmiyyah, n.d.).
Muslim, Imam, *Ṣaḥīḥ Muslim: al-Jāmiʿ al-Ṣaḥīḥ*, Abdul Hamid Siddiqi, trans. (Lahore: Sh. Muhammad Ashraf, 1987).
al-Nashshar, Ali Sami, *Nash'at al-Tafkīr al-Falsafī fī al-Islām*, 3rd edn. (Cairo: Dār al-Maʿārif, 1965).
_____, *al-Fikr al-Yahudī wa Ta'aththurihi bi al-Falsafah al-Islāmiyyah* (Alexandria: Dār al-Maʿārif, 1972).
al-Nawawī, Abū Zakariyyā Yaḥyā ibn Sharaf, *Sharḥ Ṣaḥīḥ Muslim* (Riyad: Maktabah al-Riyāḍ al-Ḥadīthah, n.d.).
Neuwirth, Angelika, "*Ṭariqāh al-Bāqillānī fī Iẓhār Iʿjāz al-Qur'ān*," *Studia Arabica et Islamica* [Arabic Section], Widad al-Qadi, ed. (Beirut: American University, 1981).
al-Qattan, Mann'a, *Mabāḥith fī ʿUlūm al-Ḥadīth* (Cairo: Maktabah Wahabah, 1987).
al-Qayrawānī, Abū Muḥammad ʿAbd Allāh ibn Abū Zayd, *Kitāb al-Jāmiʿ fī*

al-Sunan wa al-Ādāb wa al-Maghāzī wa al-Tārīkh, M. Abu al-Ajfan, Uthman Battikh, eds. (Beirut: Mu'assasah al-Risālah, 1983).
al-Qaysi, Abū Ṭālib Muḥammad Makkī, *al-ᶜUmdah fī Gharīb al-Qur'ān*, Yusuf A. al-Marᶜashili, ed. (Beirut: Mu'assasah al-Risālah, 1981).
al-Qurṭubī, Abū ᶜAbd Allāh Muḥammad ibn Aḥmad al-Anṣārī, *al-Jāmiᶜ li Aḥkām al-Qur'ān* (Cairo: Dār al-Kitāb al-ᶜArabī, 1967), vol.2.
Qutaybah, Abū Muḥammad ᶜAbd Allāh ibn Muslim ibn, *Tafsīr Gharīb al-Qur'ān*, Ahmad Saqar, ed. (Beirut: Dār al-Kutub al-ᶜIlmiyyah, 1978).
_____, *Ta'wīl Mushkal al-Qur'ān*, Ahmad Saqar, ed. (Cairo: Dār al-Turāth, 1973).
Qutb, Muhammad, *Madhāhib Fikriyyah Muᶜāṣarah*, 1st edn. (Beirut: Dār al-Sharq, 1983).
Qutb, Sayyid, *Fī Ẓilāl al-Qur'ān* (Beirut: Dār al-Shurūq, 1994).
_____, *al-Taṣwīr al-Fannī fī al-Qur'ān* (Beirut: Dār al-Shurūq, 2004).
al-Rafi, Mustafa Sadiq, *Tārīkh Ādāb al-ᶜArab* (Beirut: Dār al-Kitāb al-ᶜArabī, 1974).
al-Rāzī, Fakhar al-Dīn, *Tafsīr Mafātīḥ al-Ghayb* [known as *Tafsīr al-Kabīr*] (Beirut: Dār al-Fikr, 1978).
_____, *Iᶜtiqādāt Firāq al-Muslimīn wa al-Mushrikīn* (Cairo: Maktabah al-Nahḍah, 1938).
_____, *Asās al-Taqdīs* (Cairo: Maṭbaᶜah Muṣṭafā al-Bābī, 1935).
Rushd, Abū al-Walīd Muḥammad ibn Aḥmad ibn, *Faṣl al-Maqāl fī mā bayn al-Ḥikmah wa al-Sharīᶜah min al-Iṭṭiṣāl*, 2nd edn. (Cairo: Dār al-Maᶜārif, 1983).
_____, *Bidāyah al-Mujtahid wa Nihāyah al-Muqtaṣid* (Beirut: Dār al-Fikr, n.d.).
al-Sabat, Abdullah, *Al-Raḥmān ᶜalā al-ᶜArsh Istawā* (Kuwait: al-Dār al-Salafiyyah, 1978).
Saᶜd, Ibn, *Ṭabaqāt*, E. Schau, ed. (Leiden: Brills, 1905).
al-Ṣanᶜanī, Muḥammad ibn Ismāᶜīl al-Amīr, *Subul al-Salām fī Sharḥ Bulūgh al-Marām* (Cairo: Maktabah ᶜĪsā al-Bābī al-Ḥalabī, 1938), vol.4.
Shafi, Mufti Muhammad, *Maᶜārif al-Qur'ān* (Karachi: Idārah al-Maᶜārif, 1990).
al-Shahrastānī, Muḥammad ibn ᶜAbd al-Karīm, *Kitāb al-Milal wa al-Niḥal* (Cairo: al-Ḥalbī, 1968).
_____, *Nihāyah al-Aqdām fī ᶜIlm al-Kalām* (Beirut: Dār al-Kutub al-ᶜIlmiyyah, 2004).
Shaltut, Mahmud, *al-Islām ᶜAqīdah wa Sharīᶜah* (Cairo: Dār al-Qalam, 1966).

al-Sharqī, Aḥmad ibn Ibrāhīm ibn ᶜĪsā, *Sharḥ Qaṣīdah ibn al-Qayyim*, 1st edn. (Beirut: al-Maktab al-Islāmī, 1962).
al-Shāṭibī, Abū Isḥāq Ibrāhīm ibn Mūsā, *al-Muwāfaqāt fī Uṣūl al-Sharīᶜah*, 3rd edn. (Cairo: al-Maktabah al-Tijāriyyah al-Kubrā, 1975).
al-Shawkānī, Muḥammad ibn ᶜAlī, *Nayl al-Awtar* [known as *Tafsīr al-Shawkānī*] (Beirut: Dār al-Jīl, 1973).
_____, *al-Tuḥaf fī Madhāhib al-Salaf* (Cairo: Maṭbaᶜah al-Imām, n.d.).
Shaybah, Muḥammad ibn ᶜUthmān ibn Abī, *Kitāb al-ᶜArsh wama Ru'iya Fīhi*, Muhammad ibn Hamd al-Humud, ed. (Beirut: Dār al-Jīl, 1991).
al-Shaykh, Abd al-Rahman ibn Hasan Al, *Fatḥ al-Mājid Sharḥ Kitāb al-Tawḥīd* (Makkah: Maṭbaᶜah al-Ḥukūmah, 1967).
al-Suyūṭī, Jalāl al-Dīn, *Ṣawn al-Manṭiq wa al-Kalām*, Ali Sami al-Nashshar, Suad Ali Abd al-Razzaq, eds. (Cairo: Silsilah Iḥyā' al-Turāth, Dār al-Naṣr, 1970).
al-Ṭabarī, Abū Jaᶜfar Muḥammad ibn Jarīr, *Jāmiᶜ al-Bayān ᶜan Ta'wīl Āy al-Qur'ān*, Mahmud Muhammad, Ahmad Muhammad Shakir, eds. (Cairo: Dār al-Maᶜārif, 1954).
al-Ṭabarsī, Abū ᶜAlī al-Faḍl ibn al-Ḥasan, *Majmaᶜ al-Bayān fī Tafsīr al-Qur'ān* (Beirut: Dār Maktabah al-Ḥayāt, 1961).
al-Taftazānī, Saᶜd al-Dīn, *Sharḥ al-ᶜAqā'id al-Nasafiyyah* (Cairo: Dār Iḥyā al-Kutub al-ᶜArabiyyah, 1955).
al-Tahhan, Mahmud, *Taysīr Muṣṭaliḥ al-Ḥadīth* (Riyadh: Maktabah al-Maᶜārif, 1987).
Tamir, Arif, *Khams Rasāil Ismāᶜīliyyah* (Damascus: Dār al-Inṣāf, 1956).
Taymiyyah, Ibn, *Daqā'iq al-Tafsīr al-Jāmiᶜ lī Tafsīr Ibn Taymiyyah* (Damascus: Mu'assasah ᶜUlūm al-Qur'ān, 1983).
_____, *al-Risālah al-Madaniyyah fī Taḥqīq al-Majāz wa al-Ḥaqīqah fī Ṣifāt Allāh Taᶜālā*, 2nd edn. (Makkah: al-Maṭbaᶜah al-Salafiyyah, 1932).
_____, *Naqḍ al-Manṭiq*, 1st edn. (Cairo: Maṭbaᶜah al-Sunnah al-Muḥammadiyyah, 1951).
_____, *Majmūᶜ al-Fatāwā*, Abd al-Rahman ibn Muhammad ibn Qasim, ed. (Rabat: Maktabah al-Maᶜārif, n.d.).
_____, *Minhāj al-Sunnah fī Naqd Kalām al-Shīᶜah wa al-Qadariyyah*, Muhammad ibn Rashad Salim, ed. (Riyadh: Islamic University of al-Imam Muhammad bin Saud, 1985).
Tirmazī, Imam, *Saḥīḥ Sunan al-Tirmazī*, M. N. al-Albani, ed., 1st edn. (Gulf States: Maktabah al-Tarbiyah al-ᶜArabiyyah, 1988).
_____, *Sunan al-Timazī*, Ahmad Shakir, ed. (Beirut: Dār Iḥyā' al-Turāth al-ᶜArabī, n.d.).

al-Umri, Akram Diya, *al-Sīrah al-Nabawiyyah al-Saḥīḥah* (Qatar: Dār al-Kutub al-Qaṭariyyah, 1991).
al-Uthaymin, Mohammad ibn Salih, *al-ʿAqīdah al-Wasaṭiyyah li Ibn Taymiyyah* (Virginia: Institute of Islamic and Arabic Sciences, 1991).
al-Wazīr, Muḥammad ibn al-Murtaḍā al-Yamanī ibn, *Īthār al-Ḥaq ʿalā al-Khalq* (Cairo: Maṭbaʿah al-Adab wa al-Mu'ayyid, 1900).
Yasin, M., *al-Īmān* (Amman: Dār al-Furqān, 1985).
al-Ẓāhirī, Abū Muḥammad ʿAlī ibn Aḥmad ibn Ḥazm, *al-Muḥallā*, Ahmad Shakir, ed. (Beirut: al-Maktab al-Tijārī, n.d.).
______, *al-Faṣl fī al-Milal wa al-Ahwā' wa al-Niḥal* (Cairo: Maktabah al-Salām al-ʿIlmiyyah, n.d.).
al-Zamakhsharī, Abū al-Qāsim Mahmūd ibn ʿUmar, *Tafsīr al-Kashshāf ʿan Ḥaqā'iq Ghawāmiḍ al-Tanzīl wa ʿUyūn al-Aqāwīl fī Wujūh al-Ta'wīl* (Cairo: Muṣṭafā al-Bābī al-Ḥalabī, 1966).
al-Zindani, Abd al-Majid, *Kitāb Tawḥīd al-Khāliq* (Madinah: Maktabah Ṭayyibah, 1989).
______, *Kitāb al-Tawḥīd* (Madinah: Maktabah Ṭayyibah, 1990).

Other Sources

Abboud, Peter F., ed., *Elementary Modern Standard Arabic* (Cambridge: Cambridge University Press, 1996).
Abrahamov, Binyamin, *Anthropomorphism and Interpretation of the Qur'an in the Theology of al-Qasim ibn Ibrahim* (Boston: Brill, 1996).
______, "The *Bi-lā Kayfa* Doctrine and its Foundations in Islamic Theology," *Arabica* (November, 1995), vol.42.
Adams, Charles J., "Islamic Religious Tradition," *The Study of the Middle East*, Leonard Binder, ed. (New York: John Wiley & Sons, 1976).
______, "Islam," *Man and His Gods: Encyclopedia of World Religions*, Jeoffrey Parrinder, ed. (London: Hamlyn Publishing Co., 1971).
Agassi, Joseph, "Anthropomorphism in Science," *Dictionary of the History of Ideas*, Philip P. Wiener, ed. (New York: Charles Scribner's Sons, 1973).
Agus, Jacob B., *The Evolution of Jewish Thought* (New York: ARNO Press, 1973).
Ahmad, Imad-ad-Dean, *Signs in the Heavens: A Muslim Astronomer's Perspective on Religion and Science* (Maryland: Writers' Inc. International, 1992).

Bibliography

Ahsan, M. M., Kidwai, A. R., eds., *Sacrilege Versus Civility: Muslim Perspectives on The Satanic Verses Affair* (Leicester: The Islamic Foundation, 1991).

Albright, William F., *Archaeology and the Religion of Israel* (Baltimore: The John Hopkins Press, 1968).

_____, "Archaeology Confronts Biblical Criticism," *The American Scholar* (April, 1938), vol. VII.

_____, *From the Stone Age to Christianity*, 2nd edn. (Baltimore: The Johns Hopkins Press, 1967).

_____, *Yahweh and the Gods of Canaan* (New York: Doubleday, 1968).

Ali, Abdullah Y., trans., *The Holy Qur'an* (Madinah: King Fahd Holy Qur'an Printing Complex, 1989).

Altizer, Thomas J. J., *The Gospel of Christian Atheism* (London: Collins, 1966).

Anastos, Milton V., "Nestorius was Orthodox," *Dumbarton Oaks Papers* (Cambridge MA, 1962), vol.16.

Anawati, George C., "Attributes of God: Islamic Concepts," *Encyclopedia of Religion* (1987), vol.1.

Anderson, Hugh, *Jesus and Christian Origins* (New York: Oxford University Press, 1964).

Anderson, James N., ed., *The World Religions* (London: Frank Cass, 1965).

Andrae, Tor, *Mohammed: The Man and His Faith*, Theophil Menzel, trans. (New York: Books for Libraries Press, 1971).

Aquinas, Thomas, Summa Theologiae, H. Mcabe, trans. (New York: McGraw-Hill, 1964).

Arberry, Arthur J., *Avicenna on Theology* (Connecticut: Hyperion Press, 1979).

_____, *Revelation and Reason in Islam* (London: George Allen & Unwin Ltd., 1965).

_____, *The Koran Interpreted* (London: George Allen & Unwin, 1955), [2 vols.] [also in 1 vol., Oxford, 1964].

Armstrong, Karen, *A History of God: The 4000-Year Quest of Judaism, Christianity and Islam* (New York: Ballantine Books, 1994).

_____, *Muhammad: A Biography of the Prophet* (San Francisco: Harper Collins, 1992).

Arnold, Matthew, *Literature and Dogma* (New York: AMS Press, 1970).

Arnold, Thomas W., *Painting in Islam* (Oxford: Clarendon Press, 1928).

_____, *The Preaching of Islam* (Lahore: Sh. Muhammad Ashraf, 1979).

Asad, Muhammad, *The Message of the Qur'an* (Bristol: Book Foundation, 2003).

Bibliography

Atkinson, R. L., Atkinson, R. C., Smith, E. E., Bem, D. J., Hilgard, E. R., eds., *Introduction to Psychology* (New York; London: Harcourt Brace Jovanovich Publishers, 1990).

Augstein, Rudolf, *Jesus Son of Man*, H. Young, trans. (New York: Urizen Books, 1977).

Augustine, St., *Concerning the City of God Against the Pagans*, H. Bettenson, trans., David Knowles, ed. (Baltimore: Penguin Books, 1972).

Ayoub, Mahmoud M., *The Qur'an and its Interpreters* (Albany: SUNY, 1984).

Baab, Otto, *The Theology of the Old Testament* (New York: Abingdon Press, 1969).

Bacon, Francis, *The New Organon and Related Writings*, Fulton H. Anderson, ed. (New York: Liberal Arts Press, 1960).

Badham, Leslie, *Verdict on Jesus: A New Statement of Evidence* (New Delhi: IKON, 1995).

Baeck, Leo, "Romantic Religion," *Judaism and Christianity*, W. Kaufmann, trans. (Philadelphia: Jewish Publication Society of America, 1960).

_____, *The Essence of Judaism*, Victor Grubenweiser, trans. (New York: Schocken Books, 1961).

Baillie, Donald M., *God was in Christ: An Essay on Incarnation and Atonement* (New York: Scribner's Sons, 1948).

Balentine, Samuel, *The Hidden God: The Hidding of the Face in the Old Testament* (New York: Oxford University Press, 1983).

Baljon, J. M. S., "Qur'anic Anthropomorphism," *Islamic Studies* (Islamabad: Islamic Research Institute, 1988), vol.27.

Barbour, Ian G., *Models and Paradigms* (London: S.C.M Press, 1974).

Barnes, Barry, *Scientific Knowledge and Sociological Theory* (London: Routledge and Kegan Paul, 1974).

Barr, James, "Theophany and Anthropomorphism in the Old Testament," *Supplements to Vetus Testamentum* (Leiden: E. J. Brill, 1960), vol.17.

Barrett, Charles K., *Jesus and the Gospel Tradition* (Philadelphia: Fortress Press, 1968).

_____, *The Gospel According to St. John: An Introduction with Commentary & Notes on the Greek Text*, 2nd edn. (Philadelphia: The Westminster Press, 1978).

Barth, Karl, *The Doctrine of the Word of God* (Edinburgh: T & T Clark, 1956).

Bartsch, Hans W., ed., *Kerygma and Myth* (New York: Harper & Row, 1961).

Bauckham, Richard, *God Crucified: Monotheism and Christology in the New Testament* (Michigan: W. B. Eerdmans, 1999).
Bavinck, Herman, *Gereformeerde Dogmatiek*, 4th edn. (Kampen: Kok, 1928).
Beckwith, Francis J., Craig, William Lane, Moreland, J. P. eds., *To Everyone an Answer: A Case for the Christian World View* (Downers Grove: InterVarsity Press, 2004).
Bell, Richard, *Introduction to the Qur'an* (Edinburgh: Edinburgh University Press, 1958).
_____, *The Origin of Islam in its Christian Environment* (London: Macmillan, 1926).
Bellah, Robert, "Civil Religion in America," *Daedalus, Journal of the American Academy of Arts and Sciences* (Winter, 1967), vol.96.
Belloc, Hilaire, *The Great Heresies* (New York: Sheed & Ward, n.d.).
Berkouwer, Gerrit C., *The Second Vatican Council and the New Catholicism*, Lewis B. Smedes, trans. (Michigan: Eerdmans, 1965).
Berlin, Isaiah, *Karl Marx: His Life and Environment* (Oxford: Oxford University Press, 1963).
Berman, Lawrence V., "Maimonides, the Disciple of Alfarabi," *Maimonides, A Collection of Critical Essays*, Joseph A. Buijs, ed. (Notre Dame, Indiana: University of Notre Dame Press, 1988).
_____, "Maimonides, the Disciple of Alfarabi," *Israel Oriental Studies* (1974), vol.4.
Bethman, Erich W., *Bridge to Islam* (London: Allen & Unwin, 1953).
Bigg, Charles, *The Christian Platonists of Alexandria: The 1886 Bampton Lectures* (Oxford: Clarendon Press, 1968).
Bilezikian, Gilbert G., *The Liberated Gospel: A Comparison of the Gospel of Mark and Greek Tragedy* (Michigan: Baker, 1977).
Blau, Joseph L., *Modern Varieties of Judaism* (New York: Columbia University Press, 1966).
Bleeker, Jouco, Widengren, Geo, eds., *Historia Religionum* (Leiden: E. J. Brill, 1971), vol.II.
Boas, Franz, "Anthropology," *Encyclopedia of the Social Sciences* (New York: Macmillan, 1935).
Bodley, Ronald V. C., *The Messenger: The Life of Mohammed* (New York: Doubleday, 1946).
Boers, Hendrikus, *Who Was Jesus? The Historical Jesus and the Synoptic Gospels* (San Francisco: Harper & Row, 1989).
Boring, M. Eugene, "How May We Identify Oracles of Christian Prophets in

the Synoptic Tradition? Mark 3:28-29 as a Test Case," *Journal of Biblical Literature* (1972), vol.91.

_____, *Sayings of the Risen Jesus: Christian Prophecy in the Synoptic Tradition* (Cambridge: Cambridge University Press, 1982).

Bornkamm, Gunther, *Jesus of Nazareth* (New York: Harper & Row, 1960).

_____, *Paul, Paulus*, D. M. G. Stalker, trans. (New York: Harper & Row, 1969).

_____, *The New Testament: A Guide to Its Writings*, R. H. Fuller, Ilse Fuller, trans. (Philadelphia: Fortress Press, 1973).

Boullata, Issa J., "The Rhetorical Interpretation of the Qur'an: Iʿjaz and Related Topics," *Approaches to the History of the Interpretation of the Qur'an*, Andrew Rippin, ed. (Oxford: Clarendon Press, 1988).

Bousset, Wilhelm, *Kyrios Christos* (Nashville: Abingdon Press, 1970).

Bovon, Francois, "The Synoptic Gospels and the Noncanonical Acts of the Apostles," *Harvard Theological Review* (1988), vol.81.

Bowman, Robert M., Komoszewski, J. Ed, Bock, Darrell L., *Putting Jesus in His Place: The Case for the Deity of Christ* (Michigan: Kregal, 2007).

Brandon, Samuel G. F., ed. "Anthropomorphism," *Dictionary of Comparative Religion* (New York: Scribner's Sons, 1970).

Branscomb, B. Harvie, *The Gospel of Mark* (New York: Harper & Brothers, n.d.).

Bright, John, *The Authority of the Old Testament* (New York: Abingdon Press, 1967).

Bright, William, *The Age of Fathers* (New York: AMS Press, 1970), vol.1.

Brightman, Edgar S., "Anthropomorphism," *Collier's Encyclopedia* (New York: Crowell-Collier Educational Corporation, 1965).

Brown, David, *The Divine Trinity* (London: Duckworth, 1985).

Brown, Raymond, "Did Jesus Know He was God?," *Biblical Theology Bulletin* (1985), vol.15.

_____, "The Literal Sense of Scripture," *The New Jerome Biblical Commentary*, Raymond Brown, Joseph Fitzmeyer, Jerome Murphy, eds. (New Jersey: Prentice-Hall, 1968).

Brunner, Emil, *The Christian Doctrine of God*, Olive Wyon, trans., 11th edn. (Philadelphia: The Westminster Press, 1974).

Buber, Martin, "Religion and Reality," *Eclipes of God: Studies in the Relation Between Religion and Philosophy* (New York: Harper & Brothers, 1952).

_____, *The Prophetic Faith* (New York: Harper & Brothers, 1960).

_____, *Two Types of Faith*, Norman P. Goldhawk, trans. (New York: Macmillan, 1951).

______, *Between Man and Man*, R.G. Smith, trans. (Boston: Beacon Press, 1961).
Bucaille, Maurice, *The Bible, the Qur'an and Science* (Indiana: American Trust Publications, 1978).
______, *What is the Origin of Man?*, 9th edn. (Paris: Seghers, 1983).
Bulliet, Richard W., *Islam, The View From the Edge* (New York: Columbia University Press, 1994).
Bultmann, Rudolf K., "New Testament and Mythology," *Kerygma and Myth*, Hans W. Bartsch, ed., R. H. Fuller, trans., 2nd edn. (London: Oxford University Press, 1964).
______, *Jesus and the Word*, L. P. Smith, E. H. Lantero, trans. (New York: Charles Scribner's Sons, 1958).
______, *The History of the Synoptic Tradition*, J. Marsh, trans. (Oxford: Basil Blackwell, 1963).
Burkett, Delbert, *The Son of Man Debate: A History and Evaluation* (Cambridge: Cambridge University Press, 2000).
Burrel, David B., *Knowing the Unknowable God: Ibn Sina, Maimonides, Aquinas* (Notre Dame, Indiana: University of Notre Dame Press, 1986).
Burridge, Richard A., *What Are the Gospels? A Comparison with Graeco-Roman Biography* (New York: Cambridge University Press, 1992).
______, *Four Gospels, One Jesus? A Symbolic Reading* (Grand Rapids: W. B. Eerdmans, 2005).
Burton, John, "Those are the High-Flying Cranes," *Journal of Semitic Studies* (1970), vol.15, no.2.
______, *The Collection of the Qur'ān* (London: Cambridge University Press, 1977).
Butterworth, George W., trans., *Origen on First Principles* (London: SPCK, 1936).
Calvin, John, *Commentary on the Book of the Prophet Isaiah*, W. Pringle, trans. (Michigan: William B. Eerdmans, 1948).
______, *Institutes of the Christian Religion*, John Allen, trans., 6th American edn. (Philadelphia: Presbyterian Board of Christian Education, 1932).
Carlyle, Thomas, *Sartor Resartus and On Heroes and Hero Worship*, Introduction by W. H. Hudson (London: Everyman's Library, 1955).
Case, Shirley J., *Jesus: A New Biography* (New York: Greenwood Press, 1968).
Chadwick, Henry, *Early Christian Thought and the Classical Tradition* (New York: Dorset Press, 1967).

______, *The Early Church* (New York: Dorset Press, 1967).
______, trans., *Origen: Contra Celsum* (Cambridge: Cambridge University Press, 1965).
Champion, Selwyn G., Short, Dorothy, *Reading from World Religions* (Greenwich, USA: Fawcett Publications, 1959).
Cicero, Marcus T., *On the Nature of the Gods*, H. C. P. McGregor, trans. (Harmondsworth: Penguin, 1972).
Clair-Tisdall, St., *The Original Sources of the Quran* (London: SPCK, 1905).
Clarke, C. P. S., *Short History of The Christian Church* (London: Longman, 1966).
Clements, Robert E., *Abraham and David* (London: S.C.M. Press, 1967).
Cohen, Hermann, *Religion of Reason: Out of the Sources of Judaism*, Simon Kaplan, trans., introduced by Leo Strauss (New York: Frederik Ungar Publishing Co., 1972).
Collins, J. J., "The Son of Man and the Saints of the Most High in the Book of Daniel," *Journal of Biblical Literature* (1974), vol.93.
______, *The Apocalyptic Imagination* (New York: Crossroad, 1984).
Commentary on the Gospel of John (Book II), ch.2, http://www.newadvent.org/fathers/101502.htm.
Comte, Auguste, *The Positive Philosophy*, with a new Introduction by Abraham S. Blumberg (New York: AMS Press, 1974).
Conzelmann, Hans, *Jesus: The Classic Article From RGG Expanded and Updated*, J. R. Lord, trans., J. Reumann, ed. (Philadelphia: Fortress Press, 1973).
______, *History of Primitive Christianity*, John E. Steely, trans. (New York: Abingdon Press, 1973).
Cosslett, Tess, *Science and Religion in the Nineteenth Century* (Cambridge: Cambridge University Press, 1984).
Cragg, Kenneth, *The Call of the Minaret* (New York: Oxford University Press, 1970).
______, *The Mind of the Qur'an* (London: Allen & Unwin, 1973).
______, *The Event of the Qur'an* (London: Allen & Unwin, 1971).
______, *The House of Islam* (California: Dickenson Publishing Co. Inc., 1969).
Crone, Patricia, Cook, Michael, *Hagarism, The Making of the Islamic World* (London: Cambridge Univeristy Press, 1977).
Crosby, Donald, *Interpretive Theories of Religion* (The Hague: Mouton Publishers, 1981).
Crossan, John D., *The Historical Jesus: The Life of a Mediterranean Jewish Peasant* (San Francisco: Harper Collins 1991).

Crownfield, Frederic R., *A Historical Approach to the New Testament* (New York: Harper & Brothers, 1960).
Cullmann, Oscar, *The Christology of The New Testament*, Shirley C. Guthrie, Charles A. M. Hall, trans. (Philadelphia: The Westminster Press, 1963).
Cupitt, Don, *Christ, Faith and History: Cambridge Studies in Christology*, S. W. Sykes, J. P. Clayton, eds. (Cambridge: Cambridge University Press, 1972).
Daniel, Norman, *Islam and the West: The Making of an Image* (Edinburgh: Edinburgh University Press, 1989).
_____, Review of "Hagarism," *Journal of Semitic Studies* (1979), vol.24.
Danzger, M. Herbert, *Returning to Tradition* (New Haven; London: Yale University Press, 1989).
Darwin, Charles, *The Descent of Man* (New York: Appleton & Co., 1962).
Dashti, Ali, *Twenty Three Years, A Study of the Prophetic Career of Mohammad*, F. R. C. Bagley, trans. (London: George Allen & Unwin, 1985).
Davidson, Andrew B., *The Theology of the Old Testament*, S. D. F. Salmond, ed. (New York: Charles Scribner's, 1904).
Davies, Paul, *God and the New Physics* (New York: Simon & Schuster, 1983).
_____, *The Edge of Infinity* (New York: Simon & Schuster, 1982).
_____, *The Mind of God: The Scientific Basis for a Rational World* (London: Simon & Schuster, 1992).
Davis, Moshe, *The Emergence of Conservative Judaism* (Philadelphia: The Jewish Publication Society, 1963).
De Boer, Tijitze J., *History of Philosophy in Islam*, E. R. Jones B. D., trans. (London: Luzac & Co., 1970).
De Jonge, Marinus, *Christology in Context: The Earliest Christian Response to Jesus* (Louisville: Westminster John Knox Press, 1988).
De Moor, Johannes C., *The Rise of Yahwism: The Roots of Israelite Monotheism* (Leuvan: Peeters Press, 1990).
De Spinoza, Benedict, *The Chief Works of Benedict de Spinoza: On the Improvement of the Understanding; The Ethics; Correspondence*, R. H. M. Elwes, trans. (New York: Dover, 1955).
De Vaux, Roland, *The Bible and the Ancient Near East* (New York: Doubleday, 1971).
De Visme, Williamson Rene, *Politics and Protestant Theology: An Interpretation of Tillich, Barth, Bonhoeffer, and Brunner* (Baton Rouge: Louisiana State University Press, 1976).

Denny, Frederick M., *An Introduction to Islam* (New York: Macmillan, 1985).
Dentan, Robert C., *The Knowledge of God in Ancient Israel* (New York: The Seabury Press, 1968).
Dermenghem, Emile, *The Life of Mohamet*, A. Yorks, trans. (New York: Dial Press, n.d.).
Draenes, Stan, *Freud's Odyssey: Psychoanalysis and the End of Metaphysics* (New Haven: Yale University Press, 1982).
Draycott, G. M., *Mahomet Founder of Islam* (London: Martin Secker, 1916).
Driver, G. R., Hodgson, L., eds. and trans., *The Bazar of Heraclides Nestorius* (Oxford; New York: Clarendon Press, 1925).
Driver, S. R., *An Introduction to the Literature of the Old Testament* (Gloucester: Peter Smith, 1972).
Duggan, W. J., "Anthropomorphism," *Encyclopedic Dictionary of Religion*, Paul Kevin Meagher, Thomas C. O'Brien, Sister Consuelo M. Aherne, eds. (Washington: Corpus Publications, 1979).
Eaton, Charles Le Gai, *Islam and the Destiny of Man* (Albany: State University of New York Press, 1985).
Ehrman, Bart D., *Jesus, Apocalyptic Prophet of the New Millennium* (Oxford: Oxford University Press, 1999).
_____, *Misquoting Jesus* (San Francisco: Harper, 2005).
_____, *The Orthodox Corruption of Scriptures* (New York: Oxford University Press, 1993).
Eichrodt, Walther, *Theology of the Old Testament*, J. A. Baker, trans. (Philadelphia; Pennsylvania: The Westminster Press, 1961), vol.2.
Eilberg-Schwartz, Howard, *God's Phallus, and Other Problems For Men and Monotheism* (Boston: Beacon Press, 1994).
Eissfeldt, Otto, *The Old Testament: An Introduction*, P. R. Ackroyd, trans. (New York: Harper & Row, 1965).
Eliade, Mircea, *The Encyclopedia of Religion* (New York: Macmillan, 1987).
Engels, Friedrich, *Ludwig Feuerbach and the Outcome of Classical German Philosophy* (New York: International Publishers, 1941).
Enslin, Morton S., *The Prophet From Nazareth* (New York: McGraw-Hill, 1961).
Esposito, John L., *Islam the Straight Path* (New York: Oxford University Press, 1991).
Ettinghausen, Richard, *The Characted of Islamic Art in the Arab Heritage*, N. A. Faris, ed. (Princeton: Princeton University Press, 1944).

Fairbairn, Andrew M., *The Place of Christ in Modern Theology* (New York: Scribner's Sons, 1911).
Fakhry, Majid, *A History of Islamic Philosophy* (New York; London: Columbia University Press, 1970).
Farnel, Lewis R., *Attributes of God* (Oxford: Clarendon Press, 1925).
Farrar, Frederic W., *History of Interpretation* [Bampton Lectures] (New York: E. P. Dutton & Co., 1886), [reprinted by Baker Book House, Michigan, 1961].
al-Faruqi, Ismail R., "Divine Transcendence and Its Expression," *World Faiths* (Spring, 1979), vol.17.
_____, "Misconceptions of the Nature of the Work of Art in Islam," *Islam and the Modern Age* (May, 1970), vol.1, no.1.
_____, "On the Nature of Art in Islam," *Islam and the Modern Age* (August, 1976), vol.1, no.2.
_____, "Islam and Art," *Studia Islamica,* fasciculi XXXVII (1973).
_____, *Al-Tawḥīd: Its Implications for Thought and Life*, 2nd edn. (Virginia: International Institute of Islamic Thought, 1992).
_____, *Towards Islamic English* (Virginia: International Institute of Islamic Thought, 1986).
al-Faruqi, Ismail R., al-Faruqi, Lois L., *The Cultural Atlas of Islam* (New York: Macmillan Publishing Company, 1986).
Fedigan, Linda M., *Primitive Paradigms: Sex Roles and Social Bonds* (Montreal: Eden Press, 1982).
Ferguson, John, *Clement of Alexandria* (New York: Twayne Publishers Inc., 1974).
Ferré, Fredrick, *Basic Modern Philosophy of Religion* (New York: Charles Scribner's Sons, 1967).
_____, "In Praise of Anthropomorphism," *International Journal for Philosophy of Religion* (1984), vol.16, no.3.
Feuerbach, Ludwig, *Lectures On the Essence of Religion*, Ralph Manheim, trans. (New York: Harper & Row, 1967).
_____, *The Essence of Christianity*, E. G. Waring, F. W. Strothmann, eds. (New York: Frederick Unger, 1957).
Filson, Floyd V., *The New Testament Against Its Environment* (London: S.C.M. Press, 1963).
Firth, Raymond, *Tikopia Ritual and Belief* (Boston: Beacon Press, 1967).
Fishbane, Michael, *Biblical Myth and Rabbinic Mythmaking* (Oxford: Oxford University Press, 2003).
Fisher, George P., *History of Christian Doctrine* (New York: AMS Press, 1976).

Flinn, Frank K., ed., *Christology, The Center and the Periphery* (New York: Paragon House, 1989).
Fohrer, Georg, Sellin, Ernst, *Introduction to the Old Testament*, David E. Green, trans. (New York: Abingdon Press, 1968).
Fowler, Henry T., *The History and Literature of the New Testament* (New York: Macmillan, 1934).
Fowler, M. D., "The Meaning of *lipne* YHWH in the Old Testament," *ZAW 99* (Berlin, 1987).
Fox, Robin L., *Pagans and Christians* (New York: Alfred & Knopf Inc., 1987).
______, *The Unauthorized Version: Truth and Fiction in the Bible* (New York: Penguin Books, 1992).
Frank, Richard M., *Beings and Their Attributes, The Teaching of the Basrian School of Muʿtazila in the Classical Period* (Albany: SUNY Press, 1978).
______, "Moral Obligation in Classical Muslim Theology," *Journal of Religious Ethics* (1983), vol.11, no.2.
Fredriksen, Paula, *From Jesus to Christ: The Origin of the New Testament Images of Jesus* (New Haven: Yale University Press, 1988).
Frend, W. H. C., *The Early Church* (Philadelphia: Fortress Press, 1985).
Freud, Sigmund, *Civilization and Its Discontents*, James Starchey, trans. (New York: W. W. Norton, 1961).
______, *Moses and Monotheism*, Katherine Jones, trans. (New York: Vintage, 1967).
______, *The Ego and the ID*, John Riviere, trans. (London: Hogarth, 1927).
______, *The Future of an Illusion* (New York: W. W. Norton, 1961).
______, *The Interpretation of Dreams*, A. A. Brill, trans. (New York: Modern Library, 1950).
______, *Totem and Taboo: Some Points of Agreement Between the Mental Lives of Savages and Neurotics*, J. Starchey, trans. (New York: W. W. Norton, 1955).
Friedman, Richard E., "The Biblial Expression *master panim*," *Hebrew Annual Review* (1977), vol.1.
______, *The Disappearance of God* (Boston; New York; London: Little, Brown & Co., 1995).
______, *Who Wrote the Bible* (New Jersey: Prentice Hall, 1978).
Fromm, Erich, *You Shall Be As Gods* (Greenwich; Connecticut: Fawcett Premier, 1966).
Frye, Northrop, "The Religious Vision of William Blake," *Toward a New*

Christianity, Thomas J. J. Altizer, ed. (New York: Harcourt, Brace & World Inc., 1967).
Fueck, Johann, "The Originality of the Arabian Prophet," *Studies on Islam*, M. L. Swartz, ed. (New York: Oxford University Press, 1981).
Fuller, Reginald H., *The Foundations of New Testament Christology* (New York: Charles Scribner's Sons, 1965).
Furnish, Victor P., *Jesus According to Paul* (Cambridge: Cambridge University Press, 1993).
Gabrieli, Francesco, *Muhammad and the Conquests of Islam*, Virginia Luling, Rosamund Linell, trans. (London: Weidenfeld & Nicholson, 1968).
Gallus, Alexander, "A Biofunctional Theory of Religion," *Current Anthropology* (1972), vol.13.
Gardet, L., "God in Islam," *The Encyclopedia of Religions*, Mircea Eliade, ed. (New York: Macmillan, 1993), vol. 6.
Gardner, James, *The Faiths of the World: An Account of All Religions and Religious Sects, Their Doctrines, Rites, Ceremonies, and Customs* (London: A. Fullarton, 1858).
Gatje, Helmut, *The Qur'ān and its Exegesis*, A. T. Welch, trans. (Los Angles: University of California Press, 1976).
Geertz, Clifford, "Religion as a Cultural System," *Anthropological Approaches to the Study of Religion*, Michael Banton, ed. (London: Tavistock Publiations, 1966).
Geiger, Abraham, *Judaism and Islam*, [prolegomenon by Moshe Pearlman] (New York: KTAV Publishing House, 1970).
Geisler, Norman L., ed., *Inerrancy* (Michigan: Zondervan, 1979).
Geisler, Norman L., E. Nix, William, *A General Introduction to the Bible* (Chicago: Moody Press, 1969).
Geller, Stephen, "The Struggle at the Jabbok: The Use of Enigma in a Biblical Narrative," *JANES (Journal of the Near Eastern Society)* (1982), vol.14, p.38.
Gellner, Ernest, *Muslim Society* (Cambridge: Cambridge University Press, 1981).
______, *Postmodernism, Reason and Religion* (London; New York: Routledge, 1993).
Gerhardsson, Birger, *The Origins of the Gospel Traditions* (Philadelphia: Fortress Press, 1979).
Gersh, Harry, *The Sacred Books of the Jews* (New York: Stein and Day Publishers, 1968).

al-Ghazālī, Abū Ḥāmid, *Al-Ghazālī on The Ninety-Nine Beautiful Names of God*, David B. Burrell, Nazih Daher, trans. (Cambridge: The Islamic Texts Society, 1992).
Gibb, Hamilton A. R., *Modern Trends in Islam* (New York: Otagon Books, 1972).
_____, *Mohammedanism* (London: Oxford University Press, 1972).
_____, Kramers, Johannes H., eds., *Shorter Encyclopaedia of Islam* (Leiden: E. J. Brill, 1953).
Gibbon, Edward, *The Decline and Fall of the Roman Empire*, Dero E. Saunders, ed. (London: Penguin, 1980).
Gill, Jerry H., ed., *Christian Empiricism* (London: SPKC, 1974).
Glatzer, Nahum, *Franz Rosenzweig: His Life and Thought* (New York: Schocken Books, 1973).
Goitein, Shelomoh D., "Mohammad's Inspiration by Judaism," *Journal of Jewish Studies* (1958), vol.9.
_____, *Jews and Arabs: Their Contacts through the Ages* (New York: Schocken Books, 1955).
Goldziher, Ignaz, *Introduction to Islamic Theology and Law* (Princeton: Princeton University Press, 1981).
_____, *Muslim Studies*, S. M. Stern, ed. (London: George Allen and Unwin, 1971).
Gore, Charles, *The Incarnation of the Son of God* (New York: Scribner's Sons, 1960).
Gould, Stephen J., *Ever Since Darwin* (New York: W. W. Norton, 1977).
Graham, William A., "Qur'an as Spoken Word: An Islamic Contribution to the Understanding of Scripture," in *Approaches to Islam in Religious Studies*, Richard C. Martin, ed. (Tucson: University of Arizona Press, 1985).
Grant, Robert McQueen, ed., *Gnosticism: An Anthology* (London: Collins, 1961).
_____, *The Early Christian Doctrine of God* (Charlottesville: University Press of Virginia, 1966).
_____, *The Formation of the New Testament* (New York: Harper & Row, 1965).
_____, *The Letter and the Spirit* (London: SPCK, 1957).
Greenberg, Moshe, "Comments" [on "A Cognitive Theory of Religion" by Stewart Guthrie], *Current Anthropology* (1980), vol.21.
Greene, Oliver B., *The Second Coming of Jesus* (Greenville: Gospel Hour, 1971).

Greenstein, Howard, *Judaism, An Eternal Covenant* (Philadelphia: Fortress Press, 1983).
Greer, Rowan A., trans., *Origen: An Exhortation to Martyrdom, Prayer and Selected Works* [The Classics of Western Spirituality Series] (New Jersey: Paulest Press,1979).
Greig, J. C. G., ed., *Religions of Mankind Today and Yesterday*, Niele L. Jensen, trans. (Edinburgh; London: Oliver & Boyd, 1967).
Grillmeier, Alois, *Christ in Christian Tradition*, John Bowden, trans. (Atlanta: John Knox Press, 1975).
Grudem, Wayne, *Systematic Theology: An Introduction to Biblical Doctrine* (Michigan: Zondervan, 1994).
Grunebaum, Gustave E. von, *Islam, Essays on the Nature and Growth of a Cultural Tradition* (Chicago: American Anthropological Association, 1955).
Guillaume, Alfred, *Islam* (Baltimore: Penguin Books, 1969).
Guthrie, Donald, *New Testament Theology* (Downers Grove: InterVarsity Press, 1981).
Guthrie, Shirley C., Jr., *Christian Doctrine* (Richmond: CLC Press, 1968).
Guthrie, Stewart, *Faces in the Clouds: A New Theory of Religion* (New York: Oxford University Press, 1995).
Guttman, Julius, *Philosophies of Judaism*, David W. Silverman, trans. (New York: Holt, Rinehart and Winston, 1964).
Gwatkin, Henry M., *Studies of Arianism* (New York: AMS Press, 1978).
Habermas, Gary R., Licona, Michael R., *The Case for the Resurrection of Jesus* (Michigan: Kregal, 2004).
Halkin, Abraham S., "The Hashwiyya," *Journal of the American Oriental Society* (December, 1934), vol.54.
Hamori, Esther J., *When Gods Were Men, The Embodied God in Biblical and Near Eastern Literature* (New York: Walter de Gruyter, 2008).
Hanson, Richard P. C., *Allegory and Event* (London: S.C.M. Press, 1959).
Hardy, Edward R., Richardson, C. C., eds., *Christology of the Later Fathers,* The Library of Christian Classics (Philadelphia: The Westminster Press, n.d.), vol. III.
Harnack, Adolf V., *History of Dogma*, Neil Buchanan, trans. (New York: Dover Publications, 1961).
______, *What is Christianity?*, Thomas B. Saunders, trans. (London: G. P. Putnan's Son's, 1901).
Harris, Murray J., *Jesus as God: The New Testament Use of Theos in Reference to Jesus* (Grand Rapids: Baker Publishing Group, 1992).

Harris, Robert, *Inspiration and Canonicity of the Bible*, 5th edn. (Michigan: Zondervan, 1973).
Harvey, Van, *A Handbook of Theological Terms* (New York: Macmillan, 1964).
Haykal, Muhammad, *The Life of Muhammad*, I. R. al-Faruqi, trans. (Indianapolis: North Trust Publication, 1976).
Hebblethwaite, Brian, *The Incarnation: Collected Essays in Christology* (Cambridge: Cambridge University Press, 1987).
Heim, Karl, *God Transcendent* (London: James Nisbet & Co., 1935).
Heller, Bernard J., *Modern Jewish Thought*, J. B. Agus, ed. (New York: ARNO Press, 1973).
Helm, Paul, ed., *Divine Commands and Moral Requirements* (Oxford: Oxford University Press, 1981).
Henninger, Joseph, "Pre-Islamic Bedouin Religion," *Studies on Islam*, Marlin L. Swartz, ed. (New York: Oxford University Press, 1981).
Heschel, Abraham J., *Between God and Man, An Interpretation of Judaism*, F. A. Rothschild, ed. (New York: Free Press, 1959).
Hick, John, *Faith and Knowledge* (New York: Cornell University Press, 1966).
_____, *God and the Universe of Faiths* (London: Macmillan, 1973).
_____, ed., *The Myth of God Incarnate* (Philadelphia: The Westminster Press, 1977).
_____, *The Metaphor of God Incarnate* (London: S.C.M. Press, 1993).
Hill, Winfred F., *Learning, A Survey of Psychological Interpretations* (New York: Harper Collins, 1990).
Hirschfeld, Hartwig, "New Researches into Composition and Exegesis of the Quran," *Asiatic Monograph* (London: Royal Asiatic Society, 1902), vol. III.
Hitti, Philip K., *Capital Cities of Islam* (Minneapolis: University of Minnesota Press, 1973).
_____, *History of the Arabs*, 9th edn. (London: Macmillan, 1968).
_____, *The Arabs: A Short History* (Washington: Regnery Gateway, 1993).
_____, *The Near East in History* (New York: D. Van Nostrand Co., 1961).
Hodgkin, Edward C., *The Arabs* (Oxford: Oxford University Press, 1966).
Hodgson, Leonard, *The Doctrine of the Trinity* (London: Nisbet, 1943).
Hodgson, Marshall G. S., *The Venture of Islam* (Chicago: Chicago University Press, 1974).

Hoffmann, R. Joseph, ed., *The Origins of Christianity, A Critical Introduction* (New York: Prometheus Books, 1985).
Hoffmann, R. Joseph, Larue, Gerald A., eds., *Jesus in History and Myth* (New York: Prometheus Books, 1986).
Hoskyns, Edwyn C., Davey, Francis N., *The Riddle of the New Testament* (London: Faber & Faber, 1985).
Hume, David, *The Natural History of Religion*, H. E. Root, ed. (Stanford: Stanford University Press, 1957).
Hunt, Ignatius, *The World of the Patriarchs* (New Jersey: Prentice-Hall, 1967).
Husik, Isaak, *A History of Medieval Jewish Philosophy* (New York: Simon & Schuster, 1930).
Ibrahim, Ezzeddin, Johnson-Davies, Denys, selected and translated, *Forty Hadith Qudsī*, 6th edn. (Beirut: The Holy Koran Publishing House, 1990).
Idowu, Emanuel B., *African Traditional Religion: A Definition* (London: S.C.M. Press, 1973).
Idziak, Janine M., ed., *Divine Command Theory* (New York: Mellen Press, 1979).
Illingworth, John R., *Personality, Human and Divine* (London: Macmillan, 1899).
_____, *Divine Transcendence* (London: Macmillan, 1911).
Imschoot, Paul V., *Theology of the Old Testament*, Kathryn Sullivan, F. Bucks, trans. (New York: Descleev Company, 1954).
Ingersoll, Robert, *Some Mistakes of Moses* (New York: Prometheus Books, 1986).
Irving, Thomas B., *The Qur'an*, 3rd edn. (Vermont: Amana Books, 1988).
Irving, Washington, *Life of Mahomet* (New York: Everyman's Library, 1949).
Izutsu, Toshihiko, *Ethico-religious Concepts in the Qur'an* (Montreal: McGill University Press, 1966).
_____, *God and Man in the Koran* (New Hampshire: Ayer Co. Publishers Inc., 1987).
Jacob, Edmond, *Theology of the Old Testament*, A. W. Heathcote, P. J. Allcock, trans. (London: Hodder & Stoughton, 1958).
Jeffery, Arthur, *Islam: Muhammad and His Religion* (New York: Bobbs Merrill, 1958).
Jeremias, Joachim, *New Testament Theology*, John Bowden, trans. (New York: Charles Scribner's Sons, 1971).

Jevons, Frank B., "Anthropomorphism," *Encyclopedia of Religion and Ethics*, James Hastings, ed. (New York: Charles Scribner's Sons, 1913).
Johnson, Paul, "Peaceful Co-Existence," *Prospect London* (April, 1996), no.7.
Johnstone, Pierce de Lacy, *Muhammad and His Power* (Edinburgh: T & T Clark, 1901).
Kadushin, Max, *The Rabbinic Mind*, 3rd edn. (New York: Bloch Publishing, 1972).
Kandhalvi, Muhammad Zakariyya, *Faza'il-e-A'ama'l*, Abdul Rashid Arshad, trans. (Karachi: Darul Ishaat, n.d.).
Kaplan, Mordecai M., *Judaism as a Civilization: Toward a Reconstruction of American-Jewish Life*, 2nd edn. (New York: Schocken Books, 1967).
_____, *The Future of the American Jew* (New York: Reconstructionist Press, 1957).
_____, *The Meaning of God in Modern Jewish Religion* (New York: Reconstructionist Press, 1962).
Kasemann, Ernst, "The Problem of the Historical Jesus," *Essays on New Testament Themes* (London: S.C.M. Press, 1964).
Kasher, Rimmon, "Anthropomorphism, Holiness and Cult: A New Look at Ezekiel 40-48," *ZAW 110* (1998).
Katsh, Abraham I., *Judaism and the Koran* (New York: A. S. Barnes & Co., 1962).
Katz, Steven T., *Jewish Ideas and Concepts* (New York: Schocken Books, 1977).
Kaufmann, Yehezkel, *The Religion of Israel*, Moshe Greenberg, trans. (Chicago: The University of Chicago Press, 1960).
Kazi, A. K., Flynn, J. G., trans., *Muslim Sects and Divisions: The Section on Muslim Sects in Kitab al-Milal wa al-Nihal by Shahrastani* (London: Kegan Paul International, 1984).
Kee, Howard C., *Jesus in History: An Approach to the Study of the Gospels* (New York: Harcourt, Brace & World Inc., 1970).
_____, *What Can We Know About Jesus?* (Cambridge: Cambridge University Press, 1990).
Kegley, Charles W., ed., *Reinhold Niebhur, His Religious, Social and Political Thought* (New York: Macmillan, 1956).
Kelly, John N. D., *Early Christian Creeds* (New York: David McKay Co., 1972).
_____, *Early Christian Doctrines* (New York: Harper and Brothers, 1958).

Kelsay, John E., "Religion and Morality in Islam," [doctoral thesis] (Chalottesville: University of Virginia, 1985).

Kepler, Thomas S., ed., *Contemporary Thinking About Jesus: An Anthology* (New York: Abingdon-Cokesbury Press, 1944). [It was also published by Greenwood Press, New York, 1969].

Khadduri, Majid, *The Islamic Conception of Justice* (Baltimore: The John Hopkin University Press, 1984).

Kirk, George E., *A Short History of the Middle East*, 2nd edn. (London: Methun, 1964).

Kister, M. J., *Society and Religion from Jahiliyyah to Islam* (London, UK: Variorum; Vermont, USA: Gower Publishing Group, 1990).

Klemke, E. D., "Living Without Appeal," *The Meaning of Life* (New York: Oxford University Press, 1999).

Klubertanz, George, *St. Thomas Aquinas on Analogy: A Textual Analysis and Systematic Synthesis* (Chicago: Loyola University Press, 1960).

Knox, John, *The Humanity and Divinity of Jesus* (Cambridge: Cambridge University Press, 1967).

Koester, Helmut, "The Text of the Synoptic Gospels in the Second Century," *Gospel Traditions in the Second Century: Origins, Recensions, Text, and Transmission*, William L. Petersen, ed. (Notre Dame, Indiana: University of Notre Dame Press, 1989).

Korpel, Marjo C. A., *A Rift in the Clouds: Ugaritic and Hebrew Descriptions of the Divine* (Munster: UGARIT-Verlag, 1990).

Krasner, Barbara R., "Sublime Anthropomorphism: The Significance of Jewish Mysticism for Personal and Communal Existence," Ph.D. Dissertation, Temple University (Ann Arbor: University Microfilms International, 1975).

Kulandran, Sabapathy, *The Concept of Transcendence* (Madras: The Christian Literary Society, 1981).

Kung, Hans, Ess, Josef van, Stietencron, Heinrich von, Bechert, Heinz, eds., *Christianity and the World Religions* (London: Harper Collins Publishers, 1992).

Kung, Hans, *Judaism, Between Yesterday and Tomorrow*, John Bowden, trans. (New York: Crossroad, 1992).

______, *On Being a Christian*, E. Quinn, trans. (New York: Doubleday & Co., 1976).

Lammens, Henri, *Islam, Beliefs and Institutions*, Sir E. D. Ross, trans. (London: Cass & Co., 1968).

Lane-Poole, Stanley, *Studies in a Mosque* (Beirut: Khayats, 1966).

Latourette, Kenneth, *A History of Christianity* (New York: Harper, 1953).
Lawson, E. Thomas, McCauley, Robert N., *Rethinking Religion: Connecting Cognition and Culture* (Cambridge: Cambridge University Press, 1990).
Leaman, Oliver, *An Introduction to Medieval Islamic Philosophy* (Cambridge: Cambridge University Press, 1985).
_____, *A Brief Introduction to Islamic Philosophy* (Cambridge: Polity Press, 1999).
Leslie, John, *Universe* (London: Routledge, 1996).
Lévi-Strauss, Claude, *The Savage Mind* (Chicago: University of Chicago Press, 1966).
Levy, Reuben, *The Social Structure of Islam* (Cambridge: Cambridge University Press, 1959).
Lewis, Bernard, *The Arabs in History*, 3rd edn. (London: Hutchinson University Library, 1964).
Lewis, C. S., *The Incarnation of the Word of God, Being the Treatise of St. Athanasius*, Geoffrey Bles, trans. (London: The Centenary Press, 1944).
Lierman, John, *The New Testament Moses: Christian Perceptions of Moses and Israel in the Setting of Jewish Religion* (Tubingen: Mohr Siebeck, 2004).
Lightfoot, Robert H., *History and Interpretation in the Gospels* (London: Hodder & Stoughton, 1935).
Lightman, Alan, Brawer, Roberta, *Origins: The Lives and Worlds of Modern Cosmologists* (Cambridge: Harvard University Press, 1990).
Livingston, James C., *Modern Christian Thought* (New York: Macmillan, 1971).
Lods, Adolphe, *Israel, From its Beginnings to the Middle of the Eighth Century* (London: Routledge & Kegan Paul, 1948).
_____, *The Prophets and the Rise of Judaism* (Connecticut: Greenwood Press, 1971).
Lossky, Vladimir, *The Mystical Theology of the Eastern Church* (London: J. Clarke, 1957).
Lubac, Henri de, *The Drama of Atheist Humanism*, M. Riley, trans. and ed. (New York: Sheed & Ward, 1950).
Lull, Timothy F., ed., *Martin Luther's Basic Theological Writings* (Philadelphia: Fortress Press, 1989).
Luria, Salvador E., *Life: The Unfinished Experiment* (New York: Scribner's Sons, 1973).
Lyttkens, Hampus, *The Analogy Between God and The World: An Investigation of its Background and Interpretation of its Use by Thomas of Aquino* (Uppsala: Almquist and Wiksells Boktwyckeri AB, 1952).

Macdonald, Duncan B., *Development of Muslim Theology, Jurisprudence and Constitutional Theory* (Beirut: Khayats, 1965).

MacGregor, Geddes, *The Bible in the Making* (New York: J. B. Lippencott, 1959).

Macquarrie, John, *God-Talk: An Examination of the Language and Logic of Theology*, (London: S.C.M Press, 1967).

_____, *Thinking About God* (New York: Harper & Row, 1975).

Madelung, Wilferd, *Religious Schools and Sects in Medieval Islam* (London: Variorum Reprints, 1985).

_____, "Early Sunni Doctrine Concerning Faith," *Studia Islamica* (1970), vol.32.

Maimonides, Moses, *The Guide for the Perplexed,* M. Friedlander, trans., 2nd edn. (New York: Dover Publication Inc., 1956).

Makdisi, George, "Hanbalite Islam," *Studies on Islam*, M. L. Swartz, ed. (New York: Oxford University Press, 1981).

_____, *Ibn 'Iqil: Religion and Culture in Classical Islam* (Edinburgh: Edinburgh University Press, 1997).

_____, *Censure of Speculative Theology. An Edition and Translation of Ibn Qudāma's Taḥrīm an-Naẓar fī Kutub Ahl al-Kalām*, George Makdisi, trans. (London: Luzac, 1962).

Margoliouth, David S., *The Early Development of Mohammedanism* (London: Williams & Norgate, 1914).

Marmorstein, Arthur, *The Old Rabbinic Doctrine of God: Essays in Anthropomorphism* (London: Oxford University Press, 1937).

_____, *Studies in Jewish Theology*, J. Rabbinowitz, M. S. Lew, eds. (New York: Books for Libraries Press, 1972).

Marshall, I. Howard, *The Gospel of Luke: A Commentary on the Greek Text, New International Commentary on the New Testament* (Exeter: Paternoster Press, 1978).

Martin, Bernard, ed., *Great 20th Century Jewish Philosophers* (New York: Macmillan, 1970).

_____, *Mohammedanism* (London: Butterworth, 1912).

Martin, Richard C., *Islam, A Cultural Perspective* (New Jersey: Prentice-Hall, 1982).

_____, ed., *Approaches to Islam in Religious Studies* (Tucson: University of Arizona Press, 1985).

Martineau, James, *A Study of Religion: Its Sources and Contents* (Oxford: Clarendon Press, 1888).

Marty, Martin E., *A Short History of Christianity* (Minneapolis: Fortress Press, 1987).

Marx, Karl, "Theses on Feuerbach," *Ludwig Feuerbach and the Outcome of Classical German Philosophy*, Friedrich Engels (New York: International Publishers, 1941).

Mascall, Eric L., *Christ, The Christian and The Church* (London: Longmans Green, 1946).

Mawdudi, Sayyid Abul A'la, *Four Basic Qur'anic Terms*, Abu Asad, trans., 2nd edn. (Lahore: Islamic Publications Ltd., 1982).

_____, *Towards Understanding the Qur'an*, Zafar I. Ansari, trans. and ed. (Leicester: The Islamic Foundation, 1988).

_____, *The Meaning of the Qur'an*, Ch. M. Akbar, trans., A. A. Kamal, ed., 4th edn. (Lahore: Islamic Publications, 1983).

McAlpine, Thomas H., *Human and Divine Sleep in the Old Testament* (Sheffield: JSOT, 1987).

McDonnell, W. J., et al., eds., *New Catholic Encyclopedia* (New York: McGraw-Hill, 1967), vol.2.

McGiffert, Arthur C., *A History of Christian Thought* (New York: Charles Scribner's Sons, 1960).

McGrath, James F., *John's Apologetic Christology: Legitimation and Development in Johannine Christology* (New York: Cambridge University Press, 2001).

McInerny, Ralph M., *The Logic of Analogy: An Interpretation of St. Thomas* (The Hague: Martinus Nijhoff, 1961).

Meek, Teophile J., *Hebrew Origins* (New York: Harper & Row, 1960).

Meeks, Wayne A., *The Writings of St. Paul: A Norton Critical Edition* (New York: W. W. Norton & Co., 1972).

_____, "Moses as God and King," *Religions in Antiquity: Essays in Memory of Erwin Ramsdell Goodenough*, J. Nuesner, ed. (Leiden: E. J. Brill, 1970).

Meijering, Eginhard P., *God Being History: Studies in Patristic Philosophy* (Amsterdam: North-Holland Publishing Company, 1975).

Meloney, George S. J., *The Cosmic Christ, From Paul to Teilhard* (New York: Sheed & Ward, 1968), vol.1.

Menezes, F. J. L., *The Life and Religion of Mohammed, The Prophet of Arabia* (London: Sands & Co., 1911).

Mettinger, Trygge N. D., *In Search of God: The Meaning and Message of the Everlasting Names* (Philadelphia: Fortress Press, 1988).

Metzger, Bruce M., *The New Testament, Its Background, Growth and Content* (New York: Abingdon Press, 1965).

Meynell, Hugo, "The Intelligibility of the Universe," *Reason and Religion*, S. C. Brown, ed. (Ithaca: Cornell University Press, 1977).

_____, *The Intelligible Universe* (New York: Macmillan, 1982).
Mickelsen, A. Berkeley, *Interpreting The Bible* (Michigan: Wm. B. Eerdmans Publishing, 1963).
Miethe, Terry, Flew, Antony, *Does God Exist?: A Believer and an Atheist Debate* (New York: Harper, 1991).
Miller, John H., ed., *Vatican II: An Interfaith Appraisal* (London: University of Notre Dame Press, 1966).
Miller, Joseph H., *The Disappearance of God: Five Nineteenth Century Writer* (Cambridge: Harvard University Press, 1975).
Mir, Mustansir, "Coherence in the Qur'an: A Study of Islahi's Concept of Nazm," *Tadabbur-i Qur'an* (Indiana: American Trust Publication, 1986).
Moltmann, Jurgen, *The Trinity and the Kingdom: The Doctrine of God* (San Francisco: Harper & Row, 1981).
_____, *The Crucified God* (New York: Harper & Row, 1974).
Moore, George, *Judaism* (Cambridge: Harvard University Press, 1970).
Moore, Keith L., "Highlights of Human Embryology in the Koran and the Hadith," presented at the Seventh Saudi Medical Meeting at King Faisal University (May 3-6, 1982), [published by Muslim Students Association of US and Canada, Ottawa, Quebec, n.d.].
Moosa, Matti, *Extremist Shiites, The Ghulat Sects* (New York: Syracuse University Press, 1988).
Morey, Robert, *The Islamic Invasion: Confronting the World's Fastest Growing Religion* (Eugene: Harvest House Publishers, 1992).
Moule, Charles F. D., "A Reconsideration of the Context of Maranatha," *New Testament Studies* (1960), vol.6.
_____, *The Origin of Christology* (Cambridge: Cambridge University Press, 1977).
Muir, William, Weir, Thomas H., *The Life of Mohammad* (Edinburgh: John Grant, 1912).
Murata, Sachiko, Chittick, William C., *The Vision of Islam* (New York: Paragon House, 1994).
Nadwi, Sayyed Abul Hasan A., *Mankind's Debt to the Prophet Muhammad* (Oxford: St. Cross College, 1992).
Naish, John, *The Wisdom of the Qur'an* (Oxford: Oxford University Press, 1937).
Nasr, Seyyed Hossein, *Science and Civilization in Islam* (Cambridge: Islamic Texts Society, 1987).
_____, *A Young Muslim's Guide to the Modern World* (Chicago: Kazi Publications Inc., 1994).

_____, *Islamic Science: An Illustrated Study* (London: World of Islam Festival Pub. Co., 1976).

_____, Leaman, Oliver, eds., *History of Islamic Philosophy* (London; New York: Routledge, 1996), vol.1.

Neil, Stephen, *The Interpretation of the New Testament 1861-1961* (New York: Oxford University Press, 1966).

Netton, Ian R., *Allah Transcendent* (London; New York: Routledge, 1989).

_____, *Text and Trauma: An East-West Primer* (Richmond: Curzon Press, 1996).

Neusner, Jacob, *Death and Birth of Judaism* (New York: Basic Books, 1987).

_____, ed., *Understanding Rabbinic Judaism: From Talmud to Modern Times* (New York: KTAV Publishing House Inc., 1974).

_____, *The Incarnation of God: The Character of Divinity in Formative Judaism* (Philadelphia: Fortress Press, 1988).

Neuwirth, Angelika, "Images and Metaphors in the Introductory Sections of the Makkan Suras," *Approaches to the Qur'an*, G. R. Hawting, Abdul-Kader A. Shareef, eds. (New York; London: Routledge, 1993).

_____, *Studien zur Komposition der mekkanischen Suren* (Berlin; New York: Walter de Gruyter, 1981).

Nicholson, Reynold A., *A Literary History of the Arabs* (Cambridge: Cambridge University Press, 1953).

Niehaus, Jeffrey J., *God at Sinai: Covenant & Theophany in the Bible and Ancient Near East* (Michigan: Zondervan, 1995).

Nielsen, Kai, "Empiricism, Theoretical Constructs, and God," *Journal of Religion* (1974), vol.54.

_____, *Scepticism* (London: St. Martin's Press, 1973).

Nietzsche, Friedrich, "Thus Spoke Zarathustra," *The Philosophy of Nietzsche* (New York: Modern Library, 1954). [Thus Spoke Zarathustra has been separately translated by R. J. Hollingdale and is available from Penguin Books, Baltimore, 1964].

Nineham, Dennis E., *Saint Mark* (London: Pelican Books, 1969).

_____, *The Use and Abuse of The Bible* (New York: Macmillan, 1981).

Norris, Richard A., Jr., ed. and trans., *The Christological Controversy* (Philadelphia: Fortress Press, 1980).

Nu'mani, Shibli, *Sirat-un-Nabi*, M. T. B. Budayuni, trans. (Lahore: Kazi Publications, 1979).

Nunn, T. Percy, "Anthropomorphism in Physics," *Proceedings of the British Academy*, [Annual Philosophical Lecture, Henriette Hertz Trust] (London: Oxford University Press, 1927).

Nutting, Anthony, *The Arabs* (New York: C. N. Potter, 1964).
Obermann, Julian, "Islamic Origins," *The Arab History*, Nabih Amin Faris, ed. (Princeton: Princeton University Press, 1944).
O'Collins, Gerald, Farrugia, Mario, *Catholicism: The Story of Catholic Christianity* (Oxford: Oxford University Press, 2003).
O'Leary, De Lacy, *Arabic Thought and Its Place in History* (London: Routledge & Kegan Paul Ltd., 1968).
Orpheus, Salomon R., *A History of Religion* (New York: Livercraft Inc., 1932).
Packer, James I., *"Fundamentalism" and The Word of God: Some Evangelical Principles* (Michigan: W. B. Eerdmans, 1974).
Paivio, Allan, *Imagery and Verbal Processes* (New York: Holt, Rinehart & Winston, 1971).
Palmer, Humphrey, *Analogy* (New York: St. Martin's Press, 1973).
Parker, Theodore, *Discourse of Matters Pertaining to Religion* (Boston: C. C. Little J. Brown, 1842).
Patrick, Dale, *The Rendering of God in the Old Testament* (Philadelphia: Fortress Press, 1981).
Patton, Walter M., *Ahmad b. Hanbal and the Mihna* (Leiden: E. J. Brill, 1897).
Peake, Arthur S., "The Messiah and the Son of Man," *Bulletin of the John Rylands Library* (1942), vol.8.
Pelikan, Jaroslav, ed., *Luther's Works* (St. Louis: Concordia Publishing House, 1959), vol.22.
_____, *The Christian Tradition: A History of the Development of Doctrine* (Chicago; London: University of Chicago Press, 1971), vol.1.
Perlmann, Moshe, *Ibn Kammūna's Examination of the Three Faiths: A Thirteenth Century Essay in Comparative Study of Religion* (Berkeley, LA: University of California, 1971).
Perrin, Norman, *A Modern Pilgrimage in New Testament Christology* (Philadelphia: Fortress Press, 1972).
Peters, Francis E., *A Reader on Classical Islam* (New Jersey: Princeton University Press, 1994).
Petuchowski, Jakob J., "Reformed Judaism," *Encyclopedia Judaica* (Jerusalem: Keter Publishing House, 1971), vol.4.
Plaut, W. Gunther, *The Torah, A Modern Commentary* (New York: Union of American Hebrew Congregations, 1981).
Pollard, T. E., "The Origins of Arianism," *Journal of Theological Studies* (1958), vol.9.

Preus, J. Samuel, *Explaining Religion* (London: Yale University Press, 1987).
Prideaux, Humphry, *The True Nature of Imposture, Fully Displayed in the Life of Mahomet* (London: E. Curll, 1723).
Provine, William, "Evolution and the Foundation of Ethics," *Science, Thechnology and Social Progress*, Steven L. Goldman, ed. (Bethlehem, PA: Lehigh University Press, 1989).
Quick, Oliver C., *Doctrines of the Creed, Their Basis in Scripture and Their Meaning Today* (New York: Scribner's Sons, 1938).
Qureshi, Zafar A., *Prophet Muhammad and his Western Critics* (Lahore: Idārah Maʿārif Islāmī, 1992).
Rad, Gehhard V., *Old Testament Theology*, D. M. G. Stalker, trans. (New York: Harper, 1962).
Rahman Afzalul, ed., *Encyclopaedia of Seerah* (London: Seerah Foundation, 1981).
Rahman, Fazlur, *Islam* (Chicago: University of Chicago Press, 1979).
_____, *Islam and Modernity: Transformation of an Intellectual Tradition* (Chicago; London: University of Chicago Press, 1982).
_____, *Major Themes of the Qur'an* (Chicago: Bibliotheca Islamica, 1980).
_____, "Some Key Ethical Concepts of the Qur'an," *Journal of Religious Ethics* (1983), vol.11, no.2.
Ramsey, Ian T., *Models and Mystery* (Oxford: Oxford University Press, 1964).
_____, *Religious Language: An Empirical Placing of Theological Phrases* (New York: Macmillan, 1963).
Ramsey, Michael, ed., *Lambeth Essays on Faith* (London: The Society for Promoting Christian Knowledge SPCK, 1969).
_____, *The Resurrection of Christ: An Essay in Biblical Theology* (London: Geoffery Bles, 1962).
_____, *Jesus and the Living Past* (Oxford: Oxford University Press, 1980).
Reinhart, A. Kevin, "Islamic Law as Islamic Ethics," *Journal of Religious Ethics* (1983), vol.11, no.2.
Renan, Ernest T., *Studies in Religious History, History of the People of Israel and Religion of Antiquity* (London: Metheson & Co., 1886).
Richardson, Alan, Bowden, John, *The Westminster Dictionary of Christian Theology* (Philadelphia: The Westminster Press, 1983).
Richardson, Herbert W., ed., *Transcendence* (Boston: Beacon Press, 1969).
Riches, John K., *A Century of New Testament* (Pennsylvania: Trinity Press International, 1993).

Rickett, Margaret, *Painting in Britain, The Middle Ages* (New York: Penguin Books, 1954).

Ricoeur, Paul, "Philosophy and Religious Language," *Journal of Religion* (1974), vol.54.

Rippin, Andrew, "Rahman and the Hanifs," *Islamic Studies Presented to Charles Adams*, W. B. Hallaq, D. P. Little, eds. (Leiden: E. J. Brill, 1991).

_____, "Literary Analysis of Qur'an, Tafsir, and Sira: The Methodologies of John Wansbrough," *Approaches to Islam in Religious Studies*, Richard C. Martin, ed. (Tucson: University of Arizona Press, 1985).

_____, *Muslims: Their Religious Beliefs & Practices* (New York: Routledge, 1990), vol.1.

Roberts, J. J. M., "The Visual Elements in Isaiah's Vision in Light of Judaean and Near Eastern Sources," *From Babel to Babylon: Essays on Biblical Historyand Literature in Honour of Brian Peckham*, J. R. Wood, John E. Harvey, Mark Leuchter, eds. (New York: T & T Clark, 2006).

Robertson, Archibald, "St. Athanasius: Select Works and Letters," *A Select Library of Nicene and Post-Nicene Fathers of the Christian Church* (Grand Rapids: W. B. Eerdmans, 1957), vol. IV.

Robinson, Harold W., ed., *Record and Revelation: Essays on the Old Testament* (Oxford: The Clarendon Press, 1951).

Robinson, John M., *Introduction to Early Greek Philosophy* (Boston: Houghton Mifflin, 1968).

Rodinson, Maxime, *Muhammad*, Anne Carter, trans. (New York: Pantheon Books [Random House], 1971).

Rodwell, J. M., *The Koran*, (translated from the Arabic) with Introduction by Rev. G. Margoliouth (New York: Everyman's Library, 1950).

Rosenzweig, Franz, *The Star of Redemption*, W. W. Hallo, trans. (Notre Dame, Indiana: University of Notre Dame Press, 1985).

Roskam, Hendrika N., *The Purpose of the Gospel of Mark in Its Historical and Social Context* (Boston: Brill, 2004).

Rowley, Harold H., *The Faith of Israel: Aspects of Old Testament Thought* (London: S.C.M. Press, 1956).

_____, *The Old Testament and Modern Study: A Generation of Discovery and Research* (Oxford: Clarendon Press, 1967).

_____, *From Moses to Qumran: Studies in the Old Testament* (New York: Books for Libraries Press, 1971).

Rushdie, Salman, *The Satanic Verses* (London; New York: Viking Penguin, 1988).

Said, Edward W., *Orientalism: Western Conceptions of the Orient* (New York: Crossroads, 1985).
Sale, George, *The Koran, Commonly Called Al-Quran, with a Preliminary Discourse* (London: Fredrick Warne, 1899).
Sanders, E. P., *Jesus and Judaism* (London: S.C.M. Press, 1985).
_____, *The Historical Figure of Jesus* (New York: Penguin, 1993).
_____, *The Tendencies of the Synoptic Tradition* (Cambridge: Cambridge University Press, 1969).
Saunders, John J., *A History of Medieval Islam* (London: Routledge & Kegan Paul Ltd., 1965).
Sayers, Dorothy L., *Creed or Chaos* (New York: Harcourt, Brace & Co., 1949).
_____, *The Emperor Constantine* (New York: Harper & Brothers, 1951).
Scalise, Charles, "Origen and the Sensus Literalis," *Origen of Alexandria, His World and His Legacy*, Charles Kannengiesser, W. L. Peterson, eds. (Notre Dame, Indiana: University of Notre Dame Press, 1988).
Schaeffer, Francis A., *No Final Conflict: The Bible Without Error in All That It Affirms* (Illinois: InterVarsity Press, 1975).
Schaff, Philip, *History of the Christian Church* (Michigan: W. B. Eerdmans, 1976).
_____, Wace, Henry, eds., *The Nicene and Post-Nicene Fathers* (Michigan: W. B. Eerdmans, 1978).
Schechter, Soloman, *Aspects of Rabbinic Theology: Major Concepts of the Talmud* (New York: Schocken Books, 1961).
Schiffman, Lawrence, *From Text to Tradition: A History of Second Temple and Rabbinic Judaism* (New Jersey: KTAV Publishing House Inc., 1991).
Schleiermacher, Friedrich, *The Christian Faith*, [2nd edn. of *Der Christliche Glaube*], H. R. Mackintosh, J. S. Stewart, trans. and eds. (Edinburgh: T & T Clark, 1928.
Schoeps, Hans-Joachim, *Paul, The Theology of the Apostle in the Light of Jewish Religious History*, Harold Knights, trans. (Philadelphia: The Westminster Press, 1961).
Schweitzer, Albert, *The Mysticism of Paul the Apostle*, W. Montgomery, trans. (New York: The Seabury Press, 1968).
Seale, Morris S., *Muslim Theology: A Study of Origins with Reference to the Church Fathers* (London: Luzac & Co., 1964).
Sellers, Robert V., *The Council of Chalcedon: A Historical and Doctrinal Survey* (London: SPCK, 1961).

Seltzer, Robert M., *Jewish People, Jewish Thought* (New York: Macmillan, 1980).
Senders, James A., "Torah and Paul," *God's Christ and His People*, Jacob Jervell, Wayne A. Meeks, eds. (Oslo: Universitetsforlaget, 1977).
Serjeant, Robert B., Review of "Qur'anic Studies," *Journal of the Royal Asiatic Society* (1987).
Seters, John V., *Abraham in History and Tradition* (New Haven: Yale University Press, 1975).
al-Shahrastānī, Muḥammad ibn ʿAbd al-Karīm, *Kitab al-Milal wa al-Nihal: Book of Religious and Philosophical Sects: Part 1*, William Cureton ed. (London: Society for the Publication of Oriental Texts, 1842).
Shorrosh, Anis A., *Islam Revealed* (Nashville: Thomas Nelson Publishers, 1988).
Silver, Daniel J., *A History of Judaism* (New York: Basic Books Inc., 1974).
Simpson, Cuthbert A., *The Early Traditions of Israel: A Critical Analysis of the Pre-Deuteronomic Narrative of the Hexateuch* (Oxford: Basil Blackwell, 1948).
Skinner, Burrhus F., *The Technology of Teaching* (New York: Appleton-Century-Crofts, 1968).
______, Ferster, Charles B., *Schedules of Reinforcement* (New York: Appleton-Century-Crofts, 1957).
Smith, Dwight M., Jr., *Composition and Order in the Fourth Gospel* (New Haven: Yale University Press, 1964).
Smith, Henry P., *The Bible and Islam: Or, the Influence of the Old and New Testaments on the Religion of Mohammed* (New York: ARNO Press, 1973).
Smith, Mark S., *The Early History of God* (New York: Harper & Row, 1990).
Smith, Morton, *Palestinian Parties and Politics that Shaped the Old Testament* (New York: Columbia University Press, 1971).
Soskice, Janet M., *Metaphor and Religious Language* (Oxford: Oxford University Press, 1985).
______, "Myths, Metaphor and Narrative Theology," *Recent Developments in the Philosophy of Language* (Utrecht: Oxford University Press, 1988).
Souter, Alexander, *Text and Canon of the New Testament* (New York: Scribners', 1925).
Spear, Norman E., *The Processing of Memories: Forgetting and Retention* (New York; London: John Wiley & Sons, 1978).

Spencer, Herbert, *Illustrations of Universal Progress* (New York: D. Appleton & Co., 1870).
Steinmueller, John E., *A Companion to Scripture Studies*, 2nd edn. (New York: Joseph F. Wagner Inc., 1941).
Stevick, Daniel B., *Beyond Fundamentalism* (Richmond, USA: John Knox Press, 1964).
Stobart, James W. H., *Islam and its Founder* (London: SPCK Press, 1901).
Stroumsa, Gedaliahu G., "Form(s) of God: Some notes on Metatron and Christ," *Harvard Theological Review* (1983) vol.76.
Sturch, Richard, *The Word and the Christ: An Essay in Analytic Christology* (Oxford: Clarendon Press, 1991).
Suffrin, A. E. "God," James Hastings, *Encyclopedia of Religion and Ethics*, John A. Selbie, ed. (Edinburgh: Kessinger Publishing, 1925-1940), vol.6.
Sullivan, Francis A., *The Christology of Theodore of Mopsuestia* (Rome: University Gregorian, 1956).
Swartz, Merlin, *A Medieval Critique of Anthropomorphism: Ibn al-Jawzi's Kitab Akhbar as-Sifat* (Boston: Brill, 2002).
Swinburne, Richard, *Revelation: From Metaphor to Analogy* (Oxford: Clarendon Press, 1992).
_____, *The Coherence of Theism* (Oxford: Clarendon Press, 1977).
Sykes, S. W., Clayton, J. P., eds., *Christ Faith and History* (Cambridge: Cambridge University Press, 1972).
Tambiah, Stanley J., *Magic, Science, Religion, and the Scope of Rationality* (Cambridge: Cambridge University Press, 1990).
Taylor, Vincent, *The Names of Jesus* (London: Macmillan, 1953).
Taymiyyah, Ibn, *Essay on the Jinn*, abridged and translated by Abu Ameenah Bilal Philips (Riyadh: Tawheed Publications, 1989).
Terrien, Samuel, *The Elusive Presence* (San Francisco: Harper & Row, 1978).
Teske, Ronald J., *To Know God and the Soul: Essays on the Thought of St. Augustine* (Washington: The Catholic University of America Press, 2008).
Thackery, William M., *Letters and Private Papers*, G. N. Ray, ed. (Cambridge: Harvard University Press, 1945), vol.2.
Tillich, Paul, *A History of Christian Thought*, Carl E. Braaten, ed. (New York: Simon & Schuster, 1968).
_____, *Biblical Religion and the Search for Ultimate Reality* (Chicago: University of Chicago Press, 1955).
_____, *Systematic Theology* (Chicago: Chicago University Press, 1951), vol.1.

_____, *Systematic Theology* (Chicago: Chicago University Press, 1957), vol.2.

_____, *The Shaking of the Foundations* (New York: Scribner's Sons, 1948).

_____, *Theology and Culture* (New York; Oxford: Galaxy Books, 1964).

_____, *What is Religion?*, James L. Adams, trans. (New York: Harper & Row, 1973).

Todt, H. E., *The Son of Man in the Synoptic Tradition*, D. M. Barton, trans. (London: S.C.M. Press, 1965).

Torrey, Charles C., *The Jewish Foundation of Islam* (New York: KTAV Publishing House, 1967).

Tritton, Arthur S., *Islam, Beliefs and Practices* (London: Hutchinson University Library, 1966).

Twersky, Isadore, *A Maimonides Reader* (New York: Behrman House, 1972).

Tylor, Edward B., *Primitive Culture; Researches into the Development of Mythology, Philosophy, Religion, Language, Art and Cultures* (New York: Holt & Co., 1883).

Uehlinger, Christoph, "Anthropomorphic Cult Statuary in Iron Age Palestine and the Search for Yahweh's Cult Images," *The Image and the Book*, Karel van der Toorn, ed. (Leuvan: Peeters, 1997).

Urbach, Efraim, *The Sages, Their Concepts and Beliefs* (Massachusetts: Magnes Press Hebrew University, 1975).

Urban, Linwood, *A Short History of Christian Thought* (New York: Oxford University Press, 1995).

Vahanian, Gabriel, *The Death of God* (New York: George Braziller, 1961).

Vahiuddin, S., "Richard Bell's Dating of the Qur'an, A Critical Analysis," *Islamic Culture* (Hyderabad: Deccan, 1956), vol. XXXX, no.3.

Vanhoozer, Kevine J., *Is There a Meaning in This Text?* (Michigan: Zondervan, 1998).

Verhoeven, F. R. J., *Islam: Its Origin and Spread in Words, Maps and Pictures* (Amsterdam: Djambatan, 1962).

Vermes, Geza, *Jesus the Jew: A Historian's Reading of the Gospels* (Minneapolis: Fortress Press, 1981).

_____, *Scripture and Tradition in Judaism* (Leiden: E. J. Brill, 1973).

Vischer, Wilhelm, *The Witness of the Old Testament to Christ*, A. B. Crabtree, trans. (London: Lutterworth Press, 1949).

Vriezen, Theodorus C., *The Religion of Ancient Israel* (Philadelphia: The Westminster Press, 1967).

Wagner, Richard, *My Life* (New York: Dodd Mead, 1911).
Wagtendonk, Kees, "Images in Islam: Discussion of a Paradox," *Effigies Dei: Essays on the History of Religion*, D. Plas, ed. (New York: Brill, 1987).
Waines, David, *An Introduction to Islam* (New York: Cambridge University Press, 1995).
Walzer, Richard, *Al-Farabi on the Perfect State* (Oxford: Clarendon, 1985).
Wansbrough, John, *Quranic Studies: Sources and Methods of Scriptural Interpretation* (Oxford: Oxford University Press, 1977).
_____, *The Sectarian Milieu* (London: Oxford University Press, 1978).
Warfield, Benjamin B., *Revelation and Inspiration* (New York: Oxford University Press, 1927).
Watt, William M., *Bell's Introduction to the Qur'an* (Edinburgh: Edinburgh University Press, 1970).
_____, *Islamic Philosophy and Theology* (Edinburgh: Edinburgh University Press, 1967).
_____, *Early Islam: Collected Articles* (Edinburgh: Edinburgh University Press, 1990).
_____, "Early Discussions about the Qur'an," *Muslim World* (1950), vol. XL.
_____, *Muhammad: Prophet and Statesman* (Oxford: Oxford University Press, 1961).
_____, *Muhammad at Mecca* (Karachi: Oxford University Press, 1979).
_____, *The Formative Period of Islamic Thought* (Edinburgh: Edinburgh University Press, 1973).
_____, *What is Islam* (New York: Frederick Praeger Publishers, 1968).
Webb, Clement C. J., *God and Personality* (London: Allen & Unwin, 1918).
Weinberg, Steven, *The First Three Minutes: A Modern View of the Origin of the Universe* (New York: Basic Books, 1977).
Weinfeld, Moshe, *Deuteronomy and Deuteronomic School* (Oxford: Oxford University Press, 1972).
Wellhausen, Julius, *The Religio-Political Factions in Early Islam*, R. C. Ostle, ed., R. C. Ostle, S. M. Walzer, trans. (New York: North-Holland / American Elsevier, 1975).
Wells, George A., *Did Jesus Exist?* (London: Pemberton, 1968).
Wensinck, Arent J., *The Muslim Creed: Its Genesis and Historical Development* (New York: Barnes & Noble Inc., 1965).
Werblowsky, R. J. Zwi, "Anthropomorphism," *The Encyclopedia of Religion*, M. Eliade, ed. (New York: Macmillan, 1987).
Werner, Martin, *The Formation of Christian Doctrine*, S. F. G. Brandon, trans. (San Francisco: Harper & Brothers, 1957).

Wessels, Antonie, *A Modern Arabic Biography of Muhammad: A Critical Study of Muhammad Husayn Haykal's Hayat Muhammad* (Leiden: E. J. Brill, 1972).

Westcott, Brooke F., *A General Survey of the History of the Canon of the New Testament* (New York: Macmillan, 1896).

Westermann, Claus, *Genesis 12-36: A Commentary*, John J. Scullion, trans. (Minneapolis: Augusburg, 1985).

Whale, John S., *Christian Doctrine* (Cambridge: Cambridge University Press, 1961).

Wheeler, John A., "Forward," *The Anthropic Cosmological Principle*, J. D. Barrow, Frank J. Tipler (Oxford: Oxford University Press, 1986).

White, Leslie, *The Science of Culture: A Study of Man and Civilization* (New York: Macmillan, 1964).

Wiener, Philip P., *Dictionary of the History of Ideas* (New York: Charles Scribners' Son's, 1972).

Wigram, William A., *The Separation of the Monophysites* (London: The Faith Press, 1923).

Wildberger, Hans, *Isaiah 1-12, A Commentary*, Thomas H. Trapp, trans. (Minneapolis: Fortress Press, 1991).

Wiles, Maurice, *The Making of Christian Doctrine* (Cambridge: Cambridge University Press, 1967).

William, John A., *Islam* (New York: G. Braziller, 1961).

Williams, Wesley, "Aspects of the Creed of Imam Ahmad Ibn Hanbal: A Study of Anthropomorphism in Early Islamic Discourse," *International Journal of Middle East Studies* (2002), vol.34.

Winston, David, *Philo of Alexandria* (New York: Paulist Press, 1981).

Witherington, Ben, III, *The Christology of Jesus* (Minneapolis: Fortress Press, 1990).

______, *The Gospel of Mark: A Socio-Rhetorical Commentary* (Grand Rapids: W. B. Eerdmans, 2001).

Wolfson, Harry A., "Philosophical Implications of the Problems of Divine Attributes in the Kalam," *J.A.O.S.* (1958).

______, *Philosophy of the Kalam* (London: Harvard University Press, 1976).

______, *The Philosophy of the Church Fathers*, 3rd edn. (Cambridge, MA: Harvard University Press, 1970).

______, *The Repercussion of the Kalam in Jewish Philosophy* (Cambridge; London: Harvard University Press, 1979).

Wrede, William, *The Messianic Secret* (Greenwood: Attic Press, 1971).

Wright, Nicholas T., *The Challenge of Jesus: Rediscovering Who Jesus Was and Is* (Downers Grove: InterVarsity Press, 1999).
Young, Frances M., *From Nicaea to Chalcedon* (London: S.C.M. Press, 1983).
Zwemer, Samuel M., *The Muslim Christ Oliphant* (London: Anderson & Ferrier, 1912).

Index

Index

Index

Index

Index

Index